AQA Law

D0186579

A2

Second Edition

Emma Bateman
Guy Blundell
Nick Price
Peter Smith
Pam Whelan
John Wilman
Series editor
Richard Wortley

Nelson Thornes

Text © Emma Bateman, Guy Blundell, Peter Smith,
John Wilman and Richard Wortley 2013
Original illustrations © Nelson Thornes Ltd 2013

The right of Emma Bateman, Guy Blundell, Peter Smith, John Wilman and
Richard Wortley to be identified as authors of this work has been asserted by
them in accordance with the Copyright, Designs and Patents Act 1988.

All rights reserved. No part of this publication may be reproduced or transmitted
in any form or by any means, electronic or mechanical, including photocopy,
recording or any information storage and retrieval system, without permission in
writing from the publisher or under licence from the Copyright Licensing Agency
Limited, of Saffron House, 6–10 Kirby Street, London, EC1N 8TS.

Any person who commits any unauthorised act in relation to this publication
may be liable to criminal prosecution and civil claims for damages.

First published in 2009 by Nelson Thornes Ltd
This edition published in 2013 by:
Nelson Thornes Ltd
Delta Place
27 Bath Road
CHELTENHAM
GL53 7TH
United Kingdom

13 14 15 16 17 / 10 9 8 7 6 5 4 3 2 1

A catalogue record for this book is available from the British Library

ISBN 978 1 4085 1971 4

Cover photograph: Alamy/Image 100
Illustrations by Paul McCaffrey; additional illustrations by eMC Design Ltd

Page make-up by OKS Prepress, India

Printed in China

Acknowledgements

The editors and publisher would like to thank the following for permission to reproduce copyright material:

Text
p15 'Ex-soldier Aaron Wilkinson sentenced for killing woman' by Arj Singh, © *The Independent* 2012; p21 'Father branded a fool over quadbike death of his daughter' by Caroline Gammel, © *The Telegraph* 2008; p22 'Ellie Lawrenson's grandmother found not guilty of manslaughter'© *The Liverpool Echo* 2007; p38 'Our Stalker Hell' by Sadie Nicholas, © *The Daily Express* 2012; p47 'Devoted husband who strangled wife in his sleep walks free from court' by Steven Morris, © *The Guardian* 2009, Copyright Guardian News & Media Ltd; p54 'Cotterill jailed over Cup assault' by Sri Carmichael, *The Independent* 2007; p185 'Man admits blackmailing Coleen Rooney over lost mobile' by Helen Carter, © *The Guardian* 2011, Copyright Guardian News & Media Ltd; p194 'Mark Rothko defacement: man arrested on suspicion of criminal damage' by Ben Quinn, © *The Guardian* 2012, Copyright Guardian News & Media Ltd; p197 'London rioter jailed over furniture shop arson', © *The Telegraph* 2012; p200 'Shop worker Farrakh Nizzar jailed for £1m lottery scam bid', © Press Association 2012; p208 'Banned customer drove off without paying', © *Skegness Standard* 2008; p221 'Millionaire's daughter denies car charges', © Press Association 2012; p344 'Compensation award for car crash girl sets personal injury record at £23m' by Caroline Davies, © *The Guardian* 2012, Copyright Guardian News & Media Ltd; p346 'Unduly lenient sentence cases referred to the Court of Appeal for 2011', sourced from www.gov.uk 2012; p347 'Eddie Gillfoyle free after maintaining innocence for 18 years in jail' by Peter Walker and agencies, © *The Guardian* 2010 Copyright Guardian News & Media Ltd; p375 'Levi Bellfield gets life without parole' by Caroline Davies, © *The Guardian* 2011, Copyright Guardian News & Media Ltd.

Images
p5 Ian Hooton/Science Photo Library; p10 © 2000 Topham/FNP-STAR; p16 iStockphoto; p21 John Stillwell/PA Archive/Press Association Images; p22 Sports Illustrated/Getty Images; p25 Getty Images; pp31, 32, 36 iStockphoto; p38 PA Archive/Press Association Images; p43 Getty Images; p49 Paul Brown/Alamy; p54 Martin Rickett/PA Archive/Press Association Images; p59 David Hartley/Rex Features; p65 Rex Features; p78 Press Association; p121 Rex Features; p134 Fotolia; p170 Sean Malyon/Corbis; p171 (top) NTI Media Ltd/Rex Features; p171 (bottom) Getty Images; p172 Crown Copyright/MOD; p178 National Geographic Image Collection/Alamy; p182 Ocean/Corbis; p185 McPix Ltd/Rex Features; p193 iStockphoto; p194 Rex Features; p197 (left) Gavin Rodgers/Rex Features; p197 (right) London News Pictures/Rex Feature; p199 The Advertising Archives; p221 Rex Features; p229 David Hartley/Rex Features; pp254, 289 Getty Images; p325 Alamy; pp336, 337 (top) iStockphoto; p337 (bottom) Interfoto/Alamy; p338 (top) Bettmann/Corbis; p338 (bottom) United States Holocaust Museum; p339 Corbis; p340 Getty Images; p347 (top left) Corbis; p347 (top right) Corbis; p347 (bottom) PA Archive/Press Association Images; p356 *The Times*/NI Syndication; p375 © Mayor's Office for Policing and Crime, Metropolitan Police Service, 2012 and PA Wire/Press Association Images.

Every effort has been made to trace all copyright holders within the book, but if any have been inadvertently overlooked the publisher will be pleased to make the necessary arrangements at the first opportunity.

Contents

Introduction   vi

Table of cases   vii

Table of statutes   xv

Unit 3A
Criminal law
(fatal and non-fatal offences against the person)   1

Introduction   1

1 Murder and voluntary manslaughter   **2**
1   Murder   2
2   Voluntary manslaughter: loss of control   9
3   Voluntary manslaughter: diminished responsibility   14

2 Involuntary manslaughter   **19**
1   Gross negligence manslaughter   19
2   Unlawful act manslaughter   23
3   How to approach a question on homicide   28

3 Non-fatal offences against the person   **31**
1   Assault and battery   31
2   Sections 47, 20 and 18 of the Offences Against the Person Act 1861   35

4 Defences   **42**
1   Introduction to defences in criminal law   42
2   The defence of insanity   42
3   The defence of automatism   46
4   The defence of intoxication   48
5   The defence of consent   53
6   The defence of self-defence/prevention of crime   57

Practice questions   60
Evaluation of fatal and non-fatal offences against the person   62

Unit 3B
Contract law   80

Introduction   80

5 Formation of contract   **81**
1   Offer   81
2   Acceptance   84
3   Consideration   88
4   Privity of contract   93
5   Intention to create legal relations   95
6   Formation of contract – overview   97

6 Contract terms   **99**
1   Terms of a contract   99
2   Implied terms 1   102
3   Implied terms 2   103
4   Implied terms 3   108
5   Control of exclusion and limitation clauses: common law approaches   110
6   Control of exclusion and limitation clauses: statutory approach   113
7   Overview of contract terms   117

7 Vitiating factors   **119**
1   Misrepresentation   119
2   Types of misrepresentation   123
3   Examination techniques   127

8 Discharge of contract   **128**
1   Discharge of contract   128
2   Performance   129
3   Frustration   132
4   Breach   136
5   Overview of discharge of contract   138

9 Remedies   **140**
1   Remedies   140
2   Damages   142
3   Other remedies   146
4   Overview of remedies   147

Practice questions   149
Critical evaluation and proposals for reform of contract law   151

Unit 4A
Criminal law
(offences against property) **166**

Introduction **166**

10 Theft **167**
1 Definition and *actus reus* of theft 167
2 *Mens rea* of theft 175

11 Robbery, blackmail, burglary and criminal damage **181**
1 Robbery 181
2 Blackmail 184
3 Burglary under s9(1)(a) and (b) of the Theft Act 1968 188
4 Criminal damage 193

12 Fraud and making off without payment **198**
1 Distinguishing the areas of fraud in the specification 198
2 Fraud by false representation: s2 of the Fraud Act 2006 199
3 Obtaining services dishonestly: s11 of the Fraud Act 2006 204
4 Making off without payment 208

13 Defences **212**
1 Introduction to defences in criminal law 212
2 The defence of intoxication 212
3 The defence of duress by threats 217
4 The defence of duress of circumstances 223
5 The defence of self-defence/prevention of crime 226

Practice questions 230

Unit 4B
Tort **232**

Introduction **232**

14 The tort of negligence: general principles relating to physical damage and medical negligence **233**
1 When does a duty of care exist? 233
2 Breaching the duty of care 237
3 Causation and remoteness of damage 240
4 Defences to a claim in negligence 244
5 Claiming damages for negligence 246
6 Medical negligence 247

15 The tort of negligence: claiming psychiatric damage and economic loss **253**
1 Claiming psychiatric damage 253
2 Claiming economic loss 260

16 Product liability: liability in tort for defective goods **268**
1 Negligence 268
2 Consumer Protection Act 1987 274

17 Occupiers' liability **280**
1 Lawful visitors and trespassers 280
2 Occupiers' Liability Act 1957 282
3 Occupiers' Liability Act 1984 287

18 The tort of nuisance and the rule in *Rylands* v *Fletcher* **292**
1 Private nuisance 292
2 Public nuisance 299
3 The rule in *Rylands* v *Fletcher* 302

19 Vicarious liability **307**
1 Who is an employee? 308
2 Course of employment 311

Practice questions 316

Unit 4C
Concepts of law 318

Introduction 318

20 Law and morality 320
1 An introduction to law and morality 320
2 The relationship between law and morality 326
3 The enforcement of morality 330
4 Answering questions on the topic of law and morality 334

21 Law and justice 336
1 Theories of justice 336
2 Justice in procedural and substantive law 343
3 Answering questions on the topic of law and justice 353

22 Judicial creativity 355
1 Creativity within the doctrine of judicial precedent 355
2 Creativity within statutory interpretation 359
3 The creative role of judges 363
4 Answering questions on the topic of judicial creativity 369

23 Fault 371
1 Liability depending upon fault 371
2 Liability not depending upon fault 378
3 Should liability depend upon fault? 381
4 Answering questions on the topic of fault 385

24 Balancing conflicting interests 386
1 Theories about interests 386
2 Balancing interests in procedural law 387
3 Balancing interests in substantive law 391
4 Answering questions on the topic of balancing conflicting interests 400

Practice questions 402

Index 403

Introduction

About this book

Nelson Thornes has developed this book to ensure that it offers you the best support for your A2 course and helps you to prepare for your exams. You can be confident that this book has been reviewed by subject experts and is closely matched to the requirements of your specification.

How to use this book

The book content is divided into chapters matched to the sections of the AQA Law specification for Units 3 and 4. Units 3A (Criminal law: fatal and non-fatal offences against the person) and 3B (Contract law) cover Unit 3. Units 4A (Criminal law: offences against property), 4B (Tort) and 4C (Concepts of law) cover Unit 4.

The features in this book include:

In this topic, you will learn how to:

Each chapter is made up of two or more topics. At the beginning of each of these topics, you will find a list of learning objectives that contain targets linked to the requirements of the specification.

Key terms

Terms that you will need to be able to define and understand.

Key cases

Cases that demonstrate a key legal concept.

Link

These refer you back to other points in the book that consider similar issues.

Activity

Things for you to do that will reinforce the information you have just learned.

Study tips

Hints to help you with your study and to prepare you for your exam.

Practice questions

Questions in the style that you can expect in your exam.

You should now be able to:

A bulleted list of learning outcomes at the end of each chapter summarising core points of knowledge.

Table of cases

Key case locators are in **bold**.

A

A&W Hemphill v *Williams* (1966); (1966); [1966] 2 Lloyd's Rep 10; **314**

A and Others v *Secretary of State for the Home Department* (2004 ; [2004] UKHL 56; **364**, 365, 398

A v *National Blood Authority* (2001); [2001] 3 All ER 289; 275–276, **275**, 278

AB v *South West Water* (1993); [1993] 1 All ER 609; 299

Abdul-Hussain (1999); [1999] Crim LR 570; **220**

Abouzaid v *Mothercare* (2000); [2000] All ER (D); 2436; **274**, 277–278, **277**, 352

The 'Achilleas' (2008); [2008] UKHL 48; **143**

Adams v *Lindsell* (1818); [1818] 1 B & Ald 681, [1818] 106 All ER 250; **85**, 393

Addie v *Dumbreck* (1929); [1929] All ER 1; 352, **358**

Addis v *Gramophone Co. Ltd* (1909); [1909] AC 488; **144**

Adler v *George* (1964); [1964] 1 All ER 628; **360**

Adomako (1994); [1994] 3 All ER 79; **20**, 22, 373–374, **373**

Ahluwalia (1992); [1992] 4 All ER 889; **10**, 11, 14, 65–66

Alcock v *Chief Constable of South Yorkshire* (1991); [1991] 4 All ER 907; 254, 256–257, **256**, 377

Allen (1985); [1985] 2 All ER 641; **206**

Allen (1988); [1988] Crim LR 698; **49**, **213**

Allen v *Gulf Oil* (1981); [1981] 1 All ER 353; **296**

Alphacell Ltd v *Woodward* (1972); [1972] AC 824, [1972] 2 All ER 475; 379, 382

Amalgamated Investment v *Walker Ltd* (1977); [1976] 3 All ER 509; **133**

Ancell v *McDermott* (1993); [1993] 4 All ER 355; **236**

Andrews (1937); [1937] 2 All ER 552; 19, 20

Anglia Television Ltd v *Reed* (1972); [1971] 3 All ER 690; **144**, 163

Ashdown v *Samuel Williams & Sons Ltd* (1957); [1957] 1 All ER 35; **286**

Ashton v *Turner* (1980); [1980] 3 All ER 870; **365**

Aswan Engineering v *Lupdine Ltd* (1986); [1987] 1 All ER 135; **272**

Attia v *British Gas* (1987); [1987] 3 All ER 455; **259**

Attorney-General for Jersey v *Holley* (2005); [2005] 3 All ER 371; **355**, 364, 367

Attorney-General for Northern Ireland v *Gallagher* (1963); [1961] 3 All ER 299; **51**, **215**

Attorney-General for Ontario v *Orange Productions* (1971); [1971] 21 DLR (3d); 257; [1971] 3 OR 585 (Ontario High Court of Justice); 299

Attorney-General v *PYA Quarries* (1957); [1957] 1 All ER 894; **300**

Attorney-General's Reference (No. 2 of 1992); [1993] 4 All ER 683; **46**

Attorney-General's Reference (No. 3 of 1994); (1997); [1997] 3 All ER 936; 3

Attorney-General's Reference (No. 4 of 1980); (1982); [1981] 2 All ER 617; **26**

Attwood v *Small* (1838); [1838] 6 Cl & Flyn 232; **121**

Autoclenz Ltd v *Belcher* (2011); [2011] UKSC 41; **310**

B

B and R v *DPP* (2007); [2007] EWHC 739 (Admin); **182**

B v *DPP* (2000); [2000] 1 All ER 833; 379, 382, 391

Baillie (1995); [1995] 2 Crim App Rep 31; [1995] Crim LR 739; **10**

Bairstow Eves London Central Ltd v *Smith* (2004); [2004] EWHC 263 (QB); **116**

Baker and Wilkins (1997); [1997] Crim LR 497; 218

Balfour v *Balfour* (1919); [1919] 2 KB 571; **96**, 357

Barnes (2004); [2004] EWCA Crim 3246; 53

Barnes v *Hampshire County Council* (1969); [1969] 3 All ER 746; **236**

Barnett v *Chelsea and Kensington Hospital Management Committee* (1968); [1968] 1 All ER 1068; **248**, **376**

Barr v *Biffa Waste Services* (2012); [2012] EWCA Civ 312; **295**

Bartlett v *Sidney Marcus* (1965); [1965] All ER 753; **104**

Bateman (1925); [1925] 19 Crim App Rep 8; **19**, 20, 22

Beale v *Taylor* (1967); [1967] 3 All ER 253; **104**

Beard v *London General Omnibus* (1900); [1900–3] All ER 112; **312**

Bentham (2005); [2005] UKHL 18; **182**

Bernstein v *Pamson Motors Ltd* (1987); [1987] 2 All ER 220; 106–107, **141**

Beswick v *Beswick* (1968); [1967] 2 All ER 1197; 164

Bettini v *Gye* (1876); [1876] 1 QB 183; **100**, 136

Bevans (1988); [1988] Crim LR 236; **187**

Bhamra v *Dubb* (2010); [2010] EWCA Civ 13; [2010] All ER (D) 115 (Jan); **235**

Bird (1985); [1985] 2 All ER 513; 57–58, **57**, 77–78, 79, **227**

Bisset v *Wilkinson* (1927); [1927] AC 177; **120**, 161–162

Blaue (1975); [1975] 3 All ER 446; **4**

Blyth v *Birmingham Waterworks* (1856); [1865] 251 J Ex 212; 237, 376

Bogle v *McDonald's Restaurants* (2002); [2002] EWHC 490; **275**, 276

Bolam v *Friern Hospital Management Committee* (1957); [1957] 2 All ER 118; **238**, 248

Bolitho v *City and Hackney Health Authority* (1997); [1997] 4 All ER 771; **249**

Bollom (2004); [2004] 2 Crim App Rep 6; **39**

Bolton v *Mahadeva* (1972); [1972] 2 All ER 1322; **130**

Bolton v *Stone* (1951); [1951] 1 All ER 1078; **238,** 352, **376**

Bourhill v *Young* (1943); [1942] All ER 396; 376

Bourne (1939); [1938] 3 All ER 615; **328**

Bourne Leisure Ltd v *Marsden* (2009); [2009] EWCA Civ 671; **284**

Bowen (1996); [1996] 2 Crim App Rep 157; 219, **219**

Bradford v *Robinson Rentals* (1967); [1967] 1 All ER 267; **241**

Bramhall v *Edwards* (2004); [2004] EWCA Civ 403; 105

Brannon v *Airtours* (1999); [1999] EWCA Civ 588; **244**

Bratty (1963); [1961] 3 All ER 523; **44, 46**

Bridlington Relay v *Yorkshire Electricity* (1965); [1965] 1 All ER 264; **295**

Brinkibon Ltd v *Stahag Stahl GmbH* (1982); [1982] 1 All ER 293; 86

British Railways Board v *Herrington* (1972); [1972] 1 All ER 749; 287, 288, 323, **352, 358,** 367, **378**

Brogden v *Metropolitan Railway* (1877); [1877] 2 App. Cas. 666; **85**

Brooks and Brooks (1983); [1982] 76 Crim App Rep 66; **209**

Brown (1985); [1985] Crim LR 611; **189**

Brown (1993); [1993] 2 All ER 75; **53–54, 55,** 77, 325, 356, 392

Brown (2011); [2011] EWCA Crim 2796; 16

Brown and Others (1993); **333**

Brown and Stratton (1998); [1998] Crim LR 485; **39**

Burgess (1991); [1991] 2 All ER 769; **44**

Burrell v *Harmer* (1967); [1967] Crim LR 169; **56**

Burstow (1997); [1997] 4 All ER 225; **31,** 32, 33, **38,** 70, 71

Byrne (1960); [1960] 3 All ER 1; **14,** 15–16, 350

Byrne v *Van Tienhoven* (1880); [1880] 5 CPD 344; **83**

C

Caldwell (1982); [1981] 1 All ER 961; 362

Callow v *Tillstone* (1900); [1900] 83 LT411; **384**

Calvert v *William Hill* (2008); [2008] EWHC 454 (Ch);, [2008] All ER (D); 170 (Mar); **235**

Cambridge Water v *Eastern Counties Leather* (1994); [1994] 1 All ER 53; **304**

Camplin (1978); [1978] 2 All ER 168; **12**

Caparo v *Dickman* (1990); [1990] 1 All ER 568; **234,** 236, 251, **264,** 365, **376**

Carey (2006); [2006] EWCA Crim 17; **25**

Carlill v *Carbolic Smoke Ball Co.* (1893); [1893] All ER 127; **82,** 83, 152, 153

Carmichael v *National Power* (1999); [1999] 4 All ER 897; **310**

Carroll v *Fearon* (1998); [1998] PIQR P416; **270**

Carslogie Steamship Co. v *Royal Norwegian Government* (1952); [1952] 1 All ER 20; **242**

Cassidy v *Ministry of Health* (1950); [1951] 1 All ER 574; **249**

Castle v *St Augustine's Links* (1922); [1922] 38 TLR 615; 299

Cato (1976); [1976] 1 All ER 260; **4**

Cattle v *Stockton Waterworks* (1875); [1875] LR 10 QB 453; **261**

Central London Property Trust Ltd v *High Trees House Ltd* (1947); [1956] 1 All ER 256; **90,** 155, 366

Century Insurance v *Northern Ireland Road Transport Board* (1942); [1942] 1 All ER 491; **312,** 380

Chadwick v *British Railways Board* (1967); [1967] 2 All ER 945; **255, 256**

Chan Fook (1994); [1994] 2 All ER 552; **36,** 367

Chandler v *Webster* (1904); [1904] 1 KB 493; **134,** 393–394

Chapelton v *Barry Urban District Council* (1940); [1940] 1 All ER 356; **111**

Chappell & Co. v *Nestlé* (1960); [1959] 2 All ER 701; **88**

Charles Rickards Ltd v *Oppenheim* (1950); [1950] 1 All ER 420; **130**

Chaudhry v *Prabhakar* (1988); [1988] 3 All ER 718; **263**

Cheshire (1991); [1991] 3 All ER 670; **5,** 64, 373

Chester v *Afshar* (2004); [2004] 4 All ER 587; **251**

Christie v *Davey* (1892); [1893] 1 Ch D 316; **296,** 396

Church (1966); [1965] 2 All ER 72; 24

Clarence (1888); [1888] 22 QBD 23; 39

Clarke (1949); [1949] 2 All ER 448; 327

Clarke (1972); [1972] 1 All ER 219; **43,** 374

Clarke v *Dickson* (1858); [1858] EB & E 148; **126**

Clegg (1994); [1995] 1 All ER 334; 58–59, **58,** 78, **228,** 368

Clegg v *Olle Anderson* (2003); [2003] EWCA Civ 320; **106**

Clinton (2012); [2012] EWCA Crim 2; **12,** 66–67

Clouden (1987); [1987] Crim LR 56; **182**

Cocker (1989); [1989] Crim LR 740; 349

Cole (1994); [1994] Crim LR 582; **218**

Collins (1973); [1972] 2 All ER 1105; **189,** 190

Collins v *Godefroy* (1831); [1831] 1 B Ad 950; **91**

Collins v *Willcock* (1984); [1984] 3 All ER 374; **33**

Collister and Warhurst (1955); [1955] 39 Crim App Rep 100; **186**

Constanza (1997); [1997] Crim LR 576; **31,** 32

Conway (1989); [1988] 3 All ER 1025; **224**

Conway v *Wimpey* (1951); [1951] 1 All ER 363; **313**

Corcoran and Anderton (1980); [1980] 71 Crim App Rep 104; **183**

Corion-Auguiste (2004); unreported; **25**

Cotton v *Derbyshire Dales DC* (1994); [1994] *The Times,* 20 June; 377

Couchman v *Hill* (1947); [1947] 1 All ER 103; **101,** 112, 122

Council of Civil Service Unions v *Minister for the Civil Service* (1984), ('The GCHQ case'); [1984] 3 All ER 935; **365**

Crown River Cruises v *Kimbolton Fireworks* (1996); [1996] 2 Lloyd's Rep 533; **294**

Crowther v *Shannon Motor Co.* (1975); [1975] 1 All ER 139; **104–105**

Cunningham (1957); [1957] 2 All ER 412; 33, 39–40, 70

Cunningham (1982); [1981] 2 All ER 863; 6

Cutter v *Powell* (1795); [1795] 6 Term Rep 320; **129**

D

D & C Builders v Rees (1966); [1965] 3 All ER 837; **89**
Davidge and Bunnett (1984); [1984] Crim LR 297; **174**
Davis (2008); [2008] 3 All ER 461; 399–400
Davis Contractors Ltd v Fareham UDC (1956); [1956]
  2 All ER 145; [1972] 2 All ER 898; **133**
Davis v Johnson (1979); [1979] AC 264; 366, 367
Dawson (1985); [1985] Crim LR 383; [1985] 81 Crim
  App Rep 150; **24**
Dawson and James (1976); [1976] 64 Crim App Rep
  170; **181**
Dennis v Ministry of Defence (2003); [2003] EWHC
  793; **295, 298**, 397, 401
Denny, Mott & Dickson v James Fraser (1944); [1944]
  1 All ER 678; **132**
Denton (1982); [1982] 1 All ER 65; **195**
Derry v Peek (1889); [1889] 14 App Cas 337; **123**
Dica (2004); [2004] 3 All ER 593; **39**, 55, 71, 76, 367
Dick Bentley v Harold Smith Motors (1965); [1965] 2
  All ER 65; **101**
Dickson v UK (2007); [2007] All ER (D) 59 (Dec); 398
Dietschmann (2003); [2003] 1 All ER 897; **16–17**
Dimmock v Hallett (1866); [1866] 2 Ch App 21; **120**
*Director General of Fair Trading v First National Bank
  plc* (2001); [2001] UKHL 52; **116**
Donachie v Chief Constable of Greater Manchester
  (2004); [2004] EWCA Civ 405, [2004] All ER D 126
  April; **255**
Donoghue v Folkestone Properties (2003); [2003] 3 All
  ER 1101; **288**
Donoghue v Stevenson (1932); [1932] AC562, [1932]
  All ER 1; **19–20**, 233–234, **233**, 236, 251, 268–269,
  268, **270**, 273, 355, 376
Dooley v Cammell Laird (1951); [1951] 1 Lloyd's Rep
  271; **258**
Doughty (1996); [1986] Crim LR 625; [1986] 83 Crim
  App Rep 319; 66
DPP v A (2000); [2000] 164 JP 317; 40
DPP v Huskinson (1988); [1988] Crim LR 620; **174**
DPP v Hutchinson (1990); 2 All ER 836; 365, 366
DPP v J and others (2002); [2002] All ER (D) 260; **176**
DPP v K (1990); [1990] 1 All ER 331; **34**
*DPP v Knuller (Publishing, Printing and Promotions);
  Ltd* (1971); [1972] 2 All ER 898; **333**
DPP v Ray (1974); [1973] 3 All ER 131; **201**
DPP v Smith (2006); [2006] 2 All ER 16; 36, **38**, 367
Dunlop Pneumatic Tyre Co. Ltd v Selfridge (1915);
  [1915] AC 847; **93**
*Dunlop Pneumatic Tyre Co. v New Garage and Motor
  Co* (1915); [1915] AC 79; **145**
Dyke and Munro (2001); [2001] EWCA Crim 2184;174

E

Easom (1971); [1971] 2 All ER 945 (CA); **177**
East v Maurer (1991); [1991] 2 All ER 73; **124**
Echo and Express Publication v Tanton (1999); [1999]
  1RLR 367; **310**
Edgington v Fitzmaurice (1885); [1885] 29 Ch D 459; **120**
Edwards (2001); unreported; 21

Egan (1992); [1992] 4 All ER 470; **16**
Elliot v C (1983); [1983] 2 All ER 1005; 350
Ellis v Chief Adjudication Officer (1998); [1997]
  EWCA Civ 1642; **156**
English (1981); unreported; **14**
Entores Ltd v Miles Far East Co. (1955); [1955] 2 All
  ER 493; **86**
Errington v Errington (1952); [1952] 1 All ER 149; **83**
Esso Petroleum Co. Ltd v Customs and Excise (1976);
  [1976] 1 All ER 117; **96**, 156
Esso Petroleum Co. Ltd v Marden (1976); [1976] 2 All
  ER 5; **125**
European Commission v UK (1997); [1997] All ER
  (EC) 481; **277**
Evans v Triplex Safety Glass (1936); [1936] 1 All ER
  283; **271**

F

Felthouse v Bindley (1863); [1863] 142 All ER 1037;
  85, 153
*Fibrosa Spolka Ackyjna v Fairbairn Lawson Combe
  Barbour Ltd* (1943); [1942] 2 All ER 122; **134**
Finlay (2001); unreported; **21**
Fisher v Bell (1961); [1961] 3 All ER 731; **82**, 152
Fisher v Harrods Ltd (1966); [1966] 1 Lloyd's Rep 500;
  269, 271
Fitzpatrick v Sterling Housing Association (1999);
  [1999] 4 All ER 705; 358
Fletcher v Krell (1873); [1872] 42 LJ QB 55; **122**
Foakes v Beer (1884); [1884] 9 App Cas 605; **89**, 90
Froom v Butcher (1975); [1975] 3 All ER 520; **244**

G

G and R (2003); [2003] 4 All ER 765; 75, 325, 350, 355
Galli-Atkinson v Seghal (2003); [2003] EWCA Civ
  697; **257**
*Gamerco SA v ICM/Fair Warning (Agency); Ltd and
  Others* (1995); [1995] EWHC 1; **135**
Gammon (HK); Ltd v Attorney-General of Hong Kong
  (1985); [1984] 2 All ER 503; 379, 382, 383
Garwood (1987); [1987] 1 All ER 1032; **186**
Geary v JD Wetherspoon plc (2011); [2011] EWHC
  1506; [2011] All ER (D) 97 (Jun); 285–286, **285**
Gemmell and Richards (2003); [2003] UKHL 50; 391
George Mitchell Ltd v Finney Lock Seeds Ltd (1983);
  [1983] 2 AC 803; **114**
Ghosh (1982); 1982 2 All ER 689; 178–179, **178**, **203**
Gibbins and Proctor (1918); [1918] 13 Crim App Rep
  134; 2, 327
Gibson (1990); [1991] 1 All ER 439; 333
Gibson v Manchester City Council (1979); [1979]
  1 All ER 972; **84**
Giles v Walker (1890); [1890] 24 QBD; **303**
Gill (1963); [1963] 2 All ER 688; 220
Gittens (1984); [1984] 3 All ER 252; **16**
Gladstone Williams (1987); [1987] 3 All ER 411; 57,
  77, **227**
Gomez (1993); [1993] 1 All ER 1; **168**
Goodfellow (1986); [1986] Crim LR 468; [1986] 83
  Crim App Rep 23; 24, **26**

Goodwill v *British Pregnancy Advisory Service* (1996); [1996] 2 All ER 161; **124**, **264**

Gotts (1991); [1992] 1 All ER 832; 350

Gould (1968); [1986] 1 All ER 849; 356

Graham (1982); [1982] 1 All ER 801; **217**, 218, 219

Grant v *Australian Knitting Mills* (1935); [1936] AC 85; 269, **270**

Granville Oil & Chemicals Ltd v *Davis Turner & Co. Ltd* (2003); [2003] 1 All ER (Comm) 819; **114–115**

Greatorex v *Greatorex* (2000); [2000] 4 All ER 769; **258**

Green v *Chelsea Waterworks Company* (1894); [1894] 70 LT 547; **305**

Gregg v *Scott* (2005); [2005] UKHL 2; **250**

Griffiths v *Arch Engineering* (1968); [1968] 3 All ER 217; **272**

Griffiths v *Peter Conway* (1939); [1939] 1 All ER 685; **105**

Guthing v *Lynn* (1831); [1831] 2 B & Ad 232; **84**

H

Hadley v *Baxendale* (1854); [1854] 9 Exch 341; **142**, 163

Hale (1978); [1978] 68 Crim App Rep 415; **182**, 183

Hale v *Jennings Bros* (1938); [1938] All ER 579; **303**

Haley v *London Electricity Board* (1964); [1964] 3 All ER 185; **238**, 395

Halsey v *Esso Petroleum Co. Ltd* (1961); [1961] 2 All ER 145; 294, 301

Hamilton Jones v *David & Snape* (2004); [2003] EWHL 3147; **144**

Hancock and Shankland (1986); [1986] 1 All ER 641; **7**, 63

Hardie (1985); [1984] 3 All ER 848; 49–50, **49**, 213–214, **213**

Hardman v *Chief Constable of Avon and Somerset* (1986); [1986] Crim LR 330; **193**

Hardwick v *Johnson* (1978); [1978] 2 All ER 935; **156**

Harooni v *Rustins* (2011); [2011] EWHC 1632; [2011] All ER (D) 08 (Jul); 304

Harris v *Perry* (2009); [2008] EWCA Civ 907; **239**

Harrow London Borough Council v *Shah* (1999); [1999] 3 All ER 302; 379, 381, 383

Harry (1974); [1974] Crim LR 32; **186**

Hartley v *Ponsonby* (1857); [1857] 7 E & B 872; **91**

Harvey (1981); [1981] Crim LR 104; **187**

Harvey v *Plymouth City Council* (2010); [2010] EWCA Civ 860; [2010] All ER; **280**

Harvey v *RG O'Dell Ltd* (1958); [1958] 2 QB 78; **312**

Hasan (2005); [2005] UKHL 22; **218**, 222

Haseldine v *Daw* (1941); [1941] 3 All ER 156; **285**

Havana Railways case (1961); [1961] AC 1007; 366

Haynes v *Harwood* (1935); [1935] 1 KB 146; **245**

Haystead v *Chief Constable of Derbyshire* (2000); [2000] 3 All ER 890; **34**

Heard (2007); [2007] EWCA Crim 125; **75**

Hedley Byrne & Co. Ltd v *Heller & Partners Ltd* (1964); [1963] 2 All ER 575; **124**, 160, 161, **262**, 263

Hennessey (1989); [1989] 2 All ER 9; **47**

Herne Bay Steamboat Co. v *Hutton* (1903); [1903] 2 KB 683; **133**

Hill and Hall (1989); [1989] Crim LR 136; 195

Hill v *Baxter* (1958); [1958] 1 All ER 42; **371**

Hill v *Chief Constable for West Yorkshire* (1988); [1990] 1 All ER 1046; 351, 365

Hilton v *Thomas Burton (Rhodes); Ltd* (1961); [1961] 1 All ER 74; 382

Hinks (1998); [2000] All ER 833; **169**

Hochster v *de la Tour* (1853); [1853] 2 E & B 678; **136**

Hoenig v *Isaacs* (1952); [1952] 2 All ER 176; **130**

Holley (2005); [2005] 3 All ER 371; **13**

Hollier v *Rambler Motors (AMC); Ltd* (1972); [1972] 2 QB 71; **112**

Hollywood Silver Fox Farm v *Emmett* (1936); [1936] 1 All ER 825; **296**

Hong Kong Fir v *Kawasaki Kaisha Kasan* (1962); [1962] 2 QB 26; **100**

Horwood v *Land of Leather Ltd* (2010); [2010] EWHC 545 (Comm); 92

Hotson v *East Berkshire Health Authority* (1987); [1987] 2 All ER 909; **250**

Household Fire & Carriage Accident Insurance Co. Ltd v *Grant* (1879); [1878–9] LR 4 Ex D 216; **85**

Howard Marine v *A Ogden & Sons (Excavations) Ltd* (1978); [1978] QB 574; **125**

Howells (1997); [1997] 3 All ER 417; 382–383

Hudson and Taylor (1971); [1971] All ER 244; **220**

Hughes v *Lord Advocate* (1963); [1963] 1 All ER 705; **241**

Hunter v *Canary Wharf* (1997); [1997] 2 All ER 426; 292, **298**

Hutton v *Warren* (1836); [1836] 1 M & W 466; 99, 102

Hyde v *Wrench* (1840); [1840] 49 All ER; 83, **85**

I

Ibrams and Gregory (1981); [1981] 74 Crim App Rep 154; **9–10**

Ireland (1997); [1997] 4 All ER 225; **31**, 33, **38**, 70, 71

J

Jackson v *Horizon Holidays Ltd* (1975); [1975] 3 All ER 92; **93**, 156, **351**, 367, **368**, 393

Jaggard v *Dickinson* (1980); [1980] 3 All ER 716; **195**

JCC v *Eisenhower* (1994); [1994] 2 All ER 552; **37–38**

Jebson v *Ministry of Defence* (2000); [2000] EWCA Civ 198; 344–345, **344**, 377, 395

Jeffery v *Black* (1978); [1978] 1 All ER 555; **345**

Jewson Ltd v *Boyhan* (2003); [2003] EWCA 1030; **105**

Jolley v *Sutton London Borough Council* (2000); [2000] 3 All ER 409; **241**, 280

Jones (1986); [1987] Crim LR 123; **55**

Jones and Smith (1976); [1976] 3 All ER 54; **191**

Jones v *Padavatton* (1969); [1969] 2 All ER 616; **96**, 156

Jones v *Tower Boot Company Ltd* (1997); [1997] 2 All ER 406; **361**

Jones v *Vernon's Pools* (1938); [1938] 2 All ER 626; **96**

Jordan (1956); [1956] 40 Crim App Rep 152; **5**

K

Keane and McGrath (2010); [2010] EWCA Crim 2514 [2010] All ER (D) 185 (Oct); 78

Kelly (1998); [1998] 3 All ER 741; **171**

Kemp (1957); [1957] 3 All ER 249; **44**

Kennaway v *Thompson* (1981); [1981] QB 88; **297**

Kennedy (2007); [2007] UKHL 38; **25**

Keown v *Coventry NHS Trust* (2006); [2006] EWCA Civ 39, All ER (D) 27 (Feb); **288**

Kingston (1994); [1994] 3 All ER 353; **49**, 76, **213**, **358**

Knightley v *Johns* (1982); [1982] 1 All ER 851; **242**

Knuller v *DPP* (1973); [1972] 2 All ER 898; 366

Krell v *Henry* (1903); [1903] 2 KB 740; **132**, 394

Kubach v *Hollands* (1937); [1937] All ER 970; **271**

L

Lamb (1967); [1967] 2 All ER 1282; **23**

Lamb v *Camden London Borough Council* (1981); [1981] 2 All ER 408; **242**

Lambert v *Cooperative Insurance Society* (1975); [1975] 2 Lloyd's Rep 485; **122**

Lambie (1982); [1981] 2 All ER 776; **201**, 202

Lampleigh v *Braithwaite* (1615); [1615] 80 ER 255; **88–89**, 155

Larsonneur (1933); [1933] 24 Crim App Rep 74; 379

Latimer (1886); [1886–90] All ER 386; 34

Latimer v *AEC* (1953); [1953] 2 All ER 449; **239**

Lavender (1994); [1994] Crim LR 297; **176**

Law Society v *KPMG Peat Marwick* (2000); [2000] 4 All ER 540; **265**

Lawrence (1972); [1971] Crim LR 645; **168**

Lawrence v *Fen Tigers* (2012); [2012] EWCA Civ 26, [2011] All ER (D) 96 (Mar); **294**

Le Brun (1991); [1991] 4 All ER 673; **26**

Leaf v *International Galleries* (1950); [1950] 1 All ER 693; **126**, 162

Lennon v *Metropolitan Police Commissioner* (2004); [2004] EWCA Civ 130; **263**

L'Estrange v *Graucob* (1934); [1934] 2 KB 394; **110**

Lewis (2010); [2010] EWCA Crim 151; **25–26**

Lewis v *Averay* (1972); [1971] 3 All ER 907; **126**

Limpus v *London General Omnibus* (1863); [1862] 1 H & C 526; **312**, 380, 396

Lipman (1970); [1969] 3 All ER 410; **51**

Lister v *Hesley Hall Ltd* (2001); [2001] 2 All ER 769; **312**, **358**, 380

Litchfield (1998); [1998] Crim LR 507; **20**

Little (1992); [1993] 2 All ER 9; 31

Lloyd (1985); [1985] 2 All ER 661; **176**, 180

Lloyd v *DPP* (1985); [1992] 1 All ER 982; 195

London and North Western Railway v *Neilson* (1922); [1922] AC 263; **112**

Long v *Lloyd* (1958); [1958] 2 All ER 402; **126**, 162

Lowery v *Walker* (1911); [1911] AC 10; **280**

Lyons, Sons & Co. v *Gulliver* (1913); [1914] Ch 631; **300**

M

McDavitt (1981); [1951] 1 All ER 905; **209**

McFarlane v *EE Caledonia Ltd* (1993); (1967); [1994] 2 All ER 1; 255–256, **255**

McKew v *Holland & Hannen & Cubitts* (1969); [1969] 3 All ER 1621; **242**, 242–243

McKinnon Industries v *Walker* (1951); [1951] 3 DLR 739; **295**

McLoughlin v *O'Brian* (1983); [1982] 2 All ER 298; **257**

McWilliams v *Sir William Arrol & Co. Ltd* (1962); [1962] 1 All ER 623; **240**, **241**

Madden (1975); [1975] 3 All ER 155; **300**

Magor and St Mellons RDC v *Newport Corporation* (1950); [1950] 2 All ER 1226; 366

Mahon v *Osborne* (1939); [1939] 1 All ER 535; **249**

Majewski (1977); [1976] 2 All ER 142; **50**, 50–51, 75, 76, **214**

Malcherek and Steel (1981); [1981] 2 All ER 422; **5**

Marcic v *Thames Water* (2003); [2001] 4 All ER 326; **296**

Maritime National Fish Ltd v *Ocean Trawlers Ltd* (1935); [1935] AC 524; **133**

Marriot (1971); [1971] 1 All ER 595 (CA); 382

Marshall (1998); [1999] Crim LR 317; **171**

Martin (1989); 1 All ER 652; 223–224, **223**

Martin (Anthony Edward); (2001); [2001] EWCA Crim 2245; **58**, 58–59, 78, **228**, 229, 372, 392

Matthews and Alleyne (2003); [2003] EWCA Crim 192; **8**, 63–64

Mattis v *Pollock* (2003); [2004] 4 All ER 85; **312**

Merritt v *Merritt* (1971); [1970] 2 All ER 760; **96**, 357

Miller (1954); [1954] 2 All ER 529; **36**

Miller (1983); [1983] 2 All ER 427; 3

Miller v *Jackson* (1977); 1977 3 All ER 338; 297, **297**, 396–397, 401

Ministry of Justice (*R* on the application of Nicklinson) (2012); [2012] EWHC 304; 76–77

Misra and Srivastava (2004); [2004] *The Times*, 13 October; 22

Mitchell (1983); [1983] 2 All ER 427; **24**

M'Naghten (1843); [1843–60] All ER 229; **43**, 73

Mohammed (2005); [2005] EWCA Crim 1880; **13**

Moloney (1985); [1985] 1 All ER 1025; 7, 62–63

Moloney v *Lambeth London Borough Council* (1966); [1966] 64 LGR 644; **284**

Mondial Shipping and Chartering BV v *Astarte Shipping Ltd* (1995); [1995] CLC 1011; **86**

The Moorcock (1889); [1886–90] All ER 530; **99**, 102

Morphitis v *Salmon* (1990); [1990] Crim LR 48; **193**

Morris (1984); [1983] 3 All ER 288; **168**

Morris v *Murray* (1990); [1990] 3 All ER 801; **245**

Morrison (1989); [1989] 89 Cr App R 17 (CA); 41

Mowatt (1976); [1967] 3 All ER 47; **40**, 72

MPC v *Charles* (1976); [1976] 3 All ER 112; 201–202, **201**

Muirhead v *Industrial Tank Specialties* (1985); 3 All ER 705; **272**

Mullin v *Richards* (1998); [1998] 1 All ER 920; **238**

Murdoch v *Glacier Metal* (1998); [1998] EWCA Civ 33; **295**

Museprime Properties Ltd v *Adhill Properties Ltd* (1990); [1991] 61 P& CR 111; **121**

N

Nedrick (1986); [1986] 3 All ER 1; **7**, 41

Nettleship v *Weston* (1971); [1971] 3 All ER 581; **237**, **351**, 376

Network Rail Infrastructure v *Conarkin Group* (2011); [2011] EWCA Civ 644; **262**
Newbury and Jones (1976); [1977] 2 All ER 365; **26**
Nichols v *Marsland* (1876); [1876] LR 1 Ex 265; **305**
Nisshin Shipping Co. Ltd v *Cleaves & Co. Ltd* (2003); [2003] EWHC 2602; **94**

O

O'Brien (1974); [1974] 3 All ER 663; 327
O'Connell v *Jackson* (1971); [1971] 3 All ER 129; **244**
O'Grady (1987); 3 All ER 420; 392
Olley v *Marlborough Court Hotel* (1949); 1 All ER 127; **111, 350**
Orchard v *Lee* (2009); [2009] EWCA Civ 295; **238**
Oscar Chess Ltd v *Williams* (1957); [1957] 1 All ER 325; **101**
Oxford v *Moss* (1978); [1979] Crim LR 119; **171**

P

Page One Records Ltd v *Britton* (1967); [1967] 3 All ER 822; **147**
Page v *Smith* (1996); [1995] 2 All ER 736; **255**
Pagett (1983); [1983] Crim LR 394; **4**, 373
Palmer (1971); [1971] 1 All ER 1077; **58**, 78, **228**, 392
Paradine v *Jane* (1647); [1647] Aleyn 26; **132**
Paris v *Stepney Borough Council* (1951); [1951] 1 All ER 42; **239**, 251
Parker v *Clarke* (1960); [1960] 1 All ER 93; **95**
Parmenter (1991); [1991] 4 All ER 698; 33, **36–37, 367**
Partridge v *Crittenden* (1968); [1968] 2 All ER 421; **82**
Patchett v *SPATA* (2009); [2009] EWCA Civ 717; 263–264, **263**
Patel v *Ali* (1984); [1984] Ch 283; 164
Pearson v *Coleman Bros* (1948); [1948] 2 All ER 274; **281**
Pepper v *Hart* (1993); [1993] 1 All ER 42; 362
Perry v *Kendricks Transport* (1955); [1956] 1 All ER 154; **305**
Pharmaceutical Society of GB v *Boots Cash Chemists* (1953); [1953] 1 All ER 482; **82**, 151–152
Phipps v *Rochester Corporation* (1955); [1955] 1 All ER 129; **284**
Pinnel's case (1602); [1602] 5 Co Rep 117; **89**
Pittwood (1902); [1902] 19 TLR 37; 2, 327
Platt v *Liverpool City Council* (1997); [1997] EWCA Civ 1588; **289**
Pommell (1995); [1995] 2 Crim App Rep 607; **225**
Ponting (1985); [1985] Crim LR 318; **345**
Poussard v *Spiers* (1876); [1876] 1 QBD 410; **100**
Pretty (2002); [2001] UKHL 61; **53**

Q

Quick (1973); [1973] 3 All ER 347; 46–47, **46**

R

R v *G and another* (2003); [2003] 4 All ER 765; 195
R v *R* (1991); [1991] 4 All ER 481; **327, 367**
Rai (2000); [2000] Crim LR 192; **201**
Ramsgate Victoria Hotel v *Montefiore* (1866); [1866] LR1 EX; **83**
Ratcliff v *McConnell* (1999); [1999] 1 WLR 670; **290**

Ratcliffe v *Plymouth and Torbay Health Authority* (1998); [1998] PIQR P170; [1998] Lloyd's Rep Med 162; 42 BMLR 64 (Court of Appeal); **250**
Re A (2000); [2000] 4 All ER 961; **355**
Re McArdle (1951); [1951] 1 All ER 905; **88**, 154–155
Re Moore & Co. v *Landauer & Co.* (1921); [1921] 2 KB 519; **104**, 129, 146
Re S (1996); unreported; **368**
Re Selectmove (1995); [1995] 2 All ER 531; **90**, 155
Read v *J Lyons & Co.* (1946); [1946] 2 All ER 471; **304**
Ready Mix Concrete v *Minister of Pensions* (1968); [1968] 1 All ER 433; 309–310, **309**
Redgrave v *Hurd* (1881); [1881–2] LR 20 Ch D 1; **121**
Reeman v *Department of Transport* (1997); [1997] 2 Lloyds Rep 648; 264–265
Reilly v *Merseyside Regional Health Authority* (1994); [1994] EWCA Civ 30; **253**
Reynolds (1988); unreported; **14**
Richardson (1998); [1999] Crim LR 62; **56**, 76
Richardson and Irwin (1999); [1999] Crim LR 494; **75**
Richardson v *LRC Products Ltd* (2000); [2001] 59 BMLR 185, [2000] Lloyd's Rep Med 280; **275**
Rickards v *Lothian* (1913); [1913] All ER Rep 71; **303**
Rimmington (2005); [2006] 2 All ER 257; **300**
Ritchie v *Atkinson* (1808); [1809] 10 East 530; **129**
Roberts (1971); [1971] 56 Crim App Rep; 71; **6, 37**, 72
Robinson v *Harman* (1848); [1848] 1 Exch Rep 850; (1843–60) All ER 383; 162
Rodger and Rose (1997); [1998] 1 Crim App Rep 143; **224**
Roe v *Minister of Health* (1954); [1954] 2 All ER 131; **249**
Roles v *Nathan* (1963); [1963] 2 All ER 908; **284**
Roscorla v *Thomas* (1842); [1842] 3 QB 234; **121**
Rose v *Miles* (1815); [1815] M & S 101; 299
Rose v *Plenty* (1975); [1976] 1 All ER 97; 313–314, **313**, 383, 396
Routledge v *Grant* (1828); [1828] 130 All ER 920; **83**, 152
Routledge v *McKay* (1954); [1954] 1 All ER 855; **101**
Royal College of Nursing v *DHSS* (1981); [1981] 1 All ER 545; **365**, 367
Royscot Trust v *Rogerson* (1991); [1991] 2 QB 297; **125**
Ruxley Electronics and Construction Ltd v *Forsyth* (1996); [1995] 3 All ER 268; **143**, 163
Ryan (1996); [1996] Crim LR 320; 189–190, **189**
Rylands v *Fletcher* (1868); [1868] LR1 EX 265; LR 3 HL 330; 232, 292, 302–306, **302**, 352, **380, 382**

S

St Helens Smelting v *Tipping* (1865); [1865] HLC 642; **294**
Saunders v *Leeds Western Health Authority* (1984); [1984] 129 Sol Jo 225; **249**
Savage (1992); [1991] 4 All ER 698; 33, **36–37, 367**
Schorsch Meier GmbH v *Hennin* (1974); [1975] 1 All ER 152; 366
Scotson v *Pegg* (1861); [1861] 6 H & N 295; 91
Scott v *Associated British Ports* (2000); Court of Appeal, 22 November 2000 (unreported); **288**

Scott v *London and St Katharine Dock* (1865); [1865] All ER 246; **249**

Scott v *Shepherd* (1773); [1773] 96 All ER 525; **242**

Sedleigh-Denfield v *O'Callaghan* (1940); [1940] 3 All ER 394; **293**

Shanklin Pier Ltd v *Detel Products Ltd* (1951); [1951] 2 All ER 471; **93–94**

Sharp (1987); [1987] 3 All ER 103; 220–221, **220**

Shaw v *DPP* (1962); [1961] 2 All ER 446; **333**, **365**

Shogun Finance Ltd v *Hudson* (2003); [2001] EWCA Civ 1000; 394

Shohid (2003); [2003] All ER (D) 216; **25**

Simpkins v *Pays* (1955); [1955] 3 All ER 10; **95**

Sion v *Hampstead Health Authority* (1994); [1994] 5 Med LR 170; **257**

Slingsby (1995); [1995] Crim LR 570; **55**

Small (1987); [1987] Crim LR 777; 177–178, **177**

Smedleys Ltd v *Breed* (1974); [1974] AC 839; 327, 379, **381**

Smith (1959); [1959] 2 All ER 193; **5**, 373

Smith (2000); [2000] 4 All ER 289; 364

Smith New Court Securities Ltd v *Scrimgeour Vickers* (1996); [1997] AC 254; **124**

Smith v *Baker* (1891); [1891] AC 325; **245**

Smith v *Eric S Bush* (1990); [1990] 1 AC 831; **265**

Smith v *Chief Superintendant of Woking Police Station* (1983); [1983] 76 Crim App Rep 234; **32**

Smith v *Finch* (2009); [2009] EWCH 53 (QB); [2009] All ER (D) 158 (Jan); **244**

Smith v *Hughes* (1960); [1960] 2 All ER 859; **360**

Smith v *Leech Brain & Co.* (1962); [1961] 3 All ER 1159; 251

Sofroniou (2004); [2003] EWCA Crim 3681; **205**

Spartan Steel and Alloys Ltd v *Martin and Co. (Contractors); Ltd* (1972); [1972] All ER 245; **261**, 262, 377

Spencer v *Wincanton Holdings* (2009); [2009] EWCA Civ 1404; **243**

Spice Girls Ltd v *Aprilia World Service BV* (2000); [2002] EWCA Civ 15; **120**, 121

Spratt (1990); [1991] 2 All ER 210; 367

Spring v *Guardian Assurance* (1994); [1994] 2 All ER 129; **265**

Spurling v *Bradshaw* (1956); [1956] 2 All ER 121; **111**, 350

Steele (1977); [1977] 65 Crim App Rep 22; 327

Steer (1987); [1987] 2 All ER 833; **196**

Stennett v *Hancock and Peters* (1939); [1939] 2 All ER 578; **269**

Stevenson v *McLean* (1880); [1880] 5 QBD 346; **85**

Stilk v *Myrick* (1809); [1809] 2 Camp 317; 90–91, **91**, 155

Stone and Dobinson (1977); [1977] 2 All ER 341; **20**, 22

Storey v *Ashton* (1869); [1869] LR 4 QB 476; **314**

Storkwain (1986); [1986] 2 All ER 635; **384**

Sturges v *Bridgeman* (1879); [1879] 11 Ch D 852; **297**

Sullivan (1984); [1983] 2 All ER 673; **44**

Sumpter v *Hedges* (1898); [1898] 1 QB 673; **130**

Sutradhar v *National Environment Research Council* (2006); [2006] 4 All ER 490; **235**

Sweet v *Parsley* (1970); [1969] 1 All ER 347; 379, **382**, 384

Swinney v *Chief Constable of Northumbria* (1996); [1996] 3 All ER 449; 351

T

T v *North Yorkshire County Council* (1998); [1998] EWCA Civ 1208; 358

Tabassum (2000); [2000] Crim LR 686; **56**, 76

Tate & Lyle Industries v *Greater London Council* (1983); [1983] 1 All ER 1159; **301**

Tate v *Williamson* (1866); [1866] 2 Ch App 55; **122**

Taylor v *Caldwell* (1863); [1863] 3 B & S 826; **132**, 393

Taylor v *Laird* (1856); [1856] 1 H & N 266; **83**

Tedstone v *Bourne Leisure Ltd* (2008); [2008] EWCA Civ 654; **283**

Tetley v *Chitty* (1986); [1986] 1 All ER 663; **293**

Thake v *Maurice* (1986); [1984] 2 All ER 513; **109**

Thomas (1985); [1985] 81 Crim App Rep 331; 33

Thomas v *BPE Solicitors* (2010); [2010] EWHC 306; **86**

Thomas v *Thomas* (1842); [1842], 2 QB 851, 114 All ER 330; **88**, 154

Thorne v *Motor Trade Association* (1937); [1937] 3 All ER 157; **186**

Thornton (1996); [1992] 1 All ER 306; **10**

Thornton v *Shoe Lane Parking Ltd* (1971); [1971] 1 All ER 686; **111**

Tomlinson v *Congleton Borough Council* (2003); [2003] 3 All ER 1122; **282**, 288, **290**

Transco plc v *Stockport MBC* (2003); [2004] 1 All ER 589; **302**, **303**, 304

Transfield Shipping Inc. v *Mercator Shipping Inc. (The 'Achilleas')* (2008); [2008] UKHL 48; **143**

Treacy v *DPP* (1971); [1971] 1 All ER 110; **186**

Troughton (1987); [1987] Crim LR 138; **209**

Tuberville v *Savage* (1669); [1669] 1 Mod Rep 3; 86 Eng Rep 684; **32**

Tulk v *Moxhay* (1848); [1848] 41 All ER 1143; **94**

Turner (No.2) (1971); [1971] 2 All ER 441; 172–173, **172**, 391

Tweddle v *Atkinson* (1861); [1861] 1 BS 393; **93**, 156, 393

Twine v *Bean's Express* (1946); [1946] 1 All ER 202; 380, 396

U

Union Eagle Ltd v *Golden Achievement Ltd* (1997); [1997] 2 All ER 215; **130**

V

Vacwell Engineering v *BDH Chemicals* (1970); [1970] 3 All ER 553; **241**

Valderrama-Vega (1985); [1985] Crim LR 220; **218**

Velumyl (1989); [1989] Crim LR 299; **176**

Venna (1976); [1975] 3 All ER 788; 34

Vickers (1957); [1957] 2 All ER 741; 6, 64

Victoria Laundry (Windsor) v *Newman Industries* (1949); [1949] 1 All ER 997; **143**, 345

Vincent (2001); [2001] EWCA Crim 295; **210**

W

W v *Essex County Council* (2000); [2000] 2 All ER 237; **259**

Wacker (2002); [2002] EWCA Crim 1944; **20**

The Wagon Mound (No. 1) (1961); [1961] 1 All ER 404; **241**, 376

The Wagon Mound (No. 2) (1966); [1966] 2 All ER 709; **298**

Wain (1995); [1995] 2 Crim App Rep 660; **174**

Walker v *Crystal Palace Football Club* (1909); [1910] 1 KB 87 (Court of Appeal); **309**

Walkington (1979); [1979] 2 All ER 716; **190**

Wallbank v *Wallbank Fox Designs* (2012); [2012] EWCA Civ 25; [2012] All ER (D) 01 (Feb); **313**

Walters v *North Glamorgan NHS Trust* (2002); [2002] EWCA Civ 1 792; **258**

Warwick (1995); [1995] 2 All ER 168; **196**

Watford Electronics Ltd v *Sanderson CFL* (2001); [2001] 1 All ER (Comm) 696, [2001] All ER (D) 290 Feb; **114**

Watson (1989); [1989] 2 All ER 865; **24**

Watson v *British Board of Boxing Control* (2001); [2001] QB 1134; **235**, 376

Watt v *Hertfordshire County Council* (1954); [1954] 2 All ER 368; **239**

Webster (2006); [2006] EWCA Crim 415; **172**

Weddall v *Barchester Healthcare* (2012); [2012] EWCA Civ 25; [2012] All ER (D) 01 (Feb); **313**

Weller v *Foot and Mouth Disease Research Institute* (1965); [1965] 3 All ER 560; 261–262, **261**

Wheat v *Lacon* (1966); [1966] 1 All ER 582; **283**

White (1910); [1910] 2 KB 124; **4**, 372

White and Carter (Councils); v *McGregor* (1962); [1961] 3 All ER 1178; **145**

White v *Chief Constable of South Yorkshire* (1998); [1999] 1 All ER 1; **255**

White v *Jones* (1995); [1995] 1 All ER 691; **262**

Whiteley v *Chappell* (1868); [1868] 4 LRQB 147; **359**, 361

Williams (1991); [1992] 2 All ER 183; **6**

Williams (Gladstone) (1987); [1987] 3 All ER 411; 392

Williams v *Phillips* (1957); [1957] 41 Crim App Rep 5; **173**

Williams v *Roffey Bros & Nichols (Contractors); Ltd* (1990); [1990] 1 All ER 512; **91–92**, 133, 155, **324**, 355

Wilsher v *Essex Area Health Authority* (1988); [1988] 1 All ER 871; **250**

Wilson (1996); [1996] 2 Crim App Rep 241; 325, 334, 357, 392

Wilson v *Burnett* (2007); [2007] EWCA 1170; [2007] All ER (D) 372 (Oct); **95–96**

Wilson v *Secretary of State for Industry* (2003); [2003] UKHL 40; **362**

Windle (1952); [1952] 2 All ER 1; **45**

Winzar v *Chief Constable of Kent* (1983); [1983] *The Times*, 28 March; 379, 384

With v *O'Flanagan* (1936); [1936] 1 All ER 727; **120**

Woodman (1974); [1974] 2 All ER 955; **173**

Wood (2008); [2008] EWCA Crim 1305; **17**

Woodward v *Mayor of Hastings* (1944); [1944] 2 All ER 565; **285**

Woollin (1998); [1998] 4 All ER 103; **7–8**, 63–64

Woollins v *British Celanese* (1966); [1966] 1 KIR 438; 283–284, **283**

Worsley v *Tambrands* (2000); [2000] PIQR 95; **276**

Y

Yachuk v *Oliver Blais* (1949); [1949] 2 All ER 150; **244**

Young v *Bristol Aeroplane* (1944); [1944] 2 ALL ER 293; 356

Table of statutes

Key statutes and their locators are in **bold**.

A

Abolition of the Death Penalty Act 1965 64–65
Abortion Act 1967 328, 365, 367
Access to Justice Act 1999 343
Aliens' Order 1920 379

B

Bail Act 1976 388

C

Children Act 1960 379
Civil Partnership Act 2004 364
Consumer Protection Act 1987 152, 268, 274–279, **274**, 352, **380**, 383
Consumer Protection (Distance Selling) Regulations 2000 86–87
Contract (Rights of Third Parties) Act 1999 94, 351, 393
Contributory Negligence Act 1945 244, 395
Coroners and Justice Act 2009 9–12, 14–15, 17, 65, 67, 373
Criminal Damage Act 1971 51, 78, 193–197, 215, 350, 391
Criminal Justice Act 1967 57, 63, 391
Criminal Justice Act 1972 346
Criminal Justice Act 1988 31
Criminal Justice Act 1998 346
Criminal Justice Act 2003 389
Criminal Justice and Immigration Act 2008 78, 227
Criminal Law Act 1967 78, 391
Criminal Procedure (Insanity and Unfitness to Plead) Act 1991 42

D

Dangerous Dogs Act 1991 324
Distance Selling Regulations 2000 86–87
Domestic Violence and Matrimonial Proceedings Act 1976 366

E

Electronic Commerce (EC Directive) Regulations 2002 86
Embryology Act 1994 367

F

Fraud Act 2006 169, 170, 198–210
Frustrated Contracts Act 1943 134–135, 137, 138–139, 394

H

Homicide Act 1957 9, 14–17, 42, 45, 67, 364, 373
Human Fertilisation and Embryology Act 1994 367
Human Rights Act 1998 324, 364, 365, 397–400

I

Immigration Act 2008 78, 227
Infant Life Preservation Act 1929 328
Insanity and Unfitness to Plead Act 1991 42

L

Law Reform (Contributory Negligence) Act 1945 244, 395
Law Reform (Frustrated Contracts) Act 1943 134–135, 137, 138–139, 394
Legal Aid, Sentencing and Punishment of Offenders Act 2012 78, 228

M

Malicious Damage Act 1861 362
Matrimonial Causes Act 1973 327
Matrimonial Proceedings Act 1976 366
Minimum Wage Act 1998 324
Misrepresentation Act 1967 122, 124, 125, 160
Murder (Abolition of the Death Penalty) Act 1965 64–65

O

Occupiers' Liability Act 1957 280–291, 377
Occupiers' Liability Act 1984 287–291, 323, 377
Offences against the Person Act (1861) 25, 35–41, 44, 51, 63–64, 69–71, 371, 374, 389, 392

P

Person Act 1861 328
Police and Criminal Evidence Act 1984 348, 387
Prevention of Terrorism Act 2005 398
Protection of Freedoms Act 2012 71
Protection from Harassment Act 1997 71

R

Race Relations Act 1965 328, 361
Race Relations Act 1976 362
Rights of Third Parties Act 1999 94, 351, 393

S

Sale of Goods Act 1979 100, 102–107, 113, 129, 140–141, 146, 157–158, 268
Sale of Goods Act 1994 141
Sentencing and Punishment of Offenders Act 2012 78, 228
Sexual Offences (Amendment) Act 2000 329
Sexual Offences Act 2003 325
Street Offences Act 1958 360
Supply of Goods and Services Act 1982 100, 103, 107, 108–110, 113, 157–158, 324

T

Theft Act 1968 167–180, 181, 187, 188–192, 194, 206, 208, 210, 325

U

Unfair Contracts Terms Act 1977 100, 113–118, 158–159, 286, 350
Unfair Terms in Consumer Contracts Regulations 1999 100, 115–118, 158–159, 350

W

Wage Act 1998 324
War Damage Act 1965 324

Criminal law
(fatal and non-fatal offences against the person)

Introduction

Chapters in this unit:

1 **Murder and voluntary manslaughter**

2 **Involuntary manslaughter**

3 **Non-fatal offences against the person**

4 **Defences**

Unit 3 gives candidates a choice between the study of criminal law and contract law. The unit constitutes 50 per cent of the overall marks for the A2 section of the qualification, and 25 per cent of the overall marks for the A Level qualification. The Unit 3 examination is of 1.5 hours' duration. Candidates must answer one question. The examination paper will include both criminal law and contract law questions: Questions 1 and 2 are on criminal law and Questions 3 and 4 are on contract law. Candidates who choose criminal law will have to select one question to answer, as will candidates who have chosen contract law. Each question is divided into three parts, all of which must be answered.

Each question is worth 75 marks. Each part is worth 25 marks. Parts (a) and (b) will be a test of your ability to select and apply the law to the given scenario, and part (c) will require an evaluative discussion of a stated area of the specification. All areas of the specification, including the defences, are possible questions for a critical evaluation including proposals for reform. The one exception is that no critical evaluation question will be asked on involuntary manslaughter.

All questions require essay-style answers. In Parts (a) and (b), you should aim to include: correct identification of the issues raised by the question; sound explanation of each of the points, and clear application of the law to the facts disclosed. This may involve some consideration of alternatives where the law lacks clarity in its application to the scenario. In Part (c), illustration may be in many forms – for example, legislation, cases, research, statistics, material from the media – and these need to be put into a coherent argument to answer the question set. Study tips are provided throughout each topic.

Unit 3A comprises four chapters:

1 **Murder and voluntary manslaughter:** concerned with the law with respect to murder and manslaughter.

2 **Involuntary manslaughter:** explains the law on involuntary manslaughter.

3 **Non-fatal offences against the person:** considers the law on non-fatal offences against the person.

4 **Defences:** concerned with the defences to the offences dealt with in Chapters 1–3.

1 Murder and voluntary manslaughter

In this topic, you will learn how to:

- state the definition of murder

- explain the *actus reus* and *mens rea* of murder

- explain cases that illustrate the *actus reus* of murder

- explain the issues and rules with respect to causation and murder

- apply the rules to a given situation.

1 Murder

Murder is an example of unlawful homicide. Homicide is the killing of one human being by another. It can be lawful or unlawful. One example of lawful homicide would be where a person kills another in self-defence, using no more than reasonable force in the circumstances. Another would be the killing of the enemy by a soldier on active duty in wartime. Unlawful homicides include manslaughter, both voluntary and involuntary (see the next chapter), and murder. Murder is the most serious form of unlawful homicide.

In this chapter, we will examine the definition of murder. We will also find what must be proved in order to prove guilt in a case of murder.

Definition of murder

Murder is a common law offence, and has never been defined by statute. The most commonly accepted definition is the one given by the early 17th-century judge, Sir Edward Coke. He defined murder as:

> ... the unlawful killing of a reasonable person in being and under the King's (or Queen's) peace with malice aforethought, express or implied.

The first part of this definition, the unlawful killing of a reasonable person in being and under the Queen's peace, describes the *actus reus* of murder. The second part, with malice aforethought, express or implied, describes the *mens rea* of murder. Both elements will be discussed in detail in the course of this chapter.

The *actus reus* of murder

'Unlawful killing'

As was stated at the beginning of this chapter, some killings might be lawful. Such killings are recognised by the law as being justified. For example, a person who kills while acting in self-defence or in the prevention of a crime, provided that the force used was reasonable in the circumstances, will not be guilty of an unlawful killing. Similarly, some killings might be authorised, such as those which take place during a war, or judicial executions in countries where the death penalty is carried out.

Omissions

In the majority of unlawful killings, the action that causes the death raises few legal problems. It may be the result of shooting, stabbing, strangulation and so on. However, in some cases the death may be the result not of a positive act but of an omission, or failure to act. If the accused has a duty towards a person and fails to carry out that duty and death results, then the *actus reus* of murder may exist. As has been seen in your AS law module, there are certain situations where this may happen. These include:

- a duty arising from a relationship, for example that between parent and child, such as *Gibbins and Proctor* (1918)

- a contractual duty, such as *Pittwood* (1902)

a duty arising from the accidental creation by the defendant of a dangerous chain of events, such as *Miller* (1983). It should be noted that no one died in *Miller*, but there remains potential liability for an omission.

A 'reasonable person in being'

The idea of a 'reasonable person in being' raises the question as to the point at which someone begins, and ceases, to be classed as a human being in the eyes of the law.

A foetus in the womb, having no existence independent of its mother, is not defined in law as 'in being'. It is only considered to be such when it has been fully expelled from its mother's body. It is not clear whether this is the case if the umbilical cord remains uncut, or if it is yet to take its first breath. However, if the foetus in the womb is deliberately injured and the child dies from these injuries after having been born, then the attacker would be criminally liable. This was decided in the *Attorney-General's Reference (No. 3 of 1994)* (1997); the verdict, however, would be likely to be manslaughter (see Chapter 2: Involuntary manslaughter), rather than murder.

Doctors are permitted to switch off life support machines of people who are 'brain dead', without being liable for unlawful homicide. It would seem therefore that one who is 'brain dead' is not generally considered to be a 'reasonable person in being'. Although there are no cases directly on this point, the related cases of *Malcherek and Steel* (1981) (dealt with later under Causation) would tend to confirm this.

Under the Queen's peace'

The killing of an enemy in war is not murder, as such a person is not 'under the Queen's peace'. It would, however, be considered the *actus reus* of murder to kill a prisoner of war.

Prosecution for murder

A feature of the crime of murder is that a British citizen can be tried in the domestic courts for a murder alleged to have been committed in the United Kingdom or in any other country.

A prosecution for murder can be brought at any time after the death of the victim. However, if death occurs more than three years after the injury that caused it, the consent of the Attorney-General is required to prosecute for murder. The same is true where a person has already been found guilty of an offence that was connected to the circumstances of the death.

Causation

The principles of causation have been studied in AS Law. It has to be proved that there is a direct and unbroken link between the defendant's act and its criminal consequence. The death of the victim has to be the direct result of the defendant's conduct. There must be no intervening act breaking the chain of causation. There must be both factual and legal causation. Factual causation is that the death would not have happened but for the conduct of the defendant. Legal causation requires the act to be the operating and substantial cause of the death. If the chain of causation is broken, then there is no liability for unlawful homicide. This does not necessarily mean, however, that there is no liability for the initial act – for example, for assault occasioning actual bodily harm.

Activity

Using only the material you have read so far in this chapter, do you think that the *actus reus* of murder is present in the following cases? Give reasons for your opinions.

a Arnold and Bert are steeplejacks. High up on a factory chimney, Bert pulls out a gun, points it at Arnold, and says that he is going to kill him for having an affair with his wife. Arnold lunges at Bert to knock the gun from his hand, and in doing so causes Bert to fall backwards off the scaffolding to his death.

b Cheryl has agreed to look after her aged uncle Dennis. He is dependent on various prescription drugs, but Cheryl, tired of the responsibility towards him, deliberately fails to get them for him. As a result of this, he dies.

c Eric, during the course of an argument, stabs his pregnant girlfriend. She recovers, but gives birth to their child prematurely. As a result of the premature birth, the child dies shortly afterwards.

Key cases

White (1910): mother died of a heart attack before poison administered by her son could take effect; chain of causation was broken.

Pagett (1983): police bullet killed girl being held as a human shield by defendant; defendant responsible for her death.

Cato (1976): mutual injection of drugs was more than a minimal cause of death.

Blaue (1975): refusal of blood transfusion following stabbing not the main cause of death.

Factual causation

In **White (1910)** the defendant put poison in his mother's drink with the intention of killing her. She took a little of the drink, but died of a heart attack before the poison could take effect. There was no evidence that the heart attack was in any way the result of the poison. There was therefore no direct link between White's act and his mother's death, and he was acquitted of murder. He was, however, found guilty of attempted murder.

A more controversial case illustrating actual causation is **Pagett (1983)**. The defendant, armed with a shotgun, was attempting to resist arrest. He forcibly held a 16-year-old girl in front of him as a human shield, and fired at the police officers. Instinctively, the police fired back at him, killing the girl. Pagett was tried for murder. He argued that it was not he who fired the shot that killed the girl. This was true, but it was held that, but for his action, the girl would not have been killed. His conduct was held to be the factual cause of her death. She died and Blaue was convicted of manslaughter.

Legal causation

The cause of death in unlawful homicide can vary between the substantial and the minimal. Stabbing a victim in the chest is clearly a substantial cause of death. The problem lies with the other end of the spectrum. The law does not require conduct to be substantial, but it must be more than a minimal cause of the death. A defendant can be guilty of unlawful homicide even if his conduct only contributed to the death, or if he was only one among others who contributed to it.

There must be a more than 'slight or trifling' link. An extreme example of a minimal cause would be if a person pricks the finger of another who is in the course of bleeding to death following an accident. The further loss of blood from the pin-prick may accelerate the death, but it could only be said to be a minimal cause.

In **Cato (1976)** two drug addicts had spent the night injecting each other with a mixture of heroin and water. In the morning, both were extremely ill, and one of them died. The other was charged with his friend's manslaughter. The Court of Appeal held that the heroin need not necessarily have been the only cause of death, but it was more than a minimal cause, and one that accelerated the moment of the victim's death.

'Taking the victim as he finds him'

When considering the chain of causation, it is necessary to bear in mind that the consequences of a person's conduct might be affected by unknown circumstances. For example, an attacker might hit someone on the head with a baseball bat in the course of a robbery. Normally, this might produce no more than a sore head and bruising. Unknown to the assailant, however, the victim has an unusually thin skull, and dies of his injuries. It is no good the defendant protesting that he didn't know about the thin skull; he must take the victim as he finds him. If a person's injuries are made more serious by some unusual physical or mental condition, then a defendant is liable for such injuries. This is usually known as the 'thin skull rule'.

The case which illustrates this rule is **Blaue (1975)**. The victim, a young woman, was stabbed by the defendant. It was necessary for her to have a blood transfusion, but her religion (she was a Jehovah's Witness) did not allow this. She died, and the defendant was found guilty of murdering her. It was no good his maintaining that a blood transfusion would have saved her; he had to take his victim as he found her.

New intervening acts

It is possible for the chain of causation to be broken by some new and independent event. In this case, the defendant will no longer be responsible for the consequence, providing that the intervening event is sufficiently different and serious. The intervening event could be the result of an act by a third party, some unforeseeable happening, or the victim's own action.

A case illustrating the first of these situations is **Jordan (1956)**. The victim had been stabbed in the stomach, and following treatment in hospital, his wounds were healing well. An antibiotic was given to him, and a large intake of liquid. It had previously been found that he had an allergy to the drug, and that he shouldn't be given large amounts of liquid. He suffered a severe allergic reaction and died. It was held that the actions of the medical staff were the main means of death, not the initial stab wound. There was a sufficiently independent intervening act, and the defendant was not guilty of murder.

However, it is unusual for medical treatment to be held to break the chain of causation. The two cases of **Smith (1959)** and **Cheshire (1991)** show that medical treatment will not break the chain where the original wound is still the operating cause of death.

In *Smith*, a soldier had been stabbed in the lung during a barrack-room brawl. He was taken to the medical centre, but was dropped on the way. When he eventually got there, the medical staff attempted to give him artificial respiration by pumping on his chest. This worsened his condition and he died. Although the treatment he had received drastically reduced his chances of survival, Smith was found guilty of his murder.

In *Cheshire*, a victim had been shot in the stomach and thigh. In hospital, a tube was inserted in his throat to help him breathe more easily. As a result of rare complications following this tracheotomy, the victim died. The complications had not been noticed by the doctors. Although his wounds at the time were no longer life threatening, Cheshire was held responsible for his death.

At the beginning of this chapter, when considering 'reasonable persons in being', the cases of **Malcherek and Steel (1981)** were mentioned. Both cases involved switching off the life-support machines of victims who were considered to be 'brain dead'. *Malcherek and Steel* (1981) established that such switching off does not break the chain of causation, and therefore death is the result of the defendant's action.

Action taken by the victim

It is not difficult to imagine situations where a victim who feels threatened takes drastic action to escape, and in doing so is injured or is killed. Consider the case of a person who dies as a result of jumping from a first-storey window to escape an attacker. Does this action break the chain of causation? Is the death the direct result of the attacker's action, or the independent act of the victim? It depends, of course, on the nature and seriousness of the threat. If the threat to the victim is serious, then it would be more reasonable for him to take the evasive action that resulted in his injury. In such a case, the chain of causation would not be held to be broken. If, on the other hand, the threat was of a relatively trivial or minor nature, then drastic evasive action would be held to break the chain of causation. Two cases that illustrate this point both involve jumping out of moving cars.

	Key cases

Jordan (1956): wrong administration of drug in hospital was a new intervening act.

Smith (1959): clumsy and inappropriate treatment of a soldier following a stabbing did not break the chain of causation.

Cheshire (1991): the victim, whose wounds were no longer life-threatening, died as a result of unusual complications; no break in chain of causation.

Malcherek and Steel (1981): two separate cases raised the same point of law; turning off a life support machine was not a new intervening act so no break in chain of causation.

Malcherek established that switching off life support does not break the chain of causation, and therefore death is the result of the defendant's action

Key cases

Roberts (1971): victim jumped from moving car to avoid sexual advances; chain of causation was not broken.

Williams (1991): victim broke chain of causation because his reaction was unreasonable.

Vickers (1957): intention to cause serious bodily harm is sufficient for the *mens rea* of murder.

In **Roberts (1971)** the driver of the car turned off down a side road and subjected his passenger to unwanted sexual advances. She jumped out of the moving car in order to escape, and was injured. It was held that the defendant was liable for her injuries. There was a direct line of causation between his conduct and her injuries, which had not been broken by her act.

In **Williams (1991)** on the other hand, the victim jumped out of a moving car because he alleged that there had been an attempt to steal his wallet. Because this was held to be an unreasonable reaction under the circumstances, and disproportionate to the threat, it was held that the chain of causation had been broken by the victim's intervening act. The defendant was not liable for the victim's injuries.

Activity

What do you think the criminal liability might be in the following cases?

1. Gert is unable to tolerate her unhappy marriage to Harry any longer. After Harry has gone to bed, she takes a knife and stabs him. Unknown to her, the equally desperate Harry was already dead, having taken a large overdose of drugs half an hour earlier.

2. Mahmoud is attacked by Naseem and suffers serious, though not fatal, injuries. On its way to take Mahmoud to the hospital, the ambulance is involved in a high-speed car crash in which the driver of the ambulance and Mahmoud are killed.

3. Oona is on a fairground ride, during the course of which the person next to her attempts to indecently assault her. Desperate to get away, she jumps out and, being hit by the following car, is fatally injured.

The *mens rea* of murder

'Malice aforethought, express or implied'

'Malice afterthought, express or implied' is the *mens rea* of murder as defined by Sir Edward Coke. Case law has identified some extensions of this definition. There is no requirement for 'malice' to be present. It is possible to imagine a situation where a killing takes place from motives of love or compassion. An example might be of a parent who gives a fatal overdose of drugs to a child suffering from an intolerably painful terminal illness, as in *Gray* (1965). 'Aforethought' does not need any previous planning or thinking about it beforehand, merely that the intention to kill does not occur after the act. The *mens rea* of an unlawful killing is an intention to kill or cause grievous bodily harm.

If a defendant who kills has either of these intentions, then he is guilty of murder. Notice that this is the case even when the defendant does not expressly intend to kill his victim. The intention to cause grievous (meaning serious) bodily harm is enough for a conviction for murder.

This was established in **Vickers (1957)**, a decision confirmed by the House of Lords in *Cunningham* (1982). In *Vickers* (1957) the defendant had broken into the cellar of an old lady's shop. When she discovered him there, he attacked her savagely by punching her and kicking her in the head. She died from her injuries. The court held that an intention to inflict grievous bodily harm, resulting in the death of the victim, was enough to imply the necessary intention for murder.

Foresight of consequences

The express intention to kill is usually straightforward to identify. For example, a terrorist who puts a bomb on a passenger airliner, resulting in its blowing up at 35,000 feet, can safely be assumed to intend the death of his victims. Similarly, implied intention can often be safely inferred where the defendant clearly intended to cause serious injury, as in *Vickers* (1957).

The main difficulty arises when the defendant's main aim is not to kill or cause serious injury, but to achieve some quite different end. Several cases over the years have attempted to clarify this matter by examining the question of foresight. How far can intention to kill or cause serious injury be inferred from the defendant's foreseeing the consequences of his actions? This was considered in the cases of **Moloney (1985)**, **Hancock and Shankland (1986)** and **Nedrick (1989)**.

In *Moloney* (1985) the defendant had been drinking with his stepfather, a man with whom he was apparently on good terms. In the early hours, the two men had challenged each other as to who could be first to load his gun and be ready to fire. Moloney won, pointed his gun at his stepfather, pulled the trigger and killed him instantly. He maintained that he had no intention whatever of killing or causing injury; it was 'just a lark'. Following the direction of the judge at his trial, he was found guilty of murder. The House of Lords, however, allowed his appeal, and changed the verdict to manslaughter. They held that nothing less than the actual intention to kill or cause serious harm should constitute the necessary *mens rea* for murder. The mere foresight of probable death or serious injury was not in itself intent, though it could be evidence from which a jury might infer intention.

In *Hancock and Shankland* (1986) the House of Lords further developed the decision in *Moloney* (1985). Two striking miners had dropped large blocks of concrete from a bridge over a road into the path of a taxi with a police escort taking a non-striking miner to work. One piece of concrete hit the taxi's windscreen, killing the driver. The defendants claimed that their only intention was to block the road, not to kill or injure anyone. In allowing their appeal and substituting a verdict of manslaughter, the House of Lords ruled that in such a case the degree of probability of death or injury was of paramount importance. It was suggested that juries should be directed that:

- the greater the probability of a consequence, the more likely it is that the consequence was foreseen
- if the consequence was foreseen, the greater the probability is that it was also intended
- juries must be reminded that the decision is theirs to be reached upon a consideration of all the evidence.

In *Nedrick* (1986) the defendant had poured paraffin through the letterbox of a house, with the intention of frightening the woman who lived there. A child died in the resulting fire. The defendant's appeal against his conviction for murder was allowed. The Court of Appeal suggested that the jury members should in future consider the following:

- Do they feel that death or serious injury was the virtually certain result of the accused's voluntary act?
- Did the accused foresee that death or serious injury was the virtually certain result of his act?

If the answer to both was 'yes', then the jury could reasonably infer that the accused intended the consequences of his act.

A further development took place in the case of **Woollin (1998)**, in which the defendant lost his temper while feeding his baby son. He threw the baby against a wall, and it died of its injuries. In allowing Woollin's appeal against a conviction for murder, the House of Lords approved the direction given in *Nedrick* (1986), provided that the word 'find' was substituted for 'infer'. The jury therefore should not 'find' the necessary intention unless the answers to the two questions above are 'yes'. This

Key cases

Moloney (1985): defendant killed his stepfather in drunken game; nothing less than the actual intention to kill or cause serious harm should be the *mens rea* in murder.

Hancock and Shankland (1986): striking miners dropped concrete blocks into the path of a taxi, killing its driver; foresight of consequences may amount to intention, but it is up to the jury.

Nedrick (1986): a child died in a fire caused by the defendant; jury should ask itself two questions; if answer to both is 'yes', it may infer the probable intention.

Woollin (1998): defendant killed his baby son in a fit of temper; if the answers to the questions in *Nedrick* (1989) are 'yes', the jury must find, rather than infer, intention.

would seem to suggest that the House of Lords again found in *Woollin* (1998) that foresight of consequence amounts to intention, when in *Moloney* (1985) it had ruled that it was not necessarily so.

Foresight of consequences was again considered in **Matthews and Alleyne (2003)**, in which the defendants had thrown their victim from a bridge into a river. They knew that he could not swim, and they left the scene before he could reach safety. The victim drowned. The defendants argued on appeal that the direction given at their trial suggested that foresight of consequences was the same as intention. However, the Court of Appeal regarded foresight of consequences being the same as intention to be more as a rule of evidence. A jury in such a case is entitled to find the existence of intention, but does not necessarily have to. Despite what the Court of Appeal may have considered to be a technical misdirection, it decided that it would not have made any difference to the jury's decision. The conviction of Matthews and Alleyne was therefore upheld.

Key cases

Matthews and Alleyne (2003): victim died as a result of being thrown into a river: foresight of consequences as being the same as intention is more like a rule of evidence.

Conclusion

The best way of expressing the present position is as follows:

A person commits murder when he kills another with the necessary intent.

Intention for murder is nothing less than the intention to kill or cause serious bodily harm. The defendant's foresight of the consequences of his actions is no more than evidence from which the jury may find intent.

Activity

What do you think might be the liability for murder in the following cases? Give your reasons.

1 Peter is in severe financial trouble. He places some fake cargo in a freight plane, primed with a bomb and timed to explode in mid-air. In this way, he hopes to claim insurance on the fake goods. The plane is destroyed at 30,000 feet, and all the crew are killed as a result.

2 Quin interferes with the power steering of his girlfriend Rosie's car, with the intention of preventing her from meeting a secret lover. On leaving her drive, Rosie tries to turn into the road, but cannot avoid an approaching vehicle. The oncoming car crashes into her, and she is killed immediately.

3 Tracey, a member of an extreme terrorist group, enters a pub carrying a holdall that contains a bomb. She shouts a warning, and immediately runs out. Very shortly afterwards, the bomb explodes, killing three people who were unable to get out in time.

You should now be able to:

- state the definition of murder

- explain the *actus reus* of murder, giving cases as examples

- explain causation in relation to murder

- explain the law relating to murder

- apply the law to given scenarios.

2 Voluntary manslaughter: loss of control

Definition of voluntary manslaughter

Voluntary manslaughter arises where the definition of murder appears to have been satisfied (both *actus reus* and *mens rea*) but one of two possible defences granted by statute can be successfully pleaded. This will reduce the offence from murder to voluntary manslaughter, allowing more discretion to the judge in sentencing.

It is essential to understand that a defendant cannot be charged with voluntary manslaughter. He is charged with murder – then if, at his trial, he successfully pleads one of the two defences, he will be convicted of voluntary manslaughter.

The law on voluntary manslaughter is a mixture of statute and common law rules on interpretation. The defences are set out in the Coroners and Justice Act 2009 and the Homicide Act 1957. They are:

- loss of control
- diminished responsibility.

These defences are only available to a charge of murder, which is why they are referred to as special. Their effect is to reduce the conviction from murder to manslaughter, enabling the judge to pass a discretionary sentence instead of a mandatory life sentence.

Loss of control replaces defence of provocation

Section 54 Coroners and Justice Act 2009 abolished the defence of provocation. The defence of provocation allowed a defence in circumstances where the defendant killed whilst suffering a sudden and temporary loss of control, on account of provoking words or conduct, and acted as a reasonable person would have done in that situation. The new defence is defined under s54(1) and states:

> Where a person kills or is party to the killing of another, the defendant is not to be convicted of murder if:
>
> (i) the defendant's acts and omissions resulted from the defendant's loss of self-control
>
> (ii) the loss of self-control had a qualifying trigger
>
> (iii) a person of the defendant's age and sex, with a normal degree of tolerance and self-restraint and in the circumstances of the defendant, might have reacted in the same or a similar way.

1 The loss of self-control

Section 54(2) states that the loss of self-control doesn't have to be sudden. In other words, there may be a time delay between the qualifying trigger and the reaction of the defendant in killing the victim. However, there must still be a loss of self-control. Therefore the longer the delay, the less likely the jury is to believe that the killing resulted from a loss of self-control.

In the case of **Ibrams and Gregory (1981)** the defendants and a young woman had been harassed and threatened by the victim. The three of them devised a plan that involved the woman, who was the ex-girlfriend of the victim, luring him into bed; at this stage, the defendants would burst in and attack him. The plan was carried out four days later and the victim was killed. The defendants were found guilty of murder but appealed on the grounds that they had been provoked by the victim's threatening behaviour. Their appeal was turned down on the basis that their crime had been planned over a number of days and there was no sudden loss

In this topic, you will learn how to:

- state the definition of loss of control
- explain the elements of loss of control
- explain cases that illustrate circumstances that can amount to loss of control
- explain cases that illustrate circumstances that can fulfil the objective test
- apply the rules to a given situation.

Key cases

Ibrams and Gregory (1981): there will be no defence to murder where the defendant is motivated by a desire for revenge.

of control. Unlike the law of provocation, under which it was necessary to prove that the defendant had a sudden loss of control, the defence of loss of control does not require there to be a sudden loss of control. However, in a case where there is evidence of planning, such as in *Ibrams and Gregory* (1981), the defence would fail. The Coroners and Justice Act expressly excludes the defence where the killing is motivated by a considered desire for revenge s54 (4).

The longer the gap between the trigger and the killing, the less likely it will be for the defence to succeed, but the defendant may be able to prove that he remained out of control throughout the relevant period. A case that may assist on this point, but which was decided under the law of provocation, was the case of **Baillie (1995)**.

In this case, the defendant discovered that his sons had been supplied with drugs and threatened by a drug dealer. He took his sawn-off shotgun and cut-throat razor and drove to where the dealer lived. On the way, there was a delay because of a road accident. At the dealer's house, there was an argument and the defendant fatally shot the dealer. The defendant was convicted of murder at the trial, but his appeal succeeded on the basis that although there had been a delay between the loss of control and the killing, he did not regain control during that time. In similar cases, there would need to be some debate over whether the defendant was still suffering a loss of self-control or was acting out of revenge.

Removal of the requirement for suddenness is one of the major differences between the loss of control defence and the previous defence of provocation, where the loss of self-control had to be sudden and temporary. The main reason for the reform was that this defence was difficult to plead in the cases of women who killed their partners after suffering domestic violence. Because women, and particularly those in abusive relationships, are less likely to respond to violence immediately, claims were unlikely to succeed because of the time that elapsed. These issues were highlighted in the famous cases of Kiranjit Ahluwalia and Sara Thornton.

In **Ahluwalia (1992)** the defendant had been abused by her husband over many years. One night, after a day on which she had again suffered violence, she poured petrol on him while he slept and set him alight. Her husband died from the injuries and she was convicted of his murder. Although her appeal to reduce her conviction to voluntary manslaughter was successful, it was on the grounds of diminished responsibility because there was too long a delay between the abuse from her husband and the killing for the defence of provocation.

In **Thornton (1996)** the defendant had suffered violence at the hands of her husband over many months. One night, after he had returned home drunk and abusive, she went to the kitchen to calm down and then looked for a weapon. She sharpened a carving knife and then returned to the lounge where she stabbed and killed her husband. She was convicted of murder. At the first appeal, the defence of provocation failed because the Court of Appeal said that there was not a sudden and temporary loss of control. At her second appeal, the court recognised that it was possible to have a situation where although the final incident may not seem enough to cause the defendant to lose control, it needs to be considered in the context of the other incidents. In her case, her husband's abuse on that evening was considered the final straw in a build-up of provocation.

2 The qualifying triggers

The defendant must prove that his loss of self-control was a result of one of the triggers permitted under the Act. Section 55 identifies three qualifying triggers. They are as follows:

Key cases

Baillie (1995): Baillie was successful in pleading provocation even though there was a delay before the killing, as he remained out of control during the relevant period of time.

Ahluwalia (1992): defendant waited for her husband to fall asleep before killing him; because of this delay, provocation was not available as a defence.

Thornton (1996): defendant killed her husband after a delay following an abusive incident; 'last straw' could trigger final loss of self-control.

At Sara Thornton's second appeal against the conviction for the murder of her husband the court held that it was possible that a minor incident could act as the last straw and trigger a sudden final loss of control, following a long build-up of provocation. A retrial was ordered at which, in 1996, the jury acquitted her of murder.

Fear of serious violence from victim

The defendant will need to establish that he lost control because of a genuine fear of serious violence. This is a subjective test and it does not matter that the fear was unreasonable and it does not need to be shown that there was any actual violence. However, the jury needs to be convinced that the fear was genuine and there is likely to be an objective assessment of what 'serious' violence is. The threat of a minor assault would not be serious even if the defendant perceived it to be. The fear must be of violence against the defendant or an identifiable person, not against people in general. For example, the defendant could be afraid that the victim would use serious violence against his child, but serious violence against someone that the defendant doesn't know is insufficient. Although there is no requirement that the serious violence should be imminent, where the threat is anticipated at a much later and unspecified time, the defence is unlikely to succeed.

Loss of control from a fear of serious violence will normally be pleaded where the amount of force used is considered excessive in response to the threat. An example of this is in *Ahluwalia* (1992) where the abusive husband was actually asleep when the defendant fatally attacked him. In cases where the force used was considered reasonable, the defendant could plead the defence of self-defence. This is a total defence and leads to an acquittal. Self-defence is discussed in Chapter 4: Defences.

Things done and/or said which constituted circumstances of a grave character but also caused the defendant to have a justifiable sense of being seriously wronged

This is known as the anger trigger and is much more restrictive than the previous law, where there were no restrictions on what constituted provoking acts or words. There were concerns that very trivial acts or words could be cited as a reason for losing control, and in the case of *Doughty* (1986) a crying baby was said to amount to provocation. In order for this trigger to apply the defendant will have to satisfy two aspects: that the circumstances were of a grave character and that he had a justifiable sense of being seriously wronged. These are assessed objectively, so it is for the jury to decide what a reasonable person would think, rather than from the defendant's perspective. There may be situations where the defendant does feel aggrieved because of taunts or insults. However, this will be insufficient if the jury does not think that the circumstances are of a grave character or does not think it was justifiable to feel seriously wronged. An example of where the anger trigger would apply is in a situation where a father loses control and kills a man whom he finds raping his daughter. In such a case a jury would consider the circumstances to be of a grave character and would consider his sense of being seriously wronged to be justified.

A combination of both triggers

There may be situations where the defendant argues that a combination of factors taken as a whole, although each one would be insufficient alone, caused the defendant to lose control.

Restrictions

Section 55 of the Act also identifies restrictions on the availability of the qualifying triggers.

Incitement

The defendant's fear of serious violence is to be disregarded if the defendant himself deliberately incited the violence from the victim. This might arise where the defendant taunts the victim with abuse or threats in order to provoke the victim into saying or doing something that might justify the defendant killing him. As an example, the defendant tells the victim that he has had unprotected sex with the victim's sister in the full knowledge that he is infected with HIV. The victim then goes to attack the defendant, who responds by killing him and then argues that he acted because of fear of violence. In this case, the defendant would have incited the violence. The defence will be unavailable if the defendant incites either of the qualifying triggers.

Sexual infidelity

Sexual infidelity is also to be disregarded as a potential trigger. This is one of the controversial changes in the law, as under the law of provocation there were no restrictions. So, for example, if the defendant finds out his partner is having an affair and loses his temper, the defence of loss of control is not available to the defendant. Only the fact of sexual infidelity is disregarded; other related circumstances of an extremely grave character might still potentially amount to a qualifying trigger if they caused the defendant to have a justifiable sense of being seriously wronged. If a woman kills her husband after discovering that he paid for sex with underage girls, it could be argued that the trigger was not her husband's infidelity but her outrage at his criminal activity and lack of morality.

The question as to when a judge should put the defence to the jury in cases involving sexual infidelity was considered in the recent case of **Clinton (2012)**. This case was one of the first to go to the Court of Appeal for an interpretation of the new law. At his trial for murdering his wife, Clinton had been told that the defence of loss of control could not be put to the jury because the trigger was sexual infidelity. Clinton's wife of 16 years left him and he found sexual photographs on her Facebook pages showing she was having affairs with other men. Two weeks after leaving him, she came back to the family home, and when Clinton asked about the photographs she taunted him with details of her sexual exploits. She also said that she was leaving him for good and didn't want the children to live with her. She noticed that he had been looking at websites about committing suicide and remarked that he would not have guts to do it. The Court of Appeal decided that where sexual infidelity is not the only trigger, there is not a total exclusion and the defence can be put to the jury. It was argued that the victim's other comments – about the defendant not having the guts to kill himself, and about her not wanting their children to live with her – could be sufficient for the second trigger. Consequently, a retrial was ordered so that the defence could be put before a jury.

Revenge

The defence is not available to a defendant who acts from motives of revenge, even if the defendant loses control as a result of one of the qualifying triggers.

3 The objective test

A jury must consider whether a person of the defendant's own sex and age, with a normal degree of tolerance and self-restraint, might have reacted in the same or a similar way to the defendant in the given circumstances. In the case of **Camplin (1978)** the 15-year-old defendant killed a man who sexually attacked him, and it was decided that the age and sex of the defendant is relevant in considering the objective test.

After years of uncertainty under the previous law as to which characteristics are relevant, the position now, under the Coroners and Justice Act 2009, allows all the defendant's circumstances to be taken into account – apart from those that affect his capacity for tolerance and self-restraint. This means that a jury could consider that a defendant had a history of being abused by their partner in cases like *Ahluwalia* and

Clinton (2012): there is not a total exclusion on sexual infidelity as a trigger if there are other things done or said that contributed to the defendant's loss of control.

Camplin (1978): fifteen-year-old boy killed his tormentor with a chapati pan: 'reasonable person' test not confined to adult male.

Mohammed (2005): defendant's bad temper must be disregarded when considering what a reasonable person would have done in the same situation (objective test).

Holley (2005): alcoholism and depression are not relevant characteristics for the objective test as they affect capacity for tolerance.

Thornton, but it is insufficient that the defendant is simply bad-tempered and prone to violence. The case of **Mohammed (2005)** illustrates this point.

Mohammed was a strict Muslim father with a reputation for being violent and bad-tempered. He found his daughter in her bedroom with her boyfriend. The man ran away but Mohammed went to get a knife and stabbed his daughter to death. Mohammed's bad-tempered disposition was not relevant in deciding what a reasonable man would have done in the circumstances. This case would be decided the same under the new law, as he would be compared to someone with normal powers of restraint.

The case of **Holley (2005)** concerned an alcoholic and depressive defendant who killed his partner with an axe after finding out she had slept with another man. Unlike the new defence, under the previous law sexual infidelity could justify provocation. However, the significant factor for the objective test is that the defendant's alcoholism and depression could not be considered, as these circumstances would affect a person's capacity for tolerance and self-restraint. It is unclear as to how judges will interpret this test in situations where the defendant is being taunted about his alcoholism, for example. It would seem logical that this would then be considered as part of the circumstances, but this needs to be clarified in future case law. However, depression and alcoholism could be used to argue a defence under diminished responsibility, as they are recognised medical conditions.

In many cases where the defendant argues that he killed because of a justifiable sense of being seriously wronged, it is likely that the defence will be withheld from the jury. The reason for this is that it will only be in exceptional cases that a person of normal tolerance and self-restraint is driven to kill.

Burden of proof

The defendant must raise sufficient evidence to support the defence. If not, the trial judge can refuse to let the jury consider the defence of loss of control. If the evidence is put to the jury, the burden of disproving it beyond all reasonable doubt is on the prosecution.

When assessing the defence of loss of control, ask yourself the following questions:

- Did the defendant actually lose self-control?
- Was there a delay between the incident causing the loss of control and the killing, and if so is it relevant?
- Did the defendant lose control on account of one of the qualifying triggers, and if so which one or was it a combination?
- Did the defendant incite the victim?
- Did the defendant lose control on account of sexual infidelity, and if so are there any other factors that could be considered?
- Was the defendant acting out of a considered desire for revenge?
- Would a person with the defendant's characteristics and a normal level of tolerance have acted the way the defendant did?

You should now be able to:

- explain the law relating to loss of control
- apply the law to given scenarios.

Activities

1. Consider whether the defence of loss of control would succeed in the following three situations:

   a Sally and Mark are married. One day, Sally discovers that Mark has been having a sexual relationship with a man. Sally is so angry that she picks up a bread knife and stabs him in the chest, killing him instantly.

   b Tom is angry with Jack over a bet that he has lost, and he threatens to get his mates to sort Jack out if he doesn't forget the bet. Jack gets into his car and starts to drive at speed towards Tom, who picks up a brick and throws it at the windscreen. This causes Jack to crash his car, which leads to his death.

   c Ranjit was in a car accident in which her young son died and in which she suffered a head injury that left her unable to control her temper. On her return to work, she overhears a work colleague make a remark that Ranjit is responsible for her son's death because he wasn't properly strapped in to the car seat. In a rage, Ranjit storms out of the building and returns an hour later with a hammer. She uses it to hit her colleague, who dies later in hospital.

2. Use the internet to research the case of Andrew Lindo, who killed his partner and was convicted of murder when his defence of loss of control was unsuccessful. Work out why you think the defence failed.

In this topic, you will learn how to:

■ state the definition of diminished responsibility

■ explain the relationship of diminished responsibility

■ explain cases that illustrate circumstances that can amount to abnormality of mind and causes of abnormality of mind

■ explain cases that can illustrate circumstances that can amount to substantial impairment

■ apply the rules to a given situation.

3 Voluntary manslaughter: diminished responsibility

The defence of diminished responsibility was introduced by the Homicide Act 1957, s2. The defence of insanity (see Chapter 4) had existed before then, and still does. However, the test for insanity is too narrow to include many of the mental problems from which people can suffer. The verdict when a person successfully pleads insanity is 'not guilty by reason of insanity'. In a trial for murder, the result of successfully pleading the defence of diminished responsibility is to change the verdict to one of manslaughter. This is still the case following the Coroners and Justice Act 2009.

Section 52 of the Coroners and Justice Act 2009 replaces section 2(1) of the Homicide Act 1957 with new subsections (1) to (1B). The correct citation for diminished responsibility remains Homicide Act 1957, s2.

New definition of diminished responsibility

The 'abnormality of mind' as expressed in the previous definition prior to The Coroners and Justice Act 2009 is replaced by the words 'abnormality of mental functioning'. Section 2 of the Homicide Act 1957 now states:

> A person who kills or is party to a killing is not to be convicted of murder if the defendant was suffering from an abnormality of mental functioning which:
>
> i) arose from a recognised medical condition
>
> ii) substantially impaired the defendant's ability to do one of the following:
>
> ■ understand the nature of his conduct
> ■ form a rational judgement
> ■ exercise self-control
>
> iii) provides an explanation for the defendant's acts and omissions in doing the killing or being a party to the killing.

An abnormality of mental functioning provides an explanation for the defendant's conduct if it causes, or is a significant contributory factor in causing, the defendant to carry out that conduct.

An abnormality of mental functioning which arose from a recognised medical condition

Under the 1957 Homicide Act, 'abnormality of mind' has been held to cover many different kinds of medical condition, such as psychotic disorders (**Byrne (1960)**), clinical depression, and epilepsy. It can also be the result of post-natal depression, (**Reynolds (1988)**), pre-menstrual tension (**English (1981)**) and battered wife syndrome (*Ahluwalia* (1992)).

The Coroners and Justice Act 2009 recognises that there are many different existing lists that classify accepted physical, psychiatric and psychological conditions. Foremost among these are the World Health Organisation's international classification of diseases, and the American Psychiatric Association's diagnostic and statistical manual of mental disorders. If a jury accepts that, at the time of the killing, a defendant was suffering from a condition included in one of these lists, then the test in (a), above, will be met.

Key cases

Byrne (1960): a sexual psychopath's inability to control his perverted desires meant he could plead diminished responsibility.

Reynolds (1988): a young mother killed her mother with a hammer: post-natal depression could cause diminished responsibility.

English (1981): a woman who killed could bring evidence to show that her responsibility had been impaired enough by pre-menstrual tension to admit the defence of diminished responsibility.

Ex-soldier Aaron Wilkinson sentenced for killing woman

Gamekeeper Aaron Wilkinson, 24, was jailed for a minimum of five years at Bradford Crown Court for killing 52-year-old Judith Garnett by shooting her in the chest and head. But he will not be released until he no longer poses a threat to public safety.

Wilkinson was cleared in April of murdering Mrs Garnett but admitted manslaughter on the grounds of diminished responsibility.

At the time of the killing, Wilkinson was suffering from post-traumatic stress disorder after a tour in Afghanistan during which he witnessed three Afghan soldiers being blown up by an improvised explosive device and suffered a shrapnel wound during an intense two-day battle with the Taliban.

He has also been diagnosed with Asperger's syndrome, or a similar condition, since his return from war in 2009.

Wilkinson said he could not explain why he shot Mrs Garnett and said it was as though he was in a 'trance'. The jury accepted that the combination of Asperger's syndrome and PTSD had left Wilkinson unable to fully exercise self-control at the time of the attack.

But the judge rejected the idea that he could not exercise any [self-control] at all as Wilkinson loaded a third cartridge into the shotgun and shot Mrs Garnett in the head, having already shot her twice.

He said: 'There was an element of calculation in which you could have paused and made greater efforts to restrain yourself. After you had fired the first two shots either instinctively as you say, or with some calculation I think, you then calmly loaded a third cartridge and that is a moment where you could have made greater efforts to restrain yourself'.

The Independent, 6 July 2012

There may well be new or emerging conditions that are recognised, but that are not on one of the accepted lists. In such a case, the defence can call an acknowledged specialist whose work has been validated. It will then be up to the jury, properly directed, to consider this evidence.

Byrne (1960) was an early case following the Homicide Act 1957 that examined the issue of 'abnormality of mind'. The defendant was a sexual psychopath who strangled a young woman and then mutilated her body. At his trial, he was found guilty of murder. On appeal, however, the Court of Appeal substituted a conviction for murder for one of manslaughter.

The court said that:

> Abnormality of mind ... means a state of mind so different from that of ordinary human beings that the reasonable man would term it abnormal It seems to us to be wide enough to cover the mind's activities in all its aspects, not only the perception of physical acts and matters, and the ability to form a rational judgement as to whether an act is right or wrong, but also the ability to exercise willpower to control physical acts in accordance with that rational judgement.

Byrne was not able to resist the impulse to gratify his perverted desires, therefore the defence of diminished responsibility was available to him. (Although the verdict was changed to manslaughter, the court saw no reason to alter his sentence of life imprisonment).

Substantial impairment

The Homicide Act 1957 required that a person's mental responsibility must be substantially impaired, but did not specify in which way. The Coroners and Justice Act 2009 attempts to clarify this.

It must be shown that the abnormality of mental functioning substantially impaired the defendant's ability to understand the nature of his conduct, to form a rational judgement, or to exercise self-control. In a case where the defendant has psychopathic tendencies, as in *Byrne* (1960), the condition would affect his ability to exercise self-control. A defendant who had been suffering from depression or battered wife syndrome may argue that they were unable to form a rational judgement.

The question as to whether there was substantial impairment will be a question for the jury, and the definition remains the same as it did under the previous law (*Brown* 2011). In the case of **Egan (1992)** it was confirmed that the word 'substantial' '[means] more than some trivial degree of impairment [that] does not make any appreciable difference to a person's ability to control himself, but it means less than total impairment'.

The abnormality must provide an explanation for the killing

Under the revised definition, there is now a causal element that means the abnormality should cause, or be a significant contributory factor in causing, the defendant to kill. The defence will fail if the evidence suggests that the defendant would have killed anyway, irrespective of the abnormality. This issue as to what caused the defendant to act as he did is complicated if the defendant has been drinking alcohol or taking drugs, as mental abnormality as a result of intoxication is not included in the defence.

Abnormality and intoxication

If a defendant is suffering from an abnormality of mental functioning, and takes drugs or consumes alcohol and then kills the victim, the defence may be available even if the voluntary intoxication played a part in the decision to kill.

In **Gittens (1984)** the defendant killed his wife and stepdaughter while heavily intoxicated and suffering from depression. On appeal against his murder conviction, the Court of Appeal held that the jury should have been directed to disregard the effect of the intoxication and then consider whether his depression was sufficient to impair his mental responsibility. Because of the misdirection to the jury, the defendant's conviction was reduced to voluntary manslaughter.

The decision in *Gittens* (1984) was approved by the House of Lords in **Dietschmann (2003)**. Dietschmann had killed a man whilst suffering from a depressive condition following the death of his aunt, to whom he was very emotionally attached. The defendant had also consumed large amounts of alcohol at the time of the killing. Lord Hutton said at the appeal that the question was not simply whether the defendant would have killed had he not been intoxicated, and he gave a model direction for juries:

> Has the defendant satisfied you that, despite the drink, his mental abnormality substantially impaired his mental responsibility for his fatal acts, or has he failed to satisfy you of that?

However, Lord Hutton did go on to say that if the jury decided the defendant would not have killed without taking drink or drugs, it was

Key cases

Egan (1992): defendant killed a woman whilst suffering from an abnormality of the mind and being intoxicated; issue was whether his abnormality rather than the drink had substantially impaired his responsibility; 'substantial' does not have to mean 'total' but must be more than trivial impairment.

Gittens (1984): defendant killed while suffering from depression combined with drink and drugs; consideration was whether the depression alone was enough to impair his responsibility for the act.

Dietschmann (2003): defendant killed while suffering from a mental abnormality combined with intoxication; consideration was whether the abnormality alone substantially impaired his responsibility for the act.

Alcohol dependency syndrome is a recognised medical condition

unlikely that it would find that the abnormality on its own was sufficient to impair his responsibility.

Alcohol dependency syndrome

Alcohol dependency syndrome, which is also referred to as alcoholism, is a recognised medical condition that can be used for the defence of diminished responsibility.

The leading case on this point is **Wood (2008)**. The defendant was an alcoholic who killed his victim, while drunk, in a frenzied attack with a meat cleaver. It was agreed by medical experts that he was suffering from alcohol dependency syndrome but it was unclear whether this had actually caused brain damage. Wood was found guilty of murder at his trial and appealed to the Court of Appeal, where his conviction was reduced to voluntary manslaughter on the grounds of diminished responsibility. In cases where the defendant has an addiction, the jury has to consider the effect of the alcohol consumed because of the addiction, which is classed as involuntary drinking. If the drinking is not because of the addiction, it is classed as voluntary and its effects cannot be considered. If not all the drinking is attributable to the addiction, so there is both voluntary and involuntary, the defence can still be pleaded, but the jury must only consider the effects of the involuntary consumption. The key question then for the jury is whether this substantially impaired his mental responsibility.

Burden of proof

A defendant who raises the defence of diminished responsibility has the burden of proving it on a balance of probabilities, which is a much lower standard than beyond all reasonable doubt.

Summary of the special defences to murder

Special defences to murder

	Loss of Control – Section 54 of the Coroners and Justice Act 2009	Diminished Responsibility – Section 2 of the Homicide Act 1957
Element 1	The defendant must prove a loss of self-control.	The defendant must prove he was suffering from an abnormality of mental functioning arising from a recognised medical condition.
Element 2	There must be a qualifying trigger: ▮ fear of serious violence ▮ things done and/or said that amount to circumstances of an extremely grave character and cause the defendant to have a justifiable sense of being seriously wronged ▮ a combination of both triggers.	The abnormality of mental functioning must substantially impair the defendant's ability to do one of the following: ▮ understand the nature of his conduct ▮ form a rational judgement ▮ exercise self-control.
Element 3	The defendant must have acted like another person of the same age and sex, in the same circumstances and with an ordinary level of tolerance and self-restraint.	The abnormality must also provide an explanation for the defendant's conduct, so it must cause the defendant to carry out the killing or be a significant factor.
Burden of proof	If the defence is put to the jury, the prosecution must disprove it beyond all reasonable doubt.	The defendant must prove that he was suffering from diminished responsibility on a balance of probabilities.

Key cases

Wood (2008): alcohol dependency syndrome is a recognised medical condition that can lead to a successful plea of diminished responsibility if the other elements of the defence are satisfied.

Study tip

A question that asks you to discuss the defendant's liability for the murder of the victim (e.g., 'Discuss whether Brian can be liable for the murder of Colin') will normally be testing three areas of law:

▮ the crime of murder, including discussion of the *actus reus* and *mens rea*

▮ the defence of diminished responsibility

▮ the defence of loss of control.

When discussing murder, consider whether there are issues relating to the *actus reus* or *mens rea* that need further discussion. If causation is not raised, there is no need to consider this in detail; if the question states that Brian shot Colin, who died instantly, there is no need to spend time on causation as the examiner is likely to be testing another aspect.

It is important to carefully read the facts provided in the questions, as they may give students the scope to discuss both defences. Although you might conclude that one defence is more likely to succeed, you should give equal weight to the discussion of both. The three areas of law will be of equal importance in terms of gaining marks, so allocate your time accordingly. Remember that other defences are possible but the special defences are the most probable.

Activities

1 Consider whether the defence of diminished responsibility might be successful in the following situations:

a Andy is a 38-year-old man with the mental age of a six-year-old. When his neighbour, Beth, calls him 'stupid', he flies into a rage and stabs her to death.

b Callum suffers from paranoia and thinks that he is being followed when he goes out. One night, he goes out to the local pub, where he drinks seven pints of strong lager, followed by several whiskies. At the end of the evening, he gets into an argument with another customer, Dwayne, whom he accuses of plotting to turn everyone against him. He grabs a heavy ashtray and smashes it over Dwayne's head, killing him.

c Ellie, 16, has recently given birth in circumstances of secrecy. Suffering from stress and post-natal depression, she goes to visit her aunt Sarah. Far from being sympathetic, Sarah launches into a criticism of Ellie's lifestyle. Ellie seizes a pair of kitchen scissors and stabs Sarah to death.

2 Research recent cases on diminished responsibility on the internet. Begin by finding more details on the case of Aaron Wilkinson, and then find other recent cases where the defence has been raised.

You should now be able to:

- explain the law relating to diminished responsibility
- apply the law to given scenarios.

2 Involuntary manslaughter

Introduction

In the last chapter, we saw that the crimes of murder and voluntary manslaughter both require a particular degree of intent. The intention in both crimes is the intention to kill or cause grievous (serious) bodily harm. In voluntary manslaughter, the charge is reduced from murder if the defendant can successfully prove one of the specific defences to murder. The important difference between voluntary and involuntary manslaughter is that in involuntary manslaughter the defendant does not intend to kill or cause serious harm.

This will inevitably mean that the range of involuntary manslaughter is very wide. Death may result from an extremely dangerous act at the one end, to some relatively minor degree of carelessness at the other. The maximum sentence for involuntary manslaughter is life imprisonment. It is, however, discretionary. A judge may therefore pass a sentence that reflects the seriousness of the offence, from life imprisonment to – if such a sentence is justifiable in the circumstances – even a non-custodial one.

In this chapter, we will consider two forms of involuntary manslaughter. These are:

- gross negligence manslaughter
- unlawful act manslaughter, (sometimes called constructive manslaughter).

In this topic, you will learn how to:

- explain the meaning of gross negligence manslaughter
- explain cases that illustrate gross negligence manslaughter
- apply rules to a given situation.

1 Gross negligence manslaughter

Gross negligence manslaughter is when a person dies as a result of the negligence of another, and the degree of negligence by the defendant is sufficiently serious as to make him criminally liable for the death. It was in the case of **Bateman (1925)** that 'gross negligence' by the defendant was referred to as the basis for criminal liability.

The test stated in that case was:

> Does the conduct of the accused show such disregard for the life and safety of others as to amount to a crime against the state and conduct deserving of punishment?

In *Andrews* (1937) it was stated that where there is a charge of gross negligence manslaughter, simple lack of care that would constitute civil liability is not enough. For the purposes of the criminal law, a very high degree of negligence is required to be proved before the crime is established.

The statement in *Andrews* (1937) was made by Lord Atkin, who five years earlier, in the case of **Donoghue v Stevenson (1932)**, had formulated the test for negligence in civil cases.

In *Donoghue* v *Stevenson* (1932) it was stated that a duty of care was owed to:

> … persons who are so closely and directly affected by my act that I ought reasonably to have them in contemplation as being so affected when I am directing my mind to the acts or omissions which are called into question.

Key cases

Bateman (1925): a doctor's negligent treatment of his patient resulted in death; 'gross negligence' was the basis for criminal liability.

Donoghue v Stevenson (1932): a snail in ginger beer; key case in negligence that established the principles of duty of care and the neighbour test.

■ Key cases

Adomako (1994): a anaesthetist failed to notice disconnected tube during an operation; he was convicted of gross negligence manslaughter.

Stone and Dobinson (1977): defendants breached duty towards old lady in their care; she died and they were convicted of manslaughter.

Litchfield (1998): contractual duty of care owed towards crew by ship owner and master; three crew died when ship driven onto rocks.

Wacker (2002): fifty-eight illegal immigrants suffocated on Channel crossing; duty owed for the purposes of manslaughter, even though victims were complicit in a crime.

The leading modern case on gross negligence manslaughter is **Adomako (1994)**, in which the defendant was an anaesthetist during an eye operation. During the operation, the tube supplying oxygen to the patient became disconnected. After suffering a heart attack, the patient later died as a result of brain damage. It was testified at the trial that a competent anaesthetist should have noticed the disconnected tube within seconds. The defendant's failure to do so was described as 'abysmal'. His conviction for gross negligence manslaughter was subsequently upheld by the House of Lords.

Adomako (1994) established that the elements required to prove gross negligence manslaughter are:

■ a duty of care exists on the part of the defendant towards the victim
■ there is a breach of that duty of care, which causes death
■ the gross negligence is such as to be considered criminal by the jury.

Duty of care

Lord Mackay said in *Adomako* (1994) that the ordinary principles of negligence in civil law (as outlined in *Donoghue* v *Stevenson* (1932), above) should apply when ascertaining whether a duty of care existed, and, if so, whether it was breached.

A case illustrating this is **Stone and Dobinson (1977)**. The defendants had undertaken the care of Stone's elderly sister. She became bedridden and unable to care for herself. As the result of the defendants' failure to feed her or get medical help, the old lady died. They had owed her a duty of care because they had voluntarily agreed to look after her. The breach of this duty of care resulted in the defendants being convicted of manslaughter.

A breach of duty can also occur where there is a contractual situation, as in the case of **Litchfield (1998)** where it was held that the owner and master of a sailing ship owed a duty to the crew. The defendant sailed knowing that engine failure was likely, as the fuel was contaminated. Three crew members died when the boat was driven onto rocks. The case of *Singh* (1999) established that a duty towards tenants was owed by the defendant, who had a duty to manage and maintain property. A faulty gas fire had resulted in the deaths of some of his tenants.

The case of **Wacker (2002)** established that being complicit in a crime does not in itself prevent a duty of care being owed to the victim. The defendant had agreed to carry illegal immigrants in his lorry on a cross-channel ferry. The air vent enabling them to breathe had been closed for the duration of the crossing. The crossing took an hour longer than usual, and the result was that 58 of the immigrants died of suffocation. The Court of Appeal held that although a civil action could not arise from this situation (because the victims and defendant had been complicit in the commission of a crime), a duty of care existed for the purposes of a criminal case of manslaughter. This decision was based partly on a matter of public policy, and it may have opened the door to other duties of care being recognised in future.

Gross negligence

The cases of *Bateman* (1925) and *Andrews* (1937), mentioned at the beginning of this topic, established that the degree of negligence amounting to manslaughter must be far greater than that in a civil case. For criminal liability, the negligence has to be 'gross' and go 'beyond a mere matter of compensation between subjects' (*Bateman* (1925)).

In *Adomako* (1994) the House of Lords approved the test in *Bateman* (1925). The then Lord Chancellor, Lord Mackay, said:

The jury will have to consider whether the extent to which the defendant's conduct departed from the proper standard of care incumbent upon him, involving as it must have done a risk of death to the patient, was such that it should be judged as criminal.

It is the jury then, taking into account all the evidence, that must decide whether the breach of duty of care was serious enough to amount to gross negligence. With regard to the risk of death, did it amount to a criminal act or omission? If the jury thinks it did, then the verdict is guilty of gross negligence manslaughter. The following further cases of **Finlay (2001)** and **Edwards (2001)** illustrate this.

In *Finlay* (2001) a scout leader was in charge of a party of scouts when one of them, a ten-year-old, fell to his death on Snowdon. There was evidence that several of the proper safety procedures had not been followed, but the jury felt that the defendant's conduct did not show such disregard for life and safety as to amount to gross negligence. He was acquitted of manslaughter.

In *Edwards* (2001) a couple had allowed their seven-year-old daughter and her friend to play on a railway bridge. They had promised to warn them if a train approached, but the children were killed by a train that the defendants had not seen. They had ignored an obvious and serious danger, or had decided to take the risk, and this amounted to gross negligence. The jury found them guilty of manslaughter.

Key cases

Finlay (2001): a boy scout died on Snowdon; scout master's conduct not enough to amount to gross negligence.

Edwards (2001): parents allowed children to play on the railway; the children were killed by a train; parents held to be grossly negligent and guilty of manslaughter.

Study tip

When answering a question on gross negligence manslaughter, examine the facts of the scenario carefully and then ask yourself the following questions:

- Did the defendant owe the victim a duty of care? (See *Donoghue* v *Stevenson* (1932), above.)
- Was there a breach of that duty of care by the defendant, which directly resulted in the victim's death?

If the answer to these questions is 'yes', then the defendant was negligent. Then ask yourself:

- Was the negligence serious enough to give rise to criminal liability?

Again, if the answer to this is 'yes', and a jury would be likely to agree, then the defendant is probably guilty of gross negligence manslaughter.

When you write your answer:

- start with an introduction by way of stating the definition of the crime of gross negligence manslaughter
- briefly outline the law relating to the crime
- deal with the above points systematically in turn, illustrating them with relevant cases
- come to a reasoned conclusion.

Father branded a fool over quadbike death of his daughter

Gary Cooke, 46, pleaded guilty to the manslaughter of seven-year-old Elizabeth, who was killed on Boxing Day 2007.

She was testing out her new quadbike – a present from her parents – on the road for the first time when she was involved in a collision with a Range Rover.

She had been driving behind her father, who [had gone] to collect friends who lived less than a mile away and allowed his children to ride their new quadbikes behind his [car].

Giving Cooke a nine-month prison sentence, suspended for two years, Judge Christopher Bell QC said the defendant had acknowledged his 'stupidity' from the outset.

'I don't suppose I am alone in remembering the shock of hearing the news on the radio when this happened,' Bell said. 'I don't suppose I was alone in immediately thinking "what sort of fool would allow his child out in such circumstances".

'The roads at any time are a potentially dangerous place. At night in the depths of winter, on a quiet, narrow, country lane, to allow a seven-year-old out on a road with a powerful vehicle is folly of the highest order.'

[Prosecutor Stephen Harvey QC said], 'This tragic accident was a direct result of the defendant's gross negligence.'

Annette Henry, defending, said [Mr Cooke] had 'been punished in the most tragic way conceivable'.

The Telegraph, 20 October 2008

Risk of death

In *Adomako* (1994) Lord Mackay referred in his judgement to the 'risk of death'. The law did not originally seem to be clear on this point. In *Bateman* (1925) the test for determining whether there was a risk of death was a 'disregard for the life and safety of others', and in *Stone and Dobinson* (1977), a risk to the 'health and welfare' of the victim. Both were approved in *Adomako* (1994). However, in *Misra and Srivastava* (2004) the Court of Appeal confirmed that only risk of death will be sufficient for gross negligence manslaughter, and as a matter of policy the Crown Prosecution Service did not prosecute for anything less.

Mens rea

Since the very essence of involuntary manslaughter is that the defendant does not have the intention to kill or cause serious harm, that aspect of *mens rea* is not present. For gross negligence manslaughter the defendant is judged by his behaviour rather than his state of mind. There must be an obvious risk of death but this is judged objectively so it does not matter that the defendant did not see the risk.

Activity

Read the article, and then use the Internet to further research this case. Discuss why you think the jury decided that Jacqueline Simpson did not deserve a criminal conviction.

Ellie Lawrenson's grandmother found not guilty of manslaughter

The grandmother of dog attack victim Ellie Lawrenson was acquitted of manslaughter today.

The jury of seven men and five women at Liverpool crown court found Jacqueline Simpson, 45, not guilty after a six-day trial.

Five-year-old Ellie was killed by her uncle Kiel Simpson's pit bull terrier Reuben on New Year's Eve after Ms Simpson, who had smoked 10 cannabis joints and drunk two bottles of wine, let it in.

Ellie, who was killed at the house in Knowles House Avenue, St Helens, had 72 injuries.

[After the verdict,] Colin Davies, assistant district crown prosecutor for Merseyside, said: 'The CPS brought this prosecution on the basis that Jacqueline Simpson owed a duty of care towards her granddaughter Ellie.

'We said that she breached that duty of care by letting the dog into her house, knowing that it was potentially dangerous and capable of killing a child. Furthermore, we said that her breach of that duty of care was such that a jury would consider it to be so gross that it amounted to a crime.

'There is no doubt – and it was accepted by the defence – that Jacqueline Simpson owed a duty of care towards her granddaughter.

'However, the jury by its verdict have accepted that, if there was a breach of her duty of care, it was not such that it amounted to a crime.'

Liverpool Echo, 11 September 2007

Activity

Consider the liability for gross negligence manslaughter in the following cases.

1 Geoff is the driver of a train on a rural branch line. He is looking at the list of horses in a race that day, and so he fails to notice a red signal. Rounding a bend, the train hits a closed crossing gate and ploughs into a car. The driver of the car is killed.

2 Hank, together with his mate Ian, has stolen a car. As a result of Hank driving too fast, the car crashes. Ian is seriously injured but Hank suffers only slight bruising and whiplash. Hank runs away from the scene without summoning any medical help for Ian. Medical help would have saved Ian, but without it he dies of his injuries.

3 Jim is an electrician. He is called to Kylie's house to do some rewiring. Having double-booked himself, Jim is in a great hurry to get to another job. In his haste, he inadvertently wires up the mains electricity to the plumbing. Kylie is fatally electrocuted when she tries to turn on the tap in her kitchen.

You should now be able to:

- explain the law relating to gross negligence manslaughter
- apply that law to given scenarios.

2 Unlawful act manslaughter

Unlawful act manslaughter is when the defendant causes the victim's death whilst carrying out a criminal act that is deemed to be dangerous.

To prove that a defendant has committed unlawful act manslaughter, it is necessary to prove that he has committed an act that is:

- unlawful
- dangerous
- the one that caused death
- an unlawful act for which the defendant had the *mens rea*.

The unlawful act

The unlawful act must be a criminal offence. A civil wrong could not amount to an unlawful act for this purpose. An act that is the result of ignorance or foolishness would be insufficient, if no criminal offence is involved.

In the case of **Lamb (1967)** the defendant and his friend had been playing with a loaded revolver. There were two bullets in the chamber of the gun, but both men thought that neither bullet would fire unless it was opposite the barrel. Lamb pointed the gun at his friend and pulled the trigger. Because the cylinder revolved, a bullet from the next chamber was fired. His friend was killed. Although dangerous and fatal, the act of pointing the gun was held not to have been unlawful. His friend was not in fear of harm at the time, so there was no assault in the technical sense (see Chapter 3: Non-fatal offences against the person). Therefore there was no criminal offence, and Lamb's appeal against his conviction for manslaughter was allowed.

In most cases, the unlawful act resulting in death would be some type of physical assault. It could be some other crime, however, such as burglary, arson or criminal damage, provided that it may be likely to cause injury.

In this topic, you will learn how to:

- explain the meaning of unlawful act manslaughter
- explain cases that illustrate unlawful acts, the dangerous nature of an act and substantial cause of death
- explain the *mens rea* requirements of unlawful act manslaughter
- apply the rules to a given situation.

Key cases

Lamb (1967): man shot dead while playing dangerous game with gun; no criminal offence involved, therefore no conviction for manslaughter.

There must be an unlawful act. An omission (failure to act; see 'Causation' in Chapter 1: Murder and voluntary manslaughter) could not give rise to liability for unlawful act manslaughter. In this respect, unlawful act manslaughter differs from murder, voluntary manslaughter and gross negligence manslaughter. This was confirmed in *Lowe* (1973) where the defendant's child died from neglect.

Dangerous act

What constitutes a dangerous act? The test for this is an objective one, and can best be expressed in the words of Edmund Davis LJ in *Church* (1966). He said that:

> The unlawful act must be such as all sober and reasonable people would inevitably recognise must subject the other person to, at least, the risk of some harm resulting therefrom, albeit not serious harm.

The important points to note about this are that:

- it need not be the accused who necessarily foresaw the harm, but any 'sober and reasonable' person
- the risk may be only 'some harm', not necessarily serious harm.

The harm need not be aimed at the victim. If the defendant commits an unlawful act upon one person, and another dies as a result, he still may be guilty of unlawful act homicide. An illustration of this is the case of **Mitchell (1983)**, in which the accused punched someone during an argument in a post office queue. The man who was attacked fell back and knocked over an old lady, causing her injuries from which, shortly afterwards, she died. It was enough that the initial assault was unlawful and dangerous. It was foreseeable by a reasonable person that some injury might be caused to someone.

In the case of **Dawson (1985)** there was an attempted robbery at a petrol station by three men using pickaxes and an imitation gun. The cashier suffered from heart disease and the shock of the incident caused a heart attack from which he died. On appeal the court said that in assessing whether the reasonable person would recognise that there was a risk of some harm, the jury must imagine they possess the knowledge that the defendant had or should have had at the time of the offence. In this case, if the defendants were not aware of the heart problem then the jury could not consider this factor when assessing the risk of causing some harm.

But what if it is obvious from the outset that someone is frail and vulnerable? In that case, the 'reasonable person' would realise that harm could follow from the victim's condition. To commit an act causing fear and apprehension in such a situation might well mean a conviction for manslaughter, if death is the consequence.

In the case of **Watson (1989)** the victim was a frail old man who died from a heart attack after the defendant burgled his house. It would have been obvious to the reasonable person that some harm could come to someone in the victim's situation. However, the defendant escaped conviction for manslaughter on a point of causation as it could not be proved it was the break-in that caused the heart attack, rather than the police activity that followed the incident.

The dangerous act may not be intended to cause harm to a person. It is enough for harm to be aimed at property, if an individual dies as a result. So long as it accords with Lord Davis's description (above) then it could mean liability for dangerous act manslaughter. An example of such a case is that of *Goodfellow* (1986) (which will be dealt with later, at the end of this topic). His conviction for manslaughter was upheld on the grounds

---

Key cases

Mitchell (1983): scuffle in post office queue resulted in old lady dying after being knocked down; defendant guilty of manslaughter, despite harm not being directed at the victim.

Dawson (1985): petrol station attendant died from heart attack caused by fear; not a dangerous enough act to warrant manslaughter conviction.

Watson (1989): in determining whether the act is dangerous, the jury can consider what the defendant would have known about the victim at the time of the offence; in this case, the victim was old and frail.

that he had intentionally committed an unlawful act (arson), which any reasonable person might foresee would cause harm, and death had resulted.

Substantial cause of death

The unlawful act must be the substantial cause of death. In this respect the same general principles, such as the chain of causation and the thin skull rule, apply to manslaughter as to murder.

In **Corion-Auguiste (2004)** the defendant threw an 'air bomb' firework in a crowded enclosed bus station. In the general panic, passengers rushed for the exits and an elderly lady was knocked over in the rush. She struck her head and died later in hospital. The defendant was convicted of unlawful act manslaughter. His act was the direct and substantial cause of the victim's death.

In **Kennedy (2007)** the defendant, at the request of the victim, filled a syringe with heroin. He gave it to the victim in order for the victim to inject himself. The victim died as a result of the drug, and the defendant was found guilty of unlawful act manslaughter. The House of Lords, on quashing the conviction, held that the victim's voluntary act in injecting himself had broken the chain of causation. The unlawful act relied on by the prosecution (Offences against the Person Act (1861) s23, causing a noxious substance to be administered to the victim) could not be said to have taken place. The victim, an adult, made a voluntary and informed decision to act in the way he did. Contrast this case with *Cato* (1976) (described in Chapter 1: Murder and voluntary manslaughter, Topic 2), where the defendant and the victim injected each other.

The unlawful and dangerous act need not be the sole cause of death, so long as it was not trivial.

This principle is illustrated by the case of **Shohid (2003)**, in which the defendant was one of a group of men who attacked the victim and his friend on the platform of a railway station. The victim and his friend were forced onto the railway track, and the friend was able to climb back onto the platform. The victim, however, was prevented from doing so by some of the attackers, not including the defendant, and was killed by a train. Upholding the defendant's conviction for manslaughter, the Court of Appeal held that the original attack was sufficiently serious as to be a cause of the subsequent death, and it was not necessary that it should be the only cause.

In **Carey (2006)**, however, the original attack was not held to be serious enough to be the cause of death. Three girls started a fight, in which a fourth suffered only minor bruises. This girl later ran away but collapsed after running about 100 m. Her death was from an inherent heart disease that had been aggravated by her running. The girls who started the fight were convicted of manslaughter based on the unlawful act of affray. The convictions were quashed on appeal on the grounds that the victim had not been running away from a serious threat, but merely to get home. The only dangerous act directed at her was a single punch, which was not the cause of her death. Furthermore, the acts of violence and threats in the affray were not dangerous enough for a reasonable person to have foreseen any serious harm to the victim.

In **Lewis (2010)** the defendant chased the victim after an incident involving the defendant's car. The victim ran into the road and was run over by another vehicle. Lewis appealed against his conviction for unlawful act manslaughter, but his appeal was unsuccessful. It was decided that the assault was a continuing act and that it was the cause of death, as the victim's attempted escape in response to the assault

Key cases

Corion-Auguiste (2004): firework thrown into bus station; old lady died in panic rush; defendant's act was direct cause of death.

Kennedy (2007): victim injected himself after being given drug by defendant; chain of causation broken, and no noxious substance administered by the defendant; no manslaughter.

Shohid (2003): the original attack on victim in a railway station was serious enough to be the cause of the resulting death, even though it was not the main cause.

Carey (2006): a girl died as a result of a heart disease while running away after a fight; the original punch was held not to be the cause of her death.

Lewis (2010): victim died after being run over whilst trying to run away from the defendant; defendant's assault was held to be the cause of death.

If a victim has taken the illegal substance voluntarily, it will break the chain of causation between the supplier and the victim's death (Kennedy (2007))

was foreseeable. This meant that there was no break in the chain of causation. Furthermore, the crime satisfied the test of dangerous act as given in *Church* (1966).

What if the death of a victim is the result of a series of unlawful acts by the defendant? If it cannot be proved which particular act caused the death, it is sufficient to show that any one of them could have done. This is illustrated by **Attorney-General's Reference (No. 4 of 1980) (1982)**. The defendant pushed his girlfriend during a struggle between them and she fell over a landing rail. Thinking he had killed her, he dragged her upstairs by a rope tied round her neck and then cut up her body to dispose of it. He argued that when he pushed his girlfriend it was an accident and therefore, as this killed her, he was not guilty. However, it could not be proved at what point the victim had actually died. The Court of Appeal held that he could be convicted of manslaughter even though it could not be shown which dangerous act caused the death.

Mens rea

In order to prove unlawful act manslaughter, there must be a positive act. An omission is not sufficient. The act itself must have been intentional; it must have been accompanied by the *mens rea* to commit that act. There need not have been any intention to cause harm, as in the case of **Newbury and Jones (1976)**. The defendants were two teenage boys. As a train approached, they pushed a piece of paving stone over the parapet of a bridge. It hit the train, went through a window and killed the guard. Upholding their conviction for manslaughter, the House of Lords held that a defendant could be convicted of unlawful act manslaughter even if he did not foresee that his act might cause harm to another. He need not be aware that his act was unlawful, nor need he intend, or consider the risk of, injury. It was enough that he realised what he was doing and had the intention of doing it. Moreover, the risk of injury must have been obvious to a reasonable person of normal intelligence.

In **Le Brun (1991)** the defendant had, without intending any serious harm, hit his wife on the chin during an argument outside their house. She fell unconscious and he dragged her away in order to avoid detection. In doing so, he caused her head to hit the pavement hard enough to fracture her skull. She died as a result, and the defendant was convicted of manslaughter. Upholding the verdict, the Court of Appeal held that although the original act was not the direct cause of death, that act and the cause of her death were both part of 'the same sequence of events'. The original punch was intentional, and that was enough.

Overlap between gross negligence and unlawful act manslaughter

The case of **Goodfellow (1986)** is an example of a case where the defendant could have been found guilty of both unlawful act and gross negligence manslaughter. His intention was to set fire to his council house, a plan described by a friend whom he told about it as 'a stupid idea'. He determined to carry out the scheme anyway. He intended that the adults should rescue the children and all should escape unharmed. The fire would be blamed on a neighbour allegedly throwing a fire bomb through the window, and he and his family would be moved by the council to other accommodation. The fire spread so rapidly that three people were unable to escape, and died as a result. In addition to the unlawful act aspect, the defendant had acted in such a manner as to create an obvious and serious risk of causing physical injury or death to some person. He had recognised that risk and had nonetheless gone on to take it recklessly. In other words, he could be said to have been grossly negligent.

Key cases

Attorney-General's Reference (No. 4 of 1980) (1982): a girl died after a series of unlawful acts, any one of which could have caused death; it was not necessary to prove which particular act was responsible.

Newbury and Jones (1976): boys killed a train guard by pushing a piece of paving stone off a bridge; enough for manslaughter that the defendants realised what they were doing and intended to do it.

Le Brun (1991): defendant punched his wife, who fractured her skull and died as he dragged her away unconscious; enough that the original punch was intentional.

Goodfellow (1986): defendant deliberately set fire to his accommodation in order to get an alternative; three people died in the fire; he was convicted of unlawful act manslaughter.

Summary of involuntary manslaughter

The forms of involuntary manslaughter may be summed up as follows:

Gross negligence manslaughter	Unlawful act manslaughter
■ The defendant's conduct can be lawful or unlawful and can be an act or omission.	■ The defendant must commit an act and not an omission.
■ There must be a breach of the duty of care that causes death.	■ The unlawful act must be a criminal offence.
■ There must be an obvious risk of death.	■ The act must be dangerous but the defendant does not need to recognise this.
■ The conduct must, in the opinion of the jury, justify a criminal conviction.	■ The act must be the one that causes death.
	■ The defendant must have had the *mens rea* for the unlawful act.

Differences between the types of manslaughter

The important distinction to bear in mind is that:

■ unlawful act manslaughter requires the performance of an unlawful (criminal) activity

■ gross negligence does not.

In addition:

■ unlawful act manslaughter requires there to have been an act, not an omission

■ gross negligence can result from an omission.

Activity

Assess the liability for unlawful act manslaughter in the following scenarios.

1 In a fight outside a night club, Liam punched Matt. Matt fell to the ground, and Liam gave him a half-hearted kick to the head and walked away. Matt had a very thin skull, and died as a result of the kick.

2 Nick was trespassing on the land of Ollie, a farmer. When Ollie confronted him, Nick became aggressive. Fearful for his safety, Ollie turned to run but had a heart attack and died.

3 Paddy thought it would be amusing to drop breeze blocks from a bridge over a canal to see if he could cause a boat to sink. He dropped one block onto a narrow boat passing below. He hit Qasim, who was at the tiller, and killed him.

You should now be able to:

■ explain the law relating to unlawful act manslaughter

■ apply the law to given scenarios.

In this topic, you will learn how to:

■ apply the law to problem scenarios involving a death.

3 How to approach a question on homicide

Questions on homicide will normally be asking you to show one of the following:

■ liability of the defendant for the murder of the victim

■ liability of the defendant for the involuntary manslaughter of the victim

■ liability of the defendant for the death of the victim.

Murder

If the question asks only about the defendant's liability for murder, you will need to discuss the *actus reus* and *mens rea* of murder and also look for evidence of the special defences so that these can be considered. This was discussed in Chapter 1.

Involuntary manslaughter

If the question asks about the defendant's liability for the involuntary manslaughter of the victim, there is no need to discuss murder. The question will normally require discussion of both types of involuntary manslaughter.

Consider the following scenario:

> Having drunk a large amount of vodka and taken some drugs, Rob and other members of his gang were out late at night when they saw Vincent – a member of a rival gang. With Rob in the lead, shouting about killing Vincent, they began to chase him. After about two minutes, Vincent suddenly collapsed and fell to the ground. Rob reached him first and was about to kick him but then said to the others, 'Leave it. He looks bad. Better let someone else take care of it.' They then all ran off. Vincent was an asthmatic and the stress of the chase had triggered an asthma attack from which he died. Prompt medical treatment might well have saved his life.
>
> Discuss the possible liability of Rob for involuntary manslaughter in connection with the death of Vincent.

Although there is only one defendant and one victim in this case, the question requires discussion of both types of involuntary manslaughter:

■ unlawful act manslaughter in respect of the assault (chase)

■ gross negligence in respect of the omission to get help, based on a duty arising from creating a dangerous situation.

You need to explain and apply the key elements of each type of involuntary manslaughter, with emphasis on the particular issues raised, such as causation. Your answer should conclude which type of involuntary manslaughter is more likely to get a successful conviction for the prosecution. The defence of voluntary intoxication is also relevant here (see Chapter 4).

Now consider a different scenario with two defendants:

> Leon and his friend Phil often tested each other out by having informal wrestling matches. However, Phil was always a little worried about these matches because Leon could easily become excessively violent. During one such match, Leon suddenly succeeded in hurling Phil across the room, causing Phil to strike his head heavily against a wall. Feeling rather sick, Phil found his

way home, where he spent the next two days in bed before going to the Accident and Emergency department of his local hospital. There he was examined by Sally, an overworked doctor. After a brief examination, she concluded that he only had trivial injuries and sent him away with painkillers. In fact, he had suffered major injuries to his skull and brain, and he died the next day.

Discuss the possible liability of Leon and of Sally for the involuntary manslaughter of Phil.

In this case, there are two defendants and one victim. Leon's liability is based on the act of hurling Phil across the room and is therefore unlawful act manslaughter, and Sally's is based on her breach of duty to a patient and so is gross negligence manslaughter. Where there are two defendants and only one victim, there will be issues of causation. Neither defendant has to be the sole cause, but each must make a significant contribution to the victim's death. Leon may argue a break in the chain of causation.

Liability for the death of the victim

Sometimes, the examination question will not specify which form of homicide you need to discuss, and you will need to decide from the facts of the scenario. Study the flowchart diagram on page 30 to see the key questions that will help you to determine liability. As murder and manslaughter share the same *actus reus*, it is logical to start by establishing that the defendant was the cause of death before looking at issues of *mens rea*.

It is sometimes difficult to determine whether a defendant intended serious harm, which is sufficient for murder, or some harm, which is sufficient for unlawful act manslaughter. In these situations, your answer could discuss both possibilities. However, it is important to remember that the special defences of loss of control and diminished responsibility can only be pleaded to murder.

Consider which homicide offence is relevant in this scenario:

Following a dispute in a bar between rival gangs, which started because of insults made by Chris about Gary's sister, the two groups left the bar and a series of running fights took place. Eventually Gary, shouting about the insults to his sister, chased Henry, Chris's friend, close to a 20-metre high cliff above the town beach. Then Gary took out a knife he had been carrying and he threatened Henry, forcing him back on to the very edge of the cliff. Henry made a grab at Gary. Gary felt in danger of being pulled over the cliff and struck out at Henry with his knife. Henry lost his footing and fell on to the rocks below. Gary ran off, leaving Henry's body to be found the next day. Consider the liability of Gary in connection with Henry's death.

In this answer, you can start by discussing the *actus reus* of unlawful homicide and then discuss whether Gary has the *mens rea* of murder. As it is not possible to determine exactly what Gary's intention was, you may conclude that he did intend death or serious harm and therefore could be liable for murder, in which case the defence of loss of control could be raised. However, if you conclude that he may have only intended to threaten Henry to keep him away, then unlawful act manslaughter would be appropriate. Both these approaches are acceptable, and you could also combine the two of them. A further issue raised by the facts, which would need to be mentioned, is the defence of self-defence – this is discussed in Chapter 4.

An overview of unlawful homicide

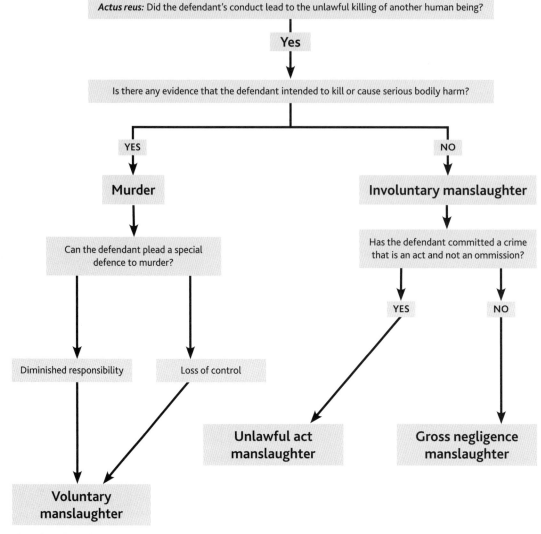

Flow chart for liability for homicide

■ Study tip

Structure your answer as follows:

■ state the general principles of the law as they relate to the question you are answering

■ apply those principles to the facts of the case

■ come to your conclusion as to likely liability.

You should now be able to:

■ answer problem questions involving death

■ construct an appropriately reasoned answer, quoting authority where necessary.

3 Non-fatal offences against the person

In this topic, you will learn how to:

- state the meaning of assault and battery
- distinguish between assault and battery
- explain cases that illustrate assault and battery
- apply the rules to a given situation.

1 Assault and battery

Assault and battery are the least serious of the non-fatal crimes. It needs to be recognised that they are two separate and distinct offences. The essential difference between the two is that the offence of assault is causing the victim to fear force (but with no requirement that harm is actually suffered) whereas the offence of battery is the actual infliction of harm. The terms assault and battery can be confusing since the word 'assault' is more normally understood to describe an act of physical harm as opposed to a mere fear of such harm.

Assault and battery were traditionally common law offences and all the principles still derive entirely from decided cases in accordance with common law principles. The offences are, however, recognised by statute law, and s39 of the Criminal Justice Act 1988 (CJA 1988) provides that they be tried summarily with a maximum sentence of six months' imprisonment or a fine. *Little* (1992) ruled that assault and battery should be considered statutory offences despite the fact that s39 does not provide any definitions, but only fixes the penalty and tariff.

It follows from the fact that assault and battery are two distinct offences that, in theory, one can be committed without the other. Both offences are committed when, in full view of the victim, the accused pulls back his fist and then punches, since harm is feared when seeing the fist pull back (the *assault*) and then inflicted with the punch (the *battery*). However, only a battery is committed if the punch is made from behind, since then the victim has not feared the harm. Conversely, only an assault is committed if the fist is pulled back but the accused misses the victim.

Assault

Actus reus

In **Ireland; Burstow (1997)** the House of Lords confirmed that an **assault** is committed when the accused intentionally or recklessly causes the victim to apprehend immediate and unlawful violence.

The *actus reus* of assault is:

- an act
- causing the victim to apprehend immediate and unlawful violence.

An act

An act or words from the defendant must cause the victim's fear. An assault cannot be committed by omission. An act might be waving a knife, or might be a gesture such as the accused running his finger across his throat to indicate slitting.

In **Constanza (1997)** the court ruled that *words alone* were sufficient for an assault. Here, the accused stalked the victim and his harassment campaign included sending her 812 letters. It was held that the contents of those letters were assaults since the victim read them clearly as threats, even though there was no reinforcing physical gesture. It follows that emails and texts and all other forms of written communication can also constitute assaults.

Key terms

Assault: intentionally or recklessly causing the victim to apprehend immediate and unlawful violence.

Key cases

Ireland; Burstow (1997): silent telephone calls can be an assault; the case for immediacy is made if the victim fears the 'possibility' of an immediate attack, and this fear does not have to be rational.

Constanza (1997): words alone can be an assault.

Silent phone calls can be an assault (Ireland (1997))

The decision in *Burstow* (1997) went even further than *Constanza* (1997) and ruled that silence could amount to an assault, in the form of silent telephone calls made by the accused to the victim.

Words spoken by the defendant will prevent an act from being an assault if the words make it clear that the accused is not intending to cause the harm that is otherwise suggested by his conduct. This principle comes from the old case **Tuberville v Savage (1669)** where the defendant placed his hand on his sword, angered by comments made to him. This might have constituted an assault, since it could cause another to fear an immediate attack, but it was accompanied by the words: 'If it were not for assize time I would not take such language.' These words meant that he was not going to use his sword because the criminal judges were in town.

Causing the victim to apprehend immediate and unlawful violence

We need to break this phrase down to examine how the courts apply this principle. There are a number of aspects to the definition that need to be considered:

Causing

This is merely the application of the principles of causation that you have studied at AS level.

Apprehend

If the victim does not *apprehend* immediate force, then an assault has not been committed. In *Lamb* (1967) two friends were playing with a revolver. One of the men was shot dead by the other, but there was no assault because the shot man had not appreciated that the gun would fire, and so could not apprehend immediate force.

The victim does not have to actually *fear* violence, and the word 'apprehend' equally means *anticipating* violence. A heavyweight boxer may not be frightened at the idea of a slap from a frail elderly woman but if he stands in front of her expecting that slap, then theoretically it qualifies as an assault.

Immediate

Traditionally, it has been held that the victim must fear *immediate* violence, and not violence at some time in the near or distant future. However, the law has now taken a more liberal view of the meaning of 'immediacy', in part to allow courts to achieve justice for victims of harassment and stalking campaigns.

In **Smith v Chief Superintendant of Woking Police Station (1983)** the victim was at home in her ground-floor flat, wearing only her night dress, when she was terrified by suddenly seeing the accused staring in at her through the window from her garden. The accused was unable to enter the flat because the doors and windows were locked, but the court ruled that the requirement of immediacy was satisfied if the victim 'did not know what the defendant was going to do next, but whatever he might be going to do ... was something of a violent nature.' This suggests that 'immediate' does not mean the same as 'instantaneous'.

In *Burstow* (1997) the House of Lords ruled that the case for immediacy was proved if the conduct of the accused caused the victim to apprehend the 'possibility' of an immediate attack. Such fear does not even have to be rational in the panic of the moment, provided that it is genuinely held.

Unlawful violence

The use of the word 'violence' can be misleading. The phrase 'apprehend immediate and unlawful force' is often used as an alternative way

■ Key cases

Tuberville v Savage (1669): words can prevent an assault if they make clear that the victim will not suffer immediate harm.

Smith v Chief Superintendant of Woking Police Station (1983): fear of what the accused might be likely to do next was sufficiently immediate for the purposes of the offence.

The victim feared an attack from the man outside, even though her doors and windows were locked (Smith v Superintendant of Woking Police Station (1983))

of stating the principle of assault, because the victim is not required to apprehend any injury, pain or harm for the purposes of proving the offence. In fact, assault can be committed even where the 'force' apprehended is a mere touch, provided that touch is unwanted. This leads on to the final requirement of unlawfulness. Generally, a lack of consent to the feared violence or force will make it unlawful, but this principle and its exceptions will be discussed below under battery.

Mens rea

The *mens rea* of assault was stated in *Savage* (1992) as an intention to cause the victim to apprehend immediate and unlawful violence, or recklessness as to whether such an apprehension is caused. The intention can be direct or oblique intention. The recklessness is *Cunningham* (1957) recklessness, so the defendant must realise that his acts or words could cause the victim to apprehend violence.

Battery

Actus reus

The *actus reus* of **battery** was stated in *Ireland; Burstow* (1997) as the application of unlawful physical force on another. The victim does not have to suffer any pain or injury.

In **Collins v Willcock (1984)** it was decided that 'any touching of another person, however slight, may amount to a battery'. In this case, a police officer had committed a battery by taking hold of the arm of a woman suspected of soliciting for the purposes of prostitution. This had been done to detain her but with no intention to make an arrest.

A slap, a kiss, throwing a drink over someone, and even touching the victim's clothes has been suggested as meeting the requirements of a battery. In *Thomas* (1985) a school caretaker rubbed the hem of a pupil's skirt and the court held that touching a person's clothes is equivalent to touching the person, and could therefore be a battery.

Unlawful physical force

The fact that the victim has not consented to the battery will usually make the act unlawful. However, genuine consent will not always make the act lawful, and this is discussed in detail – together with the other criminal defences that you will study – in Chapter 4: Defences.

Certain force is lawful even without consent, such as the reasonable force applied in self-defence. Police officers may use reasonable force in the prevention of crime, but only so far as the law deems necessary for them to carry out their duties. The officer in *Collins v Willcock* (1984) was held to have committed a battery because he was not arresting the woman and therefore had no need to take her arm.

It would be absurd to make all touching without consent an offence, as unwanted physical contact is almost unavoidable in everyday situations. Lord Goff recognised this in *Collins v Willcock* (1984):

> Most of the physical contacts of ordinary life are not actionable because they are impliedly consented to by all who move in society and so expose themselves to the risk of bodily contact. So nobody can complain of the jostling which is inevitable from his presence in, for example, a supermarket, an underground station or a busy street; nor can a person who attends a party complain if his hand is seized in friendship, or even if his back is (within reason) slapped.

However, if the contact exceeds what is generally held to be acceptable (such as a hand squeezed tightly and at length until it hurts, or a person repeatedly slapped on the back) then the *actus reus* of battery might still be established.

Key terms

Battery: intentionally or recklessly applying unlawful physical force on another.

Key cases

Collins v Willcock (1984): followed earlier cases to rule that the slightest touch (holding an arm, in this case) can amount to a battery.

Indirect batteries

Most batteries are force applied directly by one person to another. However, it has been long established that batteries can be inflicted *indirectly*. In *Martin* (1881) the accused placed an iron bar across the exit in a theatre, turned off the lights and shouted 'fire'. Several people were hurt in the ensuing crush, and the conduct was held to constitute a battery.

More recently was the case of **DPP v K (1990)** where a 15-year-old schoolboy hid sulphuric acid in a hand drier in a school toilet block. He had no intention of causing harm, and planned to remove it later. However, in the meantime, a fellow pupil used the drier and was sprayed by the acid, which caused severe scars on his face. The court confirmed that battery could be committed by an indirect act. This principle was developed further in **Haystead v Chief Constable of Derbyshire (2000)** where the accused punched a woman, causing her to drop her baby. The court held that the defendant had effectively used the woman as a weapon to injure the baby, and he was held liable. The defendant would also have been liable under the principle of transferred malice, which is discussed below in relation to *mens rea*.

Omissions

Unlike assault, a battery can be committed by an omission, but only where there is a duty to act. This limits the scenarios where omission might be relevant, but there is one interesting reported case where the defendant had created a dangerous situation and then failed to act. In *Santana-Bermudez* (2004) the accused was asked, but failed, to inform a police officer searching him that he had a hypodermic needle in his pocket. The officer was injured when she put her hand in his pocket, and the court ruled that his failure to tell her of the needle satisfied the requirements of the *actus reus*.

Mens rea

The *mens rea* of battery was confirmed in *Venna* (1976) as the intention to apply force to another, or recklessness as to whether such force is so applied. It is important to note that the intention or recklessness is only required for the act of physical contact itself, and not in respect of harm that might arise from such contact.

Remember that the defendant might be liable under the doctrine of transferred malice, as illustrated in *Latimer* (1886). In this case, the defendant intentionally hit A with his belt, but the belt rebounded and accidentally hit B. The defendant had the *mens rea* for the attack on A and this was transferred to the act upon B, which satisfied the *actus reus* of battery. The doctrine only operates where the *mens rea* and *actus reus* coincide for the same crime, as they did here.

> **Key cases**
>
> **DPP v K (1990):** confirmed that a battery can be committed by an indirect act.
>
> **Haystead v Chief Constable of Derbyshire (2000):** developed the rule that an indirect act can be a battery by finding that a woman who had dropped her baby after being punched had been used as an 'instrument' to commit the battery.

> ■ **Activity**
>
> Identify which offences might have been committed in the following scenarios and use case authorities to back your argument:
>
> **1** Alice has been sponsored for charity to hug as many people as she can in 60 minutes. She sees Ben in the street and shouts, 'I am going to give you a great big hug!' Ben does not want to be hugged by a stranger and replies, 'No thanks, not today'. Alice ignores this and hugs him anyway.
>
> **2** Ellie has recently split up from her violent boyfriend, Carl. She is sitting in a bus in a traffic jam when she receives a text from him saying, 'You are going to die'. Terrified, she looks out of the window and sees him sitting in a café on the other side of the road.

You should now be able to:

■ explain and distinguish the offences of assault and battery

■ explain the law to given scenarios.

2 Sections 47, 20 and 18 of the Offences Against the Person Act 1861

When the victim has suffered harm, depending on the degree of harm the defendant will be charged under ss47, 20 or 18 of the Offences Against the Person Act 1861 (OAPA 1861). These are statutory offences but the sections only provide the basic definitions of each offence and case law is heavily relied upon to explain the meaning of the terms used in setting out the offences.

Section 47 of OAPA 1861

Section 47 deals with the least serious cases of harm. Section 47 states:

> Whosoever shall be convicted on indictment of any assault occasioning actual bodily harm shall be liable to imprisonment for not more than five years.

The offence is triable either way, depending on the gravity of the assault.

Actus reus

As you have seen at AS, the key elements in the *actus reus* are the words:

■ assault

■ occasioning

■ actual bodily harm.

Assault

The term 'assault' under s47 means either an assault or a battery according to the cases and principles set out for assault above.

Occasioning

An assault or battery will only be charged under s47 if it *occasions* actual bodily harm. If there is no such harm, then the charge will be brought under s39 of the CJA 1988. 'Occasion' appears to mean the same as 'cause' and the normal rules of causation apply, as confirmed in *Roberts* (1971). The facts of this case were that the victim jumped from a moving car, fearing a sexual assault when the accused told her to undress and tried to remove her coat. The court needed to consider whether the victim's actions in jumping out of the car, had broken the causal chain. The court ruled that the chain was still intact since her actions could 'reasonably have been foreseen as the consequence of what he was saying or doing.' The judgement recognised that a victim will not necessarily act in a sensible manner in a moment of fright, but added that a defendant might not be held responsible if the victim does something 'daft' or unexpected that no reasonable man could be expected to foresee.

Where the accused directly physically attacks their victim, then causation is immediately established and no further discussion is required.

Actual bodily harm

The word 'actual' refers to the fact that, unlike assault or battery, there must be some form of physical or psychological injury caused to the victim. **Assault occasioning actual bodily harm** can be very minor

In this topic, you will learn how to:

■ explain the offence of assault occasioning actual bodily harm

■ explain the offence of reckless infliction of grievous bodily harm or wounding

■ explain the offence of wounding or causing grievous bodily harm with intent

■ *mens rea* of each offence

■ distinguish between each of the offences

■ explain cases that illustrate each of the offences

■ apply the rules to a given situation.

> **Key terms**
>
> **Assault occasioning actual bodily harm:** assault or battery causing an injury that is more than trivial but less than serious harm.

Key cases

Miller (1954): actual bodily harm is 'any hurt or injury calculated to interfere with the health or comfort of the victim' that is not 'transient or trifling'.

Chan Fook (1994): psychiatric harm can be deemed actual bodily harm, provided that expert evidence shows the harm is a symptom of an identifiable clinical condition and not just 'mere emotions'.

Savage; Parmenter (1991): House of Lords ruled in this combined appeal that *Roberts* (1971) was the correct law on s47, confirming the Court of Appeal judgement in *Savage* (1991) and overruling the Court of Appeal judgement in *Parmenter* (1991) that had stated that subjective recklessness was required in respect of the harm caused.

harm, and indeed was described in **Miller (1954)** as 'any hurt or injury calculated to interfere with the health or comfort of the victim', provided it is more than 'transient and trifling'.

The definition of actual bodily harm was extended to hair being cut without the consent of the victim in *DPP* v *Smith* (2006). Here, the defendant forced down the head of his former girlfriend and chopped off her ponytail. The defence tried to argue that hair could not be treated as 'bodily' harm since it was dead tissue above the scalp. The court disagreed, however, and determined that hair was to be treated as part of the body. It noted that cutting a woman's hair without her consent is a 'serious matter amounting to actual (not trivial or insignificant) bodily harm'. It was also stated, *obiter*, that if paint or a similar material was put on the hair, that could also be actual bodily harm.

Injuries such as a lost or broken tooth, loss of consciousness, minor cuts requiring medical treatment (such as stitches), minor fractures and extensive bruising would normally be charged under s47.

Psychiatric as well as physical harm can be regarded as actual bodily harm, and this was confirmed in **Chan Fook (1994)**. In this case, a victim had been subjected to aggressive interrogation and locked in a room when he was suspected of stealing an engagement ring. The Court of Appeal ruled that the term 'actual bodily harm' could cover psychiatric harm, but only if medical experts could prove that the state of mind caused in the victim was evidence of an identifiable clinical condition; 'mere emotions such as fear, panic and distress', when unrelated to such a condition, would not be considered actual bodily harm.

It needs to be noted that the definition of actual bodily harm from *Miller* (1954) is therefore not adequate as a principle to be applied to psychiatric harm cases, as these cases require a more serious degree of harm amounting to a clinical condition.

Mens rea

The combined House of Lords appeal of *Savage; Parmenter* (1991) confirmed that the *mens rea* for assault is sufficient to establish the *mens rea* for a s47 offence. Accordingly, the *mens rea* is either intention or recklessness as to causing the victim to apprehend immediate and unlawful violence, or intention or recklessness as to the application of unlawful force. The crucial point to note here is that no extra *mens rea* need be proved as regards the harm caused by the assault or battery. The accused does not have to have intended or even had foresight of the slightest bodily harm, provided that he intended or had foresight of the actual assault or battery itself and that this assault or battery caused the harm.

The facts of **Savage (1992)** explain this principle. Mrs Savage was in a pub when she spotted her husband's ex-girlfriend. Mrs Savage went over to the other women and said, 'Nice to meet you darling' and threw the contents of her glass of beer at her. But as well as being soaked by the beer, the victim's wrist was also cut by a piece of broken glass as Mrs Savage dropped the glass after throwing the beer. Mrs Savage said that she had not meant to drop the glass and insisted that she had only intended to throw the beer without any intention to injure the victim. Nor had she realised

Cutting a ponytail was held to be actual bodily harm (DPP v Smith (2006))

that there was any risk of injury. Her argument was that she could, at most, be liable under s39 for battery for covering her victim with beer, but that she could not be liable under s47 because she did not have the necessary *mens rea* for the more serious actual bodily harm that followed when the glass broke. However, the Court of Appeal decisively ruled that provided there was proof of an assault (using the assault definitions for the *actus reus* and *mens rea*) then the case for a s47 offence was made by simply proving that this assault caused (occasioned) the actual bodily harm.

This confirmed the position in **Roberts (1971)** where the defendant had the *mens rea* for the battery as he had intended to touch the girl's coat but had not intended nor had foresight even of the fact she might suffer minor injuries. He was convicted under s47 because he had the necessary *mens rea* for battery and this battery had *caused* the actual bodily harm.

Mrs Savage appealed her case to the House of Lords, which heard it together with an appeal in the case of *Parmenter* (1991), where a defendant had played with his son so roughly that he had caused injuries to him. The defendant in this case also argued that he did not have the required *mens rea* for the actual bodily harm caused by the assault. By awkward coincidence, the Court of Appeal hearings of both cases had taken place on the same day, but the judges in *Parmenter* (1991) came to a different conclusion and ruled that it was necessary to find that the defendant had been subjectively reckless not only in respect of the battery but *also* in respect of the actual bodily harm caused! Fortunately, the House of Lords established some certainty on the matter by confirming the Court of Appeal ruling in *Savage* (1992) and overruling *Parmenter* (1991) on the grounds that the law on the necessary *mens rea* for s47 was correctly stated in *Roberts* (1971).

Section 20 of OAPA 1861

Section 20 of OAPA 1861 states:

> Whosoever shall unlawfully and maliciously wound or inflict any grievous bodily harm upon any person, either with or without any weapon or instrument, shall be guilty of an offence and shall be liable ... to imprisonment for not more than 5 years.

Section 20 is a more grave offence than s47, despite the fact that the maximum sentence for both offences is five years. The offence is triable either way.

Actus reus

As has been seen at AS, the offence can be committed in either of two ways:

1 unlawful **wounding**, or

2 unlawful infliction of **grievous bodily harm**.

The defendant is charged with wounding *or* grievous bodily harm. If the wound has also inflicted grievous bodily harm, then the prosecution must choose from the two offences, depending on which reflects the true nature of the assault.

Wounding

A wound takes place when both layers of the skin are broken and there is usually blood loss. In **JCC v Eisenhower (1994)** the victim was hit in the eye with a pellet fired from an air pistol. He suffered ruptured blood vessels in his eye but the court held that there must be 'a break in the continuity of the skin' to constitute a wound for the purposes of s20 and internal bleeding was not sufficient. Scratches, abrasions and burns will not be considered wounds

---

Key cases

Roberts (1971): *mens rea* for s47 is the same as for assault and battery; no further requirement to show *mens rea* in respect of any intention or foresight as to the harm caused.

JCC v Eisenhower (1994): wound must break the continuity of the skin, and internal bleeding is not sufficient.

Key terms

Wounding: both layers of the skin are broken, usually causing blood loss.

Grievous bodily harm: injury that causes serious harm, or more than one minor injury that together cause serious harm.

Key cases

DPP v Smith (1961): grievous bodily harm means no more and no less than 'really serious harm'.

Burstow; Ireland (1997): s20 offence can be committed without an assault or battery involving either direct or indirect force, and 'inflict' should have the same meaning as 'cause'.

(unless the second layer of skin is broken) and nor will broken bones and internal ruptures. The definition of 'skin' includes the inner lining of cheeks and lips. This definition leads to the strange conclusion that a pin prick to the skin that draws blood can be classed as a wound.

Grievous bodily harm

A minor wound might be charged as a s20 offence but any other bodily harm under s20 must be 'grievous'. In **DPP v Smith (1961)** the House of Lords ruled that 'grievous' means no more and no less than 'really serious'. In *Saunders* (1985) it was held that 'serious harm' would suffice and the word 'really' was not necessary. Psychiatric harm can be grievous bodily harm provided that it is sufficiently serious (**Burstow (1997)**). Examples of serious injury include: broken bones, injuries requiring lengthy medical treatment, and injuries causing a substantial loss of blood or permanent disability or disfigurement.

Stalking Nightmare

Had the new stalking law that came into force this week existed 20 years ago, Tracey Morgan might have been spared her horrendous nine-year ordeal at the hands of Anthony Burstow, now in prison for the attempted murder of another woman.

Under this new law, those who harass others by following or spying on them can be jailed for up to six months, and those who cause their target to fear violence or force them to change the way they live face up to five years.

Nobody is more delighted than Tracey, who has campaigned tirelessly for 16 years to change the law. Her own ordeal began in November 1992 when Burstow started work at the Royal Navy base in Hampshire where Tracey was a shy, 24-year-old, married PA.

'Burstow was 32 and his wife was stationed with the Navy in Hong Kong so I felt sorry for him,' says Tracey, now 44. 'I made an effort to include him in office life. But suddenly everywhere I went he was there, even in my rear view mirror as I drove to work. One night he followed me home and when I demanded an explanation he told me to mind my own business. My bosses banned him from my office.'

Undeterred, Burstow turned up on Tracey's doorstep one Saturday while her husband Andy was out, ringing the bell repeatedly and making silent calls to the home phone. Andy reassured her they'd tackle Burstow together but neither could fathom what terror would follow. Unbeknown to them, Burstow had taken Tracey's house keys from her bag at work, had copies made and would let himself into her home at lunch times.

Tracey says: 'Underwear was taken from my drawers and draped over my car wing mirrors. There were silent calls day and night, anonymous mail and Burstow turned up wherever we were – we didn't know he'd bugged our house and my office so he overheard all our plans. I couldn't sleep and was too scared to leave the house.'

In January 1993 Tracey alerted Hampshire police. At the time there were no laws in the UK to

deal with stalking so although the police were desperate to prosecute Burstow incredibly they couldn't do so unless he physically harmed her. When he poured oil over her car twice that same year he was jailed for six months and Tracey and Andy flew to South Africa for a holiday. But while they were away Burstow appealed his sentence and was released.

'He removed the glass from the lounge window and took photos and our wedding video,' she says. 'The police later found the video in Burstow's car and he got 18 months for burglary. But even from prison he made crank calls. Chillingly, when police decoded disks found in his cell they contained details of how he'd bugged our house and tried to pay someone to kill Andy.' Petrified, they moved house but ten days later the calls started again. Sadly, Tracey's marriage broke down and she moved in with her parents.

'In February 1995, Hampshire police tried to bring a test case where Burstow would be tried for grievous bodily harm causing psychiatric injury, but the case was deemed too fragile,' Tracey explains. 'Then he stole underwear from my parents' washing line and was arrested for theft so the police attempted a second charge of GBH of the mind and in March 1996 Burstow got three years.'

Tracey joined missing estate agent Suzy Lamplugh's mother Diana, the assistant chief constable of Sussex police and two detectives to fight for a stalking law. Ten days before Burstow's early release in June 1997, the Protection From Harassment Act was introduced, making it an offence to harass another person, with a maximum five-year penalty. 'It was such a groundbreaking law that everyone seized upon it, which meant my case was in the same bracket as two neighbours rowing over a hedge,' Tracey adds. 'That's why it's such a step forward to have stalking now recognised as a serious crime.'

Express.co.uk, 27 November 2012

Bollom (2004) ruled that the victim being elderly or a child is relevant to the grievousness of the harm, since their injuries will tend to be more serious than the same injuries to a 'six-foot adult in the fullness of health'. In this case, a 17-month-old baby suffered extensive bruising and abrasions and this was treated as grievous bodily harm.

If the victim suffers minor injuries which, taken as a whole, amount to serious harm, then this has been held to constitute grievous bodily harm despite the fact that the injuries viewed separately would not satisfy the seriousness required for s20. This was decided in **Brown and Stratton (1998)**, where the victim was beaten and suffered multiple injuries including concussion, bruising, lost teeth and a broken nose, and these minor injuries were considered together to be chargeable under s20 as grievous bodily harm.

The grievous bodily harm must be 'inflicted' upon the victim. It had been argued in the past that 'inflict' has a narrower meaning than 'cause' used in s18 in respect of wounding and grievous bodily harm with intent. At its narrowest interpretation in *Clarence* (1888) 'inflict' was understood to need an assault or battery requiring the application of direct force. In this case, the court held that the defendant had not inflicted grievous bodily harm on his wife when he infected her with gonorrhoea on the basis that her consent to sexual intercourse meant that there had not been a battery.

However, in *Wilson* (1996) it was held that an offence under s20 could be committed without any need for an assault or battery. This was confirmed in **Burstow (1997)**, where the House of Lords ruled that there was no necessity to apply direct or indirect force. The prosecution only needed to prove that the defendant caused the victim to suffer grievous bodily harm. Lord Hope added that for practical purposes the words 'cause' and 'inflict' may be taken to be interchangeable.

Removing the requirement for an assault or battery under s20 led to the development of 'biological' grievous bodily harm in **Dica (2004)** where the defendant was knowingly suffering from HIV and infected two women through consensual sex. Dica was convicted and the court ruled that *Clarence* (1888) 'should have no further relevance' in cases where the defendant knows that they are suffering from HIV or some other serious sexual disease and recklessly transmits it to the unknowing victim through consensual intercourse.

Unlawfulness

The last issue to discuss is the fact that a wounding or grievous harm needs to be unlawful in order to be an offence and in most cases a simple lack of consent by the victim will render the act unlawful. However, there are instances where, even if the victim has consented, the defendant will still be liable and this is discussed in Chapter 4, Defences.

Mens rea

The wounding or grievous bodily harm must be done '**maliciously**' but it was confirmed in *Cunningham* (1957) that this merely means that the

Key cases

Bollom (2004): injuries caused to a child or elderly person will be more serious than the same injuries caused to a strong, healthy adult.

Brown and Stratton (1998): several minor injuries can amount to grievous bodily harm.

Dica (2004): recklessly transmitting a disease to an unknowing victim was ruled to be inflicting grievous bodily harm.

Study tip

Students commonly make the mistake of stating that a wound must be serious enough to satisfy the definition for grievous bodily harm, or conversely that grievous bodily harm has not been committed unless there is a wound. This is not the case: grievous bodily harm can be committed without a wound, and a non-serious wound can amount to unlawful wounding.

Key terms

Maliciously: for the purposes of s20 this means intending the harm or being reckless as to whether such harm might occur (*Cunningham* (1957)).

Key cases

Mowatt (1976): established that the defendant will be liable under s20 provided that he intended or foresaw 'some physical harm to some person, albeit of a minor character'.

defendant must intend to inflict the harm or be subjectively reckless as to whether such harm might occur.

The leading case of **Mowatt (1976)** established the crucial principle that the prosecution does not have to prove that the defendant intended or foresaw the wound or the grievous bodily harm. The case is proved provided that the defendant intended or foresaw that *some* harm *might* occur. Lord Diplock stated in his judgement:

> It is quite unnecessary that the accused should have foreseen that his unlawful act might cause physical harm of the gravity described in the section, i.e. a wound or serious physical injury. It is enough that he should have foreseen that some physical harm to some person, albeit of a minor character, might result.

Lord Diplock's words were the subject of scrutiny in *DPP* v *A* (2000) where a 13-year-old boy had mistakenly shot his friend in the eye whilst meaning to fire below knee level. The magistrates' court dismissed the s20 charge but prosecution appealed on the basis that the word 'maliciously' had been wrongly applied, and the Divisional Court allowed the appeal. The magistrates had taken their definition from *Stone's Justices' Manual* but this reputable publication had mistakenly stated that the defendant needs to foresee that the harm *would* occur as opposed to the correct interpretation that the harm *might* occur.

Section 18 of OAPA 1861

Section 18 provides:

> Whosoever shall unlawfully and maliciously by any means whatsoever wound or cause any grievous bodily harm to any person, with intent to do some grievous bodily harm to any person, or with intent to resist or prevent the lawful apprehension or detainer of any person, shall be guilty of an offence, and being convicted thereof shall be liable … to imprisonment for life.

This is a much more serious offence than s20, despite the similarities in language used to describe the assault. It is triable on indictment only, and the maximum sentence is life imprisonment.

Actus reus

The *actus reus* is unlawfully wounding or causing grievous bodily harm to the victim. The meanings of the words 'wound' and 'grievous bodily harm' are exactly the same as for s20, and the defendant needs only to 'cause' these injuries with the normal rules of causation applying.

Section 18 also covers wounding and causing grievous bodily harm when resisting arrest, and this charge will be preferred where it might be easier to prove that the defendant intended to resist arrest than prove that he intended to cause grievous bodily harm.

Again, the wound or grievous bodily harm must be unlawful and the comments above in relation to s20 apply equally to s18.

Mens rea

The vital difference between s20 and s18 is the level of *mens rea*. Recklessness is sufficient to establish *mens rea* for s20, but only intention will suffice for s18. Furthermore, it is not enough to intend *some* harm, but instead prosecution must prove that the defendant intended to cause *grievous* bodily harm. Note that when the defendant wounds the victim, the *mens rea* must be to intend grievous bodily harm. An intention to wound does not form part of the *mens rea*. If the defendant intended serious harm then he will be convicted under s18 even if the wound turns out to be a minor injury.

Study tip

It can be helpful to use the IDEA method when approaching a scenario question:

■ **Identify** the relevant offences by looking at what happened to the victim – pay attention to the words used, such as 'severe'.

■ **Define** the *actus reus* and *mens rea* for the relevant offences.

■ **Explain** the key points of the definitions, with reference to case law.

■ **Apply** the law to the facts, using all the details given in the scenario.

In respect of resisting arrest where the defendant causes serious injury the *mens rea* requirement is that the defendant must intend to resist or prevent an arrest but need not have intended serious harm. It is sufficient that the defendant intends or is reckless as to causing some harm which is the same as for s20, as stated in *Morrison* (1989).

Oblique intention as well as direct intention applies to s18. Therefore, according to the test in *Nedrick* (1986), if the defendant foresaw that grievous bodily harm was virtually certain to result from his conduct then he will be liable under s18. Oblique intention could be used to satisfy the *mens rea* of assault, battery, s47 and s20 but the prosecution is more likely to establish recklessness as this is easier to prove.

Activities

1 Raz and Kieran are enjoying an afternoon at an outdoor swimming pool when a heated argument breaks out between them. Raz tells Kieran to calm down but Kieran, now even more angry, pushes Raz into the water. As he falls, Raz cracks his head on the side of the pool and the cut requires stitches. Raz climbs out of the pool and, furious, starts to chase Kieran, who runs straight out of the swimming pool complex and onto the road where he is knocked down by a speeding car. He suffers a broken leg and ruptured spleen. Consider what offences Raz and Kieran might have committed.

2 Make up a fight scenario that will require the application of the law from both *Mowatt* (1976) and *JCC v Eisenhower* (1994) when considering whether any offence has been committed. Then provide the answer, setting out the relevant potential offences and the principles from both these cases together with any other cases you use.

3 Find an article in a newspaper or online that gives details of a court hearing where the defendant has been convicted of an offence under ss47, 20 or 18 of the OAPA 1861. Explain how the facts of the case satisfy requirement of the *actus reus* and *mens rea* for each relevant offence.

4 Read the study tip box on page 40 and use the outlined method to approach this scenario:

Andy, Gary and their friends had been drinking heavily in a bar one night when Chris and his friends came in. There was a lot of ill feeling between the two groups, and Chris began making loud and insulting remarks about Andy's girlfriend Debbie, who was also Gary's sister. While Chris's group were laughing about it, Andy suddenly threw a bottle of beer at Chris. Chris was not aware of this until the bottle struck the wall just behind him and shattered, causing him to jump away instinctively. At that moment, Edward, a customer unconnected with either group, panicked and tried to run out of the bar. However, the floor was now wet with beer and he slipped and fell straight on to the jagged edge of the broken beer bottle. The resulting damage was so severe that he lost his sight in one eye.

When applying the law to the facts, ask yourself why the scenario includes the detail that Chris was not aware of the bottle being thrown initially. What is the significance of Edward being hurt when he was not connected to the dispute? Can the fact that Edward ran away be used in the application? In this scenario, you would also need to consider the defence of voluntary intoxication (discussed in Chapter 4).

You should now be able to:

■ explain and distinguish the offence, under ss47, 20 and 18 of the Offences Against the Person Act 1861

■ explain and apply the law to given scenarios.

4   Defences

In this topic, you will learn how to:

■ outline the range of defences in the syllabus

■ explain the effect of a successful defence to a crime

■ state an appropriate method of applying a defence to problem questions.

1 Introduction to defences in criminal law

The AQA Law specification for Unit 3 sets out the defences that will be included. These are insanity, automatism, intoxication, consent and self-defence/prevention of crime. Defences become relevant when the *actus reus* of an offence has been committed with the applicable *mens rea*. Therefore, in your answers to the scenario-based questions, you are well-advised to discuss the offences and then consider the application of any relevant defence.

The defence of insanity is too narrow to include many of the mental problems from which people can suffer. This is why the Homicide Act 1957 introduced the partial defence of diminished responsibility. The verdict given when a person successfully pleads insanity is 'not guilty by reason of insanity'.

The defence of automatism requires an external factor, which distinguishes it from insanity. However, the defence will not be available if the defendant was responsible for creating the automatism.

The defence of intoxication through drink or drugs is sometimes said not to be a defence at all, but incapacity to form the *mens rea* of the crime. A defendant will be guilty of most crimes if committed whilst intoxicated, but being drunk or under the influence of drugs may mean that the necessary intent could not be formed for crimes such as murder.

Self-defence/prevention of crime are a mixture of defences that largely apply to crimes involving violence, so have important application to some of the offences within this unit.

The defences are to some extent interlinked. The challenge is to select the appropriate defence or defences for the individual problems.

You should now be able to:

■ outline the range of defences available in the AQA specification

■ understand the effect of a defence to a crime

■ understand how to approach problem questions involving a defence.

In this topic, you will learn how to:

■ explain the meaning of the defence of insanity

■ distinguish between insanity and diminished responsibility

■ explain cases that illustrate the defence of insanity

■ apply the rules to a given situation.

2 The defence of insanity

Insanity as a defence is relevant only at the time the offence was committed. Insanity after that is only of relevance in deciding whether the defendant stands trial or not. The defendant must prove that, on the balance of probabilities, he was insane at the time of the offence. If the prosecution wishes to raise the issue of the defendant's insanity, it must prove that beyond reasonable doubt. This is because everyone is presumed to be sane.

If the defence is found to exist, the defendant is not found 'not guilty', but a special verdict of 'not guilty by reason of insanity' is given. Under the Criminal Procedure (Insanity and Unfitness to Plead) Act 1991 the court has a range of options available. For the offence of murder, the court must make a hospital order restricting the defendant's discharge indefinitely. For any other offence, the court may make one of the following orders:

■ a hospital order and an order restricting discharge either for a limited or unlimited period of time

a guardianship order

a supervision and treatment order

an order for absolute discharge.

The law relating to the defence of insanity comes from the case of **M'Naghten (1843)**. This case involved the attempted assassination of the then Prime Minister, Sir Robert Peel. The defendant missed but killed Peel's secretary, Edward Drummond. Medical opinion suggested the defendant was mentally ill, and this resulted in the House of Lords setting out rules for use in such cases.

The rules were set out in the case as follows:

> That if the accused was conscious that the act was one which he ought not to do; and if the act was at the same time contrary to law, he is punishable. In all cases of this kind the jurors ought to be told that every man is presumed to be sane, and to possess a sufficient degree of reason to be responsible for his crimes, until the contrary be proved to their satisfaction: and that to establish a defence on the ground of insanity, it must be clearly proved that at the time of committing the act the party accused was labouring under such a defect of reason, from disease of the mind, as not to know the nature and quality of the act he was doing, or as not to know that what he was doing was wrong.

This sets out three key issues that must be established for the defence to succeed:

1 defect of reason

2 caused by disease of the mind

3 so that the defendant does not know the nature and quality of his act or does not know that what he was doing was wrong.

Defect of reason

The concept of defect of reason is based on an inability by the defendant to use powers of reason, rather than his failing to use his powers of reason. Thus, a person who is confused or absent minded is not insane and, indeed, may have a defence to a crime as lacking the *mens rea*. This can be seen in the case of **Clarke (1972)** where the defendant was charged with stealing from a supermarket. What had happened was that she transferred some items from the supermarket's basket to her own bag and left the shop without paying for these items. She claimed that she must have put the items in her bag in a moment of absent-mindedness, and had no intent to steal. She suffered from diabetes, a number of domestic problems and clinical depression, which could cause her to be absent minded. At her trial, the judge said this was a defence of insanity, so she quickly withdrew the defence (in 1972, there were not the current options on a finding of insanity). On appeal, the court decided that she was not deprived of reason, merely temporarily absent-minded. She was not, therefore, insane, but could be found not guilty as she lacked the *mens rea* for the offence of theft.

Caused by disease of the mind

The term 'disease of the mind' is a legal term and not a medical term. This is because the law is concerned with whether the defendant should be liable for his acts. The disease of the mind must be a physical disease, rather than one brought about by external factors such as drugs. It can be a permanent state or a temporary state – hence the fact that where the defence is successful, the defendant remains in the control of the court (for example, at a secure hospital) for an indeterminate period.

Daniel M'Naghten's case led to the M'Naghten rules on insanity

Key cases

M'Naghten (1843): this case set out the test for the defence of insanity; there are three key areas of the test – defect of reason, disease of the mind, and the defendant does not know the nature and quality of his act.

Clarke (1972): a person who is confused or absent-minded is not insane; thus an absent-minded person putting things in her own bag rather than a supermarket basket may be not guilty of theft if the jury recognises she did not have the *mens rea* for theft.

The court has attempted to decide what constitutes a disease of the mind over many years. It is perhaps best to look at relevant cases for examples of a disease of the mind, but these should not be seen as an exclusive list. The key is to distinguish the diseased mind from the unaffected mind.

In the case of **Kemp (1957)** the defendant suffered from arteriosclerosis which affected the flow of blood to his brain. This sometimes caused a temporary lack of consciousness. During one such episode, he attacked his wife with a hammer and killed her. The court decided that this was a case of insanity rather than automatism (see Topic 3) and, more importantly, established the fact that a disease of the mind could be temporary and the actual medical condition of the brain was not, in itself, relevant. Devlin J stated:

> In my judgement the condition of the brain is irrelevant and so is the question whether the condition of the mind is curable or incurable, transitory or permanent.

In **Bratty (1963)** Lord Denning approved the statement set out above from Devlin J. He added that any mental disorder that could lead to violence that was likely to reoccur was a disease of the mind. This should be seen as an additional pointer rather than a limiting factor on what amounts to a disease of the mind. Lord Denning was anxious to protect the public from people who suffered in this way. *Bratty* (1963) involved a plea of insanity and automatism by the defendant. The defendant suffered from a psychomotor epileptic seizure, during which the strangulation of a girl took place. The effect of this type of seizure, is that the victim of it may carry out purposeful acts whilst in an unconscious state. In this case, he was driving his van with the girl in the passenger seat. He took off her tights and strangled her with them. The court said that this type of seizure could amount to insanity and gave the court the opportunity to distinguish insanity from automatism.

In **Sullivan (1984)** the defendant kicked and injured his friendly elderly neighbour during a minor epileptic fit. The fact that this was only temporary did not prevent it from being a defence of insanity. It could not be a defence of automatism as that required an external factor. This, and other decisions regarding epileptic fits, demonstrates very clearly that the legal definition of insanity is very different from the medical definition.

In **Burgess (1991)** the defendant had been watching films with his friend at her flat when they both fell asleep. Burgess hit his friend across the head with a bottle and a video recorder and then grabbed her throat; when she cried out, he realised what he had done and claimed he had been sleepwalking. He was charged with s18 Offences Against the Person Act 1861 and pleaded automatism. However, the judge said the appropriate defence was insanity because his sleepwalking was caused by an internal factor, and he was ordered to be detained in a hospital. His appeal against the decision failed, confirming that if sleepwalking is caused by an internal factor it can be classed as a disease of the mind.

So that the defendant does not know the nature and quality of his act or does not know that what he was doing was wrong

The expression 'nature and quality' merely refers to the physical quality of the act. This means that the defendant proves any of the following:

- ▨ that he did not know what he was doing
- ▨ that he did not appreciate the consequences of his act
- ▨ that he did not appreciate the circumstances in which he was acting.

In these situations the defendant lacks *mens rea* but because this is a result of his insanity, the special verdict is given rather than him being acquitted.

■ Key cases

Kemp (1957): arteriosclerosis caused occasional lapses of consciousness in the defendant; whilst he was suffering from this, he killed his wife by hitting her with a hammer; this was treated as insanity.

Bratty (1963): psychomotor epileptic seizure could amount to insanity.

Sullivan (1984): minor epileptic fit can amount to insanity, rather than automatism, in law; automatism requires an external factor.

Burgess (1991): sleepwalking can be a disease of the mind if caused by an internal factor.

The idea that the defendant did not know that what he was doing was wrong means that he had the *mens rea* for the offence but because of his insanity he did not know it was wrong. This does not distinguish between legal and moral 'wrongness'. It seems that a common sense approach to this will prevail – the issue is rarely raised, although it became central in the case of **Windle (1952)**. In that case, the defendant killed his insane wife. He pleaded his own insanity, but had originally given himself up to the police saying, 'I suppose I'll hang for this!' As this showed he knew the nature and quality of his act, and that what he was doing was wrong, he was convicted of murder – a hanging offence at the time.

Conclusion

The defence of insanity is a rarely used defence today as it has a special verdict rather than an acquittal. It was a more popular defence when there was the death penalty for murder and before the introduction of diminished responsibility in the Homicide Act 1957. Defendants are not keen on the indeterminate nature of the orders made under a special verdict, and often withdraw or do not propose the defence. However, if the defendant raises evidence of his mental state by pleading diminished responsibility or automatism, the prosecution can raise insanity. The vital elements of the defence revolve around the distinction between internal and external factors and the idea of a disease of the mind.

> ### ■ Key cases
>
> **Windle (1952)**: defendant did know the nature and quality of his act, and that what he was doing was wrong, so he could not rely on the defence of insanity.

■ Activity

Consider the criminal liability of the defendant in the situation below, taken from the 2007 case of Johnson, and consider the defence of insanity to the offences that you find he has committed:

The appellant in June 2006 was leading an independent life at a block of flats in Barnes. It is plain that he was subject at the time to delusions and to clear auditory hallucinations, which the psychiatrists, who have seen him as a result of the events which we shall describe, had no difficulty in diagnosing as amounting to paranoid schizophrenia.

In another flat in the block in which he lived was a man called Alan Taylor. It is plain that he was somewhat uneasy about the behaviour of the appellant and rightly so as it transpired, for, on 20 June 2006 at about three o'clock in the afternoon the appellant forced his way into Alan Taylor's sitting room while Alan Taylor was watching television. The appellant shouted very aggressively, although it was difficult to make sense of what he was saying. He was holding a large kitchen knife, with which he stabbed Alan Taylor first in the left shoulder. When Alan Taylor tried to protect himself he suffered four deep stab wounds and many small lacerations to his fingers. The applicant then, fortunately having not caused fatal injuries, left the flat and Alan Taylor was able to call the emergency services. He was found in a serious condition, having lost a great deal of blood. After two weeks in hospital, he was happily released and it would appear, again fortunately, that he has made a good recovery.

The story of that afternoon did not end at Alan Taylor's flat, because the appellant turned up at the home of a person who considered himself to be a friend, called Russell Pidworth, at Mortlake Cemetery. Russell Pidworth was not there but his father was. There was a serious incident in the doorway of that house, when it would appear as though the appellant was seeking to obtain entry, asking for Russell. He was carrying a knife, which was clearly the knife with which he had injured Alan Taylor. He was shouting and swearing and accused Russell of 'noncing my sister'. He threatened Russell Pidworth's father, who was there at the time, but bravely, it would appear, was able to at least calm him to the extent that eventually the appellant left. It subsequently transpired that Russell had two days earlier seen the appellant in the cemetery holding a knife and thrashing out at shrubs; and when he, Russell, asked what he was doing the appellant complained at that stage about an Indian man in a shop 'who has been noncing my sister'.

www.bailii.org/ew/cases/EWCA/Crim/2007/1978.html

You should now be able to:

■ state and apply the law of the defence of insanity.

In this topic, you will learn how to:

■ explain the meaning of the defence of automatism

■ distinguish between insane and non-insane automatism

■ explain cases that illustrate the defence of automatism

■ apply the rules to a given situation.

Key cases

Bratty (1963): sets out the key definition for disease of the mind.

Attorney-General's Reference (No. 2 of 1992): automatism requires a total lack of awareness, not just partial control.

Quick (1973): highlights the distinction between automatism from external factors and insanity from internal factors when related to a diabetic condition; taking insulin is an external factor.

3 The defence of automatism

Automatism requires the defendant to show that his act was:

▨ involuntary
▨ due to an external factor.

An involuntary act

The defendant's act must be involuntary in that that his mind is not controlling his limbs in a purposeful manner. This is similar to **Bratty (1963)**, considered in insanity, where the defendant claimed that 'a blackness came over him'. In that case, Lord Denning said:

> No act is punishable if it is done involuntarily and an involuntary act means an act which is done by the muscles without any control by the mind such as a spasm, a reflex action or a convulsion; or an act done by a person who is not conscious of what he is doing, such as an act done whilst suffering from concussion or done whilst sleepwalking.

However, it should be noted that this has to be a total lack of awareness, not just partly automatic as in the case of **Attorney-General's Reference (No. 2 of 1992)** where the defendant killed two people whose car was on the hard shoulder of the motorway. He claimed he was driving his lorry 'without awareness', caused by driving for a long time on the motorway, and was in a trance-like state. The court decided that he was still partly in control so automatism did not apply.

The external factor

This requirement is that the automatism has been caused by an external factor, such as a blow on the head, rather than an internal factor, such as a disease. This has already been seen in the topic of insanity. It follows from this that the automatism must not be self-induced – this is the case with self-administered drink or drugs. Automatism is self-induced when it results from the defendant's actions or failing to take action. This can be seen in the case of **Quick (1973)**, set out below.

The difference between insanity and automatism

The distinction between insanity and automatism is key to the understanding of these defences. The basic rule is that insanity results from factors internal to the defendant and automatism arises as a result of external factors. This is sometimes known as insane automatism and non-insane automatism.

In *Quick* (1973) the defendant was a nurse alone on duty in a ward at a hospital where a paraplegic patient, unable to walk, was sitting watching television. Half an hour later, the patient had sustained two black eyes, a fractured nose, a split lip that required three stitches, and bruising of his arm and shoulders. There was undisputed medical evidence that these injuries could not have been self-inflicted.

The defendant admitted that he had been drinking and that his drinks had included whisky and a quarter of a bottle of rum, but his was not a defence of intoxication. He also said that he was, and had been since the age of seven, a diabetic, and that morning he had taken insulin as prescribed by his doctor. After taking the insulin he had had a very small breakfast and no lunch. On many occasions he had been admitted to hospital either unconscious or semi-conscious due to hypoglycaemia, which is a condition brought about when there is more insulin in the bloodstream than the amount of sugar there can cope with. At the start of the imbalance, the higher functions of the mind are affected. As the effects of the imbalance become more marked, more and more mental functions are upset. Unless the sufferer's hypoglycaemia is reversed (for example, by giving him a sugar lump) he can go into a coma. In the later stages of mental impairment a sufferer may become aggressive and violent without being able to control himself, and without knowing at the time what he is doing or having any recollection afterwards of what he has done.

As the defendant's condition arose as a consequence of an external factor (the insulin), he could rely on a defence of automatism rather than insanity.

In **Hennessey (1989)** the defendant was charged with taking a motor car without authority and driving while disqualified. He claimed that he was suffering from hyperglycaemia (high blood sugar level caused by diabetes) at the time because he had not taken any insulin to stabilise himself, nor eaten properly for days, and as a result was acting unconsciously. The court decided that the defence of automatism was not available to him as the diabetes was an internal factor. The only possible defence for a jury to consider was insanity.

> **Key cases**
>
> **Hennessey (1989):** highlights the distinction between automatism from external factors and insanity from internal factors when related to a diabetic condition; lacking insulin is an internal factor.

Devoted husband who strangled wife in his sleep walks free from court

A 'decent and devoted' husband who strangled his wife while he dreamt she was a intruder has been cleared of murder after the Crown Prosecution Service accepted he had not been in control of his actions but was not a danger to anyone else.

Father-of-two Brian Thomas killed his wife, Christine, as he was in the throes of a nightmare about a 'boy racer' who had broken into the camper van they were sleeping in. Members of the jury at Swansea crown court wept after they were ordered to formally acquit Thomas, who had suffered 'night terrors' for about 50 years without ever being treated.

Experts said afterwards that about 2% of the UK population suffered from the condition, also known as *pavor nocturnus*. It was possible that many other similar attacks were carried out, though not with fatal consequences, and so went unreported.

Thomas, a retired steelworker from Neath in south Wales, will be advised to seek treatment for his condition. Friends and family said he was devastated by the loss of his beloved wife of almost 40 years. In court he was described as a 'broken man' who might try to harm himself. Since he was a child, Thomas had been prone to sleepwalking and other sleep disorders. At home he and his wife slept in separate bedrooms but shared a double bed when they went away in their camper van.

Thomas, 59, used to take tablets for depression but stopped taking them when he and his wife, 57, went away in their van because they made him impotent.

In July last year the couple went on one of their regular jaunts in their camper van. They parked up in a carpark in the seaside village of Aberporth, west Wales but were disturbed by 'boy racers' performing wheelspins and handbrake turns at 11.30 pm.

They drove to the carpark of the Ship Inn in the village where they settled down for the night. But later Thomas made a 999 call saying he had strangled his wife in his sleep.

He told the operator: 'What have I done? I've been trying to wake her. I think I've killed my wife. Oh my God. I thought someone had broken in. I was fighting with those boys but it was Christine. I must have been dreaming or something. What have I done? What have I done? Can you send someone?'

At first police were sceptical but friends and relatives told detectives they were a loving couple. They enjoyed regular nights out, watched rugby together and had booked a Mediterranean cruise to celebrate their forthcoming 40th wedding anniversary. Tests carried out on Thomas, some while he spent ten months in prison on remand, confirmed he suffered from night terrors.

At the start of the trial, the prosecution said it was a 'unique' case. It accepted that Thomas should be found not guilty but initially called for a special verdict of not guilty due to insanity, which would have meant he could have been held in a secure psychiatric hospital. The law dictates that this is a verdict that cannot be determined by anyone other than a jury, which is why the case had to go to court.

But in the end the CPS decided to offer no more evidence and the jury returned a straightforward verdict of not guilty.

The jury had been told that Thomas's sleep disorder meant he was in a state of 'automatism' – his mind was not in control of his body. It is possible he had suffered particularly severe night terrors because he had come off his regular medication.

The Guardian, 20 November 2009

Conclusion

The defence of automatism revolves around the distinction between internal and external factors.

Application of the defences of insanity and automatism to problems in the examination

In the examination, there are often questions involving the defence of insanity or automatism. Discussion of these defences is suggested whenever a character in the scenario appears to be mentally unstable – for example, hearing voices. Automatism is the factor to consider when the character is said to be dazed, concussed or not aware of what he is doing.

Activity

Consider the scenario set out below. You should discuss both offences and possible defences.

For many years, Janine has believed that fairies and pixies live at the bottom of her garden. She now also believes that, as a result of population growth, they have expanded to inhabit parts of the garden of her neighbour, Kenneth.

Janine was looking out of her bedroom window when she saw Kenneth digging in his garden. Believing that Kenneth was destroying the fairies' and pixies' homes, she rushed into the garden. As she went out, she picked up an old shotgun that had been left behind by her first husband. She believed the gun was unloaded and she was about to take it to hand in at a weapons amnesty. She then started to shout and wave the shotgun at Kenneth. Unfortunately, the shotgun was loaded and went off, injuring Kenneth who fell to the ground.

Janine was shocked by what had happened and thought she had killed Kenneth. She began to move in a trance-like manner to where Kenneth lay. She thought Kenneth was dead so dragged him to her compost heap where she covered him in leaves. Some days later he died of exposure.

You should now be able to:

- state and apply the law of the defence of automatism
- distinguish between insanity and automatism.

In this topic, you will learn how to:

- state the definition of the defence of intoxication
- distinguish between crimes of basic and specific offence
- distinguish between the effect of voluntary and involuntary intoxication
- explain the effect of mistake when intoxicated
- explain the law relating to Dutch courage
- apply the rules to a given situation.

4 The defence of intoxication

Intoxication can be either voluntary or involuntary. In general, where the intoxication is voluntary, a person should not be excused from the consequences of their actions. This is because that person is responsible for being in the state of intoxication that impairs their judgement. However, intoxication can be used to show that the defendant could not form the necessary *mens rea* for the offence with which he has been charged. In that sense, it can provide a defence.

Voluntary and involuntary intoxication

Voluntary intoxication is where the defendant takes the drink or drugs of his own free will. Involuntary intoxication is where a person does not know he is taking alcohol or intoxicating drugs. In cases of involuntary intoxication, there will only be a defence if the *mens rea* for a crime was not formed. If this is proved, the defendant will be acquitted. Involuntary intoxication can arise where:

- the defendant's drinks were spiked with alcohol or drugs, such as when a drug is slipped into a soft drink or alcohol is added without the defendant's knowledge

■ the defendant takes drugs prescribed by his doctor in accordance with the instructions

■ the defendant takes a non-dangerous drug, although not prescribed to him, in a non-reckless way.

If involuntary intoxication is to be a defence, it must be shown that the effect of the intoxication is that the defendant was, as a result of the intoxication, unable to form the *mens rea* of the offence. This is not always possible, as can be seen in the case of **Kingston (1994)**. At a trial in the Lewes Crown Court in March 1992, the defendant, Barry Kingston, and a man named Penn were jointly indicted on a count of indecent assault on a youth aged 15. The defendant, who had paedophiliac homosexual tendencies (which he normally controlled fully), was blackmailed by two former business associates who arranged for Penn to photograph and audio-tape Kingston in a compromising situation with the boy. Sedative drugs were found in Penn's flat when it was searched and the prosecution claimed that Penn had laced the boy's drink. Kingston's defence was that Penn had also laced his drink. Kingston said that he had seen the boy lying on the bed but had no recollection of any other events that night, and had woken in his own home the next morning. He said that he would never have committed the offence had he not been affected by the drug. The House of Lords stated that involuntary intoxication was not a defence to a charge if it was proved that the defendant had the necessary intent when the offence was committed, even though he was not to blame for the intoxication. Lord Mustill saw this case as one of disinhibition – the taking of the drug (whatever it was) lowered Kingston's ability to resist temptation, so that his desires overrode his ability to control them.

If the defendant argues that he did not realise the strength of the alcohol or the drugs, this will not be classed as involuntary intoxication. This was decided in **Allen (1988)** where the defendant was charged with indecent assault but argued that he didn't realise the strength of the wine he had been given. His intoxication was classed as voluntary.

Where the defendant takes a non-dangerous drug, although not specifically prescribed to him, the taking may be treated as involuntary and may therefore provide a defence if it was not done recklessly. This can be seen in the case of **Hardie (1985)**. Here, the defendant's relationship with Mrs Hardie had broken down and she had insisted that he must leave. He did not wish to do so, but on the morning of 2 January 1982 he packed a suitcase. At about lunchtime he found two bottles of tablets in a cabinet. One contained Valium that Mrs Hardie had been prescribed in 1974.

Key cases

Kingston (1994): defendant can only use the defence of involuntary intoxication if the court is convinced that because of being intoxicated the defendant lacked the required *mens rea* for the offence; in this case, the court said that an intoxicated intent was still an intent.

Allen (1988): intoxication remains voluntary even where the defendant claims he did not know the strength of the drink or drugs.

Hardie (1985): voluntary consumption of dangerous drugs might be conclusive proof of recklessness; this is not the case with non-dangerous drugs, and a jury should have been directed to consider whether the defendant had been reckless in consuming the Valium.

Taking a prescription drug to relieve stress was classed as involuntary intoxication in Hardie (1985)

Whilst he had never taken Valium before, the defendant took one about 12 o'clock to calm him down, but it did not have much effect. He and Mrs Hardie then went shopping and he took two more in front of her. She said, 'Take as many as you like, they are old stock and will do you no harm'. He took two more shortly afterwards and when back at the house he fell into a deep sleep. From this time on, he could remember only odd periods for the rest of the day.

It was not disputed that the defendant must have started the fire, for he was alone in the bedroom when it started. Having started it, he emerged, returned to the sitting room to be with Mrs Hardie and her daughter, Tonia, and stayed there. Shortly afterwards, Mrs Hardie heard sounds from the bedroom, went there and found smoke and flames coming from the wardrobe. There was evidence that before, at the time of and after the fire the defendant was showing signs of intoxication, and that such signs might have resulted from the taking of Valium some hours earlier.

The court decided that this did not necessarily amount to voluntary intoxication. The jury should be directed that if they came to the conclusion that, as a result of the Valium, the defendant was at the time unable to appreciate the risks to property and persons from his actions, they should then consider whether the taking of the Valium was itself reckless. The courts later decided that there was a distinction between 'dangerous' drugs, including those where it is 'common knowledge' that the taker 'may become aggressive or do dangerous or unpredictable things' or those that make the defendant incapable of appreciating risks (amphetamines and LSD being well-known examples), and non-dangerous drugs such as Valium. Where the drug can be said to be dangerous, there may be recklessness in self-administering it, which would be the case when the drug was well known for causing certain negative effects.

The distinction between crimes of basic intent and specific intent

Where intoxication is voluntary, it is necessary to establish whether the crime is one of basic intent or specific intent.

Key cases

Majewski (1977): this case made the distinction between crimes of basic intent and crimes of specific intent.

The principle is that intoxication is a defence to crimes of specific intent and not those of basic intent. The key case with respect to this is **Majewski (1977)**. In that case, during the evening of 19 February 1973 the defendant and his friend, Leonard Stace, who had also taken drugs and drink, went to The Bull public house in Basildon. Stace became involved in a disturbance. Glasses were broken. The landlord asked Stace to leave and escorted him to the door. As he did so, Stace called to Majewski: 'He's putting me out.' Majewski got up and prevented the landlord from getting Stace out, and abused him. The landlord told both men to go. They refused and a brawl followed. Majewski was violent and abusive and spat in the landlord's face. When the police came, a fierce struggle took place to get Majewski out. He shouted at the police: 'You pigs, I'll kill you all, you f—— pigs, you bastards.' Majewski was charged with s47 OAPA 1861 assault occasioning actual bodily harm. His defence of voluntary intoxication was unsuccessful as s47 is a basic intent crime and so he was convicted.

The House of Lords considered the whole aspect of intoxication and came to the conclusion that self-induced intoxication can only be raised as a defence to crimes of specific intent, but not to crimes of basic intent.

This means that in crimes where the *mens rea* can only be intention, such as murder, voluntary intoxication can remove the defendant's *mens rea*; however, where the crime is one of basic intent there will be no defence. A crime of basic intent is one that only requires the prosecution to prove that the defendant has been reckless – and as the defendant's action in becoming voluntarily intoxicated is in itself reckless behaviour, the *mens rea* element is satisfied and the intoxication cannot be used as an excuse. Where the defendant is charged with a specific intent crime, he will need to prove that the intoxication meant that he did not form the necessary intent, but he may still be convicted of a lesser offence that only requires recklessness for the *mens rea*. However, not all 'specific' intent offences have a corresponding 'basic' intent offence. A typical example of this is theft.

Murder is a crime of specific intent but manslaughter is a crime of basic intent. In **Lipman (1970)** the defendant had been taking LSD a drug which causes hallucinations. The defendant believed he was being attacked by snakes and he killed his girlfriend, who had also taken the drug, by forcing a sheet into her mouth thinking he was defending himself. He was charged with murder which is a crime of specific offence but acquitted on the basis that he could not have formed the necessary *mens rea*. He was however found guilty of unlawful act manslaughter which is a crime of basic intent. On appeal it was confirmed by the Court of Appeal that voluntary intoxication could be a defence to murder if it removed the *mens rea* but cannot be a defence to manslaughter.

The offences that we have considered in this unit can be categorised as follows:

Specific and basic intent offences

Basic Intent Crimes	Specific Intent Crimes
Offences Against the Person Act 1861 s47	Offences Against the Person Act 1861 s18
Offences Against the Person Act 1861 s20	Murder
Assault	
Battery	
Involuntary manslaughter	

> **Key cases**
>
> **Lipman (1970):** voluntary intoxication was a defence to murder but not to unlawful act manslaughter.
>
> **Attorney-General for Northern Ireland v Gallagher (1963):** if *mens rea* is formed before intoxication, as in 'Dutch Courage', there will be no defence of intoxication; in this case, the defendant's intention to kill his wife was formed before he got drunk.

It should also be noted that if the *mens rea* is formed before the intoxication, as in 'Dutch Courage', there will be no defence of intoxication. This can be seen in the case of **Attorney-General for Northern Ireland v Gallagher (1963)**. In this case, the defendant decided to kill his wife. He went out and bought a bottle of whisky and a knife. He drank the whisky and became so drunk that he could not form the *mens rea* for murder (an intention to kill or cause really serious harm); then he killed his wife. As he had formed the intention to kill her before he became intoxicated, he had no defence of intoxication.

Conclusion

The first distinction is between voluntary and involuntary intoxication. Involuntary intoxication is a defence, but only where the intoxication is completely involuntary. The defence of intoxication applies differently to offences of specific intent and those of basic intent. It is essential, therefore, to understand the distinction between the two.

In the examination, there are often questions involving the defence of intoxication. Discussion of this defence is suggested whenever a character in the scenario takes an alcoholic drink or drugs, whether illegal or legal. It may well be the case that you decide, after due consideration, that the defence will be unsuccessful. Nevertheless, you must include that preliminary discussion.

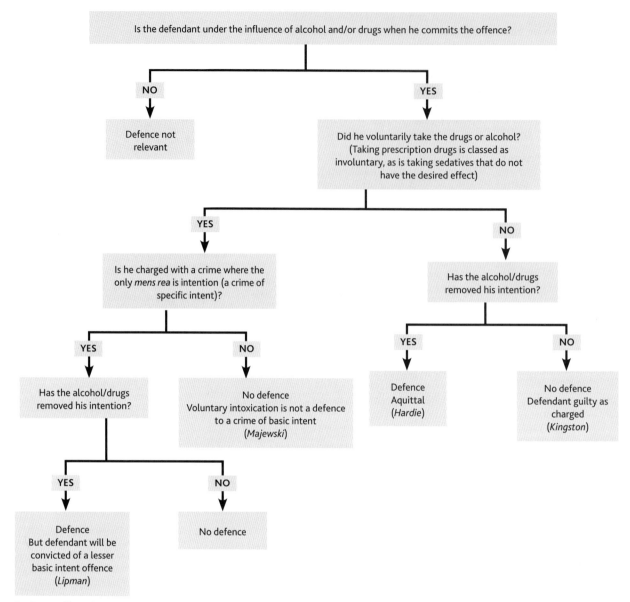

Defence of intoxication

■ **Activity**

Consider the scenario set out below. You should discuss both offences and possible defences.

Rob drank a few glasses of wine and then took a rowing boat out onto the river with Salma. Unknown to him, someone had slipped a drug into the wine and, by the time that he began rowing, he was already feeling rather confused. Tom, who was walking along the riverbank, jeered at Rob and then threw a stone at him, striking him in the chest. Rob stood up and persistently shouted and shook his fist, even though the boat was rocking dangerously. Shortly afterwards, the boat overturned and Salma, who could not swim, drowned in the river.

You should now be able to:

■ state the law of the defence of intoxication.

5 The defence of consent

The defence of consent is, in many ways, not a defence at all, as it could be argued that there has been no unlawful act. The issues are deciding what a person can consent to, and the genuineness of the consent. We will consider them in this order:

- What offences can a person consent (and not consent) to?
- Is the consent genuine?

Consent is not a defence to murder

A person cannot consent to being killed (murder) and euthanasia is against the law. Even where the victim has consented, the law does not permit this activity. This was confirmed in the case of **Pretty (2002)**. Dianne Pretty suffered from motor neurone disease, which left her paralysed. She wanted her husband to be able to assist her suicide without fear of prosecution, so that she could choose the time of her death and die with dignity. She argued that Article 2 (right to life) of the European Convention on Human Rights protects the right to life and the right to choose the manner of death.

However, the House of Lords and the European Court did not find that Article 2 created a right to die, and indeed that the need to protect vulnerable citizens justified the prohibition of assisted suicide.

Consent as a defence to non-fatal offences

There are a number of areas where the law allows consent, although the extent of the consent may be limited. This was discussed in detail in **Brown (1993)**. This case involved consenting gay men who performed sado-masochistic acts in private. Whilst at the time many perceived the acts as distasteful and immoral, the question before the court was whether the individuals could consent to these activities. The court confirmed that consent is allowed as a defence to battery but not to more serious injuries, as the law insists that there are limits to the defence of consent when injuries are more serious than assault (ss47, 20 and 18): it is not in the public interest for people to harm each other for no good reason. The court stated that the defence is not available for injuries more serious than assault unless they fell into one of the 'recognised exceptions'. A list was given, including 'properly conducted games and sports, reasonable surgical interference and dangerous exhibitions'.

Normal sports activities

Many sports involve some physical contact and the risk of injury inflicted by another. The problem comes in the extent of the consent. Clearly, a person consents to being hit and possibly to very serious injuries in a boxing match, perhaps the most famous case being that of Michael Watson in 1991. Whilst the event is being properly conducted and supervised within the rules, there is consent. When the incident goes beyond the rules and regulations of the sport, then there is the potential for criminal liability. This can be seen from the case of *Barnes* (2004). In this case, the victim suffered a serious leg injury following a tackle during an amateur football match. The Court of Appeal decided that criminal proceedings should only take place in those situations where the conduct was sufficiently serious. Most sports have their own disciplinary procedures that cover most situations, and physical injury is an inevitable risk of sport – those taking part consent to such injury.

In this topic, you will learn how to:

- state the definition of the defence of consent
- apply the rules to a given situation.

 Key cases

Pretty (2002): assisted suicide is a criminal offence and to deny a person the right to an assisted death is not a breach of the victim's human right (right to life).

Brown (1993): leading case on consent, which set out the parameters for the defence.

Before a prosecution is considered, the following needs to be taken into account:

- the type of sport
- the level at which it was played
- the nature of the act
- the degree of force used
- the extent of risk of injury
- the state of mind of the person causing the injury.

The court also noted that in the heat of the moment excessive force might be used but that was unlikely to be criminal.

Footballer jailed for assault

The Barrow defender James Cotterill was sentenced to four months in prison yesterday for breaking an opponent's jaw during an FA Cup match.

Cotterill, 24, pleaded guilty to punching the Bristol Rovers striker Sean Rigg, causing him grievous bodily harm during the first-round game on 11 November. Half an hour into the game Cotterill fractured Rigg's jaw in two places with a left-hook, Preston Crown Court heard. It must be held together with metal plates for the rest of his life.

The FA suspended Cotterill from any football-related activities after

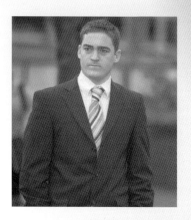

the match at Barrow's Holker Street ground. The ban lasts until 1 March. Rigg has made a recovery and is now back playing for Bristol Rovers. Cotterill was ordered to pay £270 costs.

The Independent, 18 December 2006

Normal social intercourse

This covers things such as shaking hands, tapping someone on the shoulder to draw their attention to something, hugging and so on. It should be noted that a person can withdraw their consent, thus making the action potentially criminal.

Medical procedures, dentistry, piercing, tattooing and blood tests

Most surgical treatment can be readily consented to, either expressly by signing consent forms or having the forms signed by a parent or guardian for a child, and by implied consent in emergencies. This consent can be refused or withdrawn at any time.

Patients undergoing medical procedures will be asked for their consent before treatment, and for surgical procedures this will normally be written consent. This consent means that the patient is agreeing to the harm and any associated risks, and therefore the medical practitioner cannot be charged with an offence.

With respect to piercing and tattooing, this can be consented to but is regulated by statute such as the Tattooing of Minors Act 1969.

Horseplay and sexual activities

Lord Mustill in his dissenting speech in **Brown (1993)** said, whilst discussing the law on horseplay:

> As a matter of policy the courts have decided that the criminal law does not concern itself with these activities, provided that they do not go too far. It also seems plain that as the general social appreciation of the proper role of the state in regulating the lives of individuals changes with the passage of time, so we shall expect to find that the assumptions of the criminal justice system about what types of conduct are properly excluded from its scope, and what is meant by 'going too far' will not remain constant.

This is relevant to unregulated sports and games and is a rather more physical form of social intercourse. It includes the usual pushing and shoving between friends, arm wrestling, and so on. The problem comes when it gets out of hand or is clearly not consented to, as this is bullying. A typical case is that of **Jones (1986)** where a group of boys gave another 'the bumps' by tossing him in the air. The defendants were entitled to be acquitted if the jury decided that they were indulging in 'rough' and undisciplined sport or play, not intending to cause harm, and genuinely believing that the injuries which occurred in the course of the horseplay did so with the victim's consent.

With respect to sexual activities, the law is concerned on moral grounds with respect to extreme sexual activities, however consensual, and the transmission of diseases such as AIDS. In *Brown (1993)* the victims and the defendants were involved in consensual sado-masochistic homosexual activities that did not result in permanent injury or hospitalisation. Despite the consensual nature of the activities, the defendants were found guilty – the European Court of Human Rights confirmed that there was no breach of human rights in imposing criminal sanctions for such activities. This follows the established principle that it is not in the public interest that people should cause each other actual bodily harm for no good reason.

The case of *Dica* (2004) established that it is possible to be charged with inflicting biological grievous bodily harm under s20 of the Offences Against the Person Act 1861. In this case, the defendant had unprotected sex with the victims in the knowledge that he was HIV positive. However, the case also raised issues of consent. The women had consented to sex but as they did not know that the defendant was HIV positive, they had not consented to the risk of infection. Had they known and made the decision to take the risk, then this would have provided a defence, but their lack of knowledge of his condition meant Dica was convicted.

It is important to reiterate that the defence of consent is only relevant where the *actus reus* and *mens rea* of the crime have been established. Thus, if the defendant has no *mens rea*, the defence is irrelevant. This can be seen in the case of **Slingsby (1995)** where the defendant caused internal injuries to a woman partner from the signet ring he was wearing. At the time of the incident, neither the defendant nor the victim was aware of the injury, or the cause of it, until the wound became septic and resulted in a serious medical problem. The victim's death was not the result of a criminal act as the defendant lacked the *mens rea* for unlawful act manslaughter, so the issue of consent was irrelevant.

Key cases

Brown (1993): even though the activities were fully consensual, the defendants were convicted because the acts were intentional, and, also because of the moral view taken; the conviction was not interfered with by the European Court of Human Rights, under the name of *Laskey* v *UK* (1997).

Jones (1986): where there is horseplay there will be no offence committed if the defendants were not intending to cause harm, and genuinely believed that the injuries which occurred in the course of the horseplay did so with the victim's consent.

Slingsby (1995): consent is only relevant where the *actus reus* and *mens rea* of the case has been established.

Is the consent genuine?

The fact that the victim appears to consent does not mean that the consent is genuine. If the victim is a child or is mentally challenged, then the consent may not be valid. The question is whether the victim has sufficient understanding and intelligence to give consent. This can be seen in the case of **Burrell v Harmer (1967)** where the defendant tattooed two boys who were aged 12 and 13 with their consent. The defence of consent was not allowed, as the court felt that the boys were unable to understand the pain involved whilst recognising what a tattoo was. Age in itself does not mean there is no consent, but the failure to appreciate the nature of the act does form the basis of the lack of consent.

Where the consent is obtained by fraud, it will not be a valid consent. The fraud must be as to the nature of the act. This can be seen in the case of **Tabassum (2000)** where women consented to a breast examination carried out by the defendant in the erroneous belief that he was medically qualified. The offence had taken place because the women, who had consented to being touched purely for medical purposes, had not consented for any other purpose. This seems inconsistent with **Richardson (1998)** where consent to dental treatment was accepted as a defence even though the patients did not know that the defendant had been disqualified from practice. This latter case also seems inconsistent with the case of *Dica* (2004) and so perhaps should be disregarded.

Application of the defence of consent to problems in the examination

In the examination, there are often questions involving the defence of consent. Discussion of this defence is suggested whenever a character appears to submit to the offence. It may well be the case that you decide, after due consideration, that the defence will be unsuccessful. Nevertheless, you must include that discussion.

> ### Key cases
>
> **Burrell v Harmer (1967):** a person's age does not in itself negate the defence of consent; it is the ability to appreciate the nature of the act that is important.
>
> **Tabassum (2000):** consent can be for a particular purpose only.
>
> **Richardson (1998):** concealment of facts does not amount to fraud.

> ### Activity
>
> Consider the scenario set out below. You should discuss both offences and possible defences.
>
> Emma, who was 12 years of age but looked older, paid for her tongue to be pierced and a stud inserted by Farah. Emma's tongue rapidly developed a serious infection that required hospital treatment. The treatment was administered by George, a newly qualified doctor. George misinterpreted Emma's medical record and gave her an antibiotic drug which her body could not tolerate. This resulted in her death.

You should now be able to:

■ state the law of the defence of consent.

6 The defence of self-defence/prevention of crime

Self-defence is where the defendant admits committing the *actus reus* with the necessary *mens rea*, but says he was acting in self-defence. A person may use force as is reasonable in the circumstances to defend himself or another or his property. The law recognises use of force in private defence and public defence, and the details of both are outlined below.

Private defence

The common law defence of self-defence, which provides that a person may use such force as is reasonable in the circumstances, is available to the defendant if he is:

- defending himself or his property against an actual or imminent attack, or
- defending another against such an attack.

Public defence

Section 3 of the Criminal Law Act 1967 states that a person may use such force as is reasonable in the circumstances in order to:

- prevent the commission of an offence, or
- effect a lawful arrest.

Requirements for private and public defences

The private and public defences overlap because if a person uses force against an attacker, as well as defending himself (self-defence) he is obviously also preventing a crime. Both defences have been clarified by s76 of the Criminal Justice and Immigration Act 2008, which did not aim to change the law but to put the legal principles from the case law into statutory form. The requirements for both private and public defences are the same:

- the necessity of force
- the reasonableness of force.

The necessity of force

The basic principle is that the use of force is not justified if it is not necessary. It will be necessary if it is seen to be so in the circumstances which exist or which the defendant genuinely believed existed. This can be seen from the case of **Gladstone Williams (1987)** where a man saw a woman become the victim of a robbery by a youth. This man struggled with the robber with a view to stopping him and handing him to the police. At this point the defendant appeared and thought that the man was attacking the youth, and stepped in to protect the youth. The defendant was successful in pleading prevention of crime, even though he was mistaken as to the actual facts. His defence is based on what he genuinely believed was happening.

The defence comes into operation even if the attack has not yet taken place, providing it is imminent. In other words, the defendant does not have to wait for an attack to start but can get in the first blow. The difficulty with this is establishing that the force he uses is reasonable. However, it is clear that the defendant does not have a duty to retreat as far as possible before using force, which was the case before this 1967 Act. This can be seen from the case of **Bird (1985)**. The facts of the case were that on 10 March 1984 the defendant, Debbie Bird, was celebrating her 17th birthday. There was a party at a house in Harlow. There was a guest at the party called Darren Marder, who became the victim. He and the defendant had been together as boyfriend and girlfriend for about five months the year before. That relationship had come to an end. Marder arrived at the party with his new girlfriend, and an argument broke out. The defendant told Marder to leave, and he did.

In this topic, you will learn how to:

- state the definition of the defence of self-defence/prevention of crime
- distinguish between self-defence and prevention of crime
- apply the rules to a given situation.

Key cases

Gladstone Williams (1987): defence under s3 of the Criminal Law Act 1967 is based on the genuine belief of the defendant rather than the actual facts; in this case, the defendant believed a youth was being attacked when in fact his victim was trying to arrest the youth.

Bird (1985): defendant does not have to wait for an attack to start but can get in the first blow.

A little later, Marder came back and a second argument took place. The defendant poured a glass of Pernod over Marder, and he retaliated by slapping her around the face. When she was later held up against a wall she lunged at Marder with her hand, which was the hand that held the Pernod glass. The glass hit him in the face, broke, and took out his eye. The court decided that it was unnecessary to show an unwillingness to fight and there were circumstances where a defendant might reasonably react immediately and without first retreating, as Bird did in this case. The force was not reasonable in terms of what had happened, but was reasonable with respect to what she thought might happen when she was pinned against the wall. This rule is now contained in the Criminal Justice and Immigration Act s76(6A) as amended by the Legal Aid, Sentencing and Punishment of Offenders Act 2012 s148.

The reasonableness of force

The jury has the task of deciding whether, in all the circumstances, the defendant used reasonable force. The jury, of course, can take as long as it needs to consider the facts, the facts as the defendant believed them, the circumstances of the attack, the time available to the defendant to decide on his course of action, and the risk to the defendant balanced against the risk of harm to the victim. The defendant usually does that in a split second so he may use excessive force. If that is the case, that excessive force is unlawful.

Lord Morris of Borth-y-Gest said in the case of **Palmer (1971)**:

> It is both good law and good sense that a man who is attacked may defend himself. It is both good law and good sense that he may do, but may only do, what is reasonably necessary. But everything will depend upon the particular facts and circumstances. … It may in some cases be only sensible and clearly possible to take some simple avoiding action. Some attacks may be serious and dangerous. Others may not be. If there is some relatively minor attack it would not be common sense to permit some action of retaliation which was wholly out of proportion to the necessities of the situation. If an attack is serious so that it puts someone in immediate peril then immediate defensive action may be necessary. If the moment is one of crisis for someone in imminent danger he may have to avert the danger by some instant reaction.
>
> If the attack is all over and no sort of peril remains then the employment of force may be by way of revenge or punishment or by way of paying off an old score or may be pure aggression. There may no longer be any link with a necessity of defence. Of all these matters the good sense of a jury will be the arbiter. If there has been no attack then clearly there will have been no need for defence. If there has been attack so that defence is reasonably necessary it will be recognised that a person defending himself cannot weigh to a nicety the exact measure of his necessary defensive action.

The famous cases of **Clegg (1994)**, a soldier on a checkpoint in Northern Ireland in the 1990s faced with what might be a terrorist attack, and **Martin (Anthony Edward) (2001)**, who shot and killed a 16-year-old intruder with a pump-action shotgun, demonstrate the difficulties juries face when considering what amounts to reasonable force.

In **Clegg (1994)** the defendant was a soldier on duty in Northern Ireland before the peace settlement. He was at a road checkpoint when a car came towards him at high speed. Seeing that it was not going to stop, he fired at it. His last shot hit a girl passenger in the back seat and killed her. Evidence showed that the car had already passed him when he fired that final shot. It was held that under the circumstances neither he nor anyone else was any longer in danger, therefore his plea of self-defence or defence of another should not succeed. He was found guilty of murder, a decision which was

■ **Key cases**

Palmer (1971): Lord Morris of Borth-y-Gest set out the way in which reasonable force was to be explained.

Clegg (1994) and Martin (Anthony Edward) (2001): the defendants were unsuccessful in pleading self-defence because the amount of force used was excessive. Self-defence requires the force to be reasonable.

upheld on appeal. He was, however, eventually cleared of the charge in 1999 when it was disputed whether it was his bullet that killed the victim.

In *Martin (Anthony Edward)* (2001), the defendant lived alone in an isolated farmhouse in East Anglia which had been burgled in the past. On this particular occasion, Martin, woken by the sounds of someone entering his property, took his shotgun and fired without warning into the darkness. One of the intruders, 16-year-old Fred Barras, was shot in the back and killed. Martin was found guilty of murder. On appeal his plea of self-defence was rejected on the grounds that the force he had used was unreasonable. However, his conviction was reduced to manslaughter on the grounds of diminished responsibility. He was freed in 2003.

Tony Martin, the Norfolk farmer who failed in his plea of self-defence

The question of proportionality arises in the Criminal Justice and Immigration Act 2008. Section 76 (6) makes plain that the degree of force used by a person is not to be regarded as having been reasonable in the circumstances as he believed them to be if it was disproportionate in those circumstances. Guidance as to whether the degree of force used was reasonable in the circumstances of a case can now be found in the 2008 Act, s76 (7) of which provides:

(a) that a person acting for a legitimate purpose may not be able to weigh to a nicety the exact measure of any necessary action; and

(b) that evidence of a person's having only done what the person honestly and instinctively thought was necessary for a legitimate purpose constitutes strong evidence that only reasonable action was taken by that person for that purpose.

Burden of proof

The burden is on the prosecution to prove to the jury beyond all reasonable doubt that the defendant was either:

- not acting to defend himself/herself or another;
- not acting to defend property, or not acting to prevent a crime or apprehend an offender; or
- if he was so acting, the force was excessive.

Conclusion

A person may use such force as is reasonable in the circumstances in the prevention of crime, or in effecting or assisting in the lawful arrest of offenders or suspected offenders or of persons unlawfully at large.

Application of the defence of self-defence/prevention of crime to problems in the examination

In the examination, there are questions involving the defence of self-defence. Discussion of this defence is suggested whenever a character in the scenario is reacting to a threat of violence made against him.

Activity

Consider the scenario set out below. You should discuss both offences and possible defences.

Ali, who was aged 55, had been on bad terms with Bill, aged 32, over an alleged attack by Ali on Bill's young daughter. By chance, they found themselves together in the house of a mutual friend. Bill was heard to say, 'I am going to do that pervert'. Shortly afterwards, encouraged by his friend, Colin, Bill began punching and kicking Ali. As he was falling to the floor, Ali took a knife from his pocket and slashed Bill's arm. Bill reeled backwards, bleeding heavily. Ali suffered from a broken nose and broken ribs.

You should now be able to:

- state the law of self-defence/ prevention of crime.

Practice questions

Example question 1 (AQA, January 2012)

Read this scenario and answer all **three** questions.

You should write in continuous prose, give reasoned answers, and make reference to cases, statutes and examples where appropriate.

Adrian and Ben were at home watching a 'cage fighting' (martial arts) DVD, having spent all morning drinking beer and whisky. They agreed to a fight in which they would try to copy the moves they had been watching. Adrian succeeded in securing an arm-lock on Ben, who indicated to Adrian that he accepted defeat. However, Adrian continued to apply pressure and Ben's arm was broken. The break was relatively minor, but Ben was left with a permanent restriction in movement when his arm was further damaged by poor treatment at the hospital.

Returning from visiting Ben in hospital that evening, Adrian found himself walking past Charles and Dora, who were both aged 80. By now, Adrian was tired and feeling annoyed about the day's events. He kicked away the walking stick being used by Charles. Charles fell and suffered a deep cut to his forehead, which bled a lot. Seeing this, Dora became very frightened, and had to receive treatment for anxiety and depression for months afterwards. Emma had witnessed the accident from a distance and she ran over to stop Adrian causing any further harm. However, George, another witness to the incident, had also gone to assist Charles and Dora. Emma mistook George for Adrian. She immediately slapped George twice, very hard, causing his face to sting.

1   Discuss the possible criminal liability of Adrian for the injuries to Ben.   *(25 marks + 5 marks for AO3)*

2   Discuss the possible criminal liability of Adrian arising out of his conduct in relation to Charles and Dora. Discuss the possible criminal liability of Emma for her conduct in relation to George.   *(25 marks)*

3   Despite some recent reforms, there are still criticisms to be made of the current law on murder and voluntary manslaughter. Consider relevant criticisms of that law, and suggest any reforms that might be appropriate.   *(25 marks)*

Example question 2 (AQA, January 2012)

Read this scenario and answer all **three** questions.

You should write in continuous prose, give reasoned answers, and make reference to cases, statutes and examples where appropriate.

When James repaired the brakes of the car owned by his neighbour, Harry, he was distracted by a conversation with his wife and forgot to tighten the bolts on one wheel. Shortly after Harry drove the car away, he saw his friend, Kim, walking towards him on the grass verge of the road. She was followed at a short distance by her friend, Lauren. As a joke,

Harry decided to give Kim a bit of a scare by speeding up and driving at her. Kim realised that it was Harry and began to laugh. At that moment, the car wheel came off and the car veered off the road and into Kim, causing fatal injuries. Meanwhile, Lauren had hastily flung herself into a hedge, where her face and arms were ripped by thorns, leaving permanent scars.

Afterwards, Kim's father, Mike, began to suffer from anxiety and stress and became depressed and irritable. Unknown to him, Nora, his wife, began an affair with Oliver. One day in a bar, Mike overheard Oliver boasting to some friends about his physical abuse of women, and identifying Nora as his latest woman, 'whose stupid daughter got herself run over and killed'. Stunned, Mike brooded on this for about 45 minutes before he suddenly rushed over to Oliver, pushed him off his bar stool, and stamped two or three times on his head. Oliver had a previously undetected weakness of the skull and he suffered massive damage to his brain. Doctors treating him for his injuries decided that nothing more could be done. Oliver was pronounced dead after his life-support machine was switched off.

1　Discuss the possible criminal liability of Harry for the injuries to Lauren. Discuss the possible criminal liability of Harry and of James for the involuntary manslaughter of Kim.

(25 marks + 5 marks for AO3)

2　Discuss the possible criminal liability of Mike for the murder of Oliver. *(25 marks)*

3　Despite some recent reforms, there are still criticisms to be made of the current law on murder and voluntary manslaughter. Consider relevant criticisms of that law, and suggest any reforms that might be appropriate. *(25 marks)*

3A Evaluation of fatal and non-fatal offences against the person

In this chapter, you will learn how to:

- ▪ evaluate aspects of criminal law that are covered in the AQA A2 Law specification

- ▪ state proposals for reform of those areas of the criminal law

- ▪ write an essay that is appropriate for an examination question.

Introduction

This chapter aims to consider the areas of criminal law that you have studied (apart from involuntary manslaughter, which does not require evaluation). For each topic that you need to evaluate, there are a number of points that you can use to develop your arguments. You should remember that every aspect of the law has its good and bad points. Indeed, in criminal law, these may well vary with the point of view of the person considering the law; a victim may view the law differently to the accused, and the general public may view the law differently again.

As you will appreciate, a great deal of time and care is taken by experts when drafting an Act of Parliament. Nevertheless, statutes have to be interpreted in the light of the infinite range of human behaviour, and according to the ever-changing nature of society. The common law, too, has developed to accommodate these changes. Over the years, judges refine and clarify the law to reflect the needs of the time. In many cases this is entirely successful, and adds to our understanding of what the law is on a particular point.

It also often happens, however, that a particular area of law is capable of ambiguity, and we find that conflicting decisions occur. There is a real risk that injustices might happen as a result. In these cases, there comes a point where it may be necessary to introduce reforms. These would take the form of a new precedent or new legislation, and their aim would be to:

- clarify existing areas of difficulty or ambiguity
- change the law where necessary
- introduce new laws to reflect present needs.

Each of the topics are evaluated in turn. You should be able to write an essay on each topic, in order to be prepared fully for the exam.

1 Murder

Murder

There are several aspects of the law relating to murder that are considered to be in need of change or clarification. The main ones are:

- the necessary intent
- the use of force in self-defence
- the mandatory life sentence.

Intent

In *Moloney* (1985) Lord Bridge said that in the great majority of cases it would be enough for a trial judge to ask the jury to consider whether the prosecution had satisfied them that the defendant had intended a particular consequence. In cases where there is a shooting or stabbing, there is usually no problem. However, establishing *mens rea* in cases where the prime intent was not to kill will inevitably involve problems. What did the defendant intend? What did he foresee might happen as the result of his act? Only the defendant himself can possibly know what was in his mind at the time. In some cases, even the defendant himself might not have known.

As things stand at the moment, a person who intends to cause serious bodily harm and actually causes his victim's death is guilty of murder. But should a defendant whose only intention is to cause serious bodily harm be as guilty of murder as one who deliberately sets out to kill? And what of the defendant whose main intention is not even to cause serious bodily harm? In the case of *Hancock and Shankland* (1986), which was discussed earlier on page 7, the striking miners argued that their intention had been to block the road when they threw the concrete slab from the bridge. They said that they did not intend to kill or cause serious harm to the taxi driver who was driving the non-striking miner to work, but merely to prevent the taxi from getting to the mine. They were both convicted of murder, although this verdict was changed on appeal to one of manslaughter. It is the foresight of consequences that causes the main area of concern. This is an area that subsequent cases (as considered above) have done little to clarify.

Over the years, it has often been suggested that the criminal law be **codified**. This would mean that murder would be included in new legislation. A draft criminal code was produced in 1989, in which the following definition of murder was proposed:

> A person is guilty of murder if he causes the death of another –
>
> **a** intending to cause death; or
>
> **b** intending to cause serious personal harm and being aware that he may cause death.

This would mean that a defendant who did not intend to kill, but had the intention as described in (b), above, could still be found guilty of murder. This would happen only if the jury was sure that the defendant was aware that his action could cause death. However, no such attempt at codifying the criminal law has yet been made, probably due to shortage of parliamentary time.

As to what the word 'intention' actually means, some help is provided by the Criminal Justice Act 1967. Section 8 of this Act states that:

> A court or jury in determining whether a person has committed an offence:
>
> **a** shall not be bound in law to infer that he intended or foresaw a result of his actions by reason of its being a natural and probable consequence of those actions, but
>
> **b** shall decide whether he did intend or foresee that result by reference to all the evidence, drawing such inferences from the evidence as appear proper in the circumstances.

Again, the Law Commission in its report *Offences Against the Person and General Principles* (1993) proposed that the word 'intentionally' should be defined thus:

> A person acts intentionally with respect to a result when:
>
> **a** it is his purpose to cause it; or
>
> **b** although it is not his purpose to cause it, he knows that it would occur in the ordinary course of events if he were to succeed in his purpose of causing some other result.

The introduction of this reform would go a long way towards clarifying the rather confusing situation caused by *Woollin* (1998) and *Matthews and Alleyne* (2003). In *Woolin*, the House of Lords decided that foresight

Key terms

Codify: to gather together all parts of a particular area of law so that they all exist together in a single document rather than in many different Acts of Parliament and the common law; the process is called codification.

of consequences amounts to intention, whereas in *Matthews and Alleyne* the Court of Appeal said that foresight of consequences is a rule of evidence, so the jury is entitled to find intention but is not obliged to so.

Implied malice

One of the main criticisms of murder is that the *mens rea* includes the intention to cause grievous bodily harm in addition to the intention to kill. This was confirmed in the case of *Vickers* (1957). The facts of the case were that the defendant broke into a shop intending to steal but was disturbed in the process by an elderly woman, whom he then attacked by kicking and punching. The victim died from the injuries.

The defendant's conviction for murder was upheld in the Court of Appeal, and Lord Goddard said:

> Murder is, of course, killing with malice aforethought, but malice aforethought is a term of art. If the defendant intends to inflict grievous bodily harm and that person dies, that has always been held in English law sufficient to imply the malice aforethought which is a necessary constituent of murder.

The term 'malice aforethought' is in itself misleading because no premeditation is required for murder, as its intention can arise in the heat of the moment. In relation to implied malice, it is arguably unfair for a defendant to be convicted of the most serious homicide offence when there was no intention to kill, nor the foresight of the likelihood of killing.

The word 'grievous' is interpreted as 'serious harm that does not have to be life threatening'. If, as in the case of *Cheshire* (1991), the victim died of medical complications following the initial wound, which was not itself life threatening, the defendant can be guilty of murder because he intended to cause serious harm. A murder conviction leads to a mandatory life sentence and, arguably, this sentence should be reserved solely for those who intend to kill.

The implied malice rule has been criticised by several judges and legal writers because it is argued that it extends the definition of murder too far. It is hard to justify because the fault element, meaning the intention to cause grievous bodily harm, does not correspond to the prohibited consequences, namely the death of the victim.

Mandatory life sentence

The **mandatory** life **sentence** for murder was laid down by the Murder (Abolition of the Death Penalty) Act 1965. The reason for this was that murder is generally held to be the most dreadful of crimes and deserves the maximum sentence permitted by the law. There was also an element of appeasement of those who opposed the abolition of the death penalty.

A judge must impose life imprisonment on any person aged 18 or over who is found guilty of murder. When passing a life sentence, the judge must decide on the tariff. This is the length of time that the defendant must serve in prison as a minimum before being considered for release. The length of the tariff will depend on the particular factors of the crime, such as whether it was racially motivated or had a sexual element. In some cases, the judge can order a whole of life sentence, which means that the defendant will never be released. Once the defendant has served the minimum term under the tariff he may be released, but under licence, which means that he can be made to return to prison if he doesn't comply with the terms of his release. This is therefore why it is known as a life sentence, because it remains even when the defendant is no longer in prison. A person between the ages of 10 and 17 is 'detained

Key terms

Mandatory sentence: sentence fixed by law, which the judge has no option but to impose on a defendant found guilty; an example is the mandatory life sentence for murder.

at Her Majesty's pleasure'. This means indefinitely, until such a time as it is deemed safe to return him to society.

Objections to the mandatory life sentence are often put forward, however. It is suggested that although murder is a dreadful crime and deserves to be punished, there is no flexibility for the judge to vary the sentence according to the seriousness of the killing. Murders cover varying degrees of seriousness. On the one hand, there are the cold-blooded serial killers such as Sutcliffe or the Wests, and ruthless terrorist bombers belonging to extremist groups. On the other hand, there are those who kill from motives of compassion ('mercy killers') or those like Anthony Martin who overstep the limits of reasonable force in self-defence. All convictions for murder, of whatever degree of seriousness, attract the same sentence – life imprisonment. Another objection to the mandatory life sentence is that, in order to avoid it, inappropriate verdicts of manslaughter might be returned. This has happened in the case of so-called 'mercy killings', where the defence of diminished responsibility has been accepted on the flimsiest of evidence to avoid a conviction for murder.

Suggestions for reform of the law in this matter continue to be made. If life imprisonment usually does not mean 'for life', then why call it life imprisonment, and why insist on it being passed? One suggestion is to abolish the mandatory life sentence and make it **discretionary**. Other crimes, such as manslaughter, rape, wounding with intent, and indeed attempted murder, attract a maximum of life imprisonment. It is, however, discretionary; the judge may impose any sentence up to and including life imprisonment, according to the seriousness of the offence. If the punishment for murder were to be discretionary life imprisonment, a judge would have the power to impose life (meaning for life) for the most serious murders. For other killings, a judge could impose a term of years reflecting their relative seriousness.

Another suggestion is that different degrees of murder could be introduced, as in the USA. In this way, the most serious murders would attract a mandatory life sentence. Less serious ones would attract a discretionary life sentence. The Law Commission in its recent report on homicide, (2006) recommended that voluntary manslaughter should be reclassified as 'second degree murder'.

The problem of the mandatory life sentence has been highlighted by the case of Frances Inglis in 2010, who killed her brain-damaged son as a mercy killing; she was convicted of murder and was given the mandatory life sentence

Key terms

Discretionary sentence: judge has power to pass any sentence up to and including the maximum laid down by law; for example, theft carries a maximum sentence of seven years; judge may sentence offenders to anything from absolute discharge to maximum seven years, depending on the seriousness of the offence.

2 Voluntary manslaughter

Evaluation of voluntary manslaughter requires a critical analysis of the two special defences to murder, which are loss of control and diminished responsibility.

Loss of control

The Coroners and Justice Act 2009, which came into force in October 2010, abolished the much-criticised defence of provocation and replaced it with the defence of loss of control. This requires the defendant to prove loss of control from a qualifying trigger. Despite this being a very recent reform, the new defence has already attracted much criticism.

Fear of serious violence

The first qualifying trigger attempts to address the problem faced by women who kill their partners after suffering abuse by them, illustrated in the case of *Ahluwalia* (1992). Under the law of provocation, there had to be a sudden and temporary loss of control. Women are usually physically weaker than men and are therefore less likely to react straight away when attacked by a violent partner. Ahluwalia waited until her husband was asleep, and therefore the defence of provocation was unavailable to her. The removal of the suddenness requirement is a positive change, as is the recognition that killing through fear is as justified as killing through anger. However, it is still necessary to lose self-control based on fear, and this may prove to be difficult, as people do not typically lose control when afraid. The Law Commission had argued for this requirement to be removed, which would have meant that the defence could be pleaded if the defendant acted out of a fear of serious violence, without needing to prove a loss of self-control. It remains to be seen whether this reform will achieve its intended purpose.

Things done or said

Another criticism of the law of provocation was that almost any words or conduct could be considered to have provoked the defendant to kill. The defence of loss of control identifies specific qualifying triggers to prevent situations such as that in *Doughty* (1996), where a crying baby was held to amount to provocation. Whilst it is accepted that reform was needed to prevent the defence being available in cases such as *Doughty* (1996), there has been much criticism of the exclusion of sexual infidelity as a qualifying trigger.

The second qualifying trigger defined in s55 of the Coroners and Justice Act 2009 applies if the defendant's loss of control was attributable to things done or said, or both, which constituted circumstances of an extremely grave character and caused the defendant to have a justifiable sense of being seriously wronged. However, if the things done or said constitute sexual infidelity, this has to be disregarded. Parliament's reason for passing this provision was to prevent a situation where men were provided with an excuse for killing an unfaithful partner and therefore treated more leniently. The aim of the exclusion was to make it clear that killing an unfaithful partner would always be classed as murder; however, as anticipated, this has already caused problems of interpretation.

Defining what is meant by sexual infidelity is problematic. In the recent case of *Clinton* (2012) the Court of Appeal allowed the defendant's appeal that the defence should have been put to the jury because sexual infidelity was only part of the reason for his loss of control, and there were other factors. This sets an important precedent that already dilutes the impact of the provision because in many cases the sexual infidelity is likely to be part of the context rather than the only factor and questions whether the judges have really followed the intention of Parliament. So, if a man is told by his partner that she has had an affair and the child he thought was his is her lover's child, the man may argue he has lost control because of the child and not because of the infidelity. There is, however, still the argument that sexual infidelity is one of the most likely reasons for someone to lose their self-control, and therefore it should never have been excluded in the first place.

Potential reform

Whilst the new defence of loss of control corrects some of the defects in the law of provocation, it also remains far from satisfactory. Possible reforms would be to remove the need for loss of self-control in relation to fear of serious violence, to protect abused women more adequately, as suggested by the Law Commission. Also, the controversial sexual infidelity exception may need to be removed or revised in the light of the decision in *Clinton* (2012) but some argue that the second trigger should be abolished altogether, as there can be no excuse for killing in anger. In New Zealand, following a case in which a man stabbed his girlfriend over

200 times, claiming she had provoked him, the Government decided to abolish provocation. The Justice Minister of New Zealand said:

> It effectively provides a defence for lashing out in anger, not just any anger but violent homicidal rage. It rewards lack of self-control by enabling an intentional killing to be categorised as something other than murder.

The Law Commission in New Zealand endorsed this view and the defence was abolished in 2009. Some critics of the loss of control defence in this country argue that the first qualifying trigger should be retained but the second, which allows killing in anger as a defence, should be withdrawn.

Diminished responsibility

The previous law on diminished responsibility

The original definition of the defence of diminished responsibility, under s2 of the Homicide Act 1957, was as follows:

> Where a person kills or is party to the killing of another, he shall not be convicted of murder if he was suffering from such abnormality of mind (whether arising from a condition of arrested or retarded development of mind or any inherent causes or induced by disease or injury) as substantially impaired his mental responsibility for his acts and omissions in doing or being a party to the killing.

The problems with this definition were that the terminology was vague and did not fit with medical terminology. The specified causes, listed within the brackets above, gave rise to conflicting opinions as to their meaning, and also excluded other causes. There was also little guidance for juries as to when a defendant's mental responsibility was substantially impaired, except that it had to be more than trivial but need not be total. This therefore gave a wide scope for juries to make their decisions, and led to arguments that the defence was becoming too easy to plead. On the other hand, the fact that the law was open to interpretation did allow a defence to women suffering from 'battered woman syndrome' and to defendants in mercy killing cases, who argued that they had become depressed living with a suicidal or terminally ill relative.

The new definition

The Coroners and Justice Act 2009 retained the partial defence of diminished responsibility but substituted a new definition, still under s2 of the Homicide Act 1957. The term 'abnormality of mind' has been replaced with 'abnormality of mental functioning', which the Law Commission argued was a term preferred by psychiatrists. This abnormality must come from a recognised medical condition, and this reflects the need for modern terminology and for proof of the defence to be based on medical diagnosis. In response to the problem of juries interpreting 'substantial impairment', this is now specific and the mental abnormality must substantially impair the defendant's mental responsibility to do at least one of the following: understand the nature of his conduct, form a rational judgement or exercise control. A further aspect of the new definition is the emphasis on a causal link, so that the defence should not succeed where the defendant's condition makes no difference to his behaviour, in that he would have killed in spite of his condition.

Evaluation of the new defence

In general, the new defence deals with the previous criticisms and provides more clarity and modern terminology. However, one concern over the revised defence is that it is likely to be interpreted narrowly and that some deserving cases, such as mercy killers, may find the defence unavailable to them. The problem of diagnosing people who kill in such situations is that they may be reacting to an extremely stressful situation but may not actually have a recognised medical condition. The vagueness of the previous law allowed for more flexibility in such situations, and there is a danger that by tightening the law it will lead to some injustices.

Another potential problem is the overlap between diminished responsibility and insanity. Insanity requires that the defendant must be suffering from a disease of the mind that causes a defect of reason such that the defendant does not know the nature and quality of his act. There is a great deal of similarity with diminished responsibility if the defendant is arguing that his recognised medical condition substantially impaired his ability to understand the nature of his conduct. If the defendant raises the defence of diminished responsibility, the prosecution can argue for insanity, so that there is a special verdict whereby the defendant is committed to a mental institution. Although this has always been the case under the previous law, the overlap because of the new wording could make this more likely.

One of the recommendations made by the Law Commission was to include developmental immaturity as part of the definition, which would allow children a defence, on the basis that there should be some consideration that if a ten-year-old kills (ten is the minimum age for criminal responsibility), there may be issues relating to their immaturity that could reduce a murder charge to voluntary manslaughter. However, the Government did not adopt this, which leads to the position that an adult who has the mental age of a child will be able to plead the defence but a child will not be able to use the defence because their immaturity is considered normal.

Reclassification of homicide

The 2006 report on homicide by the Law Commission suggested that voluntary manslaughter should be reclassified as 'second degree murder'. It would still attract a discretionary life sentence, as it does now. Reclassifying voluntary manslaughter as a degree of murder would recognise the fact that the killing was intentional rather than accidental.

A summary of the Law Commission's proposals is as follows:

First degree murder (mandatory life sentence) would cover:

1 intentional killing; or
2 killing with an intention to cause serious injury, in the awareness that there is a serious risk of causing death.

Second degree murder (discretionary life sentence; guidelines on minimum terms) would cover:

1 killing with intent to do serious injury
2 killing with intent to cause some injury or fear or risk of injury, in the awareness that there is a serious risk of causing death; and
3 killing with the intent for first degree murder, but where a defence of loss of control, diminished responsibility or suicide pact succeeds.

Manslaughter (discretionary life sentence) would cover the various types of involuntary manslaughter as exist at the moment, (see Chapter 2: Involuntary manslaughter).

By introducing a three-tier structure of homicide, the Law Commission suggested that it would 'give the jury in homicide trials greater power to reflect in their verdict the extent to which the offender was at fault in killing'.

As yet, no action has been taken on these proposals.

Activity

Plan and write an answer to the following question:

Despite some recent reforms, there are still criticisms to be made of the current law on murder and voluntary manslaughter. Consider relevant criticisms of that law and consider any reforms that might be available.

When writing an answer that requires you to evaluate the law, ensure that you do the following:

- briefly outline the relevant current law
- discuss the strengths and weaknesses in the law
- identify proposals for reform
- discuss how the proposals would improve the law.

Study tip

When writing a critical analysis of murder and voluntary manslaughter, it is acceptable to refer to just one of the special defences in addition to murder. If you choose to deal with both, less detail will be expected on each defence.

You should now be able to:

- evaluate the law relating to murder, loss of control and diminished responsibility
- construct an appropriate essay on these topics.

3 Non-fatal offences

It is unanimously accepted that the law on non-fatal offences is in need of reform. A Law Commission Report published in 1993 described the Offences Against the Person Act 1861 and the common law of assault and battery as 'inefficient as a vehicle for controlling violence' where 'many aspects of the law are still obscure and its application erratic'. The law on non-fatal offences is routinely criticised as being chaotic, unjust, irrational, outdated and unclear. The essential problem lies with the fact that the OAPA 1861 is Victorian legislation that was never intended to be a logical and consistent set of rules applying to non-fatal offences. Instead, it was a piece of legislation that simply brought all the then applicable laws into one Act. Hence, the sections are randomly ss47, 20 and 18 because the Act also includes other sections setting out the law on matters as diverse as poisoning and kidnapping. As a consequence, there is no uniformity of language used between the sections, nor is there a coherent hierarchy in respect of the seriousness of the offences.

Matters are made worse by the fact that the legislation suffers from poor drafting, allowing a woeful lack of explanation of *mens rea* and failure to define terms. We add to this the basic problem that the courts are having to apply a piece of legislation drafted in the reign of Queen Victoria to situations created in a very different modern society. We shall look at these criticisms in more detail before considering any proposed reforms. Much of the material that you study in this topic is ideally suited for further discussion in Unit 4C when you study Concepts of law.

Language

Key words and phrases used in ss47, 20 and 18 of the OAPA 1861 are not defined in the statute and so need to be explained through case interpretation. It is not appropriate that statutory offence terminology such as 'actual', 'grievous' and 'bodily harm' is continually evolving through cases and appeal processes, and this can only lead to inconsistent decision-making.

Another criticism is that much of the language is old fashioned, badly drafted and used inconsistently. An example is the use of the word 'maliciously', which is not defined in the Act, in ss20 and 18. It was interpreted in *Cunningham* (1957) to cover recklessness but its usual and modern meaning would usually imply bad motive and wickedness. Furthermore, whilst 'maliciously' provides the only clues as to *mens rea* under s20, it has no purpose whatsoever in s18, where the *mens rea* is made clear by the words 'with intent'.

The use of the word 'inflict' in respect of grievous bodily harm under s20, as opposed to 'cause' in s18, has also been subject to criticism. 'Inflict' was originally understood to have a narrower meaning than 'cause' and requiring an assault or battery, but it has now been established in *Ireland; Burstow* (1997) that neither is necessary and 'inflict' should be given the same meaning as 'cause'. This interpretation has been criticised for permitting liability under s20 where there is insufficient fault on the part of the defendant to justify such a serious conviction. If an assault or battery is not required then, in theory, I might be held liable for the serious psychiatric harm caused to my friend by telling her she looked a fright on her wedding day. I might not have intended to cause her harm but if I knew that she was a depressive and that this comment might severely aggravate her condition, then I could have the necessary *mens rea* of subjective recklessness. Strangely, I would not be liable if her psychiatric harm only amounted to actual bodily harm, since an assault is required under s47. It does not seem right that it is easier to prove a s20 charge than the lesser charge of s47.

The meaning of 'wounding' is also not set out in the Act, and case law has provided that it means a breaking of both layers of the skin. This does not match the normal understanding of the word and, as pointed out earlier, this means that a person can be charged under s20 for wounding by merely pricking their victim's finger with a pin. However, the Charging Standard recommends that such minor injuries, including small cuts and lacerations, would be more appropriately charged under s47. It must be remembered, however, that the Charging Standard is designed only as a set of guidelines to assist prosecutors to choose the appropriate charge. It is not legally binding upon the courts, and liability, once the charge is determined, will be decided in accordance with statute and case authority.

Hierarchy of seriousness

Section 39 of the CJA 1988 and ss47, 20 and 18 of the OAPA 1861 were not designed to work as one coherent hierarchy of offences. Accordingly, there is not a logical sentencing structure that reflects the seriousness of each offence. The legal philosopher HLA Hart wrote that this 'might bring the law into disrepute' as 'principles of justice or fairness between different offenders require morally distinguishable offences to be treated differently and morally similar offences to be treated alike'.

There is a potential for overlap between s39 of the CJA 1988 and s47 of the OAPA 1861 since the threshold of harm that qualifies as actual bodily harm is set very low and includes all harm (save for serious harm and some wounds) that is considered more than 'transient and trifling' (*Miller* (1954)). Hart would argue that injuries at the lower scale of s47, and those charged under s39 of the CJA 1988, are morally similar, and the significant disparity between the respective sentences of five years and six months is therefore unjust. Even more surprising is the fact that although grievous bodily harm is a much more serious offence than actual bodily harm, the maximum sentence for both s20 and s47 is five years. The sentence then jumps to life imprisonment for s18, which might seem a disproportionate increase when the difference between the two offences is one of motive only, as the harm requirement is the same.

Mens rea

According to *Roberts* (1971) a person is liable for actual bodily harm under s47 where there was only recklessness or intention as to causing a battery. Similarly under *Mowatt* (1976) liability for grievous bodily harm will arise where the defendant intended only minor harm or was reckless as to the fact that some physical harm might be caused to some person. This has been criticised as failing to match the punishment to the culpability of the defendant, and therefore as being unjust.

Outdated

The legislation was drafted in a different age and needs updating to modernise the language and to better reflect the concerns of modern society. Lord Steyn commented in *Ireland; Burstow* (1997) that 'the Victorian legislator … would not have in mind psychiatric illness' but illnesses affecting the mind are now an established area of medical health and legislation needs to reflect this. Remember also that the telephone was not invented in 1861, let alone e-mail and text! Judges found ways to establish liability for psychiatric harm in the stalking cases but the liberal interpretations they imposed upon the wording of the Act in order to achieve this have been the subject of much criticism. Because of the difficulties faced by the courts in dealing with stalking cases under the law of non-fatal offences, Parliament passed the Protection from Harassment Act 1997, which was recently amended by the Protection of Freedoms Act 2012. There are two offences: stalking, and stalking involving fear of violence or serious alarm or distress. This makes it easier to prosecute and convict defendants in stalking cases.

Judges also had to strain interpretation to convict the defendant for grievous bodily harm in *Dica* (2004). The Act is not suitable to deal with the prevention of the spread of AIDS or any other sexually transmitted diseases.

Reforms

Widespread criticism of the legislation governing the non-fatal offences led to the Criminal Law Revision Committee publishing proposals for reform in 1981. These proposals formed the basis of the **Law Commission Report 1993** and an attached draft Bill, which was never put before Parliament. The new Labour government produced a draft Bill in 1998, essentially in the same form as the Law Commission Bill. The **1998 draft Bill** includes the following proposals:

- Statutory definitions are provided for assault and battery.
- Section 47 is replaced by the offence of intentionally or recklessly causing injury to another person, with a maximum prison sentence of five years. Prosecution will no longer need to prove that the injury was caused by an assault or battery. 'Injury' is defined to mean 'physical injury', which includes pain, unconsciousness and any impairment of a person's physical condition, and also 'mental injury', which includes any impairment of a person's mental health.
- Sections 20 and 18 are replaced by the separate offences of recklessly causing a serious injury to another and intentionally causing a serious injury to another. The maximum prison sentences are seven years and life imprisonment respectively. There is no longer any reference to wounding, so the problem that a minor wound can be charged under these sections is removed. The troublesome word 'inflict' is removed and all references are to 'caused'.

Key terms

Law Commission Report 1993: report 'Legislating the Criminal Code: Offences Against the Person and General Principles', which includes a draft Bill.

1998 draft Bill: draft Offences Against the Person Bill issued by the government (and based upon the proposals of the Law Commission Report 1993), which is included in a Consultation Document entitled 'Violence: Reforming the Offences Against the Person Act 1861'.

▥ The harm intended or foreseen must correspond to the offence committed contrary to the *mens rea* principles in *Roberts* (1971) and *Mowatt* (1976). Accordingly, the reckless defendant will only be convicted under the new s47 if he has foresight of the *injury* as opposed to the battery that caused it, and he must have foresight of serious injury to be convicted for grievous bodily harm.

▥ Save for the offence of intentionally causing serious injury, 'physical injury' does not include disease. Therefore, a person will only be liable if he *intends* to infect another with a serious sexual disease, and reckless infection will not be an offence.

▥ Intention and recklessness are defined.

The draft Bill is clearly an improvement but has, nevertheless, attracted criticism. Such criticism includes the argument that the offence replacing s47 should also be divided into two separately punishable offences, based on recklessness or intent, as there is no logic as to why the different *mens rea* should only be relevant to serious injuries. Furthermore, the definition of 'injury' still fails to establish a clear dividing line between what might constitute an injury and what would be charged as the lesser charge of assault. 'Serious' is still not defined and the term 'assault' continues to be used to mean both an assault and a battery.

In his forward to the 1998 draft Bill, the Home Secretary pledged his government's commitment to modernising and improving the law. Regrettably, the Bill has yet to be enacted and the courts are still relying upon the OAPA 1861.

Activities

1. Using case authorities from this section, explain how the courts have interpreted the following words:
   - actual
   - grievous
   - bodily harm.

2. Write down some reasons as to why it might be a disadvantage that the words listed above are not defined in the OAPA 1861.

3. Make a table with a list of criticisms of the present law on non-fatal offences on one side, and a matching list of proposed reforms on the other.

4 General defences

The following defences will be evaluated in this topic:

▥ insanity

▥ intoxication

▥ consent

▥ self-defence.

Evaluation of the defence of insanity

A typical criticism of the defence can be found in a House of Commons debate in 1967, when Dr Winstanley said:

> These rules were formulated following the case of Daniel M'Naghten and they are still in force despite the fact that they have been almost constantly subjected to criticism and attack, not only by the medical profession but by lawyers and members of the general public.
>
> I do not need to repeat the various attacks that have been made over the years, but it is interesting to note that as long ago as 1874 the noble Lord, Lord Bramwell, giving evidence to the Select Committee on the Homicide Law Amendment Bill in June, 1874, said that the present law lays down such a definition of madness that nobody is hardly ever really mad enough to be within it. That is the kind of view which has been held by the many people who have frequently criticised this form of the law. We had much criticism at the time of the Royal Commission on Capital Punishment, since when we have had a general acceptance of the fact that the M'Naghten Rules, while they provide a basis, do not necessarily provide a satisfactory one.
>
> Briefly, the important rules – two of them; there are others which are less important today – provide that a person can only be found insane in relation to a criminal act if, first, he is unaware of the nature and quality of the act which he is doing, or, secondly, if he is so aware, that he is not aware that that particular act is wrong.
>
> Many people have held that we should alter the law to embody provisions to cover the type of mental abnormality which could result in a person, while he was aware of what he was doing, or while he might be aware that what he was doing was wrong, was none the less subject to an uncontrollable impulse or otherwise unable to control his behaviour.

Source: hansard.millbanksystems.com

There are a number of points to consider about the defence of insanity. They are:

- the shift of the burden of proof
- the definition of insanity
- the ineffectiveness of the verdict
- the scope of the defence.

The shift of the burden of proof

There is a different standard of proof depending on whether the defence or the prosecution raise the issue of insanity. This is likely to confuse a jury, or at least be deemed an irrelevant distinction by many. This also conflicts with the *Woolmington* v *DPP* (1935) principle that the burden is always on the prosecution to prove the offence, not to prove a defence.

The definition of insanity

The definition of insanity is said to be 'medically irrelevant'. The legal definition of insanity has not advanced significantly since 1843; in 1953, evidence was given to the Royal Commission on Capital Punishment that doctors even then regarded the legal definition to be obsolete and misleading. The distinction between internal and external factors relating to diabetes, and hyperglycaemia and hypoglycaemia, is particularly complicated. In any event, no one would recognise that a diabetic person was insane purely as a result of their condition!

The rules currently do not distinguish between defendants who represent a public danger (the claimed main purpose of the special verdict) and those who do not. Illnesses such as diabetes and epilepsy can be controlled by medication.

The ineffectiveness of the verdict

A finding of insanity can mean an indefinite stay in a secure mental hospital, whereas if a defendant pleads guilty to an offence he will be given a specific sentence. Even where there is a mandatory life sentence, defendants will receive a minimum tariff. Therefore, given the choice, most defendants prefer to plead guilty and receive a conviction and sentence. Added to this is the stigma attached to being labelled insane, which contributes to making this a very unpopular defence that is only raised in a small number of cases each year.

Article 5 of the European Convention on Human Rights provides that a person of unsound mind may only be detained where proper account of objective medical expertise has been taken. It is not always the case that a plea of insanity can be said to have done so. It is to be noted that there is likely to be a human rights challenge on all indeterminate sentences.

The scope of the defence

The Butler Committee recommended that proof of severe mental disorder should be sufficient to negate responsibility. This would create a presumption of no criminal responsibility where there is proof of a severe mental disorder. However, this assumes a lack of criminal responsibility simply because there is evidence of some sort of mental dysfunction, rather than establishing a standard of criminal responsibility. This may be seen to be an interesting view of fault-based liability. This then questions the application of the defence to all crimes rather than those involving *mens rea* only.

Law reform

The Law Commission's tenth programme of Law Reform includes:

Project 7: unfitness to plead and the insanity defence

1.20 The current law is based on rules formulated in the first half of the 19th century when the science of psychiatry was in its infancy. Those rules are in need of reform. There are important unresolved issues which include the scope of a trial of the facts following a finding of unfitness to plead. In addition, there is a need to reconsider the relationship between automatism and insanity and that between diminished responsibility and insanity.'

www.lawcom.gov.uk

In July 2012, the Law Commission published a Scoping Report on Insanity, which seeks to investigate how the defence is working in practice before suggesting proposals for reform. The report posed a number of questions for legal practitioners to respond to, and the closing date for responses was in November 2012. Once all the evidence has been considered, the Law Commission will set out the next stage of the project but has not yet done so at the time of writing.

Evaluation of the defence of intoxication

The defence of intoxication is a relatively modern invention – the law originally took the view that if you were intoxicated, you should be criminally responsible as you got yourself into that state. The current law does not depart significantly from this, but does distinguish between voluntary and involuntary intoxication, and between a certain basic criminal responsibility and crimes where a specific intention must be formed by the defendant.

There are a number of criticisms to make of the law in this area:

- the distinction between specific and basic intent
- the relationship of intoxication to other defences.

The distinction between specific and basic intent

The general law takes a subjective approach to *mens rea*. If there is no subjective *mens rea* there should be no liability as can be seen in the case of *G and R* (2003). The case of *Majewski* (1977) ignores this subjective approach, as it decided that even if the defendant had not actually seen the risk of his conduct he will be guilty as becoming voluntarily intoxicated is in itself recklessness. As the majority of crimes are basic intent crimes, it is questionable whether the defendant's *mens rea* should be construed in this way. For specific intent crimes, the defendant will not be guilty if the intoxication removes the intention, meaning the criminal liability is based on the defendant's mental element, but where there is a lower offence of basic intent the defendant would be convicted of the lesser charge.

The distinction also requires judges to decide whether each criminal offence is one of basic or specific intent. This seems not to be settled as can be appreciated from the appeal in the case of **Heard (2007)**. The appeal in this case was based on whether sexual assault under s3 of the Sexual Offences Act 2003 was one of specific or basic intent. The Act did not make it clear, and this highlights the difficulty created by the distinction.

There are a number of other strange anomalies – for example, attempted rape is specific intent and yet rape is a basic intent crime, meaning intoxication can be a defence to attempted rape but not to rape itself.

The relationship of intoxication to other defences

In the case of **Richardson and Irwin (1999)** the defendant students were messing around after drinking and held their friend over the balcony of his room. Unfortunately, he fell and was severely injured. The court decided that the jury should consider the effect of alcohol on the consent to this horseplay.

In the defence of insanity, if the defendant's drink or drug-taking produces a disease of the mind, he can be found insane under the M'Naghten rules. This was discussed in the early case of *Davis* (1881) and approved in both *Beard* (1920) and *Gallagher* (1963).

Law reform

The Law Commission Report on Intoxication and Criminal Liability 2009 recognised the problems of categorising offences as either specific intent or basic intent. Specific intent crimes are those requiring a specific fault requirement of intention, and basic intent crimes are all other offences that do not require a specific fault element. In effect, a crime of basic intent is any crime that is not specific intent, but this has led to a number of anomalies. Some basic intent crimes can be committed with intention, such as assault, and yet are basic intent because they can be committed recklessly. However, the term basic intent is in itself misleading because no actual intent is required. There are some specific intent crimes, such as handling stolen goods, which can be convicted on proof of knowledge or belief that the goods were stolen.

Recommendations

The Law Commission recommended keeping the general rule from the case of *Majewski* (1977) but drafted the proposals without the terms

---

Key cases

Heard (2007): the court had to decide whether the offence of sexual assault contrary to s3 of the Sexual Offences Act 2003 was one of basic or specific intent.

Richardson and Irwin (1999): the court decided that effect of alcohol should be taken into account when considering the defence of consent.

'specific intent' and 'basic intent'. In place of these terms is a list of some subjective fault elements that are known as integral fault elements:

- intention as to consequence
- knowledge as to something
- belief as to something (where this is equivalent to knowledge)
- fraud
- dishonesty.

These integral fault elements would have to be proved by the prosecution, but the *Majewski* rule would apply to all other states of mind not listed, including recklessness. This would mean that a person could not be found guilty of an offence that requires an integral fault element unless that particular state of mind could be proved.

In relation to involuntary intoxication, the Law Commission recommended that the intoxication should be relevant regardless of the nature of the fault element, which reflects the present position from the case of *Kingston* (1994). This would mean that if the defendant did not have the *mens rea*, he would not be guilty of any offence, no matter what the *mens rea* requirement.

Summary

The present rules from the case law would be put into statutory form to give more certainty and clarity.

The recommendations would remove the confusion that has been created by the terms 'specific intent' and 'basic intent' and it would be clear as to which states of mind have to be proved (integral fault elements).

Evaluation of the defence of consent

There are a number of points to consider about the defence. They are:

- the problem of informed consent
- consent and euthanasia
- individual freedom and its restriction.

The problem of informed consent

There is a lack of consistency in the decisions on cases involving the issue of informed consent. In *Richardson* (1998) the victims were the patients of a dentist who had been struck off the register, but they were unaware of this. They argued that they would not have given consent had they known he should not have been practicing, but the court decided that despite this they had consented to treatment. However, the victims in *Tabassum* (2000) and *Dica* (2004) were found not to have consented: in *Dica*, the victim consented to sex but was unaware the defendant had HIV, and in *Tabassum* the victims were tricked into allowing the defendant to touch their breasts as he had said it was for a survey on cancer. There seems to be no clear difference between these two cases, and the case of *Richardson* and this confusion needs clarifying.

Consent and euthanasia

The *Oxford English Dictionary* defines euthanasia as 'the bringing about of a gentle and easy death in the case of incurable and painful disease with the consent of the victim'. Under the current law, this is illegal. A person who helps another to die, which is sometimes referred to as a 'mercy killing', can be charged with murder, manslaughter or with assisting a suicide. The recent case of *Ministry of Justice* (2012) was an attempt to get the courts to change the law on this issue. This appeal was on behalf of Tony Nicklinson, who had for several years suffered from locked-in syndrome as a result of a stroke, and was paralysed from the neck down. He wanted the court to allow him to have an assisted death once he felt he could no longer endure his suffering and had no quality of life. The High Court rejected his appeal, stating that an issue of this importance should be left to Parliament to decide, and reaffirmed the current position that consent cannot be given to an assisted death.

There is a high level of public support for the legalisation of euthanasia, on the basis that in a civilised society people should be entitled to a dignified death when they have an incurable illness and are suffering intolerable pain. The law allows patients to refuse medical treatment and food, but this can result in a slow and painful death that is unacceptable to many. A further argument in favour of reform is that of personal autonomy, that everyone should have the freedom to make decisions about when to end their life. It is worth mentioning that suicide is not illegal, only assisted suicide, but often those who wish to die – such as Tony Nicklinson – are unable to take their own life because of their condition. However, opponents of euthanasia argue that if it were possible to consent to death, it would threaten the right to life of others, especially the elderly, the seriously ill and the disabled, whose lives may be considered to be of less value. The argument is that legalising euthanasia would undermine the sanctity of life, and it is opposed on moral and religious grounds.

Individual freedom and its restriction

It is difficult to understand that individual activities done with consent should not be lawful. However, the state does interfere where those individual freedoms are perceived to be used in an immoral manner and where the consent may not be freely given, despite appearances. This can be seen in the case of *Brown* (1993).

Law reform

In 1995, following the decision in *Brown*, the Law Commission published a Consultation Paper. The key issue raised in this paper is to what extent a person should be able to consent to injury being inflicted upon him. The Law Commission stated that the law needed clarification because of the number of conflicting decisions, and concluded that a victim's consent to personal injury should be valid except where the injury is seriously disabling or involves death, and even then there should be an exception for legitimate reasons, such as medical treatment. The proposals would appear to provide a satisfactory compromise between the need to respect the autonomy of the defendant and victim and the need to protect the victim. Where an injury is seriously disabling or worse, it is appropriate for the state to intervene, but not in cases like *Brown* where there were no long-term injuries. In *Brown* the defendants were guilty, but under the reform proposals victims could consent to such injuries.

Evaluation of the defence of self-defence

The defence of self-defence is available to all of the non-fatal and homicide offences, and is a complete defence that acknowledges that people should have the right to defend themselves, others or their property.

Arguments that the law favours the defendant

The law is to a large extent weighted towards the defendant, and even allows a defence for those who defend themselves whilst being mistaken as to the circumstances, provided the mistake is an honest one (*Gladstone Williams* (1987)). This recognises that sometimes a quick reaction is needed, or that people may not be fully rational when afraid. The law is also reasonably generous towards the defendant in other situations. There is no duty to retreat, and in *Bird* (1985) the Court of Appeal said that it was unnecessary to show an unwillingness to fight and that there were circumstances where the defendant may act without first retreating. In the case of *Beckford* (1988) Lord Griffith said:

> A man who is about to be attacked does not have to wait for his assailant to strike the first blow or fire the first shot; circumstances may justify a pre-emptive strike.

It is even possible in certain circumstances to plead the defence if the defendant was the original aggressor. In the case of *Keane and McGrath* (2010) the Court of Appeal said that the defence could be pleaded in circumstances where the victim's response to the original aggression was disproportionate, and the defendant retaliated. In such cases, the roles are effectively reversed so the victim becomes the aggressor.

Reasonable force

However, despite many aspects that favour the defendant, the key problem with the defence is the issue of reasonable force. It was recognised in the case of *Palmer* (1971) that the force does not have to be exactly proportionate. Lord Morris said:

> If there has been an attack so that the defence is reasonably necessary it will be recognised that a person defending himself cannot weigh to a nicety the exact measure of his necessary defensive action.

There have, however, been a number of high-profile cases, such as that of Lee Clegg, where the defendant has been unsuccessful because the force used was excessive. The case of the farmer Tony Martin, who shot and killed a burglar and was found guilty of murder, led to a high-profile media campaign to clarify the law. Another aspect to this case was that the defendant's characteristics could not be considered. Martin's psychiatric condition, which led to an appeal on the grounds of diminished responsibility, was not relevant for deciding whether the force was reasonable to him. One of the key criticisms of the decisions in these cases was that if the defence of self-defence fails in a murder case because it is an all-or-nothing situation, the defendant faces a mandatory life sentence. The passing of the Coroners and Justice Act 2009 has alleviated this problem by providing a partial defence, loss of control, that can be pleaded in situations where the defendant may use excessive force because of a fear of serious violence. This defence will reduce the conviction to voluntary manslaughter.

The issue of what is reasonable force is a very topical debate because of recent high-profile cases, such as that of Munir Hussain who attacked an intruder who threatened his family. His defence failed because the force was not considered proportionate, and although his sentence was reduced on appeal, the case led to renewed public concern as to what a person can do to protect their home and family.

Attempts to clarify the law

In order to clarify the common law on self-defence and the defences under the Criminal Law Act 1967, Parliament passed s76 of the Criminal Justice and Immigration Act 2008. Although this does not aim to change the law, it puts into statutory form the rules of law established through case law. It was confirmed in the Court of Appeal in the case of *Keane and McGrath* (2010) that s76 simply confirms the common law. The new provision did nothing in terms of clarifying which of the defendant's characteristics are relevant to self-defence, which was an issue in the case of Tony Martin.

In June 2011, the Government announced that it would be legislating to 'clarify' the law on self-defence. Changes were introduced by way of s148 of the Legal Aid, Sentencing and Punishment of Offenders Act 2012 (which is not in force at the time of writing). The Government explained that the purpose of s148 is to provide greater reassurance to householders about exercising their rights, by making it clear that a person can use

Munir Hussain was imprisoned for attacking an intruder in his home who had threatened his family, as he was held to have used excessive force

reasonable force to defend property (in addition to defending himself or other people or preventing crime) and that he is under no legal duty to retreat, which puts the decision in *Bird* (1985) into statutory effect.

At the Conservative Party Conference in September 2012, Justice Secretary Chris Grayling announced that he is reviewing the changes made to the law by the 2012 Act with a view to giving greater protection to householders who attack intruders. He said that any amount of force used would be acceptable unless it was 'grossly disproportionate'. An example of grossly disproportionate force would be stabbing a burglar who was already lying on the floor unconscious. Such a proposal may be well received by the general public and prove to be a vote winner for the Conservatives, but many within the legal profession feel that there is adequate clarification already and that this would be an unnecessary and problematic development.

David Farrer QC, a criminal barrister, said:

> We have seen the same populist sentiments from successive governments, however the realities are that there is no need to reform the current law. In practice, the application of the reasonable force test is perfectly straightforward and is applied to facts of each individual case. The CPS in recent years has caught the mood of the country and is making sensible decisions on bringing prosecutions in self-defence incidents.

In this statement, Farrer was referring to the fact that in recent years there have been relatively few prosecutions by the Crown Prosecution Service in situations where a householder has attacked a burglar. This means that the CPS is already exercising discretion as to whether to prosecute in the first place, rather than having to ask a jury to decide. In September 2012, Andrew Ferrie fired a gun at a burglar in his home, causing serious injuries to the burglar, but the CPS decided that he had acted with reasonable force and he was not charged.

It could therefore be argued that there is no need for the Government to change the law on reasonable force. To allow the use of any amount of force unless it was 'grossly disproportionate' could encourage vigilantes and set a dangerous precedent that is morally reprehensible.

Activity

Plan and write an answer to the following question, bearing in mind that there will be 30 minutes available in the exam to do this:

Write a critical an analysis of any two of the general defences. Include in your answer a consideration of any proposals for reform for one of your chosen defences.

You should now be able to:

- evaluate the individual defences
- state proposals for reform of the defences.

Introduction

Chapters in this unit:

5 **Formation of contract**

6 **Contract terms**

7 **Vitiating factors**

8 **Discharge of contract**

9 **Remedies**

Unit 3 gives candidates a choice between the study of criminal law and contract law. The unit constitutes 50 per cent of the overall marks for the A2 section of the qualification, and 25 per cent of the overall marks for the A Level qualification. The Unit 3 examination is of 1.5 hours' duration. Candidates must answer one question. The examination paper will include both criminal law and contract law questions: Questions 1 and 2 are on criminal law and Questions 3 and 4 are on contract law. Candidates who choose criminal law will have to select one question to answer, as will candidates who have chosen contract law. Each question is divided into three parts, all of which must be answered.

Each question is worth 75 marks. Each part is worth 25 marks. Parts (a) and (b) will be a test of your ability to select and apply the law to the given scenario, and part (c) will require an evaluative discussion of a stated area of the specification. All areas of the specification, including the remedies, are possible questions for a critical evaluation including proposals for reform. The one exception is that no critical evaluation question will be asked on discharge of contract.

All questions require essay-style answers. In Parts (a) and (b), you should aim to include: correct identification of the issues raised by the question; sound explanation of each of the points; and clear application of the law to the facts disclosed. This may involve some consideration of alternatives where the law lacks clarity in its application to the scenario. In Part (c), illustration may be in many forms – for example, legislation, cases, research, statistics, material from the media – and these need to be put into a coherent argument to answer the question set. Study tips are provided throughout each topic.

Unit 3B comprises five chapters:

5 **Formation of contract:** concerned with the formation of contract.

6 **Contract terms:** deal with the terms of a contract.

7 **Vitiating factors:** considers the law with respect to misrepresentation.

8 **Discharge of contract:** concerned with the discharge of contracts.

9 **Remedies:** examines the remedies available for a breach of contract.

5 Formation of contract

In this topic, you will learn how to:

- define an offer

- explain the nature of an offer

- distinguish between an offer and an invitation to treat

- explain when an offer is made

- describe the rules that decide when an offer comes to an end

- describe the different methods of, and importance of, communication of an offer

- apply the rules to a given situation.

Key terms

Offer: statement of intent to be legally bound by the terms of the offer if it is accepted.

Offeror: person making an offer to another person.

Offeree: person receiving an offer from the offeror.

Bilateral contract: both parties to the agreement have obligations to perform.

Unilateral contract: only one party has obligations to do something.

1 Offer

The study of the law on contract will always start with the offer. This will be followed by an acceptance (Topic 2) that creates an agreement which may become a legally binding contract if other factors are also present (Topics 3, 4, and 5). The public believe they understand the meaning of an offer but, as will be seen, it has a very specific definition in law. This topic will consider the definition of an offer, how what may appear to be an offer is not, when an offer is created/ended and, finally, how an offer is communicated.

The offer

The nature of an offer

An **offer** is the first step in the creation of a contract. For example, Rameez wishes to sell his car and tells Leanne that his car is for sale to her for £1,000. Rameez is the **offeror** and Leanne is the **offeree**. The next step is accepting the offer.

Rameez has made a statement to Leanne that is an offer. A valid acceptance by Leanne will legally bind him to the terms of the offer, which will lead to the creation of a binding contract.

It is important to distinguish between a **bilateral contract** and a **unilateral contract**.

Most contracts tend to be a bilateral contract, where one party has made a promise to the other (to transfer ownership of the car) in return for the other's promise (to make a payment of £1,000).

An example of a bilateral contract is the agreement made between Rameez and Leanne for the purchase of the car.

A unilateral contract is when one party (Party 1) has promised to pay the other party (Party 2) a sum of money if Party 2 performs a certain act but Party 2 makes no promise in return to perform the act.

An example would be if Person A promises to pay Person B £500 if he repaints her caravan on Thursday. Person A has made a promise to pay Person B, but that person is under no obligation to perform the act. If he decides on Thursday to repaint the caravan then there is an acceptance of the offer (see Topic 2), but Person A can do nothing if Person B chooses not to perform the task.

Who makes the offer in different situations

Sometimes, one party wishes to commence negotiations with the other party rather than make an offer. For example, Rameez may suggest to Claire that she should look at his car as he is thinking of selling it for about £1,000. This may seem like an offer but it is not – Rameez has merely made the first step in the negotiation process. This step is called an 'invitation to treat'. An invitation to treat may appear to be an offer but is an attempt by a party (usually a seller) to encourage the other party (the buyer) to make an offer.

■ **Key cases**

Pharmaceutical Society of GB v Boots Cash Chemists (1953): goods in a self-service store are an invitation to treat, not an offer.

Fisher v Bell (1961): a knife with a price label on it in a shop window was only an invitation to treat.

Partridge v Crittenden (1968): an advertisement in a newspaper that offered wild birds for sale was an invitation to treat, not an offer for sale.

Carlill v Carbolic Smoke Ball Co. (1893): an advertisement could contain an offer if it was clearly meant to be taken seriously and the advertisement indicated the offeree should take a particular 'course of action'.

Invitations to treat

There are many examples of invitations to treat. They include:

Self-service displays

Goods on a shelf in a supermarket are an invitation to treat and not an offer, as shown in **Pharmaceutical Society of GB v Boots Cash Chemists (1953)**. Boots was prosecuted for offering medicines for sale without a pharmacist being present. This was an offence under the Pharmacy and Poisons Act 1933. The court decided that Boots was not guilty as the offer was made by the customer at the checkout. The invitation to treat invites the customer to make an offer to buy the goods from the seller. This rule allows a shopkeeper to refuse a sale under contract law, e.g. if the wrong price has been attached to the goods or if there is no stock remaining.

Shop window displays

A shop window display is only an invitation to treat. The customer makes the offer once inside the shop, as shown in the case of **Fisher v Bell (1961)** where a shopkeeper was prosecuted under the Restriction of Offensive Weapons Act 1959 because he displayed a knife in the shop window with a ticket. He was found not guilty as he was not offering the knife for sale, it was an invitation to treat.

Advertisements

Advertisements in a newspaper or magazine are usually invitations to treat, such as in the case of **Partridge v Crittenden (1968)**.

Lots at an auction

At an auction, the auctioneer makes invitations to treat and the bidders make offers. The auctioneer then accepts the highest bid by banging his gavel. The bidder may withdraw an offer at any time up to the auctioneer's acceptance.

When an advertisement may be an offer

Sometimes what may seem like an invitation to treat may actually be an offer, such as in the case of **Carlill v Carbolic Smoke Ball Co. (1893)**.

The company advertised its smoke ball stating that if the buyer the ball correctly three times daily for two weeks caught the 'flu, the company would pay £100 in compensation. The advertisement also stated that the company had deposited £1,000 with its bank as security for the compensation. Mrs Carlill bought the product, used it, and caught the 'flu. The advertisement was an offer, which Mrs Carlill had accepted by purchasing and then using the item (the 'course of action'). The court was also influenced by the words relating to the specific compensation promised and the money on deposit, which the court decided would show to a potential buyer that the company was serious in its claims.

This case is authority for two important propositions:

- ▨ An advertisement may constitute an offer to the whole world, i.e. to anyone who reads it.
- ▨ Acceptance may not have to be communicated to the offeror (see Topic 2).

Termination of an offer

Once an offer exists, it is open for acceptance by the offeree. It may then become very important whether the offer is still in existence, as if not then no agreement can flow from it. An offer can end (be terminated) in a variety of ways, some of which are explained below.

If properly withdrawn

If the offer is properly withdrawn *before* acceptance then no offer exists. For example, Rameez may offer the car to Leanne but then withdraw the offer before she has accepted, which results in the offer terminating.

In **Routledge v Grant (1828)** a seller of a house said the house was available for purchase for six weeks. The offeror then informed the offeree that the offer had been withdrawn. The offeror was entitled to withdraw the offer before the offeree had accepted it. An example of an improperly withdrawn offer can be found in **Byrne v Van Tienhoven (1880)**.

Van Tienhoven offered goods to Byrne and then sent a letter withdrawing the offer. This letter arrived after Byrne had accepted the offer, so the withdrawal letter was not effective.

An interesting problem arises as to when an offeror may withdraw a unilateral offer. If it may be withdrawn at any time, then the offeree may have commenced acceptance – for example, returning a lost pet in response to a notice offering a reward – and the offeror may withdraw the offer just before the pet is returned, which seems unfair on the offeree. The Court of Appeal in **Errington v Errington (1952)** held it was unlikely that a unilateral offer could be validly withdrawn once the offeree had started to perform the required act.

The specified time for acceptance has passed

If the offer is stated to be open for acceptance until a particular date then it no longer exists after that date. In *Routledge v Grant* (1828) the offer would have automatically terminated after the six-week period had expired.

The offer terminates if a reasonable time has passed

In many situations, an offer has no time limit placed upon it. The court allows the offer to exist for a *reasonable* time. The court will consider all the circumstances when reaching its decision, as demonstrated in **Ramsgate Victoria Hotel v Montefiore (1866)**. In this case, the defendant offered to buy shares in the hotel on 8 June, the hotel tried to accept the offer on 23 November, but the defendant no longer wanted the shares. The court decided that the five-month gap was too long and the offer had lapsed.

It would not be reasonable to expect an offer to buy shares to exist for six months, as the value of shares fluctuates dramatically.

The offer is rejected

The rejection of an offer will terminate that offer. The making of a counter-offer is treated as a rejection (see Topic 2 and the case of *Hyde* v *Wrench* (1840)). Leanne would reject the offer by replying to Rameez that she would not buy the car, *or* by agreeing to buy the car but suggesting a price of £900.

Death of one of the parties

The general rule is that if the offeree dies, the offer terminates. However, if the offeror dies, an offeree's acceptance may still be valid (provided the death was unknown to the offeree).

By acceptance

If the offeree properly accepts the offer then the offer no longer exists, as it is now part of the agreement. If Leanne responds to the offer of Rameez by replying 'yes', the offer is ended and an agreement is created. Rameez may no longer alter the terms of the offer, as it no longer exists.

Communication of the offer

The offeror must communicate the offer to the offeree – the offeree cannot accept an offer of which he has no knowledge. There are different ways of communicating an offer:

- An offer can be to one person, a class of persons or the whole world – see *Carlill* v *Carbolic Smoke Ball Co.* (1893).
- The offer must be communicated to the offeree. **Taylor v Laird (1856)** shows that an offer cannot be accepted unless the person who is seeking to accept it knows of its existence.

Key cases

Routledge v Grant (1828): an offer can be revoked at any time even if it is said to be open for a fixed period that has not yet ended.

Byrne v Van Tienhoven (1880): if an offer is to be validly withdrawn by the offeror, then that withdrawal must be properly communicated to the offeree.

Errington v Errington (1952): if a party commences performance of their act, on reliance of a promise by an offeror in a unilateral contract, then the offeror cannot revoke that promise.

Ramsgate Victoria Hotel v Montefiore (1866): an offer made to buy shares in a company had lapsed when the company responded five months later; the person making the offer was entitled to assume the company did not want him to invest.

Taylor v Laird (1856): a captain's claim for wages failed as on return trip he worked as an ordinary crew member but did not tell the owner of his change of status.

An offer may be withdrawn at any time before an acceptance. Suppose Rameez offers his car to Leanne for £1,000 and states the offer will remain open for acceptance until 12 noon on Monday 16 June. In reliance on this statement, Leanne drives a 100-mile round trip to view the car and is so impressed with its quality that she asks her local garage to check it out for her at a cost of £50. The report is favourable but before she can accept the offer Rameez telephones her on Sunday 15 June to withdraw the offer. Even though Rameez has withdrawn the offer before the stated date, Leanne will be unable to recover any of her expenses from Rameez.

The withdrawal of an offer must be communicated to the offeree. This links in with the termination of an offer. If Rameez wishes to withdraw his offer to Leanne, he must communicate that withdrawal to her. He may either do this himself or instruct a third party on his behalf, and in either event Rameez has only to take reasonable steps to bring the withdrawal to Leanne's attention.

The terms of the offer must not be vague. The parties cannot reach agreement if the words of the offer are too vague, as demonstrated in **Guthing v Lynn (1831)**. In this case, the buyer of a horse agreed to pay the seller an extra £5 if the horse was 'lucky'; this offer was too vague to be accepted so there was no contract. This links with the rule from **Gibson v Manchester City Council (1979)** that a letter from the council stating 'it may be prepared' to sell a house to Mr Gibson was not an offer but an invitation to treat.

In the scenario, if Rameez offers his car to Leanne at a 'reasonable price' there can be no valid acceptance of such an offer.

Key cases

Guthing v Lynn (1831): the terms of offer must not be vague, as, if so, then it becomes impossible to decide precisely what the parties have agreed.

Gibson v Manchester City Council (1979): an indication by a party that they may be interested in contracting with the other party is part of negotiations and, at best, is an invitation to treat, and cannot be an offer.

Activities

1 Look at a local or national newspaper and consider whether the advertisements are offers or invitations to treat.

2 Create your own advertisements, one to be an offer and the other an invitation to treat. What are the main differences?

You should now be able to:

■ understand the nature of an offer

■ explain the rules in relation to an offer

■ apply the law to given situations.

In this topic, you will learn how to:

■ define acceptance

■ explain the different forms of acceptance

■ describe the different methods of, and importance of, communication of acceptance

■ apply the rules to a given situation.

2 Acceptance

Acceptance is the second step in the formation of a contract. If Leanne wishes to purchase the car offered by Rameez then she must communicate that acceptance to him in a positive manner. The simplest example is that she says 'Yes, Rameez, I agree to buy your car for £1,000'.

There are various rules concerning acceptance, which are set out below.

Rules concerning acceptance

The acceptance must be unconditional

A crucial element of acceptance is that it must be an agreement to all the terms of the offer. If the offeree tries to vary the terms of the offer then the offer is terminated *and* there cannot be a valid acceptance.

For example, in **Hyde v Wrench (1840)** Wrench offered his farm to Hyde for £1,000. Hyde agreed to buy the farm, but for £900, which Wrench refused. Hyde then said he would pay the original £1,000. Wrench was entitled to refuse this suggestion, as Hyde had terminated the original offer when he made his counter-offer of £900.

Request for information

An offeree may sometimes ask the offeror for information concerning the terms of the offer. This request for information does not terminate the offer. In **Stevenson v McLean (1880)** the purchaser asked if delivery of iron could be staggered. The purchaser sent a telegram to the seller accepting the offer but in the meantime the seller sold the iron to a third party, claiming the purchaser had made a counter-offer. The court decided the purchaser had made an enquiry, not a counter-offer, so the original offer still existed.

Form of acceptance

Acceptance may be in any form, e.g. it may be verbal, written or a gesture. If the offer states the acceptance must be in a specified form, then any other type of acceptance is unlikely to be valid.

Communication of acceptance

Whether an acceptance must be communicated to the offeror depends on the contract being bilateral or unilateral.

In unilateral contracts, the acceptance need not be communicated to the offeror. For example, Mrs Carlill did not have to inform the Carbolic Smoke Ball Company that she had accepted their offer. Her conduct alone was sufficient for acceptance.

In bilateral contracts, the general rule is that the acceptance must be communicated to the offeror. This can be seen in **Felthouse v Bindley (1863)**. An uncle wanted to buy his nephew's horse and wrote a letter saying 'If I hear no more about him I shall consider the horse mine for £30'. The nephew wanted to sell to the uncle so did nothing, as suggested, but told the auctioneer who held the horse not to sell it. In error, the auctioneer still sold the horse to a third party. The third party was entitled to the horse as the uncle and the nephew never had an agreement. The nephew's acceptance was never communicated to the uncle.

The rule for the communication of acceptance is sensible as it allows for there to be certainty between the parties as to whether an agreement is made or not.

Acceptance may be communicated by a party's conduct after the offer is made. In **Brogden v Metropolitan Railway (1877)**, although the latter never formally accepted the offer of Mr Brogden, the parties did deal with each other on the terms set out in the offer so acceptance was held to have taken place.

The 'postal rule'

The **postal rule** was created in the early 1800s and is an exception to the general rule concerning communication of acceptance for a bilateral contract. The rule, shown in the case of **Adams v Lindsell (1818)**, tries to balance the interests of two innocent parties. What happens if the offeree's letter of acceptance is delayed in delivery or is never delivered at all?

The postal rule was applied in **Household Fire & Carriage Accident Insurance Co. Ltd v Grant (1879)** where a company accepted the defendant's offer to buy shares by posting a properly addressed and stamped letter. Although the defendant never received this acceptance letter, the court held there was a valid acceptance at the moment the letter was posted. However, in *Holwell Securities* v *Hughes* (1974) the postal rule did not apply as the offeror had stated the acceptance must be received by 'notice in writing', so the acceptance had to be received and only placing the letter in the postbox was not sufficient.

Key terms

Acceptance: unconditional agreement to all the terms of the offer.

Postal rule: postal acceptance takes effect when the letter of acceptance is posted; 'posted' means that the letter is in the control of the Post Office or one of its employees authorised to receive letters and the letter is correctly addressed and stamped.

Key cases

Hyde v Wrench (1840): a counter-offer ends the original offer.

Stevenson v McLean (1880): an enquiry about whether credit was available did not reject the offer, which could still be accepted.

Felthouse v Bindley (1863): a statement that if nothing further was heard then a contract would be made was not sufficient to be the positive act required for acceptance.

Brogden v Metropolitan Railway (1877): even in a complicated, commercial transaction there can be acceptance of an offer just by conduct, if supported by external evidence e.g. in the form of an order placed on the terms of the agreement.

Adams v Lindsell (1818): the postal rule states that a letter of acceptance takes effect at the moment of posting.

Household Fire & Carriage Accident Insurance Co. Ltd v Grant (1879): if the postal rules apply, acceptance takes place when the letter is posted, even if does not arrive.

The probable reasons for the postal rule are based on business efficiency (i.e. what else could the offeree have done?) and acknowledgement of the practicalities of business (i.e. in balancing the rights, responsibilities and expectations of innocent parties, the postal rule is an acceptable compromise).

Problems with the postal rule in modern society

There is some uncertainty as to whether the postal rule applies to more modern methods of communication such as text messages, emails, faxes, pager messages, telexes, etc. There is case law that clarifies certain points, but not all. The case of **Entores Ltd v Miles Far East Co. (1955)** would seem to suggest that the postal rule does *not* apply to some methods of instantaneous communication, e.g. by telephone or by telex.

In *Brinkibon Ltd* v *Stahag Stahl GmbH* (1982), the court confirmed the Entores decision and stated:

> … it would seem … that the communication should take effect at the time when the [offeree] could reasonably have expected it to be read.

The courts seem reluctant to extend the postal rule to methods of communication outside the postal system itself.

The case of **Mondial Shipping and Chartering BV v Astarte Shipping Ltd (1995)** clarified two particular and important points concerning communication of acceptance. First, if an acceptance is sent out of office hours the acceptance will only be effective once office hours restart. Second, the postal rule does not apply to faxes (and, by implication, does not apply to other modern forms of communication).

This view was confirmed in **Thomas v BPE Solicitors (2010)** when the High Court stated the postal rule was inapplicable to an acceptance sent by email. The decision confirmed the comments made by Lord Wilberforce in the *Brinkibon Ltd* v *Stahag Stahl GmbH* (1982) case that the issue should be resolved by reference to:

> the intentions of the parties, sound business practice and … where the risks should lie.

Electronic Commerce (EC Directive) Regulations 2002

Under these regulations any organisation or service provider that sells goods or services on the Internet from a website must follow certain requirements in order for there to be a valid contract between the purchaser (the regulations are aimed at protecting consumers rather than businesses) and the seller.

These requirements are that the service provider must: provide receipts for orders (offers by the purchaser) without delay; allow purchasers to amend orders (offers) easily before sending the order (offer); and provide the name and address (geographical and electronic) of the service provider.

These regulations do not alter the rules on offer and acceptance outlined above, but they do allow the consumer some protection. It is the purchaser who makes the order (offer) based on the invitation to treat provided on the website. However, to protect the customer, the contract is voidable if the basic information described above is not given in the invitation to treat.

An incident in 1999 indicated the application of the common law rules of offer and acceptance to an advertisement on a website. A large electronic retailer mistakenly advertised televisions for sale at £30 when the correct price was £300. Many customers contacted the retailer 'accepting' the retailer's 'offer' but it was concluded that the advertisement was an invitation to treat, that the purchasers were making the offer and that the retailer was entitled to reject those offers.

Consumer Protection (Distance Selling) Regulations 2000

If a commercial supplier is supplying goods or services to a consumer and the contract is made, for example, by an exchange of letters, faxes, emails,

---

■ Key cases

Entores Ltd v Miles Far East Co. (1955): a telex was sent and the court decided the telex took effect when it was *received*, i.e. the postal rule did not apply.

Mondial Shipping & Chartering BV v Astarte Shipping Ltd (1995): postal rule does not apply to faxes; it should be noted that where items to which the postal rule does not apply arrive outside office hours, communication will not take place until office hours.

Thomas v BPE Solicitors (2010): the court had to decide whether an acceptance email sent by a party was communicated when it was sent or when it was read, and concluded the postal rule did not apply so the email had to be read to be an effective acceptance.

by tele-shopping or by website trading, then the consumer is entitled to a 'cooling-off' period in which the contract may be ended by the consumer.

The consumer has the right to cancel the contract within seven working days of the consumer's receipt of the goods.

The Regulations do not alter the common law rules of offer and acceptance, but do allow the consumer some protection when having made a valid contract and then having second thoughts.

Offer and acceptance problems

There may be examination questions based either wholly or partly on offer and acceptance. These questions might involve what appears to be an offer but may be an invitation to treat. This could be linked with an acceptance that may be valid but has a potential problem with communication.

The answer should identify the topics under review, state the relevant law clearly and concisely, and then apply that law to the question. Inevitably, there will be room for discussion of the application of the law and you do not necessarily need to write a definitive answer.

For example, one previous exam question was as follows:

> Brian was a member of the Alpha Wine Club. He received a letter from the Club which stated 'As one of our most valued customers, Brian, we offer you this opportunity to buy a case of French red wine at the specially low price £95. Stocks are limited, so reply within five days to be certain of getting your wine'. Brian sent an email that same day to order a case of the wine. However, though the email was received by the Club, it was accidentally deleted by a trainee customer service employee before it had been dealt with. Consequently, Brian did not receive the wine, which had sold out by the time that he queried the lack of delivery. Subsequently, Brian discovered that, had he obtained the wine, he could have re-sold it for £150 on the open market'.
>
> Taking into account the rules on formation of a contract, consider whether Brian has any rights and remedies against the Alpha Wine Club in connection with the case of red wine.

You should first deal with the communication to Brian and discuss the status of the letter. Define an offer and an invitation to treat, with examples, and discuss the different consequences if the letter is an offer or an invitation to treat, i.e. if an offer then Brian's email is an acceptance, if an invitation to treat is Brian's email an offer?

Then define an acceptance and, in particular, discuss whether the acceptance (*if* the letter is an offer of course) has been communicated, which involves a discussion of the 'postal rule', and whether it applies to the modern method of communication in this question.

> **Link**
>
> Your answer should also cover remedies, and this is dealt with in Chapter 9: Remedies.

Activities

1. Explain the postal rule and justify its existence.
2. Describe the effect of an offeree's acceptance by email that is never received by the offeror.

You should now be able to:

- understand the nature of acceptance
- explain the rules in relation to acceptance
- apply the law to given scenarios.

In this topic, you will learn how to:

■ define consideration

■ distinguish between sufficiency and adequacy of consideration

■ explain the meaning of past consideration

■ explain the situation where there is part performance and performance of an existing duty

■ describe the function of consideration

■ apply the rules to a given situation.

Key terms

Consideration: price paid by the claimant for defendant's promise – for example, the claimant pays the defendant £1,000 for the defendant's promise to transfer possession and ownership of their car to the claimant.

Adequacy: whether something is of equivalent value or comparable in price.

Sufficiency: when the consideration is real, tangible and has some value.

Key cases

Thomas v Thomas (1842): the court will not interfere with the validity of a contract just because one party may have a bad bargain, provided there is no misrepresentation by either party.

Chappell & Co. v Nestlé (1960): consideration in a contract must have some value in the eye of the law, even if that value is of a nominal amount.

Re McArdle (1951): a promise to pay for work done voluntarily after the work has been done is not consideration, as it is for consideration that is past.

Lampleigh v Braithwaite (1615): an exception to the past consideration rule may apply if one party makes a request for a service that is of such importance as to imply that a later payment will be made for it.

3 Consideration

Consideration is what passes from one contractual party to another; each party in a contract must give something of value.

Consideration is traditionally thought of as money, goods or services. However, in modern cases the courts seem willing to take a flexible approach to the traditional view of consideration.

The usual attitude of the courts to consideration (and to formation of contracts generally) is to attempt to reach a decision that allows the court to enforce what the parties have agreed. Our commercial and business world is based on contractual obligations, and the court does not like allowing parties to escape these obligations.

Consideration need not be adequate but must be sufficient

The court's view is that the **adequacy** of consideration is a matter for the parties to decide, and is best shown in the case of **Thomas v Thomas (1842)**. The court will not interfere if one party has made a bad bargain.

Mrs Thomas remained in the family home after her husband's death, provided she paid rent to Mr Thomas's estate of £1 per year; this was not a commercial rent, but the contract between Mr Thomas and his widow was valid as the adequacy of the consideration was irrelevant.

However, for consideration to be valid it must be sufficient. This means the consideration must:

■ be real (the consideration must exist)

■ be tangible (the consideration must be definite, e.g. a vague promise may not be definite enough for **sufficiency**)

■ have some value (even if of a nominal amount).

The case of **Chappell & Co. v Nestlé (1960)** demonstrates the criteria in action. In a promotion by Nestlé, customers could send in chocolate bar wrappers together with a payment in return for a record. The wrappers supplied by the customer had some economic value for Nestlé as they represented sales of chocolate bars. For tax reasons, the court had to decide whether chocolate wrappers were consideration; the court decided they were as they were real, tangible and had some value, even though Nestlé threw them away once received.

Past consideration

To be valid, consideration must be a mutual exchange of promises. If one party carries out an act voluntarily, and a second party later promises to pay for or contribute to this act, then this is called 'past' consideration. The promise to pay by the second party is not good consideration as it is a promise to pay for something that has already happened. The first party is not able to enforce the promise of the second party as there is no valid contract. In **Re McArdle (1951)** some family members redecorated the family home and other family members then promised in writing to contribute a fixed sum to the cost of redecoration, but never did. No payment was due as the promise to pay was for something that had already occurred: it was past consideration, so there was no contract.

There is an exception to this rule from the old case of **Lampleigh v Braithwaite (1615)** when Braithwaite was to be hanged for murder and requested his friend Lampleigh to obtain a pardon from the King, which Lampleigh obtained. Braithwaite promised to pay Lampleigh £100 but never did, claiming past consideration. The court held that the request for the pardon implied that a payment would be made as it was so important to Braithwaite, so the promise was valid consideration. As a result, the exception to the past consideration rule will apply when a party:

- requests a service from another, and
- the promise of payment can be implied into the request.

This exception may apply in commercial situations where the payment is implied due to the context of the facts. In *Re Casey's Patents* (1892) a manager worked on patents for a company, which then promised him a one-third share in the patents. The company then refused to share the patents, claiming past consideration. The manager was entitled to the share as it was implied that when he worked on the patents he would receive payment of some form.

Part payment of a debt in place of the whole debt gives no consideration

This rule from **Pinnel's case (1602)** is that a creditor is able to claim the remainder of a debt even if the creditor has agreed with the debtor that a part payment by the debtor will clear the debt.

In a scenario, Miriam owes Vicky £600 for costumes. Vicky may agree to accept £500 and confirm that the balance of £100 will be written off. However, under Pinnel's rule Vicky is still entitled to claim the £100. The reasoning behind the rule is that Vicky is 'giving' something to Miriam (a reduction in the debt) but what is Miriam giving in return? As Miriam is not supplying any form of consideration for the reduction in the debt there is no valid agreement as to the part payment, so the original debt is still outstanding.

In **Foakes v Beer (1884)** Foakes owed Beer £2,000 and they agreed he would repay by instalments and Beer would do nothing more. Beer then asked for interest and Foakes refused. Foakes was giving Beer no consideration to be allowed to pay by instalments, therefore Beer was entitled to sue for the whole amount and to claim interest.

The above case should be compared with **D & C Builders v Rees (1966)** when builders were owed £482 by Rees but agreed to accept £300 in full settlement as the builders were near bankruptcy. The builders were able to claim the balance of £182.

There is a subtle difference between these two cases. In *Rees* the reduction in payment had been obtained by the use of economic pressure on the builders who had a cash-flow problem. In *Foakes* there was no such pressure and the original arrangement as to payment by instalments had been reached with mutual consent. It could be argued that the *Rees* decision is correct but in *Foakes* some flexibility could, and should, have been allowed to Foakes, who was trying to resolve the dispute on terms fair to both parties.

The law appreciates that Pinnel's rule may seem harsh, so exceptions have developed.

- *Accord and satisfaction*: If the debtor agrees to pay a smaller amount on a date earlier than originally agreed *or* in cash when a cheque was originally agreed, then the debtor has provided consideration for the new agreement. Alternatively, if the creditor agrees to accept something other than money for the whole debt this is good consideration, even if the item provided is not comparable in value to the debt. This is another example of the rule about adequacy of consideration.
- *Promissory estoppel*: If one party to an existing contract (the promisor) promises to vary the contract (for the other's benefit) and the other party (the promisee) relies on that promise to vary, then the promisor cannot go back on the promise, i.e. the promisor is 'estopped' from breaking the promise.

Key cases

Pinnel's case (1602): payment of a smaller sum on the due date in satisfaction of the full debt cannot be good consideration, so the balance of the debt remains outstanding.

Foakes v Beer (1884): agreeing to pay an existing debt by instalments without further consideration means the full debt remains repayable at once.

D & C Builders v Rees (1966): economic pressure put on the claimant by the defendant meant the defendant could not rely on the agreement as it was not achieved equitably.

Key cases

Central London Property Trust Ltd v High Trees House Ltd (1947): promise intended to be binding, intended to be acted upon and in fact acted on, but without consideration from the other contracting party, is binding.

Re Selectmove (1995): confirmed the court is unlikely to extend the concept of promissory estoppel to cases other than those involving a debt.

Stilk v Myrick (1809): the captain did not have to pay extra wages as the crew only did the work they would have had to do anyway, i.e. cover for their missing colleagues.

In **Central London Property Trust Ltd v High Trees House Ltd (1947)** a landlord agreed with his tenant that the tenant need only pay half rent during World War II, as the tenant had trouble finding subtenants in London due to the bombing. After the war, the landlord claimed all the rent accrued for the period after the war had ended, and he was entitled to this rent. However, the judge Lord Denning said that the landlord would not have been entitled to the balance of rent accrued during the war, as even though there was no consideration from the tenant for the reduction in rent for the war period, the tenant had relied on the landlord's promise and the agreement was valid for the reduction in rent for the war period. Lord Denning's statement appears to be in direct conflict with the decision in *Foakes*. If Beer could break her promise not to sue, why cannot High Trees House Ltd sue in the *High Trees* case? Lord Denning's comments in *High Trees* seem to indicate consideration is not a crucial element of a contract. This was a radical view at the time, and the courts have been cautious in allowing this new principle to develop.

For promissory estoppel to apply, it is likely that the promisee must have acted to their detriment when relying on the promise (or acted 'differently' according to Lord Denning). It is also likely that the promisor is able to withdraw the promise on giving reasonable notice to the promisee.

In **Re Selectmove (1995)** a company owed tax to the Inland Revenue. An agreement was reached that the tax owed would be paid by instalments and Selectmove commenced payment. The Inland Revenue then claimed the whole debt, which would put Selectmove into liquidation. Selectmove argued that it had relied on the Inland Revenue's promise not to sue and that Lord Denning's principle from *High Trees* was applicable. The court was reluctant to extend the principle of promissory estoppel as to do so would undermine the basic principle in English law of the need for consideration so as to create a legally binding contract. The Inland Revenue was not bound by the agreement and, applying the principle from *Foakes*, the whole debt was due.

This case is of interest in that Selectmove also argued the principle from *Williams* v *Roffey Bros & Nichols (Contractors) Ltd* (1990) would allow the agreement with the Inland Revenue to stand. The Williams case is dealt with in the section below (existing duty) and is further evidence of the reluctance of the courts to extend the *High Trees* principle.

An existing duty

If a contractual party performs an existing duty (and no more) then this performance cannot be consideration for a new contract. This is shown in the case of **Stilk v Myrick (1809)**. The details here were that two members of a crew deserted, leaving eighteen, and the captain promised to share the two men's wages between the eighteen if they covered for the missing two. The eighteen agreed, but the captain refused the extra payment when they reached port. The captain did not have to pay the extra wages as the eighteen only performed what they had to anyway, i.e. cover for their colleagues.

In the scenario, Vicky has contracted to manufacture twelve costumes for £600 (contract 1). Vicky then discovers that the cost of material has suddenly increased. As a result, she asks if Miriam agrees to pay an additional £10 per costume, making a new total of £720 (contract 2). Miriam agrees but then pays only the original £600. Is the additional £120 due?

The court will ask what consideration both parties were giving for contract 2. Obviously Miriam is paying the extra £120 but Vicky is manufacturing the costumes that she was contracted to complete in any event. Vicky is merely performing her 'existing duty' and that is not sufficient to be valid consideration for contract 2. The additional £120 is not payable.

This principle was followed in **Collins v Godefroy (1831)** where the promise of payment for the performance of a public duty (attending court under a court order) was not enforceable as there was a public duty to attend court anyway.

The situation may be complicated by the involvement of a third party.

In the scenario, Miriam may have agreed that Vicky would deliver the costumes by Monday 23 June. Siobhan (the third party) supplies some of the material to Vicky for the manufacture of the costumes and has agreed with Vicky to supply the material by 20 May. Miriam wanted to ensure the costumes were ready by 23 June so agreed to pay Siobhan an extra £100 (in addition to Vicky's fee to Siobhan) if the material is supplied to Vicky by 20 May.

Miriam has agreed to pay Siobhan (a third party) to perform a duty Siobhan is already contracted to perform for Vicky. If Siobhan delivers the material on time is she entitled to the additional £100? The answer to this question is, perhaps surprisingly, yes.

This principle was set out in *Scotson* v *Pegg* (1861) when Scotson agreed with X to deliver coal to anyone nominated by X. X nominated Pegg (the third party) and Scotson made his delivery. For reasons not relevant to this topic, Scotson sued Pegg and Pegg claimed there could be no contract as Scotson was only performing a duty for Pegg that Scotson had to perform anyway under Scotson's contract with X. In this situation, it is possible to offer the same consideration to two different parties, so Scotson was successful against Pegg.

In certain circumstances, the courts have been willing to allow what appears to be an existing duty to be classed as valid consideration for a new contract. Two examples are:

1   If what is given is more than what was originally expected, as in **Hartley v Ponsonby (1857)** when 19 out of 36 crew members of a ship deserted and the unexpected increased labour and danger for the remaining 17 men meant they were entitled to extra payment.

2   If performance of the existing duty gives the other party a 'benefit'. As will be seen in the Williams case below, the court may give a wide meaning to the definition of benefit.

An important case is **Williams v Roffey Bros & Nichols (Contractors) Ltd (1990)**, when a developer contracted with a builder (Roffey) to refurbish some flats. There was a condition that if Roffey did not complete by a specified date then Roffey would have to pay daily compensation to the developer until completion. Roffey subcontracted the roofing work to a roofer (Williams) for £20,000. Unfortunately, Williams encountered labour problems and it appeared to Roffey that the roofing work would overrun the completion date Roffey had agreed with the developer. Roffey suggested to Williams that he would pay an extra £10,300 to allow Williams to employ more labour to ensure the roofing work was completed on time. Williams agreed, and managed to complete the roofing work on time so Roffey did not have to pay the developer any compensation for late completion. Roffey refused to pay the extra £10,300, arguing that Williams was merely performing an existing duty and the principle from *Stilk* v *Myrick* (1809) applied. The Court of Appeal decided the extra payment was due to Williams as Roffey was receiving benefits from Williams, namely:

■   the extra payment ensured Williams continued the roofing work and did not stop in breach of contract with Roffey

■   the extra payment allowed Williams to complete on time so Roffey avoided his potential liability to the developer for late completion

Key cases

Collins v Godefroy (1831): performing a public duty does not amount to consideration for another contract as the duty must be performed anyway.

Hartley v Ponsonby (1857): performing an existing duty may be valid consideration if that existing duty has become, for example, more dangerous or difficult.

Williams v Roffey Bros & Nichols (Contractors) Ltd (1990): an example of when performing an existing duty may be valid consideration even if the benefit obtained relates to an entirely separate contract; however, reference should be made to *Re Selectmove* (see p90).

the extra payment avoided Roffey the trouble and expense of engaging other people to complete the roofing work.

This case is seen as very significant as it has widened the limits of what the courts may consider as valid consideration.

The concept of 'benefit' created in the Williams case seemed to achieve recognition, if not support, in the case of *Horwood* v *Land of Leather Ltd* (2010). The judge, Teare J, said witness evidence acknowledged a particular payment was of 'commercial benefit' to the company and:

> ... the court should be slow to say that ... which a businessman says is a benefit is not.

Activities

1. Explain, in your words, the difference between 'adequacy' and 'sufficiency' in respect of consideration.

2. Describe two examples of when Pinnel's rule would not apply to part payment of a debt.

3. A student wants to make holiday money so visits a property without warning, mows the lawn, and weeds and cleans the paths. He then asks the owner for payment, and the owner promises him £20. Can the student insist on payment?

4. The same student has a part-time summer job as a pizza delivery driver. He is paid £100 per week but as the summer is the busiest time of year for the cafe owner, the student asks for an extra £25 per week, to which the owner agrees. At the end of the season, is the student entitled to the extra payment?

You should now be able to:

- understand the principle of consideration
- explain the rules in relation to consideration
- apply the law to given scenarios.

4 Privity of contract

The rule of privity in contract is that only those who are parties to the contract are bound by it and can benefit from it.

The justification for this rule, seen in **Dunlop Pneumatic Tyre Co. Ltd v Selfridge (1915)**, is that it would be unfair for two parties to make a contract that would bind a third person to do something, and conversely it would be unfair for that third person to be able to sue either or both of the two parties contracting under that contract.

In the *Dunlop* case, Dunlop manufactured tyres and sold some to Dew, who agreed not to resell them below a certain price. Dew resold to Selfridge on the basis of the same term not to resell below a certain price, but Selfridge then resold below this price and Dew refused to sue. Dunlop sued Selfridge but as Dunlop was not a party to the contract between Dew and Selfridge, the claim failed.

Relationship between privity and consideration

The rule of privity can be seen as based on a rule of consideration in that 'consideration must move from the promisee'.

In **Tweddle v Atkinson (1861)** two fathers agreed with each other to pay an agreed amount each to their son and daughter respectively when the couple married. The written contract stated it was made for the couple's benefit. The couple married, and the bride's father paid his agreed share, but the son's father had died by this time. The trustees of this father's estate refused to make the payment, so the son sued his late father's estate. The son lost his claim as he had provided no consideration under the contract and was not a party to the contract made between the two fathers.

This rule is seen as causing injustice and the courts have on occasions tried to ignore the rule.

In **Jackson v Horizon Holidays Ltd (1975)** Mr Jackson booked a holiday for himself and his family, which turned out to be very disappointing. Mr Jackson sued Horizon Holidays for damages for himself and his family. The Court of Appeal held that it would be unfair to limit the award of damages to Mr Jackson and so the claims of his family were allowed even though, strictly, they were not parties to the holiday contract, which was in Mr Jackson's sole name.

General exceptions – agency, collateral contracts, restrictive covenants

The courts and Parliament created certain, limited, exceptions when the rule of privity would not apply.

Agency

An agency situation arises when one person, the agent, is authorised to make a contract on behalf of another person, the principal.

In a valid agency situation, the principal will be bound by the terms of the contract even though he did not make the contract himself. The principal and the agent are treated by the courts as being one person, and that person is a party to the contract.

Collateral contracts

The court may be able to avoid the strict rule of privity by finding a second contract alongside the main agreement.

In **Shanklin Pier Ltd v Detel Products Ltd (1951)** Shanklin Pier contracted with a painter for their pier to be painted and insisted on a particular type of paint provided it would last for 7–10 years. The manufacturer of the paint (Detel) gave that assurance to the painter. The paint lasted only three months and Shanklin Pier sued Detel. On the face

In this topic, you will learn how to:
- define privity of contract
- distinguish between privity of contract and consideration
- explain the exceptions to the doctrine of privity of contract
- describe the function of the Contracts (Rights of Third Parties) Act 1999
- apply the rules to a given situation.

Key cases

Dunlop Pneumatic Tyre Co Ltd v Selfridge (1915): only a person who is a valid party to a contract can sue or be sued under that contract.

Tweddle v Atkinson (1861): a person cannot sue or be sued successfully under a contract unless that person has provided consideration under the contract.

Jackson v Horizon Holidays Ltd (1975): in limited circumstances the court will allow a claimant to be awarded losses incurred by a third party.

Shanklin Pier v Detel Products (1951): the strict privity rule can be avoided by finding a collateral contract in a case such as this.

of it, Shanklin Pier should lose the case under the privity rule as they had no contract with Detel. However, the court decided that a second (collateral) contract between Shanklin Pier and Detel existed alongside the original contract between Shanklin Pier and the painter.

Restrictive covenants

A restrictive covenant exists under land law when a purchaser of land promises the seller in the contract of purchase (the 'initial contract') that he will not do something on the land and that covenant then 'runs with the land'.

This means that all subsequent purchasers of that land are legally bound by that promise, even though they are not parties to that initial contract.

In **Tulk v Moxhay (1848)** Tulk sold a garden in Leicester Square, London, to Elms. The initial contract contained a restrictive covenant that Elms would not build on this land. Elms sold to Moxhay, who intended to build on the land. Tulk could enforce the covenant against Moxhay even though there was no direct contract between them: the covenant had run with the land and Moxhay was bound by it.

Contracts (Rights of Third Parties) Act 1999

Under this Act, someone who is *not* a party to a contract (a 'third party') may enforce the contract against either or both of the actual parties to the contract if:

1 the third party is expressly identified by name, or as a member of a class or as answering a particular description, *and*
2 the contract *expressly* provides the third party may enforce the contract, *or*
3 the contract term *purports* (intends) to confer the benefit of the term on the third party.

Point 1 means, for example, an unborn baby may use the Act if properly described.

Points 2 and 3 mean the third party may enforce the contract if the contract either states that to be the case or that is how the contract may be interpreted. In this respect, the case of **Nisshin Shipping Co. Ltd v Cleaves & Co. Ltd (2003)** confirmed the court will use the objective test of what reasonable contracting parties would have thought the relevant term(s) of the contract meant.

However, if 'on a proper construction of the contract' it appears the parties did not intend the term to benefit a third party, then the Act will not apply. The parties to the contract therefore have the right to exclude the Act from benefiting a third party. Most commercial contracts now include such a term so the impact of the Act is not as great as was anticipated.

It should be noted that if the contract contains an exclusion and/or limitation clause, then the third party may use the rules concerning the unenforceability of such clauses (discussed in Chapter 6: Contract terms, Topic 5).

> ### Key cases
>
> **Tulk v Moxhay (1848):** restrictive covenants (part of land law) are an exception to the privity of contract rule.
>
> **Nisshin Shipping Co. Ltd v Cleaves & Co. Ltd (2003):** the test for what reasonable contracting parties would have thought the terms of the contract meant is an objective test.

> ### Activities
>
> **1** Define what privity of contract means.
>
> **2** Create an example of how the 1999 Act may affect the rights of a third party.

You should now be able to:

- understand the nature of privity of contract
- explain the rules in relation to privity of contract and the exceptions
- apply the law to given scenarios.

5 Intention to create legal relations

In addition to the tests for the existence of a valid contract – namely offer, acceptance and consideration – the courts will also inquire whether the parties did really intend to create a legally binding contract.

When parties agree something with each other, they do not always believe or intend that if either breaks the agreement the other will be able to sue. It would not be possible for the courts to decide every single dispute based on all these situations.

Intention to create legal relations ('legal intent') must exist between the parties for the agreement to become legally enforceable.

If the agreement is made in a *social* or *domestic* situation then the law presumes there is *no* legal intent. The court will consider the subject matter of the agreement as much as the status of the parties involved. For example, if a father (a farmer) agrees to sell his combine harvester to his farmer son for £10,000 then the court presumes there is no legal intent but there is likely to be a valid contract once the court takes the context of the contract into account.

If the agreement is in a *commercial* or *business* situation then the law presumes there *is* legal intent unless there is evidence to the contrary.

It must be noted that these are only presumptions (i.e. starting points) for the court, and other evidence may allow the court to alter its view.

Social and domestic arrangements

Social arrangements

Agreements between friends, work colleagues or neighbours are unlikely to have legal intent, although there may be exceptions.

In **Simpkins v Pays (1955)** a lodger, her landlady and the landlady's granddaughter regularly entered 'fashion' competitions on the basis that any prize money would be shared equally. All three contributed to the entry fee and one form was sent off, containing all three entries in the sole name of the landlady. The landlady received the prize money of £750 but did not share the winnings as agreed. Although the agreement was made in a social setting, the court decided the involvement of money (both the equal contribution to the entry fee and the possibility of winning a substantial sum) had created legal intent between the parties, so the winnings had to be shared.

In **Parker v Clarke (1960)** a young couple, Mr and Mrs Parker, agreed to sell their home and move in with, and care for, an older couple (Mr and Mrs Clarke). In return, Mr and Mrs Clarke agreed to leave them their home in their wills. Mr and Mrs Parker sold their home, gave some money to their daughter to buy a flat, and moved in with Mr and Mrs Clarke. Mr Clarke altered his will to leave the property to Mr and Mrs Parker. An argument followed, and Mr and Mrs Clarke evicted the younger couple. There was legal intent between the parties, as Mr and Mrs Parker had given up their financial security by selling their home. Further, by altering his will, Mr Parker had shown that he expected to be legally bound by the agreement.

The importance of being able to prove the existence of legal intent in a social setting is shown in **Wilson v Burnett (2007)** when three work colleagues decided to split any prize money from a bingo session they would attend that night. One colleague won over £100,000 and a dispute arose over the enforceability of the agreement reached. The Court of Appeal held there was no legal intent on the basis that:

In this topic, you will learn how to:

■ define intention to create legal relations

■ distinguish between domestic and commercial agreements

■ apply the rules to a given situation.

 Key cases

Simpkins v Pays (1955): if money (usually more than a small amount) is exchanged or financial security is put at risk then there may be legal intent in an agreement made in a social setting.

Parker v Clarke (1960): evidence of legal intention can come from surrounding circumstances such as selling a home and changing a will.

Wilson v Burnett (2007): an agreement made at work on a casual basis is unlikely to have legal intent.

There were basic problems with an agreement such as this, both of definition and on the question of whether a necessarily casual conversation could be elevated into an agreement binding and enforceable in law.

Domestic arrangements

Agreements between family members are not usually legally binding, as demonstrated in **Balfour v Balfour (1919)**.

Mr Balfour went abroad to work and agreed to pay his wife £30 a month, but did not pay as agreed. There was no enforceable contract as this was a domestic agreement.

This case should be contrasted with **Merritt v Merritt (1971)** where Mr Merritt deserted his wife and agreed to pay her a regular monthly amount from which she would pay the mortgage on their former home. Mr Merritt defaulted in his payments. There was legal intent as the parties were separated when the agreement was made and it was not therefore a domestic arrangement.

In **Jones v Padavatton (1969)** a mother bought a house for her daughter to live in while the daughter studied to be a barrister. They had an argument and the mother tried to evict the daughter from the property. The daughter claimed she had an enforceable contract with her mother. There was no legal intent as this was a domestic arrangement.

The *Jones* case was a split decision in the court. There was evidence both in support of and against the existence of legal intent. The case highlighted how important the presumptions are when deciding such cases, and if the initial presumption had been the other way the court's final decision may have been different.

Commercial agreements

In the **Esso Petroleum Co. Ltd v Customs and Excise (1976)** case the company gave out world cup coins with little value with every four gallons of petrol. Customs and Excise wanted to charge tax on the coins, so the court had to decide if there was legal intent in respect of the agreement to supply the coins. Normally, promotional advertising by a company is not seen as having legal intent, but the House of Lords decided by a majority that there was legal intent. Esso did not profit directly from the supply of the coins but did profit from the increased sales of petrol as a result of the promotion.

In **Jones v Vernon's Pools (1938)** the pools company inserted a term in its competition form stating '… this agreement will not create a legal relationship and is binding in honour only'. Jones said his winning form had been lost and claimed his winnings, but there was no enforceable agreement as the 'honour clause' removed all legal intent from the agreement.

Key cases

Balfour v Balfour (1919): the court presumes no intent to create legal relations in a domestic arrangement between family members, but this presumption is rebuttable by evidence in the case that the parties intended otherwise.

Merritt v Merritt (1971): a more formal written agreement between husband and wife as to some financial arrangements following a marital split can be legally binding.

Jones v Padavatton (1969): allowing a child who is a student to live in a house bought specially by a parent is merely a domestic arrangement.

Esso Petroleum Co. Ltd v Customs and Excise (1976): an agreement made in a business setting is presumed to be legally binding unless there is evidence that shows a different intent.

Jones v Vernon's Pools (1938): it is possible to exclude legal liability by the use of an express term in the agreement to that effect.

Activities

1 What are the two presumptions used by the court to assist in deciding if there is an intent to create legal relations?

2 Give an example of a domestic agreement to which you have agreed – is it legally binding? If not, how could you try to ensure that such an agreement was legally binding?

3 Explain the reason for the different decisions in the *Esso* and *Jones* cases.

You should now be able to:

■ understand the principle of intention to create legal relations

■ apply the law to given situations.

6 Formation of contract – overview

How to approach a problem involving formation of contract

The exam question may, or may not state specifically that the question in respect of the scenario relates to the 'formation of a contract'. It is unlikely that one question will cover all five topics.

If the question involves, for example, an advert and/or negotiations and/or a delayed or failed acceptance then the question covers offers, invitations to treat and acceptance. If the scenario involves friends, relatives, work colleagues, neighbours, etc., then the question involves intention to create legal relations. If one of the parties makes a bad bargain and/or promises to pay for something after the event and/or asks for more money having already agreed to carry out the task for a lower amount then the question covers consideration. Finally, the scenario may involve a father making a contract with a builder for repair work to the house belonging to the father's son – this involves privity and whether the son may enforce the contract against the builder.

You must always identify the area(s) of law under review and then apply the relevant law to the question. This allows you to concentrate on explaining one area of law and then its application without the confusion of other rules of law, principles and cases. This also allows the examiner to evaluate the answer in a logical manner.

For example, an AQA exam question from January 2006 was:

> Paul was a talented artist with little business knowledge. He asked his brother, Richard, to assist him to promote his work for one year. Richard agreed to do so in return for a commission of 15 per cent on all sales of Paul's work during that year. After eight very successful months, Richard told Paul that he wanted 20 per cent commission for the remaining four months. Though he agreed, Paul never paid any extra commission and, at the end of the year, refused to do so.
>
> Having regard to the relevant elements in the formation of contract, consider whether Richard has any rights and remedies against Paul in connection with the unpaid extra commission.

Your first need to identify the topics involved. The reference to an agreement between brothers should immediately indicate that *intent to create legal relations* is relevant. Richard has asked for more money (the *extra* commission) and this should indicate that *consideration* is relevant and in particular *existing duty*.

Your answer should first deal with the intent to create legal relations. Explain the different presumptions that exist in commercial and family agreements (with reference to cases as examples), decide which type of agreement exists, and then outline the consequences to the parties if there is, or is not, an intent to create legal relations.

Your answer should then define consideration and the rule about performing an existing duty and whether that is good consideration or not. There are various cases to which reference should be made and you should discuss whether Richard is supplying something extra by way of a benefit, that justifies the application of the *Williams* v *Roffey* principle.

Read the question carefully and take time to consider what are the relevant topics contained within the question. It is very important to explain and apply relevant elements of contract formation. No credit will be given for a discussion of offer, acceptance or privity. The answer should also cover remedies, and this is dealt with in Chapter 9: Remedies.

In this topic, you will learn how to:

- apply the law to problem scenarios involving formation of contract

- construct an essay evaluating the law on formation of contract.

How to write an essay evaluating the law on formation of contract

The part (c) examination question is different to the (a) and (b) questions, which are based on the scenario described in the question. The typical (c) question will ask you to 'critically analyse the law of formation of a contract and include any appropriate suggestions for reform'. There are 25 marks each for questions (a) and (b) and also 25 marks for question (c) so this third question must be given the same consideration as the other two.

You should include an accurate explanation of areas of the law of contract formation, and discuss the fairness, relevance and clarity of those areas. Inevitably, all areas of law are not perfect and a description of that law and a logical criticism of that law should be included. Make sensible suggestions as to how the law could be improved or whether, in all the circumstances, reform is not appropriate or possible.

You should also explain areas of relevant law that work well, are clear and/or fair, as 'critically analyse' does not mean that all the analysis should result in suggestions for reform of bad law.

■ Activities

1. Prepare a list of the main headings for offer, acceptance, consideration, privity and intent to create legal relations.

2. Use this list to create your own examination question, covering at least two of these topics.

3. Create a further question using the remaining three topics.

You should now be able to:

■ answer problem questions involving formation of contract

■ construct an appropriate essay on these topics.

6   Contract terms

In this topic, you will learn how to:

- identify the relevant obligations in a contract

- distinguish between express and implied terms

- distinguish between conditions, warranties and innominate terms

- distinguish between exclusion and limitation clauses

- distinguish between terms and representations

- explain the relationship between common law and statute using examples of terms of a contract.

Key cases

The Moorcock (1889): if the business of the contract could not be carried on without the term and if, when the contract was made, an independent third party (the 'officious bystander') had asked the parties if a particular term should be in the contract and both parties would have replied 'Oh, of course', then that term will be implied into the contract by the court.

1   Terms of a contract

The terms of a contract are what the parties have agreed between themselves. They define the extent and limit of the parties' respective obligations.

Mike is a car dealer and has advertised a moped for sale in his local newspaper for £1,750 (an invitation to treat). James visits Mike to view the moped, considers its condition and makes an offer of £1,250 that Mike rejects. James asks for confirmation that the moped is a 2006 model, that it only has one previous owner (Mike) and that it will be supplied with a full tank of petrol. During the negotiations, Mike confirms the above three points and states the price of the moped is now at a reduced price of £1,500. James makes an offer to buy the moped for £1,500, which Mike accepts. James pays in cash and drives the moped away.

There are terms of this contract that James will pay £1,500 for the moped and in return Mike will transfer ownership and possession of the moped to James.

Basic terminology

Express and implied terms

The terms of a contract are usually what the parties have expressly agreed between themselves and are stated in the contract (whether verbally or written). In the scenario, one express term is that the price for the moped is £1,500. However, sometimes the law will imply a term or terms *into* a contract or *cancel* a term or terms in a contract whether or not the parties agree.

A term can be implied *into* a contract in four different ways:

1   The 'business efficacy' and the 'officious bystander' tests

The court will imply a term into a contract if the term is *necessary* to make sure the contract works on a businesslike basis. Two tests were set out in **The Moorcock (1889)** as being required before a term is implied in this way.

In *The Moorcock* (1889) the defendant owned a harbour and hired out moorings for boats to unload their cargo. A boat owner hired a mooring and paid the fee. It was accepted that both parties realised the boat would rest on the seabed when the tide was out. The boat landed on sharp rocks under the mooring, and sank. There was no express term in the contract about the safety of the mooring so the boat owner could not sue for breach of contract. The court implied a term into the contract to cover the mooring's safety, so the boat owner succeeded in the claim for breach of contract. The court decided a term about the safety of the mooring was necessary for the contract to be effective and both parties, if asked, would have agreed such a term was required.

2   Terms implied by custom

A term may be implied into a contract if such a term would exist as a matter of custom. For example, it was the agreed farming practice that a tenant farmer, on being given notice to quit by the landlord, would be allowed compensation for the seeds and labour he had put into the land and from which the landlord would benefit (*Hutton* v *Warren* (1836)). That term would be implied in such a contract.

3 Terms implied by the Sale of Goods Act 1979

See Topics 2, 3 and 4.

4 Terms implied by the Supply of Goods and Services Act 1982

See Topics 2, 3 and 4.

A term may be *excluded* in one of three ways:

a If the term is not incorporated in the contract
See Topic 5.

b Terms prohibited by the Unfair Contracts Terms Act 1977
See Topic 6.

c Terms prohibited by the Unfair Terms in Consumer Contracts Regulations 1999
See Topic 6.

Conditions, warranties and innominate terms

Once it is decided there is a particular term in a contract (whether it is expressly agreed or implied) it is necessary to evaluate which of the three types of term it is.

Condition

A **condition** is a term that is fundamental to the contract, i.e. a breach of condition deprives a party of a main benefit. When a condition is breached, such as in **Poussard v Spiers (1876)** the victim may repudiate the contract (end the contract) if desired and/or sue for damages (compensation).

Warranty

A **warranty** is a minor term of the contract. When a warranty is broken the victim may sue *only* for compensation and the contract will continue, shown in the case of **Bettini v Gye (1876)**.

Innominate (indeterminate) terms

Sometimes it is difficult to tell if a term is a condition or a warranty and these are known as **innominate terms.** Here, the court will look at the consequences of the breach of the term and then decide. For example, if the breach has a serious result then it is likely to be classed a condition so the victim may repudiate the contract and/or sue for damages.

In **Hong Kong Fir v Kawasaki Kaisha Kasan (1962)** a company hired a cargo boat for two years and a term was that the boat was 'fitted for ordinary cargo service'. During the two years' hire the boat was out of action for repairs for 18 weeks (17 per cent of the hire period). The court could not tell from the wording of the contract if the term was a condition or warranty. By looking at the result of the breach the court concluded the time lost was not too serious so the term was a warranty and only compensation could be claimed.

Exclusion and limitation clauses

An *exclusion* clause is a term of the contract that tries to exclude the liability of one of the parties if that party breaches another contractual term.

A *limitation* clause is a term of the contract that tries to limit the extent of that liability rather than exclude liability entirely.

Courts believe that parties to a contract should be allowed to agree to whatever terms of a contract they wish – even if such a term excludes or limits one party's rights against another. However, the courts are also aware that when contracts are negotiated one party may be at a disadvantage to the other – for example, a consumer dealing with a large commercial company. The result of such terms may prove harsh on the

---

■ Key terms

Condition: term that is fundamental to the contract, i.e. without that term the contract would have been pointless.

Warranty: minor term of the contract, i.e. the contract would have been made without the term.

Innominate terms: term in a contract that can be treated as either a condition or a warranty depending on the nature of the breach of the term.

■ Key cases

Poussard v Spiers (1876): Poussard's inability to sing the lead role in an opera for the first six days of performance was a breach of condition; the opera promoter was able to end the contract and replace the singer.

Bettini v Gye (1876): a singer contracted to attend rehearsals and the actual performances of a show, missed some of the rehearsals but attended all the performances; this was a breach of warranty so the theatre could only claim compensation and the singer could continue the contract.

Hong Kong Fir v Kawasaki Kaisha Kasan (1962): this case is an example of the courts considering an innominate term.

victim so over the years courts have developed rules limiting the creation of these types of terms.

Further, Parliament has created Acts and Regulations to restrict the validity and/or extent of such terms in certain circumstances.

Distinction between terms and representations

Representations

Before a contract is agreed, the parties will usually have negotiated the terms of the contract. One party may have made a statement (a 'representation') on which the other party is relying, but the representation is never included in the final contract (whether oral or in writing). The victim will wish to claim the representation is a term of the contract, while the party in breach will claim it is just a statement with no legal effect.

In the scenario, Mike stated during negotiation that the moped had only one previous owner (himself), which James later finds to be untrue. That statement was never included in the final contract (for whatever reason) so James is unable to sue for breach of a term of the contract. He may be able to sue under Misrepresentation (see Chapter 7: Vitiating factors) but this is more complicated and less easy to prove than a breach of contract. The court has developed guidelines to help it decide whether a statement made in negotiations has actually become a term of the contract or remains a mere representation.

Is the statement a representation or a term?

The guidelines are as follows:

1 The importance attached to the representation

In **Couchman v Hill (1947)** an auction catalogue stated that a heifer (a young female cow) was unserved (was not mated). Before bidding started a farmer asked the seller and auctioneer for confirmation of this, as it was important to him. They both confirmed, so the farmer bought the heifer. However, it was pregnant and died while calving. The statement made to the farmer was so important it became a term of the contract, so the farmer could claim for breach of contract.

2 Special knowledge or skill of the party making the representation (the Representor)

In **Oscar Chess Ltd v Williams (1957)** a private seller sold his car to a dealer, stating it was a 1948 model (which he believed) but it was actually a 1939 model. The contract did not refer to the age of the car and as the seller had no expertise in selling cars, and the dealer relied on their own skill, the statement was not a term of the contract.

The above should be contrasted with **Dick Bentley Ltd v Harold Smith Motors (1965)** when a car dealer stated a car had done 20,000 miles when it had actually done 100,000 miles. The contract made no mention of mileage. The statement had become a term of the contract as the dealer had special knowledge/skill, so the buyer could sue for breach.

3 The time between making the representation and the contract

In **Routledge v McKay (1954)** a seller of a motorbike said it was a 1942 model when it was actually a 1930 model. The written contract was made seven days after this representation and did not refer to the year of the bike, so the representation did not become a term of the contract.

4 Is the agreement is in writing?

As in *Routledge*, if the parties have taken the time and trouble to put the contract into a written form then the court presumes everything the parties wanted is in the written contract.

Key cases

Couchman v Hill (1947): the more important the statement, the more likely it will become a term of the contract rather than just a representation.

Oscar Chess Ltd v Williams (1957): the court is more likely to decide representation has become term of contract if representor has special knowledge or skill.

Dick Bentley v Harold Smith Motors (1965): a dealer had special knowledge that made the representation a term of the contract.

Routledge v McKay (1954): sometimes, the time gap between the representation and the making of the contract is so long that the court considers it would be unfair to make the representation part of the contract.

The relationship between common law and statutory aspects of the law

In relation to the terms of a contract, you should understand and apply the common law rules and the statutory rules and how both aspects relate.

For example, in relation to express and implied terms, it should be noted that: there are two ways in which the common law may imply a term into a contract (points 1 and 2 on p99); there are two ways that statute implies a term into a contract (points 3 and 4 on p100); there is one way common law may prohibit a contract term (point a on p100); and there are two ways statute may prohibit a contract term (points b and c on p100).

- The common law is *not limited* to the type of term to be implied. As can be seen from the *Moorcock* and *Hutton* v *Warren* cases, terms were implied into the respective contracts to cover the 'safety' of the mooring and the 'loss of profit' when leaving tenanted land.
- Statute is *limited* as to the type of term to be implied. Topics 2, 3 and 4 cover the relevant statutes in detail but, in summary, the statutes imply terms as the quality of goods when sold or transferred and/or the standard of services supplied and the time for completion of the contract.
- The common law may exclude *any type* of term from a contract if the requirement of point **a** on p100 (incorporation) is not followed.
- Statute is *limited* to prohibiting exclusion and/or limitation terms (absolutely or allowing the term if reasonable) or, in consumer contracts only, prohibiting *any type* of term if 'unfair'.

Activities

1. Mike and James did not expressly agree that the registration documents for the moped would be handed over on payment of the £1,500. Would this term be implied into the contract? If so, how?

2. Mike stated the moped had only one previous owner (himself) but this was never made a term of the contract. If James discovers there is more than one previous owner, would this statement be a representation or become a term of the contract?

3. The parties agreed that the moped would be supplied with two new tyres. James discovers the tyres are second-hand and worn. This is a breach of contract by Mike – but is it a breach of condition, warranty or an innominate term?

You should now be able to:

- understand the principles behind contract terms.

In this topic, you will learn how to:

- state the limits of the syllabus for implied terms

- distinguish between Sale of Goods and Supply of Goods and Services.

2 Implied terms 1

Your study will be limited to ss13, 14(2) and 14(3) of the Sale of Goods Act 1979 ('the 1979 Act') and to the study of ss3, 4, 13 and 14 of the Supply of Goods and Services Act 1982 ('the 1982 Act').

Scope of Sale of Goods Act 1979

One of the most important principles of contract law is that parties are allowed to make whatever contract they like (unless, for example, the contract is for an illegal purpose). This principle is called 'freedom of contract'.

This principle means that a party may, if they wish, make a bad bargain and the court will not intervene. This may sometimes be unfair, especially if one party is financially weaker than the other. Parliament decided that statute should protect this weaker party, and passed the 1979 Act. This Act implies certain terms into contracts for the *sale of goods* that will protect the consumer should the goods, for example, prove defective.

Scope of Supply of Goods and Services Act 1982

Parliament also wanted to protect parties in contracts for the *supply of work and materials* linked to the work, and so passed the 1982 Act. Where such a contract involves the transfer of goods to a party, similar terms to the 1979 Act are implied as to description, quality and fitness for purpose of the goods. In relation to the work provided (services), there are terms implied that the services will be carried out with reasonable care and skill and, unless the contract specifies a certain period, the work will be completed within a reasonable time.

Activities

1. James drives the moped away and the engine immediately seizes due to an internal defect. Even though the contract did not specifically refer to the quality of the moped, a term is implied that the moped will be of 'satisfactory quality'. James may now sue Mike under that implied term. What else could prove wrong with the moped that would mean it was not of satisfactory quality?

2. James may return the moped to Mike for its annual service. If the contract makes no reference to the quality of Mike's work and no time limit is specified for the work, does James have any remedy if the service is inadequate and Mike takes three weeks to complete the job? If James has a claim, under which Act would it be made?

You should now be able to:

- understand the distinction between Sale of Goods and Supply of Goods and Services.

3 Implied terms 2

Section 2(1) of the 1979 Act defines a contract for the sale of goods as 'a contract by which a seller transfers or agrees to transfer the property in goods to the buyer for a money consideration, called the price'.

The relevant terms implied in the sale of goods contract are set out in ss13–14 of the 1979 Act.

Sale of Goods Act 1979 s13 – meaning and application

Section 13 of the 1979 Act states when goods are sold by description or by sample, there is an implied condition that they will correspond with the description or sample.

If the buyer examines and selects the goods then s13 will still apply.

This implied term about description is a condition, so a breach of that term allows the buyer to repudiate (terminate the contract) and/or claim damages (compensation).

This term is implied into *all* contracts for the sale of goods, whether the sale is private or commercial.

In this topic, you will learn how to:

- explain the meaning of ss13, 14(2) and 14(3) Sale of Goods Act 1979

- distinguish between ss13, 14(2) and 14(3) Sale of Goods Act 1979

- apply ss13, 14(2) and 14(3) Sale of Goods Act 1979 to given situations

- describe and apply the remedies available where ss13, 14(2) and 14(3) Sale of Goods Act 1979 have been breached.

■ Key cases

Beale v Taylor (1967): description is given a wide meaning and applies to colour, size, age, weight, etc.

Re Moore & Co. v Landauer & Co. (1921): s13 is applied strictly with apparently harsh results.

Bartlett v Sidney Marcus (1965): s14(2) applies to both new and second-hand goods.

Crowther v Shannon Motor Co. (1975): the court took the view that satisfactory quality related to normal expectations relating to the goods sold.

■ Key terms

Satisfactory quality: goods that meet the standard that a reasonable person would regard as satisfactory, taking account of any description of the goods, the price (if relevant) and all other relevant circumstances.

In **Beale v Taylor (1967)** the seller advertised a car as 'Herald, convertible, white 1961' but the car was actually two cars welded together and only the back half was a 1961 model. The advertisement was a description, and as the car did not conform to this description there was a breach of s13. This was a breach of a condition so the buyer could repudiate (reject the car) and/or claim damages (compensation).

Section 13 may sometimes result in what appears to be a harsh decision. In **Re Moore & Co. v Landauer & Co. (1921)** tinned fruit was described as being in cases of 30 tins per case. Some cases contained 24 tins but the buyer received the correct number of tins in total. The seller was in breach of s13 and so the buyer could reject the goods and/or claim damages.

Because of this unfairness, the Sale and Supply of Goods Act 1994 (the 1994 Act) created a new s15(A) of the 1979 Act so that a breach of the implied term will be treated as breach of warranty if:

■ the buyer is a business (i.e. not a consumer); *and*
■ the breach is so slight that it would be unreasonable to allow the buyer to reject the goods.

A breach of warranty will allow the buyer to claim damages only and the contract will continue so the goods may not be rejected.

Sale of Goods Act 1979 s14 (2) – meaning and application

Section 14(2) of the 1979 Act states when goods are sold by a seller *in the course of a business* there is an implied condition that they will be of '**satisfactory quality**'.

The 1994 Act replaced the word 'merchantable' in the 1979 Act with the word 'satisfactory' but the pre-1994 cases are still helpful guidelines on the application of s14(2). It should be noted that s14(2) does *not* apply to a private sale.

The quality of goods includes their state and condition, and the following (among others) are aspects of the quality of goods:

■ fitness for all the purposes for which the goods of the kind in question are commonly supplied
■ appearance and finish
■ freedom from minor defects
■ safety and durability

In **Bartlett v Sidney Marcus (1965)** a buyer purchased a second-hand Jaguar, being told that the clutch needed repair. The clutch needed more work than anticipated but the court held there was no breach of s14(2). The court held that the car was still usable and that defects were to be expected in such second-hand cars.

This decision can be contrasted with the case below when more could be expected of a second-hand car.

In **Crowther v Shannon Motor Co. (1975)** the car had covered over 82,000 miles at purchase, and after another 2,300 miles the engine broke. The court held such a car should reach 100,000 miles, so there was a breach of s14(2) as when sold the car was near the point of failure.

Under the Sale and Supply of Goods to Consumers Regulations 2002 (which came into force on 31 March 2003) relevant circumstances may now include:

> … any public statements on the specific characteristics of the goods made … by the seller, the producer or his representative, particularly in advertising or on labelling.

This means that statements made in national advertising and/or by manufacturers may affect a seller's liability under s14(2).

An example of the application of 'relevant circumstances' is *Bramhall v Edwards* (2004), when a motor-home was a few inches wider than allowed by regulations. The buyer claimed the goods were of an unsatisfactory nature and therefore in breach of s14(2). Evidence was given that the authorities ignored such minor matters, so the claim was unsuccessful. This decision shows that the court is willing to take all relevant matters into account when deciding whether a breach has occurred or not.

Sale of Goods Act 1979, s14(3) – meaning and application

Section 14(3) of the 1979 Act states that when goods are sold by a seller *in the course of a business* and the buyer expressly or impliedly makes known to the seller any particular purpose for which the goods are being bought, there is an implied condition that the goods are reasonably fit for that purpose.

Section 14(3) applies whether or not the purpose made known by the buyer is the purpose for which goods of that particular type are commonly supplied.

However, s14(3) will not apply if:

▓ the buyer does not rely on the skill or judgment of the seller, or

▓ it was unreasonable for the buyer to rely on the skill and judgment of the seller.

These exceptions may occur if, for example, the buyer specifically told the seller that he did not want the seller's advice on the suitability of the goods for the stated purpose, or examined the goods and that examination would have made it clear that the goods were unsuitable.

In **Griffiths v Peter Conway (1939)** a buyer of a Harris tweed coat had very sensitive skin but did not tell the seller this fact. The coat caused dermatitis. The buyer did not claim under s14(2) as the coat was of satisfactory quality (it could be worn) but claimed the coat was not fit for its purpose for the buyer. As the seller had no knowledge of the buyer's circumstances (the extra sensitive skin), the coat was fit for its purpose.

The rule to be drawn from this decision is that for s14(3) to apply, a buyer should ensure the purpose for the goods is clearly stated *and* the seller must be informed of any unusual circumstance surrounding the use of the goods by the buyer.

Section 14(2) would appear to have a wider application than s14(3) in this respect. The Court of Appeal has stated s14(2) is concerned with the basic quality of the goods supplied while s14(3) is limited to a case where the claimant has relied on the seller's skill and judgment.

In **Jewson Ltd v Boyhan (2003)** the seller supplied boilers for the buyer's flats. Unfortunately, the boilers affected the energy efficiency rating of the flats and their value fell. The buyer claimed under ss14(2) and 14(3) but both claims were unsuccessful. The boilers were satisfactory as boilers for flats and the buyer had not relied on the seller's judgment of the suitability of the boilers for these particular flats.

This recent decision confirms the comment made above about *Griffiths* v *Peter Conway* (1939).

Remedies available for breach of ss13, 14(2) and 14(3) of the Sale of Goods Act 1979

Under ss13, 14(2) and 14(3), the victim may repudiate the contract and/or sue for damages.

▓ **Key cases**

Griffiths v Peter Conway (1939): there is relationship between s14(2) and s14(3); goods may be of satisfactory quality and yet not fit for their purpose.

Jewson v Boyhan (2003): the court decided that the buyer had not relied on the seller's skill and judgement.

Repudiation

The claimant may choose to terminate the contract due to the breach of the implied condition. In effect, the claimant is entitled to the return of the price paid but must return the goods that do not fit their description, are not of satisfactory quality or are not fit for their purpose. This remedy may prove attractive to the claimant as he may then recommence his search for the appropriate goods with his financial position restored to its original position.

The right to reject the goods may be lost if, for example, the goods have been *accepted* by the claimant. Under s11(4) of the 1979 Act, where a buyer has accepted goods a breach of condition will *not* allow the buyer to repudiate the contract and reject the defective goods. This could cause unfairness as the buyer may purchase an item and not use it for some time. If, when used, the item is found to be in breach of ss13 and/or 14, the buyer's only remedy would be damages.

The 1994 Act amended the 1979 Act to redefine when the buyer is held to have 'accepted' goods. Sections 35(1) and 35(4) of the 1979 Act define acceptance as when:

- the buyer tells the seller the goods are accepted, or
- the buyer does something inconsistent with the seller's ownership of the goods, or
- the buyer keeps the goods without telling the seller they are rejected within a reasonable time.

A case showing the unfairness of the original section is *Bernstein* v *Pamson Motors Ltd* (1987) when Bernstein purchased a new car but only managed to drive it 142 miles before he fell ill and the car was not then used for three weeks. When next used, the car was found to have serious defects and Bernstein was stranded in an isolated part of the country. Bernstein claimed a breach of the implied conditions under the 1979 Act and attempted to claim repudiation and to reject the car. As Bernstein had retained the car for three weeks, this was long enough for Bernstein to have accepted the car and the right to reject was lost.

The decision in this case raised controversy. It was felt that the innocent claimant was left unable to claim a rejection of an expensive item that failed to meet any of the requirements of the implied conditions of the 1979 Act. Bernstein's only claim was for damages (see Damages below).

This point was reconsidered in **Clegg v Olle Anderson (2003)** when Clegg purchased a new yacht in August 2000 and was told immediately that the keel was substantially heavier than specified in the contract. Clegg negotiated with the seller and then rejected the yacht by letter in March 2001. The court confirmed that the *Bernstein* (1987) case was no longer good law and that Clegg was entitled to reject the yacht under the 1979 Act as amended by the 1994 Act.

As a general rule, therefore, a buyer with a claim under ss13, 14(2) or 14(3) should reject the goods as soon as possible so that repudiation has a practical and positive result for the buyer.

Damages

As an additional or sole remedy, the claimant may choose to claim damages (i.e. compensation for the losses incurred due to the breach of one or more of the implied conditions).

Damages are explained in detail in Topic 2 of Chapter 9: Remedies, but to summarise: the aim of contractual damages is to put the claimant in the position he would have been in had the contract been performed properly. In the scenario, if the moped is not delivered then James may elect to repudiate (reclaim the £1,500 paid to Mike) and then to claim the

Key cases

Clegg v Olle Anderson (2003): explained that the Bernstein case is no longer good law and the rule as to reasonable time for rejection is looked at by the courts more sympathetically.

Activities

1. Section 15(A) of the 1979 Act: What effect does this section have on a business if the goods supplied do not fit their description? How has the law been changed? Does this new law apply to a buyer who is a consumer?

2. Section 14(2D) of the 1979 Act: How has this section assisted a buyer in succeeding in a claim under s14(2?)

3. Sections 35(1) and 35(4) of the 1979 Act: How have these two sub-sections benefited a buyer who wants to repudiate the contract and reject the goods?

expense incurred in purchasing an equivalent moped. For example, James may now have to pay an extra £250 for an equivalent moped.

In the *Bernstein* (1987) case, the claimant recovered the cost of making his way home, the loss of a full tank of petrol, £150 for a 'totally spoilt day comprising nothing but vexation' and compensation until he (Bernstein) purchased a replacement car.

Sales of Goods Act 1979 and Supply of Goods and Services Act 1982

Sale of Goods Act 1979	Supply of Goods and Services Act 1982
Section 13: In all contracts for the sale of goods, there is an implied condition that the goods will fit their description or sample. S13 applies even if the buyer examines and selects the goods.	Section 3: In all contracts when one party agrees with another for the supply of a service, which includes the transfer of ownership of goods, there is an implied condition that the goods will fit their description.
Section 14(2): If the goods are sold in the course of a business, there is an implied condition that the goods will be of satisfactory quality. The court will consider various factors, e.g. safety, durability, appearance and finish.	Section 4: When one party agrees with another in the course of a business for the supply of a service, which includes the transfer of ownership of goods, there is an implied condition that the goods are of satisfactory quality and fit for their purpose.
Section 14(3): If the goods are sold in the course of a business and the buyer expressly or impliedly makes known to the seller a particular purpose for which the goods are bought, there is an implied condition that the goods will be reasonably fit for that purpose.	
	Section 13: When one party agrees with another in the course of a business for the supply of a service, there is an implied term that the service will be performed with reasonable care and skill.
	Section 14: When one party agrees with another in the course of a business for the supply of a service, there is an implied term that the services will be performed within a reasonable time.

Remedies:

Condition: Breach of condition allows the buyer/customer to repudiate [end the contract] and/or claim damages

Warranty: Breach of warranty allows the buyer/customer to claim damages only

Innominate: If the court cannot decide if the term is a condition or a warranty then it considers the consequences of the breach to classify the term as one or the other

Activities

1. In relation to the scenario in the activity on p103, what if the moped is described as having a complete service history but Mike is unable to provide any documentation? Which, if any, of the 1979 Act's sections may assist James?

2. James has purchased the moped, uses it for ploughing his allotment, and the moped's engine seizes. Which, if any, of the 1979 Act's sections may assist James?

3. The problems listed in the activities above have occurred but Mike was not a dealer and the moped sale was a private sale. What difference, if any, would this situation make to your answers?

You should now be able to:

- understand the operation of ss13, 14(2) and 14(3) of the Sale of Goods Act 1979.

In this topic, you will learn how to:

■ explain the meaning of ss3, 4, 13 and 14 of the Supply of Goods and Services Act 1982

■ distinguish between ss3, 4, 13 and 14 of the Supply of Goods and Services Act 1982

■ apply ss3, 4, 13 and 14 of the Supply of Goods and Services Act 1982 to given situations

■ describe and apply the remedies available where ss3, 4, 13 and 14 of the Supply of Goods and Services Act 1982 have been breached.

4 Implied terms 3

This topic covers a discussion of terms implied into a contract when a service is being supplied and/or goods are transferred by one party to another.

Dan is the owner of a garage that sells cars and car parts and carries out repairs. Aimee agrees for Dan to fit four new tyres to her old car. This is a contract for the supply of a service (the fitting of the tyres) *and* the transfer of goods (the new tyres). Dan finds four *used* tyres and fits them, but takes five weeks to complete the task and then forgets to tighten the wheel nuts, with the result that Aimee crashes.

Aimee would have various claims under the 1982 Act, which are discussed below.

Supply of Goods and Services Act 1982 s3 – meaning and application

Section 3 of the 1982 Act states:

> … where, under a contract for the transfer of goods, the transferor transfers … the goods by description … there is an implied condition that the goods will correspond with the description.

This means that where one party contracts with another party for the supply of services that includes the transfer of ownership of goods, the 1982 Act implies a condition into the contract that the goods will fit their description.

The principles involved are very similar to those for s13 of the 1979 Act. It must be noted that s3 is effective for *all* contracts, not just those made between a consumer and a business.

An example of a s3 situation would be if Aidan (a bricklayer) agreed with his customer Craig that he would build a new garden wall with reclaimed red brick, and Craig accepted Aidan's quote for the job but Aidan built the wall using new red bricks. Craig would have a claim for breach of a condition of the contract, as the goods transferred to Craig (the bricks) do not correspond with their description.

Supply of Goods and Services Act 1982 s4 – meaning and application

Section 4 of the 1982 Act states:

> … where, under … a contract [for the transfer of goods], the transferor transfers the property in goods in the course of a business, there is an implied condition that the goods supplied under the contract are of satisfactory quality and/or are fit for their purpose.

The principles involved are very similar to those for s14(2) and (3) of the 1979 Act above. Note that s3 is effective *only* for contracts made in the course of a business.

An example of a s4 situation would be as above but, instead of being new, the bricks were crumbling, lopsided and damaged. Craig would have a claim under s4 as the goods were supplied in the course of a business, with a service, and they are not of satisfactory quality nor fit for their purpose.

Supply of Goods and Services Act 1982 s13 – meaning and application

Section 13 of the 1982 Act states:

> In the contract for the supply of a service where the supplier is acting in the course of a business, there is an implied term that the supplier will carry out the service with reasonable care and skill.

This term will only be implied where the service is supplied in *the course of a business*.

The implied term is equivalent to the standard of care expected in a claim in tort, i.e. has the supplier of the service achieved a *reasonable* level of care and skill in performing the work?

In Thake v Maurice (1986) a surgeon who performed a vasectomy that proved unsuccessful was not liable under s13, as he had used reasonable care and skill. The court accepted that some vasectomies naturally heal.

It is important to note that the patient in the *Thake case* could have made a contract with the surgeon that contained an *express* term confirming a successful vasectomy. Here, the patient would succeed and would not require s13. The victim only requires the implied term of s13 if there is no express term in the contract that covers the situation.

Supply of Goods and Services Act 1982, s14 – meaning and application

Section 14 of the 1982 Act states:

> In the contract for the supply of a service where the supplier is acting in the course of a business, there is an implied term that the supplier will carry out the service within a reasonable time.

Note again this term will only be implied where the service is supplied *in the course of a business*.

Section 14 assists a consumer when there is no specific term in the contract as to the time to be taken for the service to be completed, and the service has not been completed or has taken longer than expected to complete.

Remedies available for breach of ss3, 4, 13 and 14 of the Supply of Goods and Services Act 1982

It is important to note that ss3 and 4 of the 1982 Act refer to the implied terms *as conditions*. This means a breach of such a term allows the claimant to claim repudiation and/or damages. However, the same principles as stated above for the 1979 Act will apply, and the right to repudiate (and therefore to reject the goods) may be lost if the goods are accepted.

However, ss13 and 14 do not refer to conditions but to implied *terms*. This implied term will be treated as an innominate term, and the claimant of a breach of such a term will only be able to repudiate the contract if the consequences of the breach are serious.

As a result, under ss13 and 14 of the 1982 Act the claimant can *always* claim damages but may only claim repudiation successfully if the consequences of the breach are serious. For a discussion of innominate terms, see Topic 1: Terms of a contract and for repudiation and damages see Topic 3: Implied terms 2.

Key cases

Thake v Maurice (1986): if a person claims to have a particular expertise then the level of skill shown must be at the level supplied by the reasonable person in that profession, i.e. this question is an objective test based on the reasonable person.

Activities

1 In the scenario, there was no agreed contractual term as to when Dan would complete the fitting of the tyres so s14 applies. The court would decide whether five weeks to fit four tyres was a reasonable period or not. It seems an excessive period but what test would the court use to decide on Dan's potential liability?

2 Dan has supplied four used tyres rather than new tyres. Would Aimee's claim in this respect be under the 1979 or 1982 Act? Justify your decision.

You should now be able to:

- understand the operation of ss3, 4, 13 and 14 Supply of Goods and Services Act 1982.

In this topic, you will learn how to:

- explain the general principles behind exclusion and limitation clauses

- explain the concept of incorporation

- describe the main purpose rule

- explain the operation of overriding oral statements

- apply the rules in a given situation.

Key cases

L'Estrange v Graucob (1934): courts are not keen on interfering with the terms of a contract voluntarily made between parties.

5 Control of exclusion and limitation clauses: common law approaches

Exclusion and limitation clauses (terms) are briefly explained in Topic 1: Terms of a contract.

The general principle of control

A valid and enforceable exclusion or limitation clause will seriously affect a claimant's right to bring any successful claim against the party in breach of contract.

In **L'Estrange v Graucob (1934)** a café owner bought a cigarette vending machine and signed a contract that she did not read. One term stated that if the machine did not work then no claim could be made under the Sale of Goods Act 1893 (the equivalent to the current 1979 Act). The machine did not work and even though the implied term of the contract as to fitness for purpose of the goods had been breached, the exclusion clause meant the café owner's claim failed.

The courts wished to protect those who have agreed to a term, or terms, in a contract that are prejudicial to them. In consequence, for an exclusion or limitation clause to be valid it must comply with strict rules. These rules allow the courts to *control* the validity of such clauses.

Incorporation

To become part of the contract, the exclusion or limitation clause must be effectively 'incorporated' into the contract like any other term, i.e. it must become a valid and enforceable contractual term. The courts have considered various ways in which such 'terms' may succeed or fail in becoming part of the contract:

1 Signature

2 Notice

3 Previous course of dealing

1 Signature

If a party has signed a contract, then that party is bound by all the terms within that contract, whether or not the party has read the contract or not. That is the situation that applied in *L'estrange* v *Graucob* (1934) (see above).

2 Notice

This form of incorporation of the clause in the contract may occur in two situations:

a An exclusion/limitation clause is set out, or referred to, in a document that is handed to the party *when* the contract is made *and* that party either knew or should have known that the document contained such a clause.

In **Chapelton v Barry Urban District Council (1940)** Chapelton sat on one of the council's deckchairs, paid the fee when the attendant arrived and was given a 'receipt', on the reverse of which was an exclusion clause. The chair collapsed, Chapelton was injured and the council denied liability, claiming a valid exclusion clause. The clause was not part of the contract of hire as it was contained in a mere receipt, which Chapelton would not have expected to contain such a clause.

A different scenario occurred in **Olley v Marlborough Court Hotel (1949)** when Mr and Mrs Olley checked into a hotel, paid in advance and went back to their bedroom. Mrs Olley then saw a notice on the back of the bedroom door that excluded the hotel's liability for any personal property stolen from the hotel. Mrs Olley's fur coat was taken from her room due to the hotel's negligence. The hotel was liable as notice of the exclusion clause was not drawn to Mrs Olley's attention when the contract was made at the reception desk.

b The exclusion/limitation clause is displayed *where* the contract is made *and* reasonable notice of its existence is given to that party.

This manner of incorporation is difficult to identify if it is not clear when the contract is actually made. A good example is **Thornton v Shoe Lane Parking Ltd (1971)**. Thornton decided to use the Shoe Lane car park for the first time, where a notice outside the entrance stated 'All cars parked at owner's risk' ('notice 1'). Thornton then drove his car to the car park barrier, paid his fee and was given a ticket from the machine that contained, in small print, a notice: 'This ticket is issued subject to the conditions of issue displayed on the premises' ('notice 2'). Inside the building was another notice that stated Shoe Lane Parking was not liable for any property damage or personal injury ('notice 3'). When collecting his car, Thornton was injured due to the negligence of Shoe Lane Parking. Thornton's contract with Shoe Lane Parking incorporated 'notice 1', as Thornton had notice of it before making the contract, but 'notice 2' was not sufficient as it was too vague, and 'notice 3' was not incorporated as Shoe Lane Parking had not taken sufficient steps to draw Thornton's attention to it.

Thornton (1971) is an example of a case where the exemption clause is not displayed when or where the contract is made ('notice 3' was displayed inside the car park, when the contract had already been made) and no reasonable notice has been given (the small print on the barrier ticket – 'notice 2' – was not sufficient for this purpose).

3 Previous course of dealing

In **Spurling v Bradshaw (1956)** the parties had previously contracted when the victim had received notice of the other party's exclusion clause but had never bothered to read it. In the final contract, the claimant did not receive notice of the clause until after the contract was made. The other party lost the goods that were the subject matter of the clause, and relied on the exclusion clause. The parties had a previous course of dealing so the claimant was aware of the other party's standard exclusion clause and was therefore bound by it.

> ### Key cases
>
> **Chapelton v Barry Urban District Council (1940):** for an exclusion term to be valid, it must be contained or referred to in something that can be regarded as having contractual significance.
>
> **Olley v Marlborough Court Hotel (1949):** for an exclusion term to be effective, it must be brought to the party's attention either before or when the contract is made.
>
> **Thornton v Shoe Lane Parking Ltd (1971):** reasonable notice of the terms must be given to the claimant; a series of notices needs to be clearly referred to.
>
> **Spurling v Bradshaw (1956):** exclusion/limitation case may be validly incorporated into a contract if the parties have previously entered into contracts where such a clause was included.

Key cases

Hollier v Rambler Motors (AMC) Ltd (1972): a term may not be incorporated in a contract by a series of previous dealings if the court considers that previous dealings were on an irregular basis.

LNWR v Neilson (1922): the main purpose rule can override an exclusion clause.

Couchman v Hill (1947): an exemption or limitation clause may be overridden by express promise given before, or at the time of, the making of the contract.

However, this case should be contrasted with **Hollier v Rambler Motors (AMC) Ltd (1972)** where a customer had previously dealt with a garage on three to four occasions in five years, when an exclusion clause had been part of the garage's contract. There was no such clause in the contract in dispute, and the Court of Appeal decided the clause was not incorporated under the 'previous course of dealings' principle.

Main purpose rule

Even if the clause is incorporated into the contract, the courts may not allow the exclusion or limitation clause to be effective if that clause affects the main purpose of the contract.

A classic example would be in a contract for the carriage of goods. The term as to the route would be fundamental to the contract, as the importance of the time for delivery of the goods is crucial. The goods may deteriorate and/or lose value and/or be required for a specified purpose, and if a different route is used, time may be wasted. Because of this importance, any exclusion or limitation clause would have no affect on a breach of the term as to the specified route.

In **London and North Western Railway v Neilson (1922)** some important theatrical properties were to be delivered by railway by a certain route. The address labels became detached and the stationmaster innocently sent the items to various wrong destinations. The railway company was unable to rely on its exclusion clause as the main purpose of the contract was the delivery of the items by a specified route, and that obligation could not be excluded.

The courts accept that it is not always possible to identify the 'main purpose' of a contract, so the use of this rule by a victim of a breach of contract is not always successful.

Overriding oral statement

The rule of overriding oral statement is only effective if 'an express specific oral promise' is given which is inconsistent with the exclusion or limitation clause.

The **Couchman v Hill (1947)** case was dealt with in Topic 1 (Terms of a contract). The auction particulars gave notice of the exclusion clause so it was incorporated into the contract. The clause was not effective as the 'express specific oral' promises by the auctioneer and seller overrode the clause.

Activity

Danielle is the owner of a rundown and badly maintained car park in the centre of town. Entry to the car park is by payment at a barrier and then through a dimly lit archway to the car park. The car park has many potholes and rubble, including broken glass, tin cans and fast food cartons. Danielle has placed a handwritten sign at the far end of the archway, which states:

'Danielle hereby gives notice that she is not liable for any harm or injury suffered by any user of this car park.'

James is a regular visitor to town and always parks his moped in Danielle's car park. On this occasion he pays the fee at the barrier but cannot see the notice as a large branch from a tree covers it. As he parks his moped in the car park, a broken bottle cuts one of the tyres. His moped swerves and he falls off, breaking his arm. His moped is badly damaged.

1. Discuss whether Danielle's notice contains an exclusion or limitation clause.

2. Presuming the notice is an exclusion clause, has it been incorporated into James' contract with Danielle – and, if so, how?

3. Presuming the exclusion clause is incorporated, do you think James can rely on either the 'main purpose rule' or the 'overriding statement rule' to successfully claim the clause is not effective? What are the reasons for your conclusion?

You should now be able to:

- understand and explain the common law approach to exclusion and limitation clauses
- apply the law to problem situations.

6 Control of exclusion and limitation clauses: statutory approach

If the exclusion or limitation clause passes the common law tests in Topic 5 then it is incorporated into the contract. Parliament has created rules that give further protection to the victim of a breach of contract who may have no claim, or a limited claim, due to the valid exclusion or limitation clause. The clause is a valid and enforceable term of the contract but *may* become invalid and unenforceable due the relevant Act of Parliament and/or Regulation.

Control within the Sale of Goods Act 1979

The relevant sections of the 1979 Act are:

- **Section 13:** In *all* contracts when goods are sold by description or by sample, there is an implied condition that they will correspond with the description or sample. If the buyer examines and selects the goods then s13 will still apply.
- **Section 14(2):** When goods are sold by a seller *in the course of a business,* there is an implied condition that they will be of 'satisfactory quality'.
- **Section 14(3):** When goods are sold by a seller *in the course of a business* and the buyer expressly or impliedly makes known to the seller any particular purpose for which the goods are being bought, there is an implied condition under s14(3) that the goods are reasonably fit for that purpose. This is the case whether or not the purpose made known by the buyer is the purpose for which goods of that particular type are commonly supplied.

Control within the Supply of Goods and Services Act 1982

The relevant sections of the 1982 Act are:

- **Sections 3 and 4:** These sections are the equivalent to ss13, 14(2) and 14(3) respectively of the 1979 Act but cover goods transferred under a contract of service.
- **Section 13:** In a contract for the supply of services, when the supplier is acting in the course of a business, there is an implied term that the supplier will carry out the service with reasonable care and skill.
- **Section 14:** In a contract for the supply of a service, when the supplier is acting in the course of a business, there is an implied term that the supplier will carry out the service within a reasonable time.

General control within the Unfair Contract Terms Act 1977

Despite its title, the Unfair Contracts Terms Act 1977 (UCTA) does not cover all contracts or unfair terms but concentrates on exclusion and limitation clauses in an attempt to protect **consumers** and others who may be unjustly prejudiced by such clauses. UCTA covers areas of law not within the AQA specification and this study is limited to the relevant sections of the 1979 and 1982 Acts outlined above.

In this topic, you will learn how to:

- explain the operation of the Sale of Goods Act 1979
- explain the operation of the Supply of Goods and Services Act 1982
- explain the operation of the Unfair Contract Terms Act 1977
- explain the operation of the Unfair Terms in Consumer Contract Regulations 1999
- apply the above to problem scenarios.

Key terms

Consumer: (a) someone who neither makes the contract in the course of a business nor holds himself out as doing so; and (b) the other party does make the contract in the course of a business; and (c) the goods passing under or in pursuance of the contract are of a type ordinarily supplied for private use or consumption.

UCTA invalidates *any* exclusion or limitation clause inserted in a consumer contract to cover breaches of:

■ the implied conditions of description (s13), satisfactory quality (s14(2)) and fitness for purpose (s14(3)) in the Sales of Goods Act 1979

■ the equivalent implied terms under ss3 and 4 of the Supply of Goods and Services Act 1982.

It is therefore essential that the claimant must satisfy the requirement of being a consumer.

If the buyer of the goods does *not* deal as a consumer, UCTA allows the implied conditions above to be excluded or limited by the seller, but only to the extent that the exclusion or limitation satisfies the 'reasonableness' requirement of UCTA.

Section 11 of UCTA states the requirement of reasonableness is satisfied if:

> … the term shall have been a fair and reasonable one to be included having regard to the circumstances which were, or ought reasonably to have been, known to or in the contemplation of the parties when the contract was made.

Factors the court will consider are:

■ the relative strength of the parties' bargaining positions

■ whether the customer was given any inducement to agree to the exclusion or limitation term

■ whether the customer should have known of the term

■ whether the goods were altered or adapted at the customer's request.

It should be noted that any contractual term excluding or limiting liability for death or personal injury due to negligence is automatically ineffective.

A term excluding or limiting liability from either s13 or s14 of the Supply of Goods and Services Act 1982 is valid. However, if the claimant is a consumer, or the claimant has made the contract on the other party's written standard terms of business, then the exclusion or limitation term is only valid if it is reasonable.

In this area of contract law, where reasonableness is under scrutiny, each case must be decided on its own facts and it is difficult to identify a common thread or trend in the decisions. However, the following cases do give some guidance in this respect.

In **George Mitchell Ltd v Finney Lock Seeds Ltd (1983)** the purchaser agreed to buy a particular white cabbage seed but the seller provided the wrong seed and the purchaser's crop failed, causing a loss of £63,000. The contract contained a clause limiting the seller's liability to £200, that being the price of the seed. The House of Lords decided the clause was unreasonable as the sellers could have protected themselves by insurance without increasing the cost of the seed, and it was the general practice in the trade not to rely on such clauses.

The above decision should be compared to **Watford Electronics Ltd v Sanderson CFL (2001)** when computer software did not function properly and caused the purchaser losses. The sales contract included a clause excluding liability and a clause limiting liability to a refund of the purchase price. The Court of Appeal decided both clauses were reasonable. The contract had been the subject of much negotiation so the purchaser was fully aware of the clauses and their possible impact. Also, there was no real difference in bargaining power between the parties, and the purchaser had used similar clauses in his contracts when selling products to others.

The Court of Appeal confirmed in **Granville Oil & Chemicals Ltd v Davis Turner & Co. Ltd (2003)** that, in general, the Court of Appeal

■ **Key cases**

George Mitchell v Finney Lock Seeds (1983): the clause was unreasonable as company relying on clause could easily have been insured against the excluded losses.

Watford Electronics Ltd v Sanderson CFL (2001): a much-negotiated exclusion clause was reasonable.

Granville Oil & Chemicals Ltd v Davis Turner & Co. Ltd (2003): in general, the court would not wish to interfere with a freely negotiated commercial contract.

would not wish to interfere with the terms of a commercial agreement negotiated between parties of equal bargaining power, i.e. an exclusion and/ or limitation clause in such a contract is likely to be classed as reasonable.

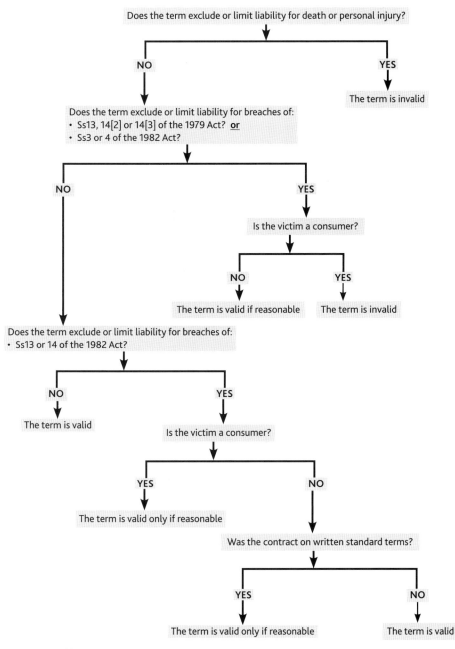

Exclusion and limitation causes

General control within the Unfair Terms in Consumer Contract Regulations 1999

These regulations replaced the regulations made in 1994. The 1999 Regulations (UTCCR) are applied alongside UCTA and cover *every* term in a contract made between a *consumer* and a *seller or supplier*, not just exclusion or limitation clauses. If UTCCR consider a term to be *unfair* then that term will not be contractually binding. However, UTCCR only protect a consumer.

Regulation 3(1) states: A consumer is '… a natural person … acting for purposes which are outside his trade or profession'.

This definition means that, unlike under UCTA, a business can *never* be a consumer under UTCCR.

Regulation 3(1) states: A seller or supplier is '… any natural or legal person who, in contracts covered by these Regulations, is acting for the purposes of his trade, business or profession …'.

Contracts covered by these regulations means contracts made between a consumer and a seller or supplier, containing terms that have not been 'individually negotiated'.

A term will not have been *individually negotiated* if the contract was prepared in advance and the consumer had no opportunity to influence the wording and meaning of the term. It is for the seller or supplier to prove the term was individually negotiated.

Regulation 5(1) states:

> Unfairness is '… any term which [is] contrary to the requirement of good faith [and] causes a significant imbalance in the parties' rights and obligations arising under the contract, to the detriment of the consumer'.

Schedule 2 of UTCCR lists, as examples, certain factors to be considered by the court:

- the relative bargaining strength of the parties
- a term requiring the consumer to pay a disproportionately high amount of compensation for a breach
- a term requiring the consumer to complete obligations even if the seller or supplier does not perform his
- special requirements placed on the consumer.

N.B. Regulation 6(2) states UTCCR will *not* apply if the term is in plain, intelligible language *and* relates to:

- a core contractual term *or*
- the adequacy of the price or remuneration for goods or services provided.

The reasoning here is that the purpose of UTCCR is to protect consumers from hidden injustice. This exception is likely to be interpreted restrictively by the courts to ensure consumers are still protected.

There are only a few cases that show how the senior courts have interpreted and applied UTCCR. As with UCTA, each case is decided on its own facts and will only give a limited indication of how the courts view the regulations. The main area for discussion will be on what is, and what is not, regarded as an unfair term.

In **Director General of Fair Trading v First National Bank plc (2001)** the consumer signed the supplier's pre-typed standard contract that included a term that interest on outstanding amounts would be charged even after a court judgement. This meant that even if a court reduced the contractual instalments, the balance of the debt would still attract interest at the original rate. The Director General issued the claim on behalf of many complainants and The House of Lords decided the term was not unfair. The three main reasons for this decision were that payment of interest on a judgment debt was not unusual, a lender would be expected to want its loan repaid plus interest and the particular term was set out clearly within the contract.

This decision should be compared with **Bairstow Eves London Central Ltd v Smith (2004)** when an estate agent's commission agreement

Key cases

Director General of Fair Trading v First National Bank plc (2001): a clearly set out term with respect to interest payments to a bank was fair.

Bairstow Eves London Central Ltd v Smith (2004): a term doubling estate agent's commission in the event of late payment was unfair.

stated that if payment was late, the commission would increase from 1.5 per cent to 3 per cent. The High court decided this term was unfair even though the original commission was for 3 per cent and the reduced commission of 1.5 per cent only applied if payment was made early.

Activities

Zoë and Mitch are the owners of an electricians' business ('Z and M') and supply electrical goods and services. Elissa visits their shop to purchase an expensive light fitting which is described as 'silver'. Elissa arranges for Z and M to put in the fitting but unfortunately Mitch omits to earth the fitting and Elissa is badly electrocuted. Elissa then discovers the fitting is only made of cheap steel and the internal wiring is defective. Elissa complains but is referred to the reverse of her pre-printed contract with Z and M, which states in small print that there is no liability for any goods or services provided by Z and M.

1 Elissa is unhappy about the fitting being steel, not silver, and she now realises Mitch did not wire the fitting satisfactorily. Outline under what statutory provisions Elissa could bring a claim against Z and M.

2 Discuss whether you think the term in the contract excluding liability is effective to protect Z and M from Elissa's claims.

3 List the major differences between UCTA and UTCCR.

You should now be able to:

■ understand and explain the statutory approach to exclusion and limitation clauses

■ understand the interaction of the common law and statutory approaches

■ apply the law to problem situations

■ construct an appropriate essay on these topics.

7 Overview of contract terms

How to approach a problem involving contract terms and exclusion clauses

The exam scenario will usually involve one party being unhappy with what is provided by the other party. You are therefore made aware that the topics under review are those covered in this chapter, i.e. express or implied terms, the three types of term, exclusion and limitation clauses and whether a statement is a term or a representation. It is unlikely that a question will cover all these topics.

If the question involves, for example, negotiations between the parties and/or an exclusion clause or an apparently unfair term, then the question covers representations and terms, UCTA and UTCCR. If the scenario involves a party breaching what is clearly a term, the answer should explain and discuss the types of term and the different rights the claimant may have. A question on terms will often be linked with a question on formation of a contract, so one, or some, of the topics in Chapter 5: Formation of contract may be relevant.

You must always identify the area(s) of law under review and then apply the relevant law to the question. This allows you to concentrate on explaining one area of law and its application without the confusion of other rules of law, principles and cases. This also allows the examiner to evaluate the answer in a logical manner.

In this topic, you will learn how to:

■ apply the law to problem scenarios involving terms of contract

■ construct an essay evaluating the law on terms of contract.

For example, one previous exam question in January 2008 was as follows:

> Sara was at a family party when she mentioned to her cousin, Tom, that she needed to rent a car for a fortnight's touring holiday. Tom ran a car repair business and he said he would provide her with a car. In return, she agreed that she would do some urgent secretarial work for him at his garage when her holiday was over. The car broke down on the second day of Sara's holiday. When she learned that it would take a further two days to repair, and that Tom could not supply a replacement car, Sara told Tom that the deal was off and she hired a car for the remainder of her holiday at a cost of £250. Tom had to pay £300 to employ a secretary from an agency to do the urgent secretarial work.
>
> Taking into account the rules on formation of a contract and on terms in a contract, consider what rights, duties and remedies, if any, are available to Sara and to Tom arising out of their agreement in connection with the car and the secretarial services.

You must first identify the topics involved. Sara wanted a car for touring so what type of term relates to the supply of the car – a condition, perhaps? What is the effect of the breach of that term by Tom – repudiation and/or damages for Sara? Perhaps Sara is in breach and, if so, to what is Tom entitled?

The question could have referred to an exclusion clause and the answer could then have discussed whether the clause was incorporated and whether UCTA and UTCCR affected the validity of the clause.

The remainder of the question relates to intention to create legal relations, as Sara and Tom are related, and consideration (is secretarial work good consideration for the hire of a car?), which are topics from Chapter 5: Formation of contract.

The answer should also cover remedies, and this is dealt with in Chapter 9: Remedies.

How to write an essay evaluating the law on contract terms and exclusion clauses

The part (c) examination question is different to the questions (a) and (b) which are based on the scenario described in the question. The typical (c) question will ask you to 'critically analyse the law of contractual terms and exclusion clauses and to include any appropriate suggestions for reform'. There are 25 marks each for questions (a) and (b) and also 25 marks for question (c), so this question must be given the same time and attention as the other two.

You should include an accurate explanation of relevant areas of the law. There must also be a discussion of the fairness, relevance and clarity of those areas. Inevitably, all areas of law are not perfect and a description of that law and a logical criticism of that law are required. You should also give sensible suggestions as to how the law could be improved, or say whether, in all the circumstances, reform is not appropriate or possible.

Explain areas of relevant law that work well, are clear and/or fair, as 'critically analyse' does not mean all the analysis results in suggestions for reform of bad law.

You should now be able to:

- answer problem questions involving terms in a contract
- evaluate the law relating to terms in a contract
- construct an appropriate essay on these topics.

Activities

1. Briefly outline in your own words, with headings, the rules on incorporation and the effect of UCTA and UTCCR.

2. How would you simplify UCTA and UTCCR?

7   Vitiating factors

In this topic, you will learn how to:

- state a definition of misrepresentation
- explain the definition of misrepresentation.

Key terms

Misrepresentation: untrue statement of fact made by one party to a contract to the other, during negotiations, which induces the other party to enter the contract but which is not a term of the contract.

Representor: party that makes the untrue statement to the other party.

Representee: party that receives the untrue statement and becomes the victim in the case.

1   Misrepresentation

Misrepresentation is when a party to a contract has made an untrue statement during negotiations, on which the other party has relied, but the content of the statement does not become a term of the contract. If the statement proves to be untrue the claimant has no claim as the statement is not a contractual term.

This situation is clearly unfair on the claimant so common law, and statute, have created the modern law of misrepresentation. The claimant, in the situation described above, is now able to claim that the untrue statement forms the basis of a claim and may be awarded damages and/or a remedy called rescission, which is explained below.

The nature of misrepresentation

Adam is thinking about replacing his moped as he has obtained a new job, which pays a higher salary, but he must now commute twenty miles per day. Adam is concerned that his current moped will not prove reliable enough, so he looks in the local paper for suitable second-hand mopeds. He finds an advert describing what appears to be a suitable replacement.

Adam makes an appointment to view this moped and meets with the seller, Tristan. Adam asks for confirmation that the moped is reliable and that there is a full service history, which Tristan confirms. Adam agrees to purchase the moped and both parties sign a short contract that states the names of the parties, the moped's registration and the agreed sale price. Adam hands over the cash and receives a bundle of papers from Tristan.

On Adam's trip home, the new moped breaks down and Adam discovers that the bundle of papers contains an incomplete service history. The moped is checked by a local garage that states the moped was in for regular repairs when owned by Andy, who sold it to Tristan. Adam is very unhappy that the moped has a history of unreliability and has an incomplete service history and asks Tristan for his money back. Tristan refuses, saying there is nothing in the contract about 'reliability' or 'full service history'. Tristan is correct so Adam cannot sue for breach of contract and is left with a moped that is almost valueless. What can he do? If it had not been for Tristan's statements, Adam would not have purchased the moped.

What are Adam's losses?

- He has wasted the cost of buying the moped.
- He will either lose his job or have to pay for a taxi to and from his new job until he manages to purchase an adequate replacement.

Case law has developed that allows a party in Adam's position to succeed in a claim. Parliament has also become involved in this area and created the Misrepresentation Act 1967. A person (the **representor**) who makes untrue statements to another (the **representee**) may be liable for those statements even if the statement does not form part of the contract – this is called misrepresentation.

Statements made before, or at the time of, the contract are called 'representations'. It should be noted that representations may, in certain circumstances, become terms of the contract and lead to a claim for breach of contract (see Chapter 6: Contract terms, Topic 1: Terms of a contract). This topic is only concerned with representations that *do not* form part of the contract.

An untrue representation is called a misrepresentation. The result of a misrepresentation is that the contract is voidable, i.e. the claimant has the choice of continuing with the contract or not.

Untrue statement

To be a misrepresentation, the statement must be untrue. However, when can silence be classed as a misrepresentation?

First, a representor may make a statement that is true but does not continue with the statement to reveal the whole truth. The maker of the statement has a duty to continue and reveal the whole truth of the situation.

In **Dimmock v Hallett (1866)** a seller of land told the purchaser there were tenants on the land (which the purchaser wanted) but failed to complete the statement by saying that all the tenants had handed in notices to quit and were leaving. This part truth was a misrepresentation.

Second, if a statement by the representor is true when made, but becomes untrue or inaccurate before the contract is made, then the representor must clarify the change. If the representor remains silent, this can be a misrepresentation, as the original statement is misleading the claimant.

In **With v O'Flanagan (1936)** a GP told the purchaser of his practice that it produced a certain annual income. However, between the statement and the contract the GP fell ill and many of the patients left the practice, making the original statement inaccurate. The non-disclosure by the GP of the drop in annual income was a misrepresentation.

Material fact

The statement must be one of material fact and will not be a misrepresentation if it is an opinion or merely an advertising 'puff'. In **Bisset v Wilkinson (1927)** during negotiations a farmer told the purchaser of his land that he thought the land would graze 2,000 sheep, which proved to be inaccurate. As the farmer had never grazed sheep on the land and the purchaser knew this, the statement was one of opinion and so could not be a misrepresentation.

A statement of intention to act in a particular way in the future may be a statement of fact if the representor did not have that intention when making the statement. In **Edgington v Fitzmaurice (1885)** a company issued a prospectus to encourage investment in the business, stating the money invested would be used in a particular way (which the company never intended to do). This statement of intent was an untrue statement of fact and therefore a misrepresentation.

Finally, a misrepresentation does not have to be in words but may also be made by actions or conduct as shown in **Spice Girls Ltd v Aprilia World Service BV (2000)**. All five members of the Spice Girls took part in the filming of a promotion for Aprilia that was to form part of an advert for Aprilia scooters, but one of the group left, making the promotion and the contract worthless. The group knew when making the promotion that one of the group would be leaving, and this was a misrepresentation by conduct.

■ **Key cases**

Dimmock v Hallett (1866): the maker of a statement has a duty to continue and reveal the whole truth of the situation.

With v O'Flanagan (1936): the maker of a statement has a duty to clarify any change to the truth of the statement before the contract is made.

Bisset v Wilkinson (1927): pure conjecture is a statement of opinion and therefore cannot be a misrepresentation.

Edgington v Fitzmaurice (1885): a statement of future intention is, generally, not a misrepresentation unless it can be proved the representor had no intent of fulfilling the statement.

Spice Girls Ltd v Aprilia World Service BV (2000): misrepresentation does not have to be in words but may also be made by actions or conduct.

All five members of the Spice Girls took part in the filming of a promotion but one of the group left, making the promotion and the contract worthless. The group knew when making the promotion that one of the group would be leaving, and this was a misrepresentation by conduct

Made by a party to the contract to the other

The statement must be made by one party to another. There is no misrepresentation when the untrue statement is made by a third party, i.e. someone not a party to the contract.

During negotiations

In **Roscorla v Thomas (1842)** after a contract had been made for the sale of a horse, the seller said to the purchaser that the horse was '… sound and free from vice' but the horse was uncontrollable. The purchaser had no claim as the statement was made after the contract had been made.

Induces the other party to enter the contract

It is not enough for the claimant to prove the statement is untrue as the statement must be important to the making of the contract.

In **Attwood v Small (1838)** the seller of a mine made an untrue statement to the purchaser about the earning capacity of the mine. The buyer instructed a surveyor to confirm the earning capacity of the mine, which the surveyor did (incorrectly). The purchaser bought the mine and then discovered the statement to be untrue. There was no misrepresentation as the purchaser relied on the survey report and not the seller's statement.

It is not a defence for the maker of the statement to claim:

- the claimant could have discovered the truth by taking reasonable steps
- the claimant was unreasonable in relying on the untrue statement.

An example of the first situation is in **Redgrave v Hurd (1881)** when the seller of a business misled the purchaser as to the true earnings of the business. The purchaser had documents available to him before he signed the contract that showed the statement to be untrue, but the purchaser chose not to read them and relied on the seller's statement. It was irrelevant that the purchaser could have discovered the untruth by reading the documents supplied, and this was still a misrepresentation.

An example of the second situation is **Museprime Properties Ltd v Adhill Properties Ltd (1990)** when the purchaser of property relied on inaccurate statements made in auction particulars. The defendant argued that no 'reasonable' purchaser would have relied on these statements, as the statements should have raised doubts about the sense of purchasing the property. The only relevant question was whether the purchaser had

Key cases

Roscorla v Thomas (1842): the statement must be made before, or at the time of, the contract; if made after the contract, it cannot be a misrepresentation.

Attwood v Small (1838): the claimant must show the statement induced him to enter the contract.

Redgrave v Hurd (1881): the claimant can rely on statements made by defendant rather than rely on documents given by defendant that would have disclosed the truth.

Museprime Properties Ltd v Adhill Properties Ltd (1990): the only relevant question was whether purchaser had relied on statements.

relied on the statements (which he had): what the reasonable person would, or would not, have done was irrelevant.

Is not a term of the contract

The statement must *not* be intended to form part of the contract. If the statement is intended to be legally binding then it becomes a term of the contract and cannot remain a representation. If the term is untrue then this forms a claim for breach of contract. It should be noted that claims for misrepresentation and breach of contract are mutually exclusive. However, s1 of the Misrepresentation Act 1967 does now allow a claimant to bring a claim for both misrepresentation and breach of contract.

See *Couchman* v *Hill* (1947), mentioned in Chapter 6: Contract terms, Topic 1: Terms of a contract, when the statement about the 'unserved' heifer was so important that it became a term of the contract, so the buyer did not have to rely on misrepresentation.

Silence and misrepresentation

English law is, generally, based on the principle that a party to a contract should be allowed to profit from their superior knowledge and is under no positive obligation to reveal the truth unless asked for a particular piece of information.

In **Fletcher v Krell (1873)** a woman applied for a job of governess. She was not asked, and did not volunteer, that she was a divorcée (which, due to the morals of the period, would mean she would not be offered the position). There was no misrepresentation as the applicant was under no duty to disclose her status and she was not asked about it.

Exceptions (i.e. when silence may be a misrepresentation)

Relationship of trust

If a relationship is based on trust, then silence by the representor may prove to be a misrepresentation. This trust will exist in relationships between lawyer and client, parent and child, and in other similar situations.

In **Tate v Williamson (1866)** a financial adviser advised his client to sell some land at an undervalue to clear debts. The adviser then purchased the land at half its value but did not tell his client. The silence by the adviser that he was to buy the land was a breach of trust and was a misrepresentation.

Contracts of 'utmost good faith'

An example of a contract of 'utmost good faith' is an application for insurance, when non-disclosure would result in the insurance company charging a lower premium than would otherwise be the case.

In **Lambert v Cooperative Insurance Society (1975)** a woman renewed her jewellery insurance without telling the insurance company her husband had recently been convicted of conspiracy to steal. This was an important fact that would have affected the insurer's decision whether to renew the insurance and, if so, at what premium. The silence of the woman was a misrepresentation and the company was entitled to declare the policy void.

> ### Key cases
>
> **Fletcher v Krell (1873):** there is no obligation to disclose information that has not been requested, and silence will not be a misrepresentation.
>
> **Tate v Williamson (1866):** in a situation based on a party trusting the other due to their relationship, then silence may be a misrepresentation.
>
> **Lambert v Cooperative Insurance Society (1975):** silence of claimant with respect to material facts for a contract of insurance was a misrepresentation.

> ### Activity
> Study some classified advertisements in the media and consider if they contain mere representations or terms of the contract.

You should now be able to:

■ understand the meaning of misrepresentation.

2 Types of misrepresentation

When the representor makes an untrue statement of fact before a contract is entered into, there are various alternatives as to what that person will have been thinking at the time of making the statement. The law of misrepresentation has developed in an attempt to cover these different situations, and there are now three main types of misrepresentation:

- fraudulent misrepresentation: when the representor has intentionally lied about a fact or been reckless as to its truth
- negligent misrepresentation: when the representor has been careless about the truth of a statement
- innocent misrepresentation: when the representor honestly believes the statement is the truth.

Re-read the scenario at the start of Topic 1. First, Tristan may have known the moped was unreliable and did not have a full service history, but lied to Adam in order to obtain the best sale price possible. Second, Tristan may have made the statements off the top of his head without checking if they were true or not. Finally, Tristan may have genuinely, but mistakenly, believed the statements he made to be true.

Fraudulent misrepresentation and remedies

This type of misrepresentation has its origins in the common law and is called the 'tort of deceit'. This is when the representor has made a statement that he knows to be untrue or is reckless as to whether it is true or not, i.e. the representor has been fraudulent in respect of the truth of the statement. Consider what was in Tristan's mind in the first part of the scenario described above.

In **Derry v Peek (1889)** a tram company used horses to pull its trams. The directors of the company believed that under a recent Act of Parliament the Board of Trade would consent to the company using motor-driven trams, and that this consent was a formality, but did not check. The use of motor-driven trams would make the company more profitable and the directors advertised for investors for the company on this basis. The company did not obtain the consent and the company shares dropped in value. The purchasers of the shares sued for their losses but this was not a fraudulent misrepresentation as the directors were only careless as to whether what they said was true.

Remedies for fraudulent misrepresentation

The victim of a fraudulent misrepresentation will be very unhappy with the position in which they find themselves. For example, Adam has lost out financially and will also incur future expenses. The law has developed two remedies available in a claim for misrepresentation.

Rescission

This is an equitable remedy, which means the court will only award it if it is fair to do so in all the circumstances. Rescission means the parties are returned to the positions they were in before the contract was made. The justification for this rule is that the misrepresentation means the contract was entered into by the claimant under a misapprehension of the true situation, i.e. if the claimant had known the truth there would have been no contract.

Damages

Damages is the title of the order made by the court that one party should pay the other money as a form of compensation for losses and harm suffered. There are two principles to consider:

In this topic, you will learn how to:

- define the different types of misrepresentation
- distinguish between the different types of misrepresentation
- apply the rules in a given situation.

Key cases

Derry v Peek (1889): fraudulent misrepresentation is when the person making the statement has made a statement that he knows to be untrue, or is reckless as to whether it is true or not.

First, because the claim is based on the 'tort of deceit' the court will award damages against the defendant even if the losses are not foreseeable, provided causation can be proved.

In **Smith New Court Securities Ltd v Scrimgeour Vickers (1996)** the victim had been induced by an untruthful statement to buy shares in a company for 82p per share when their true market value was 78p. The victim discovered the lie and sold the shares, now worth only 30p–49p per share. The question was whether the award of damages was limited to those foreseeable at the time (i.e. the difference between the price paid and the true value of the shares) or based on the actual loss to the claimant. The court awarded the victim damages based on the difference between the amount paid of 82p and the final sale price, which is more than the usual award of damages in a contractual situation.

Second, the calculation of contractual damages is usually based on putting the claimant in the position they would have been in had the contract been completed properly. Damages based on misrepresentation aim to put the claimant in the position they were in before the misrepresentation occurred. However, the court seems willing to take the view that contractual damages may be appropriate in certain circumstances.

In **East v Maurer (1991)** the representor sold his hairdressing business to the victim, stating he would not open another salon in the same area which he then did. The claimant suffered a loss of profit that was only recoverable under breach of contract, not misrepresentation. The court decided the claimant would have purchased a different business if the truth had been known. The calculation of damages awarded him the profit he would have earned from that business.

Negligent misrepresentation and remedies

This type of misrepresentation is when the representor has been careless and in breach of duty as to whether a statement is true or not. There are two types of negligent misrepresentation:

- common law
- Misrepresentation Act 1967.

Common law

Until 1964, the common law gave the claimant no remedy for a negligent misrepresentation as the only claim allowed was that for fraudulent misrepresentation.

In **Hedley Byrne & Co. Ltd v Heller & Partners Ltd (1964)** the claimant asked the bankers for a company named Easipower for a financial reference in respect of Easipower. The bankers supplied the reference, which had been negligently prepared and which stated Easipower to be in a good financial position. The claimant relied on this reference and entered into a contract with Easipower. Easipower then went into liquidation, owing the claimant money. The victim sued the bankers for these losses and, in principle, the bankers were liable to the claimant for these losses.

Various conditions were set out by the House of Lords before such a claim could be successful. These conditions have been considered and refined by later decisions. The two main conditions, and the ones that cause the most difficulty, are that there must be a 'special relationship' and 'proximity' between the claimant and the representor.

In **Goodwill v British Pregnancy Advisory Service (1996)** a married man (M) had a vasectomy and was told he need take no further contraceptive precautions. M had an affair with Miss Goodwill (G), who followed the advice and took no precautions herself. G fell pregnant and sued the BPAS for negligent misrepresentation. The court decided the claim would

---

Key cases

Smith New Court Securities Ltd v Scrimgeour Vickers (1996): because the claim is based on the 'tort of deceit' the court will award damages even if they are not foreseeable to the defendant.

East v Maurer (1991): calculation of damages awarded claimant the profit he would have earned from that business.

Hedley Byrne & Co. Ltd v Heller & Partners Ltd (1964): a claim for a misrepresentation based on negligence was allowed for the first time.

Goodwill v British Pregnancy Advisory Service (1996): for a successful claim under negligent misrepresentation, there must be proximity between the parties, i.e. a close relationship.

fail as, amongst other reasons, there was no special relationship between the BPAS and G. The BPAS was not employed to confer a benefit on M's future sexual partners.

However, in **Esso Petroleum Co. Ltd v Marden (1976)** Esso let a garage to Mr Marden and told him during negotiations that the garage would sell 200,000 gallons of petrol per year. Esso did not check with the local council and under planning law the road layout around the garage had to be altered so the petrol sales were a lot lower than stated. Esso was liable because it had been careless and there was proximity between the parties as they were involved in negotiations for a contract.

Misrepresentation Act 1967

Section 2(1) of the Misrepresentation Act (the '1967 Act') created a statutory liability for negligent misrepresentation that does not require there to be a 'special relationship' or 'proximity' between the parties. All that is needed is for there to be a false statement that results in a contract and the claimant suffering loss.

An important aspect of the 1967 Act is that once the claimant has proved there was a false statement, the onus is then on the representor to prove that there were reasonable grounds to believe the statement was true. This reverses the burden of proof in civil cases, when it is for the claimant to prove the case. As a result, the 1967 Act is preferable for the claimant to use than *Hedley Byrne* (1964).

In **Howard Marine and Dredging Co. Ltd v A Ogden & Sons (Excavations Ltd) (1978)** a company wanted to hire barges to carry earth and asked for advice about capacity. It was told by the representor that the barges carried 1,600 tons when the correct capacity was 1,055. The company relied on the advice and it took longer than anticipated to complete the job. The company proved a misrepresentation and the representor did not prove it had reasonable grounds to believe its statement was true.

Remedies for negligent misrepresentation

The remedies for negligent misrepresentation are:

▪ rescission (see fraudulent misrepresentation on p123) and/or

▪ damages

Under *Hedley Byrne* the damages are based on tort and are those that are reasonably foreseeable. However, there is some confusion about damages under the 1967 Act. The case below shows the principle applied by the Court of Appeal and, although criticised by academics and queried in other cases, the stated principle appears to be the current law for damages under s2(1). The principle is that damages under s2(1) are not subject to the reasonable foreseeability rule, and are based on how damages are measured under fraudulent misrepresentation.

In **Royscot Trust Ltd v Rogerson (1991)** a car dealer negligently misrepresented to a finance company the amount of a deposit paid for a car by a purchaser. The finance company lost money when the purchaser defaulted on the hire-purchase agreement. The Court of Appeal confirmed that the damages for negligent misrepresentation under the Act are based on tort, and also confirmed that the reasonable foreseeability test does not apply to s2(1) damages.

Innocent misrepresentation and remedies

Innocent misrepresentation is when the representor genuinely believes the statement to be true and is not at fault.

> ### Key cases
>
> **Esso Petroleum Co. Ltd v Marden (1976):** there was proximity between the parties as they were involved in negotiations for a contract between them.
>
> **Howard Marine and Dredging Co. Ltd v A Ogden & Sons (Excavations Ltd) (1978):** under the 1967 Act, once the claimant has proved there was a misrepresentation, the burden of proof shifts to the person making the representation to prove that there were reasonable grounds to believe the statement was true.
>
> **Royscot Trust v Rogerson (1991):** damages for negligent misrepresentation under the Act are based on tort.

For an innocent misrepresentation, rescission or damages may be awarded, but not both remedies (as for fraudulent and negligent misrepresentation). They are therefore alternative remedies.

Rescission as a remedy

In certain situations, rescission may no longer be available to the claimant. Rescission is an equitable remedy and the court will always use discretion when deciding if this remedy is appropriate or not.

Impossibility of restitution

In **Clarke v Dickson (1858)** the representor misled the claimant about the shares in a partnership. By the time the claimant discovered the true facts, the partnership had been converted into a limited company. Rescission was not available as the claimant could not return a partnership to the representor.

The contract is affirmed

The claimant may choose to affirm the contract in some way even though they are aware of the misrepresentation. In these circumstances, the claimant is no longer able to claim the contract as he has himself affirmed its existence.

In **Long v Lloyd (1958)** a seller misrepresented that a lorry had a certain fuel consumption. The purchaser discovered the misrepresentation and returned the lorry for repairs, to which the seller agreed to contribute. Rescission was not allowed as the purchaser had affirmed the contract by returning the lorry for repair.

Delay

A delay (for whatever reason) in bringing the claim for misrepresentation to court will mean rescission is not available as a remedy.

In **Leaf v International Galleries (1950)** a seller misrepresented a painting as a Constable but the purchaser only became aware of the misrepresentation when trying to sell it five years later. Rescission was not allowed due to delay.

Third party has gained rights

If a third party has gained an interest in the goods then rescission will not be granted as this would be unfair on the innocent third party.

In **Lewis v Averay (1972)** a seller of a car was misled by the purchaser as to the purchaser's true identity. As a result, the seller allowed the purchaser to take the car before the cheque cleared. In the meantime, the purchaser sold the car to an innocent third party and the purchaser's cheque then bounced. The seller's only effective remedy was to claim rescission and to ask for the car to be returned to him by the third party. The seller's claim for rescission failed, as in the circumstances it would be unfair to deprive the innocent third party of the car purchased in good faith.

■ **Key cases**

Clarke v Dickson (1858): rescission is not allowed if the parties cannot be restored to their pre-contractual position.

Long v Lloyd (1958): the claimant had affirmed contract even though aware of the misrepresentation and so could not claim rescission.

Leaf v International Galleries (1950): delay in bringing the claim for misrepresentation to court will mean rescission is not available as a remedy.

Lewis v Averay (1972): where a third party has gained an interest in the goods, rescission will not be granted.

■ **Activity**

An exam question may require the additional application of another area of law, e.g. a question involving misrepresentation will often also contain a question about breach of contract relating to the same scenario.

Use the scenario on p119 to decide the following points:

1 What misrepresentations, if any, have been made by Adam? If any, what type of misrepresentation?

2 Which of the misrepresentations, if any, have become terms of the contract? If so, why?

You should now be able to:

■ understand the different types of misrepresentation

■ apply the law to problem situations.

3 Examination techniques

In your exam answer, it is essential that you state the relevant law of misrepresentation before you apply it to the situation. Your answer should start with the definition of misrepresentation, and an explanation of any part of the definition that you consider may be of particular relevance to the question. For example, the question could refer to the representor making a statement that may be of opinion. Specific reference should be made to this area of the definition, with case(s) used in support of the law.

The answer should then explain the three types of misrepresentation. You should be able to identify when reading the question which type(s) of misrepresentation is/are involved. The exam scenario will rarely involve a question about innocent misrepresentation. It is likely the representor will have made the statement intentionally, knowing it was untrue, or else was careless as to the truth of the statement. You therefore need to explain the rules about fraudulent misrepresentation and/or negligent misrepresentation in some detail, with reference to cases. You must take particular care to differentiate between common law and statutory negligent misrepresentation, and explain the shift in the burden of proof in the latter.

You should now be in a position to apply the law stated in your answer. The definition should be applied to ensure all the component parts of misrepresentation are present. For example, if there was confusion over whether the statement was one of fact or opinion then the rule and relevant case should be discussed and a justified conclusion reached.

You should then decide which type of misrepresentation applies, explain why, and state whether the claim is likely to succeed or not.

Exam questions may often refer to 'rights' and 'remedies', and you must ensure enough time is allowed for an explanation and application of appropriate remedies at the end of the answer.

Even if the conclusion to the answer is that the claim will fail, the remedies for misrepresentation need to be mentioned. Rescission and damages should both be explained. Rescission may be unavailable if, for example, there has been a delay in making the claim and the test of foreseeability of loss must be mentioned.

You should include a clear, concise and accurate explanation and application of the relevant law. It is worth spending a little time when reading the scenario to note those aspects of the law that strike you as important – for example, which type of misrepresentation is involved? This makes the stating of the law more relevant and saves time overall.

You should now be able to:

- answer problem questions involving misrepresentation

- evaluate the law relating to misrepresentation

- construct an appropriate essay on these topics.

In this topic, you will learn how to:

■ state a definition of the term discharge of contract

■ outline the different ways in which a contract may be discharged

■ explain the effect of discharge of contract.

Key terms

Discharge of a contract: end of a contract; the contract will have created obligations with which the parties must comply, and when completed the contract is discharged.

Frustrating event: event that makes completion of the contract 'radically different' from what was originally agreed between the parties; it must be an event that is unforeseen *and* is not the fault of either party.

1 Discharge of contract

Chapter 5 dealt with the formation of a contract, and this chapter deals with the end of a contract. The majority of contracts will end by the parties performing all their respective obligations, in which case the law will not become involved.

However, sometimes a contract will be ended by one of the parties not performing some or all of their primary obligations. This may result in secondary obligations being imposed on the party at fault – for example, by the payment of damages. This chapter will cover three ways in which a contract may end, and explain and discuss the impact of each in turn.

The meaning of discharge of contract

Imagine Kurtis (a self-employed decorator) has contracted with Simon to paint Simon's conservatory for a fee of £1,000. It is agreed that the painting will be completed by Friday. Apart from Kurtis completing the contract, there are three possible ways in which the contract may be **discharged**.

First, Kurtis commences painting the conservatory on the Monday, paints the ceiling and three of the walls over the course of the week, but leaves the job incomplete on Friday. Kurtis arrives on Saturday morning and apologises to Simon for the non-completion of the contract. Kurtis asks for £800 as he has completed 80 per cent of the work. The contract has not been completed by Kurtis and the basic rule is that if a party has not completed their side of the bargain they are unable to claim *any* payment. This is called the strict rule of 'performance'. Kurtis is obviously not entitled to the £1,000 and may not be entitled to the £800. The contract would have been 'discharged' had Kurtis completed the entire contract.

Second, Kurtis has made the same contract as above. He commences painting on the Monday but through no one's fault, and without warning, the conservatory burns down, so Kurtis is unable to complete the contract. Kurtis is now unable to claim full payment although he has done nothing wrong. This situation is called the 'frustration' of a contract. The **frustrating event** discharges the contract.

Third, Kurtis has made the same contract as above. The painting must be completed by Friday as Simon is holding his engagement party on Saturday and the conservatory is required. Kurtis commences the painting but works rather slowly, so the work is not completed by Friday evening. Simon calls in another decorator to complete the work on Saturday morning. Kurtis has breached (broken) a term of the contract. If the breach is of a term fundamental to the contract, then the term is a condition, and Simon may sue Kurtis for damages (for example, the extra cost of employing the second decorator) and/or for repudiation (i.e. the contract is discharged and obligations under the contract are ended).

To summarise the above:

1 Complete *performance* discharges a contract.

2 A *frustrating event* discharges a contract.

3 A *breach* of a condition discharges a contract (if the victim so chooses).

The discharge of a contract ends the contract and the parties' respective obligations to each other are terminated. The court regards the contract as valid from the date of creation up to the time of discharge.

If both parties complete the contract satisfactorily then the contract is discharged. This chapter is not concerned with that scenario. The three rules stated above will also terminate a contract, and because the contract has not been completed, the court has to decide to what, if anything, the disappointed party (or parties, in the case of frustration) is/are entitled?

If Kurtis has only *performed* part of the contract, to what, if anything, is he entitled? If Kurtis cannot complete the contract due to an *unforeseen incident*, which may be a frustrating event to what are Simon and Kurtis entitled? Finally, if Kurtis *breaches* a condition of the contract, to what is Simon entitled?

2 Performance

When all parties have performed their obligations under a contract, that contract is completed and is therefore discharged (i.e. terminated).

The strict rule

The strict rule can be seen to be unfair.

In **Cutter v Powell (1795)** Cutter was a crew member and was to be paid as second mate on a trip from Jamaica to Liverpool. The boat left Jamaica on 2 August and was due in Liverpool on 9 October. Cutter died on 20 September. His widow sued for his wages from 2 August to 20 September. The claim was dismissed as Cutter had signed up to complete the entire trip and clearly had not completed all his obligations.

The application of the strict rule does seem unfair but was confirmed in *Re Moore & Co.* v *Landauer & Co.* (1921) when tinned fruit was sold and described as being in cases of 30 tins per case. The purchaser received the correct number of tins in total but some cases contained 24 tins in a case. The seller had not completed the contract (i.e. there was incomplete performance) so the purchaser could reject the cases.

It should be noted that s15(A) of the Sale of Goods Act 1979 might now mean a different decision would be reached. A business purchaser is not entitled to reject goods when they are only slightly different from the contractual description and it would be unreasonable to reject them.

As these cases show, the strict rule of performance can operate harshly and as a result the courts have developed exceptions to the strict rule.

Divisibility

If a contract can be seen as comprising separate parts then non-completion of one part is *not* a breach of the whole contract, e.g. a salary is described as yearly but is **divisible** into monthly payments so an employee leaving after three months is still entitled to three months' salary. The employee in this example may, of course, still be in a breach of contract if the contract was for a fixed period and the employee left early without authority, but that does not terminate the employee's right to the three months' salary.

In **Ritchie v Atkinson (1808)** a ship-owner agreed to carry a specific cargo at an agreed rate per ton. He carried only a part of the cargo. The ship-owner was entitled to be paid for the part cargo carried (the contract was divisible as it specified a price to be paid per ton) but was liable in damages for breach of contract for not carrying the remainder of the delivery.

Activity

Create three scenarios, each with one type of discharge of contract.

You should now be able to:

- understand the meaning of discharge of contract.

In this topic, you will learn how to:

- define the strict rule as to performance
- distinguish between substantial and part performance
- explain the importance of time for performance of a contract
- state the remedies for failure to perform
- apply the rules in a given situation.

Key terms

The strict rule: if the agreement is that payment will be made on completion of the contract, then the strict rule for performance is that there must be 100 per cent completion of a party's obligations under the contract for that party to be entitled to payment.

Divisibility: if a contract specifies that payment is due from time to time as performance of a particular part of the contract is completed, then this is a 'severable' contract.

Key cases

Cutter v Powell (1795): if the contract has not been completed and some obligation(s) remain outstanding, then no payment is due at all.

Ritchie v Atkinson (1808): the contract was divisible as it specified a price to be paid per ton.

Substantial or part performance

There are two further exceptions to the strict rule:

1 If a party has completed a '*substantial*' amount of work under the contract then that party is entitled to be paid for the work done

2 If a party accepts a *partial* performance of the contract.

In both exceptions, the party 'at fault' may be entitled to payment based on **quantum meruit**, as shown in the case of **Hoenig v Isaacs (1952)**. In this case, a decorator contracted to decorate and supply furniture for £750, but supplied two pieces of defective furniture that could be repaired for £55; the contract was substantially completed on a financial basis (93 per cent) so the decorator was entitled to be paid for what he had done on a *quantum meruit* basis, less the cost of repairing the furniture.

The question arises as to what 'substantial' means, and this was considered again in **Bolton v Mahadeva (1972)** when a builder contracted to install a central heating system for £560. His installation was defective and repairs cost £170 (i.e. on a financial basis he had carried out 69 per cent of the work). The builder was entitled to nothing, as there was no substantial completion of the contract.

If one party has agreed that the other party need not complete the entire contract, then the strict rule will not apply. However, the consent must be in the form of a specific acknowledgement that the defaulting party is entitled to be paid for what they have completed so far.

In **Sumpter v Hedges (1898)** a builder contracted to build two houses for £565, completed some work, then ran out of money. The customer completed the outstanding work. The builder was not entitled to be paid for the work done, as the customer had no alternative but to take the benefit of half-completed work and had to complete the outstanding work himself.

Time of performance

Generally, failure to complete a contract on time is treated as a breach of warranty, so a claim can only be made for damages and the contract will continue. The court will only regard time as a condition (known as making '**time of the essence**'), which allows the victim to claim the contract is repudiated (terminated) and/or damages, if:

▪ the parties have *expressly stated* in the contract that time is of the essence, or

▪ *in the circumstances*, time for completion is critical, or

▪ one party has failed to perform on time and the other has insisted on a *new date for completion* as 'time of the essence'.

The **Union Eagle Ltd v Golden Achievement Ltd (1997)** case is an example of the first situation in which time is of the essence. Here, a contract for the sale of a flat specified the time of completion of the contract as 5.00pm and time was expressly stated to be 'of the essence'; the purchaser delivered the purchase price at 5.10pm and the seller repudiated the contract; the seller was entitled to repudiate as the time for completion had been made a condition of the contract. However, what would happen if a contract specified time was of the essence but the parties agreed to extend the time for completion indefinitely? Could either party subsequently insist on a new date for completion as making time of the essence again? This occurred in the case of **Charles Rickards Ltd v Oppenheim (1950)** when the original date for the supply of a car (date 1) was of the essence but the parties agreed to extend the date. The purchaser then became impatient with the continuing delay and gave 28 days' notice of a new date for completion (date 2), which the supplier

Key terms

Quantum meruit: basis for an award made by a court whereby one party claims reasonable payment for a benefit given or for work done.

Time of the essence: when time for performance of the contract is important.

Key cases

Hoenig v Isaacs (1952): if a party has not completed their obligations under the contract, the court may order payment for the work that has been done if a substantial proportion of the work has been completed.

Bolton v Mahadeva (1972): as there was no substantial completion of the contract, the claimant was entitled to nothing.

Sumpter v Hedges (1898): if the innocent party has no option but to take the benefit of the work done, then there is no consent to part performance.

Union Eagle Ltd v Golden Achievement Ltd (1997): if the contract states 'time is of the essence' then late performance by a party means the contract may be repudiated by the other party.

Charles Rickards Ltd v Oppenheim (1950): a party to contract who has waived a term as to time can later make it 'of the essence' again.

failed to meet. The court held date 2 had made time of the essence again and the purchaser was entitled to reject the car when it was delivered after this new date.

Remedies for failure to perform

The innocent party in this type of case has to deal with a contract that is only partly performed, or is performed but not in accordance with the terms agreed. Chapter 9: Remedies covers the different remedies available to a claimant in detail, but an outline of the remedies that may be appropriate for non-performance is set out below.

In the first scenario, Kurtis has only completed 80 per cent of the work within the agreed time span. Kurtis admits he is in the wrong but is demanding 80 per cent of his fee for the work completed (which is not defective in any way). The remedy for Kurtis is to seek damages to compensate him for the work done based on *quantum meruit*.

Simon, meanwhile, has been left with a partially decorated conservatory and a decorator who is unwilling or unable to complete the work. Simon may consider three possibilities.

First, he may try and insist Kurtis returns to complete the outstanding 20 per cent of the work. The court may order a party to complete a contract in limited circumstances – this is called an order for 'specific performance'. This type of order is not used to order the completion of personal services, as the court is unable to monitor the continuing situation in what is already a tense atmosphere.

Simon's more realistic alternative is to deny that Kurtis is entitled to any payment, relying on the strict performance rule. No doubt Kurtis would argue that one of the exceptions applies – probably that he has 'substantially' performed the contract. An argument would then occur as to whether the work completed by Kurtis is substantial or not.

Finally, Simon may sue Kurtis for breach of contract, as the work was not completed on time. This situation overlaps with the third scenario. If time is *not* of the essence then Simon may only claim a breach of warranty and damages as a remedy – probably the cost of another decorator completing the 20 per cent of uncompleted work, less the balance of £200 Simon would have paid Kurtis for this work anyway. If time *is* of the essence, Kurtis has breached a condition so Simon may sue for damages and/or claim that the contract is repudiated. As Kurtis does not wish to return, and it is unlikely Simon would want him to, repudiation is rather meaningless.

Activities

1. Define the strict rule of performance and explain why it may be an unfair rule.
2. Create a scenario where one exception to the strict rule may be applied.

You should now be able to:

- understand the importance of performance of a contract
- understand the consequences of failure to perform
- apply the law to problem situations.

In this topic, you will learn how to:

- define the term frustration of contract
- explain the elements of the definition
- explain the importance of frustration as a means of discharge of contract
- state the remedies for failure to perform
- apply the rules in a given situation.

Key cases

Paradine v Jane (1647): confirmed the common law rule that in the circumstances the contract must continue, even though this might be unfair on one of the parties.

Taylor v Caldwell (1863): decided that there is an implied term in all contracts that if an unforeseen event occurs before completion of the contract that makes completion impossible, then the parties have no further obligations to each other; the contract will be valid and enforceable up to the frustrating event, but after the event all future obligations are cancelled.

Denny, Mott & Dickson v James Fraser (1944): government ban on contracts such as the one in existence – the ban being made after the contract is made – will frustrate the contract for subsequent illegality.

Krell v Henry (1903): if the main reason for the contract is based on a particular event or purpose, and that event or purpose will not take place, then the contract may be frustrated.

3 Frustration

A *frustrating event* occurs when, before a contract can be completed, something happens that makes the contract impossible, illegal or pointless. The *frustrating event* must be unforeseeable to the parties and be no one's fault.

The general principle

In **Paradine v Jane (1647)** a tenant was evicted from his land due to an invading army. The landlord sued for rent arrears and the court held the rent had to be paid even though the tenant was no longer in occupation of the land and it was impossible for him to return.

The decision in *Paradine* seems harsh on the tenant. As a result, the courts developed a principle called frustration to allow fairer decisions to be made in such circumstances.

In **Taylor v Caldwell (1863)** an owner contracted to rent out his music hall to a hirer so that musicals could be performed. Due to no one's fault, and before the musicals could take place, the music hall burned down. The hirer had spent money advertising the musicals, for which he would be paid on completion of the contract. The hirer wanted reimbursement of these expenses. The court decided that as it was now impossible to complete the contract, it was frustrated. This terminated the parties' future obligations to each other under the contract, so the owner did not have to pay the hirer for the expenses.

The courts have now defined frustration as occurring when an event makes the performance of the contract 'radically different' from what was originally agreed between the parties.

Types of frustrating events

- **Impossibility:** if the frustrating event makes the contract impossible to perform then the contract is frustrated.
- **Subsequent illegality:** if the frustrating event makes the contract illegal to perform then it is frustrated.
- **Radical change in circumstances:** if, having made the contract, the reason for the contract ends then the contract is pointless and is frustrated.

Impossibility

If it is impossible for the contract to be completed, because for example the subject matter of the contract is destroyed, then the contract may be frustrated.

This applies to *Taylor* v *Caldwell* (1863), as can be seen from the facts described above, the contract was impossible to complete due to the destruction of the music hall.

Subsequent illegality

If, due to a change in the law, the purpose for which the contract was made becomes illegal, then the contract may be frustrated. This occurred in **Denny, Mott & Dickson v James Fraser (1944)** where a contract was made for the sale of timber, but before the contract was completed the government banned the sale of this type of timber. The court held the contract was frustrated as the main purpose for the contract was now illegal.

Radical change in circumstances

In **Krell v Henry (1903)** a guest hired a hotel room in order to view Edward VII's coronation procession. The King became ill and the coronation was postponed. The room had to be paid for on the day of the coronation, and the guest refused to pay. The court decided the contract was based on the viewing of the coronation procession and as this would not occur the contract was frustrated, so the guest did not have to pay for the room.

In **Herne Bay Steamboat Co. v Hutton (1903)**, Hutton hired a boat in order to see the fleet when the King viewed it after his coronation, as in the *Krell* case above. The King became ill, so Hutton claimed the contract to hire the boat had become pointless. However, the court held the contract was not frustrated as one reason for the contract still remained (to view the fleet). Hutton had to pay for the boat hire.

When frustration may not apply

Generally, courts wish parties to complete their contractual obligations and will only allow frustration to interfere with the contract in the three situations listed above. Other situations may arise when frustration seems applicable but is not accepted by the courts.

Self-induced frustration

In **Maritime National Fish Ltd v Ocean Trawlers Ltd (1935)** a fishing company owned two trawlers and contracted to hire a third for the purpose of commercial fishing. The company needed a licence for all fishing vessels and was only allowed two, which it allocated to its own trawlers. The company then claimed frustration of the hire contract, as it could no longer use the hired trawler (a radical change in circumstances). The court decided frustration did not apply and the contract was still valid. The 'frustrating' event was within the company's control, and classed as self-induced frustration, as it could have allocated one licence to the hired trawler.

The contract has become less profitable

In **Davis Contractors Ltd v Fareham UDC (1956)** builders contracted to build houses for the UDC for £94,000 but then discovered it would cost £115,000 to complete the contract due to labour shortages. The builders claimed frustration of the contract but were unsuccessful, as the contract was not radically different to what the parties had originally intended, just less profitable.

This decision should be compared with *Williams* v *Roffey Bros & Nichols (Contractors) Ltd* (1990) (Chapter 5: Formation of contract, Topic 3: Consideration) when an extra payment, caused by labour shortage problems, was enforceable. It is accepted that there is inconsistency in the decisions but the cases do have subtle differences. For example, in *Davis* (1956) the houses had been built and the builder then asked for extra payment, while in *Williams* (1990) the roofing work *had not been completed* and it was the builder who *offered* the extra payment to the sub-contractor.

The 'event' was either a 'foreseeable' risk or referred to in the contract itself

In **Amalgamated Investment v Walker Ltd (1977)** a buyer contracted to buy a building for redevelopment for £1.7m. Unknown to both parties, the government then restricted any planning development for the building, so its value dropped to £200,000. The court decided this was not a frustrating event as the listing of old buildings was a foreseeable risk, and the original price had to be paid.

Key cases

Herne Bay Steamboat Co. v Hutton (1903): unlike *Krell* v *Henry*, the main purpose of the contract still existed so the contract was not frustrated.

Maritime National Fish Ltd v Ocean Trawlers Ltd (1935): self-induced frustration is not frustration where the 'frustrating event' arose due to the voluntary decision of one of the parties.

Davis Contractors Ltd v Fareham UDC (1956): merely because a contract becomes less profitable and/or more difficult to complete it does not frustrate the contract.

Amalgamated Investment v Walker Ltd (1977): if the event was foreseeable, or was specifically described in the contract, then if that event occurs it does not frustrate the contract.

Key terms

Self-induced frustration: when non-completion of the contract is due to an event that is under the control of that party.

The listing of a building was judged to be a foreseeable risk prior to its purchase, and so was not classed as a frustrating event

Remedies for frustration

In common law, the frustrating event automatically terminates the contract at the time of the event. Obligations already existing must be completed, but future obligations are terminated. This explains why the customer in *Krell* v *Henry* (1903) did not have to pay for the room, as the payment was an obligation that only had to be performed when the room was actually used.

This decision should be compared to **Chandler v Webster (1904)** where the facts are the same except the room had to be paid for in advance when the room was booked. The court decided the contract was frustrated but the man still had to pay for the room. His obligation to pay (when booking the room) arose before the frustrating event (the postponement of the coronation).

The courts felt there was unfairness between these two cases so in **Fibrosa Spolka Ackyjna v Fairbairn Lawson Combe Barbour Ltd (1943)** the House of Lords decided that if there had been a total failure of consideration then money already paid could be recovered (this case may be referred to as the *Fibrosa* case).

However, in a contractual situation it is rare for there to be a total failure of consideration. A party to a contract is likely to have provided something under the contract, no matter how negligible, which means the precedent of the *Fibrosa* case would not be commonly applicable.

Law Reform (Frustrated Contracts) Act 1943

The rule of frustration was created to help innocent parties, but caused its own problems (see *Chandler* v *Webster* (1904) above). Parliament therefore passed the 1943 Act to cover what happens *once* a frustrating event has occurred, i.e. to help decide who would owe what and to whom.

The Act does *not* affect the law in the situations *when* frustration may occur; it *only* applies to situations where frustration is found to exist.

The Act replaces the common law rules and covers three areas:

1 Money already paid over (e.g. a deposit) is recoverable, and money already due under the contract (as in *Chandler*) is not payable.

2 The court can use its discretion to order compensation to be paid for work done and expenses incurred under the contract before the frustrating event (provided there was an obligation to pay money before the frustrating event). The quantification of the amount

Key cases

Chandler v Webster (1904): under common law, an obligation created before the frustrating event will remain outstanding.

Fibrosa Spolka Ackyjna v Fairbairn Lawson Combe Barbour Ltd (1943): under common law, if there had been a total failure of consideration by one party before the frustrating event then the other party had no obligation to perform existing duties under that contract.

due is based on the principle of *quantum meruit* (see p126 for the definition).

3 The court may order compensation to be paid for any valuable benefit one party may acquire under the frustrated contract.

In **Gamerco SA v ICM/Fair Warning (Agency) Ltd and Others (1995)** the promoters of a concert by the band Guns' n Roses had paid the band $412,500 in advance of the concert and the band had incurred expenses in preparation. The concert was then cancelled as the stadium was found to be unsafe. The court allowed the claim by the promoters for the return of their advance payment but held, in the circumstances and using its discretion, the band was not entitled to its expenses.

Conclusion

A frustrating event may only occur if the event is not due to the fault of any party and the event is unforeseen. A frustrating event will terminate the contract immediately, and future contractual obligations of the parties are cancelled. The 1943 Act allows the court some discretion to decide which party owes what amount to another party.

In the scenario on p128, Kurtis is unable to complete the contract because the conservatory is destroyed. This event was the fault of neither Kurtis nor Simon, so it is a frustrating event. As a result, the contract is discharged. Kurtis may be entitled to be paid for the work he has completed and may receive compensation for the expenses he has incurred so far, e.g. the cost of materials used. Simon does not have to pay for the remainder of the contract.

Key cases

Gamerco SA v ICM/Fair Warning (Agency) Ltd and Others (1995): the court confirmed that the 1943 Act allowed it 'to do justice' in a situation covering work done and expenses incurred before a frustrating event, so the court had a discretion whether or not to make an award for these heads of claim and, if so, in what amount(s).

Activities

1 Explain the difference in the attitude of the courts to the cases of *Paradine* v *Jane* (1647) and *Taylor* v *Caldwell* (1863).

2 Invent a situation when a frustrating event has occurred, and then invent a further situation when it seems a frustrating event has occurred but the court decides the contract remains valid and enforceable.

3 Rameez is the owner of a garden nursery business specialising in the supply of rare plants from Spain. Claire agrees to buy five rare plants from Rameez for a total of £500, and pays a deposit of £50. Rameez has one plant in stock and supplies it to Claire and places an order with his Spanish contact for the remainder. The EU then bans the import and sale of these types of plants. Advise both Rameez and Claire as to their rights and remedies under the contract.

4 Would your answer be different if the EU had not banned the import and sale of these plants but Rameez had delayed placing his order so that all available plants had been sold, which meant Rameez had none to supply to Claire?

You should now be able to:

■ understand the importance of frustration of contract

■ understand the consequences of frustration of contract

■ apply the law to problem situations.

In this topic, you will learn how to:

■ explain the nature of breach

■ distinguish between the effects of breach of condition and breach of warranty

■ explain the meaning of the term anticipatory breach and outline its effect

■ distinguish between breach and frustration

■ state the remedies for breach of contract

■ apply the rules in a given situation.

■ **Key terms**

Breach: when a party fails to perform an obligation in the contract, which allows the other party to sue; the obligation may be of a serious nature (condition) or of a minor nature (warranty).

Repudiation: when a party breaches a condition in a contract, the claimant may choose to terminate the contract, which brings obligations under the contract to an end.

Anticipatory breach: when one party to a contract gives notice, whether expressly or impliedly by conduct, that he will not complete his obligations under the contract.

■ **Key cases**

Hochster v de la Tour (1853): anticipatory breach takes place before the due date for performance; it allows the claimant to take legal action for the breach immediately, without waiting for the due date to see if performance does unexpectedly take place then.

4 Breach

When a party fails to perform an obligation under a contract, then that party may be sued for **breach** of contract.

The nature of breach

The claimant will always be entitled to claim damages, but the contract will only be terminated depending on the type of term that has been breached (see Chapter 6: Contract terms, Topic 1: Terms of a contract).

The different effects of breach of condition and warranty

Conditions

When a condition is breached (broken), the claimant may **repudiate** (terminate) the contract if they wish and/or sue for damages, such as in the case of *Poussard* v *Spiers* (1876), seen in Chapter 6: Contract terms.

Warranties

When a warranty is breached, the claimant may sue *only* for damages and the contract continues, as seen in *Bettini* v *Gye* (1876), in Chapter 6: Contract terms.

A condition is an important term of the contract. A breach of condition by a defendant means the claimant may treat the contract as repudiated, i.e. terminated, and/or make a claim for damages. Before repudiating the claimant *must* be sure the breached term is a condition and not a warranty, as if it is a warranty and the claimant tries to repudiate then the claimant will be in breach of contract as there was no right to repudiate! The defendant may then sue for breach by the claimant, as the claimant has repudiated (terminated) the contract for no good legal reason.

Anticipatory breach

An **anticipatory breach** occurs when a party to a contract gives notice in advance to the other party that they will not be performing/completing the contract. The claimant in this situation has a choice *either* to sue immediately for breach of a condition (i.e. to treat the contract as repudiated and/or to claim damages) *or* to wait for the time for performance of the contract and to sue then.

In **Hochster v de la Tour (1853)** the claimant agreed to work for the defendant as a courier on a tour that was to start in June. In May, the defendant told the claimant he no longer required the claimant's services. The claimant was entitled to sue the defendant immediately and did not have to wait until the *actual* breach of contract (which would have occurred in June).

The choice the claimant has in this situation is of importance. The claimant may sue the defendant on receiving notice of the anticipatory breach (as in *Hochster* v *de la Tour*) or may choose to sue when the *actual* breach occurs (in the *Hochster* case this would be when the victim would have been taken on as the tour guide in June). However, what if the claimant chooses to delay suing but before the actual breach occurs the contract is discharged by a frustrating event? The claimant in this situation has no contract on which to sue as frustration ends the contract.

This is important as an examination question could involve one party giving advance notice of a breach (anticipatory breach), the claimant choosing to wait for the actual breach to sue, and a frustrating event occurring in the meantime. The claimant may then have lost the right to sue for breach.

In scenario on p128, what if, having made the contract with Kurtis, Simon warns Kurtis that he no longer requires the painting of the conservatory? In the meantime, Kurtis has purchased materials for the job but he decides to wait until the start date of the contract to sue Simon. Before then, however, the conservatory burns down. Kurtis is now in a dilemma. He can no longer sue for breach as the contract is discharged by the frustrating event, and he may only claim under the Law Reform (Frustrated Contracts) Act 1943.

Remedies for breach

This topic must be read in conjunction with Chapter 6: Contract terms, Topic 1: Terms of a contract, which outlines the three types of term in a contract.

There are two possible remedies available to a victim of a breach of contract:

1 repudiation, and/or

2 damages.

Anticipatory breach

If the claimant claims an *anticipatory breach* then he may choose to repudiate the contract when the consequences are that he is released from future contractual obligations and is no longer bound to perform any obligations under the contract. The claimant could also claim damages *immediately*. These damages are to put the claimant in the position he would have been, had the contract been completed.

Actual breach

The claimant may choose not to accept the anticipatory breach but to see if the defendant commits an actual breach at the time that performance is due. Here, the claimant may claim repudiation and/or damages that would be assessed at the time when performance should occur and, if the losses have increased due to a change in market factors, the loss will be increased. Alternatively, an event may occur that discharges the contract (e.g. frustration), which results in the claimant losing his rights under the anticipatory breach (see the scenario above when Kurtis waited for the actual breach of contract by Simon).

It must be remembered that for a breach of *condition* the right of the claimant is to claim for repudiation and/or damages. Repudiation is defined on page 128, and contractual damages are based on putting the claimant in the position they would have been had the contract been completed.

For a breach of warranty, the claim is limited to damages – based on putting the claimant in the position he would have been had the contract been completed.

Activities

1 What are the three types of contractual term? Create example scenarios to illustrate each type.

2 Explain an anticipatory breach and how it is different to an actual breach, again inventing scenarios to show this.

3 Under the heading 'Anticipatory breach' an example is given, from the scenario, of Kurtis choosing to wait for the actual breach by Simon. What effect does the burning down of the conservatory have on the contract, and how does this affect any claim Kurtis may have against Simon for his breach?

4 In this scenario, Simon's anticipatory breach is clearly a breach of condition entitling Kurtis to repudiate the contract and/or claim damages. What if Simon's anticipatory breach was only a breach of warranty – what rights does Kurtis have?

You should now be able to:

■ understand when breach of contract occurs

■ understand the effect of breach of contract

■ apply the law to problem situations.

In this topic, you will learn how to:

■ apply the law to problem scenarios involving discharge of contract

■ construct an essay evaluating the law on discharge of contract.

5 Overview of discharge of contract

How to approach a problem involving discharge of contract

The examination question may or may not specify the topic required. For example, frustration *and* breach may be referred to. This could involve an anticipatory breach (discussion of which must include the choice of the victim to sue immediately or wait for the actual breach) and then a frustrating event that would affect the victim's right to claim for actual breach, as the contract is terminated by the frustrating event.

Frustration questions are usually identifiable as when the contract becomes impossible or illegal, or the purpose for the contract disappears. You should give a definition of frustration, with examples of all three types of frustrating event. The Law Reform (Frustrated Contracts) Act 1943 must then be explained as to how the court will attempt to apportion loss. Explain anticipatory breach, including a discussion of the remedies available to the victim of the breach and the effect the frustrating event has on these remedies.

Alternatively, one party may not have completed the entire contract. Here, you should include a discussion of the strict rule of performance *and* breach. An exception to the strict rule may be possible (e.g. substantial performance) and this must be explained and discussed. The non-completion may also be a breach of contract (probably of a condition) so you should give an explanation and application of relevant law.

Finally, the question may involve parties who have made a contract and one, or both, have then failed to perform a respective obligation. You need to explain the three types of term (condition, warranty and innominate), apply the law to each breach, and explain and discuss the remedies available.

You may need to talk about remedies as well as rights available to the parties. Include a discussion of damages, repudiation and/or the 1943 Act.

One previous exam question, in June 2008, was:

> Nick decided to set up in business on his own. He entered into a contract with Perry, who owned a fleet of taxis, to carry out repairs to all of Perry's current vehicles. The total price agreed was £5,000. Of this, £1,000 was to be paid immediately and the remainder on completion of the work. Nick spent £1,500 on materials and on other preparation for the work. However, shortly before the work was due to begin, the local authority removed Perry's licences for most of his taxis because of persistent problems with Perry's drivers. Perry refused to go ahead with the contract with Nick and demanded the return of the £1,000 already paid.
>
> Taking into account the rules on frustration and on breach of contract, consider the rights and remedies of Nick and Perry in relation to the contract for the repairs to the fleet of taxis.

You should first deal with the breach of contract by Perry. Explain that this is an anticipatory breach that entitles Nick to repudiate the contract and/or claim damages immediately or to wait for the actual breach to claim breach (with reference to cases as examples). Mention the danger to Nick in waiting for actual breach. Define and explain repudiation and damages. There should be some discussion of whether Perry's breach is of a condition or warranty, and the effect this has on Nick's position.

You should then define frustration, explain its effect on the contract, and *outline* the three situations when frustration may occur. Choose the relevant situation and apply the law to the question (probably 'radical change in circumstances'). There are various cases to which reference should be made, and you should discuss whether there is frustration (as some of Perry's taxis are still in business). Mention that perhaps the frustrating event was self-induced, as Perry did not control his drivers and this caused the removal of the licences.

Make sure you focus on the explanation and application of *relevant* elements of breach and frustration. No credit will be given for a detailed discussion of other situations when frustration may occur. You *must* read the question carefully and take time to consider which are the relevant topics contained within the question.

Your answer should also cover remedies, and this is dealt with in Chapter 9: Remedies. For frustration, mention should always be made of the 1943 Act and the effect this will have on both the positions of the claimant *and* the defendant.

You should now be able to:

■ answer problem questions involving discharge of contract.

9 Remedies

In this topic, you will learn how to:

- distinguish between legal and equitable remedies
- outline the different remedies available
- outline the purpose of different remedies.

> ### Key terms
>
> **Remedy:** award made by a court in favour of a claimant in relation to non-performance of a term, or all terms, of a contract by a defendant.

1 Remedies

The purpose of the law of contract is to fulfil the reasonable expectations of the parties. However, the contract may only be partly performed, or not at all, by one party. The other party will no doubt be very disappointed and may ask the court to rectify the situation. What that party is asking the court for is called a **remedy**. The court cannot award whatever remedy it considers appropriate, but must be guided by the type of claim (e.g. is it a breach of contract or frustration?) and the range of remedies available in the circumstances of the dispute.

Legal and equitable remedies

There are various remedies available to the court, and they may be defined as being either *legal* or *equitable* remedies.

Legal remedies

A claim for damages (compensation – see Topic 2 of this chapter) is *always* available, *as of right*, to the claimant when a contractual term has been broken. This means that if the claimant has not suffered any loss the court *must* still make an award of damages – but the amount ordered to be paid would be nominal (i.e. a small amount).

Equitable remedies

Equitable remedies are dealt with in detail in Topic 3 of this chapter. As a general rule, equitable remedies *may* be awarded by the court where damages alone would not prove an adequate remedy and justice would not be served.

Equitable remedies are therefore at the *discretion* of the court. Even though there may be a breach of contract or a misrepresentation, the court will only award an equitable remedy (for example, specific performance or rescission) if it is fair in all the circumstances for it to do so.

Remedies relating specifically to goods

The Sale of Goods Act 1979 allows the buyer to sue for damages if the seller of the goods either fails to deliver the goods or breaches a contractual warranty. If the seller breaches a condition, the buyer will be able to treat the contract as ended (repudiation), to *reject* the goods and/ or claim damages. However, once the buyer has *accepted* the goods, the right to treat the contract as ended and to reject the goods is lost, and only the right to claim damages will remain.

The content below is a repeat of Chapter 6: Contract terms, Topics 3 and 4, but is essential knowledge. It is highly likely that an exam question will ask for an explanation and discussion of the possible remedy of repudiation in a sale or transfer of goods scenario (which may allow the victim to reject the goods and reclaim the purchase price and/or damages).

Under ss13, 14(2) and 14(3) of the 1979 Act, the claimant may repudiate the contract and/or sue for damages.

Repudiation

The claimant may choose to terminate the contract due to the breach of the implied condition. In effect, the claimant is entitled to the return of the price paid but must return the goods that do not fit their description, are not of satisfactory quality or are not fit for their purpose. This remedy may prove attractive to the claimant as he may then recommence his search for the appropriate goods with his financial position restored to its original position.

The right to reject the goods may be lost if, for example, the goods have been *accepted* by the claimant. Under s11(4) of the 1979 Act, where a buyer has accepted goods a breach of condition will *not* allow the buyer to repudiate the contract and reject the defective goods. This could cause unfairness as the buyer may purchase an item and not use it for some time. If when used, the item is found to be in breach of ss13 and/or 14, the buyer's only remedy would be damages.

The 1994 Act amended the 1979 Act to redefine when the buyer is held to have 'accepted' goods. The 1994 Act defines acceptance as when:

- the buyer tells the seller the goods are accepted, or
- the buyer does something inconsistent with the seller's ownership of the goods, or
- the buyer keeps the goods without telling the seller they are rejected after a reasonable time.

A case showing the unfairness of the original section is **Bernstein v Pamson Motors Ltd (1987)** when Bernstein purchased a new car but only managed to drive it 142 miles before he fell ill and the car was not then used for three weeks. When next used, the car was found to have serious defects and Bernstein was stranded in an isolated part of the country. Bernstein claimed a breach of the implied conditions under the 1979 Act and attempted to claim repudiation and to reject the car. The right to reject the car was lost as Bernstein had retained the car for three weeks and this was long enough for Bernstein to have accepted the car.

The decision in this case raised controversy. It was felt that the innocent claimant was left unable to claim rejection of an expensive item that failed to meet any of the requirements of the implied conditions of the 1979 Act. Bernstein's only claim was for damages.

In **Clegg v Olle Anderson (2003)** Clegg purchased a new yacht in August 2000 and was told immediately that the keel was substantially heavier than specified in the contract. Clegg negotiated with the seller and then rejected the yacht by letter in March 2001. The court confirmed that the *Bernstein* (1987) case was no longer good law and that Clegg was entitled to reject the yacht under the 1979 Act as amended by the 1994 Act.

As a general rule, therefore, a buyer with a claim under ss13, 14(2) or 14(3) should reject the goods as soon as possible so that repudiation has a practical and positive result for the buyer.

Similar principles and rules apply to claims made under ss3 and/or 4 of the Supply of Goods and Services Act 1982 in respect of the transfer of goods rather than their sale.

Damages

As an additional or sole remedy, the claimant may choose to claim damages (i.e. compensation for the losses incurred due to the breach of one or more of the implied conditions).

Damages are explained in detail in Topic 2 of this chapter, but to summarise: the aim of contractual damages is to put the claimant in the position he would have been in had the contract been performed properly.

In the *Bernstein* (1987) case, the claimant recovered the cost of making his way home, the loss of a full tank of petrol, £150 for a 'totally spoilt day comprising nothing but vexation', and compensation until he (Bernstein) purchased a replacement car.

> ### Key cases
>
> **Bernstein v Pamson Motors Ltd (1987):** confirmed that when the buyer has accepted the goods, or part of them, the right to reject goods and the contract as repudiated is lost.
>
> **Clegg v Olle Anderson (2003):** confirmed the amended rules on acceptance applied to a claim under ss13, 14(2) and 14(3) of the 1979 Act.

Activity

Create one scenario where goods are 'accepted' by the buyer and another scenario where the goods are not accepted. Explain the reason(s) for the difference between the two results.

You should now be able to:

■ understand the purpose of remedies.

In this topic, you will learn how to:

■ explain the purpose of damages in the law of contract

■ explain the rules relating to remoteness of damage

■ explain the way in which the law quantifies damages

■ state the basis for an assessment of damages

■ apply the rules in a given situation.

Key terms

Damages: an award made by the court that one party should pay compensation to the other to place the other party in the same position they would have been, had the contract been completed.

Key cases

Hadley v Baxendale (1854): defendant will be liable for losses caused if claimant can satisfy the court of either of the following two tests: (i) would a reasonable person foresee the loss as a consequence of the breach of contract (the objective test?); or (ii) what potential losses were in the minds of the parties when the contract was made (the subjective test?).

---

2 Damages

Damages is a technical expression in law for an award of money by the court to be paid by one party to another for losses suffered (i.e. compensation).

The purpose of damages in the law of contract

The purpose of damages in contract law is to put the injured party (the victim or claimant) in the position he would have been in had the contract been completely performed by the defendant.

The court is therefore looking forward to what should have happened.

For example, James is a computer games creator and has contracted with Mike (a computer games manufacturer) that James will design a new computer game called 'The Whiz' for the computer games convention in London on 30 June. Mike has provided James with a design studio and all the computer hardware and software required. Unfortunately, James is distracted by his career in accountancy and does not complete the design in time for the convention. James is in breach of contract and Mike may sue for damages. The court will try and estimate what profit Mike would have made from the game and order James to pay that amount as damages.

This scenario throws up a problem in the calculation of damages, which is dealt with under 'Bases of assessment' on page 143.

Remoteness of damage

In the scenario above, for what do you think James should be responsible?

What if Mike would have produced the computer game for £400,000 and would have sold 50,000 units at £20 each, leaving a net profit of £600,000? It probably seems reasonable that James should be liable for this loss, as he caused it. However, what if, as a result of James' breach of contract, Mike was unable to expand his business empire into nightclubs and lost the opportunity of buying suitable premises (which were available after June when the profit from 'The Whiz' should have been received)? Do you think James should also be liable for these losses?

A breach of contract may have far-reaching consequences, and the court has developed a rule to restrict the defendant's liability. The leading case below sets out the principle of 'remoteness of damage' in contractual situations.

In **Hadley v Baxendale (1854)** a crankshaft in the claimant's mill broke so the claimant contracted for a carrier (the defendant) to take the shaft to the makers, who would use it to model a new shaft. The carrier breached the contract by taking longer than agreed to deliver the shaft, which meant the mill was out of action for longer than anticipated and the claimant lost profit over this extra period. The carrier had not been told the mill would be out of action until the new shaft arrived. The carrier was not liable for the loss of profit as he was entitled to assume the mill owner had a spare shaft or could borrow one.

This case outlined the two alternative tests available to a claimant who, if *either is proved*, will satisfy the court that the losses were not too remote and therefore that the defendant should be liable.

The rules were considered and applied in **Victoria Laundry (Windsor) v Newman Industries (1949)** when the defendant was five months late in delivering a boiler to the laundry company (the claimant), which the defendant knew was needed by the claimant to run its business. The claimant sued for its usual loss of profits for this period (claim 1) and for the loss of profit on a special government contract it had just obtained that gave higher laundry fees (claim 2). The defendant was liable for claim 1 under the objective test, but claim 2 failed under both tests.

The two tests for remoteness were considered by the House of Lords in **Transfield Shipping Inc. v Mercator Shipping Inc. (The 'Achilleas') (2008)** when a hired ship was returned nine days late. The owner claimed damages based on the loss of a very lucrative contract, which it said was foreseeable, whereas the hirer argued the damages should be based purely on the difference between the fees paid under the contract and any extra fees the owner could have charged for this nine-day period. The House of Lords overturned the decision of the Court of Appeal by allowing the owner's claim, stating that in the scenario of the shipping industry the higher loss was foreseeable.

It must be remembered that the application of the two alternative tests is *at the time when the contract is made*. What the reasonable person or the actual defendant may discover after the contract is made is irrelevant.

In the scenario with James and Mike it can be seen that James is liable to Mike for the loss of net profit of £600,000 as, at the time the contract was made, this loss would have been foreseeable to a reasonable person (and it may also have within the knowledge of James). However, Mike is unlikely to be able to prove either that a reasonable person (objective test) or James (subjective test) knew of the loss of profit from the potential nightclub business, so James would not be liable for this loss.

Bases of assessment

Presume in the scenario above that James is in breach of contract and the loss suffered by Mike is foreseeable. The next question is how Mike's losses are calculated, i.e. the basis for assessment of the losses.

Assessment may be classed under two types:

▦ expectation loss (or loss of bargain)
▦ reliance loss.

Expectation loss (or loss of bargain)

This approach attempts to put the claimant in the position they would have been had the contract been performed, i.e. in the position the victim *expected* to be in. In Mike's case, he expected to receive a net profit of £600,000 so that would be the basis for calculating his damages. In a case of non-delivery of specified goods (e.g. 12 apple trees) the loss is any *extra* cost of obtaining 12 apple trees elsewhere.

The calculation (assessment) in the two examples above is relatively straightforward. However, problems may occur in other situations. In the case of **Ruxley Electronics and Construction Ltd v Forsyth (1996)** there was a clear breach of contract, and the loss was foreseeable, but the assessment of the loss caused the court problems (see 'Quantification of damages' on p144).

Key cases

Victoria Laundry (Windsor) v Newman Industries (1949): application of the two alternative tests of foreseeability is at the time when the contract is made.

Transfield Shipping Inc. v Mercator Shipping Inc. (The 'Achilleas') (2008): the two tests of *Hadley v Baxendale* (1854) are still the standard rule, but *The 'Achilleas'* allows the court to take a different approach (either more generous or more restrictive) if the circumstances of the case justify it.

Ruxley Electronics and Construction Ltd v Forsyth (1996): even where there is a clear breach of contract with foreseeable loss, assessment of the loss can be difficult, particularly where it is for loss of amenity.

Key cases

Anglia Television Ltd v Reed (1972): reliance loss basis of assessment is used when it is difficult to calculate the claimant's future loss because the amount of that loss is problematic.

Addis v Gramophone Co. Ltd (1909): in general, courts do not award compensation for injured feelings in contract cases.

Hamilton Jones v David & Snape (2004): exceptions to the rule that courts do not award compensation for injured feelings in contract cases include a contract which is based on pleasure, relaxation or peace of mind.

Ruxley Electronics and Construction Ltd v Forsyth (1996): confirmed that damages are to compensate for an established loss and are not to provide an unwarranted benefit for the unhappy party.

Reliance loss

As a rare alternative to the expectation basis for loss, it is possible to claim compensation calculated on the expenses incurred by the claimant before the breach.

In **Anglia Television Ltd v Reed (1972)** Anglia TV spent a lot of money preparing for a film, including paying fees to the director, designer and stage manager. Reed agreed to be the main actor but then pulled out and a suitable replacement could not be found, so the film was not made. Anglia TV could not predict what its profit on the film would have been (the success of films is very problematic) so the court awarded damages based on reliance loss. Reed must have known that such expenditure would have been incurred, and was liable for the expenses incurred by Anglia TV both before and after the contract with him was made.

Quantification of damages

The quantification (calculation) of the damages to be paid is closely related to the basis of assessment. Once the basis for assessment is decided, then the quantification of damages may be obvious. However, in some situations the quantification of the loss is complicated or difficult. There are four examples of such complicated or difficult situations:

- non-pecuniary loss
- loss of amenity (loss of a benefit)
- mitigation of loss
- liquidated (fixed) damages.

Non-pecuniary loss

On occasions, a claimant may suffer upset and distress caused by the breach of contract. In general, courts do not award compensation for injured feelings in contract cases. In **Addis v Gramophone Co. Ltd (1909)** the claimant was dismissed by his employer in a way that was described by the House of Lords as 'harsh and humiliating'. The claimant's claim for distress failed.

The courts have developed some exceptions to this rule – for example, if the contract is based on pleasure, relaxation or peace of mind, and so on. In **Hamilton Jones v David & Snape (2004)** a solicitor acting for the mother failed to stop a father taking the children abroad permanently, and the client suffered distress. This was a contract based on peace of mind so the client was awarded damages for her distress.

Loss of amenity (loss of a benefit)

On some occasions, a claimant may have suffered a breach of contract but the expectation loss (loss of bargain) basis of assessment will produce an unfair or absurd result. The court was faced with this difficulty in **Ruxley Electronics and Construction Ltd v Forsyth (1996)** where the contract for a swimming pool stated the depth as seven feet six inches, but the builder completed the pool with a depth of six feet nine inches. There was nothing wrong with the pool apart from the depth, it was still worth its cost, it did not affect the value of the property as a whole and F could still use the pool as he originally intended. The cost to correct the pool was £21,650, which was equivalent to the original cost. The House of Lords confirmed that in building contracts there are two bases for quantification of damages, namely the 'cost of reinstatement' and the 'difference in value'. The cost of reinstatement was totally unreasonable in this case and there was no real difference in value so F was entitled to nothing. However, he had not received that which he had contracted for, and so the court awarded him £2,500 for loss of amenity (i.e. loss of benefit).

There is no rule that assists the court to quantify the damages in such a case, and the court appears to have discretion to award whatever amount it considers appropriate, providing it is modest. If, for example, the pool had been built for a developer, who was to sell the property in any event, then no award would be made for, loss of amenity as the developer would not suffer any loss.

There was discussion that the *Ruxley* (1996) decision was another example of an exception to the 'non-pecuniary loss' rule (see above). However, the following case confirmed that was not true.

In *Farley* v *Skinner* (2001) the prospective purchaser of a house instructed a surveyor and specifically asked about aircraft noise. The surveyor failed to investigate properly and the purchaser's enjoyment of the house was affected, although there was no reduction in its market value. The House of Lords confirmed the award of £10,000 was for the loss of a benefit that had been contracted for, rather than for discomfort and upset caused as in the *Ruxley* (1996) case.

Mitigation of loss

Once a breach has occurred, the claimant is not entitled to sit back and allow the losses to increase. There is an obligation on the claimant to take *reasonable* steps to mitigate (reduce) the losses. For example, if James breaches the contract Mike should look in the market place to see if another computer games creator is able to create the product James did not. If Mike does not take that reasonable step then he may not recover some or all of his losses.

However, if there is an anticipatory breach (see Chapter 8: Discharge of contract, Topic 4: Breach) then there is no duty to mitigate.

The **White and Carter (Councils) v McGregor (1962)** decision is seen as harsh. The defendant had contracted to buy advertising space on the claimant's litter bins, but the defendant cancelled the contract, which was an anticipatory breach. The claimant did not accept the breach and went ahead with the contract for three years, then sued the defendant for its fee. The House of Lords held that in this situation the claimant had no duty to mitigate, and the claimant recovered its loss in full.

Liquidated (fixed) damages

The parties may fix in the contract what the amount of damages will be if there is a breach of contract, and the court will enforce that agreement. In the case of **Dunlop Pneumatic Tyre Co. v New Garage and Motor Co. (1915)** the defendant agreed to pay £5 to the claimant for every tyre sold below list price, which was held to be a valid fixed damages term as it was a genuine attempt to estimate the loss that might occur.

Key cases
White and Carter (Councils) v McGregor (1962): if there is an anticipatory breach, the claimant is under no duty to mitigate the loss.
Dunlop Pneumatic Tyre Co. v New Garage and Motor Co. (1915): parties may agree in the contract what the amount of damages will be if there is a breach of contract.

Activity

1. Create a scenario where the claimant suffers two areas of loss due to a breach of contract: one based on expectation loss and the other on non-pecuniary loss.

2. Create a scenario where the claimant has suffered losses, part of which are recoverable under the *Hadley* v *Baxendale* tests and part of which are too remote.

You should now be able to:

- understand the law relating to an award of damages in contract

- apply the law to problem situations.

In this topic, you will learn how to:

■ explain the purpose of each of the remedies, apart from damages, in the law of contract

■ explain the rules relating to rescission

■ explain the rules in relation to rejection of goods

■ explain the rules with respect to remedies against the goods themselves

■ apply the rules in a given situation.

3 Other remedies

Rejection is, like damages, a common law remedy, which means that if the claimant is successful in proving a breach of condition he will be entitled to reject the goods, provided the goods have not been accepted. There are also three equitable remedies that the court has discretion to award if damages is not an appropriate remedy:

▥ rescission
▥ injunction
▥ specific performance.

Rejection

As was discussed in Chapter 6: Contract terms and earlier in this chapter in Topics 1 and 2 (Remedies and Damages respectively), if there is a breach of a term implied by ss13, 14(2) or 14(3) of the 1979 Act or ss3 and/or 4 of the 1982 Act, the buyer/hirer has the right to treat the contract as ended (repudiation) and to return the goods, i.e. to *reject* the goods. The implied terms from the 1979 and 1982 Acts are conditions, the breach of which allows the claimant to repudiate the contract and/or claim damages.

However, under s15A of the 1979 Act, if the buyer is *not* a consumer (i.e. is a business) and there is a breach of any of the terms mentioned above but 'the breach is so slight that it would be unreasonable for him to reject the goods', then damages are the only remedy available.

This section will affect a case on similar facts to those in *Re Moore & Co. v Landauer & Co.* (1921) (see Chapter 6: Contract terms, Topic 3). In this case, the claimant was entitled to reject the goods for not fitting their description (a specific number of tins of fruit per case) but it is arguable that this breach would now be seen as insufficient to justify rejection of the goods.

It is emphasised that s15A does not affect those buying for personal use or consumption.

Equitable remedies

Rescission

This remedy is found mainly in cases of misrepresentation. The effect of this remedy is that the parties are placed in their pre-contractual position and if that is not possible then rescission is not granted. In the scenario, if James had made a misrepresentation then Mike may claim that any advance payments made by Mike to James would be repaid to Mike and any information or goods given by James to Mike would have to be returned to James.

Apart from the general rules that rescission will only be awarded if fair, and damages are not appropriate, there are other examples of when this remedy may not be awarded (for those examples see Chapter 7, Vitiating factors, Topic 2, Types of misrepresentation).

Injunction

An **injunction** is usually awarded when damages are not an adequate remedy and the rights of the claimant need protecting.

For example, if James had contracted that all his development of the game 'The Whiz' would be owned by Mike, and Mike discovered James was to sell the development to another competitor, Mike may be awarded an injunction to stop James releasing that information. Mike wants to

Key terms

Injunction: a court order instructing a party *not* to perform an action; occasionally, an injunction will order a party to perform an action.

acquire the development information rather than obtain damages against James on this point.

An injunction will not be awarded for a party to complete a personal service, as the court is unable to supervise such an order. In **Page One Records Ltd v Britton (1967)** a pop group sacked their manager and were in breach of contract. The pop group's manager claimed an injunction to stop the group employing any other manager, but failed as this would mean the group could only employ the claimant, which was impractical. The court awarded the claimant damages.

Specific performance

The court may order a party who is in breach to complete their side of the contract. This is a very rare remedy and will only be awarded when the subject matter of the contract is unique and an award of damages would be an inadequate remedy, e.g. a contract for the sale of land or a Picasso painting.

As described for an injunction, specific performance will *not* be awarded if damages are an adequate remedy, if supervision of the contract would be required, if the order would cause hardship or if the contract involves the provision of personal services.

Specific performance must be a remedy available to *both* parties for it to be awarded to either party, *and* the party claiming specific performance must have acted equitably (fairly) before and during the contract.

> ### Key cases
>
> **Page One Records Ltd v Britton (1967):** an injunction will not be awarded for a party to complete a personal service, as the court is unable to supervise such an order.

> ### Activity
>
> Define injunction and specific performance, and give examples of when they would, and would not, be granted by the court.

You should now be able to:

- understand the remedy of rejection, and when it may and may not apply
- understand the three equitable remedies, and when they may or may not apply
- apply the law to problem situations.

4 Overview of remedies

How to approach a problem that should include a discussion of remedies

An exam question will often, but not always, ask for an explanation and application of the relevant remedies that may be available to a named party in the question.

Make sure that after answering the question based on the relevant law (e.g. misrepresentation), you then continue to complete the answer by explaining and applying the remedies, e.g. damages and/or rescission. This is an easy thing to forget as the excitement of knowing some or all of the relevant law can distract you from continuing with the possible remedies available.

Once the relevant law has been explained and applied, then you need to consider the suitable remedy or remedies. Even if your conclusion is that the claimant has no claim, an explanation and application of the

In this topic, you will learn how to:

- apply the law to problem scenarios involving remedies
- construct an essay evaluating the law on remedies.

possible remedy or remedies is still needed. This part of the answer could commence as follows:

> However, if the claimant did have a valid claim under fraudulent misrepresentation then rescission and/or damages could be claimed. Rescission is when the court will return the parties to their pre-contractual positions, so in this case the purchaser will have the purchase price returned and the car will be returned to the seller.
>
> Rescission is only awarded if …
>
> Rescission is not awarded if …
>
> Alternatively, the buyer could claim damages, which are to ….

The examiner will be expecting an explanation and application of the relevant remedy or remedies, but a good discussion is sufficient and no definite decision need be reached as to whether a particular remedy would be successful or not.

Write an essay evaluating remedies

The part (c) examination question is different to the questions (a) and (b), which are based on the scenario described in the question. The typical (c) question will ask you to:

> … critically analyse the remedies available under contract and consumer law and include any appropriate suggestions for reform of those remedies.

There are 25 marks each for questions (a) and (b) and also 25 marks for question (c), so this question must be given the same consideration as the other two.

You should give an accurate explanation of the different remedies discussed in this chapter. You also need to discuss the fairness, relevance and clarity of those remedies. Inevitably, all aspects of these remedies are not perfect and you should include logical criticism with your description of each remedy. Make sensible suggestions as to how the remedies could be improved or give your opinion that, in all the circumstances, reform is not appropriate or possible.

You should also explain the remedies that appear to work well and are clear and/or fair, as 'critically analyse' does not mean that all your analysis should result in suggestions for reform of weak or inadequate remedies.

Activity

1 Define contractual damages, rejection and rescission.

2 Outline two situations that show the inadequacy of damages, and explain how another remedy would be preferable.

You should now be able to:

- answer problem questions involving remedies
- evaluate the law relating to remedies
- construct an appropriate essay on these topics.

Practice questions

■ Example question 1 (AQA, January 2012)

Read this scenario and answer all **three** questions.

You should write in continuous prose, give reasoned answers, and make reference to cases, statutes and examples where appropriate.

Anna saw an advertisement in which Quickstep, a dance academy, promised personal tuition in small groups by highly qualified and experienced dance teachers. Anna later signed a contract by which she agreed to pay £300 for 12 lessons in ballroom dancing. The contract included a clause which stated that Quickstep would not be liable for any personal injury or damage to property that occurred during the lessons. Anna was very disappointed to find that, after three lessons, she had made little progress. She felt that this was because the group was very large and the teacher, who seemed very young and inexperienced, tended to concentrate on those who already showed good dancing skills. Towards the end of the third lesson, the teacher did attempt to demonstrate part of a dance with her. However, moving too quickly for her to keep in step, he succeeded only in causing Anna to fall. In doing so, she hurt her back and tore her dress.

To help Anna over her disappointment, Cal, her father, bought her a new coat costing £200 from Barleys Fashion Store (BFS). BFS did not have in stock Anna's preferred colour in her size, so the coat had to be ordered in Anna's name, and delivered to her house. When Anna tried it on, she discovered that the colour was of a slightly different shade. BFS supplied a replacement but charged a delivery fee of £15. The replacement coat was of the right shade but did not fit well. Additionally, the seams on the sleeves appeared to be poorly stitched. Because Cal had spent over £150, he was given a voucher promising a 10% discount on his next purchase from BFS. No time limit was stated on the voucher, but when Cal attempted to use it a month later, he was told that the discount was now no longer available.

1 Consider the rights, duties and remedies of Anna and of Quickstep, in view of the statements in Quickstep's advertisement and Anna's experience in the first three lessons. *(25 marks + 5 marks for AO3)*

2 Taking into account that it was Cal who purchased the coat, discuss Anna's rights and remedies against BFS. Discuss Cal's rights and remedies against BFS in connection with the discount voucher. *(25 marks)*

3 Consider what criticisms may be made of the current rules on making an agreement in contract (offer and acceptance issues) and suggest any appropriate reforms. *(25 marks)*

■ Example question 2 (AQA, January 2012)

Read this scenario and answer all **three** questions.

You should write in continuous prose, give reasoned answers, and make reference to cases, statutes and examples where appropriate.

Eric was a plumber who had often done work for his neighbour, Dave, sometimes for payment, and sometimes as a favour for the cost of the materials only. Whilst Dave was away on business for a few days and no one was in the house, water pipes froze and then burst. Eric was unable to contact Dave, but he had a key to the house. He vacuumed up water with hired equipment and repaired the burst pipes. On his return, Dave promised to pay Eric £350. Dave also said that he thought that installing an outside tap would be a good idea. Eric asked him how much he would pay for the tap, and Dave said, 'not more than £150'. Without consulting Dave any further, Eric installed the outside tap the next day, whilst Dave was out. When he returned home, Dave was so annoyed to discover that the work had been done that he not only refused to pay anything for it, but also refused to pay the £350 that he had promised for the earlier work.

Eric agreed with Fastbuild that he would install the plumbing in six flats that they were shortly to begin building. He was to be paid £10,000 for the work. £1,000 was to be paid immediately and the remainder on completion. In preparation, Eric bought materials from Plumbserve at a cost of £2000. Shortly after Fastbuild began digging the foundations, it was discovered that the site contained toxic deposits and all work was stopped indefinitely. It was about a month before Eric inspected the materials that he had bought from Plumbserve. When he did so, he found that many had surface and superficial damage, though all would function properly. Plumbserve refused his request for replacements, on the grounds that a notice, prominently displayed at their sales counter, informed all purchasers that any complaints about materials must be made within two weeks of purchase.

1 Consider the rights and remedies, if any, of Eric against Dave in connection with the work arising out of the burst pipes, and the installation of the tap.

(25 marks + 5 marks for AO3)

2 Discuss the rights, duties and remedies of Eric and of Fastbuild arising out of the indefinite stopping of the building work, and discuss Eric's possible rights and remedies against Plumbserve. *(25 marks)*

3 Consider what criticisms may be made of the current rules on making an agreement in contract (offer and acceptance issues) and suggest any appropriate reforms. *(25 marks)*

3B Critical evaluation and proposals for reform of contract law

In this chapter, you will learn how to:

■ evaluate aspects of the law of contract that are covered in the AQA A2 law specification

■ state proposals for reform of those areas of the law of contract

■ write an essay that is appropriate for an examination question.

This chapter considers those topics of contract law that may be the subject of the evaluation question. The question will not specifically cover discharge of contracts or misrepresentation, but reference to misrepresentation is acceptable when evaluating remedies, for example. For each topic that you need to evaluate, there are a number of points that you can use to develop your arguments. You should remember that every aspect of the law has its good and bad points. Indeed, in contract law, these may well vary with the point of view of the person considering the law; a consumer may view the law differently to a business, and a claimant may view the law differently to a defendant.

As you will appreciate, a great deal of time and care is taken by experts when drafting an Act of Parliament. Nevertheless, statutes have to be interpreted in the light of the infinite range of human behaviour, and according to the ever-changing nature of society and the way in which business operates. The common law, too, has developed to accommodate these changes. Over the years, judges refine and clarify the law to reflect the needs of the time. In many cases this is entirely successful, and adds to our understanding of what the law is on a particular point.

It also often happens, however, that a particular area of law is capable of ambiguity, and conflicting decisions occur. There is a real risk that injustices might happen as a result. In these cases, there comes a point where it may be necessary to introduce reforms. These would take the form of a new precedent or new legislation, and their aim would be to:

■ clarify existing areas of difficulty or ambiguity

■ change the law where necessary

■ introduce new laws to reflect present needs.

Each of the topics are evaluated in turn. You should be able to write an essay on each topic, in order to be prepared fully for the exam.

1 Offer and acceptance

The current law of offer and acceptance can be critically evaluated in the following areas:

■ the confusion between an offer and an invitation to treat

■ what comprises a 'course of action' in an advertisement

■ the unfairness of the rules of offer and acceptance and the difficulties created by the 'postal rule'.

The confusion between an offer and an invitation to treat

The differences between an invitation to treat and an offer can, on occasions, be very slight. As a result, it may be difficult and confusing for the public. For example, most customers in a *Pharmaceutical Society of GB* v *Boots Cash Chemists* (1953) (item on shelf) situation will believe the availability of the goods and their status comprises an offer, which they are able to accept to make a valid contract. A suggestion is that all invitations to treat should be treated as offers so that the law mirrors the public's belief in the situation. However, this would interfere with the process of opening and proceeding with negotiations, and would also allow contracts to be created when against the wishes of a party, usually a seller of goods or services.

For example, in the *Boots* case if the item on the shelf had the status of an offer, then once the item is placed in the customer's basket a contract would be made, and the customer would then be bound to pay for the item. However, customers may wish to change their minds and in the suggested scenario this would be a breach of contract. Another problem would arise if the shop owner had made a mistake in pricing the item. If the contract were to be made at the shelf, then the shop owner would have no opportunity to correct this mistake – which would be unfair. This is clearly inappropriate and so the only viable option is for such items to be classed as invitations to treat.

In the *Fisher* v *Bell* (1961) case, the invitation to treat was the shop window display of the flick-knives. The justification for this decision is based on the traditional view in English law of 'freedom of contract', i.e. a party may choose with whom they wish to contract. To allow the shop window display to be classed as an offer would remove the shop owner's right to decide whether to contract with that particular customer or not. If the display was an offer, the customer could enter the shop and accept the offer and create a legally binding contract. The shop owner may not wish to sell to that customer for many reasons (e.g. age, attitude) but would not have the opportunity to decline the sale.

The principle of freedom of contract is in conflict with the criminal law, however. Under s20 of the Consumer Protection Act 1987, it is an offence to 'mislead' a consumer as to the price of goods. Most shop owners will not insist on their right not to sell the goods at the advertised price in order to maintain good relations with their customers *and* so there is no criminal offence under the 1987 Act. There is, therefore, an argument justifying a change to the rule about shop window displays being invitations to treat, on the basis that the rule is artificial and does not relate to the reality of commercial life.

What comprises a 'course of action' in an advertisement

The advertised promise in the case of *Carlill* v *Carbolic Smoke Ball Co.* (1893) appears to be an invitation to treat but was given the status of an offer by the court. The advertisement is asking the potential customer to take a course of action and something is promised at the end of that action. There is no clear definition as to what comprises a 'course of action' and what will convert an invitation to treat into an offer. For example, what if there had been no mention of the £1,000 on deposit – would the promise of £100 be enough for the advertisement to be classed an offer?

The *Carlill* decision created a wide definition as to which situations may be classed an offer. There are now more statutory and common law safeguards to protect innocent purchasers of faulty goods and/or services, so perhaps the case would be decided differently in modern times. Further, commerce and business have assimilated the principles of *Carlill*, and rarely will an advert now contain specific promise(s) that result in a genuine advert (or 'advertising 'puff') becoming an offer capable of acceptance.

The unfairness of the rules of offer and acceptance and the difficulties created by the 'postal rule'

An offer may be stated to be open for acceptance for a set period, the offeree may rely on that statement and yet the offeror may withdraw the offer within the stated period – *Routledge* v *Grant* (1828). It may be argued this is grossly unfair on the offeree. The law could be reformed to ensure that an offer, expressed to be open for a set period, must remain open for acceptance for that entire period. A breach of that provision by an offeror would lead to a claim by the offeree for damages and/or specific performance.

The courts claim the law on formation of contracts will consider what the parties intended (a 'subjective' approach). However, what the courts actually consider is what the 'reasonable' person would think of the facts (an 'objective' test). The objective test may result in unfairness as, for example, in *Felthouse* v *Bindley* (1863) (see p185) where an uncle (the offeror) and his nephew (the offeree) both wished for there to be a contract, and there was independent evidence to confirm this – the nephew had contacted the auctioneer holding the horse to remove the horse from the auction. However, the court held against the uncle and nephew as, from an objective viewpoint, there was no evidence of an acceptance from the nephew. This is, of course, arguable, as there was evidence of the nephew instructing the auctioneer to withdraw the horse from the auction.

The justification for this decision is that for the court to declare there to be a valid and legally enforceable contract there should be clear and identifiable evidence. For example, the offer has to be communicated (see Chapter 5, Topic 1: Offer) so why not the acceptance? Silence as a form of acceptance could create many problems, which is partly why the Unsolicited Goods and Services Act 1971 states that, for example, where goods are received without request there can be no contract unless the acceptance is communicated by the sender. This will be so even if the letter accompanying the unsolicited goods states that the receiver will be liable to pay for the goods unless they are returned within a certain period.

It should be noted that the need to communicate an acceptance may be waived (see the *Carlill* case) but the uncle did not waive this need – he merely stated that the nephew's silence would be acceptance, which it cannot be.

Unless the contract involves the purchase of a simple item (a newspaper) or service (a train ticket), most contracts involve some form of negotiation about the contractual terms. There is often a small distinction between a counter-offer and a request for information. The former terminates the offer, while the latter leaves the offer open for acceptance. It is unlikely that a party to negotiations (unless a commercial lawyer) would be able to draw such a fine distinction between the two, but the difference is crucial.

To create consistency, the law could be reformed so a counter-offer could have no affect on the existence of the original offer and negotiations would then continue, both parties knowing all previous offers (unless withdrawn) still existed. In a simple negotiation this may prove a fair result, but in a complicated negotiation confusion would occur. Under the present law, the parties terminate previous offers by making counter-offers, so there is only one offer in existence from one party at any one time. If all offers stayed open for acceptance, despite counter-offers, then a party could accept an offer that was made at the commencement of negotiations, which may be minutes, hours or even days beforehand. An accurate record of all offers would be required to ensure there was no misunderstanding over what was being accepted. This would be an impractical way to run commercial life in the UK so the current law seems the only alternative.

The postal rule has always created argument as to whether it is fair or not. The rule appears to be unfair on an offeror who may never receive the letter of acceptance, or receive it much later than expected. The offeror is a party to a legally binding contract without realising so. The offeror may have contracted with another party in the meantime, so the courts have to deal with three innocent parties and can make a decision that will only be satisfactory to two parties, or perhaps even just one party.

The postal rule is justified for two reasons. First, the offeree is entitled to expect the postal system to work efficiently and for the letter to arrive. Second, the offeror has the opportunity and power to protect him/herself in this situation. The offeror could, for example, state that the acceptance had to be received or must be by face-to-face communication, which would mean the postal rule could never apply. The postal rule therefore seems a fair compromise when balancing the interests of the offeror and offeree.

The *Entores* (1955), *Brinkibon* (1982) and *Mondial* (1995) cases indicate the courts' unwillingness to expand the postal rule to more modern methods of communication. This unwillingness may be due the courts' belief that an offeree should take reasonable steps to ensure the acceptance is received and that the postal rule is outdated in any event and should be restricted to the post. Clarification has been given that an offeree is entitled to assume the acceptance will be read within a reasonable time (for example, within office hours) and it is suggested this is a justifiable and fair rule.

2 Consideration

The current law on consideration can be critically evaluated in the following areas:

- that consideration must be sufficient but need not be adequate
- the fairness of certain rules of consideration
- the willingness of the court to be flexible when interpreting. consideration in certain areas but not in others.

That consideration must be sufficient but need not be adequate

A rule of consideration is that it must be sufficient. As decided in the *Nestlé* (1960) case, a chocolate wrapper is sufficient for consideration as it is real, tangible and has some value. However, in the view of a member of the public this would be seen as an irrational decision, as the chocolate wrapper has no value in the real world. The justification for this rule is the courts' willingness to validate an agreement made by parties to an agreement. If a party wishes to give something to another party and this is to form the basis of the agreement, then the court will always attempt to allow the agreement to exist and be enforceable. To do so, the consideration must have some value, and chocolate wrappers do represent value to Nestlé as evidence of their product being purchased.

The fairness of certain rules of consideration

A party to a contract may have made a bad bargain but the court will not be concerned to protect the party who has made that bad decision. If a party chooses to make a bad bargain (provided there is no illegality involved – for example, a misrepresentation) then that is the party's choice and risk. The court, rightly so, will not act as a mediator or arbitrator to decide what a *fair* consideration could or should have been. The decision in *Thomas* v *Thomas* (1842) is a fair decision as it supports the agreement made between the parties (the subjective test) and is not concerned with whether a reasonable person (the objective test) would see the consideration as a *fair* amount or not.

The willingness of the court to be flexible when interpreting consideration in certain areas but not in others

Re McArdle (1951) confirmed that promising to pay for something that has already occurred is not good consideration (known as 'past consideration is not valid consideration'). In that case, certain members of the family promised to contribute to work already completed by other members of the family.

Although this rule may seem unfair (allowing a party to break a promise), there is logic in the decision as to enforce the promise would be to validate an agreement that does not have simultaneous consideration from both parties. A contract is very important and may impose serious obligations on a party. To allow a contract to exist when there are no simultaneous promises of consideration would 'open the floodgates' to too many inappropriate claims.

Further, an exception does exist (see *Lampleigh* v *Braithwaite* (1615)) when, under certain conditions, past consideration will be valid consideration. This exception is sufficient to cover any possible unfairness in the 'past consideration' rule.

In *Stilk* v *Myrick* (1809) the crew members did not receive the promised extra payment as they were only carrying out an existing duty. Despite the captain breaking his promise there is sense and fairness in this decision, as there was an implied threat from the crew that if the captain did not promise the extra payment the remaining crew members would all desert. In *Williams* v *Roffey* (1990) there was no such pressure and, in fact, it was the defendant builder who offered the extra payment to the claimant roofer.

The decision in *Williams* v *Roffey* (1990) is to be welcomed, as it shows the court is able to review the true realities of the situation and find consideration where previously it may have been ignored. The court is now not limited to looking just to the consideration within the contract, but may now also consider factors outside the contract (e.g. the benefit to the builder of not being sued by the developer).

Again, as with promissory estoppel, the court is not keen to extend the principle from *Williams* v *Roffey* (1990) to other cases (again, see *Re Selectmove* (1995)).

If one party to an existing contract makes a promise to vary the contract, but the other party provides no consideration for that promise, then there can be no alteration. This does not seem fair, as a party is being allowed in law to break a promise, which may seem immoral (but is consistent with the decision in *Re McArdle* (1951) (above)). The case of *Central London Property Trust Ltd* v *High Trees Ltd* (1947) attempts to take a moral view by allowing the promise to be enforceable despite the lack of reciprocal consideration (called 'promissory estoppel').

Lord Denning, who stated this principle in *Central London Property Trust Ltd* v *High Trees Ltd* (1947), believed the rule should apply to all contractual situations. In effect, he was saying that consideration was not always a necessity for a valid contract. There is a conflict here between morality (breaking a promise) and the strict rule of law (consideration is required for a valid contract).

The courts are not keen to extend the principle of promissory estoppel and it will certainly not apply to cases based on pure debt (*Re Selectmove* (1995)).

3 Privity

The current law on privity in contract can be critically evaluated in that the 1999 Act, although a welcome addition to the law on privity, may have been unnecessary and may be non-effective in commercial situations.

The original rule was that a person who did not provide consideration to a contract could not enforce it, as they were not a party to that contract (see *Tweddle* v *Atkinson* (1861)). The decision in this case is, arguably, unfair on both the bride and bridegroom. The 1999 Act attempted to make this aspect of contractual law fairer by allowing third parties to the contract to enforce the contract in certain circumstances.

However, the 1999 Act is open to criticism. First, the parties to the contract may specifically exclude the application of the 1999 Act. Potentially, a carefully drafted contract will not allow a third party to obtain the benefit of the contract, so the law pre-*Tweddle* will apply. Second, it is believed that the majority of commercial contracts in the UK contain such an exclusion. Third, it could be argued the law was developing to allow third parties to enforce contract where necessary and/or appropriate. The exceptions referred to in Chapter 5, Topic 4: Privity of contract, together with the decision in *Jackson* v *Horizon Holidays Ltd* (1975) would, arguably, cover any situation where a third party may wish to enforce a contract against one of the contractual parties.

The 1999 Act does not affect the common law rule that a contract cannot impose liabilities on a third party. This rule seems appropriate, as it does not appear fair to impose contractual obligations on a person who is not a party to the contract and who has not given consent to that imposition.

4 Intention to create legal relations

The current law on intention to create legal relations can be critically evaluated in the following areas:

- the overlap between the two presumptions
- the conflicting case law
- whether this factor is required for a valid contract.

The overlap between the two presumptions

The two presumptions created by the courts have proved helpful when deciding if an agreement has legal validity or not. However, the court will always consider all the circumstances surrounding the case and, particularly in respect of social and domestic arrangements, the final decision will not always be certain. The case of *Jones* v *Padavatton* (1969) divided the Court of Appeal as to the existence of legal intent.

The conflicting case law

Sometimes, there may be different results in similar cases. This can be seen in the cases of **Hardwick v Johnson (1978)** and **Ellis v Chief Adjudication Officer (1998)**.

In *Hardwick* v *Johnson* (1978) there was legal intent in the contract between a mother who purchased a house as the home for her son and daughter-in-law on condition they paid her £7 per week to clear the purchase price. In comparison, there was no legal intent in *Ellis* v *Chief Adjudication Officer* (1998) when a mother gifted a flat to her daughter on condition the daughter cared for the mother.

These cases show the fine difference as to whether an enforceable contract exists or not. The presumption against legal intent for social and domestic arrangements is understandable, but by considering the surrounding circumstances the courts will, inevitably, reach inconsistent decisions. As a basis for precedent and an indication for future decisions, the cases are of little use.

In a business or commercial setting, there can still be uncertainty as to whether there is legal intent or not. In *Esso Petroleum Ltd* v *Customs and Excise* (1976) a minority of the House of Lords felt the offer of a gift of a free coin should *not* be regarded as a business matter. The majority

Key cases

Hardwick v Johnson (1978): legal intent was held to exist in the agreement between a mother and her son and daughter-in-law in relation to a house for occupation.

Ellis v Chief Adjudication Officer (1998): there was no legal intent between a mother and daughter in relation to a gifted flat.

considered that the context of the offer of the free coin was enough to allow the presumption for legal intent to remain. The situation of legal intent is not clear even in a commercial situation.

It could be argued that by taking the case to court, this would be evidence of at least one party's view that legal intent exists. This would not be conclusive evidence either way, however. On the contrary, there are certain contracts made in a commercial setting when neither party would consider taking the dispute to court (for example, a missed appointment at a hairdressing salon). The taking, or non-taking, of legal action is, of itself, little assistance in deciding the question of legal intent.

Whether this factor is required for a valid contract

There is an argument that there should be no need to prove legal intent. Offer, acceptance and consideration are the foundations on which a contract is made. If there are these three elements and *no* clear statement that the agreement is *not* to be legally binding, then it should be a valid contract.

This principle could be linked in with an objective test as to the intention of the parties. Such a test would probably find most social and domestic arrangements not legally enforceable because the reasonable person would not find them so. This would allow the two 'presumptions' to be set aside, and legal intent as an element of contract in itself to be ignored.

5 Implied terms aimed at consumer protection

There is overlap with the evaluation of remedies that can usefully be considered when looking at this topic.

There are three types of contractual term:

- condition: breach of which allows the claimant to repudiate the contract and/or claim damages
- warranty: breach of which only allows the claimant to claim damages
- innominate: breach of which may permit repudiation, depending on the seriousness of the consequences of the breach.

These lead to confusion and unfairness, as will be seen below.

Implied conditions in respect of goods

The implied conditions in respect of goods under the 1979 and 1982 Acts allow the consumer to reject the goods and/or claim damages. This appears to be an effective and powerful remedy. However, the right in non-consumer sales is restricted under s15(A) of the 1979 Act to those cases where rejection is reasonable. This compromise seems to create a fair and justifiable system for dealing with dissatisfied customers whether they are consumers or businesses.

The right to reject for defective goods

The right to reject defective goods is an important and powerful remedy for a consumer and, to a lesser extent, for a business. However, it may be argued that the party in default is prejudiced. Should the seller not be allowed a reasonable opportunity (as of right) to replace or repair the defective goods? This is certainly arguable if the defect is of a minor nature and is easily and quickly repairable. However, is a change in the law actually required, as most consumers would expect and request a repair in any event? For businesses, the right to reject is now restricted so the opportunity to repair and/or offer compensation is available to the seller.

Losing the right to repudiate the contract

An area of confusion for both sellers and buyers is when the right to repudiate the contract, and therefore the right to reject the goods, is lost. Section 11(4) of the 1979 Act states the right is lost when the buyer has 'accepted' the goods. The law was altered in the buyer's favour in 1994. The *Bernstein* (1987) case brought matters to a head, and the court will now take a more lenient view of when goods have been accepted and the right to reject is lost. A case showing the development of the law in this respect is *Truk (UK) Ltd* v *Tokmakidis GmbH* (2000), when the owner of a Ford chassis contracted with Truk that Truk would fit appropriate lifting equipment. The lift was installed and was not checked for six months, when the defect in installation was discovered. The owner claimed a breach of condition, repudiated the contract and rejected the goods. The court held the owner was entitled to do so.

The law of repudiation (including the right to reject) has now been made clearer and is certainly more generous to the purchaser than it previously was. This development is to be welcomed for consumers in general.

However, the detailed and overlapping rights and remedies available to both consumers and businesses in receipt of defective goods are confusing. It is recommended that there should be a consolidation and simplification of these matters, which would benefit all those involved in the sale and transfer of ownership of goods.

It should also be noted that there is concern that although there is more consumer protection than ever, members of the public are unaware of their basic rights – for example, under the implied terms of the 1979 and 1982 Acts. Further, consumers are either unwilling or financially unable to access good legal advice to pursue valid claims.

Finally, the implied terms under ss13 and 14 of the 1982 Act are not automatically conditions, as for the implied terms in the Sale of Goods Act 1979, and are less effective. Further, they can even be excluded from a consumer contract if it is reasonable to do so – depriving consumers of protection.

6 Control of exclusion and limitation clauses

We will now consider how exclusion and limitation clauses are controlled by both common law and statute.

Common law controls

The courts have attempted to control the creation of exclusion and limitation clauses by the rules of incorporation, whether by the signing of a contract, by the display of a prominent notice stating the clause, or by the parties having had a previous course of dealing. These rules seem to work well and protect the unwary, whether a consumer or business. However, an exclusion or limitation clause may still be created if, for example, notice was given in the required form but the claimant did not read the relevant document or notice.

It is suggested that English law should include, from the principles of European contract law, a duty on *all* contracting parties to act 'in accordance with good faith and fair dealing', and that such a duty could *never* be excluded or limited.

Statutory controls

The Law Commission, in its report on Unfair Terms in Contracts (LC No 298; SLC No 199), included a draft Bill to consolidate the law currently in force under UCTA and UTCCR. The report set out various criticisms of the current law, with recommendations for reform. The summary of the report is only four pages, is very readable and gives more detail on the points below.

Criticisms in the report include:

- UCTA and UTCCR contain inconsistent and overlapping provisions, using different language and concepts to produce similar but not identical results. UCTA only covers exclusion and limitation clauses, while UTCCR apply to all terms but only for consumer contracts. Under UCTA, some terms are automatically invalid while under UTCCR no term is automatically unfair.
- UCTA is written in a particularly dense style, which even specialist lawyers find difficult to follow.
- UTCCR use European concepts that are unfamiliar to English lawyers.
- UTCCR allow the Office of Fair Trading (OFT) to go to court to clarify a term, and this is very helpful for consumers and businesses, but this power is rarely exercised.

To resolve this there are a number of proposals. These include:

- A new Unfair Contract Terms Act to replace UCTA and UTCCR.
- To maintain that terms excluding basic matters of quality, and fitness of goods are invalid.
- In claims brought by consumers the burden of proof lies on the business to show the term was fair; this is justified as the business will have greater resources than the consumer.
- The OFT will have additional powers to demand, for example, that a sign in a store car park saying 'no liability is accepted for injury' is taken down.

7 Misrepresentation

Making an untrue statement can be a misrepresentation, but remaining silent will only be a misrepresentation in limited circumstances.

General principle

Misrepresentation imposes a duty on a representor not to tell untruths, but does not impose a duty to tell the truth, i.e. it is a duty of a negative nature. In the scenario in Chapter 7: Vitiating factors, Tristan had a duty not to tell an untruth to Adam because he had been asked a specific question about reliability and service history. If Adam had never asked about these matters Tristan is under no duty to tell the truth.

There are some exceptions to this rule of silence not being a misrepresentation, but could it not be argued that all parties negotiating should have a duty to disclose all relevant matters to the other – whether detrimental to that party's bargaining position or not.

There is a justification for this rule about silence. The classical view of the English law of contract is that of 'freedom of contract'. This means that parties who wish to negotiate and contract with each other should be left alone by the court and allowed to make whatever agreement they wish. The court should not intervene just because one party is poor at negotiation and makes a bad bargain. The court's view is that if the information not disclosed was of such importance, then the party should have asked about it. If the truth followed, then the representee could

Study tip

Misrepresentation may be incorporated into an examination question as appropriate, but will **not** be the specific focus of any evaluation question.

decide whether to proceed with the contract and, if an untruth followed, the representee would have a claim for misrepresentation.

This classical view of contract law should be compared to the law in other countries. For example, in the French Civil Code there is a positive obligation of 'good faith and fair dealing' when following a contractual term. Should not the English courts take a view that honest and unselfish behaviour should be expected from all parties both during negotiations and after negotiations are completed? During negotiations, one party may not be asked about a fact relating to the contract and, currently, there are only limited circumstances when silence by that party will be a misrepresentation.

Distinction between types of misrepresentation

In the scenario given in Chapter 7: Vitiating factors, Tristan may have known the moped was unreliable and there was an incomplete service history. Tristan would have intentionally made an untrue statement of fact, and this would be classed as fraudulent misrepresentation. It is often difficult to ascertain if a representor has intentionally lied, and the claimant may have evidential problems in this respect. From the information provided in the scenario, it would be unlikely Adam would succeed in such a claim.

Negligent misrepresentation exists in two forms:

1 The common law claim based on *Hedley Byrne & Co. Ltd* v *Heller & Partners Ltd* (1964)

2 The Misrepresentation Act 1967.

To succeed under the common law claim, Adam must prove there was a 'special relationship' and 'proximity' between him and Tristan. Probably, the fact that they were negotiating a contract between them would be enough to satisfy these two conditions. However, if Adam fails to prove both conditions his claim for negligent misrepresentation under *Hedley Byrne* would fail, even if the statement were untrue. Adam would have to prove that Tristan was careless as to the truth of the statement, i.e. that Tristan did not act as the reasonable person would have done in those circumstances.

The 1967 Act does not require a 'special relationship' or 'proximity' between the parties, and Adam has only to prove that Tristan made an untrue statement to him. The burden of proof then shifts from Adam to Tristan, who is liable 'unless he proves that he had reasonable ground to believe, and did believe up to the time the contract was made, that the facts represented were true'. Obviously, this is more likely to prove successful for Adam than the common law claim.

Finally, Tristan may have believed his statements to be true and had reasonable grounds for that belief. Adam would be able to succeed in a claim for innocent misrepresentation, but his remedies would be limited.

The remedies available for a misrepresentation indicate that the court is taking a moral view on the actions of the representor. If the representor has made a fraudulent misrepresentation (i.e. has lied about a fact to the claimant), then the claimant is entitled to claim damages without the limiting rule of reasonable foreseeability. One purpose of this rule is to make the award of damages a fair amount, and to limit the defendant from potentially unlimited liability. It is generally considered that the purpose of damages in civil law is to compensate the victim for losses incurred, and it is not the purpose of damages to punish the defendant – that is regarded as the responsibility of a criminal court when passing sentence.

By allowing a successful claim under fraudulent misrepresentation, to ignore the rule of reasonable foreseeability is drifting into the area of punishment. This criticism has another factor, in that a claim for negligent misrepresentation under the 1967 Act does not specify whether the reasonable foreseeability rule applies to a successful claim. Judicial decisions are unclear, but indicate that the rule does not apply. As a result, a representor who has been careless will be ordered to pay compensation on the same basis as a representor who has lied – which seems inequitable.

Remedies for misrepresentation

There are two possible remedies for a misrepresentation: rescission and damages.

Rescission means to restore the parties to their original position before the contract. If Adam were successful in this claim, he would return the moped to Tristan and in return receive the price he paid.

Damages under misrepresentation are unusual for a claim relating to a contractual situation. Contractual damages are usually based on the principle of compensating the claimant by putting him, financially, in the position he would have been in had the contract been properly completed. Damages under misrepresentation, however, are based on tort on the principle of compensating the claimant by returning him, financially, to the position held before the misrepresentation was made.

Rescission and/or damages are available for fraudulent misrepresentation and negligent misrepresentation (both common law and under the 1967 Act). However, for innocent misrepresentation damages will be awarded in lieu of rescission if it is equitable to do so according to s2(2) of the 1967 Act.

In the scenario if the claim were for fraudulent misrepresentation or negligent misrepresentation under the 1967 Act, Adam would be able to claim for losses even if not reasonably foreseeable to Tristan, e.g. for the cost of transport to and from Adam's new job until a replacement moped is purchased.

The test of foreseeability does apply to damages awarded under common law negligent misrepresentation and innocent misrepresentation.

Under *Hedley Byrne* (1964) liability is difficult to prove, as there are various requirements to be met. The 1967 Act made the law easier for claimants of a negligent misrepresentation, as once the representee has proved the statement was untrue the burden of proof is transferred to the representor, who must prove he had reasonable grounds for making the statement. This reverses the traditional rule that in a civil claim it is for the claimant to prove the case and losses on the balance of probabilities, and that the defendant does not have to prove anything. The same principle applies in criminal cases, as the prosecution must prove the case beyond reasonable doubt (a higher standard than for civil cases). There seems no justification for the 1967 Act reversing this traditional rule for negligent misrepresentation. One argument may be that as society now recognises consumers should have protection when making a contract, anyone who misleads another into making such a contract should be held responsible as the representor has superior knowledge and is abusing his position.

In *Bissett* v *Wilkinson* (1927) the representor was not liable for stating that he believed the land could graze 2,000 sheep. It could be argued this decision is unfair and the definition of misrepresentation should be altered to include statements of opinion as well as fact. The justification for this reform would be that if a representor is willing to make a comment to encourage a party to enter a contract, then the representor should be liable for that comment if it proves to be untrue. It is sometimes difficult to differentiate between an opinion and a fact, which may lead to unfairness for the representee. For example, in the scenario Tristan could argue that his statement that the moped was reliable was his opinion and not a fact. How would the court decide this? Tristan's standards may be different to those of Adam, so whose definition of 'reliability' would the court use? Would it not be fairer that all statements, whether of fact or opinion, are caught by misrepresentation? A problem with this suggestion is that although the statement would now be classed as a misrepresentation Tristan could still argue the statement to be true as, under his standards, the moped was reliable.

Rescission (to put the parties in their pre-contractual positions) is a fair remedy, but should still be allowed even when the innocent party has delayed in bringing the claim. In the case of *Leaf* v *International Galleries* (1950) the claim for rescission failed, as the innocent party only discovered the misrepresentation five years after the contract. The delay in bringing the claim was not the fault of the representee, so why should this delay prejudice the claim of the representee? One argument for the rule of delay is that for the court to hold a contract as void after a five-year delay would be unfair (even to a wrong-doer) as all parties are entitled to presume a contract is certain after a reasonable period of time. Of course, the representee will still be liable for damages. However, rescission is lost if the representee has affirmed the contract. In the case of *Long* v *Lloyd* (1958) the representee was penalised by returning the lorry for repair. This appears to be unfair, as what difference has this made to the representor? If the representee chooses to allow the representor at least one chance to remedy the problem, why should the representee then lose the opportunity to claim rescission?

There are some positive points to raise about the law of misrepresentation. For example, the three types misrepresentation now cover all possible eventualities in relation to the making of an untrue statement by a representor, i.e. lying, carelessness or innocence. There are two remedies usually available, and rescission is a very satisfactory result for a representee as they are restored to their original pre-contractual position. The current definition of misrepresentation covers most situations where a claim should be allowed and the 1967 Act allows a claim for rescission to be made, even if the misrepresentation has become a term of the contract.

8 Remedies

The following remedies will be evaluated in turn:

- damages
- injunction
- specific performance
- remedies against goods.

Damages

English courts have decided that the purpose of contractual damages is:

> '… that where a party sustains a loss by reason of a breach of contract, he is, so far as money can do it, to be placed in the same situation, with respect to damages, as if the contract had been performed' (Parke B in *Robinson* v *Harman* (1848))

This basic principle supports the freedom of contract values on which our commercial world is based, i.e. the profit on a contract is as good as earned when the contract is made. It is not acceptable to have that expectation of profit disrupted by a breach of the contract. The court has developed principles to assist in the calculation of contractual damages, and these need review.

The remoteness of damage

In *Hadley* v *Baxendale* (1854) it was confirmed that the innocent party's claim in respect of losses caused by the defendant's breach would be limited to those that are not too remote. This means that if the innocent party would have made an exceptional gain if the contract had been performed, or made an exceptional loss due to a breach of contract, the party at fault is not liable.

This appears unfair, as the defendant's breach has caused the victim's loss. The House of Lords confirmed in *The Heron* (1969) that the party at fault should not be liable for consequential losses that are merely possible or pretty unlikely. The justification for this is that without the remoteness rule, parties in the commercial world would be less inclined to enter contracts, and that even if they did the chance of obtaining adequate insurance to cover the risk of breach would either not be unavailable or would be unaffordable.

The basis of assessment of damages

The two main bases for assessment of damages cover most of the situations where a claim for damages is made. As a general rule, the claimant can choose whether to claim on loss of expectation (loss of bargain) or on reliance. Provided the claimant avoids overlapping claims, there is no reason why a claim for both cannot be made.

Reliance loss allows the court to award damages in an amount that may more accurately reflect the claimant's losses than an award based on loss of expectation – see *Anglia Television Ltd* v *Reed* (1972).

The quantification of damages

The difficulty faced by the court when attempting to quantify a victim's claim was highlighted in the *Ruxley Electronics and Construction* v *Forsyth* (1996) case. There was no doubt the builder had breached the contract by building a swimming pool with the incorrect depth, and therefore Mr Forsyth was entitled to damages. The difficulty was the quantification of those damages. Should the calculation be based on the cost of cure (£21,560 being more than the original contract price) or loss of market value (nil as the property suffered no loss in value). The House of Lords used its discretion and made the award of £2,500 based on loss of amenity, which is widely seen as the sensible decision.

However, the Court of Appeal had ordered damages in the full sum of £21,650. This shows the risks involved in allowing the court to make an award based on its discretion. If the parties had not been able to fund the appeal to the House of Lords, the Court of Appeal's decision would be the precedent to be followed today. This shows how arbitrary and random the courts' decisions may be, which creates uncertainty in the English legal system.

Further, with a few exceptions, no award is made for mental distress and upset following a breach of contract. In many cases, the worry of the consequences of a breach of a commercial contract may be devastating to an innocent party, especially if that party is a small business that may fail due to the breach.

Further, damages may be awarded in due course but are unlikely to take account of loss of business, which may be crucial to the claimant. Damages do not cover all losses and harm caused by a breach. The cost and time required to achieve a successful outcome in court is exhausting and there is no guarantee that the defendant will be able to pay the damages awarded, especially if there is no insurance cover.

Finally, the Law Commission considered the question of damages when the party in default profited from the breach in its report *Aggravated, Exemplary and Restitutionary Damages* (1997). The Commission concluded it was preferable for the court to apply the law, using its discretion where appropriate, rather than for Parliament to set out the law. The courts are therefore trusted to make awards of damages by applying the rules set out in this chapter and by using discretion despite the risks (as set out in the discussion of the *Ruxley* (1996) case).

Injunction

If appropriate, the court may order a party in breach of contract *not* to do something. There is no 'balance of convenience' test between the parties, which there would be if the injunction were to order a party *to do* something.

The making of an injunction will be rare because, as for specific performance, the court will always consider damages as the first alternative. An injunction may be an appropriate remedy if the claimant wishes the party at fault not to carry out a certain act when damages would not be a satisfactory remedy. In some situations, the court may award the claimant an injunction ordering the defendant *to do* something. However, this is unusual.

The court treats the breach of an injunction very seriously, as it is a contempt of court. The final sanction for breach of an injunction is a custodial sentence. The impact and effect of an injunction may well provide the claimant with a satisfactory resolution to the dispute.

Specific performance

There will be few situations when specific performance is required or is appropriate, but as a remedy it does allow the court to achieve justice in a case.

As explained, specific performance covers those situations where damages are either inadequate or inappropriate. This allows the court to award the claimant a remedy or remedies that adequately covers the claimant's needs and requirements, and does not allow the defendant to escape from responsibility for the breach.

For example, in *Beswick* v *Beswick* (1968) a nephew purchased his uncle's coal merchant's business and, as part of the contract, agreed to pay his uncle £6.50 per week until he died and then pay his aunt £5 per week if she survived her husband. After his uncle's death, the nephew refused to pay his aunt. She could not sue him personally, as she was not a party to the contract, but sued him in her capacity as trustee of the uncle's estate. The estate's claim was for nominal damages (it made little difference to the estate if his widow received the money or not) but the Court of Appeal awarded specific performance of the contract. This would ensure the aunt would receive her full entitlement.

If severe hardship would be caused by the order of specific performance then it is unlikely to be granted, even if the hardship arises after the contract is made. In the case of *Patel* v *Ali* (1984) there was a four-year delay after the making of the contract in the completion of the sale of a house, through no one's fault. The purchaser wanted specific performance rather than damages. However, during the delay the seller's wife had become disabled, and the sale would cause her serious hardship as she would lose her network of help, so specific performance was not ordered.

Remedies against goods

There are three types of contractual term:

1 condition: breach of which allows the claimant to repudiate the contract and/or claim damages
2 warranty: breach of which only allows the claimant to claim damages
3 innominate: breach of which may permit repudiation, depending on the seriousness of the consequences of the breach.

The critical analysis of contractual remedies overlaps with the critical analysis of the implied terms aimed at consumer protection. For the purpose of evaluating remedies, reference should be made to the sections 'Implied conditions in respect of goods', 'The right to reject for defective goods' and 'Losing the right to repudiate the contract', set out on pages 157–158.

Conclusion

With all the areas of contract law that need criticism, it should also be noted that there are positive aspects as well as negative aspects of that criticism. You should be aware of that in constructing your essay for the part (c) question in the exam. You should also note that any question on evaluation of contract law will specify which topic or topics are to be evaluated.

You should now be able to:

■ evaluate aspects of the law of contract

■ understand proposals for reform of those aspects.

Activities

1 Create a table of the areas of contract law subject to critical analysis and evaluation, listing positive and negative criticisms for each area.

2 Plan an essay based on evaluating each of the areas that you have listed above.

UNIT
4A Criminal law
(offences against property)
Introduction

Chapters in this unit:

10 Theft

11 Robbery, blackmail, burglary and criminal damage

12 Fraud and making off without payment

13 Defences

Unit 4 gives you a choice between the study of criminal law and the law of tort. The unit constitutes 50 per cent of the overall marks for the A2 section of the qualification, and 25 per cent of the overall marks for the A Level qualification. The Unit 4 examination is of 2 hours' duration. You must answer one question on criminal law or tort, and write an essay for the Concepts of law unit. The first part of the examination paper will include both criminal law and tort questions: Questions 1 and 2 are on criminal law and Questions 3 and 4 are on tort. You will choose one question to answer, from either criminal law or tort. Each question is divided into two parts, both of which must be answered. These questions are similar in style and expectation to those in parts (a) and (b) of Unit 3. There are no questions involving critical evaluation of the substantive law studied in Unit 4, as critical evaluation forms the basis of the separate essay on concepts of law.

Each question on criminal law is therefore worth 50 marks. Each part is worth 25 marks. These two parts will be a test of your ability to select and apply the law to the given scenario.

All questions require essay-style answers. In parts (a) and (b), you should include: correct identification of the issues raised by the question; sound explanation of each of the points; and clear application of the law to the facts disclosed. This may involve some consideration of alternatives where the law lacks clarity in its application to the scenario. Study tips are provided throughout each topic.

Unit 4A comprises four chapters:

10 Theft: concerned with the explanation of the law with respect to theft.

11 Robbery, blackmail, burglary and criminal damage: explains the law on robbery, blackmail, burglary and criminal damage.

12 Fraud and making off without payment: considers the law on fraud and making off without payment.

13 Defences: concerned with the defences to the offences dealt with in Chapters 10–13.

10 Theft

In this topic, you will learn how to:

- state the definition of theft
- explain the *actus reus* of theft
- explain cases that illustrate the *actus reus* of theft
- apply the rules to a given situation.

Key terms

Theft: dishonest appropriation of property belonging to another with the intention of permanently depriving the other of it.

1 Definition and *actus reus* of theft

Introduction

Theft is one of the most commonly understood crimes. Everybody recognises stealing as theft, and would include shoplifting as one of the examples of theft. However, there are other situations that may be theft, even though the crime is not always obviously committed. Compare the situation between finding a 10p piece on the pavement, a £20 note, and a diamond ring. When, and in what situations, would you consider each finding to be theft? Or is none of them theft? Is it theft to keep additional goods sent to you by mistake by a supplier? Can you steal your own property?

The definition of theft

Theft is defined in the Theft Act 1968, s1:

1 A person is guilty of theft if he dishonestly appropriates property belonging to another with the intention of permanently depriving the other of it; and 'thief' and 'steal' shall be construed accordingly.

2 It is immaterial whether the appropriation is made with a view to gain, or is made for the thief's own benefit.

3 The five following sections of this Act shall have effect as regards the interpretation and operation of this section (and, except as otherwise provided by this Act, shall apply only for purposes of this section).

There are five things to be proved to secure a conviction of theft: three of these form the *actus reus* of the offence, and two the *mens rea*. They are summarised in the table below.

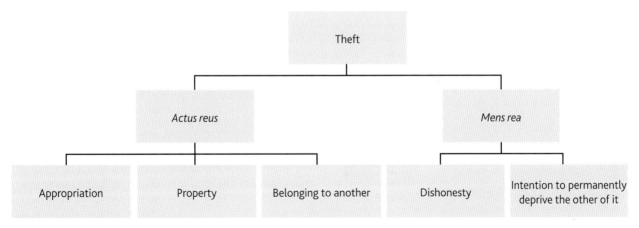

Elements of the offence of theft

Actus reus

Element 1: Appropriation

Appropriation is defined in s3 of the Theft Act 1968 as follows:

> 1 Any assumption by a person of the rights of an owner amounts to an appropriation, and this includes, where he has come by the property (innocently or not) without stealing it, any later assumption of a right to it by keeping or dealing with it as owner.
>
> 2 Where property or a right or interest in property is, or purports to be, transferred for value to a person acting in good faith, no later assumption by him of rights which he believed himself to be acquiring shall, by reason of any defect in the transferor's title, amount to theft of the property.

There are therefore a number of aspects of appropriation that need to be investigated.

Appropriation means assuming the rights of the owner of the property. In many cases of theft this will amount to taking property from the owner, however appropriation has a much wider meaning and includes any act where the defendant has done something to the property that only the owner can do. A person who owns property can do anything he likes with it (subject to the general law). For example, he can lend it to someone else, hire it to someone else, damage or destroy it. It is not necessary that all the rights of the owner need to be assumed, it is sufficient for appropriation if any of the rights are assumed. When a person has lent or hired something to someone, they retain the right of ownership. That right can therefore be the subject of theft by the person to whom the thing was lent. Appropriation can therefore be interpreted to include any situation where the defendant treats the goods as his own.

The case that confirms that a range of activities can amount to appropriation is **Morris (1984)**. In that case, the defendant dishonestly switched the labels on goods in a supermarket so as to show lower prices. He then acquired the goods by paying only the lower price at the checkout – this was his intention. The switching of the labels and placing the goods in the basket or trolley forms the appropriation.

The issue as to whether there can be appropriation when the owner has given consent was raised in the case of **Lawrence (1972)**. In that case, Lawrence was a taxi driver. A foreign student got in his taxi and asked to be taken to a hotel. The real fare was quite small. The student had little spoken English and offered a bank note to pay for the trip. Lawrence said that it was not enough. The student then offered Lawrence his wallet, and indicated he should take the right amount. Lawrence took money out of the wallet, but about 20 times as much as the fare justified. Lawrence's defence was that he had not appropriated any money, within the terms of the Act. He claimed that although he may have been dishonest, there was no appropriation. However, Lawrence was guilty of theft as the court decided that the appropriation need not be without the consent of the owner. This is clearly consistent with other cases and a sensible approach, even though there are alternative offences available under the Fraud Act 2006.

Another case on this point is **Gomez (1993)**. In that case, the defendant was an assistant manager at an electrical store. His accomplice asked to be supplied with £16,000 worth of goods, using two worthless cheques. The defendant knew the cheques were worthless but asked the manager to authorise the sale. The manager asked the defendant to contact the bank about the cheques, which the defendant pretended to do. The defendant then lied to the manager that the cheques were valid. The cheques were later returned by the bank unpaid.

Key terms

Appropriation: any assumption by a person of the rights of the owner.

Property: includes money and all other property, subject to the later exceptions in the Theft Act 1968.

Key cases

Morris (1984): appropriation of goods includes a variety of activities, including switching labels on goods in a supermarket.

Lawrence (1972): appropriation can take place even where the property has been handed over with the consent of the owner; there is often a link between the appropriation and the fact that it is done dishonestly.

Gomez (1993): issue of consent occurred here in relation to releasing goods against worthless cheques; it was decided that there can be an appropriation even if the goods are released with the owner's consent.

Study tip

There is often an overlap between theft and fraud in these situations. A case such as *Morris* (1984) can be considered to include a false representation as to the price to be paid for the goods under s2 of the Fraud Act 2006. You should look out for this overlap and discuss it in your answers.

The defendant was convicted of theft, but there was an appeal on the grounds that there had been no 'appropriation' of the goods because the manager had willingly released them. (This would not have been a problem if the defendant had been charged with a deception offence under what is now the Fraud Act 2006).

The House of Lords had to decide on the question as to whether an appropriation can take place even if the owner appears to have consented. It was decided that the decision in *Lawrence* was correct and that there could be appropriation with consent and the defendant's conviction for theft was reinstated. Although the consent had been obtained by fraud in the case of *Gomez*, the decision has wider implications and extends the scope of the meaning of appropriation. It now means that there may be an appropriation by carrying out any act to the property, with or without the owner's permission.

A twist on the idea of consent arose in the case of **Hinks (1998)**. In this case, Hinks, a single mother, became very friendly with Mr Dolphin, a naïve, gullible, middle-aged man of low intelligence, a month after his father died. She effectively took over the running of his life. He withdrew sums of £300 (the maximum permissible under the rules for his account), almost every day. On each occasion, he was accompanied by Hinks, and she placed the money in her account. After seven months, £60,000 had been moved out of his account and into her account. This was almost all of his money that he had inherited from his father. The House of Lords upheld Hinks's conviction for theft, even though all transactions appeared to be a voluntary gift. The House of Lords stated that the issue of consent was related to dishonesty rather than appropriation.

> **Key cases**
>
> **Hinks (1998):** appropriation can take place even where there is a voluntary gift.

Element 2: Property

The Theft Act 1968 s4 deals with property. The general principle is set out in s4(1) as:

> 1 'Property' includes money and all other property, real or personal, including things in action and other intangible property.

Real property includes land and buildings (but there are limitations when it can be stolen under s4 (2)), and personal property includes all moveable items such as cars, handbags, jewellery and mobile phones. Intangible property does not exist in a physical sense and a thing in action is a right that can be enforced against another person. An example is the owning of shares in a company where the owner of the shares has the right to sell them. Further examples include copyrights and trademarks.

The Act itself, in s4, goes on to include some further explanation and exceptions. These are set out in s4(2), (3) and (4) as follows:

> 2 A person cannot steal land, or things forming part of land and severed from it by him or by his directions, except in the following cases, that is to say –
>
> a when he is a trustee or personal representative, or is authorised by power of attorney, or as liquidator of a company, or otherwise, to sell or dispose of land belonging to another, and he appropriates the land or anything forming part of it by dealing with it in breach of the confidence reposed in him; or
>
> b when he is not in possession of the land and appropriates anything forming part of the land by severing it or causing it to be severed, or after it has been severed; or

c when, being in possession of the land under a tenancy, he appropriates the whole or part of any fixture or structure let to be used with the land. For purposes of this subsection, 'land' does not include incorporeal hereditaments; 'tenancy' means a tenancy for years or less period and includes an agreement for such a tenancy, but a person who, after the end of a tenancy, remains in possession as statutory tenant or otherwise is to be treated as having possession under the tenancy, and 'let' shall be construed accordingly.

This means, subject to exceptions, that you cannot steal land or part of it – such as the soil, rocks, plants or buildings. The first exception occurs in s(2)(a): a person can commit theft of land where he has the ability to transfer the ownership (or other rights over land) to another person and the land or rights being transferred are not his to transfer. This can occur where he transfers the land in a way that he is not expressly authorised to do. The Act refers to a range of situations where this can occur but, using the *ejusdem generis* rule of statutory interpretation, the words 'or otherwise' means the list is not exclusive. An example of this occurs where I am the trustee of a house and other property; this could arise under a will, particularly where the dead person's assets are left to children under the age of 18 or to a very old and infirm person. As trustee I would manage the assets, including the house (land). I might well have the right to sell the house, but would have to do so for the benefit of the children or old person. If I were to sell it for a very low price to my wife, or keep some of the sale money for myself, it could form the basis of the offence of theft. Equally, it could be theft if I lived in the house without paying any rent, although there is more likely to be an offence under the Fraud Act 2006.

The exception in s(2)(b) means that a person can commit theft of things forming part of the land that the owner of the land has not allowed the thief to possess. This, therefore, includes soil, rocks, gravel, buildings (or part of the building, such as lead on a church roof) and crops. Clearly a tenant farmer (who rents the land to grow crops and perform other farming activities) can harvest the crops he has grown without it being theft, and the landowner or anyone else cannot. Thus, it is theft for anyone who is not the owner or tenant, and is therefore not in possession, to take apples from an orchard or from someone else's garden. Severing means detaching something from the land. This will apply even when a tree overhangs your land or a public road. If the apples fall onto your land (without your help), it is not theft.

The exception in s(2)(c) refers to tenants of land, whether a tenant farmer or a student in a rented house. The section also refers to other technical aspects of land law that we do not need to explore. The tenant can be guilty of theft where he removes 'fixtures'; this would include a shed or separate garage, and parts of a house such as plumbing, electrical cables or light fittings. This is one reason why a person should be very careful before signing an inventory on renting a house or flat, as if the items they have signed for are not there at the end of the tenancy there could be an offence of theft committed.

3 A person who picks mushrooms growing wild on any land, or who picks flowers, fruit or foliage from a plant growing wild on any land, does not (although not in possession of the land) steal what he picks, unless he does it for reward or for sale or other commercial purpose. For purposes of this subsection 'mushroom' includes any fungus, and 'plant' includes any shrub or tree.

This means that a person foraging for wild food is not guilty of theft unless he does so to sell it to someone else or the person has been paid to collect the wild food. This is why people who collect wild mushrooms

It is not theft to pick wild blackberries if they are not intended for sale

for restaurants need to get permission from the landowner first, but the person collecting blackberries from the hedgerow for himself is not guilty of theft of the blackberries. Foraging is just picking from a plant. Removal of the whole plant can still form the basis of the offence of theft. It should be noted that some wild plants are protected under other Acts of Parliament, and their removal might amount to an offence.

4 Wild creatures, tamed or untamed, shall be regarded as property; but a person cannot steal a wild creature not tamed nor ordinarily kept in captivity, or the carcase of any such creature, unless either it has been reduced into possession by, or on behalf of, another person and possession of it has not since been lost or abandoned, or another person is in course of reducing it into possession.

This means that a person who traps a wild rabbit is not guilty of theft. However, once someone else has caught the wild animal, it can then be stolen. Thus, it is theft to take away a deer if it has been shot by someone else and that person is waiting to take it away. It is also theft to take away a pet, such as a cat, or a zoo animal.

Despite the expansion of the potential for an offence in this section, there remain situations where the court has had to decide whether there has been theft as a result of the nature of the property involved. This has come up with some surprising results.

In **Oxford v Moss (1978)** a student 'borrowed' an examination paper for the purpose of obtaining the information on the forthcoming exam. He copied the paper and then returned it. The student was charged with theft of the information contained on the exam paper. (He was not charged with theft of the paper as there was insufficient evidence that he intended to permanently deprive the owner of the paper; however, it could be argued that there was theft of the paper as its value reduced when the information was no longer confidential.) The court decided that the confidential information was not property and so there was no offence of theft. This is similar to copyright issues such as have occurred in music file sharing and video streaming cases. There are, however, other potential offences committed here, and the owner of the paper would have civil remedies available too.

Another problem arose in the case of **Marshall (1998)**, leading to a controversial decision. In late 1996, the defendant (and others) were video-recorded obtaining London underground tickets or travel cards from members of the public passing through the barriers, and then reselling them to other potential customers. The travellers were asked if they had finished with their card and, if they had, were asked if the defendant might have the card. Where the traveller had finished with his card, he often handed it to the defendant rather than throw it away. The cards often had some value left on them, being a day pass for a particular travel zone. The defendant then resold them at a reduced rate to persons intending to travel. London Underground Limited did not receive the revenue that it might have expected to receive from those persons who had bought the tickets from the defendant (and others). The court decided that the tickets belonged to London Underground and not to the travellers, who merely used them as evidence of the right to travel. This principle could be applied to prepaid car park tickets.

An interesting problem arose in the case of **Kelly (1998)**. Kelly, an artist, had removed a number of human body parts from the Royal College of London without its permission and without the intention of returning them. Usually, there is no property in a corpse. However, in this case, the body parts had been preserved and most of them had been the subject

Christine Hemming, wife of MP John Hemming was found guilty in 2011 of the theft of a kitten belonging to her husband's lover

Key cases

Oxford v Moss (1978): confidential information is not property within the meaning of the Theft Act 1968: in this case, an examination paper.

Marshall (1998): the court took into account the value (the intangible property in a travel card) when convicting defendants who had resold tickets that travellers had given them.

Kelly (1998): the court decided that body parts could be property for the purposes of theft, even though the common law is that there is no property in a corpse.

Tickets were held to belong to London Underground and not the traveller in Marshall (1998)

of further dissection so as to reveal the inner workings of the body. The court decided that that the parts of a corpse could be 'property' if they had acquired different attributes by virtue of the application of skill, such as dissection or preservation techniques, for exhibition or teaching purposes. This has particular implications for those working in hospital mortuaries, undertakers and crematoriums, and for the potential use of donor organs.

Element 3: Belonging to another

The Theft Act 1968 s5 deals with the 'belonging to another' element of the *actus reus* of theft. The general principle is set out in s5(1) as:

> 1 Property shall be regarded as belonging to any person having possession or control of it, or having in it any proprietary right or interest (not being an equitable interest arising only from an agreement to transfer or grant an interest).

This means that at the time the property is appropriated it must belong to another. This clearly involves rights that are less than ownership, as the Act refers to concepts such as possession and control. There are a number of areas of this section that have been the subject of cases with, usually, sensible results.

The first concepts to consider are of possession and control. A person who owns property has the fullest rights over it. Possession is the physical ability to enjoy the property. In the case of tangible property such as this book, it would be holding it and using it. With intangible property, an owner has the fullest rights to use the benefits of the property, such as spending a credit balance (money in an account) by transferring it to someone else. Possession of the intangible right is having the ability to access the use of the property.

Ownership of property may be separated from possession. If I lend you a book, I still own it but you will possess and control it. Your rights over the book are less than mine. I can still sell it (subject to any rights you may have as to possession), but you cannot sell it without my permission or it is likely to be theft. If I hire a car, I do not own it, but will have possession and control of it. This can be seen in the case of **Webster (2006)**. The case involved a medal, the Operation Telic medal for service in Iraq. The medal was awarded to Captain Gill, regional administration officer of the King's Royal Hussars, who received such a medal in early 2005. In September 2005 he received a duplicate medal. It was engraved with his name and details and was sent from the medals office that was responsible within the Ministry of Defence for the administration and issuing of medals. It is not known how the duplicate came to be sent, as Captain Gill had not applied for one. Webster was Captain Gill's staff support assistant. Captain Gill handed the medal over to Webster, who advertised it on eBay and sold it for £605.

The defendant accepted that the proper thing to do would have been to return to the medal to the medals office, though he did not believe that he was legally required to return it, thinking he had a mere moral obligation to do so. It was argued that as it was only a moral obligation to return the medal, there was no longer ownership by the Secretary of State. There was no dispute that normally when a medal is given it becomes the property of the member of the forces to whom it is given. However, the court decided that the medals office did retain a proprietary interest in the medal, and was entitled to call for the return of the duplicate medal. Therefore, the defendant could be convicted of theft.

There are other rights less than ownership that a person can acquire in various ways. This can include the right to retain possession of goods until a bill has been paid, which can be seen in the case of **Turner (No.2) (1971)**. In that case, the defendant, using his spare keys, removed his

Key cases

Webster (2006): where duplicate property has been delivered to the defendant by mistake, the defendant cannot keep the second item; it remains the property of the person who sent it in error.

Turner (No.2) (1971): a person can be convicted of theft where he steals another person's rights over goods; in this case, it was the right to retain possession of the goods until a repair bill had been paid; the defendant appears to have been convicted of stealing his own car, but in fact it was the right over the car that was stolen.

Operation Telic medal

car from outside the garage at which it had been repaired, so as to avoid having to pay for the repair. The garage was entitled to keep possession of his car until the repairs had been paid for, so the defendant was convicted of theft. It should be noted that making off without payment might be a more appropriate offence.

It is also the case that a person could be convicted of stealing stolen goods from a thief who had possession of the stolen goods. Whilst the original thief does not own the stolen goods, he is in possession of the goods. The court decided in *Kelly* (1998) (the body parts case discussed earlier) that s5(1) does not include the word lawful, so any form of possession, even unlawful, will suffice.

A person can be in control of property even though he does not know that he possesses it. In **Woodman (1974)** the defendant took a van to a disused factory near Bristol and removed a quantity of scrap metal. The disused factory still belonged to a company and the scrap metal at the factory was sold to another company, who removed much of it. That company left behind some metal that was difficult to remove, and it remained there for over a year behind a barbed wire fence and with warning notices, until the defendant removed it. Even though the owner of the disused factory did not know the metal remained on its premises, it was still in control of the site, as could be seen from the barbed wire and warning notices, so the defendant could be convicted of theft of the metal that the factory owners did not know was there.

Where property is abandoned, there is no owner of that property. The real problem is as to what amounts to abandonment. If I lose my wedding ring, I have not abandoned it – I wish to keep it and will look for it, thus retaining ownership but not actual possession. A finder who keeps it could be guilty of theft. However, if I deliberately leave a magazine on a train, I will be abandoning it, as I do not want it any more and do not care what happens to it, but perhaps hope someone will find it and take it. However, just because I throw something out, it does not mean it has become abandoned property. Rubbish placed in a dustbin for the council to collect becomes owned by the council. This explains why assistants at household recycling sites cannot just take things left there for themselves, but, subject to council regulations, may ask if they can keep the item personally. This can be seen in the case of **Williams v Phillips (1957)** where refuse collectors were convicted of the theft of refuse as they removed it from commercial premises. Their employers had posted notices providing that any proceeds from selling refuse had to be shared with the council, and warned of criminal prosecutions. The defendants had collected and sold on sacks of rags and wool they had collected without telling the council. Similarly, 'lost' golf balls on a golf course belong to the golf course owner and are not abandoned goods, so can be stolen. However, those lost on public land, such as a road alongside the golf course, are probably abandoned and have no ownership and therefore cannot be stolen.

Where property has been given to be dealt with in a particular way and that is not done, there can be theft. This is seen from s5(3) of the Act, which states:

> 3 Where a person receives property from, or on account of another, and is under an obligation to the other to retain and deal with that property, or its proceeds in a particular way, the property or other proceeds shall be regarded (as against him) as belonging to the other.

This means that the Act recognises that there are obligations in existence that may not be quite as formal as a trust, but that still give rise for the opportunity to commit the offence of theft. Cases on this usually involve

> ### Key cases
>
> **Woodman (1974):** a person can be in control of property he does not know he possesses; in this case, scrap metal in a disused factory.
>
> **Williams v Phillips (1957):** property that has been abandoned by its owner may become the property of those that remove it; in this case, the council owned rubbish left for collection.

Key cases

Davidge and Bunnett (1984): where money or cheques are given for a particular purpose, they must be used for that purpose or there can be a conviction for theft.

DPP v Huskinson (1988): where money or cheques are given for a particular purpose, there can be a conviction for theft only if there is a legal and not merely a moral obligation to use the proceeds for that purpose.

Wain (1995): when collecting charitable donations there is an obligation to repay the amount collected, although not the actual notes and coins that were donated.

money being given to someone for a particular purpose. One such case is **Davidge and Bunnett (1984)**. In that case, the defendant shared a flat with several others, who gave her cheques on the understanding that their communal gas bill would be paid with the proceeds of the cheques. In fact, she spent the proceeds on Christmas presents and left the flat without giving notice. As she was under a legal obligation to use the proceeds of the cheques for the payment of the gas bill, the cheques were regarded as property belonging to another under s5(3). She was convicted of theft.

However, it seems from the case of **DPP v Huskinson (1988)** that this will only apply if there is some form of legal, rather than moral, obligation to deal with the money in a particular way. In that case, the defendant was sent a cheque for housing benefit even though he stated he wanted his rent to be paid direct. He used some of the proceeds of the cheque to pay arrears of rent, but spent some on himself. As there was no legal requirement to use the money to pay rent arrears, he was not convicted of theft.

The case of **Wain (1995)** involved charity fundraising. People running an event were required to complete a registration form and return it to a television company. Once the form was returned to the charity (Telethon Trust), according to their usual practice they sent out a whole package of documents that provided help in organising events, a recommendation that the money be paid into a separate bank account, and information on where to obtain collecting boxes, balloons and such like. In this case, the defendant said that he had never received such a package from Telethon Trust, but nonetheless he did in fact open a separate bank account in the name of the Scarborough Telethon Appeal. The amount raised was £2,833.25. He was invited along to Yorkshire Television Headquarters, where he presented a dummy cheque to a television celebrity. He did not in fact pay over the money, claiming he was still getting it in. When pressed for payment, he gave various cheques drawn on various accounts that were worthless. His appeal against conviction for theft was rejected by the Court of Appeal. McCowan LJ stated: 'It seems to us that by virtue of s5 (3), the appellant was plainly under an obligation to retain if not the actual notes and coins, at least their proceeds, that is to say, the money credited in the bank account which he opened for the trust with the actual property. When he moved the money credited to that account over to his own bank account, it was still the proceeds of the notes and coins donated which he proceeded to use for his own purposes, thereby appropriating them.'

The final aspect of this element of the *actus reus* of theft occurs where property is received by mistake, such as an overpayment of wages or two items being sent instead of one ordered and paid for. The relevant part of the Act is s5(4), which states:

> **4** Where a person gets property by another's mistake, and is under an obligation to make restoration (in whole or in part) of the property or its proceeds or of the value thereof, then to the extent of that obligation the property or proceeds shall be regarded (as against him) as belonging to the person entitled to restoration, and an intention not to make restoration shall be regarded accordingly as an intention to deprive that person of the property or proceeds.

This simply means that, where you are given something by mistake and have a legal obligation to give it back, keeping it may be theft.

Conclusion

There are three elements to the *actus reus* of theft: appropriation; property; belonging to another. All three elements have particular aspects that need to be considered when discussing liability under s1 of the Theft Act 1968.

Activity

Identify and consider the issues with respect to the *actus reus* of theft, so far as Alan is concerned, in the following situation:

Alan went into a newsagent's shop and picked up a copy of *Law* magazine. He was not sure if he wanted the magazine so put it down. Beth looked at the magazine and, thinking it was *Claw* magazine, decided she wanted it, but had no money, so stole it. When she discovered the content was about law and not cats, she put the magazine in a rubbish bin. Alan saw the magazine in the bin and took it from the bin.

You should now be able to:

- understand the *actus reus* of theft
- apply the *actus reus* of theft to a given situation.

2 *Mens rea* of theft

The *mens rea* of theft has two elements:

- dishonesty
- **intention to permanently deprive** the other of the appropriated property.

Both elements must be proved for the offence to be committed. It is this element of *mens rea* that distinguishes normal transactions from theft. It should be noted that the Theft Act 1968 points out in s1(2) that it is 'immaterial whether the appropriation is made with a view to gain, or is made for the thief's own benefit'. This means that a person could be convicted of theft when destroying another person's property, even though he would normally be prosecuted for criminal damage.

The prosecution must prove the elements beyond reasonable doubt and this can sometimes prove difficult. It is logical to consider the elements in the reverse order. Whilst the overriding element of theft is **dishonesty**, a person can intend to permanently deprive someone of an item honestly. It is therefore preferable to consider this element first.

Element 1: Intention to permanently deprive the other of the appropriated property

As a general rule, merely borrowing something does not form an intention to permanently deprive. This therefore provides a possible excuse for criminals, who can argue when caught that they intended to give the property back eventually. Evidence is required that the defendant intended to permanently deprive the owner of the property. In most cases, intention can be inferred from the surrounding circumstances.

In this topic, you will learn how to:

- explain the *mens rea* of theft
- explain cases that illustrate the *mens rea* of theft
- apply the rules relating to both the *actus reus* and *mens rea* of theft to a given situation.

Key terms

Intention to permanently deprive: occurs where a person's intention is to treat the thing as his own to dispose of, regardless of the other's rights.

Dishonesty: this is set out in the Ghosh test on page 179.

Study tip

Be aware of the possible overlap of theft and criminal damage when answering examination questions.

Section 6(1) helps explain the meaning of 'intention to permanently deprive the other of the appropriated property'. It states:

> 1 A person appropriating property belonging to another without meaning the other permanently to lose the thing itself is nevertheless to be regarded as having the intention of permanently depriving the other of it if his intention is to treat the thing as his own to dispose of regardless of the other's rights; and a borrowing or lending of it may amount to so treating it if, but only if, the borrowing or lending is for a period and in circumstances making it equivalent to an outright taking or disposal.

There are two aspects of this definition:

1 disposing of the property regardless of the other's rights

2 a borrowing or lending making it equivalent to outright taking or disposal.

This can be seen in the case of *Marshall* (1998), which was considered in the previous topic. In that case, the idea that the underground ticket remained the property of London Underground meant that the subsequent sale to another traveller was a disposal, regardless of the company's rights. This would apply equally, for example, to re-using a cinema ticket that had not been collected.

In **DPP v J and others (2002)** the defendant took and broke his victim's headphones and then gave them back. Here, the question of whether there was an intention to permanently deprive arose, and it was considered that there was such an intention.

The aspects of borrowing have led to some difficulties. In **Lloyd (1985)** the defendant worked as a projectionist at a cinema and was responsible for looking after the films. He took films from the cinema to be copied, but the films were only out of the cinema for a few hours and were always back in time for their projection to take place at the advertised times to those people who attended the cinema to see them. Remarkably, he was not convicted of theft, although there are potentially other offences with which he could be charged.

In other cases, defendants have not been so fortunate. In **Velumyl (1989)** the defendant, without any authority from the company and contrary to the company's rules, took £1,050 from the safe at his place of work on Saturday evening, and lent it to a friend. It was a condition of that private loan that his friend should return it on Monday. A spot check took place before the money was returned. The court asked whether he intended to permanently deprive the owner of the money and concluded that he had no intention to return the same actual bank notes, just the equivalent amount of money. This satisfies this part of the *mens rea* but there is still an issue as to dishonesty.

This wider approach to the idea of depriving permanently was used again in the case of **Lavender (1994)**. In this case, the defendant lived with his girlfriend at 37 Royce Road, Spalding. His girlfriend was the tenant of the council house. She asked the council to replace damaged doors at that property, but the council refused because she was responsible for any damage to the doors. The council would have replaced the doors if she paid £400, which she did not do. The council also owned 25 Royce Road, which was unoccupied because it was undergoing repair. The defendant took two doors from 25 Royce Road to replace the damaged doors at 37 Royce Road. His intention was to use the doors at 37 Royce Road for as long as he remained there and leave them there when he eventually left that address. He argued that swapping the doors did not amount to theft because he was not permanently depriving the council of them. This argument failed and he was convicted, the court saying that the

Key cases

DPP v J and others (2002): taking and destroying of property can amount to an intention to permanently deprive; in this case it was headphones that were taken and then returned.

Lloyd (1985): removal of films from a cinema for a short time so they could be illegally copied did not amount to an intention to permanently deprive.

Velumyl (1989): defendant had intended to permanently deprive the owner of his property as he clearly did not intend to return the same notes and coins, even if he returned items of a similar value.

Lavender (1994): wider approach to the interpretation of intention to permanently deprive was taken here so as to convict a person who swapped internal doors from another council house to his council house.

defendant intended to treat the doors as his own and was thus regardless of the council's right. Those rights included the right not to have the doors at 25 Royce Road removed, and to require the tenant at 37 Royce Road to replace or pay for the damaged doors.

Conditional intent

A defendant has conditional intent in a situation where he intends to steal something if there is anything worth stealing. It was decided in the case of **Easom (1971)** that this is insufficient for the *mens rea* of theft, and the intention to permanently deprive can only be formed once the defendant has decided there is something worth stealing.

In *Easom* (1971) the defendant picked up a woman's handbag in order to see if the contents were worth stealing. When he discovered there was nothing of value in the bag, he put it back. He was found not guilty of theft on the basis that he did not have the intention to permanently deprive the owner of the handbag or any of its contents.

Element 2: Dishonesty

The meaning of dishonesty is not defined in the Theft Act 1968. It was assumed by the draftsmen of the Act that everyone would know what the word meant and therefore a jury or magistrates would be able to decide easily enough. The word was used so as to have no specific legal meaning other than its natural meaning. The Act did, however, give three specific situations in s2(1) where a person would be deemed not to be dishonest, whilst noting in s2(2) that a person may still make a dishonest appropriation even though he is willing to pay for the property.

Section 2 reads as follows:

1 A person's appropriation of property belonging to another is not to be regarded as dishonest –

   a if he appropriates the property in the belief that he has in law the right to deprive the other of it, on behalf of himself or a third party; or

   b if he appropriates the property in the belief that he would have the other's consent if the other knew of the appropriation and the circumstances of it; or

   c (except where the property came to him as trustee or personal representative) if he appropriates the property in the belief that the person to whom the property belongs cannot be discovered by taking reasonable steps.

Before discussing the meaning of dishonesty, we need to consider the exceptions in s2(1).

The first exception requires an honest, but not necessarily reasonable, belief by the defendant of his right to take the item. This is a subjective test, so the sole concern is for the defendant to convince a jury that he reasonably held that belief. An example of this is where an employee is instructed to collect certain goods from a third party. The employee honestly believes he has the legal right to do so (having been told to so by his boss) and therefore will not be dishonest in taking the goods even if, in fact, there is no such right to do so.

An example of this can be seen in the case of **Small (1987)** where the defendant noticed an old and very scruffy car parked in the road for over a week, with the key in the ignition. Parts were missing, and there was no petrol in it. The defendant thought the car had been dumped and therefore decided to get it going and drive it. His defence to stealing the

Key cases

Easom (1971): conditional intent is not sufficient for s6 of the Theft Act 1968. The defendant replaced the woman's bag because the contents were of no value, and he was not guilty of theft.

Small (1987): example of s2(1)(a) of the Theft Act 1968 operating to prevent the conviction of the defendant, who genuinely believed that the car he had taken was abandoned.

In the case of Small *(1987) the defendant was not guilty of theft because he thought the car had been abandoned*

car was that he believed it had been abandoned by its owner and therefore he had a legal right to take it, even though the owner could have been found from the registration number (this is why this case is different to one falling within the third exception). In fact, this was not the case; nevertheless, he was not guilty of theft.

The second exception requires an honest belief that the owner of the goods would consent if he knew of the circumstances. An everyday example of this is borrowing a person's pen without asking, and later returning it, or continuing a normal practice of borrowing tools and machinery between neighbours.

The third exception most usually applies in situations of finding items and then keeping them. This again requires an honest belief by the defendant that the owner cannot be found by taking reasonable steps. An example of this would be finding a £1 coin in the street. There is usually an honest belief that the owner could not reasonably be found, but that would not be so if the defendant had just seen someone pull the coin out of their pocket along with a handkerchief. Clearly, the more valuable the item, the less likely the owner cannot reasonably be found.

Where these exceptions do not apply, the courts have developed a test for dishonesty. There is usually little argument about whether an act is dishonest – for example, shoplifting is obviously dishonest and a jury would have little difficulty with that. However, defendants from time to time claimed that they had not been dishonest and there was no standard test that should be applied. Examples include borrowing from the petty cash at work without permission and contrary to the company rules, but intending to replace the money the next day, or borrowing from the till and leaving an IOU.

The matter was resolved in the case of **Ghosh (1982)**. In that case, the defendant was a surgeon acting as a consultant at a hospital. He claimed that he had himself carried out a surgical operation to terminate a pregnancy and that payment for the operation was due to himself or an anaesthetist for such an operation, when in fact the operation had been carried out by someone else and/or under the National Health Service provisions. His defence was that he had not been dishonest, as the sums paid to him were due for consultation fees that were legitimately payable under the regulations, or, alternatively, were the balance of fees already owed to him. In other words, he was alleged to have claimed money for work he had not done even though he was in fact owed money for work he had done.

The Lord Chief Justice set out the test for dishonesty:

> In determining whether the prosecution has proved that the defendant was acting dishonestly, a jury must first of all decide whether according to the ordinary standards of reasonable and honest people what was done was dishonest. If it was not dishonest by those standards, that is the end of the matter and the prosecution fails.

> If it was dishonest by those standards, then the jury must consider whether the defendant himself must have realised that what he was doing was by those standards dishonest. In most cases, where the actions are obviously dishonest by ordinary standards, there will be no doubt about it. It will be obvious that the defendant himself knew that he was acting dishonestly. It is dishonest for a defendant to act in a way which he knows ordinary people consider to be dishonest, even if he asserts or genuinely believes that he is morally justified in acting as he did.

Key cases

Ghosh (1982): set out the definitive test for what amounts to dishonesty; the two-part test is: (1) Would the defendant's behaviour be regarded as dishonest by the standards of reasonable and honest people? (If the answer is 'no', the defendant is not guilty of theft as he has not been dishonest). If the answer is 'yes', the second question is: (2) Was the defendant aware that his conduct would be regarded as dishonest by reasonable and honest people?

Link

You can usefully link this test, and much of the law of theft, to Chapter 20: Law and morality.

This test is a two-part test, known as the Ghosh test, and can be stated as follows:

1 Would the defendant's behaviour be regarded as dishonest by the standards of reasonable and honest people?

(If the answer is 'no', the defendant is not guilty of theft as he has not been dishonest.)

If the answer is 'yes' the second question is:

2 Was the defendant aware that his conduct would be regarded as dishonest by reasonable and honest people?

It can be seen that the first part of the test is objective and the second part of the test is subjective. If both parts of the test are satisfied, the defendant fulfils the criteria for being dishonest.

Conclusion

All five elements of theft must be proven, including the two *mens rea* elements – which are dishonesty and an intention to permanently deprive. Dishonesty is not defined under the Theft Act 1968 but there are three statutory exceptions that might apply. If not, the Ghosh test must be applied. The intention to permanently deprive has two aspects: disposing of property regardless of the other's rights and issues with respect to borrowing or lending.

Application of the elements of theft to problems in the examination

In the examination, there are often questions involving the elements of theft. In such cases, the best practice is to outline the *actus reus* and *mens rea* of the offence, but concentrate on the application of the law to the problem that has been set. At A2, the application is as important as the statements of law, and it is essential to focus on the issues that need discussion rather than those that are virtually self-evident from the facts in the scenario.

Consider this scenario from the AQA January 2007 examination:

> Uma and Violet were employed by Warren. One day at work, Uma discovered that Violet had left her purse in the toilets. Uma removed a fitness club membership card from the purse and then put the purse in the wastepaper bin (from which it was later removed and returned to Violet by a very alert colleague). Uma subsequently used the membership card to get herself a training session at the fitness club, for which she would normally have had to pay £10. She quietly dropped the card at the reception desk when she left.

There are a number of issues with respect to theft that arise from this situation. The mark scheme refers to:

> Theft of the purse and the membership card – explanation, in particular, of *mens rea* issues involving dishonesty and intention permanently to deprive.

The mark scheme focuses on the *mens rea* issues, as the *actus reus* of the crime requires little explanation. The fact that under s1 of the Theft Act 1968 the *actus reus* involves the appropriation of property belonging to another must be stated in the answer. Because this is so obvious, the application needs only to state that when Uma took the purse from the toilet she was appropriating (taking) property (the purse and its contents) belonging to another (Violet). There is no need to spend a great deal of time explaining aspects of the law of theft relating to any other aspect of the *actus reus* of theft.

With respect to the *mens rea*, however, much more needs to be said. Though discussion of dishonesty in the *mens rea* is certainly relevant, the fact that Uma removed the membership card and put the purse in a bin is clearly dishonest. Both parts of the Ghosh test are present – Uma's behaviour would be regarded as dishonest by the standards of reasonable and honest people, and Uma would surely be aware that her conduct would be regarded as dishonest by reasonable and honest people. The real issue is the meaning and application of intention permanently to deprive, given the contrast between the disposal of the purse and the disposal of the card.

Here, you need to consider what deductions about intention to permanently deprive can be made from the way in which Uma disposed of the two different items. It is not really possible to deduce intention to permanently deprive from the *use* of the card to get the training session. The use of the card is much more relevant to appropriation, though not really needed as there was an assumption of the rights of owner involved in taking the card. The use of the card is relevant for offences involving fraud that will be considered in Chapter 12.

With respect to intention to permanently deprive, the disposal of the purse in the bin shows no intention to return the item to the owner, who is clearly a known person from the contents of the purse. This therefore fulfils the criteria for theft. It is entirely fortuitous that the purse is found and returned.

As regards the membership card, it could be argued that Uma had no intention to permanently deprive Violet of the card because she handed it back to the reception when leaving. Section 6 states that borrowing is not theft unless it is for a period, and in circumstances, which make it equivalent to an outright taking. In *Lloyd* (1995) Lord Lane said:

> A mere borrowing is never enough to constitute the necessary guilty mind unless the intention is to return the thing in such a changed state that it can be truly said that all its goodness or virtue has gone.

In this case, although Uma treated the card as her own by getting a training session, it is unlikely that taking the card for a short period would be classed as an outright taking as the card is still of value when it is returned.

Activities

1. Consider the elements of theft in relation to the scenario set out below for both Darren and Evan:

   One day, Darren was in an open park when he came across a mountain bike, which was lying on the ground near a path. Although he waited for 15 minutes, he did not see anyone else, so he rode off on the bike. A week later, Evan saw the bike parked outside a house. Though there were significant differences in colour and other features, he immediately believed it to be his own bike, which had been stolen a few weeks before. He had just put his hands on the handlebars and was about to jump onto it when Darren came out of the house. Evan ran off. In reality, it was not Evan's bike.

2. Go back to the questions posed at the very start of this chapter and reconsider your answers now you have studied the topic of theft.

The actus reus *here is Uma taking Violet's purse*

You should now be able to:

- understand the *mens rea* of theft
- apply the *actus reus* and *mens rea* of theft to a given situation.

11 Robbery, blackmail, burglary and criminal damage

In this topic, you will learn how to:

- state the definition of robbery
- explain the *actus reus* and *mens rea* of robbery
- explain cases that illustrate the law on robbery
- apply the rules to a given situation.

Key terms

Robbery: an offence where force is used or threatened in order to steal.

Blackmail: if a person makes an unwarranted demand with menaces, with a view to gain for himself or another or with intent to cause harm to another, he is guilty of blackmail.

Key cases

Dawson and James (1976): force is required for robbery, but the word has no special meaning; it is up to the jury to decide whether the defendant's actions amounted to force.

1 Robbery

Robbery can be seen very simply as theft with force. Robbery covers a wide range of offences, from bank robberies to pushing someone to take their mobile phone.

The definition of robbery

The offence of robbery is defined in the Theft Act 1968, s8(1) as:

> A person is guilty of robbery if he steals, and immediately before or at the time of doing so, and in order to do so, he uses force on any person or puts or seeks to put any person in fear of being then and there subjected to force.

Robbery is, therefore, an aggravated form of theft. The *actus reus* is:

- the *actus reus* of theft, and
- using or threatening force immediately before or at the time of theft.

The *mens rea* is:

- the *mens rea* of theft, and
- intent or recklessness as to the use or threat of force in order to steal.

Therefore, all the limitations to the offence of theft, such as the limits on what can be stolen, are equally applicable. There are a number of points to be considered apart from the elements of theft discussed in the previous chapter. These are:

- What amounts to force on a person?
- What amounts to a threat of force on a person?
- When does the force or threat of force have to take place?
- What connection must there be between the force and the theft?

It is essential that the offence of theft has been committed before there can be a conviction for robbery.

What amounts to force or threat of force on a person?

The word 'force' is not defined in the Act. However, the force, or threat of force, must be sufficient to be noticeable, but not necessarily to the victim. Thus, waving a knife at someone who is blind would probably be sufficient. What would not be sufficient would be the threat of future violence, as that would not fulfil the definition of 'fear of being then and there subjected to force'. Such activity may be the basis of a charge of **blackmail**.

The word 'force' is given its ordinary meaning; indeed in the case of **Dawson and James (1976)**, the Court of Appeal specifically stated that the word was an ordinary word, and the jury could decide if what had occurred amounted to force. This could be jostling, as in *Dawson and James* (1976) where the defendants stood around the victim and one of them nudged the victim. This made the victim to lose his balance so that his wallet could be easily taken.

In Clouden (1987) force to the victim's bag was sufficient for a conviction of robbery

■ Key cases

B and R v DPP (2007): as long as the defendant's intention is to put the victim in fear of violence, it does not matter whether he in fact does so.

Clouden (1987): force does not have to be direct force on the victim; in this case, it was to her bag.

Bentham (2005): so long as there is the intention to create fear, it does not matter that the threat was not real; in this case, the defendant used fingers inside his jacket to make it look like he was holding a gun.

Hale (1978): the act of stealing can be a continuing act; the jury can decide when the appropriation is complete.

■ Study tip

Whenever there is the slightest push or jostle in a scenario where theft is present, you should also consider robbery.

It appears that it does not matter whether the victim is actually put in fear or not: it is the defendant's intention that matters. The fact that the victim was not afraid does not mean that the defendant did not attempt to put him in fear. This is sufficient for the offence, as can be seen from the case of **B and R v DPP (2007)**. In that case, five boys stopped the victim and asked if he had a mobile phone or some money. The victim said he did not, and was then asked which school he attended. He said where he went to school and he was then asked for his mobile phone and money. Whilst that was happening, about five or six more males ran to join the group. The eleven or twelve boys all surrounded the victim and when he did not hand over his telephone and money, his drink was taken and a packet of crisps was snatched from his hands. A number of the boys went into his pockets and took his wallet from his inside pocket, his watch from an outside pocket and his travel card. A £5 note was removed from the wallet; the wallet was then thrown to the ground. The victim said he did not feel 'particularly threatened' or 'scared' and he was not physically assaulted. He said he was 'a bit shocked'. The boys were convicted of robbery.

It also appears that there does not have to be direct force on the victim. The word 'force' is all that is required, so the jury can decide if it was sufficient. In **Clouden (1987)**, the defendant was seen to follow a woman who was carrying a shopping basket in her left hand. He approached her from behind, wrenched the basket down and out of her grasp with both hands, and ran off with it. This was sufficient force for a conviction for robbery.

It is also the case that the threat does not have to be as the victim imagines if it is intended to cause fear. In the case of **Bentham (2005)** the defendant positioned his fingers, concealed within his jacket, in such a way as to give the appearance of a gun that he was pointing at the victim. This amounted to a threat of force for the purposes of robbery, although not of possessing an imitation firearm.

When does the force or threat of force have to take place?

The importance of this question is that the definition requires the force or threat of force to take place immediately before, or at the time, of stealing. This deliberately makes the time when the force is used fairly fluid within the overall time that the crime took place. This has been made clearer by the case of **Hale (1978)** where burglars entered a house and took a jewellery box. They then tied up the occupant before leaving. The court decided that appropriation (and therefore theft) was still continuing when the occupant was tied up. The court took the view that the appropriation, and therefore the stealing, was a continuing act and the jury could decide when the theft was complete.

In his judgement in *Hale* (1978), Eveleigh LJ said:

> In the present case there can be little doubt that if the appellant had been interrupted after the seizure of the jewellery box the jury would have been entitled to find that the appellant and his accomplice were assuming the rights of an owner at the time when the jewellery box was seized. However, the act of appropriation does not suddenly cease. It is a continuous act and it is a matter for the jury to decide whether or not the act of appropriation has finished. Moreover, it is quite clear that the intention to deprive the owner permanently, which accompanied the assumption of the owner's rights was a continuing one at all material times. This court therefore rejects the contention that the theft had ceased by the time the lady was tied up. As a matter of common sense the appellant was in the course of committing the theft; he was stealing.

In some cases, the actual stealing and appropriation may be very brief. In **Corcoran and Anderton (1980)** the robbery was committed at the point of appropriation even though the robber failed. The court decided that a robbery was committed where the victim's handbag was wrestled from her grasp, even though it then fell to the ground and the robber ran off without it.

At the other end of the scale, a line must be drawn even though continuing possession of the goods stolen would appear to make it a continuing act. Eveleigh LJ's common sense approach can be used to come to a conclusion on this matter. In *Hale* (1978) the appropriation would probably end when the robbers left the house and were in the street outside. This is consistent with the theft case of *Atakpu* (1994) where the defendant hired expensive cars abroad to sell in England. The defendant successfully argued that no appropriation had taken place in England and therefore the case was not triable in England. The theft was complete long before the cars were brought into England.

What connection must there be between the force and the theft?

The force, or threat of force, must be used in order to steal. If the force or threat of force is used for a different purpose (such as rape), then it is not robbery. Where the force is used to allow the theft to happen, for example to obtain the keys to a building or safe, then it can be robbery. This can be seen from the case of *Hale* (1978) where tying up the victim allowed the successful completion of the theft.

Conclusion

The offence of robbery requires consideration of the offence of theft. If there has been no theft, there can be no robbery. The question then remains whether there was force or threat of force that, immediately before or at the time of stealing, was used in order to steal.

Application of the elements of robbery to problems in the examination

In the examination, there may be questions involving the elements of robbery. As with all problem questions, the key is to focus on the issues that require discussion and analysis, and minimise the time spent on descriptions that do little to advance the issues. Consider this extract from a past question:

> Andy went to the West Hotel to enquire about prices. Whilst the reception area was unstaffed, Andy reached over the reception counter to see what he could find in the drawer. He removed a plastic card which could be used by the hotel to 'cut' a room key. He then went to the bar and spent two hours drinking. To 'pay' for the drinks, he claimed to be a guest by showing the barman, Barry, the card and giving a room number. Barry made out the bill to the room and did not ask for any money there and then.
>
> Andy became quite drunk and began to attract attention by eating all the free snacks placed at the bar for hotel guests. Eventually, Barry tried to stop him taking yet another plate of snacks. Resisting Barry's attempt, Andy threw a pint of beer at him, which missed Barry and soaked the carpet. Andy then ran off with the plate of snacks but without having paid for any of the drinks.

Key cases

Corcoran and Anderton (1980): knocking a handbag out of the victim's grasp with force was sufficient for there to be a robbery, even though the robber did not take the bag.

Study tip

Look for the continuing act and raise the issue of when the theft is complete, following the principles laid down in *Hale* (1978).

There are a number of offences that have been committed here, as well as the issue of intoxication. At this stage, we will just concentrate on the aspect of robbery. There is the possibility that Andy stole the bar snacks, as it can be argued that he had no right to eat them because he was not a *bona fide* guest and was deliberately not paying for his drinks. The snacks are provided for guests or for those paying for drinks and Andy fell into neither category. Aspects of theft that need to be considered are, therefore, consent and appropriation and, briefly, dishonesty. If Andy was guilty of theft of the bar snacks, then his efforts to resist Barry's attempts to stop him, by throwing beer at him, could amount to the use of force for the purpose of committing the theft, and so introduce the offence of robbery. There then remains the question whether the force was used merely for the purpose of escape or actually to assist in the commission of the theft, thus leading to robbery.

■ Activity

Consider the following situation and consider whether Jason has committed robbery or not:

Jason was playing with a penknife whilst he repeatedly asked George, who was a couple of years younger, for a go on his bike. George let him. Jason rode off, was chased by an adult, dumped the bike and ran off. George says he only let Jason have the bike because he was scared of him as he had a knife.

You should now be able to:

■ understand the law relating to robbery

■ apply that law to given scenarios.

In this topic, you will learn how to:

■ state the definition of blackmail

■ explain the *actus reus* and *mens rea* of blackmail

■ explain cases that illustrate the law on blackmail

■ apply the rules to a given situation.

Key terms

Unwarranted demand: demand for something that the defendant is not legally entitled to.

2 Blackmail

Introduction

Blackmail involves a threat from the blackmailer to do something if the victim does not agree to his demand. The threat doesn't have to be something illegal, and it doesn't even have to be true. An example of blackmail could be threatening to publicise someone's criminal record when he doesn't want it made public, and demanding money in order not to do so.

The definition of blackmail

Blackmail is defined in s21 of the Theft Act 1968 as:

1 A person is guilty of blackmail if, with a view to gain for himself or another or with intent to cause loss to another, he makes any **unwarranted demand** with menaces; and for this purpose a demand with menaces is unwarranted unless the person making it does so in the belief –

   a that he has reasonable grounds for making the demand; and

   b that the use of the menaces is a proper means of reinforcing the demand.

2 The nature of the act or omission demanded is immaterial, and it is also immaterial whether the menaces relate to action to be taken by the person making the demand.

The *actus reus* of blackmail, therefore, has two aspects:

1 unwarranted demand

2 **menaces**.

The *mens rea* of blackmail has three aspects:

1 an intention to make a demand with menaces

2 doing so with a view to gain for himself or another or with intent to cause loss to another

3 either –

   a not believing he has reasonable grounds for making the demand, or

   b not believing that the use of the menaces is a proper means of reinforcing the demand.

There are, therefore, a number of points that need to be considered for the offence of blackmail. These are:

▩ What amounts to an unwarranted demand?

▩ What amounts to 'menaces'?

▩ The defendant's view to gain or loss.

▩ The defendant's belief as to reasonable grounds for making the demands.

▩ The defendant's belief that use of the menaces is a proper means of reinforcing the demand.

Key terms

Menaces: these can be threats of violence, including threats of any action detrimental to or unpleasant to the person addressed; they may also include a warning that, in certain events, such action is intended.

Man admits blackmailing Coleen Rooney over lost mobile

A man has pleaded guilty to blackmailing Coleen Rooney, the wife of the Manchester United striker Wayne Rooney.

Lee Platt, 28, admitted blackmail during an appearance at Manchester crown court on Tuesday. Platt, from Manchester, also pleaded guilty to a charge of handling stolen goods. He was arrested after Coleen Rooney lost her mobile phone during a concert at the MEN Arena in May.

The phone apparently contained family snaps of the couple's son, who cannot be identified as a section 39 order was made by a judge preventing his identification.

She was later contacted with a demand for money to have the phone returned. Instead of paying up, she contacted police.

Coleen Rooney

Two other co-defendants, Jennifer Green, 25, and Steven Malcolm, 42, also from Manchester, deny the same charges. Platt will be sentenced at Manchester crown court at a later date.

The Guardian, 30 August 2011

Key cases

Collister and Warhurst (1955):
the demand in blackmail can
be implied as well as expressed;
it will be implied when a jury
(the reasonable man) can see
from the attitude, actions and
circumstances that the defendant
is making a demand.

Treacy v DPP (1971): a demand is
made when the defendant has
done all he can to communicate
the demand.

**Thorne v Motor Trade Association
(1937):** provides an explanation
as to the meaning of the word
'menaces'; it includes threats of
violence or threats of anything
unpleasant or detrimental.

Garwood (1987): the victim was
very timid; as the defendant knew
that was the fact, his threat could
amount to menaces even though
the reasonable person would not
be affected by the threat.

Harry (1974): example of threats
so mild as not to amount to
menaces; case involved a letter
to shopkeepers on a rag week
procession route that sought
contributions to the charities to
avoid 'inconvenience'.

What amounts to an unwarranted demand?

The demand can be made either expressly or impliedly. Usually the demand is made expressly, such as an oral or written demand for a sum of money for not exposing some possible scandal. It also appears that the demand can be made impliedly. In **Collister and Warhurst (1955)** the defendants were two policemen. They indicated to the victim that he would be reported for a sexual offence, but that they would hold back the report until they met him the next day. The next day, the defendant policemen asked if he had anything for them. The victim handed over £5. Whether this amounted to a demand was a matter for the jury. The test is whether the evidence shows that, even though there was no express demand or threat, the attitude of the accused and the circumstances of the case were such that an ordinary reasonable man would understand that a demand for money was being made.

The demand is made when the defendant has done all he can to communicate the demand. In the case of **Treacy v DPP (1971)** this was when a letter was posted. This is presumably the same when an e-mail is sent (that does not bounce) or a text message is sent, assuming there is no evidence of a failure to deliver the message.

The demand made must be unwarranted. A demand will be unwarranted unless the defendant believes that he is entitled to make the demand – for example, in a situation where he has lent money to the defendant and is demanding its repayment. Thus, a demand is not unwarranted if it is for money legally owing to the defendant. It would also not be unwarranted if the claimed debt turned out not to be legally enforceable. This is because the defendant would believe he had reasonable grounds for making the demand.

What amounts to 'menaces'?

The word 'menaces' has always had a broad interpretation. In **Thorne v Motor Trade Association (1937)** Lord Wright said:

> I think the word menace is to be liberally construed, and not as limited to threats of violence, but as including threats of any action detrimental to or unpleasant to the person addressed. It may also include a warning that, in certain events, such action is intended.

Blackmail will not normally be proved unless the menaces are sufficient to influence an ordinary person to submit to the demand. It is not necessary to prove that the victim was affected by the threat. However, if the person to whom the threat is made is known by the defendant to be particularly timid, then threats that would not affect the reasonable person can still be taken as menaces. This can be seen from the case of **Garwood (1987)** where the victim was unusually timid and the defendant knew that fact.

An example of threats that do not amount to menaces can be seen in the case of **Harry (1974)**. The defendant was a member of a university rag week committee, and he had written to shopkeepers on the route of a rag procession, saying that they could be excluded from 'inconvenience' by supporting the rag week charities. This was seen to be essentially trivial and, at the time, was probably standard practice during rag weeks.

The defendant's view to gain or loss

In s34(2) of the Theft Act 1968 there are definitions:

2 For purposes of this Act –

a 'gain' and 'loss' are to be construed as extending only to gain or loss in money or other property, but as extending to any such gain or loss whether temporary or permanent; and –

i 'gain' includes a gain by keeping what one has, as well as a gain by getting what one has not; and

ii 'loss' includes a loss by not getting what one might get, as well as a loss by parting with what one has.

This means that the intended result of the blackmail involves some money or property rather than something of no monetary value such as a kiss. Things of economic value, such as a morphine injection to get pain relief from a doctor, are sufficient for blackmail. This was seen in the case of **Bevans (1988)**.

The defendant's belief as to reasonable grounds for making the demands, and that the use of the menaces is a proper means of reinforcing the demand

The defendant will not be guilty of blackmail if he believes he is justified in making the demand and if he believes that the use of threats is the proper way of enforcing the demand. The belief must be genuinely held and can be a moral rather than a legal belief, but a belief that would generally be viewed as immoral is no defence. This can be seen from the case of **Harvey (1981)** where a drug deal left the defendant having paid £20,000 for something worthless. He then kidnapped the seller's wife and child and threatened to maim and rape them if the money was not returned. He was convicted of blackmail even though he believed he was justified in making the threats.

Conclusion

The offence of blackmail is one that requires a consideration of situations where a person makes unwarranted demands with menaces. A defendant will not be guilty of blackmail if he believes he has reasonable grounds for making the demand and he believes that the use of menaces was a proper means of reinforcing the demand.

Application of the elements of blackmail to problems in the examination

In the examination, there may be questions involving the elements of blackmail. The questions could focus on the issues surrounding the making of the demand and whether it was, in fact, unwarranted. As with other areas of the specification, answers should concentrate on the areas that are less clear in the scenario, rather than those that are almost self-evident.

Key cases

Bevans (1988): gain or loss requires something of some economic value; in this case, it was a painkilling injection.

Harvey (1981): defendant's threat of serious violence will not be a proper means of reinforcing the demand.

Activity

By chance, Tom met a former friend of his, called David. Their friendship had ended when David had sexually assaulted him. Tom now threatened David that he would report the sexual assault to the police unless David gave him £50. David ignored the threat and walked off.

Consider whether Tom could be found guilty of blackmail.

You should now be able to:

■ understand the law relating to blackmail

■ apply that law to given scenarios.

In this topic, you will learn how to:

■ state the definition of burglary

■ explain the *actus reus* and *mens rea* of burglary under s9(1)(a) and (b) of the Theft Act 1968

■ explain cases that illustrate the law on burglary under s9(1)(a) and (b) of the Theft Act 1968

■ apply the rules to a given situation.

Key terms

Burglary: entry as a trespasser with intention to commit one or more of the stated offences; or, whilst trespassing, committing one of the stated offences.

Study tip

Whenever someone enters any premises or goes somewhere he would not normally be allowed, you should consider the prosecution of burglary.

3 Burglary under s9(1)(a) and (b) of the Theft Act 1968

Burglary is a well-known crime, although many people do not recognise the range of activities that can amount to burglary; it is not just entering a house and stealing something.

The law on burglary is divided into two parts: s9(1)(a) of the Theft Act 1968 is concerned with going into a building as a trespasser with intent to commit one or more of a number of specified offences; s9(1)(b) of the Theft Act 1968 is concerned with committing one of a specified range of offences after an entry has been made to a building as a trespasser. There are a number of aspects of the definitions that need to be discussed.

The definition of burglary in s9(1) of the Theft Act 1968

The Theft Act 1968 defines the offence of burglary as follows:

1 A person is guilty of burglary if:

  a he enters any building or part of a building as a trespasser and with intent to commit any such offence as is mentioned in subsection (2) below; or

  b having entered any building or part of a building as a trespasser he steals or attempts to steal anything in the building or that part of it or inflicts or attempts to inflict on any person therein any grievous bodily harm.

2 The offences referred to in subsection (1)(a) above are offences of stealing anything in the building or part of a building in question, of inflicting on any person therein any grievous bodily harm therein, and of doing unlawful damage to the building or anything therein.

There are, therefore two distinct offences, the first under s9(1)(a) and the other under s9(1)(b).

Burglary under s9(1)(a)

The offence has a number of elements that need to be considered.

The *actus reus* has three elements:

1 enters
2 a building or part of a building
3 as a trespasser.

The *mens rea* has two elements:

1 knowledge or recklessness as to his entering as a trespasser
2 with intent to commit theft, grievous bodily harm or damage to the building or its contents.

Burglary under s9(1)(b)

The *actus reus* has four elements:

1 enters
2 a building or part of a building
3 as a trespasser
4 *actus reus* of theft or grievous bodily harm, or attempted theft/grievous bodily harm therein.

The *mens rea* has two elements:

1 knowledge or recklessness as to his entry as a trespasser
2 *mens rea* for theft or grievous bodily harm or attempted theft/grievous bodily harm therein.

The basic distinction between the two offences is that the first offence is entry with an ulterior intent – to steal, cause grievous bodily harm or cause damage; the second offence is the commission of theft or grievous bodily harm (or an attempt to do so) once entry as a trespasser has taken place.

Common elements

There are a number of common elements to theft:

1 enters
2 building or part thereof
3 as a trespasser
4 knowledge or recklessness as to his entering as a trespasser.

Common element 1: Enters

Entry is done when what is called 'effective' entry has taken place. This is a question of fact and depends on whether enough of the defendant is in the building to achieve the ulterior intent (s9(1)(a)) or commit the crime or attempt crime (s9(1)(b)). Three cases illustrate this point.

The first case is **Collins (1973)** where the defendant, having discovered that a woman was lying asleep and naked on her bed, stripped off his clothes (apart from his socks) and climbed up a ladder on to the window sill of the bedroom and leaned in. At this moment the woman awoke and, mistakenly believing that the naked form at the window was her boyfriend, beckoned the defendant in. The defendant then got into her bed and it was only after the defendant had intercourse with her that the woman realised her error. At the trial, the defendant was convicted of burglary (entering as a trespasser with intent to commit rape (this was an ulterior offence for burglary until the Sexual Offences Act 2003), contrary to s9(1)(a)). One question the court had to decide was whether there was entry, as he had leaned in the window before being beckoned to come in. On appeal, the question raised was whether he had entered as a trespasser. As the girl invited him in, he could only be guilty of burglary if he had entered through the window before the permission was given. The court stated that the entry had to be substantial and effective, and his appeal was allowed because the jury had not been directed correctly at the trial.

The second case is **Brown (1985)**. In that case, the defendant was seen partially inside a shop window. The top half of his body was inside the shop window, as though he were rummaging inside it. The witness assumed that his feet were on the ground outside, although his view was obscured. The defendant was convicted of burglary as he had effective entry – he could handle the goods inside the shop window.

The third case is that of **Ryan (1996)**. Here, the victim, an elderly householder, found the defendant stuck in a downstairs window of his house in the early hours of the morning. The defendant's head and right arm were inside the window, which had fallen on his neck and trapped him. The rest of his body was outside

Key cases

Collins (1973): entry, for the purpose of burglary, needs to be effective; this means that it enables the crime to be committed, not that the defendant's body was wholly inside the building.

Brown (1985): defendant was seen with his head and shoulders inside a broken shop window; this was enough for effective entry to the shop.

Ryan (1996): entry is effective even if the crime intended cannot be committed; in this case, a would-be thief got trapped in a window, but he was still convicted of burglary.

Ryan *(1996)*

the window. He appealed against his burglary conviction on the grounds that there had not been an entry, but his appeal was rejected on the grounds that his partial entry was sufficient, even though he could not have actually stolen anything. This would then suggest that the entry need not be sufficient nor effective. There is no requirement of a successful theft, etc. to have taken place for there to be a conviction under s9(1)(a).

One final point to note is that it is probably the case that standing with a fishing rod through a letter box or using some other remote device to steal will amount to burglary, as the device is likely to be considered as an extension of the defendant's body.

Common element 2: Building or part thereof

There is no formal definition of a building, but it must be a fairly permanent structure. This would appear to exclude a tent, so theft from a tent at a music festival remains theft and not burglary. The Theft Act 1968, s9(3) expands a little on this:

> **3** References in subsections (1) and (2) above to a building shall apply also to an inhabited vehicle or vessel, and shall apply to any such vehicle or vessel at times when the person having a habitation in it is not there as well as times when he is.

This effectively means that burglary only applies to fixed structures or substantial portable structures that are designed for living in. It seems that a motor caravan would be capable of being burgled whilst being used to live in, but not when simply used as a vehicle or parked up over winter. It remains to be seen whether a sleeper cab of a lorry is classified as a caravan and whether theft from an attached trailer would be burglary.

For the purposes of burglary it is only necessary to enter part of a building as a trespasser. This is because a person often has permission to enter parts of a building but not others – this can be seen with signs in shops stating 'staff only'. In the case of **Walkington (1979)** the defendant went into Debenhams department store in Oxford Street, London, during opening hours. He moved around the shop and then went into a three-sided partition that surrounded a till on the middle of the shop floor. He stood inside the partitioned area and opened the till drawer to see if it contained any money for him to steal. The defendant was convicted under s9(1)(a) of entering part of a building as a trespasser with intent to steal – he entered the sectioned-off part as a trespasser as it was impliedly a staff-only area.

Common element 3: As a trespasser

As has been seen in *Walkington* (1979) trespass includes entry to a part of a building that the defendant does not have express or implied permission to enter. Trespass can be defined as occurring when a person intentionally or recklessly enters a building in the possession of another without permission or a legal right to do so. In *Collins* (1973) the defendant could not be guilty of burglary if he was outside the building before the permission to enter was given as he would not then enter as a trespasser. It is a different matter whether the permission was given by mistake in that case.

Permission is given either expressly ('go into my garage and get my tools') or impliedly from the circumstances. A pupil at a school has implied permission to enter the common areas of the school, designated classrooms at designated times, and other areas with permission. A sign on a staff room door that reads 'Knock and wait' suggests no general permission to enter the staff room. A pupil who has been suspended from school also has his permission to enter the school suspended, so entry on the school premises would be entry as a trespasser.

Key cases

Walkington (1979): part of a building may include a partitioned-off part of a shop; in this case, the partition sectioned off the till and that was sufficient to make it burglary.

A person who is given permission to enter for one purpose, but in fact enters for another purpose, is entering as a trespasser. A person who has a key to my house to come in and feed the cats enters as a trespasser if that person uses the key to gain entry to steal my computer. This can be seen from the case of **Jones and Smith (1976)** where the defendants took two television sets from Smith's father's house without his knowledge or consent. In the early hours of 10 May 1975, a police officer saw a car with the two appellants inside and a television set protruding from the boot of the car, and another officer saw Jones sitting on the back seat with a second television set behind him. Smith was in the front of the car. The defendants were convicted of burglary contrary to s9(1)(b) Theft Act 1968, despite evidence given by the father that his son 'would never be a trespasser in my house'.

The underlying principle is that if a person enters a building with intent to steal, cause grievous bodily harm or criminal damage, he does so as a trespasser – except in the unlikely event of the occupier giving him permission to do so.

Common element 4: Knowledge or recklessness as to his entering as a trespasser

We have already seen that trespass is defined as occurring when a person intentionally or recklessly enters a building in the possession of another without permission or a legal right to do so. This entry must be voluntary, not forced or purely accidental. For this purpose, the recklessness is *Cunningham* (1957) – subjective recklessness that is where the defendant knows there is a risk, is willing to take it and takes it deliberately.

> **Key cases**
>
> **Jones and Smith (1976):** defendants were convicted of burglary because they had knowingly exceeded their permission to be in the house; permission was not given to enter and steal things.

The different elements of s9(1)(a) and (b) of the Theft Act 1968

The first difference between s9(1)(a) and s9(1)(b) of the Theft Act 1968 is that for the offence under s9(1)(a) the defendant does not have to have committed that offence. He only has to have had the *mens rea* of intention to commit either theft, grievous bodily harm or damage to the building or its contents. The essential feature is that the defendant formed the intention before he entered the building as a trespasser. This intent can be a conditional intent – for example, to steal jewellery if there is some jewellery inside the building.

For the offence under s9(1)(b) to be committed, the defendant must commit or attempt to commit theft or grievous bodily harm. Thus, the offence requires the full *actus reus* and *mens rea* of those offences to be committed. So far as grievous bodily harm is concerned, this can be either s18 or s20 of the Offences Against the Person Act 1861. This means that the *mens rea* of s20 (maliciously) can suffice. As Lord Diplock stated in *Mowatt* (1968), it is enough that the defendant foresaw that some physical harm to some person, albeit of a minor character, might result.

Conclusion

The offence of burglary is one that requires a consideration of two possible situations where a person enters a building as a trespasser. The Theft Act 1968 s9 divides the offence into two: the first offence being committed where the defendant forms the intention to commit the ulterior crime before entry, and the second where the intention is formed after entry.

Application of the elements of burglary to problems in the examination

In the examination, there are often questions involving the elements of burglary. You should spend time identifying the issues, as you will avoid wasting time describing aspects of the offence that are not raised by the facts. Consider this extract from a past question:

> Gwen engaged Ben, an electrician, to repair the electrical wiring in the downstairs living room of her house. Ben owed £1,000 to Reggie, a violent man. Reggie knew that Ben was working at Gwen's house. Reggie told Ben that there would be big trouble for him and his family unless he stole from Gwen in order to reduce the debt. The following day, while Ben was working in Gwen's living room, she left the house to go shopping. Ben immediately remembered Reggie's threat and went upstairs to see if there was anything worth stealing. While searching Gwen's bedroom he found and decided to keep £50 and a black rubbish bag containing some old but expensive clothes that Gwen had decided to throw out. When Gwen suddenly returned and confronted Ben in the bedroom, he pushed her over as he ran out with the money and the rubbish bag. Gwen fell heavily against a wardrobe and broke her arm.

Discuss Ben's possible criminal liability for property offences arising out of his activities.

There are three property offences raised in this question: theft, robbery and burglary. As burglary includes theft as part of the analysis, it is best to start with the theft offence first.

■ In relation to the £50 and the black bag, all the five elements of theft need to be considered briefly but a key issue here is whether the clothes belong to another or whether they have been abandoned. Even though they are intended for a charity shop or to be thrown away, the clothes are still under Gwen's control and would not be abandoned.

■ When Gwen confronts Ben, this raises the possibility of robbery, as Ben pushes Gwen to get away. The main point of discussion here is whether the force was used in order to steal and whether it was at the time of the theft. It can be argued that the appropriation is a continuing act, based on the decision in *Hale* (1979), which takes a flexible approach on this issue.

■ In respect of the crime of burglary, both offences under s9(1)(a) and s(9)(1)(b) can be considered. When Ben goes upstairs, he does so intending to steal so he could be charged with s(9)(1)(a). There needs to be a discussion of the fact that he was not originally a trespasser in Gwen's house but he is now entering part of a building as a trespasser. Ben can also be charged with s9(1)(b) as, having entered as a trespasser, he commits theft and also grievous bodily harm on Gwen, as she breaks her arm. It would need to be established that he had *mens rea* in relation to causing the grievous bodily harm.

■ Activity

Consider the following situation:

Chereem dismissed David from his employment without notice and without paying him for work he had done. David was very angry about this, so the day after he left work, he returned on the excuse of collecting some possessions and photocopied important information about Cherreem's business, intending to sell it to one of Chereem's rivals. As David was leaving the building, he pushed over a security guard who was trying to see what documents David had with him.

You should now be able to:

■ understand the law relating to burglary under s9 of the Theft Act 1968

■ apply that law to given scenarios.

4 Criminal damage

Criminal damage consists of three separate offences that cover a range of activities from minor vandalism to arson. All the offences are dealt with in the Criminal Damage Act 1971.

The three offences are:

- basic criminal damage
- aggravated criminal damage (correctly called 'destroying or damaging property with intent to endanger life')
- arson.

The basic offence of criminal damage

The basic offence is set out in s1(1) of the Criminal Damage Act 1971 as:

> 1 A person who without lawful excuse destroys or damages any property belonging to another intending to destroy or damage any such property or being reckless as to whether any such property would be destroyed or damaged shall be guilty of an offence.

The *actus reus* of the offence has the following elements:

- destroy or damage
- property
- belonging to another
- without lawful excuse.

The *mens rea* of the offence is either:

- intention to destroy or damage property belonging to another, or
- recklessness as to whether such property is destroyed.

The actus reus

Destroy or damage

Destruction or damage is a question of fact and degree, including temporary or permanent physical harm to property, reduction in value or usefulness. Damage is not defined by the Act. The courts have construed the term liberally. In one case, smearing mud on the walls of a police cell was considered to be criminal damage. What constitutes damage is a matter of fact and degree and it is for the court, using its common sense, to decide whether what occurred is damage. It is also the case that the damage need not be visible or tangible if it affects the value or performance of the property.

There are a number of aspects to this. One case is **Hardman v Chief Constable of Avon and Somerset (1986)**, which decided that there was criminal damage where a pavement had been painted with water-soluble paint and chalks, even though the natural elements would eventually remove all trace of the paint on the pavement.

In **Morphitis v Salmon (1990)** a scaffold post that was being used to block the entrance to a road was removed by the defendant, so that he could gain access to the road – in doing so, the scaffold post became scratched. However a scratch on a metal scaffolding bar could not amount to criminal damage because it did not reduce its usefulness or value. However, the removal of the scaffold bar impaired the usefulness of the roadblock, and that would amount to criminal damage.

Dumping of rubbish on land may amount to criminal damage if the owner of the land will be put to expense in removing it. However, spitting

In this topic, you will learn how to:

- state the definitions of the three offences of criminal damage
- explain the *actus reus* and *mens rea* of the three offences of criminal damage
- explain cases that illustrate the law on the three offences of criminal damage
- apply the rules to a given situation.

Criminal damage

Key cases

Hardman v Chief Constable of Avon and Somerset (1986): the meaning of damage within the Criminal Damage Act 1971 includes temporary damage that will naturally disappear; in this case, it involved water-soluble paint on a pavement.

Morphitis v Salmon (1990): decided that there must be some reduction in usefulness or value of an item to amount to criminal damage; a scratch to a scaffold pole was, therefore, insufficient.

on a person's clothing is not criminal damage, however unpleasant it might be, unless the clothing is damaged by the spittle.

Destruction of property includes crushing a car or setting it on fire killing an animal or killing plants or crops.

Mark Rothko defacement: man arrested on suspicion of criminal damage

A man has been arrested in connection with the police investigation into the defacement of a Mark Rothko mural at the Tate Modern on Sunday evening.

The 26-year-old, who was arrested on suspicion of criminal damage, was detained in Worthing by officers from Sussex police, who were acting on behalf of the Metropolitan police.

The Tate Modern was closed briefly on Sunday after a person inscribed what appeared to be the words 'Vladimir Umanets, A Potential Piece of Yellowism' in black ink in a corner of Rothko's 1958 canvas Black on Maroon.

Vladimir Umanets, a Russian-born artist, later said that he had written on the canvas as an artistic gesture in order to draw attention to developments in contemporary art and the concept of 'yellowism', an idea he and a partner had conceived.

'I believe that if someone restores the [Rothko] piece and removes my signature the value of the piece would be lower but after a few years the value will go higher because of what I did,' he said, comparing himself to Marcel Duchamp, the French artist who shocked the art establishment when he signed a urinal and put it on display in 1917.

'I didn't destroy the picture. I did not steal anything. There was a lot of stuff like this before. Marcel Duchamp signed things that were not made by him, or even Damien Hirst.'

The Guardian, 8 October 2012

Property

Section 10(1) of the Criminal Damage Act 1971 defines property as:

> ... property of a tangible nature, whether real or personal, including money and –
>
> **a** including wild creatures which have been tamed or are ordinarily kept in captivity, and any other wild creatures or their carcasses if, but only if, they have been reduced into possession which has not been lost or abandoned or are in the course of being reduced into possession; but
>
> **b** not including mushrooms growing wild on any land or flowers, fruit or foliage of a plant growing wild on any land.
>
> For the purposes of this subsection 'mushroom' includes any fungus and 'plant' includes any shrub or tree.

This is similar to the definition of property that we considered under the Theft Act 1968 s4 in the previous chapter as it includes land itself, but excludes wild plants.

Belonging to another

This is much the same as in s5 of the Theft Act 1968 and is set out in s10 of the Criminal Damage Act 1971. The main difference is that criminal damage requires custody and control of property rather than possession or control. The effect is that there can be an offence of criminal damage whenever some person has any rights over property, but it is not possible to cause criminal damage to abandoned property. Also, for the purposes of the basic offence a person cannot generally be guilty if they destroy or damage their own property because it must belong to another.

■ Study tip

Every time something gets damaged or destroyed in a scenario, consider the prosecution of criminal damage.

Without lawful excuse

This is set out in s5 of the Criminal Damage Act 1971. Section 5(2) defines lawful excuse where there is belief in consent or belief in the immediate necessity to protect property. Section 5(3) makes it clear that the belief is subjective and must be honestly held. This has led to some interesting cases involving this defence to a charge of criminal damage.

In **Jaggard v Dickinson (1980)** the defendant, having been drinking, took a taxi to 67 Carnach Green, South Ockendon – a house occupied by Mr RF Heyfron, with whom she had a relationship such that, in the words of the magistrates, she had his consent at any time to treat his property as if it was her own. She got out of the taxi and entered the garden but was asked to leave by a Mrs Raven, whom she did not know. She carried on trying to get into the house, and in doing so broke the glass in the hallway of the house. She then went to the back door, where she broke another window and got in to the house, damaging a net curtain in the process. She then realised that the house was not 67 Carnach Green but 35 Carnach Green, a house that looked identical, occupied by Mrs Raven. There was lawful excuse here as the defendant honestly believed she had consent.

In the case of **Denton (1982)** the defence was successfully used where the defendant set fire to his employer's factory, having been asked to do so as part of an insurance fraud. The way that the employer put it was: 'There is nothing like a good fire for improving the financial circumstances of a business'! Denton was not guilty of criminal damage (arson) despite causing £40,000 of damage to the premises. He could have been found guilty of other offences relating to the fraud.

With respect to protection of property, this covers events such as emergency services damaging property to get in to fight a fire, as where they push a badly parked car out of the way with a fire engine. Although the test for belief that the property needs protecting is subjective, meaning what the defendant honestly believed, the question as to whether there was an immediate necessity to do so is judged objectively. Thus, removing a wheel clamp on a car which has been illegally parked is criminal damage as in the case of *Lloyd* v *DPP* (1985), where Lloyd had parked in a private car park without permission, and returned to find his car clamped. He refused to pay the £25 fee to have the clamp removed, instead returning later that night to remove it with a disc cutter. He was subsequently prosecuted, and convicted of criminal damage.

In *Hill and Hall* (1989), the defendants appealed against their convictions for criminal damage at an American military base. They had pleaded lawful excuse saying they were protecting nearby houses that could be threatened by an attack on the base. The Court of Appeal decided that it must first be established that the defendants believed the properties were in need of protection (subjective) and second whether cutting the fence would actually lead to protecting the houses. On the second point it was concluded that the threat was unlikely and despite their belief in the need for protection, the defence failed.

The mens rea

This is straightforward – either intention to destroy or damage property belonging to another or recklessness as to whether such property is destroyed. In both cases the recklessness is subjective recklessness following the case of *R* v *G and another* (2003).

The aggravated offence of criminal damage

This offence is set out in s1(2) of the Criminal Damage Act 1971 as:

> ### Key cases
>
> **Jaggard v Dickinson (1980):** defence of lawful excuse to a charge of criminal damage is effective if the defendant honestly believes that he has consent of the owner to carry out the damage; in this case, it was damaging property to get into a house.
>
> **Denton (1982):** defendant's employer asked him to set fire to his business premises as part of an insurance fraud; this raised the defence of lawful excuse because he had the owner's consent; it did not matter that the owner was not honest.

> ### Study tip
>
> When any criminal damage sets up a potentially dangerous situation, consider the aggravated offence.

> **2** A person who without lawful excuse destroys or damages any property, whether belonging to himself or another –
>
> **a** intending to destroy or damage any property or being reckless as to whether any property would be destroyed or damaged; and
>
> **b** intending by the destruction or damage to endanger the life of another or being reckless as to whether the life of another would be thereby endangered;
>
> shall be guilty of an offence.

The key aspects of this more serious offence are the intention or recklessness as to endanger life. It should also be noted that a person can be guilty if he destroys or damages his own property with intent to endanger life – for example, cutting the brake lines of your car before someone else borrows it. There is no need to prove that a life was in fact endangered.

The *mens rea* is not just the intention to damage or destroy property or be reckless thereto; the defendant must also have intended or been reckless as to endangering life. This can be seen in the case of **Steer (1987)** where, in the early hours of the morning, the defendant went to the bungalow of his former business partner, David Gregory, against whom he bore some grudge. He was armed with an automatic .22 rifle. He rang the bell and woke Mr and Mrs Gregory, who looked out of their bedroom window. The defendant fired a shot aimed at the bedroom window. He then fired two further shots, one at another window and one at the front door. Fortunately, no one was hurt. It was never suggested that the first shot had been aimed at Mr or Mrs Gregory.

The prosecution had to prove that the danger to life resulted from the actual destruction of, or damage to, property. In this case, the shooting, not the broken window, endangered life, so the defendant was not guilty of the aggravated offence.

However, the defendant may be guilty either if he intended to endanger life by the damage, which was intended to be done, or was reckless that life would be endangered by the damage. This can be seen from the case of **Warwick (1995)** where the defendant was a passenger in a stolen car. He threw bricks at a pursuing police car, smashing a window and showering a policeman with glass. As this could cause the driver to lose control, it would endanger the life of the driver and any passengers. Therefore, there was a conviction under s1(2) of the Criminal Damage Act 1971.

Thus, if a person drops something from a bridge onto cars passing below, or throws missiles at, or rams, police cars, there can be a conviction for the aggravated offence. If the intent is to break the windscreen or window, a jury is entitled to infer that there was an intention to shower the driver or passengers with glass and that as a result control could be lost, thereby endangering life. The danger would be caused, and intended to be caused, by the broken glass.

Finally, it should be noted that the defence of lawful excuse does not apply to the aggravated offence.

Arson

This offence is set out in s1(2) of the Criminal Damage Act 1971 as:

> **3** An offence committed under this section by destroying or damaging property by fire shall be charged as arson.

Whenever the damage is caused by fire, the defendant can be charged with arson; this includes the basic and aggravated offence.

Key cases

Steer (1987): aggravated criminal damage offence must arise from the damage caused rather than the cause of the damage.

Warwick (1995): aggravated criminal damage offence requires that the defendant's act was done with the intention or recklessness as to endanger life by the damage done.

Rioter who burned historic furniture store jailed for 11 years

Gordon Thompson, 34, who boasted of setting fire to the House of Reeves furniture store in Croydon on Aug 8, was jailed for 11 and a half years for what the judge described as a 'deliberate, wilful act of shocking vandalism'.

Thompson, who received the longest sentence handed down to any of last summer's rioters, apologised through his lawyer for his 'reckless actions'.

The court heard that Thompson went on the rampage through Croydon on Aug 8, looting shops before turning his attention to the Reeves store.

Following other looters into the building he stole a laptop, before borrowing a lighter and setting fire to a sofa cushion.

As the blaze caught hold, it spread to buildings on the opposite side of the road, forcing residents to flee.

Monika Konczyk, originally from Poland, had to jump to safety from the building where she lived. She said later she was so traumatised by the experience that she was too frightened to leave her home alone.

Thompson was jailed for 11 and a half years for the arson, two years each for two counts of burglary, and three years for a third count of burglary, to run concurrently.

Judge Peter Thornton told him: 'This was a deliberate, wilful act of shocking, dangerous vandalism. The Reeves family lost their historic business, something they, and generations before, had lived and worked for all their lives. Their loss is priceless. The trauma they have suffered is inestimable.'

The deputy chief crown prosecutor for London, Jenny Hopkins, said: 'Thompson's callous actions recklessly endangered the lives

Gordon Thompson (left) *and the House of Reeves furniture store* (right)

of many innocent people, not least the firefighters who bravely extinguished the blaze.

'Few will forget the terrifying ordeal of Monika Konczyk, whose flat overlooked the store. She had to throw herself from her blazing flat into the arms of those same firefighters.

'A much-loved and memorable local building was razed to the ground and the efforts of five generations of hard working members of the Reeves family to build up their family business were destroyed.'

The Telegraph, 11 April 2012

Conclusion

The offences contain some common elements in that they all concern damaging or destroying property belonging to another, with the *mens rea* requirement of intention or subjective recklessness as to causing the damage. However, the aggravated offence can be committed by damaging your own property and also requires the defendant to intend or be reckless as to endangering another's life. Arson is where the criminal damage is caused by fire. The main reason for the separate offence of arson is the potential seriousness of the consequences.

Application of the elements of criminal damage to questions in the examination

In the examination, there are often questions involving the elements of criminal damage. A typical part of a scenario is:

> Dave got into a race with another car and threw a bottle at it as it passed. The bottle broke the car's windscreen, causing the driver to swerve across the road and into the grass verge *on the opposite side.*

Here, you need to be able to differentiate between basic and aggravated criminal damage. Explain precisely how damaging a car windscreen might endanger life, so that a charge of aggravated criminal damage might be made against Dave. This would require proof that Dave foresaw the risk of endangering life by the damage.

Activity

Consider the following situation:

Gary had a grudge against Henry. Whilst Henry was busy, Gary loosened the wheel nuts on a bicycle that Henry frequently used. When Henry next rode the bicycle, the wheel worked loose and Henry fell off the bicycle, narrowly avoiding a serious accident.

You should now be able to:

- understand the law relating to criminal damage

- apply that law to given scenarios.

Fraud and making off without payment

In this topic, you will learn how to:

- outline the law relating to fraud

- distinguish between fraud by false representation and obtaining services dishonestly.

Key terms

False representation: false or misleading statement of fact or law which may also be done by conduct.

---

1 Distinguishing the areas of fraud in the specification

The Fraud Act 2006 came into being as a direct result of the need to overcome problems with the old law and to simplify the law. In February 1998, the Institute of Chartered Accountants suggested that business fraud was a growing problem that affected everyone, both as individuals and corporately in the country. The cost was huge, and the damage to the country's business reputation was increasing. Individual fraud was (and is) on an alarming scale, with billions of pounds being defrauded from credit companies, insurance companies and the state benefits system. Fraud trials tended to be long and complex, with some suggesting that jurors could not understand the evidence. There were few successful major fraud trials.

This background is surprising as everyone can recognise dishonest behaviour that is not theft, burglary or robbery. It is dishonest to claim an item of property has been lost or damaged to an insurance company when it has not. It is dishonest to claim the cost of goods supplied as part of building work is more than the real cost. It is dishonest for your solicitor to bill you for more hours worked than was in fact the case. It is dishonest for a garage to claim to have fitted new parts to a car when that is not the case.

The Fraud Act 2006 creates a general offence of fraud with different ways of committing it. The AQA Law specification includes fraud by **false representation** and obtaining services dishonestly only. Making off without payment continues under the Theft Act 1978. There are, therefore, two statutory offences to understand:

- fraud by false representation (s2 of the Fraud Act 2006)
- obtaining services dishonestly (s11 of the Fraud Act 2006).

The elements of the offence under s2 of the Fraud Act 2006 are that the defendant:

- makes a false representation
- dishonestly
- knowing that the representation was or might be untrue or misleading
- with intent to make a gain for himself or another, to cause loss to another or to expose another to risk of loss.

The elements of the offence under s11 of the Fraud Act 2006 are that the defendant:

- obtains for himself or another
- services
- dishonestly
- knowing the services are made available on the basis that payment has been, is being or will be made for, or in respect of, them or that they might be and
- avoids or intends to avoid payment in full or in part.

This offence replaces obtaining services by deception in s1 of the Theft Act 1978.

Where statutory interpretation is needed, as much of the law is new, the courts will use cases decided under the previous law to help interpret the Fraud Act 2006.

You should now be able to:

■ understand the scope of the specification

■ understand the key elements of the fraud offences.

2 Fraud by false representation: s2 of the Fraud Act 2006

Fraud by false representation is defined under s2 of the Fraud Act as:

1 A person is in breach of this section if he –
  a dishonestly makes a false representation, and
  b intends, by making the representation –
    i to make a gain for himself or another, or
    ii to cause loss to another or to expose another to a risk of loss.
2 A representation is false if –
  a it is untrue or misleading, and
  b the person making it knows that it is, or might be, untrue or misleading.
3 'Representation' means any representation as to fact or law, including a representation as to the state of mind of –
  a the person making the representation, or
  b any other person.
4 A representation may be express or implied.
5 For the purposes of this section a representation may be regarded as made if it (or anything implying it) is submitted in any form to any system or device designed to receive, convey or respond to communications (with or without human intervention).

In this topic, you will learn how to:

■ state the definition of fraud by false representation

■ explain the *actus reus* and *mens rea* of fraud by false representation

■ explain cases that illustrate the law on fraud by false representation

■ apply the rules to a given situation.

Benefit fraud is a common form of fraud by misrepresentation

There are four elements to consider:

1 makes a false representation
2 dishonestly
3 knowing that the representation was or might be untrue or misleading
4 with intent to make a gain for himself or another, to cause loss to another or to expose another to risk of loss.

We will look at each element of the offence in turn.

■ **Study tip**

Whenever a person in a scenario makes a statement that is untrue, consider the prosecution of an offence under s2 of the Fraud Act 2006.

1 Makes a false representation (the *actus reus*).

This is explained in subsections (2)–(5) of s2 of the Act, which are set out above. A number of aspects of this definition need to be considered. The first point is that fraud is a conduct crime. This means that no particular end result has to be proved. Therefore, no one has to believe the false representation that has been made. Just making the false representation is enough. The crime is complete as soon as the defendant makes the false representation provided that it is made with the necessary dishonest intent (the *mens rea*). It differs from the old deception offences in that it does not matter whether or not any one knows of the representation, is deceived, or any property is actually gained or lost.

Shop worker Farrakh Nizzar jailed for £1m lottery scam bid

A shop worker has been jailed for 30 months for trying to claim a winning £1 million lottery ticket belonging to a pensioner couple.

Farrakh Nizzar, 30, told Maureen Holt her EuroMillions ticket was a loser – and asked her if she wanted the ticket back.

Mrs Holt, 78, and her husband Fred, 80, who knew Nizzar by his nickname of 'Lucky', told him to bin the worthless ticket.

In fact when Nizzar had scanned the ticket at his cousin's Best One shop in Oldham, Greater Manchester, where he worked, the terminal told him the holder should contact Camelot.

Nizzar, kept the ticket and later called the lottery company himself in an attempt to keep the prize.

But the firm became suspicious when he was unable to answer questions about the winning ticket.

Camelot checked CCTV and traced the rightful owners of the ticket using Mr Holt's Tesco Clubcard to unite the couple with their £1 million prize.

Nizzar pleaded guilty last month to one charge of fraud by false representation committed on May 31 this year.

The Independent, 20 August 2012

The Act, in s2(2), makes it clear that 'false' means untrue or misleading, but the word 'representation' is not defined. The Act does, however, explain what the representation must be about and how it may arise. In the law of contract, the word 'misrepresentation' is defined; the 'mis-' merely means it is false. We may therefore explain the word 'representation' as a factual statement made by one party in order to induce another party to do something.

Section 2(3) helps by stating that a 'representation' means any representation as to fact or law. This means that the argument as to whether something is a statement of fact or law is irrelevant; both suffice for fraud. A statement of fact is straightforward. It could be something such as the statement that a piece of jewellery is silver when it is in fact silver plated only. A statement of law may be a statement about the effect of a legal document, such as a loan agreement that is in fact a mortgage and not an unsecured loan.

A difficulty arises where the representation is a statement of opinion. If the statement is not the genuine opinion of the person making it, it can amount to fraud, but often the victim will prefer to take civil action to recover his money, only resorting to criminal law when there is little prospect of succeeding. Thus, a statement that a car is in good condition is often made by car sales persons. This will only give rise to legal rights when the seller knows that is not the case or could not possibly have held that view. In such cases, the victim will have rights under the law of contract, but there may also be the offence of fraud by false representation.

However, it should be noted that where the representation was true when made, but later becomes false, the offence can be committed by not telling of the change. Thus, in the example of selling a car that is stated to be in good condition, the potential purchaser who returns later must be told of any change that would make the car no longer in 'good condition'. This can be seen in the cases of **DPP v Ray (1974)** and **Rai (2000)**.

In *DPP* v *Ray* (1974) the defendant was a student, and he and his friends went to the Wing Wah Restaurant in Gainsborough, Lincolnshire, and ordered a meal. At the time he entered the restaurant the defendant had only 10p on him but one of his friends had agreed to lend him some money to pay. He ate the meal and they then decided not to pay and to run out of the restaurant. They did so some 10 minutes later. No payment was offered or made, and no money was left, for the meals served. The court decided that there was an implied representation that payment would be made when the meal was ordered and that, so far as the waiter was concerned, the original implied representation made to him must have been a continuing representation so long as the defendant remained in the restaurant. (Note: this case is also one of making off without payment).

In the case of *Rai* (2000) the defendant was the owner of a property. On about 7 June 1996, he applied to Birmingham City Council for a grant towards providing a downstairs bathroom at his house for the use of his elderly and infirm mother. The council approved a grant, and on 29 July 1997 the defendant was told of this. Two days later, on 31 July, his mother died. He did not tell the council of the changed circumstances, and used the grant of £9,500 for the agreed modifications to his house. The representation that was true when made became false. As it was a continuing representation, it could be the basis of an offence that, today, would be fraud by false representation.

The representation as to the state of mind of a person can also be sufficient for criminal liability. Section 2(3) states '… including a representation as to the state of mind of the person making the representation or any other person.' If you were to go to your father to ask for £10 to help buy this textbook, but you really want the £10 to go to the pub, you would be falsely representing your state of mind. If you were to go to your father to ask for £10 to help your brother buy this textbook, but you really want the £10 to go to the pub, you would be falsely representing the state of mind of 'any other person'.

Under s2(4), a representation may be express or implied. It can be expressly made in many ways; the Act puts no limit on this. It could, for example, be written or texted, spoken directly or by phone or radio, posted on a website, put on a podcast or sent by e-mail. A representation can be implied by conduct. This could occur when a person uses a credit card or purports to make a payment from his bank account, for example, by cheque or debit card. By using the card, a person represents that he has the authority to use it for that transaction. He would not have the authority to use if the card was stolen or over its credit limit. This can be seen from the cases of **MPC v Charles (1976)** and **Lambie (1982)**.

In *MPC* v *Charles* the defendant went to the Golden Nugget club, a gaming club, and in the course of the night he used all the cheques in

Key cases

DPP v Ray (1974): representation can be a continuing representation, and therefore any change of the situation must be notified if the previously true representation is not to become false and the offence committed; in this case, the representation was the intention to pay for meals ordered at a restaurant.

Rai (2000): defendant's representation was true when it was made, but it became false when his mother died and he failed to notify the council.

MPC v Charles (1976): giving a cheque makes the implied representation that he has the authority to use the cheque; in this case, the cheque was to a casino and backed by a cheque guarantee card; as the account was overdrawn beyond its agreed limit, this could be fraud.

Lambie (1982): use of a credit card is an implied representation that the user has authority from the credit company to use the card; in this case, the fact that the transaction would take the card over its limit meant there was no such authority from the credit card company, so an offence of fraud could be committed.

his new cheque book for the purchase of chips for gaming. He used his cheque card in relation to each cheque. The bank had consequently to honour all the cheques, with the result that he went hugely over his overdraft limit. This was sufficient for the defendant to be convicted under an offence equivalent to fraud by false representation. In the House of Lords, Viscount Dilhorne said:

> The reality is in my view that a man who gives a cheque represents that it will be met on presentment, and if a cheque is accepted by the payee, it is in the belief that it will be met ... His use of a cheque card to secure acceptance of his cheque can in my opinion amount to a representation that he has the authority of the bank to use it in relation to that cheque for that purpose, and as a matter of fact will ordinarily do so. He is authorised by the bank to give its undertaking to pay ... a cheque if the stipulated conditions are fulfilled. But the authority given to him is not unlimited. ... He is not authorised to use it to secure the acceptance of a cheque which he knows would not be met by the bank if the cheque card had not been used.

This principle was extended to cover credit cards in *Lambie* (1982). In that case, the defendant had a Barclaycard (a credit card) that was issued subject to the Barclaycard current conditions of use. It was an express condition of the card's issue that it should be used only within the given credit limit. The defendant knew her credit limit was £200, as this had been notified to her in writing when the card was issued and appeared on each statement. Between 18 November 1977 and 5 December 1977, she used the card for at least 24 separate transactions amounting to £533. The bank became aware of this debt and requested the card be returned. On 6 December 1977 the defendant agreed to return the card on 7 December 1977, but she did not do so. By 15 December 1977 she had used the card for at least 43 further transactions, incurring a total debt to the bank of over £1,000. The House of Lords decided that the representation arising from the presentation of a credit card is a representation of actual authority to make the contract with the shop or other figure to whom the payment is to be made.

A representation can be made through a gesture, such as a nod of the head, or by presence in a restricted area that implies the right to be there. This would include wearing a uniform or an identification badge that implies a certain status or right to be present. A representation can also be about a person's identity, and will be relevant for identity fraud. All these become possible because of the meaning of 'false' being 'untrue or misleading'.

This is all confirmed in the explanatory notes to the Act, which state:

> 15. A representation may also be implied by conduct. An example of a representation by conduct is where a person dishonestly misuses a credit card to pay for items. By tendering the card, he is falsely representing that he has the authority to use it for that transaction. It is immaterial whether the merchant accepting the card for payment is deceived by the representation.

> 16. This offence would also be committed by someone who engages in 'phishing': i.e. where a person disseminates an e-mail to large groups of people falsely representing that the e-mail has been sent by a legitimate financial institution. The e-mail prompts the reader to provide information such as credit card and bank account numbers so that the 'phisher' can gain access to others' assets.

Finally, s2(5) makes it clear that the offence can be committed by making a representation to a machine such as an ATM (automated ticket machine).

2 Dishonestly (first part of the *mens rea*)

This is the crucial element of the offence of fraud by false representation. Throughout the passage of the Fraud Act 2006, it has been considered that the Ghosh test applies. This has been studied in Chapter 10: Theft, Topic 2 and you should review the details now.

This test came from the case of **Ghosh (1982)**. It is a two-part test, known as the Ghosh test, and can be stated as follows:

1 Would the defendant's behaviour be regarded as dishonest by the standards of reasonable and honest people?

(If the answer is 'no', the defendant is not guilty of theft as he has not been dishonest.)

If the answer is 'yes', the second question is:

2 Was the defendant aware that his conduct would be regarded as dishonest by reasonable and honest people?

It can be seen that the first part of the test is objective and the second part of the test is subjective. If both parts of the test are satisfied, the defendant fulfils the criteria for being dishonest.

It should be noted that the three statutory beliefs or defences under s2 of the Theft Act 1968 do *not* apply to fraud offences.

> **Key cases**
>
> **Ghosh (1982):** set out the definitive test for what amounts to be dishonesty; the two-part test is: (1) Would the defendant's behaviour be regarded as dishonest by the standards of reasonable and honest people? (If the answer is 'no', the defendant is not guilty of theft as he has not been dishonest); If the answer is 'yes', the second question is: (2) Was the defendant aware that his conduct would be regarded as dishonest by reasonable and honest people?

3 Knowing that the representation was or might be untrue or misleading (second part of the *mens rea*)

As we have seen, a representation is defined as 'false' if it is untrue or misleading. The person making the false representation must know that it is, or might be, untrue or misleading, but makes a decision to make it anyway. The words 'might be' do not mean recklessness. Actual knowledge that the representation might be untrue is required, rather than an awareness of a risk that it might be untrue. The first point is that the statement must, in fact, be untrue or misleading. The defendant cannot be convicted if the statement is, in fact, true. If it is the case that the statement is untrue or misleading, then the defendant must know that is the case.

4 With intent to make a gain for himself or another, to cause loss to another or to expose another to risk of loss (third part of the *mens rea*)

This part of the *mens rea* has the key words 'with intent to'. This means that there is no need for anyone to have suffered any actual loss or be exposed to any loss, or even that the defendant makes a gain. This is all about what the defendant intends by carrying out his act.

Gain and loss are defined in s5 of the Fraud Act 2006 as only including money or other property, but the gain or loss can be temporary or permanent. This is similar to the definition under the law of blackmail discussed in Chapter 11.

Conclusion

In many cases fraud will overlap with theft. However, the *actus reus* requirement for fraud is not as difficult to prove. It is also not necessary to prove or demonstrate any consequences of fraud, and fraud does not require any intent permanently to deprive.

Application of the elements of s2 of the Fraud Act 2006 to problems in the examination

Consider this problem:

> Carlos was in a hotel where a conference was being held, but he was not part of that conference. He helped himself to some coffee and biscuits. Later, when the delegates at the conference went to the restaurant to get some lunch, he went into the restaurant as the delegates went in and said to the food server – 'I am with them' and was given a plate of food, which he ate.

Here, we find Carlos has committed two offences: theft, and fraud by false representation. The theft relates to the coffee; note also that if the coffee was in a room reserved for delegates at the conference only, there could be an offence of burglary too. When he goes into the restaurant, he fulfils the elements of fraud by false representation:

■ makes a false representation – that he is a delegate at the conference

■ dishonestly – he fulfils the Ghosh test

■ knowing that the representation was or might be untrue or misleading – he knows it is untrue to imply that he is a part of the conference

■ with intent to make a gain for himself or another, to cause loss to another or to expose another to risk of loss – the intention is to get free food.

In relation to the lunch Carlos could also be charged with theft as, although he was given the food, there can still be appropriation with consent as in the cases of *Lawrence* (1972) and *Gomez* (1993).

You should now be able to:

■ understand the law relating to fraud by false representation

■ apply that law to given scenarios.

Activity

Luke had a contact in the entertainment industry from whom he could obtain event tickets, which he sold to his friends at a profit. Pierre asked Luke to get him two tickets for a forthcoming concert. Luke had told him that he would get them for £300 from his contact. In fact, the contact had previously told Luke that tickets for this concert were already sold out. Pierre gave £300 to Luke to buy the tickets but Luke used the money to pay for a holiday.

Consider which property offences may have been committed by Luke.

In this topic, you will learn how to:

■ state the definition of obtaining services dishonestly

■ explain the *actus reus* and *mens rea* of obtaining services dishonestly

■ explain cases that illustrate the law on obtaining services dishonestly

■ apply the rules to a given situation.

▋3 Obtaining services dishonestly: s11 of the Fraud Act 2006

Section 11 of the Fraud Act 2006 sets out the offence:

> 1 A person is guilty of an offence under this section if he obtains services for himself or another –
>
> a by a dishonest act, and
>
> b in breach of subsection (2).
>
> 2 A person obtains services in breach of this subsection if –
>
> a they are made available on the basis that payment has been, is being or will be made for or in respect of them,
>
> b he obtains them without any payment having been made for or in respect of them or without payment having been made in full, and
>
> c when he obtains them, he knows –
>
> i that they are being made available on the basis described in paragraph (a), or
>
> ii that they might be,
>
> but intends that payment will not be made, or will not be made in full.

It should be noted that, in many cases, the defendant will also have committed an offence under s2 of fraud by making a false representation, the false representation being that payment will be made or, where only part payment has been made, will be made in full.

We will now look at each element of the offence in turn.

1 Obtains for himself or another

Unlike the offence under s2, this offence is a result crime, as there must be proof that the services have actually been obtained. No act of deception is needed, and there is no need to prove that the service provider has been deceived. An example would be climbing a wall to see a football match. This would be accessing a service (the football match, entertainment) that is normally provided only on payment of a fee (the ticket price).

It should also be noted that the offence can be committed where the person performing the act does not do so for his own benefit. This could, therefore, possibly include lifting someone over a fence to get into a music festival.

2 Services

The offence applies to services that are 'made available on the basis that payment has been, is being or will be made for or in respect of them'. This means that where a service is being provided without charge, there cannot be an offence under this section. The word 'services' is not defined within the Act, but the Crown Prosecution Service gives a number of examples of services that would fall within this section:

- obtains chargeable data or software over the internet without paying
- orders a meal in a restaurant knowing he has no means to pay
- attaches a decoder to his TV to enable him to access chargeable satellite services without paying
- uses the services of a members' club without paying and without being a member.

These examples raise some interesting points. Chargeable data would include music or video downloads; ordering the meal without the means to pay would also suggest an offence under s2; accessing the chargeable satellite services would presumably mean there was a separate offence each time a service was accessed; if a person got access to the club, but did not use the services (for example, a gym), would there still be an offence if the sole purpose of access was to get warm on a cold day?

There is one case that helps with respect to banking services – **Sofroniou (2004)**. This is a case of identity theft. The defendant falsely pretended to be Andrew Cole, John Groves or Andrew Narramore to deceive, or attempt to deceive, banks into providing him with banking services, credit card companies into providing him with credit cards, and retailers into providing him with goods. The Court of Appeal decided that for there to be a service, interest must be payable on loans and credit cards, and they could not be 'interest free'. The defendant was guilty of obtaining services by deception under the previous law, which was abolished by the Fraud Act 2006 and replaced with obtaining services dishonestly.

It should, therefore, be noted that if the banking services obtained are free, s11 cannot be the appropriate offence. However, the same restriction does not apply to s2, nevertheless it may be difficult to establish under that section that a defendant had a view to gain or intent to cause loss.

Study tip

Note that ss2 and 11 of the Act sometimes overlap. It would be better to discuss both where that is the case.

Key cases

Sofroniou (2004): banking services fall within the definition of services but free banking services cannot form the basis of an offence under s11, only s2.

3 Dishonestly

This is exactly the same use of the *Ghosh* test as there was for s2. It is worth repeating that the examples of things that are not dishonest in s2 of the Theft Act 1968 do *not* apply here.

4 Knowing the services are made available on the basis that payment has been, is being or will be made for or in respect of them

In most cases, awareness that a service necessitates payment will not be a problem, as it is self-evident that the service is one for which payment is normally made – either in advance of the service, at the time of the service, or afterwards. The defendant must get the service either by not paying for it, or not paying in full, if there is to be a conviction under s11.

5 Avoids or intends to avoid payment in full or in part

Whilst avoiding payment is the gist of this offence, it is sufficient that the defendant intends to avoid payment. This means that the defendant must intend to avoid payment for the service provided in full or in part, and have that intention at the time that the service is obtained. Presumably, with banking services, this is a continuing act and so a later intention, whilst the service continues, will be sufficient.

It would appear that the intent must be never to pay the sum involved. This means that an honest belief that credit is being given will mean the offence is not being committed. This would be consistent with the existing law with respect to making off without payment, and with the case of **Allen (1985)**. Here, Allen, booked a room at a hotel and finally left on 11 February 1983 without paying his bill of over £1,200. He telephoned two days later to explain that he was in financial difficulties because of some business transactions, and arranged to return to the hotel on 18 February 1983 to remove his belongings and leave his Australian passport as security for the debt. He was arrested on his return and said that he genuinely hoped to be able to pay the bill, and denied he was acting dishonestly. On 3 March 1983, he was still unable to pay the bill. He said he had acted honestly and had genuinely expected to pay the bill from the proceeds of various business ventures. The House of Lords agreed, and stated:

> Anyone who knows that payment on the spot is expected or required of him and who then dishonestly makes off without paying as required or expected must have at least the intention to delay or defer payment. It follows, therefore, that the conjoined phrase 'and with intent to avoid payment of the amount due' adds a further ingredient – an intention to do more than delay or defer – an intention to evade payment altogether.

Conclusion

This offence is quite straightforward but has some subtle distinctions between it and s2. Section 11 is a result crime and it needs to be established that a service was in fact obtained, whereas for s2 the requirement is only that the defendant intends to make a gain or cause a loss. There is no need to actually achieve this result. A further difference is that s11 only relates to services that require payment, whereas s2 could be used if the defendant makes a false representation in order to benefit from a free service.

> **Key cases**
>
> **Allen (1985):** intent not to pay means an intent not to pay permanently, so a mistaken but honest belief as to credit being given will mean the offence has not been committed.

Application of the elements of s11 Fraud Act 2006 to problems in the examination

Consider this problem:

> Janet and John decided to go an art gallery in the city where they were having a break. When they got there, they discovered that this was a private art gallery, and, unlike public art galleries, there was an entry fee. As they were short of money, Janet claimed to be a student and showed an old, out-of-date student card whilst holding her fingers over the date, and said that John was unemployed although, in reality, he was in full-time employment. On the basis of this, the art gallery gave them concessionary tickets that were half the normal price.

The defendant used an out-of-date student card to gain reduced-price entry

Look at the elements of the offence:

▓ obtains for himself or another – Janet for herself and for another (John)

▓ services – entry to the art gallery

▓ dishonestly – this is self-evident

▓ knowing the services are made available on the basis that payment has been, is being or will be made for or in respect of them or that they might be – whilst there might often be no payment required at art galleries, Janet knows that payment is required and still decides to go in

▓ avoids or intends to avoid payment in full or in part – the lies about their status are designed to avoid full payment

Note also that there is the offence of fraud by false representation.

You should now be able to:

■ understand the law relating to obtaining services dishonestly

■ apply that law to given scenarios.

▓ **Activity**

Consider the following situation and consider the offences that have been committed:

Ed bought an iPod for his girlfriend's birthday and wanted to download some music onto it. He logged onto cheapycheaptunes.com and downloaded a number of tunes using his father's credit card, without his father's knowledge.

In this topic, you will learn how to:

■ state the definition of making off without payment

■ explain the *actus reus* and *mens rea* of making off without payment

■ explain cases that illustrate the law on making off without payment

■ apply the rules to a given situation.

4 Making off without payment

This offence, which is not a fraud offence as it does not require deception, occurs in situations such as where the defendant fills up his car with petrol and drives off without paying, or has a meal in a restaurant and walks out without paying. It is a crime that commonly takes place at petrol stations and has been the focus of police targets. Despite this, offences still take place such as the one reported below.

Banned customer drove off without paying

Annoyed that staff had switched off the fuel supply to a diesel pump he was using, Oliver Pidgley drove off without paying for £3.11 worth of fuel, magistrates heard.

Pidgley, 25, of Krattigen, Eastville Road, Toynton St Peter, admitted making off from Partney Filling Station without giving payment. He also admitted using his mother's vehicle without insurance.

Skegness magistrates fined him £50 for making off and ordered him to pay £3.11 compensation.

He was fined £200 for the no insurance offence and ordered to pay £60 costs and a £15 surcharge. Six penalty points were endorsed on his licence.

Prosecutor Jim Clare told the court Pidgley had previously been barred from using the filling station because of a previous incident and so the fuel supply was switched off.

Later, in a police interview he said he had planned to put £10 worth of fuel in his mother's car but when the pump was switched off he was annoyed and drove off without attempting to pay.

Liz Warwick, representing Pidgley, said her client had been on his way to football training. He was low on fuel and did not believe he had enough diesel to get to another garage.

Pidgley had an insurance policy for his own vehicle and had believed he was covered to drive his mother's car, said Miss Warwick. It had been a genuine mistake, she said.

Skegness Standard, 9 April 2008

The offence of making off without payment is defined in the Theft Act 1978, s3 as:

1 Subject to subsection (3) below, a person who, knowing that payment on the spot for any goods supplied or service done is required or expected from him, dishonestly makes off without having paid as required or expected and with intent to avoid payment of the amount due shall be guilty of an offence.

2 For purposes of this section 'payment on the spot' includes payment at the time of collecting goods on which work has been done or in respect of which service has been provided.

3 Subsection (1) above shall not apply where the supply of the goods or the doing of the service is contrary to law, or where the service done is such that payment is not legally enforceable.

This has the following elements:

■ goods supplied or services done

■ makes off from the spot

■ fails to pay on the spot as required or expected

- dishonesty
- knows that payment on the spot is required or expected
- intention to avoid payment permanently.

The first three of these are the *actus reus* and the last three form the *mens rea* of the offence.

We will look at each element of the offence in turn.

1 Goods supplied or services done

The key point here is that the goods must be supplied. This requires the goods to be delivered to the defendant, or the defendant being allowed to take the goods – as at a petrol filling station or from a self-service shop. If that is not the case, the offence is theft. Where the goods are taken from the self-service shop, both theft and making off without payment are committed.

Where services are involved, the services must be done. This includes examples such as repairing a bicycle, supplying a meal or renting a car. In the case of *Allen* (1985), considered in the previous topic, it was the provision of a hotel room. This, therefore, includes the use of a facility such as a car park. There will be no crime committed if the service has not been completed or if the goods have not been supplied. In **Troughton (1987)** the defendant, who was drunk, called a taxi to take him home. He did not give the taxi driver his exact address, only the approximate area. The taxi driver tried to get the details of the exact location but, when failing to do so, he drove to the police station. When he stopped the vehicle, the defendant ran off without paying.

On appeal it was decided that, as the defendant had not actually been taken home, there was no liability to pay.

2 Makes off from the spot

The idea of making off is just one of departing. There is no need to be seen to be running away or surreptitiously leaving when no one is looking, even though that behaviour often occurs. The important thing is that the departure is dishonest. This can be seen from the case of **Brooks and Brooks (1983)** where it was said the words 'dishonestly makes off' are words easily understandable by any jury. In that case, the defendants had a meal in the upstairs room of a restaurant. The first defendant left the restaurant in a hurry. The second defendant also tried to leave but was caught by the manager. There was clearly making off in that case.

In **McDavitt (1981)** the defendant and three friends had a meal at a restaurant. The friends left, but the defendant stayed at the table. The bill was presented by a waiter and an argument started, and the defendant refused to pay. He went to the door to try and leave, but the exit was blocked and he was kept in the restaurant until the police arrived. It was decided that 'making off' refers to 'a departure from the spot where payment is required or expected'. Where that spot is, is a matter for the jury to decide, depending on the circumstances. Here, the defendant did not actually leave the spot, but merely attempted to do so. This is why shoplifters are usually arrested outside the shop as the offence of making off without payment (and theft) will definitely be complete then, rather than being an attempt to commit the crime.

It is therefore clear that 'the spot' covers a wide range of places, but usually means the area controlled by the person to whom payment should be made.

Key cases

Troughton (1987): if the service – in this case, a taxi journey – has not been completed, there will be no liability to pay.

Brooks and Brooks (1983): expression 'making off' is to be interpreted simply as departing; what is important is not the manner in which the defendant departs, but whether he does so dishonestly.

McDavitt (1981): 'making off' refers to 'a departure from the spot where payment is required or expected'; where that spot is, is a matter for the jury to decide, depending on the circumstances.

3 Fails to pay on the spot as required or expected

Normally, failure to pay on the spot is at the end of a meal in a restaurant or before leaving a shop with goods. The key point is that the departure is made without paying as required or expected. This, therefore, depends on the normal relationship between the defendant and the victim.

In **Vincent (2001)** the defendant left two hotels in which he had stayed, without paying his bills. He was charged with making off without payment but argued that he had made an agreement at both hotels that he would settle his bill at a later date, and therefore payment on the spot was no longer a requirement. At the trial, the judge directed the jury that if this agreement had been made dishonestly it should not be considered, and Vincent was convicted. However, the Court of Appeal quashed his conviction on the basis that there had no longer been an expectation to pay on the spot, and whether or not the defendant had been dishonest in making the agreement was not relevant for the purposes of s(3) of the Theft Act 1978. Although not guilty of this offence, there is the possibility of an offence under the Fraud Act 2006 if he was dishonest about his intention to pay in the future.

4 Dishonesty

Dishonesty is the first part of the *mens rea* and relates to the making off. The test is the *Ghosh* test, as previously discussed. Thus, a defendant who honestly believed he had been given credit for the goods supplied or service done would not be guilty.

5 Knows that payment on the spot is required or expected

In many situations, it is standard practice to pay on the spot, and it will be difficult for a defendant to argue otherwise. However, if a defendant genuinely did not know that payment on the spot was required, he will not be guilty of an offence.

6 Intention to avoid payment permanently

Here the intent must be never to pay the sum involved. This means that an honest belief that credit is being given will mean the offence is not being committed. This has already been seen in the case of *Allen* (1985).

Conclusion

There are six elements of the offence of making off without payment which is a relatively straightforward crime to identify and explain. Most of the cases suggest that a common-sense approach is taken. There are, however, alternative offences where the defendant's behaviour does not fall within the requirements of the offence.

Identifying property offences in exam questions

Ken left some jackets for cleaning at Norma's dry cleaners. A week later, while he was walking to Norma's to collect the cleaned jackets, Ken decided to take them without paying the cleaning charge. This was because he was annoyed that Norma had overcharged him for previous dry cleaning. When Norma placed the jackets on the counter, Ken grabbed them and headed for the door. Norma tried to stop him going through the door, but Ken pushed her out of the way and ran off. Norma was not injured.

This question raises a number of property offences:

■ **Theft of the jackets:** this requires a particular discussion of whether the jackets were 'property belonging to another' and whether Ken could argue that he was not dishonest, as he thought he had a right to

---

■ **Key cases**

Vincent (2001): defendant agreed to pay his hotel bills at a later date, so there was no longer an expectation for payment to be made on the spot, and he was not guilty of making off without payment.

take the jackets because he had been overcharged previously. This is one of the statutory beliefs under s2(1)(a) of the Theft Act 1968.

■ **Robbery:** as Ken pushes Norma on his way out, this raises the possibility of robbery. It is necessary to discuss whether the force was in order to steal and immediately before or at the time of the theft. Reference should be made to the case of *Hale* (1978)

■ **Making off without payment:** this offence is relevant as a service has been provided and Ken has made off from the spot where payment was expected. Applying the Ghosh test, it could be considered whether the reasonable man would find it to be dishonest based on the previous overcharging.

■ **Fraud by false representation:** it would also be possible to argue that by asking Norma for the jackets, Ken was making a representation that he would pay and yet he had already decided that he was not going to pay before asking for them. (Obtaining services dishonestly would not be an appropriate offence as there is no evidence that he was dishonest when he originally left the jackets to be cleaned a week earlier.)

■ **Burglary:** as Ken entered the dry cleaners intending not to pay for the jackets, this could be charged as s9(1)(a) burglary. Based on the principle of *Jones and Smith* (1976) it could be argued that Ken did not have permission to enter if he was intending to steal. Because Ken does actually carry out a theft, he can also be charged with s9(1)(b) of the Theft Act 1968.

Activity

Consider the following situation and consider the offences that have been committed:

Farah had a row with her boyfriend and ran out of the flat she shared with him, intending to go to her mother's house. She knew she had very little money in her purse. She flagged down a passing taxi and asked to be driven to the local cinema complex. When the taxi stopped at traffic lights opposite the railway station, she leapt out of the taxi without paying and ran into the station. She used her credit card, which had already reached its credit limit, to buy a ticket to the town where her mother lived.

You should now be able to:

■ understand the law relating to making off without payment

■ apply that law to given scenarios.

13 Defences

In this topic, you will learn how to:

- outline the range of defences in the syllabus

- explain the effect of a successful defence to a crime

- apply a defence to a problem question.

1 Introduction to defences in criminal law

The AQA Law specification for Unit 4 sets out the defences that are included.

The defences are:

- intoxication
- duress by threats
- duress of circumstances
- self-defence/prevention of crime.

Defences become relevant when the *actus reus* and *mens rea* of an offence have been committed. Therefore, in your answers to the scenario-based questions you are well-advised to discuss the offences and then consider the application of any relevant defence.

The defence of intoxication through drink or drugs is sometimes said not to be a defence at all, but incapacity to form the *mens rea* of the crime. If this is considered as an idea, then it is obvious that the defence will not be of universal application. In any event, since some offences involve intoxication (being drunk in a public place or driving whilst unfit through drink or drugs), it is logical that the defence of intoxication will be of limited application.

Duress occurs where an individual carries out the crime unwillingly, because of either threats made to him (the lesser of two evils in the defendant's mind), or because the circumstances in which he finds himself suggest to the defendant that he has no other option. There are obviously going to be limits as to the application of these defences too. These defences are known as duress by threats and duress of circumstances.

Self-defence/prevention of crime covers a mixture of defences that largely apply to crimes involving violence, and so have limited, but important, application in the offences within this unit.

> **Key terms**
>
> **Duress:** occurs where the defendant is forced to perform the criminal act by someone else.

You should now be able to:

- outline the range of defences available in the AQA specification

- understand the effect of a defence to a crime

- apply a defence to a problem question.

In this topic, you will learn how to:

- state the definition of the defence of intoxication

- distinguish between crimes of basic and specific offence

- distinguish between the effect of voluntary and involuntary intoxication

- explain the effect of mistake when intoxicated

- explain the law relating to 'Dutch Courage'

- apply the rules to a given situation.

2 The defence of intoxication

Intoxication can be either voluntary or involuntary. In general, where the intoxication is voluntary, a person should not be excused from the consequences of their actions. This is because that person is responsible for being in the state of intoxication that impairs their judgement. However, intoxication can be used to show that the defendant could not form the necessary *mens rea* for the offence with which he has been charged. In that sense, it can provide a defence.

Voluntary and involuntary intoxication

Voluntary intoxication is where the defendant takes the drink or drugs of his own free will. Involuntary intoxication is where a person does not know he is taking alcohol or intoxicating drugs. In cases of involuntary intoxication, there will only be a defence if the *mens rea* for a crime was not formed. If this is proved, the defendant will be acquitted.

Involuntary intoxication can arise where:

- the defendant's drinks were spiked with alcohol or drugs, such as when a drug is slipped into a soft drink or alcohol is added without the defendant's knowledge
- the defendant takes drugs prescribed by his doctor in accordance with the instructions
- the defendant takes a non-dangerous drug, although not prescribed to him, in a non-reckless way.

If involuntary intoxication is to be a defence, it must be shown that the effect of the intoxication is that the defendant was, as a result of the intoxication, unable to form the *mens rea* of the offence. This is not always possible, as can be seen in the case of **Kingston (1994)**. At a trial in Lewes Crown Court in March 1992, the defendant, Barry Kingston, and a man named Penn were jointly indicted on a count of indecent assault on a youth aged 15. The defendant, who had paedophiliac homosexual tendencies (which he normally controlled fully), was blackmailed by two former business associates, who arranged for Penn to photograph and audio-tape Kingston in a compromising situation with the boy. Sedative drugs were found in Penn's flat when it was searched, and the prosecution claimed that Penn had laced the boy's drink. Kingston's defence was that Penn had also laced his drink. Kingston said that he had seen the boy lying on the bed but had no recollection of any other events that night, and had woken in his own home the next morning. He said that he would never have committed the offence had he not been affected by the drug. The House of Lords stated that involuntary intoxication was not a defence to a charge if it was proved that the defendant had the necessary intent when the offence was committed, even though he was not to blame for the intoxication. Lord Mustill saw this case as one of disinhibition – the taking of the drug (whatever it was) lowered Kingston's ability to resist temptation, so that his desires overrode his ability to control them.

If the defendant argues that he did not realise the strength of the alcohol or the drugs, this will not be classed as involuntary intoxication. This was decided in **Allen (1988)** where the defendant was charged with indecent assault but argued that he didn't realise the strength of the wine he had been given. His intoxication was classed as voluntary.

Where the defendant takes a non-dangerous drug, although not prescribed to him, in a non-reckless way, the taking may be treated as involuntary and may therefore provide a defence. This can be seen in the case of **Hardie (1985)**. Here, the defendant's relationship with Mrs Hardie had broken down, and she had insisted that he must leave. He did not wish to do so, but on the morning of 2 January 1982 he packed a suitcase. At about lunchtime he found two bottles of tablets in a cabinet. One contained Valium that Mrs Hardie had been prescribed in 1974.

Whilst he had never taken Valium before, the defendant took one about 12 o'clock to calm him down, but it did not have much effect. He and Mrs Hardie then went shopping and he took two more in front of her She said, 'Take as many as you like, they are old stock and will do you

Key cases

Kingston (1994): defendant can only use the defence of involuntary intoxication if the court is convinced that, because of being intoxicated, the defendant lacked the required *mens rea* for the offence; in this case, the court said that an intoxicated intent was still an intent.

Allen (1988): intoxication remains voluntary even where the defendant claims he did not know the drink's or drug's strength.

Hardie (1985): the voluntary consumption of dangerous drugs might be conclusive proof of recklessness; this is not the case with non-dangerous drugs, and a jury should have been directed to consider whether the defendant had been reckless in consuming the Valium.

no harm'. He took two more shortly afterwards and, when back at the house, he fell into a deep sleep. From this time on, he could remember only odd periods for the rest of the day.

It was not disputed that the defendant must have started the fire, for he was alone in the bedroom when it started. Having started it, he emerged, returned to the sitting room to be with Mrs Hardie and her daughter, Tonia, and stayed there. Shortly afterwards, Mrs Hardie heard sounds from the bedroom. She went there, and found smoke and flames coming from the wardrobe. There was evidence that before, at the time of and after the fire the defendant was showing signs of intoxication, and that such signs might have resulted from the taking of Valium some hours earlier.

The court decided that this did not necessarily amount to voluntary intoxication. It said the jury should be directed that, if they came to the conclusion that, as a result of the Valium, the defendant was at the time unable to appreciate the risks to property and persons from his actions, it should then consider whether the taking of the Valium was itself reckless. The courts later decided that there was a distinction between 'dangerous' drugs, including those where it is 'common knowledge' that the taker 'may become aggressive or do dangerous or unpredictable things' or those that make the defendant incapable of appreciating risks (amphetamines and LSD being well-known examples), and non-dangerous drugs such as Valium. Where the drugs can be said to be dangerous, there may be recklessness in self-administering it, which would be the case when the drug was well known for causing certain negative effects.

The distinction between crimes of basic intent and specific intent

Where intoxication is voluntary, it is necessary to establish whether the crime is one of basic intent or specific intent.

The principle is that intoxication is a defence to crimes of specific intent and not those of basic intent. The key case with respect to this is **Majewski (1977)**. In that case, during the evening of 19 February 1973 the defendant and his friend, Leonard Stace, who had also taken drugs and drink, went to The Bull public house in Basildon. Stace became involved in a disturbance. Glasses were broken. The landlord asked Stace to leave and escorted him to the door. As he did so, Stace called to Majewski: 'He's putting me out.' Majewski got up and prevented the landlord from getting Stace out and abused him. The landlord asked both men to go. They refused and a brawl followed. Majewski was violent and abusive, and spat in the landlord's face. When the police came, a fierce struggle took place to get Majewski out. He shouted at the police: 'You pigs, I'll kill you all, you f— pigs, you bastards'. Majewski was charged with s47 OAPA 1861 assault occasioning actual bodily harm. His defence of voluntary intoxication was unsuccessful as s47 is a basic intent crime and so he was convicted.

The House of Lords considered the whole aspect of intoxication and came to the conclusion that self-induced intoxication can only be raised as a defence to crimes of specific intent, but not to crimes of basic intent.

This means that in crimes where the *mens rea* can only be intention, such as murder, voluntary intoxication can remove the defendant's *mens rea*; however, where the crime is one of basic intent there will be no defence. A crime of basic intent is one that only requires the

Key cases

Majewski (1977): made the distinction between crimes of basic intent and crimes of specific intent.

prosecution to prove that the defendant has been reckless – and as the defendant's action in becoming voluntarily intoxicated is in itself reckless behaviour, the *mens rea* element is satisfied and the intoxication cannot be used as an excuse. Where the defendant is charged with a specific intent crime, he will need to prove that the intoxication meant that he did not form the necessary intent, but he may still be convicted of a lesser offence that only requires recklessness for the *mens rea*. However, not all 'specific' intent offences have a corresponding 'basic' intent offence. A typical example of this is theft.

The offences that we have considered in this unit can be categorised as follows:

Specific and basic intent offences

Basic Intent Crimes	Specific Intent Crimes
	Theft
	Burglary
	Blackmail
	Fraud under s2 Fraud Act 2006
	Fraud under s11 Fraud Act 2006
	Making off without payment
Criminal Damage under s1(1) Criminal Damage Act 1971	Criminal Damage under s1(2) Criminal Damage Act 1971

It should also be noted that if the *mens rea* is formed before the intoxication, as with the notion of 'Dutch Courage', there will be no defence of intoxication. This can be seen in the case of **Attorney-General for Northern Ireland v Gallagher (1963)**. In this case the defendant decided to kill his wife. He went out and bought a bottle of whisky and a knife. He drank the whisky and became so drunk that he could not form the *mens rea* for murder (an intention to kill or cause really serious harm); then he killed his wife. As he had formed the intention to kill her before he became intoxicated, he had no defence of intoxication.

Conclusion

The first distinction is between voluntary and involuntary intoxication. Involuntary intoxication is a defence, but only where the intoxication is completely involuntary and it removes the defendant's *mens rea*. The defence of intoxication applies differently to offences of specific intent and those of basic intent. It is essential, therefore, to understand the distinction between the two.

> **Key cases**
>
> **Attorney-General for Northern Ireland v Gallagher (1963):** if the *mens rea* is formed before the intoxication, as in 'Dutch Courage', there will be no defence of intoxication; in this case, the defendant's intention to kill his wife was formed before he got drunk.

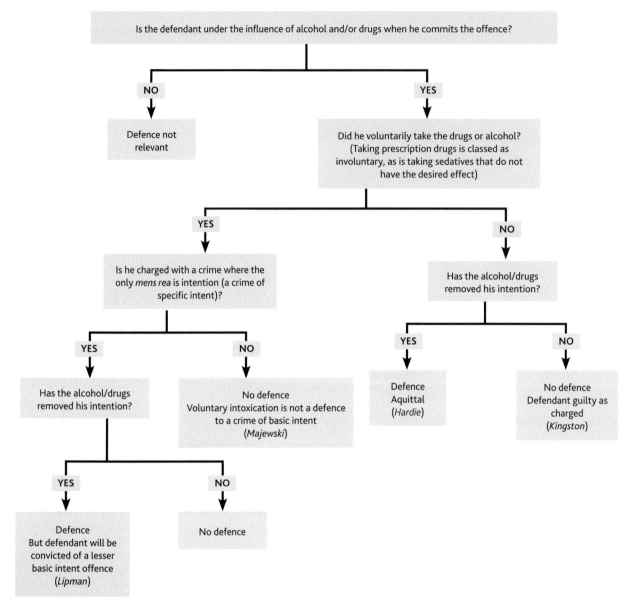

Defence of intoxication

Application of the defence of intoxication to problems in the examination

In the examination, there are often questions involving the defence of intoxication. Discussion of this defence is suggested whenever a character in the scenario takes an alcoholic drink or drugs, whether illegal or legal. It may well be the case that you decide, after due consideration, that the defence will be unsuccessful. Nevertheless, you must include that preliminary discussion.

Consider the following scenario and the offences and the defence involved:

> Ken visited a bar and sat at the table next to Toby. After Ken had drunk several lagers and after Toby had left the bar, Ken picked up off the floor Toby's bank card, which had fallen out of Toby's pocket. Ken memorised the details on the card before handing it in to the owner of the bar. On returning home, Ken used Toby's card details to buy a new mobile phone on the internet for £200, which came out of Toby's bank account.

This question scenario raises the issue of theft, fraud by false representation and intoxication.

- **Theft:** it needs to be considered whether there was theft of the bank card, the money in Toby's account and the mobile phone. It is not possible to steal the card details, as stated by the decision in *Oxford* v *Moss*.

- **Fraud by false representation:** by using the card to obtain the mobile phone, Ken is making a representation by his conduct that he is authorised to do so. His representation was made via the internet but a representation can be made to a machine (Fraud Act 2006, s2(5)). If Ken was ordering a phone contract and not just a phone, it could also be argued that he could be charged with obtaining a service dishonestly.

- **Intoxication:** it is important to describe the key elements of the defence before applying to the facts – this includes the distinction between voluntary and involuntary, and the meaning of specific and basic intent offences in relation to intoxication. Theft and fraud are specific intent crimes, and so it would need to be argued whether the voluntary intoxication had removed the *mens rea* elements required for the offences. It is important to consider all the facts carefully when applying the law, as the fact that Ken was capable of memorising the card details may suggest that he was not too intoxicated (from drinking the lagers) to form the *mens rea*.

You should now be able to:

- answer problem questions that include the defence of intoxication.

Activity

Plan an answer to the following question, breaking it down into the three areas of law that are raised.

Vinny was sitting in a bar, having his fifth glass of whisky. Warren, who had also been drinking for some time, was standing behind him, excitedly discussing a film with some friends. Warren lost his grip on his pint of beer, which spilled all over Vinny's light-coloured suit jacket. Vinny was outraged and threatened to break every bone in Warren's body if Warren did not immediately pay him £100 to 'cover the damage'. Warren took one look at Vinny, and, with the help of his friends, paid him the money.

Discuss the possible criminal liability of Vinny and Warren for the incidents in the bar.

3 The defence of duress by threats

Duress occurs where the defendant feels compelled to perform the criminal act. Duress is now split into two parts: duress by threats, and also duress of circumstances. Duress is a defence available to all crimes except murder; therefore it is available to all crimes within the AQA specification for this unit. The more recent legal development of duress of circumstances is dealt with in the next topic.

The test for duress can be stated as follows:

1 Was the defendant impelled to act as he did because he feared death or serious physical injury?

2 If so, did he respond as a sober person of reasonable firmness sharing the characteristics of the defendant would have done?

The test comes from the case of **Graham (1982)**. In that case, the defendant lived with his wife and also his gay lover, who was called King. King was a very violent and jealous man, of whom both Graham and his wife were afraid, as he had attacked Graham's wife when he saw them together. King finally decided that he wanted to get rid of Graham's wife for good, and he took a flex from an electrical appliance and put it around her neck. He told Graham to hold one end of the flex, and pressure was exerted until Mrs Graham was strangled to death. In his defence, Graham argued that he had only complied because he was afraid of King as he was so violent. Graham argued the defence of intoxication, as he had been drinking alcohol and taking Valium for anxiety, and also the defence of duress. Graham's conviction for murder was upheld on the basis that the threat was not a sufficiently serious one and the taking of drugs and drink was irrelevant for the defence of duress. Although this may have made him more susceptible to threats, he had to be compared to a reasonable sober person.

In this topic, you will learn how to:

- state the definition of the defence of duress by threats

- explain how the law balances the seriousness of the harm threatened and the offence committed

- explain how the law deals with the issues of immediacy, means of escape and self-induced duress

- apply the rules to a given situation.

Key cases

Graham (1982): set out the test for duress as: (1) Was the defendant impelled to act as he did because he feared death or serious physical injury? (2) If so, did he respond as a sober person of reasonable firmness sharing the characteristics that the defendant would have done?

Aspects of the defence of duress

There are a number of issues that need to be considered when considering the defence of duress:

- the nature of the threat
- the threat must be made in connection with the offence committed
- the characteristics of the defendant
- the effect of intoxication
- the immediacy of the threat and possible escape
- self-induced duress.

The nature of the threat

The *Graham* test states the defendant must have 'feared death or serious physical injury'. Thus, the threats must be as to serious physical harm, however minor the offence committed. Thus, 'I will kill you if you do not break Emma's pencil', could give rise to a defence of duress to a charge of criminal damage. 'I will tap you on the hand with my pen if you do not break Emma's pencil' will not give rise to the defence against a charge of criminal damage arising from breaking the pencil. There is no defence if the threat is to damage or destroy property, although there can be a defence of self-defence relating to this, which we shall consider in Topic 5 of this chapter.

What exactly amounts to serious physical injury is unclear. Certainly, psychological harm will not suffice as in *Baker and Wilkins* (1997). In this case, duress was not available to a woman who broke down the door of her ex-husband's house, believing that he had abducted their child. She had argued unsuccessfully that there had been a threat to her mental health.

Threats that come outside the scope of the defence, because they are not of death or serious injury, will be considered as a mitigating factor when the judge passes sentence. These include threats to expose a sexual affair or a person's particular sexual practices. These aspects are to be disregarded in any consideration of duress even when they appear to be increasing the pressure caused by the threat. This can be seen from the case of **Valderrama-Vega (1985)**, where a cocaine smuggler for Colombian drug dealers had been threatened with death or serious injury to himself and his family if he did not take part in importing drugs. He was also under financial pressure and had been threatened with disclosure of his homosexuality. As there had been a threat to his family, the defence succeeded, but it would have failed had duress been argued just on the basis of the financial pressures and the threat of revealing the defendant's homosexuality.

It should also be noted from *Valderrama-Vega* (1985) that the threat can be made to a member of the defendant's immediate family. The same applies in the case of a person for whose safety the defendant would reasonably regard himself as responsible. This can be seen in the specimen directions to juries set out by the Judicial Studies Board, which were specifically approved in **Hasan (2005)**.

The threat must be made in connection with the offence committed

The defence can only be relied on where there is a connection between the threats made to the accused and the offence committed in response to the threats. Thus, it is no defence to say I was threatened with death if I did not burn down a factory to a charge of breaking a totally unconnected person's arm. In the case of **Cole (1994)** the defendant robbed several building societies, and he claimed moneylenders had threatened to harm

Key cases

Valderrama-Vega (1985): only relevant factors are threats of death or serious personal injury; in this case, financial pressure and the threat to disclose the defendant's homosexuality were irrelevant factors to the defence of duress.

Hasan (2005): defence of duress can be used where the threats are made with respect to a person for whose safety the defendant would reasonably regard himself as responsible.

Cole (1994): there must be a connection between the threats made to the accused and the offence committed in response to the threats; there was no sufficient connection between armed robberies committed by the defendant and failure to repay a debt to a moneylender.

him and his girlfriend if he did not repay money he had borrowed from them. The threat related to consequences if the money was not repaid, not if he did not commit the armed robberies. The threat must be to commit a specific offence in order to plead duress for that offence.

The characteristics of the defendant

The second leg of the test, 'If so, did he respond as a sober person of reasonable firmness sharing the characteristics of the defendant would have done?', requires a consideration of the effect of the threats on the reasonable man sharing the characteristics of the defendant.

The key case on characteristics with respect to duress is **Bowen (1996)**. In this case, the defendant pleaded duress to a charge of obtaining services by deception. He had visited electrical shops on a number of occasions and bought goods on credit, which he resold to make money. He then stopped making the payments to the finance companies to which he owed the money. In his defence, he said he had been acting under duress, as two men had threatened to petrol-bomb him and his family if he didn't obtain the goods for them. It was argued that the defendant had a low IQ of only 68 and that his low intelligence made him more likely to succumb to threats. However, the court decided that this was not a characteristic that should be considered, and said:

> We do not see how low IQ, short of mental impairment or mental defectiveness can be said to be a characteristic that makes those who have it less courageous and less able to withstand threats and pressure.

The court then went on to consider the characteristics that would be relevant for a jury to consider when the defence of duress is raised:

> The defendant may be in a category of persons who the jury may think less able to resist pressure than people not within that category. Obvious examples are age, where a young person may well not be so robust as a mature one; possibly sex, though many women would doubtless consider that they have as much moral courage to resist pressure as men; pregnancy, where there is added fear for the unborn child; serious physical disability, which may inhibit self-protection; recognised mental illness or psychiatric condition such as learned helplessness … Characteristics due to self-induced abuse, such as alcohol, drugs or glue-sniffing, cannot be relevant.

This therefore means that the following characteristics are relevant:

- age and sex
- physical disability
- pregnancy
- mental illness or psychiatric condition.

However, the following characteristics are not relevant:

- low intelligence
- the fact that the defendant might be timid or more vulnerable to threats than an ordinary person
- characteristics that are self-induced through alcohol, drugs or glue-sniffing.

The effect of intoxication

It would appear from the cases of *Graham* (1982) and *Bowen* (1996) that intoxication is not a relevant factor if the effect is to make the defendant more vulnerable to threats, although it may be a defence in its own right. However, if the intoxication is involuntary then arguably it could be considered, as in Bowen the reference was to self-induced abuse.

Key cases

Bowen (1996): sets out the characteristics that can be relevant for the defence of duress.

The immediacy of the threat and possible escape

The defence of duress can only be used where there was no safe means of escape and therefore no way of avoiding the threat other than carrying it out. This can be seen in the case of *Gill* (1963) where the defendant was told to steal his employer's lorry and was threatened with violence if he failed to do so. At his trial for theft, it was stated that as there was sufficient time between the threat and the commission of the crime to go to the police, the defence of duress was not available.

The question as to whether the threat could have been avoided raises the issue of the immediacy of the threat. The defendant can only successfully plead the defence if the threat was operating on his mind at the time he committed the offence. A threat can be considered to be imminent even if it cannot be carried out at the time of the crime. In the case of **Hudson and Taylor (1971)** the defendants, who were girls aged 17 and 19, had witnessed a fight in a pub and were the key prosecution witnesses at the trial of the men involved in the fight. However, when they were called to give evidence in court, they lied when asked to identify the attacker. They were charged with perjury and admitted that they had given false evidence, but their defence was that they had been threatened before the trial by a group of violent men and had seen a member of the gang in the public gallery whilst giving evidence. The Court of Appeal decided that although the threat could not have been carried out at the time they gave their evidence, as they were in court, it was nevertheless an imminent threat.

The same principle was discussed in **Abdul-Hussain (1999)**, a case about aircraft hijackers who were Shiite Muslims who had fled from Southern Iraq – and the persecution of Saddam Hussein – to Sudan, but had overstayed in Sudan and feared being returned to Iraq to face torture and execution. Despite the lack of immediacy of the threat, the court decided that defence of duress (of circumstances in this case) was allowed.

Despite a generous interpretation of 'immediate' in the cases of *Hudson and Taylor* and *Abdul-Hussain*, it seems likely that the courts will apply a stricter interpretation following the case of *Hasan* (2005) (facts are discussed in the next section) where the House of Lords disapproved the decision in *Hudson and Taylor*. Lord Bingham said:

> I can understand that the Court of Appeal in R v Hudson and Taylor had sympathy with the predicament of the young appellants but I cannot, consistently with principle, accept that a witness testifying in the Crown Court at Manchester has no opportunity to avoid complying with a threat incapable of execution then or there.

Self-induced duress

The defence is unlikely to be available where the defendant has voluntarily put himself in a situation where he is likely to be subjected to threats of violence in order to make him commit a crime. This is consistent with other defences such as intoxication, where the voluntary nature of the defendant's behaviour usually means he has no defence. This can occur where the defendant joins a criminal group likely to subject him to such threats, or gets involved with crime and thus with other criminals likely to subject him to such threats if he lets them down or came to owe them money. From the defendant's point of view, the problem often arises when he wishes to end the association.

This can be seen in a number of cases. For example, in **Sharp (1987)** in August 1984 the defendant and two others, both of whom were armed with sawn-off shotguns, held up a sub-post office in Hounslow. They wore wigs. One of the others threatened the wife of the postmaster, whereupon the postmaster himself pressed the alarm. All three then ran off to the getaway car empty-handed. One of the others tried to fire his gun in the air in order to discourage anyone who was minded to pursue them.

Key cases

Hudson and Taylor (1971): duress is available even when the threat cannot be carried out immediately, as long as the threat is operating on the defendant's mind at the time of committing the offence.

Abdul-Hussain (1999): even though there was a lack of immediacy of the threat, the court decided that the possibility of death could overbear their minds and therefore might be available to the defendant as a defence.

Sharp (1987): where a person has voluntarily, and with knowledge of its nature, joined a criminal organisation or gang that he knew might bring pressure on him to commit an offence, and was an active member when he was put under such pressure, he cannot use the defence of duress.

In September 1984 the sub-post office at Wraysbury, near Staines, was the subject of an attack by them. The others (not the defendant) again carried loaded sawn-off shotguns. Sharp was responsible for locking the post office door after the three of them had entered. Unfortunately, the postmaster was shot and killed. Sharp admitted that he had been invited to take part in these robberies and had willingly done so. He regarded one of the others as a 'nutcase'. He did not wish any weapons to be used, or so he said. He claimed that he panicked when he saw the guns being loaded into the car, because he knew from the first robbery that the others were prepared to fire them. He wanted to pull out, but he lost his nerve and he carried on despite his wish to withdraw because one of the others pointed a gun at him and threatened to blow his head off if he did not carry on with the plan to rob the post office. The court did not allow the defence of duress because he had voluntarily got into the situation by his association with the other criminals.

Activity

Read the article below and list the reasons why the defence of duress was not accepted in this case.

Millionaire's daughter denies riot charges

A millionaire's daughter accused of taking part in last summer's riots was not acting under duress, a court was told on Monday. Laura Johnson, 20, drove looters around and was seen putting a box into the front seat of a car she was driving, a jury at inner London crown court heard.

Johnson, of Orpington, south-east London, denies three counts of burglary and three alternative counts of handling stolen goods relating to the riots last August.

Sandy Canavan, prosecuting, said: 'The prosecution say that any talk of duress is no more than a red herring in this case.

'This is a young lady who exercised extraordinarily bad judgment that night. She knew what she was doing, she did it for whatever reason seemed good to her at the time, but not under duress.'

Canavan said that just after midnight on Tuesday 9 August, a man called Raymond Johnson was driving from Chingford, in east London, to Orpington when he came off the A2 near a large retail park near the O2 leisure park in Greenwich.

He noticed that people were running to and from various stores carrying items, and pulled over to see what was going on. His attention was drawn to a black car

Laura Johnson

driven by Laura Johnson, who was no relation of his.

He saw a man run from Currys with a box with Goodmans written on it, which he threw into a nearby bush before running back to Currys. 'The white female driver of the car, we say that's Ms Johnson, went over, picked up the Goodmans box and put it in the front seat of her car.'

Mr Johnson called the police. 'He remembers seeing three men running backwards and forwards to the car, putting things in it,' Canavan said.

The people then got into the car and Ms Johnson drove off, followed by Mr Johnson, she went on.

At one point he took a picture on his phone, and Ms Johnson did not appear to be particularly distressed.

Finally, Mr Johnson went on to Orpington, but on his way back to Chingford later he drove past the retail park again, and saw the car, which had been stopped by police. He went over and spoke to police, telling them what he had seen, and arrests were made.

Ms Johnson started to rev the engine with a view to driving off, but police smashed the windscreen to stop her.

Ms Johnson told police that three males jumped into her car and told her where to go and what to do, Canavan said.

She said she was a bit concerned, and had not expected to be driving around people she did not know, the prosecutor added.

But Johnson said in her defence case statement that there was talk of stabbing people, of a gun, and one man had been playing footage on a mobile phone of someone being tortured.

Canavan said: 'The prosecution say, if what you are saying is true, the time to have said it is when you were safely with the police. Getting out and helping yourself to the Goodmans box discarded by one of the other individuals is hardly the action of someone who is being forced to drive around.'

The Guardian, 20 March 2012

■ **Key cases**

Hasan (2005): in cases of self-induced duress where the defendant voluntarily associates with others who engage in criminal activity, the defence will be excluded if the defendant foresaw, or ought reasonably to have foreseen, the risk that he might be subjected to any compulsion by threats of violence.

The defendant does not have to join a gang; merely associating with others engaged in criminal activity will suffice. This is particularly likely when there is involvement with drug dealers, as in the case of **Hasan (2005)**. Here, the defendant became involved with a violent drug dealer. The girlfriend of the drug dealer was a prostitute and Hasan worked as a driver and bodyguard, taking her to clients' homes. The defendant, acting on instructions from the drug dealer and armed with a knife, carried out a burglary on a house where there was known to be a safe containing a large amount of money, but he was caught and charged with aggravated burglary. Hasan pleaded duress on the basis that he had received threats of violence to himself and his family, which would have been carried out had he not committed the burglary. He was convicted at his trial, but in the Court of Appeal his conviction was quashed. However, the prosecution appealed to the House of Lords on a point of law to establish when a defendant loses the protection of the defence in cases where it is self-induced. The House of Lords said that a defendant could not plead duress when he had foreseen, or ought to have foreseen, that his voluntary association with a known criminal involved the risk of being subjected to any compulsion by acts of violence. This is not restricted to compulsion to commit crimes of the kind with which he was charged. The defendant loses the benefit of a defence based on duress if he ought reasonably to have foreseen the risk of coercion. A person voluntarily associating with known criminals should foresee the risk of future coercion. As a matter of policy, the law must discourage association with known criminals. As a result of the appeal, the conviction was reinstated.

Conclusion

Duress applies to excuse a defendant where his crime has been committed so as to avoid death or serious injury threatened to him or others if he did not commit the crime. The courts attempt to limit the scope of the defence by limiting the category of persons against whom the threats must be made. There are also limits set where the defendant has the opportunity to escape from the threats but does not do so when he could, and when he puts himself in a position in which he was likely to be subjected to threats – usually by his criminal association.

Application of the defence of duress by threats to problems in the examination

In the examination, there are often questions involving the defence of duress. Discussion of this defence is suggested whenever a character in the scenario is put under some sort of pressure by threats.

Consider the following scenario, and the offences and the defence involved:

> Until recently, Dave had been Gina's partner, and he was very upset that Gina had now begun to live with Fred. When he discovered that Eric had been invited to Fred and Gina's engagement party at Fred's house, Dave threatened to 'beat up' Eric unless Eric took the opportunity to smash the engagement presents brought by guests. Eric was very frightened of Dave and he agreed to do so. At the party, Fred thought that Eric was behaving strangely and followed him upstairs to a bedroom where the presents had been left. Realising that he was being watched as he was about to begin smashing the presents, Eric tried to rush past Fred. In the struggle that followed, Fred fell downstairs and broke his leg.

The scenario has three aspects to be dealt with:

1 Burglary under s9(1)(a) – this raises issues of entry as a trespasser and the intention to cause criminal damage.

2 Burglary under s9(1)(b) – this again raises issues of entry as a trespasser and subsequent infliction of grievous bodily harm.

3 Duress as a defence to both charges above – possible prior association between Dave and Eric; threat of death or serious injury; possibility of avoiding implementation of the threat; application of the objective test.

Eric's initial entry into the house was as a trespasser, notwithstanding his invitation to the party, because he intended from the outset to exceed the scope of any permission he had been given. It could also be argued that Eric entered the bedroom as a trespasser, on the basis that it was a part of a building into which he had no permission to go. Thus, s9(1)(a) burglary had been committed because Eric entered (the house or the bedroom) intending to commit criminal damage.

The broken leg suffered by Fred when he fell downstairs in consequence of the struggle with Eric could itself have amounted to grievous bodily harm, which would raise the issue of s9(1)(b) burglary. Eric might be able to assert a defence of duress on account of the threats made to him by Dave.

You should now be able to:

- answer problem questions involving the defence of duress by threats.

4 The defence of duress of circumstances

Duress of circumstances differs from duress by threats in that in duress by threats the defendant claims he is forced to commit an offence, whereas in duress of circumstances the defendant believes he, or those with him (for example, in a car), would suffer death or serious injury if he did not escape by doing what he did. In this sense, it is a little like self-defence which is considered in the next topic.

In **Martin (1989)** Simon Brown J summarised the position as follows:

First … duress … can arise from other objective dangers threatening the accused or others. Arising thus it is conveniently called 'duress of circumstances'.

Secondly, the defence is available only if, from an objective standpoint, the accused can be said to be acting reasonably and proportionately in order to avoid a threat of death or serious injury.

Third, assuming the defence to be open to the accused on his account of the facts, the issue should be left to the jury, who should be directed to determine these two questions: first, was the accused, or may he have been, impelled to act as he did because as a result of what he reasonably believed to be the situation he had good cause to fear that otherwise death or serious physical injury would result? Second, if so, may a sober person of reasonable firmness, sharing the characteristics of the accused, have responded to that situation by acting as the accused acted. If the answer to both those questions was 'yes', then the jury would acquit: the defence of necessity would have been established.

The case of *Martin* (1989) involved a charge of driving whilst disqualified. The defendant's wife had suicidal tendencies and had attempted suicide on a number of occasions. Her son had overslept, was bound to be late for work, and was at risk of losing his job unless, so it was claimed, the defendant drove him to work. The defendant's wife was distraught. She was shouting, screaming, banging her head against a wall and she was

Activity

Consider the following scenario and discuss the offences and defences involved:

Helen ran the finances for Irma's art gallery and had authority to sign cheques drawn on Irma's account. Jamal told her that if she did not write out a cheque payable to him for £1,000 that he believed Irma owed him, he would make sure she never saw her children again. Helen, a very timid person, was so frightened that she gave Jamal a cheque for £1,000. Jamal was still very angry despite getting the cheque and unscrewed the rear light covers of Irma's car, removed the bulbs, and then replaced the covers. He put the light bulbs in Irma's bin.

In this topic, you will learn how to:

- state the definition of the defence of duress of circumstances

- explain how the law balances the seriousness of the harm threatened and the offence committed

- explain how the law deals with the issues of immediacy and means of escape

- apply the rules to a given situation.

Key cases

Martin (1989): set out the principles behind duress of circumstances.

threatening suicide unless he drove the boy to work. The defence had a statement from a doctor that expressed the opinion that in view of her mental condition it is likely that Mrs Martin would have attempted suicide if her husband did not drive her son to work. The defendant believed that his wife would carry out that threat unless he did as she demanded. Despite his disqualification, he therefore drove the boy to work. He was in fact stopped by the police within about a quarter of a mile of the house.

From this case, it can be seen that the test is very similar to that of duress by threats. There are a number of elements to consider:

- the objective nature of the threat
- reasonable and proportionate action
- the nature of the test
- limits to the defence.

The objective nature of the threat

The fact that the threat must be seen objectively means that this is the view that a reasonable man – in other words, the jury – would take. This is the same as in the defence of duress by threats, and therefore requires consideration of the same characteristics of the defendant as we considered in the previous topic and in the case of *Bowen* (1996).

Reasonable and proportionate action

The requirement of 'reasonable and proportionate action' acts to limit the circumstances in which the defence may be pleaded. This is not just proportionate action, but action that would only be taken given the very serious nature of the threats made. This can be seen in the case of **Conway (1989)** where the defendant, having been attacked by two men whilst he was in a vehicle a fortnight previously, saw two men approaching his car. He drove off recklessly as, he claimed, he feared another attack. In fact, the two men were plain clothes policeman about to arrest a passenger in his car. The jury would have to consider whether the defendant's behaviour was proportionate.

The nature of the test

The test is exactly the same as the test for duress by threats, with the obvious changes:

1 Was the accused, or may he have been, impelled to act as he did because as a result of what he reasonably believed to be the situation he had good cause to fear that otherwise death or serious physical injury would result?

2 If so, may a sober person of reasonable firmness, sharing the characteristics of the accused, have responded to that situation by acting as the accused acted?

An application of the test can be seen in the case of **Rodger and Rose (1997)**. In that case, the defendants were serving terms of life imprisonment for murder. Their original tariff set by the trial judge, of 12 and 20 years respectively, had since been increased to 17 years and indeterminate respectively. They claimed they became angry and depressed and had begun to consider suicide. This, they claimed, prompted them to break out of prison. The defence was not allowed as the circumstances that caused the action were internal to themselves, and not extraneous circumstances as in all the other cases.

Key cases

Conway (1989): defendant, fearing a repeat attack, drove off recklessly; the court could consider whether this was a proportionate and reasonable behaviour so as to amount to the defence of duress of circumstances.

Rodger and Rose (1997): defence is not available where the circumstances are internal to the defendant; to do so would be a license for anyone to commit a crime based on some evidence of 'suicidal thoughts'.

Limits to the defence

The defence has the same limitations on it as duress by threats. This was specifically stated in the case of **Pommell (1995)** where the Court of Appeal made it clear that the defence was not just limited to driving offences. In that case, the police entered the defendant's house at about 8.00am on 4 June 1993 to execute a search warrant. The defendant was found lying in bed with a loaded gun in his right hand. He was asked if the gun was his and he replied, 'I took it off a geezer who was going to do some people some damage with it'. In the same bedroom police officers found a bag containing ammunition. When interviewed, the defendant was asked to explain his possession of the gun, and he said:

> Last night someone come round to see me, this guy by the name of Erroll, and he had it with him with the intention to go and shoot some people because they had killed his friend and he wanted to kill their girlfriends and relatives and kids, and I persuade him, I took it off him and told him that it's not right to do that.

The defendant went on to say that Erroll had called between 12.30am and 1.00am and, after he left, he took the gun upstairs and kept it from his girlfriend and took the bullets out of it. He then decided to wait until morning and decided to put the bullets back into it. He was lying in bed with the gun against his leg because, he said, he did not want his girlfriend to see it. He said that he was going to hand the gun to his brother so that he could hand it to the police because his brother gets on with the police and had handed in guns in the past.

The question then remains whether the jury would believe the story and excuse the defendant by finding him not guilty.

Key cases

Pommell (1995): the Court of Appeal specifically extended the defence of duress of circumstances to all crimes, as in duress by threats.

Conclusion

Duress of circumstances now has very similar principles as duress by threats, but you still need to be able to distinguish the two and apply them accurately.

Application of the defence of duress of circumstances to problems in the examination

In the examination, there are often questions involving the defence of duress. Discussion of this defence is suggested whenever a character in the scenario is put under some sort of pressure by the circumstances in which he finds himself.

Consider the following scenario, and the offences and the defence involved:

> David cycled into the countryside with his 12-year-old daughter, Ellie, who suddenly suffered serious breathing problems. Fred was passing in his car but, though he stopped, he refused to take David and Ellie to a hospital because he had an important appointment. Whilst Fred was standing holding the car door, David jumped in with Ellie and slammed the door shut, causing Fred to stumble and fall. David then drove Ellie to hospital, abandoning the car on yellow lines outside. The journey used a quarter of a tank of petrol.

The scenario has three aspects to be dealt with:

1   *Actus reus* issues in theft and robbery – property (the car, the petrol), appropriation, the use of force, purpose.

2   *Mens rea* issues in theft and robbery – dishonesty, intention permanently to deprive (applied to the car and to the petrol), intention or recklessness as to the use of force.

3   Duress of circumstances issues – subjective and objective tests, involving imminent threat of death or serious injury and reasonableness of response.

This question raises issues of theft (Theft Act s1) and of robbery (Theft Act s8) by David in connection with the taking of Fred's car and the use of the petrol during the journey. However, it was also very important to note that David's actions were prompted entirely by his concern for the safety of his daughter, Ellie. Thus, the defence of duress of circumstances can be offered in order to justify or excuse his conduct.

It should be noted that robbery applies not only in relation to the theft of the car but also to the theft of the petrol. The whole question of dishonesty is raised as it must be shown that David would be regarded as dishonest according to the ordinary standards of reasonable and honest people. This might not be the case if his motive in taking the car was to get treatment for his daughter when she was experiencing serious breathing problems.

The requirement of an intention permanently to deprive can be seen from the abandoning of the car, although the fact that it would readily be found, identified and returned might counteract that. This is not an issue with the petrol.

These facts give rise to a possible defence of duress of circumstances as there is ample evidence on which David could argue that he reasonably feared that Ellie might suffer serious injury or death, that no other course of action was open to him to avert that risk, and that a sober person of reasonable firmness would have responded in the same way.

Activity

Consider the case of *Backshall* (1998) set out below, and decide whether the defendant could successfully plead duress of circumstances. What could Howell be charged with?

Backshall had been driving his car (a Ford Mondeo) when his co-accused, Howell, attempted to overtake. It was alleged that Backshall drove his vehicle from side to side and applied his brakes several times before Howell overtook him. That was the first driving incident.

Both vehicles stopped and a fight ensued, during which it seemed Howell was the aggressor. Howell went to his car and returned with a hammer. He smashed the Mondeo's windscreen and front side windows while Backshall sat in the driver's seat.

Backshall drove away at speed, pursued by Howell. Backshall reversed from a side street into a major road and stopped, facing the wrong direction in traffic. That was the second incident. Backshall was charged with dangerous driving.

You should now be able to:

- answer problem questions involving the defence of duress of circumstances.

In this topic, you will learn how to:

- state the definition of the defence of self-defence/ prevention of crime

- distinguish between self-defence and prevention of crime

- apply the rules to a given situation.

5 The defence of self-defence/prevention of crime

Self-defence is where the defendant admits committing the *actus reus* with the necessary *mens rea*, but says he was acting in self-defence. A person may use force as is reasonable in the circumstances to defend himself or another or his property. The law recognises use of force in private defence and public defence, and the details of both are outlined below.

Private defence

The common law defence of self-defence, which provides that a person may use such force as is reasonable in the circumstances, is available to the defendant if he is:

▦ defending himself or his property against an actual or imminent attack, or

▦ defending another against such an attack.

Public defence

Section 3 of the Criminal Law Act 1967 states that a person may use such force as is reasonable in the circumstances in order to:

▦ prevent the commission of an offence, or

▦ effect a lawful arrest.

Requirements for private and public defences

The private and public defences overlap because if a person uses force against an attacker, as well as defending himself (self-defence) he is obviously also preventing a crime. Both defences have been clarified by s76 of the Criminal Justice and Immigration Act 2008, which did not aim to change the law but to put the legal principles from the case law into statutory form. The requirements for both private and public defences are the same:

▦ the necessity of force

▦ the reasonableness of force.

The necessity of force

The basic principle is that the use of force is not justified if it is not necessary. It will be necessary if it is seen to be so in the circumstances which exist or which the defendant genuinely believed existed. This can be seen from the case of **Gladstone Williams (1987)** where a man saw a women become the victim of a robbery by a youth. This man struggled with the robber with a view to stopping him and handing him to the police. At this point the defendant appeared and thought that the man was attacking the youth, and stepped in to protect the youth. The defendant was successful in pleading prevention of crime, even though he was mistaken as to the actual facts. His defence is based on what he genuinely believed was happening.

The defence comes into operation even if the attack has not yet taken place, providing it is imminent. In other words, the defendant does not have to wait for an attack to start but can get in the first blow. The difficulty with this is establishing that the force he uses is reasonable. However, it is clear that the defendant does not have a duty to retreat as far as possible before using force, which was the case before the 1967 Act. This can be seen from the case of **Bird (1985)**. The facts of the case were that on 10 March 1984 the defendant, Debbie Bird, was celebrating her 17th birthday. There was a party at a house in Harlow. There was a guest at the party called Darren Marder, who became the victim. He and the defendant had been together as boyfriend and girlfriend for around five months the year before. That relationship had come to an end. Marder arrived at the party with his new girlfriend, and an argument broke out. The defendant told Marder to leave, and he did.

A little later, Marder came back and a second argument took place. The defendant poured a glass of Pernod over Marder, and he retaliated by slapping her around the face. When she was later held up against a wall she lunged at Marder with her hand, which was the hand that held the

> ### Key cases
>
> **Gladstone Williams (1987):** defence under s3 of the Criminal Law Act 1967 is based on the genuine belief of the defendant rather than the actual facts; in this case, the defendant believed a youth was being attacked when in fact his victim was trying to arrest the youth.
>
> **Bird (1985):** defendant does not have to wait for an attack to start but can get in the first blow.

Pernod glass. The glass hit him in the face, broke, and took out his eye. The court decided that it was unnecessary to show an unwillingness to fight and there were circumstances where a defendant might reasonably react immediately and without first retreating, as Bird did in this case. The force was not reasonable in terms of what had happened, but was reasonable with respect to what she thought might happen when she was pinned against the wall. This rule is now contained in the Criminal Justice and Immigration Act s76 (6A) as amended by the Legal Aid, Sentencing and punishment of Offenders Act 2012 s148.

The reasonableness of force

The jury has the task of deciding whether, in all the circumstances, the defendant used reasonable force. The jury, of course, can take as long as it needs to consider the facts, the facts as the defendant believed them, the circumstances of the attack, the time available to the defendant to decide on his course of action, and the risk to the defendant balanced against the risk of harm to the victim. The defendant usually does that in a split second so he may use excessive force. If that is the case, that excessive force is unlawful.

Lord Morris of Borth-y-Gest said, in the case of **Palmer (1971)**:

> It is both good law and good sense that a man who is attacked may defend himself. It is both good law and good sense that he may do, but may only do, what is reasonably necessary. But everything will depend upon the particular facts and circumstances … It may in some cases be only sensible and clearly possible to take some simple avoiding action. Some attacks may be serious and dangerous. Others may not be. If there is some relatively minor attack it would not be common sense to permit some action of retaliation which was wholly out of proportion to the necessities of the situation. If an attack is serious so that it puts someone in immediate peril then immediate defensive action may be necessary. If the moment is one of crisis for someone in imminent danger he may have to avert the danger by some instant reaction.
>
> If the attack is all over and no sort of peril remains then the employment of force may be by way of revenge or punishment or by way of paying off an old score or may be pure aggression. There may no longer be any link with a necessity of defence. Of all these matters the good sense of a jury will be the arbiter. If there has been no attack then clearly there will have been no need for defence. If there has been attack so that defence is reasonably necessary it will be recognised that a person defending himself cannot weigh to a nicety the exact measure of his necessary defensive action.

The famous cases of **Clegg (1994)**, a soldier on a checkpoint in Northern Ireland in the 1990s faced with what might be a terrorist attack, and **Martin (Anthony Edward) (2001)**, who shot and killed a 16-year-old intruder with a pump-action shotgun, demonstrate the difficulties juries face when considering what amounts to reasonable force.

In *Clegg* (1994) the defendant was a soldier on duty in Northern Ireland before the peace settlement. He was at a road checkpoint when a car came towards him at high speed. Seeing that it was not going to stop, he fired at it. His last shot hit a girl passenger in the back seat and killed her. Evidence showed that the car had already passed him when he fired that final shot. It was held that under the circumstances neither he nor anyone else was any longer in danger, therefore his plea of self-defence or defence of another should not succeed. He was found guilty of murder, a decision which was upheld on appeal. He was, however, eventually cleared of the charge in 1999 when it was disputed whether it was his bullet that killed the victim.

■ **Key cases**

Palmer (1971): Lord Morris of Borth-y-Gest set out the way in which reasonable force was to be explained.

Clegg (1994) and **Martin (Anthony Edward) (2001):** the defendants were unsuccessful in pleading self-defence because the amount of force used was excessive. Self-defence requires the force to be reasonable.

In *Martin (Anthony Edward)* (2001), the defendant lived alone in an isolated farmhouse in East Anglia which had been burgled in the past. On this particular occasion, Martin, woken by the sounds of someone entering his property, took his shotgun and fired without warning into the darkness. One of the intruders, 16-year-old Fred Barras, was shot in the back and killed. Martin was found guilty of murder. On appeal his plea of self-defence was rejected on the grounds that the force he had used was unreasonable. However, his conviction was reduced to manslaughter on the grounds of diminished responsibility. He was freed in 2003.

Tony Martin, the Norfolk farmer who failed in his plea of self-defence

The question of proportionality arises in the Criminal Justice and Immigration Act 2008. Section 76 (6) makes plain that the degree of force used by a person is not to be regarded as having been reasonable in the circumstances as he believed them to be if it was disproportionate in those circumstances. Guidance as to whether the degree of force used was reasonable in the circumstances of a case can now be found in the 2008 Act, s76 (7) of which provides:

(a) that a person acting for a legitimate purpose may not be able to weigh to a nicety the exact measure of any necessary action; and

(b) that evidence of a person's having only done what the person honestly and instinctively thought was necessary for a legitimate purpose constitutes strong evidence that only reasonable action was taken by that person for that purpose.

Burden of proof

The burden is on the prosecution to prove to the jury beyond all reasonable doubt that the defendant was either:

▨ not acting to defend himself/herself or another;

▨ not acting to defend property, or not acting to prevent a crime or apprehend an offender; or

▨ if he was so acting, the force was excessive.

Conclusion

A person who may use such force as is reasonable in the circumstances in the prevention of crime, or in effecting or assisting in the lawful arrest of offenders or suspected offenders or of persons unlawfully at large.

Application of the defence of self-defence/prevention of crime to problems in the examination

Self-defence is most likely to occur in exam questions involving robbery or burglary.

Consider which property offences Alex could be charged with, and any relevant defence.

> Alex was invited by his friend, Ben, to spend the weekend at the house of Ben's parents. Because of a flood on the previous evening, which meant workmen had to be called in to carry out repairs, Alex was able to walk into a room that had previously been locked. There, he forced open a locked drawer and took out all the contents, but put them all back after deciding that none was of any interest. However, he had just picked up a small heavy paperweight from a desk, and decided to keep it, when Ben's father, Colin, came into the room and saw him do so. Colin roughly took hold of Alex, who immediately hit him with the paperweight before running away. Colin suffered bad concussion.

Activity

Make a table of the defences, as a revision aid. Include in your table the key elements and cases for each defence.

You should now be able to:

■ answer problem questions involving the defence of self-defence/prevention of crime.

Practice questions

Example question 1 (AQA, June 2011)

Read this scenario and answer **both** questions.

You should write in continuous prose, give reasoned answers, and make reference to cases, statutes and examples where appropriate.

When Eddie was walking to a local football match, he decided to carry out violent attacks on supporters during the game. After buying his ticket, Eddie entered the stadium, a structure made of brick with a metal roof. As Dan, one of the rival supporters, was running down the steps during the half-time interval, Eddie pushed him. Dan fell heavily onto one of the steps and was knocked unconscious. Eddie, pretending to help, took Dan's wallet from his coat, intending to keep it. However, when a stadium official came to help Dan, Eddie put the wallet back. He then went to the stadium bar and put a foreign coin into a vending machine for a bar of chocolate, but the machine rejected the coin.

Dan's brother, Colin, ordered a meal in a restaurant. During the meal, he drank several glasses of wine. When he was presented with the bill at the end of the meal, he suddenly realised that he had left his money at home. While the waiter was not looking, Colin left the restaurant without settling the bill. When he got to his car, which he had parked in a nearby street, he found that it had been blocked in by a badly parked van. As a result, he was unable to drive away. To 'get his own back' on the driver of the van, Colin loosened the nuts on one of the van's wheels.

1 Discuss Eddie's possible criminal liability for **property offences arising out of his activities in connection with the football stadium.** *(25 marks)*

2 Discuss Colin's possible criminal liability for **property offences arising out of his activities in connection with the restaurant and the van.** *(25 marks)*

Example question 2 (AQA, June 2010)

Read this scenario and answer **both** questions.

You should write in continuous prose, give reasoned answers, and make reference to cases, statutes and examples where appropriate.

Vladic was a member of a gang of violent criminals, led by Luca. Vladic developed a very close friendship with Edna, his elderly neighbour, who tried to encourage him to become more law-abiding. As a result, Vladic had begun to regret his association with the gang. Luca became impatient with Vladic's increasing lack of interest in the gang's activities, and told him to 'get some money off Edna quick or I'll beat her up'. The following day, Edna gave £500 in cash to Vladic to pay into her bank account. Vladic assured Edna that he would do so but, fearing that Luca would carry out his threat, Vladic handed over the money to Luca on his way to the bank.

Freda, another of Edna's friends, asked George, her neighbour, to water the plants in her kitchen while she was away on holiday, but told him not to go into her living room. The following day, however, George, having watered the plants, went into Freda's living room in order to watch television, and opened and ate a box of chocolates, which he intended to replace later. He then fell asleep on Freda's sofa, leaving a cigarette burning in an ashtray, which fell onto the carpet and set it alight. Suddenly waking, George used a chair cushion to extinguish the fire. The cushion was only slightly damaged but the carpet was badly burnt.

1   Discuss Vladic's possible criminal liability for **property** offences arising out of his dealings with Edna and Luca.

(25 marks)

2   Discuss George's possible criminal liability for **property** offences arising out of his activities in Edna's house.

(25 marks)

UNIT

4B Tort

Introduction

Chapters in this unit:

14 The tort of negligence: general principles relating to physical damage and medical negligence

15 The tort of negligence: claiming psychiatric damage and economic loss

16 Product liability: liability in tort for defective goods

17 Occupiers' liability

18 The tort of nuisance and the rule in *Rylands* v *Fletcher*

19 Vicarious liability

Unit 4 gives candidates a choice between the study of criminal law and the law of tort. The unit constitutes 50 per cent of the overall marks for the A2 section of the qualification, and 25 per cent of the overall marks for the A Level qualification. The Unit 4 examination is of 2 hours' duration. You must answer one question on tort or criminal law, and write an essay from the Concepts of law unit. The first part of the examination paper will include both criminal law and tort questions: Questions 1 and 2 are on criminal law and Questions 3 and 4 are on tort. You will choose from either criminal law or tort. Each question is divided into two parts, both of which must be answered. These questions are similar in style and expectation to those in parts (a) and (b) of Unit 3. There are no questions involving critical evaluation of the substantive law studied in Unit 4, as critical evaluation forms the basis of the separate essay on concepts of law.

Each question on the law of tort is therefore worth 50 marks. Each part is worth 25 marks. These two parts will be a test of your ability to select and apply the law to the given scenario.

All questions require essay-style answers. In parts (a) and (b), you should include: correct identification of the issues raised by the question; sound explanation of each of the points; and clear application of the law to the facts disclosed. This may involve some consideration of alternatives where the law lacks clarity in its application to the scenario. Study tips are provided throughout each topic.

The nature and method of response for the concepts of law question is described before Chapter 20, Law and morality.

Unit 4B comprises six chapters:

14 The tort of negligence: general principles relating to physical damage and medical negligence: looks at the principles of negligence in the context of a claim for physical loss (personal injury and damage to property). The chapter also considers the principles of negligence in the context of a claim for clinical negligence.

15 The tort of negligence: claiming psychiatric damage and economic loss: considers the principles of negligence in relation to losses other than straightforward physical damage.

16 Product liability: liability in tort for defective goods: looks at the contribution of tort law to compensating the consumer for losses caused by defective goods.

17 Occupiers' liability: examines the duty which an occupier of premises owes to both his lawful visitors and to his unlawful visitors (trespassers).

18 The tort of nuisance and the rule in *Rylands* v *Fletcher*: considers the liability of those whose activities interfere with the smooth running of the lives of others. The chapter considers both public and private nuisance and the rule in *Rylands* v *Fletcher*.

19 Vicarious liability: examines the nature of an employer's liability for the torts of his employees committed during the course of employment.

The tort of negligence: general principles relating to physical damage and medical negligence

Introduction

If one person is injured or suffers physical damage to his property through the carelessness of another, he may be able to bring an action in negligence. Negligence is a tort (or civil wrong) and it is one of the commonest and most important civil actions.

To win a claim for negligence, the claimant must show that:

■ the defendant owed a duty of care to the claimant – examined in Topic 1 of this chapter

■ the defendant breached that duty of care – examined in Topic 2 of this chapter

■ by breaking the duty of care, the defendant caused loss to the claimant – examined in Topic 3 of this chapter.

Once the claimant has established his claim in negligence, it is open to the defendant to show a defence, and we consider this in Topic 4 of this chapter before examining remedies open to the claimant in Topic 5.

Finally, Topic 6 of this chapter considers the principles of negligence – duty, breach and the causation of damage – in the context of medical negligence.

In this topic, you will learn how to:

■ explain what is meant by the term 'duty of care'

■ identify and explain the 'neighbour test' and the *Caparo* three-part test for identifying when a duty of care exists

■ identify an omission.

Key terms

Duty of care: duty that the law says one person owes to another to take proper care of the other.

Key cases

Donoghue v Stevenson (1932): a person owes a duty to anyone who is his 'neighbour'; a neighbour is a person the defendant should reasonably be thinking of when considering his actions.

1 When does a duty of care exist?

'**Duty of care**' is a legal phrase which means that one person has a responsibility to take proper care not to injure or cause loss to another.

Although the idea of negligence has existed for a long time, there was originally no single test to decide when one person owed a duty of care to another. Instead, the law contained a limited set of individual liabilities based on specific relationships or circumstances. Examples included the relationship between a ferry company and its passengers, the responsibilities of an innkeeper, and the duty owed by those handling weapons and ammunition. This state of affairs became increasingly difficult to manage, not least because there was no good reason why some categories of people were able to claim while others were not.

The House of Lords therefore developed a single test to decide when one person should owe a duty to another. This step was taken in the case of **Donoghue v Stevenson (1932)**, when Lord Atkin stated:

> The rule that you are to love your neighbour becomes in law: You must not injure your neighbour; and the lawyer's question: Who is my neighbour? receives a restricted reply. You must take reasonable care to avoid acts or omissions which you can reasonably foresee would be likely to injure your neighbour. Who, then, in law is my neighbour? The answer seems to be persons who are so closely and directly affected by my act that I ought reasonably to have them in contemplation as being so affected when I am directing my mind to the acts or omissions which are called in question.

The effect of this test is that a person owes a duty to take care of another whenever it is reasonable for them to think about the consequences of their actions on others. The importance of *Donoghue v Stevenson* (1932) in the development of English law is that it effectively established a single action for negligence.

The courts were quick to recognise that this new duty of care existed in a number of commonly occurring circumstances. These include:

■ A manufacturer of goods owes a duty to the ultimate consumer of the goods. This, of course, was established by the decision in *Donoghue* v *Stevenson* (1932) itself. The claimant had fallen ill after drinking ginger beer bought for her by her friend. The ginger beer was poisoned because it contained a decomposed snail, but the claimant had not seen this, as the bottle containing the drink was made of opaque glass. The House of Lords decided that, assuming the facts could be proved, the claimant could sue the manufacturer of the ginger beer as the manufacturer owed a duty to ensure that its products were safe to drink. Chapter 16: Product liability examines consumer protection law in more detail.

■ A user of the road owes a duty to other users of the road. This means that drivers, passengers, cyclists and pedestrians should all behave to keep each other safe. A common consequence of a road traffic accident is an action in negligence against the person whose carelessness caused it.

■ A professional person, such as a solicitor, an accountant or a surveyor, owes a duty to his client to practise his profession properly. Professional negligence is an expanding area of liability, and most professional people are required to have appropriate insurance. Frequently, there is an overlap with contract law as the client will have engaged the services of his adviser; however, this is often not the case with doctors, whose services are provided by the state. Negligence is therefore particularly important in this respect, and we will examine the liability of doctors later in this chapter, in Topic 6.

■ An employer owes his employees a duty to keep them safe in the workplace. This duty has been largely supplanted by health and safety legislation, but a claim for an accident at work usually includes a claim for negligence.

Establishing a duty of care in new sets of circumstances

While most claims in negligence fall into one of the established categories, the courts are clear that the duty of care can be extended to cover new circumstances. The test to be used is set out in **Caparo v Dickman (1990)** (a case involving the negligent preparation of accounts, which we consider in Chapter 15). The House of Lords stated that a duty of care exists if:

1 it is reasonably foreseeable to the defendant that his negligence will cause injury, damage or loss to the claimant;

2 there is a relationship of sufficient proximity between the two; and

3 it would be fair, just and reasonable to impose liability.

This three-part test thus represents a set of guidelines to help a court reach a sensible decision as when to extend liability in negligence. In particular, the House of Lords emphasised that the approach is 'incremental'. This means that liability will only be extended to new areas step-by-step, and by comparison with existing areas of similar liability. This should therefore prevent a future litigation 'free for all', leading to large increases in the types of loss that can be claimed for.

Factors the court might take into account include:

■ whether the defendant undertook a responsibility to the claimant, for instance in a professional capacity

■ which party is in the better position to buy insurance

■ whether it is likely that a new duty will prevent accidents in the future, or whether it will simply discourage people from undertaking normal activities for fear of being sued

Key cases

Caparo v Dickman (1990): the modern test for establishing whether a duty of care exists in a new set of circumstances is based on reasonable foreseeability, proximity and fairness.

Study tip

When discussing whether a duty of care exists, use the three-part framework laid down in *Caparo* v *Dickman* as a guideline for your answer.

- whether any new duty will lead to a large and unpredictable increase in liability
- the extent that a claimant has a responsibility to look after himself.

Two examples of cases in which the courts were prepared to recognise a duty of care are:

- **Watson v British Boxing Board of Control (2001):** The claimant was a boxer, whose injuries following a fight were made worse because medical treatment was not immediately available at the ring side. The match, including the medical provision, had been run according to rules written by the defendant in its role as the sport's governing body. The court decided that the defendant owed a duty to the claimant because injuries in a boxing match were reasonably foreseeable, and because the defendant had taken on a responsibility towards professional boxers by insisting that matches were run according to their rules.
- **Bhamra v Dubb (2010):** The claimant attended a Sikh wedding banquet, the food for which was prepared by the defendant caterer. For religious reasons, the food should not have contained egg, but one dessert did. The claimant, who knew that he had a serious allergy to eggs, ate this dessert and died as a result of a severe allergic reaction. The court decided that while a caterer did not owe a general duty to those with food allergies, as they had a responsibility to look out for themselves, in the particular circumstances of this case the defendant did owe a duty to the claimant, as the claimant would have been off-guard because of the religious prohibition against eggs.

By contrast, two examples of cases where the courts were not prepared to recognise a duty of care are:

- **Sutradhar v National Environment Research Council (2006):** The claimant lived in Bangladesh and had fallen ill after drinking water poisoned by arsenic. He sued the NERC on the ground that one of its agencies had produced a report on water resources in Bangladesh and, he claimed, had given the impression that the water was safe to drink. The court held that no duty existed for a variety of reasons: the defendant had not in fact said that it was declaring the water safe, the defendant had no responsibility for the water supply, the information was publicly available and therefore there were many potential claimants, and the effect of any liability would be to discourage anyone from making information generally available.
- **Calvert v William Hill (2008):** The claimant suffered financial ruin after his gambling addiction ran completely out of control. He sued the defendant, a well-known bookmaker, for damages, saying that it owed a duty to 'problem' gamblers to offer them help and to prevent them from further gambling. The court rejected this argument on the grounds that it was impossible for a bookmaker to identify from among its customers the small number of gamblers with an uncontrollable habit, and that the claimant had a responsibility for his own actions.

Omissions

If a defendant owes a duty of care, it is because he has chosen to undertake a particular activity, such as drive a car or manufacture ginger beer. The duty is then a duty not to cause harm to others, such as other road users or the consumer of the ginger beer, while undertaking that activity. In these circumstances, the defendant will be liable for both his acts (such as pulling out of a side road or mixing in dangerous ingredients) and his **omissions** (such as not stopping at a red light or failing to check the bottling process for snails).

Key cases

Watson v British Board of Boxing Control (2001): a duty of care exists where injury is reasonably foreseeable and where the defendant has undertaken a responsibility towards the claimant.

Bhamra v Dubb (2010): a duty of care exists where a claimant, who should normally take care for himself, is off-guard for reasons known to the defendant.

Sutradhar v National Environment Research Council (2006): no duty of care exists when the defendant has not taken on a responsibility and where there were a very large number of potential claims.

Calvert v William Hill (2008): no duty of care exists when it is impracticable for a defendant to take action and when any claimant has a responsibility towards himself.

Key terms

Omission: failure to act; defendant is not normally liable for failing to act to protect others unless there is an existing relationship between the two.

However, negligence does not normally impose a general duty of care whereby a person is under a duty to look out for everyone around him and to prevent harm coming to them. In these circumstances, if a person fails to act there is no liability for this omission. If a person is walking through the park and sees a small child in danger of drowning in a paddling pool or a teenager about to climb an electricity pylon, he has no obligation to intervene, even to save life at no risk to his own.

Thus, in **Ancell v McDermott (1993)**, when the claimant was killed in a road accident caused by an oil spillage on the road, of which the police were aware, there was no liability as the police owed no general duty of care to warn motorists. The exception to this rule is if there is a pre-existing relationship between the claimant and the defendant, so that the defendant does owe a duty to act in order to prevent harm. A school, for instance, owes a duty to protect the children in its care: whereas a member of the public can walk past and not assist a child drowning in a paddling pool, the teacher in charge of the class should act. An example is **Barnes v Hampshire County Council (1969)** where a school was liable when it released the children early, before the parents arrived, and one of the children was injured on the road. A member of the public would have had no duty to ensure the children's safety on the road, but the school did.

Topic illustration

Think about the following scenario and consider whether Malcolm owes a duty of case to Nina. We will consider other aspects of the case in later topics of this chapter:

> Malcolm, in order to celebrate passing his driving test earlier in the day, drove to his local pub and drank four pints of beer. He then set off for home, driving at speeds in excess of 50mph through a built-up area, and collided with a car being driven by Nina. The police accident investigation established that Malcolm was over the drink-drive limit, that Nina had been using her mobile telephone at the time of the accident, and that both vehicles had strayed into the middle of the road. Malcolm stated that he did not realise the effect the alcohol would have on him. Nina is particularly upset because she had to abandon her car by the roadside overnight, and an unknown person stole her wheels.

If Nina wants to sue Malcolm in negligence, she must first show that Malcolm owes a duty of care.

This should be straightforward. The fact that one road user owes a duty of care to others is one of the best examples of a duty of care under the principles in *Donoghue* v *Stevenson* (1932).

If there is any doubt, Nina should be able to establish the existence of a duty under the principles in *Caparo* v *Dickman* (1990). These include for instance, the fact that injury was reasonably foreseeable and that Malcolm and Nina had a sufficient degree of proximity as they were using the same road.

Key cases

Ancell v McDermott (1993): even the police do not owe a general duty to protect the general public in the absence of a pre-existing relationship.

Barnes v Hampshire County Council (1969): school owes a duty to safeguard the children in its care, although a member of the general public would owe no such duty, as the school has a pre-existing relationship with its students.

Link

To read more about *Donoghue* v *Stevenson* (1932), see p19.

To read more about *Caparo* v *Dickman* (1990), see pp264 and 376.

Malcolm and Nina

■ **Activities**

1 Thinking about omissions, consider why it is that the law does not require a person to take care of those around him. Ideas might relate to cost, freedom of action and proximity to the claimant. Do you think a person should be required to intervene to save another's life when there is no risk to himself?

2 Consider this scenario, which has been adapted from a past AQA exam paper:

Maxbuild, a construction company, was demolishing a building and two of its employees, Tim and Vic, were working on the site. Tim was removing brick rubble from an upper floor. To save time, he did not set up a chute for the rubble, as he had been instructed to do. Thinking that workers below had gone for a break, he did not check before throwing bricks down. In fact, Vic was still below and his eyesight was severely damaged when a brick shattered and fragments entered his eyes. Discuss whether Tim owes a duty of care to Vic, and give reasons for your answer.

You should now be able to:

■ identify situations in which a duty of care exists

■ explain the reasoning used by judges when deciding whether a duty of care exists in new circumstances.

2 Breaching the duty of care

Once the claimant has established that a duty of care exists, he must then go on to show that the defendant has breached the duty. The court will use the 'reasonable person' test: did the defendant's actions fall below those of the reasonable person in the same circumstances? The famous, and slightly more formal, statement of this test is found in *Blyth* v *Birmingham Waterworks* (1856):

> Negligence is the omission to do something which a reasonable man, guided upon those considerations which ordinarily regulate the conduct of human affairs, would do, or doing something which a prudent and reasonable man would not do. (Alderson B)

Note, however, that if the defendant did act as the reasonable person would have done, then he is not liable even though the claimant has suffered an injury or a loss. English law recognises that there can be a genuine accident for which no one is to blame.

The **'reasonable person' test** is objective: in other words, the defendant's actions are measured against the standard of the reasonable person (objective), and not against his own personal standards (subjective). It is not a sufficient defence for the defendant to say that he was doing his best, if his best is below what the reasonable person would have done. In **Nettleship v Weston (1971)** a learner driver was held liable when she caused an accident, as her driving was not up to the standard of the reasonable qualified driver, even though the court accepted that she had been driving to the best of her ability. This decision may seem harsh, given that all drivers are beginners at some point and given that the defendant could do no more than she did. However, it is the right decision, as it ensures that the claimant was not left without compensation just because he had the bad luck to be injured by a learner.

The 'reasonable person' test raises two questions: who is the reasonable person, and how does he act?

In this topic, you will learn how to:

■ identify and explain the test for establishing when a duty of care has been breached

■ describe the characteristics of the reasonable person

■ explain how the reasonable person behaves.

■ **Key terms**

'Reasonable person' test: in deciding whether a defendant has broken a duty of care that he owes, the court will ask whether he did all that the reasonable person would have done in the same circumstances.

■ **Key cases**

Nettleship v Weston (1971): reasonable person test is objective; this means that the defendant will be measured against the standard of the reasonable person rather than against his own personal standard.

Who is the reasonable person?

The law says that the reasonable person is of average intelligence and self-control, and he possesses average skill and experience. The defendant cannot escape liability by saying either that he cannot make a proper decision because he is not very bright or, as we saw in *Nettleship* v *Weston* (1971), that he is a learner or beginner. In addition, the reasonable person has knowledge of other people, and will take into account their reasonably foreseeable frailties. In **Haley v London Electricity Board (1964)** the claimant, a blind man, was injured when he fell in a trench that the defendant had dug and left unfenced. The court decided that the reasonable electric company would have fenced the hole, as blindness was not so uncommon as to be unforeseeable.

The 'reasonable person' test accepts a lower standard in two instances. If the defendant is disabled, the law requires a standard of behaviour that is reasonable for a person with that disability. In return, however, a disabled person must not exceed the reasonable limits for a person with that disability. In addition, if the defendant is either very old or very young then the court will measure his behaviour against a reasonable person of the same age. In **Mullin v Richards (1998)** the claimant and the defendant were 15-year-old schoolgirls engaged in a mock sword fight with plastic rulers. One of the rulers splintered and the claimant was injured in the eye. The defendant was not liable as she had shown the standard of care of the reasonable 15-year-old, even though the reasonable adult might have been more careful.

A second example is **Orchard v Lee (2009)**. The defendant, a 13-year-old boy playing tag with a friend in their school playground, collided with the claimant, an adult playground supervisor, causing her to be injured. He was not liable as he had acted according to the standards of an ordinary and prudent 13-year-old. He had broken no school rule, he had acted within the normal parameters of a game of tag (he had certainly not been careless to the very high degree that the Court of Appeal felt would have been necessary for him to have been liable), and he had not foreseen the risk of this type of injury as it was not normally associated with a game of tag.

By contrast there is one instance where the 'reasonable person' test expects a higher standard. A professional person practising his profession will be judged not by the standards of the ordinary reasonable person, but by the standards of a reasonable member of the profession. One example, in a medical context, is **Bolam v Friern Hospital Management Committee (1957)**, and we will discuss this principle further when we consider medical negligence in Topic 6.

How does the reasonable person behave?

In deciding how the reasonable person will behave in a given situation, the court will try to strike a balance between protecting individuals and not imposing too high a burden on those who owe a duty of care. This is recognised by s1 of the Compensation Act 2006, which states that a court may take into account whether imposing liability might prevent or discourage desirable activities in the future.

The following are examples of factors that the court may take into account:

1 Likelihood of injury

The less likely an accident is to happen, the more justified the defendant is in ignoring the risk. In contrast, if an accident is more likely to happen, then the reasonable person will take precautions against it. In **Bolton v Stone (1951)**, the claimant was injured when she was struck on the head by a cricket ball that had been hit over a 17-foot-high fence, 78 yards from the wicket. The evidence was that in 28 years only six balls had

---

■ Key cases

Haley v London Electricity Board (1964): a reasonable person takes account of the weaknesses and frailties of others.

Mullin v Richards (1998): if very young or very old, a defendant will be judged by the standards of a reasonable person of the same age.

Orchard v Lee (2009): a child will not be liable for simply playing a game according to the standards of a reasonable and prudent child of the same age.

Bolam v Friern HMC (1957): a professional person will be judged by the standards of a reasonable member of the profession.

Bolton v Stone (1951): a reasonable person does not take precautions against very unlikely occurrences.

■ Study tip

Remember that the rule in *Bolton* v *Stone* (1951) can be used both ways: just as a reasonable person does not take precautions against unlikely risks, so he does take precautions against risks that may well occur.

gone over the fence, and that this was the first to have hit someone. The claimant's case failed, as the defendants had acted reasonably in not taking further precautions against such an unlikely risk.

2 The seriousness of the consequences

The more serious the consequences, the higher the defendant's duty of care. In **Paris v Stepney Borough Council (1951)** the defendant employer was liable when the claimant was blinded in one eye when a splinter flew up from his work. The job was not normally one for which an employer would supply goggles. However, the claimant only had sight in one eye to begin with, so the defendant should have taken greater care, as for the claimant to lose an eye in those circumstances is very much more serious.

3 The value of the conduct

If what the defendant is doing is socially valuable, then that may justify him taking extra risks. In **Watt v Hertfordshire County Council (1954)** the claimant fireman was injured when, on his way to a road traffic accident to rescue a woman trapped under a bus, the lifting gear shifted and squashed him. The accident happened because the lorry was not the correct vehicle for the lifting gear, but the claimant failed because the court decided that the reasonable fire brigade would respond to an emergency quickly rather than waste time trying to find the correct lorry. In the long run, more people would be protected.

4 Cost of precautions

The easier, cheaper and more practicable it is for the defendant to minimise or eliminate a risk, the more likely he is to be negligent if he does not do so. In **Latimer v AEC (1953)** the claimant, an employee of the defendant, broke his leg when he slipped at work on floors made wet by overnight flooding. The defendant was not liable because they had carried out all reasonable precautions, such as sweeping away surface water and putting down straw.

A good example of a case that considered whether a duty of care had been broken is **Harris v Perry (2009)**. The claimant, an 11-year-old boy playing on an inflatable bouncy castle, suffered a fractured skull and a serious brain injury when he was struck on the forehead by the heel of a much larger 15-year-old boy who was doing a somersault. He claimed that the defendant, a mother who had organised the castle for her children's birthday party, had not offered a sufficient level of supervision because she was overseeing both the castle and another activity, and had been temporarily distracted by the other activity at the time of the accident. The Court of Appeal recognised that minor injuries on something like a bouncy castle were quite likely, and that some form of supervision was necessary. However, the court decided that the defendant had not breached the duty of care she undoubtedly owed when supervising other people's children, as the defendant's level of attention was appropriate to the level of foreseeable risk. The severity of the injury was unforeseeable, and even if the defendant had given her undivided attention to the castle she probably could not have prevented the accident. It was not in the interests of society to impose liability for what was a freak accident.

Topic illustration

Consider again the scenario concerning the collision between Malcolm and Nina:

> Malcolm, in order to celebrate passing his driving test earlier in the day, drove to his local pub and drank four pints of beer. He then set off for home, driving at speeds in excess of 50mph through

Key cases

Paris v Stepney Borough Council (1951): a reasonable person takes extra care if any damage caused by his actions is likely to be particularly serious.

Watt v Hertfordshire County Council (1954): a reasonable person takes risks in an emergency.

Latimer v AEC (1953): a reasonable person does not take every possible precaution.

Harris v Perry (2009): defendant will not be liable for a freak accident as long as he took appropriate care given the level of foreseeable risk.

Activities

1 Thinking about s1 of the Compensation Act 2006, give two examples of desirable activities that might be prevented or discouraged in the future if the courts set too high a standard when considering whether a duty of care has been broken. For each activity, consider what might reasonably be required of a person who owes such a duty and what further requirements might discourage such a person from undertaking the activity.

2 Remind yourself of the facts of the scenario relating to Tim and Vic (Activity 2 on p237). Assuming that Tim does have a duty to Vic, consider whether he broke the duty. Which cases might be relevant?

In this topic, you will learn how to:

■ identify and explain the difference between causation and remoteness

■ explain the 'but for' test in relation to causation, and the reasonable foreseeability test in relation to remoteness

■ identify and explain the effect of an intervening cause.

Key terms

Causation: relationship between two events, whereby the first caused the second to happen.

'But for' test: test for determining whether causation exists: if the defendant had not acted negligently would the damage still have occurred? If so, then something other than the negligence caused it, and there is no causation.

---

a built-up area, and collided with a car being driven by Nina. The police accident investigation established that Malcolm was over the drink-drive limit, that Nina had been using her mobile telephone at the time of the accident, and that both vehicles had strayed into the middle of the road. Malcolm stated that he did not realise the effect the alcohol would have on him. Nina is particularly upset because she had to abandon her car by the roadside overnight, and an unknown person stole her wheels.

Having established that Malcolm owes her a duty of care, Nina must now show that he breached the duty. The following factors might be taken into account:

■ The test is based on what the reasonable person would do. This test is objective: the fact that Malcolm does not know of the effects of alcohol is irrelevant, as the reasonable person would.

■ Equally irrelevant is the fact that Malcolm is a very inexperienced driver. The standard of care required is that of the reasonable driver. The reasonable driver does not drive too fast and does not stray into the middle of the road.

■ Nina will be able to use cases such as *Bolton* v *Stone* (1951) (the reasonable person takes precautions against foreseeable risks) and *Paris* v *Stepney Borough Council* (1951) (the reasonable person takes extra care if any damage is likely to be serious).

You should now be able to:

■ understand the role of the reasonable person test

■ explain the factors that impact how the reasonable person acts.

---

3 Causation and remoteness of damage

The claimant must prove that the breach of duty by the defendant and the loss suffered as a result are sufficiently closely linked. This must be answered in two parts:

▨ Causation: was the damage caused by the defendant's breach of duty, or was it actually caused by something else?

▨ Remoteness of damage: is the loss suffered too far removed from the defendant's breach of duty as to be unforeseeable?

Causation

Causation is decided by the **'but for' test**: but for the defendant's breach, would the loss have occurred? A different way of putting this is to ask whether, if the defendant had done all that he should have, the loss would still have occurred. If the answer is that the loss would still have occurred, then it must have been caused by something other than the defendant's negligence, and the defendant is therefore not liable. In **McWilliams v Sir William Arrol & Co. Ltd (1962)** the claimant, a scaffolder who had not been supplied by his employer with the correct safety harness, fell and was killed. The defendant employer clearly owed a duty of care (the duty owed by an employer to an employee) and had equally clearly breached the duty by not supplying the harness. Nevertheless, the claim failed because the employer was able to show that that claimant would not have worn the harness even if it had been supplied, as experienced workers in the industry usually did not. In other words, had the employer done all that it should have, the claimant would still have been killed.

Remoteness of damage

Only losses that are not too remote, or too far removed from the original negligence, are recoverable. The test for **remoteness of damage** is whether a loss is a **reasonably foreseeable** consequence of the defendant's negligence. If a loss is not reasonably foreseeable then it is not recoverable. This approach was established by the decision in **The Wagon Mound (No. 1) (1961)**. Due to the defendant's negligence, oil had been spilled in the water of a harbour, and the oil had drifted across to the claimant's wharf where welding work was being carried out. Having taken advice that it was safe to do so, the claimant continued welding secure in the knowledge that oil in the sea at sea temperature is not flammable. Nevertheless, the oil ignited, and the ensuing blaze badly damaged the claimant's property. However, the claimant's action failed as although pollution damage is a reasonably foreseeable consequence of spilling oil in the sea, fire damage is not.

There are, however, three instances when damage can be claimed even if it is not entirely reasonably foreseeable:

1 a claimant may recover damages when the specific losses that occurred are not foreseeable, as long as the general category or type of loss is foreseeable

2 a claimant may recover damages if the loss is foreseeable, but the precise manner in which it happened is not

3 a claimant may recover damages if the type of loss is foreseeable but the full extent of the loss is not.

1 Type of damage caused

If the general type of damage is reasonably foreseeable, then it does not matter that the precise form that occurred was not. In **Bradford v Robinson Rentals (1967)** the claimant was a van driver sent out by his employer on a very cold day. His van was unheated and he suffered frostbite. Although frostbite in this country is not reasonably foreseeable, the claimant's action succeeded, as some sort of cold weather harm was reasonably foreseeable.

2 Sequence of events is not foreseeable

If the damage that occurred was reasonably foreseeable, it is not necessary to foresee the precise sequence of events that led to the damage. In **Hughes v Lord Advocate (1963)** the defendant left unguarded an open manhole surrounded by paraffin lamps. The claimant, a young boy, was investigating when he knocked one of the lamps into the hole and was burned in the subsequent explosion. His claim succeeded because burn injuries caused by an unattended lamp were foreseeable, even if what actually happened was not. A similar outcome occurred in **Jolley v Sutton London Borough Council (2000)**. The defendant council, in breach of is duty, left a derelict boat on waste ground for more than two years. The claimant, a child, was badly injured when he propped up the boat in order to try and repair it and the boat collapsed on him. His claim succeeded because it was reasonably foreseeable that children would be injured in some manner if they played on the boat, even if what actually happened was not.

3 Extent of the damage

Provided that some of his damage is reasonably foreseeable, the claimant can claim for the full extent of his loss. In **Vacwell Engineering v BDH Chemicals (1970)** the defendant negligently supplied a chemical to the claimant without a warning that the chemical was liable to explode if it came into contact with water. The claimant placed some of the chemical in a sink and the resulting explosion extensively damaged its premises.

Key terms

Remoteness of damage: defendant is not liable for losses that are too far removed from his actions.

Reasonable foreseeability: test for remoteness of damage; if an item of damage is not a reasonably foreseeable consequence of the defendant's negligence, then the claimant cannot claim for it.

Key cases

McWilliams v Sir William Arrol & Co. Ltd (1962): defendant will not be liable, even though he has breached a duty of care that he owes, if the claimant would have suffered the same loss even if the defendant had done everything he should have.

The Wagon Mound (No. 1) (1961): test for remoteness of damage is reasonable foreseeability.

Bradford v Robinson Rentals (1967): as long as the type of damage is reasonably foreseeable, it does not matter that the specific loss is not.

Hughes v Lord Advocate (1963) and **Jolley v Sutton London Borough Council (2000):** the specific sequence of events leading to a loss does not have to be foreseeable as long as the nature of the resulting damage is.

Vacwell Engineering v BDH Chemicals (1970) and **Smith v Leech Brain & Co. (1962):** provided that some damage is foreseeable, then the full extent can be claimed.

Study tip

When discussing remoteness of damage, think carefully about the three rules outlined. Usually, at least one will be relevant.

Key terms

Intervening cause: something or someone forming a link between the actions of the defendant and the loss suffered by the claimant.

Key cases

Carslogie Steamship Co. v Royal Norwegian Government (1952): an intervening cause in the shape of a natural event breaks the chain of causation.

Lamb v Camden London Borough Council (1981): an intervening cause in the shape of a criminal third party breaks the chain of causation.

Knightley v Johns (1982): an intervening cause in the shape of a negligent third party may well break the chain of causation.

Scott v Shepherd (1773): an intervening cause in the shape of an innocent third party does not break the chain of causation.

McKew v Holland & Hannen & Cubitts (1969): whether a claimant's own actions break the chain of causation, thus releasing the defendant from further liability, depends on whether those actions were reasonable.

The claimant was able to claim for its full loss as the explosion was foreseeable even if the scale was not. This rule applies if, in a personal injury case, the extent of injuries is made worse by a hidden and unforeseen frailty on the part of the claimant (the 'thin skull' rule). In **Smith v Leech Brain & Co. (1962)** the claimant, through his employer's negligence, suffered a burn to his lip. This caused a cancer, due to a medical condition that made him vulnerable to this sort of illness. The claimant died as a result, and his estate was able to claim both for the burn and for the death.

Intervening causes

Sometimes the law will not impose liability for negligence, even though damage is reasonably foreseeable, because the defendant's negligence does not cause the loss directly but instead sets the scene for something or someone else to inflict the loss. The something or someone else is called an **intervening cause**, and the law has to decide which intervening causes are sufficiently significant as to free the defendant from liability – in other words, which intervening causes break the chain of causation.

A natural event as an intervening cause will normally free the claimant from further liability. In **Carslogie Steamship Co. v Royal Norwegian Government (1952)** the defendant negligently caused damage to the claimant's ship. The ship's schedule was therefore changed to bring it home for repairs, and this meant that it was at sea when it would otherwise not have been. While at sea, the ship sustained further damage in a severe storm but the claimant, while liable for the original damage, was not liable for the storm damage.

If the intervening cause is the actions of a third party, whether the defendant is freed from further liability normally depends on how blameworthy the third party is. If the third party is a criminal, then the chain of causation is normally broken and the defendant is not liable for further losses. In **Lamb v Camden London Borough Council (1981)** the defendant council's negligence led to the claimant's house being flooded. The claimant vacated the property, but squatters moved in and caused considerable damage. The defendant, however, was not liable for this damage as causation had been broken.

Equally, a grossly negligent third party can also break the chain. In **Knightley v Johns (1982)** the defendant negligently caused a road accident in a tunnel. The police attended, and a police motorcycle rider was instructed to drive against the flow of traffic in the tunnel to close it from the other end. Not surprisingly, the motorcyclist caused a second accident, but the defendant was not liable for the losses caused by that accident as the negligence of the police had broken the chain of causation.

By contrast, the actions of a third party acting without blame or even instinctively will not free the defendant from the further consequences. In **Scott v Shepherd (1773)** the defendant threw a lit firecracker into a crowded market. The firework was thrown on by two further people, before exploding and injuring the claimant. The defendant was liable for the injuries of the claimant, even though he had not thrown the firecracker at him directly, because the two middlemen were acting instinctively in an effort to protect themselves.

A final example of an intervening cause is when the claimant suffers damage over and above that caused by the defendant's negligence because of the claimant's own subsequent actions. The claimant will be able to claim for such further damage, but only if his own actions were reasonable. In **McKew v Holland & Hannen & Cubitts (1969)** the defendant's negligence injured the claimant's leg in such a way that the leg was liable to give way without warning. The claimant was further injured when he attempted to walk down some stairs that had no handrail and he fell because his leg gave way. The defendant was not liable for the second set of injuries because it was unreasonable for the claimant to have acted in the way that he did, given his injuries.

If, however, the claimant's subsequent actions are reasonable, but he undertook them in a risky way, the court should ask whether it is 'fair' for the defendant to be liable for the subsequent injury. In **Spencer v Wincanton Holdings (2009)** the claimant suffered an amputation of one leg above the knee after an accident at work caused by the negligence of the defendant, his employer. The claimant then attempted to fill his car at a petrol station while not using either crutches or a false leg, and he fell and was further injured. The defendant was liable for this further injury because the claimant's actions were reasonable and therefore it was fair that the defendant should be liable for them. However, the claimant did not recover for the whole of his loss as one-third of his damages were deducted to reflect his own contributing negligence. (We consider fully the defence of contributory negligence in the next topic.)

Topic illustration

Consider again the scenario concerning the collision between Malcolm and Nina:

> Malcolm, in order to celebrate passing his driving test earlier in the day, drove to his local pub and drank four pints of beer. He then set off home, driving at speeds in excess of 50mph through a built-up area, and collided with a car being driven by Nina. The police accident investigation established that Malcolm was over the drink-drive limit, that Nina had been using her mobile telephone at the time of the accident, and that both vehicles had strayed into the middle of the road. Malcolm stated that he did not realise the effect the alcohol would have on him. Nina is particularly upset because she had to abandon her car by the roadside overnight, and an unknown person stole her wheels.

Given that Malcolm both owed a duty of care and breached that duty, Nina now needs to consider the issues of causation and remoteness:

- Causation should not be a problem, as Malcolm's actions led to the accident.

- With respect to remoteness, Nina can claim all reasonably foreseeable losses. Some damage to her car and to the contents of the car is foreseeable, as is some personal injury. Nina should therefore be able to claim all her losses, even though they were not specifically foreseeable, using the rules from cases such as *Hughes* v *Lord Advocate* (1963) and *Smith* v *Leech Brain & Co.* (1962).

- However, it is unlikely that Nina can claim for the stolen wheels. Although Malcolm's actions led to the loss of the wheels, there was an intervening cause in the form of a criminal third party.

You should now be able to:

- understand the concepts of causation and remoteness

- apply the 'but for' and reasonable foreseeability tests

- identify situations where causation may not be broken.

Key cases

Spencer v Wincanton Holdings (2009): defendant will escape liability for further damage caused by the claimant's own actions if that is a fair outcome.

Activities

1 Thinking again about the scenario relating to Tim and Vic (Activity 2 on p237), apply the tests for causation and remoteness of damage and decide whether each is satisfied in relation to Vic's injuries. Are Vic's injuries entirely foreseeable, and does it affect his claim if they are not?

2 Consider this scenario, adapted from a recent past paper:

Dr West, who worked in the casualty department at the local hospital, was directed by the hospital to drive to another of the hospital's sites in order to treat the victims of a serious accident. On the way, he failed to stop at a red light while Tariq was crossing the road. Tariq just managed to avoid Dr West's car by hurling himself on to the pavement but, owing to his heart condition and the stress of the situation, he had a major heart attack and was in hospital for weeks.

Does Dr West owe Tariq a duty of care? If so, did he behave as a reasonable driver, given the circumstances of his journey? Are Tariq's injuries too remote given that Dr West's car did not actually collide with Tariq and given that Tariq's heart condition was not obvious or visible?

In this topic, you will learn how to:

■ identify and explain the defence of contributory negligence

■ identify and explain the defence of consent.

Key terms

Contributory negligence: claimant's loss is caused in part by his own actions and not solely by the actions of the defendant.

Consent: defence that can be used when a claimant is aware that the defendant may act negligently but agrees to the risk.

Study tip

Never, in your answer to a legal problem, jump straight to the defence, however obvious it may seem. Always describe the liability of the defendant first, because without that there is nothing for the defence to be a defence against.

Key cases

Brannon v Airtours (1999): ignoring warnings can amount to contributory negligence.

Yachuk v Oliver Blais (1949): if the claimant is a child, he will be judged by the standards of a reasonable child of the same age when deciding the issue of contributory negligence.

Froom v Butcher (1975) and **O'Connell v Jackson (1971):** failing to take basic precautions can amount to contributory negligence.

Smith v Finch (2009): contributory negligence does not apply, even if the claimant did not take reasonable precautions, if the lack of precautions made no difference to the damage suffered.

4 Defences to a claim in negligence

A defence allows a defendant to escape liability even where all the elements of the tort in question exist. Two possible defences to a claim in negligence are contributory negligence, which allows the court to apportion blame between the two parties, and consent (sometimes known as *volenti non fit injuria*) which is a complete defence thus resulting in the defendant paying nothing by way of damages.

Contributory negligence

Contributory negligence in its modern form was introduced by the Law Reform (Contributory Negligence) Act 1945.

Contributory negligence can be applied in two different ways. The first is where the claimant is partly to blame for the accident taking place. In deciding this, the court will use the same principles that it uses when deciding whether a defendant has broken a duty of care. An example is **Brannon v Airtours (1999)**. The claimant, a holidaymaker, was at a party night organised by the defendant. The claimant was injured when he climbed onto a table in order to get out, and collided with a low fan hanging from the ceiling. The defendant was held to be negligent in arranging the room in such a way as to make it difficult for people to get out without climbing over the furniture, but the claimant was found to be partly to blame for actually standing on a table despite warnings not to do so.

A contrasting example, where the claimant was not partly to blame, is **Yachuk v Oliver Blais (1949)**. The claimant, a nine-year-old boy, bought petrol from the defendant and was then burned while playing a game with the petrol. The defendant was liable in negligence for selling such a dangerous item to so young a child, and the claimant's own actions did not contribute to the accident as he had behaved according to the standards of the reasonable nine-year-old who would be unaware of the dangers.

The second way in which contributory negligence can be applied is where the claimant was not to blame for the accident, but his actions made his injuries or losses worse than they should have been. Two obvious examples are not wearing a seatbelt in a car (**Froom v Butcher (1975)**) and not wearing a crash helmet on a motorbike (**O'Connell v Jackson (1971)**). A contrasting example is **Smith v Finch (2009)** where the claimant, a cyclist, was injured when the defendant's motorcycle collided with him. Although the claimant was not wearing a cycle helmet, his actions did not contribute to his losses because the accident was such that his injuries would have occurred anyway.

If the defendant is successful in establishing contributory negligence, then the court will reduce the claimant's damages to reflect his own carelessness. The basic principle is that if the court feels that the claimant is, for example, 30 per cent to blame for the losses that he suffered, then his damages will be reduced by 30 per cent. The claimant in *Brannon* v *Airtours* (1999) thus lost 50 per cent of his damages, and in *Froom* v *Butcher* (1975) it was stated that someone who does not wear a seatbelt can typically expect to lose 15–25 per cent of their damages.

Consent

Consent, as a defence, applies when the claimant knows that there is a risk of the defendant acting in a negligent way and freely consents to take

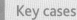

that risk. This is illustrated by **Morris v Murray (1990)**. The claimant and the defendant had spent several hours drinking, and then decided to go for a trip in the defendant's light aircraft. The plane crashed, the defendant was killed and the claimant badly injured. The claimant's subsequent action against the estate of the pilot for his undoubted negligence failed, as the claimant was fully aware of the risk of negligence on the part of the defendant, yet decided to get into the plane anyway.

The fact that consent must be freely given can lead to the defence failing. In **Smith v Baker (1891)** the claimant was an employee working on a railway line when he was injured by material falling from a crane that swung overhead. The defendant argued the defence of consent, on the ground that the crane had been swinging overhead in such a fashion for many weeks, but that the claimant had continued to work and had therefore consented to the risk. The court rejected this because simply knowing of the risk did not amount to consent, particularly where the claimant had little choice but to continue to work as he needed the job. In **Haynes v Harwood (1935)** the defendant's negligence had allowed a horse to run amok in a busy street. The claimant was injured when he tried to stop the horse. The defence of consent, made on the ground that the claimant had chosen to get involved, failed because the consent was not freely given as the claimant had felt morally obliged to try and help people in danger.

If consent is successfully pleaded by the defendant, its effect is to act as a complete defence so that the claimant receives no damages. This 'all or nothing' outcome is one reason why the defence is less commonly used today, as judges much prefer the flexibility of contributory negligence and the opportunity it gives to them to apportion blame between the parties.

Topic illustration

Consider once again the scenario concerning the collision between Malcolm and Nina:

> Malcolm, in order to celebrate passing his driving test earlier in the day, drove to his local pub and drank four pints of beer. He then set off for home, driving at speeds in excess of 50mph through a built-up area, and collided with a car being driven by Nina. The police accident investigation established that Malcolm was over the drink-drive limit, that Nina had been using her mobile telephone at the time of the accident, and that both vehicles had strayed into the middle of the road. Malcolm stated that he did not realise the effect the alcohol would have on him. Nina is particularly upset because she had to abandon her car by the roadside overnight, and an unknown person stole her wheels.

It is likely that Nina can successfully bring an action in negligence against Malcolm as she can show that he owed a duty, that he breached it, and that this led to reasonably foreseeable damage. However, Nina too is at fault, and Malcolm may wish to raise the defence of contributory negligence.

- Malcolm needs to show that Nina was also below the standard of the reasonable driver. Presumably he can do this, as Nina was using a mobile telephone and had strayed into the middle of the road.

- Malcolm also needs to show that Nina's actions were, at least in part, the cause of the accident. It might be that if Nina had been concentrating fully she could have braked sooner, thus ensuring that the collision was less severe.

- If Malcolm is able to show contributory negligence, then Nina's damages will be reduced in proportion to her contribution to the accident.

Key cases

Morris v Murray (1990): defence of consent will be established if the claimant knows that there is a risk that the defendant will act in a negligent way and consents to that risk.

Smith v Baker (1891): defendant cannot establish the defence of consent on the basis of the claimant's knowledge of the risk alone; he must show that the claimant freely consented to the risk.

Haynes v Harwood (1935): defence of consent is not available if the claimant felt morally obliged to act.

Activities

1 Consider whether the decision in *Haynes* v *Harwood* (1935) was correct.

2 Referring back to the accident involving Tim and Vic (Activity 2 on p237), consider whether Tim can raise either the defence of contributory negligence or the defence of consent against Vic.

You should now be able to:

- explain when a defence to a claim in negligence applies
- identify the behaviour on the part of a claimant that may allow the defendant to establish such a defence

---

In this topic, you will learn how to:

- identify and explain the principles relating to the calculation of damages in a claim for negligence.

5 Claiming damages for negligence

The basic rule governing the calculation of damages for a claim in negligence is that the damages should restore the claimant to the position that he was in before the accident happened, at least as far as money can.

Damages for loss to property

Compensation for damage to property is usually straightforward to calculate. A court will normally award the cost of repairing the property unless this exceeds the value of the property, in which case that will be paid instead. Thus, if the claimant's car is damaged in an accident, the defendant will be liable for the cost of the repairs or for the value of the car – whichever is the less. The claimant can also recover any associated losses, provided that they are foreseeable. If, for instance, the claimant's taxi is damaged and needs to spend a week in a garage for repairs, the claimant should be able to recover a week's lost fares.

Damages for personal injury

Although damages for personal injury caused by negligence use the same basic principle, the rules are more complex. This is because of the complicated nature of the loss, and because some categories of loss are difficult to translate into money terms. Damages for personal injury are divided into special damages and general damages.

Special damages cover the claimant's out-of-pocket expenses from the date of the accident to the date of the judgement. These can normally be calculated exactly. Examples include loss of wages, medical expenses (such as prescriptions or the hire of a wheelchair), and cost of travel to medical appointments.

General damages cover the claimant's injury and his losses for the future. These can be complex to calculate, but examples of categories of loss for which the claimant might receive damages include: pain, suffering and loss of amenity; future medical care and personal assistance; and loss of future earnings.

Pain, suffering and loss of amenity

The award for **pain, suffering and loss of amenity** compensates the claimant for his actual injury and for his physical and mental suffering. To ensure consistency, the Judicial Studies Board has laid down a framework detailing how much compensation each type of injury attracts. Factors the court should also consider include: length of time in

Key terms

Pain, suffering and loss of amenity: part of an award for damages that compensates a claimant for his injuries and for the consequent reduction in the quality of life.

hospital, loss of life expectancy, cosmetic injuries and depression. Loss of amenity is also included in the award. This means the reduction in the quality of life of the claimant, and can include any impact on the claimant's ability to look after himself and on his ability to enjoy his hobbies and interests.

Future medical care and personal assistance

This heading covers the cost of future care required by the claimant. It can include a claim for loss of wages by a relative who gives up their job to care for the claimant.

Loss of future earnings

This heading can lead to very awkward calculations, but the basic principle is that the claimant is awarded the amount of the reduction in his annual net earnings multiplied by the number of years he had left before he retired. Reductions are made if the claimant is receiving certain types of social security payments, and also for the fact that he is receiving a lifetime's earning in one lump sum and therefore can earn extra money by investing his compensation. Whether the claimant would, for instance, have received promotions (and therefore pay rises) in the future is, of course, speculative, but the court must make the best decision that it can, using such evidence as is available.

| Claimant's net annual loss (the multiplicand) | × | Number of earning years left, less deduction for use of capital | = | Damages for future loss of earnings |

Loss of earning calculator

Activity

Thinking one last time about Vic's accident on the building site (Activity 2 on p237), make a list of the items of special and general damages he might be able to claim.

You should now be able to:

- explain briefly the principles governing an award of damages in a negligence claim
- explain how those principles apply in a case of personal injury.

Key terms

Medical or clinical negligence: negligence on the part of a doctor, consultant or other supplier of medical services when treating a patient.

6 Medical negligence

Medical or clinical negligence refers to carelessness on the part of medically qualified practitioners such as nurses, family doctors or consultants at a hospital. Examples might include failing to diagnose an illness properly or at all, prescribing or administering the wrong drugs, failing to follow correct procedures during an operation, or failing to give proper advice to a patient so that he could make an informed choice. Such negligence can lead to personal injury, and, as such, is governed by the ordinary principles of negligence – duty of care, breach and causation – discussed in this chapter. What follows is an application of those principles in a medical context.

In this topic, you will learn how to:

- apply the rules relating to negligence to the specific case of medical negligence
- identify the standard that applies to members of the medical profession.

Duty of care and omissions

There is no doubt that a doctor treating a patient owes the patient a duty of care to practise his profession properly. By agreeing to take the patient, the doctor assumes responsibility for the patient, and it is reasonably foreseeable that a failure to exercise reasonable care could lead to personal injury. The existence of a duty of care promotes medical safety, minimises the risk of injury, and gives a patient an opportunity for compensation. In response to the duty, doctors, like most professionals, take out professional insurance so that a claimant can be sure that he will receive his damages.

As explained in Topic 1, having chosen to take on a patient, a doctor is liable both for what he does (for instance, prescribing the wrong drug) and for what he does not do (for instance, failing to consider an X-ray). However, a doctor, like anyone else, is not under a duty as a member of the public to assist if he should come across someone in need of help.

One exception to this appears to be the casualty department of a hospital. In **Barnett v Chelsea and Kensington Hospital Management Committee (1968)** the claimant presented himself in the defendant's casualty department, vomiting and feeling extremely unwell. The doctor on duty refused to examine him because he too was feeling unwell, and sent him away. The court decided that the hospital did owe a duty to anyone arriving in casualty. This presumably means that a hospital cannot pick and choose which casualty patients to treat and therefore which patients to whom they owe a duty.

Breaching the duty of care

In order to satisfy the duty of care to his patient, a doctor must display the standard of care of a normal person practising his profession. The standard, therefore, will be different for a family doctor and for a consultant at a hospital. In both cases, the duty is to exercise reasonable competence and skill: if a doctor makes an error of judgement, there is no liability if a reasonable member of the profession would have made the same error.

In **Bolam v Friern Hospital Management Committee (1957)** the claimant received electric shocks as part of a treatment for psychiatric problems, and sustained fractures as a result. The risk of fractures would have been all but eliminated if the claimant had been given relaxant drugs beforehand. Some doctors would have done so, but the defendant, in line with a different body of medical thought, had chosen not to because the drugs carried their own risks. The trial judge explained that:

> A doctor is not negligent, if he is acting in accordance with a practice accepted as proper by a responsible body of medical men skilled in that particular art, merely because there is a body of such opinion that takes a contrary view.

This test has two consequences. The first is that if the medical profession is split, as in the *Bolam* case, the court will refuse to choose between the two sides. As long as some reasonable practitioners would follow the defendant's course of action then the defendant is not negligent, even if his side of the profession is in a minority. This is because a judge does not have the necessary knowledge to be able to make a decision, and he cannot simply choose whichever side is in the majority as that would stifle innovation given that every new technique starts as a minority. The defendant doctor in *Bolam* was thus not liable.

The second consequence appeared to be that a doctor could escape liability if he could show that he had complied with the generally accepted practice of reasonable members of his profession. This raised the

Key cases

Barnett v Chelsea and Kensington Hospital Management Committee (1968): a hospital casualty department cannot choose which patients to treat; it owes a duty to everyone who comes though its doors.

Bolam v Friern Hospital Management Committee (1957): a doctor is not negligent if he acts in accordance with a practice accepted as proper by a responsible body of medical men.

question of what happened if the whole profession was acting below what should be an acceptable standard. The issue was addressed in **Bolitho v City and Hackney Health Authority (1997)**, when the House of Lords said that a court should enquire as to whether a generally accepted practice had a logical basis and whether the profession had weighed up the risks and benefits of the practice and reached a proper conclusion. In theory, therefore, it is possible for a court to find a doctor liable in negligence even though he did what any other doctor would have done, but in practice it will be rare for the court to hold that an entire profession is acting below a proper standard, not least because if the leading experts in a particular field believe that a practice is the correct thing to do then that in itself suggests that the practice is a reasonable one.

A different issue relating to whether a medical defendant has broken his duty of care is the problem of medical technology advancing between the date of an alleged instance of negligence and the date of the resulting trial in court. The courts have decided that the relevant standard of care to apply is reasonable practice as it was at the time of the facts of the case. In **Roe v Minister of Health (1954)** the claimant was paralysed when he was given an injection that had been contaminated by a chemical leaking into the syringe. Medical technology at the date of the trial was able to explain how the accident had happened and how to prevent it, but the defendant escaped liability as the court judged him by the standard of the reasonable doctor who, at the time of the original incident, would not have known of the danger.

A final issue relating to breach of duty in a medical context is the problem of proving negligence. In any negligence case, the burden of proof is on the claimant to show that the defendant breached the duty of care. But this can be difficult in a medical context if the details of the accident are unclear and the claimant is unsure of what happened, perhaps because he did not understand matters or because he was unconscious or too ill at the relevant time. The claimant cannot then formally prove the sequence of events.

In these circumstances, the claimant may be able to use the principle of **res ipsa loquitur** ('the thing speaks for itself'). The principle applies if:

- the thing that caused damage was under the defendant's control at the relevant time, and
- what happened would not normally happen unless negligence was involved somewhere.

The principle was explained in **Scott v London and St Katharine Dock (1865)**. The claimant was hit by some bags of sugar that had fallen from the defendant's warehouse. He was able to recover damages, even though he could not prove the sequence of events that had led to bags falling, as the bags were under the control of the defendant, bags do not normally crash onto the street without negligence, and the defendants were unable to offer an alternative explanation.

The effect of *res ipsa loquitur* is to establish a preliminary case in negligence against the defendant on the ground that, although the claimant cannot prove negligence, the very facts of the case suggest that negligence must have been present. It is then open to the defendant to show an alternative explanation for the events. If the defendant can do this, then the claimant must prove negligence in the ordinary way.

In a medical context, the application of the principle is likely to be limited to clear-cut cases, such as removing the wrong kidney or amputating the wrong leg. Three case law examples are: **Mahon v Osborne (1939)**, in which a swab was left inside a patient after an operation; **Cassidy v Ministry of Health (1950)**, in which the claimant, having been treated for a condition of the hand that had restricted

Key cases

Bolitho v City and Hackney Health Authority (1997): a court should enquire whether a medical practice can be justified on the basis of relevant risks and benefits.

Roe v Minister of Health (1954): when judging the standard of care of a doctor, a court should consider the state of medical knowledge at the time of the events of the case rather than at the time of the trial.

Scott v London and St Katharine Dock (1865): negligence was established because the facts of the case themselves suggested that at some point the defendant must have been negligent.

Mahon v Osborne (1939), Cassidy v Ministry of Health (1950) and **Saunders v Leeds Western Health Authority (1984):** all demonstrate that negligence can be established, even in the absence of clear evidence, if the facts of the case suggest that negligence must have occurred at some point.

Key terms

Res ipsa loquitur: facts of a case themselves suggest that negligence must have occurred.

movement in two fingers, was unable to use any of the four fingers on that hand properly; and **Saunders v Leeds Western Health Authority (1984)**, in which a child with a healthy heart suffered a cardiac arrest during a routine anaesthetic.

However, the principle is likely to be of less relevance where the facts are not clear-cut and where there is a realistic explanation other than negligence. In **Ratcliffe v Plymouth and Torbay Health Authority (1998)** the claimant, after a successful operation on his ankle, had been given a spinal injection to relieve pain, but the injection had led to neurological problems. Neither side was able to prove what had actually happened or why this injury had occurred. However, the defendant was able to show by way of expert evidence that the state of the claimant's back was such that the injury might have occurred even if there had been no negligence. Given that the defendant had now shown that there was a possible alternative explanation, it was down to the claimant to prove actual negligence. He was unable to do this, and thus his claim was unsuccessful.

Causation

Like any other negligence case, the claimant in a medical negligence case must be able to show that his claim satisfies the 'but for' test – in other words, the negligence on the part of the defendant was what caused the loss, rather than something else. We illustrated this with the decision in *McWilliams* v *Arrol Ltd* (1962) in Topic 3 (see p241). A further example, in a medical context, is provided by *Barnett* v *Chelsea and Kensington Hospital Management Committee* (1968), which we discussed earlier in this topic. In that case, the doctor, in breach of the duty owed to treat anyone presenting himself in the casualty department of the hospital, had sent the claimant home. The claimant died, but the legal action against the doctor for his negligence failed because even if the doctor had done all that he should, the claimant would still have died as he was suffering from an untreatable arsenic poisoning. In other words, it was not the negligence that caused the death.

The courts have taken a strict approach in their application of the 'but for' test in situations where there are a number of possible causes. In **Wilsher v Essex Area Health Authority (1988)** the claimant suffered blindness as a result of events surrounding his birth. There were six possible causes: five relating to various medical conditions, and the sixth relating to the negligence of the hospital. The House of Lords sent the case to be tried again, stating that the claimant, using the normal civil standard of balance of probabilities, had to prove that it was more likely than not that it was the negligence rather than the medical conditions that had caused the blindness.

A similarly strict approach has been taken in the 'loss of chance' cases – in other words, incidents where medical negligence increased the chances of permanent damage in circumstances where there was already a risk because of the nature of the medical condition. In **Hotson v East Berkshire Health Authority (1987)** the claimant fell and was taken to hospital, but an injury to his hip was not discovered for five days, by which time there was permanent damage. The evidence was that there was a 75 per cent chance that the damage would have occurred even if the injury had been properly diagnosed. On that basis the House of Lords refused a claim for damages as the claimant was unable to show, on the balance of probabilities, that it was more likely than not that the negligence had contributed to the loss. A similar approach was taken in **Gregg v Scott (2005)**. The defendant's negligence led to a cancer going undetected for nine months longer than it should have done. The

Key cases

Ratcliffe v Plymouth and Torbay Health Authority (1998): principle of *res ipsa loquitur* is likely to be of limited use where any alleged negligence is not clear-cut.

Wilsher v Essex Area Health Authority (1988): if a loss suffered by a patient could have been caused by a number of things, not all of which are negligence on the part of the doctors, the claimant needs to prove that it was more likely than not that it was the negligence that was the cause.

Hotson v East Berkshire Health Authority (1987) and **Gregg v Scott (2005):** courts are reluctant to award damages on the basis that medical negligence may have reduced a patient's chances of recovery.

result was that the claimant's chances of being alive and disease-free in ten years' time were reduced from 42 per cent to 25 per cent. Again the House of Lords refused to allow a loss of chance to form the basis of liability.

A different scenario is illustrated by **Chester v Afshar (2004)**. The defendant operated on the claimant's spine, having failed to warn her that there was a 1–2 per cent risk of paralysis. Although the operation was carried out with proper care, the claimant was left paralysed. She sued for negligence, not in the carrying out of the medical procedure, but rather in the failure to warn. She said that if she had known of the risk she would not have had the operation at that time (although she may have had the operation at a later date when she would have faced the same risk). Using the normal 'but for' test, her claim would fail as, even if the doctor had done all that he should, the claimant could still have been left paralysed. However, the House of Lords allowed the claim for damages on the ground that if they refused the claim then the doctor's duty to inform his patients of any risks would have no practical effect, as there would be no consequence if it were broken.

Topic illustration

Consider the following scenario:

> Shortly after undergoing abdominal surgery at the Royal Foxton Hospital, Gertrude began to suffer stomach pains. An investigation revealed that one of the clips used in her operation had been left inside when it should have been removed. Gertrude was booked in for surgery the next day, and given some tablets to take overnight to help her symptoms. Gertrude did not take the tablets as directed, with the result that the operation was more difficult than it should have been, and Gertrude took longer to recover. In addition, she also suffered some further temporary, but unusual, complications.

Gertrude has a potential claim in negligence against the hospital, but in order to be successful she will need to have regard to each of the following points:

▧ Firstly, she needs to establish that the hospital owes a duty of care. This should be straightforward, using a simple application of the principles in *Donoghue* v *Stevenson* (1932) and *Caparo* v *Dickman* (1990).

▧ Secondly, she needs to show that the hospital breached the duty of care. Presumably, the reasonable hospital does not leave clips inside a patient, and we can illustrate this by citing cases such as *Paris* v *Stepney Borough Council* (1951), which states that where any damage is likely to be severe, the reasonable person takes extra care. In this case, Gertrude may have to rely on the principle of *res ipsa loquitur* if she is unable to prove the actual sequence of events that led to the accident.

▧ There is little doubt that causation is satisfied: the hospital's breach of duty caused Gertrude's problems. With respect to remoteness of damage, Gertrude will need to prove that her problems were a reasonably foreseeable consequence of the hospital's actions, and she will perhaps rely on the rule in *Smith* v *Leech Brain & Co.* (1962) that, provided some damage is foreseeable, she will be able to recover damages for the full extent of her injuries, including the unusual complications.

▧ Finally, there is the issue of the defence of contributory negligence. The hospital will want to show that Gertrude's own actions made her problems worse than they might have been.

Key cases

Chester v Afshar (2004): a doctor has a duty to explain risks of surgery to a patient.

Study tip

When considering medical negligence, it is important to discuss the normal rules of negligence first before trying to apply them in a medical context.

■ **Activities**

1 In the UK, damages in most successful claims for medical negligence are paid by the taxpayer. Consider whether this a good use of public funds.

2 Simon was admitted to Leafytown General Hospital to have his tonsils removed. Due to a mix-up, the surgeon actually removed Simon's appendix. In the confusion surrounding the accident, the hospital's team failed to notice for four days that Simon had picked up a serious infection since being admitted. The delay meant that his chances of making a full recovery from the infection were reduced from 40 per cent to 10 per cent. Advise Simon on his chances in making a claim for negligence against the hospital.

You should now be able to:

■ explain when a doctor will have broken the duty of care that he owes to his patients

■ identify, in a medical context, examples of the rules relating to causation.

15 The tort of negligence: claiming psychiatric damage and economic loss

Introduction

In Chapter 14, we discussed the principles of ordinary negligence in relation to a claim for physical damage – in other words, personal injury and damage to property.

Negligence also allows claims for psychiatric damage and economic loss. As with any claim in negligence, the claimant must show that:

- the defendant owes a duty of care;
- the defendant has breached the duty of care; and
- the breach of the duty has caused reasonably foreseeable loss to the claimant.

However, for a variety of reasons, the courts are much more reluctant to allow claims for psychiatric damage and economic loss than for straightforward physical damage. Consequently, in both cases, the courts have adopted a **restrictive approach** as to when a duty of care is owed, and the range of potential claimants is much narrower than for physical damage.

This chapter considers the narrow rules relating to the duty of care in these instances of psychiatric damage and economic loss. It does not discuss breach and causation, as they remain the same as for physical damage and need to be demonstrated by the claimant in the normal way.

1 Claiming psychiatric damage

What is psychiatric damage?

Psychiatric damage, which is also known as nervous shock, means a recognised psychiatric illness that can be independently verified on the basis of the medical evidence. It represents the long-term psychiatric consequences of a shocking event that was experienced by the claimant. The most common example is post traumatic stress disorder. This occurs when the claimant is involved in, or witnesses, an event which is so disastrous or catastrophic as to be outside the normal range of human experiences. Typically, the event threatens death or serious personal injury to the claimant or another, and leaves the claimant feeling extreme fear or helplessness. Symptoms are very diverse, but examples are irritability, sleep problems, flash-backs, and problems with memory and concentration. Symptoms are persistent and leave the claimant unable to carry out ordinary work, family or social activities in a normal way.

By contrast, the definition of psychiatric injury excludes grief, emotional distress, ordinary shock or anything else that is not a recognisable psychiatric illness. In **Reilly v Merseyside Regional Health Authority (1994)**, for instance, the claimants were unable to recover damages in respect of their claustrophobia and anxiety after they were trapped in a lift.

When can psychiatric damage be claimed?

In addition to demonstrating that he is suffering from a recognisable psychiatric illness, the claimant must also show that he is either a primary victim or a secondary victim. These are the only two categories of people to whom a duty of care in relation to psychiatric damage is

---

Key terms

Restrictive approach: idea that fewer claimants will be able to recover for psychiatric or economic loss than for physical loss because the courts define the duty of care more narrowly.

In this topic, you will learn how to:

- explain what is meant by the term 'psychiatric damage'
- identify and explain the categories of claimant that can claim for psychiatric harm
- define and discuss the qualifying criteria required by someone who wishes to claim as a secondary victim.

Key terms

Psychiatric damage: long-term mental consequences of being involved in, or witnessing, a horrific event.

Key cases

Reilly v Merseyside Regional Health Authority (1994): a claimant may only recover damages in respect of a recognisable psychiatric illness.

Study tip

In an A Level Law exam, you cannot be expected to comment in detail on psychiatric illnesses. Briefly outline what is required and continue with your answer.

owed. Both these categories are defined very narrowly, and if the claimant cannot show that he falls within one or other of them then the defendant does not owe him a duty of care and the claim fails.

There are several reasons why the courts take such a restrictive approach as to who can claim for psychiatric damage. They include a traditional unwillingness to treat mental injuries as seriously as physical injuries, the difficulty of diagnosis, and the risk of fraudulent claims. In addition, there is a fear of 'floodgates': the idea that a single accident can lead to an unknown and unpredictable amount of liability. This is because the number of people who might suffer psychiatric damage by witnessing a dreadful event or hearing about it could be very large, especially given modern media such as television. One illustration of this is the Hillsborough Stadium disaster, when, as a result of the police's negligent management of a crowd at a football match, ninety-six people were crushed to death and many more were injured. In addition to the claims for death and personal injury, there were a large number of claims for psychiatric damage by those who witnessed the events in and around the stadium, and by those who had followed events through live television coverage. Two of these cases reached the House of Lords: *Alcock* v *Chief Constable of South Yorkshire* (1991), which dealt with claims brought by family and friends of those killed or injured; and *White* v *Chief Constable of South Yorkshire* (1991), which dealt with claims brought by individual police officers on duty in the stadium that day. As we will see in the following paragraphs, in both cases the House of Lords narrowly defined the rules governing recovery for psychiatric injury, in order to avoid nearly impossible levels of liability in respect of the thousands of people affected by the incident.

We now turn to the question of which claimants might qualify as either a primary or a secondary victim.

Claims were brought by individual police officers who were on duty in the stadium on the day of the Hillsborough disaster

Primary victims

A **primary victim** is someone who is injured or fears he will be injured and who suffers psychiatric harm as a result. In the former case, of course, he can claim for both his physical loss and his psychiatric damage.

There are two key examples of a primary victim: someone who is directly involved in an accident and someone who goes to help those involved in an accident (a **rescuer**).

1 Those involved directly in an accident

A person involved directly in an accident can claim for psychiatric damage even if he escaped physical injury, provided that he feared for his own safety. In such circumstances it does not matter that psychiatric harm specifically was not reasonably foreseeable, as long as some sort of harm, either physical or psychiatric, was reasonably foreseeable. In **Page v Smith (1996)** the claimant was involved in a road traffic incident caused by the defendant's negligence. He escaped physical injury, but the accident re-triggered the ME (myalgic encephalomyelitis, or chronic fatigue syndrome) from which he had suffered in the past and which rendered him unable to work. The House of Lords decided that his psychiatric damage was claimable, even though psychiatric damage itself was not reasonably foreseeable, as injury of some sort was a reasonably foreseeable consequence of the defendant's negligence in causing the road accident. The case is also an illustration of the 'thin skull' rule (see p242). The accident was comparatively minor (which is why the claimant probably escaped physical injury), and most people would probably not have suffered long-term psychiatric consequences as a result. But the claimant, although he had a 'thin skull' personality, was able to claim for all his injury, even though the full extent was not reasonably foreseeable.

Although most cases of this type will relate to a claimant who is directly involved in an accident, the courts have made it clear that a primary victim can exist in other situations. One example is **Donachie v Chief Constable of Greater Manchester (2004)**. The claimant was a police officer who was required to attach a tracking device to the underside of a car belonging to a suspected gang of criminals, while the gang members were drinking inside a public house. Through the negligence of the police force, the tracking device was defective and the claimant had to make nine trips to the car before the device would work. He suffered psychiatric damage because the risk grew greater on each occasion he returned to the car that he would be discovered and would suffer serious injury at the hands of the gang.

2 Rescuers

The House of Lords confirmed in **White v Chief Constable of South Yorkshire (1998)** that someone who is not involved in an accident, but who attends the scene as a rescuer, can qualify as a primary victim if they suffer psychiatric damage as a result of their experiences. In order to claim, such a person must be engaged in rescue activities and must fear for their own safety during such activities.

In *White v Chief Constable of South Yorkshire* (1998) the claimants were police officers attending the scene of the Hillsborough stadium disaster. Although they undoubtedly witnessed horrific scenes, and suffered psychiatric damage as a result, their claims failed as they themselves never feared for their own safety.

A similar example is **McFarlane v EE Caledonia Ltd (1993)**. The claimant was on board a supply ship near to the Piper Alpha oil rig when there were a series of catastrophic gas explosions that killed 164 men,

Key terms

Primary victim: someone who is directly involved in an incident and either is, or could have been, physically injured.

Rescuer: person who goes to the aid of another and by doing so places himself at risk of physical injury.

Key cases

Page v Smith (1996): as long as physical injury is foreseeable as a result of an accident, the claimant can claim for psychiatric injury, even in the absence of physical injury.

Donachie v Chief Constable of Greater Manchester (2004): a primary victim may be someone other than a person directly involved in an accident.

White v Chief Constable of South Yorkshire (1998): in order to claim for psychiatric harm, a rescuer must take part in the rescue work and must be in personal physical danger as a result.

McFarlane v EE Caledonia Ltd (1993) and **Chadwick v British Railways Board (1967)** are cases that illustrate the rule later confirmed in **White v Chief Constable of South Yorkshire (1998)**.

Study tip

When identifying whether the characters in a problem are primary or secondary victims, be careful to consider whether they went to help a victim of any accident.

Key terms

Secondary victim: person who witnesses a horrific event, but who is not personally endangered.

Close tie of love and affection: relationship between claimant and another is so close that if that other person is injured it is reasonably foreseeable that the claimant will suffer psychiatric damage.

Key cases

Alcock v Chief Constable of South Yorkshire (1991): in order to qualify as a secondary victim, a claimant must satisfy a series of conditions.

Bourhill v Young (1943): a witness with no connection to an accident victim is unlikely to be able to claim for psychiatric damage.

and injured many others. The claimant helped prepare his ship to receive the injured, for instance by bringing blankets, but his claim for psychiatric damage caused as a result of what he saw and experienced failed: he was neither a rescuer nor in immediate physical danger himself.

A contrasting example is **Chadwick v British Railways Board (1967)**. The claimant, a member of the public, attended the scene of a fatal train crash that occurred near his home. His claim for psychiatric injury succeeded: he was engaged as a rescuer and he had placed himself in danger.

Secondary victims

A **secondary victim** is someone who was not in personal physical danger, but who witnessed the accident or its aftermath. As a single incident has the potential to give rise to multiple claimants, the rules on who qualifies as a secondary victim are very tightly drawn. A claim must satisfy all of the following four controls:

1 the claimant must comply with the rules in *Alcock*'s case
2 the injury must be caused by a sudden shock
3 the claimant must be of reasonable fortitude
4 no claim can be made if the victim of an accident was the person who caused the accident.

The rules in Alcock's case

The leading case on the definition of a secondary victim is **Alcock v Chief Constable of South Yorkshire (1991)**. The case was actually a series of cases brought by relatives and friends of football fans killed or injured at the Hillsborough Stadium disaster. The House of Lords was acutely aware of the potential for unlimited liability arising from this type of case. It therefore established three qualifying criteria, all of which a claimant must satisfy before being able to claim as a secondary victim.

1 The claimant must have a close tie of love and affection

The claimant must have a sufficiently **close tie of love and affection** with the person killed, injured or endangered, such that it is reasonably foreseeable that they would suffer psychiatric harm. As a result of *Alcock*, the courts are prepared to assume that the parent, child or spouse of a victim will have such a close tie, but it is possible that a judge might find that such a tie did not exist if the evidence suggests otherwise. One example might be a married couple who have lived apart for many years.

It is open to a claimant who has a relationship with the victim other than that of parent, child or spouse to prove that he had an equally close tie of love and affection. However, this is very hard to do and in *Alcock* (1991) itself grandparents, siblings, uncles and close friends all failed in their claims. It may be that a fiancé(e), a grandparent who has brought up a grandchild, or an identical twin might succeed.

Clearly, therefore, a bystander who has no link at all with the victim is very unlikely to succeed in claiming damages. In **Bourhill v Young (1943)** the claimant heard a crash in which a motorcyclist was killed. Although she was never in any personal danger, she suffered, among other things, psychiatric damage. However, her claim failed as it was not reasonably foreseeable that someone in her position would be affected by the negligence of the motorcyclist. However, the House of Lords in *Alcock* (1991) did leave open the possibility that even an unrelated bystander could claim if he witnessed something truly and unimaginably horrific. One example given was a petrol tanker careering into a playground full of small children and exploding.

2 The claimant must be close to the accident in time and space

The claimant should be present at the scene of the accident in order to claim. In *Alcock* (1991) itself it was decided that this requirement excluded both a claimant who had been in a different part of the stadium at the time and a claimant who was sitting in a coach outside the ground, following events on a television in the vehicle, and who went to look for his son when he realised what was happening.

The courts are prepared to relax this rule slightly to allow a claim by a person who did not witness the event itself, but who did witness its **immediate aftermath**. In **McLoughlin v O'Brian (1983)** the claimant was a mother who was told that her husband and three of their children had been involved in a serious road accident. She went straight to the hospital to be told that one child had been killed, and that her husband and the two other children were seriously injured. She saw the surviving members of her family in various states of great distress and covered in blood and dirt. She suffered psychiatric damage as a result of what she had seen and heard. Her claim was allowed by the House of Lords on the ground that, although she had not witnessed the accident itself, she has witnessed the immediate aftermath – in other words, consequences of the accident that were so close to the accident, so reminiscent of the scene of the accident, that her shock and upset were as if she had witnessed the accident.

One difficulty is that the words 'immediate aftermath' have an uncertain definition: which consequences count as immediate aftermath and which do not? In *Alcock* (1991), for instance, the House of Lords decided that identifying a body in a mortuary was not sufficiently close to the scene to allow a claim for psychiatric damage. By contrast, in **Galli-Atkinson v Seghal (2003)** the claimant was a mother who, having realised that her daughter had not come home, went out to look for her. She came across the scene of a road traffic accident at which the emergency services were already in attendance. The claimant realised that the victim was her daughter, but did not see her until she was asked to identify her daughter's body in the mortuary a little later. Her claim for psychiatric harm was successful as what she had seen, from the police cordon at the scene of the accident to her daughter's body in the mortuary, amounted to the immediate aftermath of the accident.

3 The accident must be perceived by the claimant with his own senses

The claimant must directly perceive the accident with his own senses. This can include sight, hearing and even touch. However, it is not enough to be told about the offence or to hear about it on the television or the radio. Some of the claimants in the *Alcock* case failed in their claims as they had learned about the disaster from those who had been there and through the media rather than witnessing it for themselves.

One possibility that remains unclear is a claimant who witnesses events as they unfold by being in touch via mobile 'phone, particularly a 'phone with video images.

The injury must be caused by a sudden shock

A secondary victim must show that any psychiatric damage was caused by a **sudden shock** (an 'assault on the senses'). This will occur if the claimant witnesses a single, sudden event such as an accident, rather than experiencing a growing realisation that something dreadful is happening ('slow shock'). In **Sion v Hampstead Health Authority (1994)**, the claimant suffered psychiatric damage as a result of watching his son die over a period of days from road traffic injuries which it was alleged had been negligently treated by the defendant hospital. The claim failed as there was no sudden shock, but rather a growing awareness.

Key terms

Immediate aftermath: sights, sounds and experiences present immediately after an accident.

Sudden shock: sudden realisation rather than a growing awareness that something dreadful has happened.

Key cases

McLoughlin v O'Brian (1983): a witness who sees the immediate aftermath of an accident can be said to have been present at the scene of the accident.

Galli-Atkinson v Seghal (2003): the immediate aftermath of an accident can include witnessing scenes at the site of an accident together with identifying a body at a mortuary.

Sion v Hampstead Health Authority (1994): a secondary victim can only claim if their psychiatric damage is caused by a sudden shock and not by a growing realisation.

Study tip

When applying the rules in *Alcock v Chief Constable of South Yorkshire* (1991), consider each separately and try to reach a conclusion for each.

One of the Court of Appeal judges in that case had this to say on the definition of shock:

> I understand 'shock' in this context to mean the sudden sensory perception – that is, by seeing, hearing or touching – of a person, thing or event, which is so distressing that the perception of the phenomenon affronts or insults the plaintiff's mind and causes a recognisable psychiatric illness. (Staughton LJ)

The courts are, however, prepared to take a realistic view of the meaning of the word 'event' when deciding if there was a single shocking incident that led to psychiatric damage. In **Walters v North Glamorgan NHS Trust (2002)** the claimant was the mother of an infant who had been negligently misdiagnosed by a hospital in South Wales. The baby suffered a fit, and was transferred by ambulance to a hospital in London, where he died. The court decided that, although it had been 36 hours from the initial fit to the death, this amounted to a single event with one step leading inevitably to the next and which had led to the claimant's psychiatric damage.

Reasonable fortitude

A secondary victim must show that his psychiatric damage was reasonably foreseeable and that a person of **reasonable fortitude** ('customary phlegm') would have sustained the injury. He cannot claim if he has a 'thin skull' personality and consequently suffers psychiatric damage when a person of reasonable fortitude would not have done.

However, a person with a 'thin skull' personality can claim for the full extent of his injury if the circumstances are such that a person of reasonable fortitude would have suffered some psychiatric damage.

A primary victim owes no duty to a secondary victim

In the cases we have looked at so far, the secondary victim (claimant), the victim of the accident and the defendant have been three different people.

However, it might be that the victim of the accident and the defendant are the same person. In this circumstance, the defendant does not owe a duty, and the secondary victim's claim will fail. The reason for this is that an individual does not owe a duty to anyone to look after himself so as to avoid predicaments that might cause distress to another. This would infringe personal liberty and the right of an individual to do with his life as he wishes.

One example is **Greatorex v Greatorex (2000)** when the defendant was badly injured in a road traffic accident caused by his own negligent driving. By chance, his father was one of the fire and rescue officers attending at the scene, and he suffered psychiatric damage as a result of realising that the victim of the accident was his own son. His claim failed as the defendant owed no duty to look after himself in case it caused distress to another.

Who else might claim for psychiatric damage?

At the fringes of the law relating to psychiatric damage, there are a number of cases which are, at best, difficult to fit into the established categories of primary victim and secondary victim. The courts have made it clear that they will allow claims in appropriate circumstances.

One example is a person who suffers psychiatric damage because of a mistaken belief that his actions have led to the death, injury or endangerment of others, when in fact the accident was caused by someone else's negligence. In **Dooley v Cammell Laird (1951)** the claimant, a crane operator, feared that he had injured his colleagues when his crane dropped its load into the hold of a ship where he knew they were working. The accident was in fact caused by his employer's negligence but the claimant suffered psychiatric damage, for which he was able to claim damages, because he believed it was his fault.

Key cases

Walters v North Glamorgan NHS Trust (2002): for the purposes of psychiatric damage, a shocking event need not be an instantaneous occurrence, but can be prolonged over several hours.

Greatorex v Greatorex (2000): a person does not owe a duty of care to look after himself so that those close to him do not suffer psychiatric harm in the event that he is injured because of his own carelessness.

Dooley v Cammell Laird (1951): a claimant may be able to claim for psychiatric harm if he believes that his own actions have injured a work colleague when in fact the accident occurred because of the employer's negligence.

Key terms

Reasonable fortitude: strength and resilience shown by an ordinary person.

Another difficult case is **W v Essex County Council (2000)**. The claimants, who had four children of their own, fostered a teenager, having been assured, wrongly, by the defendant council that he was not a known or suspected sexual abuser. The foster child seriously abused the claimants' own children, and the parents suffered psychiatric damage, not least because they felt responsible for having brought their own children into contact with someone who would abuse them. The defendant asked the courts to strike out the claim on the ground that there was no arguable chance of success given the definitions of primary and secondary victims. The House of Lords refused to do this: they felt that the definitions were sufficiently uncertain that there was a possibility that a trial court, having established the facts, might find that the claimants qualified as secondary victims or even primary victims (perhaps because the claimants felt personal responsibility for the harm to their children, much as the claimant felt personal responsibility for the accident in the *Dooley* case). In the event, the case settled out of court, but the comments of the House of Lords will almost certainly give rise to future litigation in unusual sets of facts.

A final example of psychiatric damage in unusual circumstances is **Attia v British Gas (1987)**. The claimant had contracted with the defendant to install gas central heating. Due to the defendant's negligence, the house caught fire, and it and its contents were severely damaged. The claimant was uninjured and had not been in personal danger, but she suffered psychiatric harm and was successful in her claim for damages for this. It might seem surprising that she was able to claim, since she only witnessed property being destroyed, when others have failed in their claims even though they witnessed people being injured. The explanation might be that the claimant and the defendant had a legal link before the negligence was committed, in that they had a contract.

Topic illustration

Consider this scenario, adapted from a past AQA exam paper:

> Nabeela (aged 11) had been trespassing in a derelict building owned by Lister Properties when she fell from an upper floor and became trapped in debris. She suffered serious back and leg injuries, and her screams were heard by Oliver, a police officer who was walking past the building. As soon as he saw her, he telephoned for an ambulance, and then tried to remove rubble from her and to comfort her. Meanwhile, other children had run to tell Nabeela's aunt, Pat, who lived close by. Pat arrived just in time to see paramedics sedating Nabeela and putting her into the ambulance. Both Oliver and Pat found it very difficult to recover from the experience, and both were away from work for prolonged periods of time with anxiety and depression. Discuss the rights available to Oliver and to Pat against Lister Properties.

Any claim will be against Lister Properties for their negligence in allowing Nabeela to play in the building in the first place. However, Oliver and Pat have not suffered any kind of physical loss, whether personal injury or damage to property, and therefore you need to consider the rules relating to psychiatric damage.

■ The first element is a discussion of whether Oliver and Pat have suffered psychiatric damage. You should discuss rules relating to a recognisable psychiatric illness, but you don't need to decide whether the claimant has actually suffered such an injury.

■ The second element is to discuss whether either Oliver or Pat qualifies as a primary victim. There might be an argument for Oliver, as he is a rescuer, but only if he placed himself in personal danger. It is difficult

Key cases

W v Essex County Council (2000): future claims for psychiatric loss may arise out of events other than an accident.

Attia v British Gas (1987): liability may exist, in the right circumstances, for witnessing damage to property.

to see how Pat can be a primary victim, as she only arrived later when the ambulance was leaving.

■ We then need to discuss if either Oliver or Pat are secondary victims, and this requires a discussion of the rules in *Alcock* (1991). Key issues include whether either has a close enough relationship to Nabeela, whether either was at the scene of the accident or (in Pat's case) at the immediate aftermath, and whether either suffered psychiatric damage through sudden shock.

Activities

1 What reasons might there be for allowing a claim for psychiatric damage in the case of a rescuer who is unconnected to any of the victims? Should professional rescuers, such as fire crew or ambulance staff, be able to claim even if they are not in personal danger?

2 The rules relating to recovery for psychiatric damage in the case of secondary victims have been widely criticised for being too narrow. Would you reform the rules? If so, how would you do so in order to prevent unlimited liability?

3 Malcolm was driving to work in an absent-minded way, as he was worried about some of that day's meetings. His car mounted the pavement and struck some scaffolding around a building. Part of the scaffolding collapsed, narrowly missing Norma, but trapping her behind the debris. Oscar, a bystander, rushed across to help Norma even though he could see that the remainder of the scaffolding was wobbling dangerously. Peter, Norma's brother, who had been shopping with Norma and had gone on ahead, heard the crash and dashed out of a shop to see scaffolding collapsing where Norma had been standing. Norma, Oscar and Peter all suffered long-lasting mental problems as a result of their experiences. Discuss Malcolm's liability in connection with these mental problems.

You should now be able to:

■ explain the nature of psychiatric damage, and discuss how liability for it differs from liability for physical damage

■ identify situations when a defendant owes a duty of care to a claimant for psychiatric damage

■ explain whether a claimant satisfies the requirements for a primary victim or a secondary victim.

In this topic, you will learn how to:

■ explain what is meant by the term 'economic loss'

■ identify and explain the requirements needed in a claim for negligent misstatement.

Key terms

Economic loss: financial loss rather than physical loss.

2 Claiming economic loss

What is economic loss?

Economic loss is financial loss rather than physical loss such as personal injury or damage to property. It represents 'damage to the wallet' of the claimant, as the defendant's negligence has left the claimant less well off than he would have been if the negligence had not occurred. Examples include a loss in profits, an unwise investment, a loss of a financial benefit and a loss in value of items.

There are two types of economic loss: consequential economic loss and pure economic loss. The distinction is important because, subject to exceptions, a claimant can recover for consequential economic loss, but not for pure economic loss.

Consequential economic loss occurs when the claimant suffers a money loss because he has suffered an item of physical loss – in other words, the economic loss is consequential on the physical loss. Examples include a worker who loses wages because he has been injured by the defendant's negligence, or a taxi driver who loses fares because his taxi has been damaged by the defendant's negligence. In both cases, the defendant's negligence causes physical loss or injury that in turn leads to a money loss for the claimant.

By contrast, **pure economic loss** is a stand-alone economic loss: there is no item of physical loss. An example would be if the defendant's negligence causes a traffic accident that closes the road, thus preventing people getting to the claimant's café, and the claimant, as a result, loses several hours' worth of takings. The claimant has suffered a money loss, but no physical loss or injury, and therefore his loss is a purely economic loss.

The difference between consequential economic loss and pure economic loss is illustrated by the facts of **Spartan Steel and Alloys Ltd v Martin and Co. (Contractors) Ltd (1972)**. The defendant was carrying out road works when, negligently, it severed the electricity cable that supplied power to the claimant's smelting works. At the time the power was shut off, the claimant was producing a consignment of ingots (in a process called a 'melt'). In order to protect its furnace, the claimant had to remove the metal by prematurely cooling it, but this in turn meant that the metal was damaged. The claimant suffered three losses:

- Damage to the metal: this was a physical loss in the form of damage to property.
- Loss of profit, because the damaged metal could not now be sold: this was an economic loss consequential on the physical loss to the metal.
- Loss of profit on four further melts that had been planned for the period when the electricity was off: this was an economic loss not associated with any physical loss (a pure economic loss) as the metal that was scheduled to be used was undamaged by the incident.

When considering to what extent the law allows recovery for pure and consequential economic losses, we need to distinguish between economic losses caused by a negligent act and economic losses caused by a negligent misstatement.

Liability for economic loss caused by a negligent act

The rule relating to the recovery of economic loss caused by a negligent act is that consequential economic loss is always recoverable, as long as the claimant can satisfy the normal rules on causation and remoteness, but that pure economic loss is not recoverable.

This rule can be traced back to the decision in **Cattle v Stockton Waterworks (1875)**. The claimant was building a tunnel for a fixed price for a third party, when the tunnel was flooded due to the defendant's negligence. The claimant lost money on his building contract because it was now more difficult and more expensive to complete the tunnel, but he could not pass the cost on to the third party because of the fixed price clause in the contract. When the claimant sued the defendant for his losses, the court refused the claim as the claimant had suffered an economic loss without any physical loss.

An example of the courts refusing a claim for pure economic loss caused by a negligent act is **Weller v Foot and Mouth Disease Research Institute (1965)**, in which the defendant's negligence caused an escape of the foot and mouth virus. To prevent the disease from spreading, the authorities banned the movement of animals, which in turn damaged

Key terms

Consequential economic loss: economic loss that occurs because the claimant has also suffered physical loss.

Pure economic loss: when a claimant suffers an economic loss but no physical loss.

Key cases

Spartan Steel and Alloys Ltd v Martin and Co. (Contractors) Ltd (1972): economic loss caused by a physical loss can be recovered, an economic loss that stands alone cannot be.

Cattle v Stockton Waterworks (1875) and **Weller v Foot and Mouth Disease Research Institute (1965):** claimant cannot recover for a pure economic loss.

the business of the claimants who were livestock auctioneers. The claim for loss of profit failed as it was a pure economic loss: the claimants had suffered no physical loss.

By contrast, an example of a successful claim for a consequential economic loss caused by a negligent act is **Network Rail Infrastructure v Conarkin Group (2011)**. The claimant owned a railway line that was blocked for five days by rubble that had fallen from a bridge because of negligence on the part of the defendant's lorry driver. As a result, the claimant had had to pay out compensation to train companies who were unable to use the railway. This economic loss was recoverable because it was consequential on the physical damage done to the railway.

Spartan Steel and Alloys Ltd v *Martin and Co. (Contractors) Ltd* (1972) itself provides a final example. The claimant successfully recovered for the first two of its losses: the damage to the metal (physical loss), and the loss of profits that should have been made on the sale of the metal (consequential economic loss). But the claimant failed in its third claim, as the loss of profits on the planned melts was a pure economic loss.

As with liability for psychiatric damage, the principal reason why the courts take such a restrictive approach to the recovery of pure economic loss is the fear of 'floodgates', and the danger that a single accident could lead to an unknown and unpredictable amount of liability. Suppose, for example, that the contractor in the *Spartan Steel* case had negligently severed the electricity cable supplying an entire city: it would be virtually impossible to work out the economic losses that would be suffered by all the city's businesses during the time that the power was off.

Nevertheless, there are a small number of cases, with very particular facts, where the courts have been prepared to allow a claim for pure economic loss caused by a negligent act. A well-known example is **White v Jones (1995)**. Following a family argument, the testator had cut his two daughters, the claimants, out of his will. The family then settled its differences, and the testator gave instructions to his solicitor, the defendant, for a fresh will, leaving bequests to both the claimants. The solicitor was negligent as he delayed drawing up the will and the testator died before he could execute it. This meant that the existing will, which excluded the claimants, took effect and the claimants thus lost their gifts. The House of Lords was prepared to allow the claimants to recover their loss, even though it was a pure economic loss. There was no 'floodgates' problem because there was no threat of unlimited liability: the negligent solicitor would know which beneficiaries would lose and by how much.

Liability for economic loss caused by negligent misstatement

A defendant may be liable if he makes a statement to someone to whom he owes a duty of care but, due to his negligence, the statement is inaccurate and it causes the claimant a reasonably foreseeable pure economic loss. Such a statement is a **negligent misstatement**: it can be written or verbal, and can be in any form that conveys information to the claimant. Examples include a report, a reference, professional advice, a survey, a set of accounts and a map.

The possibility of liability existing for a negligent misstatement was first recognised in **Hedley Byrne v Heller (1964)**. The claimant was an advertising agency that was about to book, at its own financial risk, a large amount of advertising space on behalf of a client. The claimant asked the defendant, the client's bank, for a financial reference relating to the client, as the claimant wanted reassurance that the client would be able to pay for the advertising space. The financial reference was negligently prepared: it suggested that the client was in a much stronger financial position than was actually the case. As a result, the

■ **Key cases**

Network Rail Infrastructure v Conarkin Group (2011): a claimant may recover a consequential economic loss caused by a negligent act.

White v Jones (1995): pure economic loss caused by a negligent act may be recoverable if there is no danger of unlimited liability.

Hedley Byrne v Heller (1964): a claimant can recover pure economic loss caused by a negligent misstatement if there is a special relationship between him and the defendant.

■ **Key terms**

Negligent misstatement: statement that is inaccurate because of the negligence of the person who made the statement.

claimant booked the space, but the client never paid for it as it went into liquidation shortly afterwards, and the claimant lost its money. The claimant therefore sued the bank for its negligence in preparing the reference. In the event, the defendant won the case because it had included in the reference a clause excluding liability, but the House of Lords made it clear that, in the absence of such an exclusion clause, liability for a negligent misstatement could exist.

As with any other example of pure economic loss, negligent misstatement, raises the risk of an unknown and unpredictable liability – for instance, a newspaper publishing careless investment advice that many thousands of readers then rely on. Therefore, in *Hedley Byrne* v *Heller* (1964) the House of Lords made it clear that, for the purposes of negligent misstatement, a defendant owes a duty of care only to someone with whom he has a '**special relationship**'. The effect of this is to greatly restrict the number of potential claimants and thus avoid the risk of unlimited liability.

The case law is not entirely clear as to what the precise requirements for a special relationship are, but it is possible to identify five key elements:

1 The defendant possesses a skill or expertise.
2 The defendant voluntarily assumes responsibility for his statements.
3 The defendant knows who will use his statement.
4 The defendant knows for what purpose his statement will be used.
5 The claimant relies on that statement in circumstances in which it is reasonable to do so.

1 The defendant possesses a skill or expertise

The defendant is in possession of a skill or an expertise that the claimant needs. Normally, the defendant in a negligent misstatement case will be a professional adviser. Good examples are an accountant preparing a set of accounts, a surveyor writing a report on a building, and a solicitor giving legal advice. However, liability can be extended to a non-professional adviser. In **Lennon v Metropolitan Police Commissioner (2004)** the claimant, a policeman transferring between forces, asked a clerical officer in the defendant's personnel department for advice on his eligibility for a housing allowance. Liability was established as the clerk gave wrong information with the result that the claimant lost financial payments to which he would otherwise have been entitled.

Liability has even been extended to a social setting. In **Chaudhry v Prabhakar (1988)** the defendant, who had some knowledge of cars, helped the claimant, a friend, choose a second-hand car, but failed to notice that the car had been in an accident. He was held liable for the money the claimant wasted purchasing the car when shortly afterwards the car was found to be unroadworthy and therefore valueless.

2 The defendant voluntarily assumes responsibility for his statements

If the defendant **voluntarily assumes responsibility** for his statements, it means that he is effectively saying to the claimant that he is prepared for the claimant to rely on any advice, and that he (the defendant) will take responsibility for the advice. As was pointed out in *Hedley Byrne* v *Heller* (1964), a defendant does not have to give advice: he can either decline altogether or give any advice subject to a disclaimer as to liability (as of course happened in *Hedley Byrne* itself).

One example of a case in which the court decided that a defendant had not voluntarily assumed responsibility is **Patchett v Swimming Pool and Allied Trades Association (2009)**. The claimant, wanting to engage a reputable contractor to build a swimming pool in his garden, consulted

Key terms

Special relationship: link of sufficient closeness between a defendant and a claimant that liability for a negligent misstatement can be imposed.

Voluntary assumption of responsibility: defendant chooses to take responsibility for advising the claimant.

Key cases

Lennon v Metropolitan Police Commissioner (2004): a person does not need to be a professional adviser in order to possess the skill or expertise necessary for liability in negligent misstatement.

Chaudhry v Prabhakar (1988): a special relationship for the purposes of negligent misstatement may exist in a social setting.

Patchett v SPATA (2009): a defendant is not liable for a negligent misstatement when it is clear that he had not intended to assume responsibility.

the defendant trade association's website. The website, by way of a drop-down menu, suggested various contractors – including the company that the claimant eventually chose. The website did not make it clear that this particular contractor was not a full member of the trade association and therefore was not covered by the defendant's guarantee. When the contractor became insolvent part way through the construction, the claimant lost several thousand pounds that he had paid by way of instalments. The claimant sued for his loss on the basis that the website constituted a negligent misstatement. However, the defendant was not liable as it was clear that it had not intended to assume responsibility for the contents of the website – the website itself said that any reader should make further enquiries and should obtain the defendant's information pack, which would have made the true position clear.

3 Known user

A defendant will normally only be liable if he knows or should know, when making a statement, the identity of the particular person or class of persons who will rely on the statement. In **Caparo v Dickman (1990)** an accountant prepared a company's annual accounts. One of the shareholders, on the basis of the accounts, took the company over and then discovered that it had lost a lot of money, as the company was not worth what the accounts had suggested that it was. The claimant's action for negligent misstatement failed as the accounts were prepared for the shareholders as a class to use in the interests of the company, rather than for an individual shareholder to use in his own interests. A similar case, but with a different result, is Morgan Crucible v Hill Samuel Bank (1990). The claimant was bidding to take over a company, and based its plans on accounts and other financial statements prepared by the defendant accountant. This time, however, the defendant was liable for the negligent misstatements contained in the accounts because the defendant knew, when it made its misstatements, that there was a confirmed bidder and that it would be relying on the accounts.

A very different example is **Goodwill v British Pregnancy Advisory Service (1996)**. The defendant charity had carried out a vasectomy on a client, but had not warned him that there was a small chance that the procedure could reverse itself naturally. Three years later, the client entered into a relationship with the claimant, who fell pregnant. She sued for the economic losses caused by the costs of bringing up a child, but her claim failed. The defendant did not owe a duty to someone who was not their client, particularly when the defendant could not know that its statements would be passed to the claimant or how she would use them.

4 Known purpose

Similarly, a defendant will normally only be liable if he knows or should know, when making a statement, for what purpose his statement will be used. This was another reason why the claim failed in **Caparo v Dickman (1990)**: the accounts were drawn up for the purposes of complying with company law and of allowing the shareholders as a group to exercise control over their company. The accounts were not drawn up for the purpose of a takeover.

A second example is *Reeman v Department of Transport* (1997). The claimant had bought a boat on the strength of a seaworthiness certificate issued by one of the defendant's inspectors. The certificate had been negligently prepared, and the boat was unsafe and therefore of little value, particularly compared with what the claimant had paid for it. However, the claim for negligent misstatement failed on the ground

Key cases

Caparo v Dickman (1990): with reference to 'known user', liability for negligent misstatement only exists if the maker of the statement can identify the person or class of persons who will be relying on the statement. With reference to 'known purpose', liability for negligent misstatement only exists if the maker of the statement knows to what use his statement will be put.

Goodwill v British Pregnancy Advisory Service (1996): a defendant will not be liable for negligent misstatement when he cannot know to whom his statement will be passed.

that the certificate had been produced for the purpose of complying with regulations designed to promote safety at sea, not for the purpose of putting a commercial value on the boat.

A contrasting example is **Law Society v KPMG Peat Marwick (2000)**. The defendant was a firm of accountants that had prepared the annual accounts for a firm of solicitors. The accounts did not pick up the fact that large amounts of client money were being stolen. When the true picture emerged, the claimant's compensation fund had to pay out to the victims of the fraud, and the claimant sued to recover the loss from the defendant. The defendant was liable, even though it had prepared the accounts for the solicitors' firm rather than the claimant, because of two key facts that it knew or should have known. First, the defendant knew who would be using the accounts, as the regulations governing the solicitors' profession required that the accounts be passed to the claimant. And, second, it knew that the purpose for which the claimant would use the accounts would be to make a decision as to whether to intervene in this particular solicitors' practice to stop fraud and minimise claims against the compensation fund.

5 Reasonable reliance

Finally, the claimant must demonstrate that he actually did rely on the misstatement and that it was reasonable in the circumstances for him to do so. One common example is the contrast between a business appointment and a drinks party: it is reasonable to rely on advice given by a professional person at a formal consultation; it is not reasonable to take advice given by someone late in the evening and after several drinks.

In **Smith v Eric S Bush (1990)** the claimant was the purchaser of a house who had approached a lender for a mortgage. As is common practice, the lender asked the defendant, a surveyor, to prepare a report on the house, and then passed the resulting survey to the claimant. The claimant relied on the survey, rather than paying for her own, and subsequently suffered an economic loss when the house partially collapsed because of defects that the survey had negligently failed to identify. The House of Lords decided that it was reasonable for the claimant to have relied on the survey: the defendant knew that the survey would be passed to her; there was not an unknown liability as both the identity of the claimant and the amount of any loss were known in advance; and the alternative was to insist that the claimant should also get a survey at the same time as the lender, which was an unnecessary duplication of effort.

Liability for a misstatement relied on by a third party

In each of the negligent misstatement cases discussed above, the defendant made a statement to the claimant upon which the claimant relied. A different scenario is when the defendant makes a negligent misstatement to a third party, and the third party relies on it, thus causing the claimant an economic loss.

This possibility was considered in **Spring v Guardian Assurance (1994)**. The claimant's case was that he had failed to obtain a new job because of a negligent reference prepared by the defendant, upon which the prospective employer had relied. The House of Lords decided that there could be liability where a third party had relied on a negligent misstatement (although in the case itself the claimant then faced the further problem of proving that he would actually have got the job had the reference been accurate).

Key cases

Law Society v KPMG Peat Marwick (2000): liability for negligent misstatement can exist when the defendant should know that his statement will be passed to a third party and for what purpose that third party will use it.

Smith v Eric S Bush (1990): a claimant can only recover for a pure economic loss caused by a negligent misstatement if he can show that he relied on the statement and that it was reasonable for him to do so.

Spring v Guardian Assurance (1994): a defendant may be liable for a negligent misstatement that was relied on by a third party and thus caused the claimant an economic loss.

Study tip

Include in your answer a full discussion of whether a special relationship exists. Use the five elements discussed in the text as a framework for your answer.

Topic illustration

Consider this scenario, taken from a past AQA exam paper:

> An article in the IT pages of the *Herald*, a national newspaper, described and recommended Safestore, a security software package. After reading the article, Gordon bought a copy of Safestore and installed it on his computer's hard disk, hoping to protect his clients' confidential business information. In fact, the article had failed to explain that the version of Safestore on public sale was less comprehensive than the version reviewed. Gordon's security was breached two months later while he was online. In consequence, he had to pay a total of £30,000 to clients affected by the breach and he stopped receiving orders for his services.

Negligent misstatement

Gordon has suffered a loss as a result of the *Herald*'s article, and any discussion of his claim against the paper would need to cover the following points:

▓ First, you would need to discuss the nature of Gordon's loss. He has suffered no physical loss, whether personal injury or damage to property, but rather his loss is purely economic.

▓ You might then discuss the fact that pure economic loss cannot be claimed unless it is the result of a negligent misstatement. An article in a newspaper is a statement.

To claim for negligent misstatement, Gordon needs to establish a special relationship between himself and the newspaper, and this will require a discussion of the various factors. Particularly relevant will be whether the newspaper has a skill or expertise, whether it knew that Gordon would rely on the article and whether it was reasonable for Gordon to rely on the article.

Activities

1   Consider the cases discussed earlier in relation to the elements required to establish the special relationship needed for a negligent misstatement. To what extent is each element present in every case?

2   Amelia writes a weekly financial column that she sells to various newspapers and journals, and that is widely respected for its accurate assessment of investment opportunities. One column was very positive about an investment in a new mining company, and Bart, having read the article, invested heavily in the mining company. Callum also read the article and telephoned Amelia to speak to her directly about the mining company, after which he too invested heavily. Both Bart and Callum lost all the money they had invested when the mining company collapsed because of a fundamental and obvious flaw in its business plan that Amelia had failed to spot. Meanwhile, Dirk, an internet engineer, while carrying out work in the office next door to Amelia's, wrongly reconnected various cables. The result was that Amelia's column for that week, unknown to her, was not sent to her subscribers, and she was therefore not paid for it. Consider Amelia's liability to both Bart and Callum, and Dirk's liability to Amelia for the losses suffered.

You should now be able to:

- distinguish between consequential economic loss and pure economic loss and explain the significance of the difference

- explain the purpose of a special relationship in the context of a negligent misstatement

- identify the elements that a claimant must demonstrate in order to show a special relationship.

16 Product liability: liability in tort for defective goods

Introduction

In a modern economy, consumers are able to buy and use a wide variety of goods. However, the manufacturers and suppliers of those goods are often large companies with great economic power, whereas the individual consumer is an ordinary person without the knowledge or the resources necessary to secure appropriate contracts to protect himself against faulty goods and the damage they might do.

There are, therefore, several legal protections to ensure that a consumer has a remedy if things go wrong. Criminal law, for instance, includes offences relating to things such as unsafe goods or food unfit for consumption. In contract law, the Sale of Goods Act 1979 gives a remedy to a consumer who buys goods from a business and finds that the goods do not match a description or a sample, are not of satisfactory quality or are not fit for purpose.

This chapter, however, is concerned with the contribution of tort law to consumer protection. This takes two forms: an action in negligence and an action brought under the Consumer Protection Act 1987.

In this topic, you will learn how to:

- identify the duty of care in negligence in the context of defective goods

- explain factors the court might use when deciding if the duty has been broken

- consider which types of loss might be recoverable.

Key cases

Donoghue v Stevenson (1932): a manufacturer owes a duty of care to the consumer of his goods.

Key terms

Duty of care: duty that the law says one person owes to another to take proper care of the other.

1 Negligence

A claimant suing in negligence in respect of defective goods must show, as with any action in negligence, that the defendant owes a duty of care, that the defendant has breached the duty of care and that reasonably foreseeable damage has resulted. In doing this, the claimant will use the same principles that we discussed in Chapter 14, in the context of a claim for physical damage. Here, we will consider the application of those principles to a claim for defective products.

The duty of care

Donoghue v Stevenson (1932) itself was, of course, a case about defective goods. Having considered the general principles as to when a **duty of care** might exist (the neighbour test), Lord Atkin went on to consider the position with specific reference to manufacturers. His conclusion was that a manufacturer of goods owes a duty of care to the consumer of those goods when he intends those goods to reach the consumer in the form in which they left the factory, and without further examination or preparation by any intermediate person. In relation to the facts of the case, a manufacturer of ginger beer, which is supplied in a sealed bottle made of opaque glass, owes a duty of care to the consumer of the drink to take reasonable care to ensure that the ginger beer does not injure the consumer or damage her goods.

The claimant

Donoghue v *Stevenson* (1932) stated that the duty of care was owed to the consumer of the defective goods, and the case itself is an example of a consumer who was able to recover damages even though she had not bought the ginger beer. Subsequent cases have widened the scope of the duty to cover any person who buys or uses the goods, or is affected by them.

In *Grant* v *Australian Knitting Mills* (1935) the claimant was a purchaser who bought for himself woollen underpants manufactured by the defendant. The fabric of the garments contained sulphites, and this contamination caused the claimant to suffer dermatitis when he tried to wear them. The defendant was held to be negligent as the underpants contained a hidden defect that could not be reasonably discovered by a purchaser or wearer.

In **Stennett v Hancock and Peters (1939)** the defendant was a garage that had repaired the wheel of a lorry. Two hours later, while the lorry was being driven along the road, part of the wheel came off and hit the claimant, a pedestrian, who was injured. The claimant was not the owner or user of the wheel, and had not asked the defendant to repair it. Nevertheless, as a bystander affected by the defendant's negligence in repairing the goods, she was able to claim.

The defendant

Donoghue v *Stevenson* (1932) stated that the duty of care is owed by the manufacturer of goods. This too has been widened by subsequent cases so that today anyone who is involved in supplying goods, and whose actions might reasonably foreseeably affect the consumer, owes the duty of care.

Donoghue itself provides an example of a manufacturer being found liable, but in *Stennett* v *Hancock* (1939), above, the defendant was not a manufacturer but a repairer.

A different example is **Fisher v Harrods Ltd (1966)**. The claimant attempted to open a bottle of jewellery cleaning fluid given to her by a friend who had bought it from the defendant's store. The fluid contained a mixture of chemicals that caused pressure to build up in the bottle, so that when the claimant removed the screw cap, the stopper underneath flew out and some of the fluid squirted into the claimant's eye, injuring it. The defendant, as retailer, was liable, as it was aware that there had been problems with the bottles and therefore it should have investigated further, as that is what the reasonable retailer would have done. Had the defendant done so, it would have discovered that the manufacturer was inexperienced in preventing leaks and had created the hazard by putting a stopper in the bottle.

Finally, we can note that the duty of care exists in respect of all types of goods and the packaging in which they come.

> ### Key cases
>
> **Stennett v Hancock and Peters (1939):** claimants other than consumers may be able to bring an action in negligence for defective goods.
>
> **Fisher v Harrods Ltd (1966):** defendants other than manufacturers may be liable in an action in negligence for defective goods.

> ### Study tip
>
> When discussing possible liability in negligence for defective products, begin by identifying the claimant and the defendant. This will help you to identify and discuss how any duty has been broken and what losses might be recovered.

Fisher *v* Harrods Ltd *(1966)*

Key terms

'Reasonable manufacturer' test: if a manufacturer did not do as the reasonable manufacturer would have done in the circumstances, then it has broken the duty of care that it owes to the consumer.

Study tip

Your discussion as to whether the duty of care has been broken will be one of the more important parts of your answer. Often it is obvious that a duty is owed and that the actions of the defendants have caused the losses complained of. What is more difficult is deciding whether the defendant acted as the reasonable person would have done.

Key cases

Grant v Australian Knitting Mills (1935) and **Carroll v Fearon (1998):** where it is clear from the facts of a case that there was negligence at some point in the manufacturing process, liability will exist even though the claimant is unable to prove the exact nature of the negligence.

Donoghue v Stevenson (1932): a defendant manufacturer owes a duty to the ultimate consumer of his goods when it is clear that no third party will check the goods before they are delivered to the claimant.

Breaching the duty of care

When deciding whether a manufacturer has breached the duty of care it owes to the consumer, the court will ask whether the manufacturer acted as the **reasonable manufacturer** would have done in the same circumstances. We now need to discuss examples of factors that might be relevant.

Faulty manufacturing process

A common cause of faulty goods is that a defect occurs because of a lack of care in the manufacturing process. Under the normal rules relating to the burden of proof, it would be the responsibility of the claimant to prove how the defendant had fallen below the standard of the reasonable manufacturer. This clearly is very difficult for an ordinary person who has no knowledge or experience of the relevant manufacturing process. The courts have therefore stated that they are prepared to find liability where it is clear from the facts of the case that carelessness must have been involved even though it is very difficult to pinpoint precisely where.

An example of this is **Grant v Australian Knitting Mills (1935)** which we discussed earlier. The very fact that the underpants left the defendant's factory containing the sulphites indicated that negligence was present somewhere in the manufacturing process, as a reasonable manufacturer would have taken proper care to ensure that the goods were not sent out from the factory in such a state.

A more modern example is **Carroll v Fearon (1998)**. The claimants were injured in a car accident caused by a tyre manufactured by the defendant. Liability was found to exist, even though the claimants were unable to demonstrate how the defendants were negligent. The court found that the very fact that the tyre was defective was enough to demonstrate negligence on the part of the defendant in the absence of an alternative explanation. This is similar to the principle of *res ipsa loquitur*, which we discussed in Topic 6 of Chapter 14 in the context of medical negligence.

Intermediate examination

The defendant should take reasonable steps to protect any person into whose hands his goods might come if he knows that there is no reasonable expectation that any third party will check the goods before they reach the hands of the claimant. One example of this is **Donoghue v Stevenson (1932)** itself: the manufacturer of the ginger beer should have taken reasonable precautions to ensure that the drink was safe as he knew that it would not be checked by any intermediate third party before it reached the hands of the person who would drink it.

A second example is *Griffiths* v *Arch Engineering* (1968). The defendant hired out a grinding machine that had been fitted with a wheel that was too large for the speed at which the machine was set. The hirer lent the machine to the claimant, an employee of another company, who was injured when he attempted to use the machine and the wheel shattered. The court decided that the defendant was liable for failing to take reasonable precautions to protect any person into whose hands the machine might come, on the ground that the defendant had no reason to believe that any third person would check the machine before it was used.

Instructions and warning labels

If goods present a danger unless used in a particular way, then the manufacturer should give proper instructions for use and an appropriate warning. Common examples include labels on goods that state they should not be allowed to come into contact with the eye or that they should not be eaten. If an appropriate warning is not given, then the manufacturer may be liable in negligence. One example is *Fisher* v *Harrods Ltd* (1966), in which the cleaning fluid represented a foreseeable hazard to eyes. In addition to being found negligent for not carrying out proper investigations, as discussed above, the defendant was also found negligent for not having attached an appropriate label warning of the danger.

A second example is **Kubach v Hollands (1937)**. A manufacturer of chemicals had supplied them to a shop with a warning that they should be tested before use. The shop resold the chemicals to a school for use in a chemistry class, but without passing on the warning. The chemicals were not, in fact, what they were supposed to be. They exploded and injured the claimant, a pupil at the school, when she attempted to heat them. The claimant recovered damages against the shop because it had acted negligently in supplying chemicals without the relevant warning. However, the claimant failed in her action against the manufacturer because it had given an appropriate warning when selling the goods, and had acted as the reasonable manufacturer would have done.

Causation

As with any negligence case, the claimant must show that the defendant's breach of duty caused the damage complained of. This might be difficult if there is more than one explanation for an accident, as the claimant must then show – using 'balance of probabilities' as the ordinary civil standard of proof – that it was more likely than not that it was the defendant's negligence, rather than something else, that caused the damage.

One example of this is **Evans v Triplex Safety Glass (1936)**. The claimant, who had bought his car a year earlier, was injured when his car windscreen, which had been manufactured by the defendant, shattered through no obvious cause. He sued the defendant for his injuries but was unable to show on the balance of probabilities that it had been any negligence on the part of the defendant that had caused the accident. Factors that the court took into account included: firstly, the length of time between the purchase of the car and the accident; secondly, the possibility that the glass may have been put under strain when it was screwed into its frame; and, thirdly, something other than a defect in the manufacture may have caused the glass to break.

Damage

A claimant suing in respect of defective goods can recover damages for his personal injuries and for damage to other property of his that was caused by the defective goods. However, unlike a claim for breach of contract, he cannot claim for either the value of the defective item itself or for the cost of any repairs. This illustrates a key principle of the tort of negligence: a claim can only be brought when damage has actually been caused. If defective goods cause no damage but simply sit there, not working properly, then there is no claim.

Thus, if I am given a toaster as a birthday present, and the toaster is so faulty that it catches fire when I try to use it, I can sue the manufacturer in negligence (assuming I can show negligence on the part of the manufacturer) for any personal injury to me or damage to my kitchen, but not for the value of the toaster itself. Had I bought the toaster for myself, I could have sued the seller for breach of contract and recovered damages both for the value of the toaster and for any damage that it had caused.

The reason why the value of the defective goods themselves cannot be claimed is that such a loss is seen as a pure economic loss, because the

Key cases

Kubach v Hollands (1937): instructions, labels and warnings will be taken into account when deciding if a defendant breached the duty of care.

Evans v Triplex Safety Glass (1936): a claimant must be able to show on the balance of probabilities that it was the defendant's action which caused the loss complained of.

Study tip

When discussing breach of duty, you may find that there are arguments both for and against the defendant.

claimant has suffered a reduction in the value of his assets and is therefore worth less than he should have been. As we discussed in Chapter 15, in the context of claims for economic loss, a claimant cannot normally recover damages for a pure economic loss caused by a negligent act.

An illustration of this is **Muirhead v Industrial Tank Specialties (1985)**. The claimant was a fish farmer who had engaged contractors to install pumps made by the defendant to ensure a flow of oxygenated water in his lobster tank. The pumps did not work properly because they were fitted with French motors incompatible with British voltages, and as a result the claimant lost an entire consignment of lobsters. The defendant, as the manufacturer, was liable in negligence because it had breached its duty to the claimant, as the user of the pumps, by not ensuring that its electrical products would work properly in the UK. However, although the claimant won damages in respect of the lost lobsters, as that was damage caused by the defective goods to other property, he could not claim for the money he had spent on buying the pumps in the first place, as that was a pure economic loss.

Given that a claimant can sue for damage to other property but not for the loss of the defective item itself, the law needs to be able to draw a line between the two. This is straightforward in both the toaster example and the *Muirhead* case, but not all examples are as easy. The issue was raised in **Aswan Engineering v Lupdine Ltd (1986)**. The claimant had bought a quantity of a waterproofing compound, contained in plastic pails manufactured by the defendant. The waterproofing compound was lost because the pails, while stacked on a quayside in Kuwait, had collapsed in the heat. The claimant sued in negligence for the defective pails, but lost its case as the damage suffered was not reasonably foreseeable.

However, if the damage had been foreseeable, the issue would then have been which losses the claimant could have recovered damages for. Clearly, it would not have been able to recover damages for the pails themselves, as they were the defective goods, but it was unclear whether it could have claimed damages for the lost waterproofing compound on the ground that this counted as damage to other property. The judges of the Court of Appeal were unable to reach an agreed conclusion, but they did discuss several examples in relation to components and packaging.

■ Where an assembled item is damaged by a single defective component within that item, the issue is whether a claimant can sue for physical damage to the rest of the item on the ground that that counts as damage to other property. One example is whether the owner of a car can claim for damage to the car caused by a defective tyre that led to an accident and, in particular, whether it would make a difference if the both the car and the tyre were brand new and supplied together or if the tyre was a replacement for a worn-out tyre on an existing car.

■ Where goods are contained in defective packaging, the issue is whether a claimant can sue for damage to the goods caused by the packaging on the ground that that counts as damage to other property. This was the problem in *Aswan* itself. Other examples discussed by the judges (with no agreed conclusions) were whether a manufacturer of a cork would be liable for the loss of a bottle of wine if it were contaminated by a defect in the cork, or whether a manufacturer of a carrier bag supplied at a supermarket or a jeweller's shop would be liable for the contents of the bag if the bag gave way and damaged the goods inside.

Defences

The normal negligence defences, contributory negligence and consent, apply to an action in respect of defective goods. One example is **Griffiths v Arch Engineering (1968)**. The claimant lost 20 per cent of

> ### Key cases
>
> **Muirhead v Industrial Tank Specialties (1985):** action in negligence for defective goods does not allow the recovery of damages for the value of the defective goods themselves.
>
> **Aswan Engineering v Lupdine Ltd (1986):** it is unclear whether a claimant can claim for the value of goods supplied with the defective item.
>
> **Griffiths v Arch Engineering (1968):** a defendant may be able to raise a defence of contributory negligence to a claim for defective goods.

his damages on the ground that his injuries may well have been less severe if he had gripped the grinding machine with both hands, given that it was clearly a two-handed tool.

Topic illustration

Alf was given a new television set, manufactured by Consumer Electricals Ltd, as a birthday present from his mother, Bertha. When Alf unpacked the television, he found that the set was slightly dusty, so he wiped it down with a wet cloth. Alf then plugged the television in and switched it on. The set exploded, injuring Alf and damaging various items of furniture in the vicinity. An investigation revealed that the explosion occurred because some of the wires had not been properly fitted, but that the situation had been made worse because of water that had leaked into the back of the set from Alf's cloth. There was a user's manual at the bottom of the box in which the television had been packed, warning users not to use a wet cloth, but Alf had not read it.

Alf has a potential claim in negligence against Consumer Electricals Ltd, and a discussion of that claim would cover the following points:

▪ First, we need to identify the duty of care that Consumer Electricals owes to Alf, and to be able to explain why the former is the defendant and the latter is the claimant. This is a straightforward application of *Donoghue* v *Stevenson* (1932).

▪ Secondly, Alf needs to establish a breach of that duty. This requires an application of the standard of the reasonable manufacturer of electrical equipment, and might involve a discussion of factors such as a faulty manufacturing process, the likelihood (or otherwise) that someone would inspect the television before it was first plugged in, and the lack of a more prominent warning against wet cloths.

▪ Causation and remoteness of damage are straightforward, but there is the possibility of a defence of contributory negligence. We need to discuss whether Alf acted as a reasonable person in wiping an item of electrical equipment with a wet cloth, and whether he should have read the user's manual as a very first step.

Activities

1 Compile a table showing, for each of the cases in this topic:

- what type of person each claimant is (for instance, a consumer or a bystander)
- what type of person each defendant is (for instance, a manufacturer or a repairer)
- which factors the court took into account when deciding if the duty of care was broken.

2 Sylvia owns a large casserole dish, which was recently given to her as a birthday present by her mother. Sylvia warned her cleaning lady, Tanya, that the dish, which was sitting on top of the stove, contained a very hot stew that Sylvia had just taken out of the oven. When Tanya, who was talking to her sister on her mobile phone, came to move the dish in order to clean the top of the stove, the handle snapped and hot stew spilled out. This scalded Tanya and damaged the kitchen floor, and the casserole dish itself was badly dented in the accident.

Discuss whether the manufacturer of the casserole dish might be liable in negligence to Sylvia, Tanya or both. You should consider whether a duty of care is owed, whether any duty has been broken, which losses might be claimed by either lady and whether there is any defence.

You should now be able to:

- identify situations in which a duty of care exists
- explain the reasoning used by judges when deciding whether the duty of care has been broken.

In this topic, you will learn how to:

- identify the liability for defective products under the Consumer Protection Act 1987
- define the categories of defendant under the Act
- explain what is meant by 'defect' and 'damage'.

Key terms

Consumer Protection Act 1987: Act that imposes strict liability for defective goods as an alternative to any action in negligence.

Key cases

Abouzaid v Mothercare (2000): actions in negligence and under the Consumer Protection Act 1987 for defective goods require the claimant to prove different levels of fault.

2 Consumer Protection Act 1987

As an alternative to negligence, a person suffering loss caused by defective goods may be able to bring an action under the provisions of Part I of the **Consumer Protection Act 1987** (CPA 1987). The CPA 1987 was enacted in order to bring UK law into line with the requirements of a European Union directive concerning product liability. The key difference between the two types of action is whether the claimant needs to prove fault on the part of the defendant. In the case of an action in negligence, which is fault based, the claimant needs to show that the defendant fell below the standard of the reasonable person. But in the case of an action brought under the CPA 1987, liability is strict and the claimant does not have to prove any fault at all on the part of the defendant.

An example of this is **Abouzaid v Mothercare (2000)**. The claimant, a child, suffered a serious eye injury when he was hit in the face by a buckle. The buckle was part of a pram accessory and it was attached to an elastic strap that had sprung back when it had slipped from the grasp of the claimant. The defendant argued that there should be no liability because at the time that the product has been supplied no one, including child safety experts, was aware of the risk posed by the accessory. The court, however, found the defendant strictly liable under the Act on the ground that the accessory was clearly unsafe, but found no liability in ordinary negligence because the defendant had done all that the reasonable supplier of children's products would have done given that the risk was unknown at the time.

Nature of the liability under the CPA 1987

By s2(1) of the CPA 1987, a claimant may sue if he suffers damage that is caused wholly or partly by a defect in a product.

We now turn to consider who can be liable under the Act, and that is meant by the words 'product', 'defect' and 'damage'.

Defendant

The CPA 1987 imposes liability on four different classes of defendant:

1 By s2(2)(a), the producer of a product. 'Producer' is defined by s1(2) as:

   a The person who manufactured the product. In **Bogle v McDonald's Restaurants (2002)**, which we discuss later, a restaurant was held to be the producer of cups of coffee that it served.

   b The person who won or abstracted a substance (such as sand, gravel, coal or minerals).

   c The person who carried out a process that gave a product one of its essential characteristics (such as canning or freezing fruit and vegetables, cooking meat or dyeing cloth).

2 By s2(2)(b), a person who holds himself out to be the producer of a product by putting his name on the product or by using a trademark or other distinguishing mark in relation to the product. The best example is a supermarket that sells own-brand products that are actually made by a different company.

3 By s2(2)(c), a person who has imported a product into the European Union in order to supply that product as part of a business.

4 By s2(3), a supplier of a product who, when asked by a claimant, fails to identify any person falling within the first three classes of defendant. Any request by the claimant must be made a reasonable time after the damage occurs, and at a time when it is not reasonably practicable for the claimant to identify the defendant for himself.

If more than one person is liable, then, by s2(5), each is liable for the full amount, and the court will need to apportion liability between them.

Product

By s1(2), a **product** is any goods (including electricity) and includes any product within a product, such as a component or raw materials. The Act states in s45(1) that 'product' includes substances, crops, things attached to land, and ships, vehicles and aircraft. Buildings are included if any damage or injury is caused by defective materials, but are excluded if the loss is caused by poor workmanship.

In **A v National Blood Authority (2001)** the court decided that human blood to be used in transfusions is a product covered by the Act. Presumably this would extend to body parts, such as hearts and corneas, to be used in transplant operations.

Defect

By s3 CPA 1987, there is a **defect** in a product if the safety of the product is not such as persons generally are entitled to expect in the circumstances.

In **Richardson v LRC Products Ltd (2000)** a condom failed at the moment of the man's ejaculation, and the claimant became pregnant as a result. The claimant failed in her action for the cost of bringing up the resulting child because, among other reasons, the condom was held not to be defective. Its safety was of a standard that people are entitled to expect, as it is widely known that such a product does not offer a complete guarantee.

The meaning of 'defect' was also considered in **A v National Blood Authority (2001)** (mentioned above). The claimant contracted the hepatitis C virus from contaminated blood given during a blood transfusion. The court decided that people generally expect a blood

Key cases

Bogle v McDonald's Restaurants (2002): a restaurant is a producer of the drinks and meals that it serves.

A v National Blood Authority (2001): a product for the purposes of the Consumer Protection Act 1987 includes human blood. With regards to defect, an item is defective if there is a general expectation that goods of that type will always be entirely safe.

Richardson v LRC Products Ltd (2000): an item is not defective where there is a general expectation that goods of that type will occasionally fail.

Study tip

Be careful to identify all possible defendants. There will often be more than one.

Key terms

Product: any goods, raw materials and crops.

Defect: product is defective if its safety is not such as persons generally are entitled to expect in the circumstances.

transfusion to be entirely safe, and in the event that it causes injury or loss then the supplier of the blood is liable under the Act.

Section 3 goes on to outline a number of factors that the courts should take into account when deciding if a product is defective.

■ **The marketing of the product:** relevant factors might include the target of any advertising (such as products for children or for those with diabetes) and any claims made by the advertising (for instance, that goods have been tested to a higher standard than is normal).

■ **Instructions provided with goods:** there are many examples of goods that are safe only if used properly. In those cases, whether the courts decide that an item is defective will depend on whether any instructions as to use or warning labels provide adequate information as to the dangers and how to avoid them. Examples include household medicines, DIY tools and chemicals used for clearing drains. In **Worsley v Tambrands (2000)** the defendant, a manufacturer of tampons, was not liable for the consequences of toxic shock syndrome suffered by the claimant, a user of its products, because the box carried a clear warning.

■ **Reasonable expectations as to how the product is used:** for example, a properly constructed bath is suitable for taking baths, but no action would exist for losses caused if the bath were used in an attempt to cross the English Channel.

■ **Time of supply:** as technology progresses, products will become safer. The Act is therefore careful to say that just because subsequent versions of a product are safer, that does not mean that older versions are necessarily defective.

Another factor that might be taken into account is the consumer's reasonable care for his own safety. In **Bogle v McDonald's Restaurants (2002)** the claimants were scalded by very hot drinks that were packaged in strong paper cups with lids, but that were knocked over on trays or on tables so that the lids came off, allowing the hot liquid to pour out and cause injuries. The court held that the drinks were not defective as they were of a safety that people generally are entitled to expect in the circumstances, even though the lids came off. This was because sufficient precautions had been taken (the cups and their lids were of adequate strength, and the staff had been trained to put the lids firmly on the cups) while still allowing customers to receive what they wanted (drinks served at near-boiling temperatures, and removable lids so that they could sip from the cups). In these circumstances, people knew that there was a risk, and that extra care should be taken – particularly around children.

The Act, however, does not cover products that are faulty but which do not cause any damage or injury. If a person's new radio does not work, but is otherwise harmless and causes no damage, then he has no action.

Damage

By s5 of the CPA 1987, a claimant is able to sue for the following categories of damage caused by a defective product:

■ death or personal injury
■ damage to property, including damage to land.

However, the following may not be claimed:

■ damage to property when the damage is worth less than £275
■ damage to the defective item itself, or to any item supplied with the defective item
■ damage to any goods that are being used other than for personal use – for instance, a business use.

> ### Key cases
>
> **Worsley v Tambrands (2000):** instructions, labels and warnings will be taken into account when deciding if a product is defective.
>
> **Bogle v McDonald's Restaurants (2002):** what a consumer might reasonably be expected to do to look after himself will be taken into account when deciding if a product is defective.

Therefore, the Act cannot be used by someone who is not a consumer, such as the claimant in *Muirhead* v *Industrial Tank Specialties* (1985) (discussed above). However, it is unclear whether there can be a claim for a defective item that is used partly for domestic purposes and partly for commercial purposes – for instance, a claim by someone who earns his living as a self-employed caterer and who suffers a loss caused by defective kitchen equipment used both for family meals and for his work.

Defences

The CPA 1987 sets out a number of defences to an action for a defective product. The most controversial of these is the development risks defence, which we will consider first before moving onto other defences covered by s4(1) and, finally, contributory negligence.

The development risks defence

By s4(1)(e) CPA 1987, it is a defence to a claim brought under the Act in respect of a defect in goods if the defendant can show that the state of scientific and technical knowledge at the time of the supply of the product was not advanced enough to allow a producer of goods of that type to discover the defect.

The **development risks defence** is controversial because it dents the Act's strict liability. Strict liability should mean that, in order to protect a claimant, a defendant is liable even if he is not at fault, but the defence allows the defendant to escape liability. If, therefore, a claimant suffers injury or loss as a result of something like a new medicine, cosmetic or food item that turns out to have unforeseen and harmful effects, he may not have a legal action. He cannot use negligence because if the defect is undiscoverable then the defendant will have done all that he reasonably could, given the state of scientific and technical knowledge; and he cannot use the Act because of the existence of the defence.

In applying the defence, the key issue is what is meant by 'the state of scientific and technical knowledge'. The following three cases give some guidance.

In **European Commission v UK (1997)** the European Court of Justice (ECJ) said that only scientific and technical knowledge that was accessible should be taken into account. If knowledge is not accessible, then a defendant will escape liability. This raises the question as to what 'accessible' means. One example given during the case was that research published in Chinese in an obscure journal in Manchuria would not be accessible. Presumably, therefore, research published in the West would be accessible, and a defendant would not be able to use the defence even though he himself was unaware of the research.

The case reached the ECJ because it was thought that the version of the defence that appears in the UK Act was wider than the version in the original EU directive. The UK Act allows the defence when scientific and technical knowledge in the relevant industry is unaware of the defect, whereas the EU directive allows the defence only when general scientific and technical knowledge – whether inside the industry or elsewhere – is unaware of the defect. The court decided that the UK version was not necessarily incompatible with the directive, but that any future case should interpret the defence according to EU law principles, including the accessibility test.

The defence was raised in **Abouzaid v Mothercare (2000)**, discussed earlier. The defendant's argument was that the defence should apply as even child safety experts had not identified the risk posed by a buckle attached to an elastic strap. The court rejected this argument on the ground that the defence was available only where the fault was

---

Key terms

Development risks defence: defence that allows a defendant to escape liability when a defect in a product is unknown and cannot be discovered given the current state of scientific and technical knowledge.

Key cases

European Commission v UK (1997): for the purposes of the development risks defence, scientific and technical knowledge only includes information that is accessible.

Abouzaid v Mothercare (2000): development risks defence is not available in respect of defects that are discoverable but that no one had thought to investigate.

undiscoverable by existing scientific and technical knowledge, rather than simply because no one had thought to test for this particular problem.

The defence also failed in **A v National Blood Authority (2001)**, in which the claimant had contracted the hepatitis C virus from contaminated blood given during a blood transfusion. The defendant argued that although the risk of such an infection was known, there was no known way to test individual batches of blood to see which were infected. The court rejected this argument, saying that the development risks defence is only available when a risk is unknown – not when it is known but cannot be identified in individual products.

Other defences available under s4(1) of the CPA 1987

There are five further defences listed by s4(1) CPA 1987. They are:

1   **Compliance with the law (s4(1)(a)):** it is a defence if a product is defective because the law said that it had to be made in a particular way. One example might be that a warning label on a dangerous product has to be in a particular form to comply with regulations, but the warning is in fact inadequate.

2   **Non-supply of the product (s4(1)(b)):** a defendant will escape liability if he can show that he has never supplied the product in question. One example may be if experimental goods are stolen, and sold on by the thieves.

3   **Any supply was non-commercial (s4(1)(c)):** there is no liability if the defendant supplied the goods without a view to a profit. Examples include donating items to a jumble sale and giving a prize to be used in a charity raffle.

4   **The defect did not exist when the goods were put into circulation (s4(1)(d)):** there is no liability if the defendant can show that any defect only came into existence after the goods were supplied by him. Examples would be a third party deliberately adding a contaminant to a jar of jam after it had left the factory, or a toaster becoming dangerous because someone has accidentally dropped it down the stairs.

5   **Subsequent products (s4(1)(f)):** a defendant will escape liability if he supplies a component to a manufacturer who incorporates the component into a larger product and the larger product is defective, provided that the defect has appeared either because of the design of the larger product or because the defendant followed the instructions of the manufacturer of the larger product.

Contributory negligence

Section 6(4) CPA 1987 preserves the defence of contributory negligence in relation to liability under the Act, so that if injury or damage to property occurs partly as a result of the actions of the claimant, the court will be able to reduce the amount of damages payable by the defendant to reflect the level of the claimant's contribution to his losses.

Topic illustration

Consider again the scenario concerning Alf and his new television:

> Alf was given a new television set, manufactured by Consumer Electricals Ltd, as a birthday present from his mother, Bertha. When Alf unpacked the television, he found that the set was slightly dusty, so he wiped it down with a wet cloth. Alf then plugged the television in and switched it on. The set exploded, injuring Alf and damaging various items of furniture in the vicinity. An investigation revealed that the explosion occurred because some of the wires had not been properly fitted, but that the situation had been made worse

Key cases

A v National Blood Authority (2001): development risks defence is only available in respect of risks which are unknown and not those which are known but which cannot be identified in any particular item.

Study tip

Once you have considered whether the defendant is liable, don't forget to go on to think about possible defences. However, you should not jump straight to the defences in your answer. Make sure you establish the main liability first.

because of water that had leaked into the back of the set from Alf's cloth. There was a user's manual at the bottom of the box in which the television had been packed, warning users not to use a wet cloth, but Alf had not read it.

In addition to any claim in negligence, Alf might also be able to claim under CPA 1987. Any discussion of that claim should cover the following points:

- Firstly, you will need to explain why Alf is the claimant and why Consumer Electricals is the defendant.

- Secondly, you will need to discuss whether the television is a 'product' and whether the fault it contains amounts to a 'defect'.

- Next, you will need to discuss for which losses Alf can recover damages. Clearly, he can claim for the injury to himself, but he cannot claim for the value of the television. Whether he can claim for damage to other property will depend on whether that damage exceeds £275.

- Finally, as with the claim in negligence, you should discuss whether the defendant can use the defence of contributory negligence.

Activities

1. Compile a table to compare and contrast the rules governing liability for defective products in negligence and under the Consumer Protection Act 1987. Entries might include: rules relating to the identity of the claimant and the defendant, the definition of a defective product, the level of fault the claimant must prove, the types of damage that can be claimed, and defences available.

2. Carla bought a bottle of own-brand drain cleaner from her local supermarket, and poured it down the plughole of her bath. The chemicals reacted with water in the drain, causing the plughole to erupt in Carla's face, burning her skin and damaging some towels.

   Discuss whether Carla might have an action under the Consumer Protection Act 1987. Issues you may need to consider include: the identity of the defendant, the packaging of the bottle, and what Carla might be able to claim for.

You should now be able to:

- consider the reasoning a court might use when deciding if liability under the Consumer Protection Act 1987 exists

- identify and explain defences that might exist to a claim under the Act.

Occupiers' liability

Introduction

The occupier of premises owes a duty to keep safe lawful visitors to those premises. The duty is imposed by the Occupiers' Liability Act 1957, which we will abbreviate in this chapter to 'OLA 1957'.

The occupier may also owe a second (and different) duty to protect trespassers who enter his premises. This duty is contained in the Occupiers' Liability Act 1984, and we will abbreviate the name of that Act to 'OLA 1984'.

As a first step, therefore, it is important to know whether an entrant to premises is a lawful visitor or a trespasser.

In this topic, you will learn how to:

- define a lawful visitor and a trespasser

- identify and explain these concepts where a visitor has implied permission to enter or exceeds his permission to enter.

Key terms

Lawful visitor: a person who enters premises with either express or implied permission.

Key cases

Lowery v Walker (1911): a frequent entrant, to whom the occupier does not object, may have implied permission to be on the premises.

Harvey v Plymouth City Council (2010): an occupier does not owe a duty under OLA 1957 to a visitor who exceeds any implied permission.

Jolley v Sutton London Borough Council (2000): if premises contain something which is an attraction to children, then the children will have implied permission to enter if the occupier does nothing to prevent them from investigating.

1 Lawful visitors and trespassers

Lawful visitors

A **lawful visitor** is someone who has permission to enter, and this can be either express or implied. If a person has express or stated permission to enter, there is normally no doubt that he is a lawful visitor. More difficult is when a person appears to be a trespasser, but the law implies permission for him to enter, thus ensuring that he is a lawful visitor and one who is covered by OLA 1957. Four examples can be given:

1 Repeated visits

If the occupier knows, or should know, that people are repeatedly visiting his land, and he does nothing about it, then permission may well be implied. In **Lowery v Walker (1911)** villagers were in the habit of taking a shortcut across the defendant's field to reach the railway station. The defendant, without warning, placed a wild horse in the field and it attacked one of the villagers. The court held that the villager was a lawful visitor, and therefore owed a duty by the defendant, as the defendant had known of the shortcut but had done little to discourage people from using it.

However, a claimant will not be able to use OLA 1957 if he exceeds his implied permission. In **Harvey v Plymouth City Council (2010)** the claimant, in order to avoid paying for a taxi, ran drunkenly across some open land in the dark, tripped over a very low fence and fell down a five-metre drop, sustaining serious head injuries. His claim that the defendant council, the owner of the land, owed him a duty under OLA 1957 as a visitor, on the ground that the defendant knew that children and teenagers frequently used the land for meeting, drinking and general recreational activities, was rejected because any implied permission did not extend to reckless and dangerous activities, such as drunkenly running about in the dark.

2 The doctrine of allurement

The doctrine of allurement states that a child will not be a trespasser if he wanders on to land to investigate something that is both dangerous and attractive to children. In *Cooke* v *Midland Great Western Railway* (1909) the allurement was a railway turntable, and in **Jolley v Sutton London Borough Council (2000)** the attraction was an abandoned boat left on waste ground. In both cases, the child was able to claim, as a lawful visitor, for injuries sustained on the attractive item.

3 Entry in order to communicate

There is implied permission to walk up the front path of a house to the front door with the purpose of communicating with the occupants (*Robson v Hallett* (1967)). This permission does not extend beyond the front door, even if it should be open, and it does not cover any person who is forbidden to enter by a notice on a gate (for instance hawkers, canvassers and salesmen). If asked to leave, the visitor remains a lawful visitor as long as he leaves within a reasonable time and by a reasonable route.

4 Statutory powers of entry

There are a large number of circumstances when a person is authorised by a statutory power to enter the premises. Examples include an electricity meter reader, a postman, a fireman and a policeman with a search warrant. In such a case, the entrant will be a lawful visitor even if the occupier objects to his presence.

Trespassers

A **trespasser** is any person:

■ who enters without an invitation, and
■ whose presence is either:
  – unknown to the occupier, or
  – known to the occupier, but the occupier has objected to it in some practical fashion (for instance, a sign, a locked gate or a verbal warning).

Trespass is a strict liability tort: it is irrelevant that the trespass is inadvertent or unintentional. The motive is also irrelevant: a child on an adventure or a walker who has lost his way are trespassers in the same way as a burglar or a poacher.

Sometimes a person who begins his visit as a lawful visitor can become a trespasser. This will occur if the visitor's permission to enter the land is limited or restricted in some way, and he oversteps that limit. Three examples can be given:

1 Limit as to area

It is commonplace for a visitor to premises not to have permission to wander at will throughout those premises. A student at school probably should not enter the staffroom or the head teacher's study without an invitation, and a visitor to a stately home or a museum should not go through a door marked 'Authorised Personnel Only'.

If the limits of the permission are unclear, the court will give a claimant the benefit of the doubt. In **Pearson v Coleman Bros (1948)** the claimant, a young girl, was visiting a circus with her family. While looking for the toilet, she wandered into the zoo area and was mauled by a lion. She was able to claim as a lawful visitor as it was not at all clear that she should not have been where she was – for instance, there was a lack of signs and barriers.

2 Limit as to time

A visitor who stays longer than they should becomes a trespasser. A student at school or someone visiting a museum will become a trespasser if they linger after closing time.

3 Limit as to purpose

A visitor who is invited to premises for a particular purpose, but then chooses to undertake a different activity, also risks becoming a trespasser. The most famous judicial statement to this effect is as follows (although

---

Study tip

■ When answering a question relating to occupiers' liability, as a first step always identify whether the claimant is a lawful visitor or a trespasser and be prepared to explain your answer.

■ Consider whether an entrant on to the premises is a regular visitor: if he is, and if the occupier has done nothing about it, then he may well be a lawful visitor.

Key terms

Trespasser: someone other than a lawful visitor; he or she has no permission to enter.

Key cases

Pearson v Coleman Bros (1948): if it is unclear where on premises a visitor may go, the visitor will be given the benefit of the doubt.

the case itself was about navigation and the proper use of a shipping channel):

> When you invite a person into your house to use the staircase, you do not invite him to slide down the banisters, you invite him to use the staircase in the ordinary way in which it is used. (Scrutton LJ *The Carlgarth* (1927))

In **Tomlinson v Congleton Borough Council (2003)** the claimant visited a country park owned by the defendant council. He chose to dive into a lake despite the presence of a sign forbidding swimming. At that point the claimant became a trespasser, as he had moved from activities he was permitted to undertake to an activity he was not permitted to undertake. Consequently, when he was injured in the lake, his claim was brought under OLA 1984, as a trespasser, even though he had started as a lawful visitor.

Key cases

Tomlinson v Congleton Borough Council (2003): if a lawful visitor exceeds the permission he has to enter, then he becomes a trespasser.

Study tip

When considering an examination scenario relating to occupiers' liability, identify the visitor and the purpose for his visit, and then ask yourself whether the visitor is in fact now doing something different to that purpose.

Activities

1. Given that trespassers can include everyone from playing children to burglars, consider the advantages and disadvantages of a legal duty to safeguard those entering without permission. Should occupiers be allowed to maintain defences such as broken glass embedded in the top of a wall or barbed wire?

2. How is the difference between a sign that says 'Keep Out' and one that says 'Slippery Footpath – Be Careful' relevant to the decision as to whether an entrant is a lawful visitor or a trespasser?

You should now be able to:

- identify which entrants to premises are owed the duty under the Occupiers' Liability Act 1957 and which are owed the duty under the Occupiers' Liability Act 1984

- explain the difference between express permission to enter and implied permission to enter.

In this topic, you will learn how to:

- explain what is meant by the term 'duty of care' in the context of the Occupiers' Liability Act 1957

- define key terms such as 'occupier' and 'premises'

- consider when a duty of care has been breached and when the occupier might have a defence.

2 Occupiers' Liability Act 1957

A claim under OLA 1957 works in much the same way as a claim for negligence: the claimant must show that the defendant owes him a duty of care, that the defendant has breached the duty and that the breach has led to damage. In turn, there are a number of possible defences open to the defendant.

The duty

Establishing the existence of a duty of care is straightforward. By s2(1) of OLA 1957, an occupier of premises owes a duty of care to all his lawful visitors.

The duty of care

According to s2(2) of OLA 1957, the duty of care is:

> a duty to take such care as in all the circumstances of the case is reasonable to see that the visitor will be reasonably safe in using the premises for the purposes for which he is invited or permitted by the occupier to be there.

This definition makes heavy use of the idea of 'reasonableness'. The occupier should act only with reasonable care and he should ensure that his visitor is reasonably safe. The duty is also a duty to keep visitors, rather than the premises, safe. This is because sometimes the economic cost of making premises safe would be unreasonable. If land contains dangerous cliffs, crumbling archaeological ruins or deep wells, it is more sensible to put up fences and warning notices than to try to eliminate the danger.

Occupier

OLA 1957 does not define who an **occupier** is, but it is clear from the cases that an occupier is any person who controls the premises (or the relevant part of the premises) to such an extent that his carelessness could lead to a visitor suffering loss. The obvious example is the owner of the premises, but others might include a tenant, the organiser of a stall at a fairground, the main contractors in a large building project and a local authority that has taken possession of a house.

Possession need not be exclusive, and it is possible for premises to have more than one occupier. In **Wheat v Lacon (1966)** the first defendant was the manager of a pub owned by the second defendant. The first defendant lived in a flat over the premises and, with the permission of the owner, took in paying guests in his private accommodation. One guest was killed when he tripped and fell down the back stairs. The court decided that both the manager and the brewery owed the guest a duty under OLA 1957 (although in the event the claim failed as the claimant was unable to show negligence against either). When more than one person is an occupier, the duties of the different occupiers may vary according to the degree of control they exercise, perhaps as to different parts of the building – including different parts of the fabric of the building.

Premises

Premises include land and any buildings on the land. By s1(3)(a) of OLA 1957, the term also includes any fixed or moveable structure – for instance, a shed, a bridge or scaffolding and any vessel, vehicle or aircraft.

Discharging the duty

To avoid liability, the occupier must show that he acted as the reasonable occupier would have done in the same circumstances. This is the same standard as in ordinary negligence, which we discussed in Topic 2 of Chapter 14, so cases such as *Bolton* v *Stone* (1951), *Paris* v *Stepney Borough Council* (1951), *Watt* v *Hertfordshire County Council* (1954) and *Latimer* v *AEC* (1953) will be relevant.

An example is **Tedstone v Bourne Leisure Ltd (2008)**. The claimant, while using the defendant's spa facilities, slipped on a pool of water close to a Jacuzzi and was injured. The evidence showed that the accident happened at a place where water had not been known to gather before, that the water had not been there five minutes before the accident, and that the sheer volume of water meant that something unusual – such as a malfunction – had occurred. In these circumstances, the defendant was not liable as no reasonable system of checking for spillages and other problems could have picked up on this problem in time to prevent this accident.

Warnings

The duty of care is to keep the visitor, rather than the premises, safe. To this end, s2(4)(a) of OLA 1957 states that the occupier may be able to carry out his duty by providing **reasonable warnings**. These might be implied warnings, such as a fence or a locked door, or express warnings, such as a notice warning of dangers. Any notice should be clear in explaining the danger, and should be visible. In **Woollins v British Celanese (1966)** the defendant was liable as, although it had put up a

> ### Key terms
>
> **Occupier** of premises: person whose control of those premises is such that his actions can prevent or cause risk to visitors.
>
> **Premises:** made up of land and the features on that land, both natural and man-made.
>
> **Reasonable warning:** anything that indicates to a visitor the presence of a danger or a risk; such a warning should be clear in meaning and visible.

> ### Key cases
>
> **Wheat v Lacon (1966):** there can be more than one occupier of premises at any one time.
>
> **Tedstone v Bourne Leisure Ltd (2008):** an occupier can only be expected to take reasonable precautions.
>
> **Woollins v British Celanese (1966):** a defendant cannot rely on a warning notice if the notice was placed so that the claimant could not see it.

notice warning of a dangerous roof, the notice was behind a door so that it was not easily visible to anyone working in the area.

The occupier's duty is varied in two particular circumstances:

■ children
■ a specialist visitor undertaking his job.

Children

By s2(3)(a) of OLA 1957, an occupier must be prepared for children to be less careful than adults. Consequently, it is not a defence for an occupier to say that any precautions he took would have been adequate to protect an adult, if the reasonable occupier would have taken further precautions to protect a child. In **Moloney v Lambeth London Borough Council (1966)** a four-year-old child slipped through the banisters lining a staircase in a block of flats. The defendant council was liable as it was foreseeable that small children would be using the staircase and it was no defence that the gaps in the banisters were too small for an adult to fall through.

Young children present a particular difficulty to occupiers: almost anything can be dangerous to them and they rarely understand written notices warning of danger. However, when deciding what precautions need to be taken, an occupier is entitled to expect that parents will take appropriate care of young children. In **Phipps v Rochester Corporation (1955)** a five-year-old boy fell into a substantial trench dug by the defendant on its own land. The child was held to be a lawful visitor, as the defendant knew children played on the site but had done nothing to prevent them from doing so. However, the child's claim failed on the ground that reasonable parents would not allow their children to be placed in a dangerous situation without proper supervision and protection.

Similarly, in **Bourne Leisure Ltd v Marsden (2009)** the defendant, the owner of a caravan park, was not liable when the claimant, a two-year old boy, wandered away from his parents, who had been momentarily distracted, and drowned in an unfenced pond. The parents had been given, on arrival, a site map that indicated features such as roads and ponds, and they knew that the site as a whole would be unsafe for unaccompanied children of their son's age. The court was careful to say that the parents were not to blame, but that in turn did not mean that the occupier was to blame.

A specialist visitor undertaking his job

By s2(3)(b) of OLA 1957, an occupier may expect that a specialist visitor will be aware of, and will protect himself against, risks within his own specialism. If an occupier knows that the electrics in his house are unsafe, and he calls out an electrician to deal with the problem, then the occupier may take fewer precautions with respect to the danger as the electrician should know what he is doing. In **Roles v Nathan (1963)** two chimney sweeps died after they were overcome by carbon monoxide fumes when cleaning out part of the defendant's heating system. The claim brought under OLA 1957 failed, as the chimney sweeps had been properly warned about the danger, and the risk was one they should have been familiar with and known how to have dealt with.

Causation and remoteness

As with any negligence-based action, once the claimant has shown that a duty of care exists and that it has been broken, he must then go on to show that the defendant's actions caused his loss – and that any loss is not too remote a consequence of the negligence. These rules were described in Topic 3 of Chapter 14.

Key cases

Moloney v Lambeth London Borough Council (1966): the occupier of premises should take appropriate extra care if he knows that small children will be using the premises.

Phipps v Rochester Corporation (1955): the occupier of land is entitled to assume that small children will be properly supervised.

Bourne Leisure Ltd v Marsden (2009): when considering liability in respect of a child, the fact that parents are not to blame does not necessarily mean that the occupier is to blame.

Roles v Nathan (1963): a specialist visitor to premises can be expected to guard against risks related to his specialism.

Study tip

Having identified that an occupier owes a duty under the Occupiers' Liability Act 1957, make sure that you discuss whether he has breached the duty, and remember to focus on relevant factors: there is little point in giving a full discussion of children if the entrant is an adult.

Defences

An occupier may use the following defences to a claim brought under OLA 1957:

- independent contractors
- contributory negligence
- consent
- excluding liability.

Independent contractors

By s2(4)(b) of OLA 1957, the occupier is not liable if the visitor is injured by something dangerous that was created by faulty workmanship on the part of an outside contractor, provided that it was reasonable for the occupier to have brought in an **independent contractor**, and provided that the occupier took reasonable steps to ensure that the contractor was competent and that the work had been properly done.

This means that an occupier will not be liable if his property is dangerous because of work done by an outside contractor if the work is beyond the knowledge and expertise of an ordinary reasonable person either to complete for himself or to check. Examples might include rewiring the electrics or fitting a satellite dish. In **Haseldine v Daw and Son Ltd (1941)**, the claimant was injured when, while visiting the defendant's premises, the lift in which he was travelling fell to the ground. The defendant was not liable because a reasonable person would ask a reputable contractor to maintain a lift and would not be in a position to check the work.

However, if the work could have been completed or checked by the occupier himself, then he will be liable even if he chooses to ask an outside contractor to do it. Examples might include cleaning a floor so that it is not left in a slippery state, or fitting a carpet so that the edges are loose and there is a danger of someone tripping over. In **Woodward v Mayor of Hastings (1944)** an outside contractor swept snow from the steps of a school but failed to deal with the frozen snow underneath, so that the steps were left in a slippery condition. The claimant, a pupil of the school, fell and was badly injured. The defendant was liable, because a reasonable person ought to be able to check whether steps are safe even if they had asked someone else to sweep them.

Contributory negligence

Section 2(3) states that when considering a claim brought under OLA 1957, the court should consider both the care and lack of care that would ordinarily be looked for in a visitor. This is the defence of contributory negligence, and it works in the same way against an action brought under OLA 1957 as it does against an action in ordinary negligence. You should therefore be familiar with the principles relating to the defence, which we discussed in Topic 4 of Chapter 14, and be prepared to use them when discussing OLA 1957.

Consent

Similarly, an occupier can use the defence of consent (as discussed in Topic 4 of Chapter 14) if faced with an action under OLA 1957. By s2(5) of the Act, he owes no obligation to a visitor in respect of risks that the visitor willingly accepts.

One possible example is **Geary v JD Wetherspoon plc (2011)**. The claimant, a customer in the defendant's bar, attempted to slide down the banisters of the large open staircase, but fell onto the marble floor four metres below and was very seriously injured. Her claim failed because she admitted that she was aware of the obvious risk in sliding down the banisters, and that she chose to take the risk. In those circumstances, the

Key terms

Independent contractor: someone who is not an employee but who is carrying out a service in exchange for a fee.

Key cases

Haseldine v Daw and Son Ltd (1941): an occupier is not liable for risks created by an independent contractor, provided that the risk is something that the occupier could not be expected to check for himself.

Woodward v Mayor of Hastings (1944): an occupier will be liable for the actions of an outside contractor if he could have completed or checked the work for himself.

Geary v JD Wetherspoon plc (2011): an occupier does not owe an obligation to a visitor in respect of risks that the visitor willingly accepts.

Study tip

The defence of contributory negligence is often relevant. Ask yourself whether the visitor himself acted reasonably and sensibly at all times.

defendant did not have a duty to protect her. (Arguably, the claimant was a trespasser at the moment of the accident as she had exceeded the limits of her permission, but the judge made it clear that the position was the same whether the claimant was a lawful visitor or a trespasser.)

Excluding liability

By s2(1) of OLA 1957, an occupier may restrict or exclude altogether the duty of care owed to his visitors. This might be done by putting up a sign saying that he does not accept responsibility for the safety of anyone visiting the premises, although any such sign should be clearly worded and clearly visible. In **Ashdown v Samuel Williams & Sons Ltd (1957)** the claimant was in the habit of taking a shortcut to her workplace across the railway goods yard belonging to the defendant. She was hit by some railway trucks that were being shunted negligently, but her claim under OLA 1957 failed because there were clear signs saying that people took the shortcut at their own risk.

The rule allowing exclusion of liability has been substantially modified in the case of business premises by the provisions of the Unfair Contract Terms Act 1977 (UCTA 1977). By s2(1) of that Act, liability cannot be excluded for the death or personal injury of a visitor where that loss is caused by negligence; and by s2(2), liability for other types of loss caused by negligence can only be excluded if it is reasonable for the occupier to do so.

However, by s1(3)(b) of UCTA 1977, the occupier of business premises is able to exclude liability in respect of visitors admitted for a recreational or educational purpose that is outside the occupier's business. An example might be a farmer who allows a class from the local school to conduct a nature trip in one of his fields.

Remedies

A successful claimant can claim damages for death and personal injury. By s1(3) of OLA 1957, he can also claim damages for damage to property (including damage to the property of someone other than himself) and any consequential economic loss resulting from damage to property, such as the costs of recovery.

Topic illustration

Consider this scenario, taken from a past AQA exam paper:

> Gordon engaged Ian to repair damage to a wall in his house. While doing so, Ian cut through an electricity cable and fused the power supply. Gordon was out, so Ian opened the locked door to the cellar with a key hanging from a nail on a nearby wall. As he went down the cellar stairs to find the electricity unit, a rotten stair gave way under his weight and he fell, breaking his leg and ripping his clothes.

In discussing Ian's possible claim under OLA 1957, we would need to consider the following issues:

- The first issue is whether Ian is a lawful visitor. He was clearly an invitee to the premises when he arrived to repair the wall, and you could argue that he remained a lawful visitor when he entered the cellar as it was a necessary, if unexpected, part of his job.

- Assuming Ian is a lawful visitor, you need to establish whether Gordon owed a duty of care to Ian on the ground that he is an occupier and that the house is within the definition of premises.

- The next issue is whether Gordon broke the duty he owes to Ian. Did he act as the reasonable occupier would have done? You can discuss issues such as whether there was a need for a warning in

Key cases

Ashdown v Samuel Williams & Sons Ltd (1957): an occupier may exclude any liability he might have under the Occupiers' Liability Act 1957 by giving proper notice to the visitor.

the circumstances and whether the presence of a locked door was adequate protection.

- There is little to discuss on the issues of causation and remoteness: Ian's losses are reasonably foreseeable. However, there may be an issue of contributory negligence given that Ian went somewhere unusual without checking with the occupier, and perhaps with no light.

- Finally, there is the issue of remedies. As this is OLA 1957, Ian can claim both for personal injury and for damage to property (his clothes).

Activities

1 In *Searson* v *Brioland* (2005) the claimant was an 82-year-old lady attending the wedding reception for her granddaughter at the defendant's banqueting venue. As she was leaving through the exterior door, she tripped over the raised threshold, which had a height of 2.8cm. The Court of Appeal allowed her claim for damages for the injuries she had sustained on the grounds that the claimant's mind was on other matters, there was no warning of a raised step and it is unexpected to step *up* when leaving a building (as distinct from entering a building). Do you agree that liability should exist in such circumstances?

2 Consider this scenario, which has been adapted from a past AQA exam paper:

Jarvis opens his large house and gardens to the public. On one particular day, despite torrential rain, Liam visited the house and paid the entrance fee. Jarvis's gardens were laid out on a number of levels, the path between two levels consisting of steep steps. Down one side of the steps was a low spiked fence, to which a handrail was attached. A notice at the top of the steps warned that extra care was necessary in wet weather. Liam slipped and overbalanced while running down the steps holding the handrail, and was jerked round onto the spikes of the fence badly cutting his face.

Why is Liam a lawful visitor? What factors might the court take into account when deciding whether Jarvis breached the duty he owed under the Act? If Jarvis is found to have breached the duty, can he rely on any defence?

You should now be able to:

- identify factors that a court might take into account when deciding whether an occupier has breached the duty of care he owes to a visitor

- identify and explain possible defences to an action brought under the Occupiers' Liability Act 1957.

3 Occupiers' Liability Act 1984

A trespasser is not a lawful visitor and is therefore not protected by OLA 1957. Originally, the law offered such a person little, if any, protection, but this was a harsh approach and could be very unfair if, for instance, a wandering child was involved. The House of Lords therefore modified the law in *British Railways Board* v *Herrington* (1972). The claimant, a child aged six, was badly injured when he trespassed onto an electrified railway line owned by the defendant. The railway line ran next to a field open to the public, where the defendant knew that it was common for children to play. The fence between the field and the line had been trodden down for some time, but the defendant had done nothing about it. The House of Lords held that the defendant was liable because common sense and common humanity suggested that if a company were to build something as dangerous as an electric railway line in the vicinity of an area in which children played, they should take measures to protect the children – particularly where the danger, as here, was not obvious to a small child. However, this duty of 'common humanity' was uncertain in its scope, so Parliament clarified the position with the enactment of the Occupiers' Liability Act 1984.

In this topic, you will learn how to:

- identify the limited circumstances in which the duty under the Occupiers' Liability Act 1984 is owed

- explain the nature of the duty and the standard expected of an occupier.

When is the duty under OLA 1984 owed?

A potential claimant under OLA 1984 must overcome two preliminary hurdles before he can show that the occupier of premises owes him a duty under the Act at all.

The first is that the claim must arise out of the dangerous state of the premises rather than the dangerous activities of the claimant himself. If the premises are safe, but the accident was caused by the claimant acting unwisely, then the duty under OLA 1984 does not arise. In **Keown v Coventry NHS Trust (2006)** the claimant was an 11-year-old boy playing with other children on land around a building owned by the defendant. At that stage, the claimant was a lawful visitor, as the defendant knew that children played there, but he became a trespasser when he overstepped the limit of any implied permission by climbing 'monkey fashion' up the underside of a metal fire escape attached to the outside of the building. The claimant fell and was badly injured, but his claim failed as the accident happened through his own dangerous activities and not because of any fault with the building. A similar example is *Tomlinson* v *Congleton Borough Council* (2003), discussed on p290. The defendant owed no duty as the premises in question, the lake, were not unsafe as far as lakes go.

The second hurdle is the provisions of s1(3) of OLA 1984, which states that an occupier owes a duty in respect of a danger on his premises if:

- he is aware of the danger or has reasonable grounds to believe that it exists
- he knows or has reasonable grounds to believe that someone else is in the vicinity of the danger or may come into the vicinity of the danger
- the danger is one against which, in all the circumstances, he may reasonably be expected to offer some protection.

If the claimant cannot show that these three conditions all exist, then the defendant owes no duty of care and the claim fails. One illustration of this is **Donoghue v Folkestone Properties (2003)**. In the middle of a winter's night, the claimant dived into a harbour owned by the defendant and broke his neck when he collided with an underwater piling. The claimant was a trespasser, but the defendant was held not to owe a duty under OLA 1984 because it had no reasonable ground to believe that anyone would be in the vicinity of the danger. It could not be anticipated that anyone would want to dive into a harbour at that time of the night and at that time of the year.

A more complex example is **Scott v Associated British Ports (2000)**, in which the defendant was the occupier of a railway line. There had been two instances of 'train surfing' (youngsters attempting to jump onto goods trains as they moved slowly past) both of which had led to the participant losing a limb. The accidents were a number of years apart. With respect to the first, the defendant did not owe a duty under OLA 1984 as they had not known that trespassers were present. In the second case, this was not so because of the defendant's knowledge of the first incident. (In the event, the defendant was not liable as the court decided that even if the area had been properly fenced, the claimant would still have got in and thus causation was not proven.)

When considering whether the danger is one which the occupier should offer some protection against, possible factors include whether the occupier would take precautions for himself, whether the danger is obvious (particularly given the likely age of any trespasser) and whether the duty of 'common humanity' discussed in *BRB* v *Herrington* (1972) suggests that he should take action.

Key cases

Keown v Coventry NHS Trust (2006): an occupier does not owe a duty under the Occupiers' Liability Act 1984 when the risk is created by the dangerous activities of the entrant rather than the state of the premises.

Donoghue v Folkestone Properties (2003): an occupier will not owe a duty under s1(3) Occupiers' Liability Act 1984 if he cannot be expected to know that trespassers will be in the vicinity of a danger at that time.

Scott v Associated British Ports (2000): a court may decide that a defendant has the relevant knowledge because of previous incidents on the premises.

Scott v Associated British Ports *(2000) demonstrates the rules of the OLA with regard to trespassers train surfing*

The Duty under OLA 1984

By s1(4) of OLA 1984, the duty owed by an occupier to a trespasser is to take such care as is reasonable in all the circumstances to see that the trespasser does not suffer injury on the premises because of the danger.

By s1(2) of OLA 1984, the terms 'occupier' and 'premises' have the same meaning as they do for the purposes of OLA 1957. Similarly, a trespasser is someone who is not a lawful visitor for the purposes of OLA 1957.

Discharging the duty

Having established that the defendant owes a duty under OLA 1984, the claimant must then show that the defendant broke that duty by not taking reasonable care to protect the claimant. Case law suggests that the courts will often decide this issue in favour of the defendant, as in many circumstances there is a limit to what the reasonable person would do to protect someone who should not be there.

Factors that the judge might take into account include:

- likelihood of trespass
- seriousness of injury risked
- cost and practicality of precautions
- likely age of any trespasser
- visibility and attractiveness of any danger
- relative obviousness of the danger
- reason for trespass – malicious or otherwise
- common sense
- the idea that an occupier should not have to guard against an irresponsible minority.

In **Platt v Liverpool City Council (1997)** the claimant, a child, was killed when the derelict building in which he was trespassing collapsed. The defendant was held not liable on the ground that there was nothing more that the council could reasonably have done: it had secured the building with an eight-foot-high metal fence with wooden posts set in concrete. The court recognised that it is impossible to guard against a determined and irresponsible minority.

Study tip

Unlike the duty under the Occupiers' Liability Act 1957, the duty under the 1984 Act is not automatic. There will be instances where the occupier owes no duty at all.

Key cases

Platt v Liverpool City Council (1997): an occupier may have done all that is reasonable even if he cannot guard against a determined and irresponsible minority.

> **Key cases**
>
> **Tomlinson v Congleton Borough Council (2003):** clear and visible signs warning of a danger may be all that an occupier needs to do to satisfy his duty under the Occupiers' Liability Act 1984.
>
> **Ratcliff v McConnell (1999):** an occupier owes no duty in respect of risks willingly accepted by the trespasser.

As with OLA 1957, the occupier may be able to discharge his duty by taking such steps as are reasonable in all the circumstances of the case to give warning of the danger concerned or to discourage persons from incurring the risk (s1(5) of OLA 1984). This might include clear and visible warning signs, fences and secured entrances. In **Tomlinson v Congleton Borough Council (2003)** you have already seen why the occupier did not owe a duty. However, the House of Lords stated that even if a duty had been owed, the occupier, by putting up signs forbidding swimming, had done enough to discharge the duty.

With respect to what an occupier might need to do to discharge his duty, *Tomlinson* is also interesting for further remarks made by the House of Lords. The defendant had made known its plans to prevent such an accident happening again by turning the beach, from which the claimant had dived, into marshy ground so that people would be unable to get close to the lake. The House of Lords said that such action was unnecessary: it would be very expensive, it would be a measure needed to stop only a small number of irresponsible people, and it would deprive the vast majority of visitors of the use of a beach.

Defences

Contributory negligence

Although OLA 1984 makes no specific mention of a defence of contributory negligence, it is clear that judges will accept the defence. As with OLA 1957, the defence works in the same way as it does for a claim in ordinary negligence.

Consent

Section 1(6) of OLA 1984 states that the defendant owes no duty in respect of risks willingly accepted by the trespasser.

In **Ratcliff v McConnell (1999)** the claimant, an adult student at the defendant college, dived one night into an outdoor swimming pool owned by the defendant, but misjudged his actions and suffered very serious injuries when he broke his neck. The claimant was a trespasser as he had ignored signs prohibiting use of the pool and had clambered over a fence to get to it. The court decided that the defendant did not owe a duty under OLA 1984 as the claimant was aware of the risk of diving into a pool in the dark, and had accepted that risk.

Excluding liability

The law is not clear whether an occupier of premises can exclude any duty he might owe under OLA 1984 by, for instance, putting up a sign stating that people enter at their own risk. The question is not dealt with in either the Occupiers' Liability Act 1984 or the Unfair Contract Terms Act 1977, and there appears to be no case law decision either.

It might be that an occupier can exclude the duty, but within the same limits relating to business premises as exist for OLA 1957. Alternatively, given that OLA 1984 was a result of the House of Lords establishing a duty of common humanity in the *British Railways Board* v *Herrington* (1972) case, it might be that the duty is an unexcludable minimum: it is owed in all circumstances because common decency and humanity suggests that it should be. If this latter approach is correct, then it is probably also correct to say that in those circumstances where an occupier is able to exclude his duty under OLA 1957, he will in fact be unable to exclude his liability altogether, but will instead owe the lower duty under OLA 1984. Otherwise, lawful visitors would be left in a worse position than trespassers.

Remedies

A successful claimant can claim damages for death and personal injury, but, by s1(8) of OLA 1984, he cannot claim damages for any loss to his property.

Topic illustration

Consider again the scenario concerning Ian and Gordon:

> Gordon engaged Ian to repair damage to a wall in his house. While doing so, Ian cut through an electricity cable and fused the power supply. Gordon was out, so Ian opened the locked door to the cellar with a key hanging from a nail on a nearby wall. As he went down the cellar stairs to find the electricity unit, a rotten stair gave way under his weight and he fell, breaking his leg and ripping his clothes.

On this occasion, we are discussing Ian's possible claim under OLA 1984:

- The first issue remains whether Ian is a lawful visitor. Although he first entered Gordon's house as a lawful visitor, there is an argument that he became a trespasser when he exceeded his permission to be there, either by trying to do something he wasn't engaged to do (switching off the electricity) or by going somewhere Gordon did not expect him to go (the issue of the locked door and the key is relevant).

- Assuming Ian is an unlawful visitor, we need to establish whether Gordon owed a duty of care to Ian under OLA 1984. Our discussion would focus on s1(3), and on questions such as whether Gordon knew that Ian would go into the cellar and whether he knew that the step was rotten.

- If Gordon does owe the duty, we need to define the duty and discuss whether Gordon did take such care as is reasonable in all the circumstances.

- Finally, as with OLA 1957, there is the issue of a possible defence in contributory negligence and the question of remedies (damages for personal injury only).

Activities

1. Several of the cases discussed in this section involve people diving into shallow water and sustaining extremely serious and permanent injuries. Can anything realistically be done to prevent such accidents?

2. Consider this scenario, which has been adapted from a past AQA exam paper:

   Following recent embarrassing revelations, Andrew was being pursued by investigative journalists from the national press. He retreated to his weekend cottage, and engaged Charles, a local joiner, to fit shutters to the outside of all windows to protect his privacy. While doing so, Charles fell from a ladder and broke his arm, when a rotten window sill on which he had placed his foot gave way under his weight. David, one of the reporters, climbed a wall at night to get into the grounds of the cottage. When he jumped down, he landed on an old glass frame left under the wall and suffered a very bad cut to his leg.

   In relation to both Charles and David, consider the issues of whether Andrew owed a duty, whether he breached any duty owed and whether any defences and remedies may be available.

Study tip

When referring to the Occupiers' Liability Act, make sure you always state whether it is the 1957 or 1984 Act to which you refer.

You should now be able to:

- explain the duty contained in the Occupiers' Liability Act 1984 and when it might apply

- consider factors that a court might take into account when deciding if an occupier has breached the duty owed to trespassers

- identify possible defences.

18 The tort of nuisance and the rule in *Rylands* v *Fletcher*

Introduction

This chapter is about liability for activities that interfere with another person's land or that cause a nuisance to the public at large. Such liability exists in four types:

1 **Private nuisance:** an activity that interferes with a person's ability to use his own land in a reasonable way.
2 **Public nuisance:** an activity that impacts on the public at large.
3 **The rule in *Rylands* v *Fletcher* (1868):** a specific type of nuisance that covers an escape of a dangerous substance.
4 **Statutory nuisance:** there are a number of statutes covering matters such as clean air, an escape of oil or chemicals, water pollution, radioactive substances and public health and hygiene.

We consider only the first three types, as statutory liability is outside the scope of the A Level specification.

In this topic, you will learn how to:

- explain and define what is meant by private nuisance

- outline the factors a court will use when deciding if an activity is lawful

- identify defences and remedies appropriate to a claim in private nuisance.

Key terms

Private nuisance: activity which interferes for a substantial length of time with the claimant's right to enjoy his land in a reasonable way.

Legal interest: formal ownership or control of land – for instance, the freehold or a tenancy.

Key cases

Hunter v Canary Wharf (1997): to sue in private nuisance, a claimant must have a legal interest in the land affected.

1 Private nuisance

Private nuisance is a tort. It exists whenever there is an unlawful interference for a substantial length of time with a person's right to enjoy his land in a reasonable way.

A claimant in an action for private nuisance must show that:

- he has the right to bring an action and the person he is suing is capable of being a defendant

- there is an interference in the form of either physical damage to the land or a loss of amenity (convenience) in using the land

- the interference is sufficiently serious in all the circumstances to be unlawful.

If the claimant is successful in all of these, the defendant may show one of the defences available in any action for private nuisance, but if that fails the claimant will be entitled to a remedy from the court usually in the form of damages or an injunction or both.

The parties to an action for private nuisance

Claimant

To be able to bring an action in private nuisance, a claimant must be someone with a **legal interest** in the affected land, such as an owner or a tenant. This rule was confirmed by the House of Lords in **Hunter v Canary Wharf (1997)**. The case was brought by a number of claimants who were complaining about things such as dust and interference with television reception caused by the building works relating to the Canary Wharf development in London's Docklands. Some of the claimants were unable to pursue their claims because they lacked any legal interest in the affected land, one example being a wife who did not jointly own the family home with her husband.

The reason for this rule is that private nuisance is a tort relating to interference with land and the possible impact that this might have on the value of the land. Therefore, the proper claimant is the person who might suffer a financial loss. In addition, if the law protected people other than owners (for instance, lodgers), it might be very difficult for someone who is creating a nuisance to reach an out-of-court settlement with all the various interested parties.

Defendant

The obvious defendant is the creator of the nuisance.

In addition, the occupier of the land – if he is a different person from the creator of the nuisance – can also be a defendant if he adopts or continues the activities of the creator. One example is **Sedleigh-Denfield v O'Callaghan (1940)** where a trespasser installed a pipe in a ditch on the defendant's land. Three years later, the pipe became blocked and the subsequent flooding damaged the claimant's land. The defendant was liable, even though he had not installed the pipe, as he knew of its existence.

Finally, it is possible for a landlord to be liable for the activities of a tenant if he authorised or approved those activities. In **Tetley v Chitty (1986)** a local council was liable for the noise and disturbance caused by a go-kart club after the council leased land to the club for the express purpose of developing a race track.

Interference

Claims in private nuisance cover two types of interference with, or loss to, the affected land: physical damage, and loss of amenity enjoyment.

1 Physical damage

Private nuisance covers **physical damage to land**, damage to plants and crops growing in the land, and probably damage to goods stored on the land. However, private nuisance does not allow the recovery of damages for personal injury: in those circumstances, a claimant should bring an action in negligence.

Examples of physical damage include: gases from a factory killing or damaging flowers, oil smuts from a refinery covering washing pegged on a line or damaging paintwork, and damage to foundations caused by vibrations from a generating plant.

2 Loss of amenity/enjoyment

Nuisance also covers cases where there is no physical damage, but where the claimant's ability to use or enjoy his land is restricted by the activities of the defendant. This is known as **loss of amenity**. Examples include: excessive noise preventing the claimant from getting a good night's sleep, or unpleasant smells and fumes preventing the claimant from opening his windows.

Unlawfulness

When will an interference be unlawful?

The function of private nuisance is to balance the conflicting interests of neighbours. In general, people do have the right to use their own land as they wish, and it might be that their neighbours have to put up with the occasional late-night party or with the noise from the building of a conservatory.

However, there is a limit beyond which activities become unlawful. The test that the courts use in deciding when this limit has been reached is whether the nuisance interferes with ordinary existence – in other words,

> ### Key cases
>
> **Sedleigh-Denfield v O'Callaghan (1940):** a person can be liable for a private nuisance which he did not create, if he adopts the activity in question.
>
> **Tetley v Chitty (1986):** a person can be liable for a private nuisance that he does not create but that he authorises.

> ### Key terms
>
> **Physical damage to land:** actual damage to land or to buildings and plants on the land.
>
> **Loss of amenity:** interference with the claimant's ability to use his land in a reasonable way.

whether the impact on the claimant is so unreasonable that he should not be expected to put up with it.

To help it make this decision, the court will consider a number of factors when balancing the conflicting interests of the claimant and the defendant. One interesting result of this balancing of the factors is that certain activities will be lawful in some sets or circumstances but not in others, so that we can say that nuisance has a variable standard. One example is that playing very loud music through the night is not a problem in an isolated farmhouse but would be a problem in a block of flats.

The following are factors that the court might take into account when balancing the conflicting interests of neighbours:

1 the locality of the events
2 the duration of the nuisance
3 the degree to which the activity interferes with neighbours
4 the sensitivity of the claimant
5 the reasons for the defendant's activities and whether they have a useful function
6 the motive behind the defendant's activities and whether he is acting simply out of malice.

1 Locality

The location of the nuisance is important as a wider range of activities are acceptable in, for instance, industrial zones than in residential areas. In **Halsey v Esso Petroleum Co. Ltd (1961)** the defendant oil company was found liable for the activities of its oil depot, which was located in the middle of a housing area. Part of the nuisance was the constant coming and going of oil tankers by day and by night, which would have been less of a problem on an industrial estate.

Locality was relevant in **Lawrence v Fen Tigers (2012)** when the noise from the defendant's motor racing circuit was held not to amount to a nuisance. The Court of Appeal decided that the character of the locality had been altered by the local authority planning permission for the circuit and the long-established use of the land for motor racing. This meant that the noise from the track was an established part of the character of the locality, and should be taken into account when deciding whether the activity amounted to a nuisance.

However, locality is irrelevant where the nuisance causes physical damage. This can be seen in **St Helens Smelting v Tipping (1865)**. The claimant complained that fumes from the defendant's copper smelting works were damaging trees and crops on the claimant's land. The claimant was successful, even though the location was a manufacturing area, because the courts will act to prevent physical damage.

2 Duration

The more often something happens, the more likely it is to be nuisance. The Court of Appeal confirmed in *Barr* v *Biffa Waste Services* (2012), which is discussed below, that duration is an important, if not decisive, element. In the *Barr* case, one of the key factors in establishing a nuisance was that the strong smells had been continuing off and on for five years.

However, in the right circumstances, even a single event can amount to nuisance. In **Crown River Cruises v Kimbolton Fireworks (1996)** the defendant was liable in nuisance for burning debris that originated in a 20-minute firework display and that damaged the claimant's river boats.

Key cases

Halsey v Esso Petroleum Co. Ltd (1961): industrial activities are more likely to be a nuisance in a residential area.

Lawrence v Fen Tigers (2012): activity can become part of character of a locality through planning permission and long-established usage of the land for this purpose.

St Helens Smelting v Tipping (1865): even in an industrial zone, a defendant does not have the right to carry out activities that inflict physical damage on his neighbours' properties.

Crown River Cruises v Kimbolton Fireworks (1996): even a single incident can amount to a nuisance.

3 Degree of interference

The more serious or worse an interference, the more likely it is to be a nuisance. How serious an interference is can depend on the time of day. Building works that are acceptable at three o'clock in the afternoon might not be acceptable at three o'clock in the morning.

If physical damage is involved, then relatively small nuisances are actionable. If a loss of enjoyment is involved, the threshold is higher. The Court of Appeal in **Barr v Biffa Waste Services (2012)** restated that there must be a real interference with comfort or convenience of living, as judged by the standards of the average man. In that case, the defendant's storage of mostly organic material in a landfill site amounted to a nuisance as it had led on many occasions, particularly in warmer weather, to very strong and unpleasant garbage smells that had affected the ordinary enjoyment of the claimants' houses and gardens.

By contrast, in **Murdoch v Glacier Metal (1998)** the claimant complained that the constant low-level droning noise from the defendant's factory was keeping her awake at night, but the court held that there was no nuisance as no one else had complained. It also stated that in any event there was a considerable amount of noise from a nearby road, so any noise from the factory would not interfere with ordinary existence.

4 Sensitivity

If the claimant is using his property for an extra-sensitive use, he is not entitled to sue in circumstances where a reasonable use would not need protection. In **Bridlington Relay v Yorkshire Electricity (1965)** the claimant's complaint was that the defendant's overhead electric power cables were interfering with transmissions from the claimant's television mast. The court dismissed the claim on the ground that the power cables would not have interfered with any ordinary user of the land, and that the only reason the claimant had suffered damage was because of the very sensitive nature of his activities.

If the defendant's activities would have interfered with an ordinary use of the claimant's land, then the claimant can claim for the full extent of his loss even though the loss was partly caused by the extra-sensitive nature of his use. In the Canadian case of **McKinnon Industries v Walker (1951)** the claimant could claim for the full damage caused to delicate orchids by gas emitted from the defendant's factory, as even flowers of ordinary sensitivity would have been affected.

5 Social utility of the defendant's conduct

The usefulness to society of the defendant's conduct has a bearing on whether it is reasonable for the claimant to have to put up with it. One example is that the noise and dust from a building site over a limited period of time is allowable because it is useful to have new buildings, whereas in other circumstances the noise and the dust might be a nuisance.

Often, social utility does not prevent what is a clear nuisance from being a nuisance, but it does have a bearing on remedies. In **Dennis v Ministry of Defence (2003)** the claimant lived in a large house in the country, but his peace was regularly destroyed by RAF training jets flying overhead. The court found that the noise did amount to a nuisance and awarded damages, but it was not prepared to grant an injunction as the flights were a necessary part of this country's defence preparations.

6 Malice on the part of the defendant

If a defendant deliberately does something with no purpose other than to annoy the claimant, the defendant's **malice** can make unlawful something that might not otherwise be a nuisance. This can be most

---

Key cases

Barr v Biffa Waste Services (2012): nuisance is an activity that materially interferes with the ordinary existence of the claimant.

Murdoch v Glacier Metal (1998): a claim in private nuisance will fail if activity does not interfere with ordinary existence.

Bridlington Relay v Yorkshire Electricity (1965): a claim in private nuisance will fail if claimant's use of his land is so sensitive that even ordinary activities on the part of the defendant create an interference.

McKinnon Industries v Walker (1951): a claimant can sue for the full extent of his loss, even though his use of his land is extra-sensitive, if defendant's activities would have disturbed even a normal use.

Dennis v Ministry of Defence (2003): if an activity is in the public interest, the claimant may fail to win an injunction.

Key terms

Malice: deliberate intent to cause some sort of injury or upset.

Key cases

Hollywood Silver Fox Farm v Emmett (1936) and **Christie v Davey (1892)**: malice on the part of the defendant can convert a lawful activity into an unlawful activity.

Allen v Gulf Oil (1981): defendant will escape liability in private nuisance if his activities have been authorised by Parliament.

Marcic v Thames Water (2003): defendant will escape liability in private nuisance if Parliament has created an alternative remedy for any claimant.

Study tip

In an exam, when discussing whether an activity is sufficiently unreasonable as to amount to a private nuisance, do not waste time discussing factors which are clearly not relevant. Concentrate on relevant material and be sure to apply the rules to the facts of any problems and to cite cases where you can.

Key terms

Statutory authority: permission given by Parliament to create a private nuisance.

clearly seen in **Hollywood Silver Fox Farm v Emmett (1936)**. The claimant farmed silver foxes. The defendant, as part of an ongoing feud, deliberately fired shotguns within the boundaries of his own land so as to startle the foxes and cause them to miscarry. In normal circumstances, firing a shotgun in the countryside would probably not amount to a nuisance, but the malicious motive in this case made it unlawful.

A second example of malice is **Christie v Davey (1892)**. The defendant lived next door to a house in which various people gave piano and singing lessons. To show his annoyance, he began to whistle, shriek and bang tin trays on the walls whenever a lesson was taking place. The court imposed an injunction against him because it was clear that his activities were done deliberately to disrupt and to upset. After a careful consideration of evidence relating to number, length and timings of lessons, the judge also found that the original music-making was not a nuisance.

Christie *v* Davey *(1892)*

Defences to an action in private nuisance

There are two specific defences available to an action for private nuisance: statutory authority and prescription.

Statutory authority

Statutory authority means that the nuisance is created by a public body acting under a legislative duty or power. As long as the activity is carried out without negligence and with reasonable regard to, and care of, the interests of others, a person affected will not be able to sue in nuisance as the nuisance has effectively been authorised by Parliament. An example is **Allen v Gulf Oil (1981)**: the House of Lords decided that the defence was arguable in the case of an oil refinery that had been built under powers contained in an Act of Parliament, and that was causing a nuisance to its neighbours in the form of fumes and noise.

It is also a defence for a public body to show that Parliament has created an alternative remedy. In **Marcic v Thames Water (2003)** the claimant sued for private nuisance as a result of the flooding of his land caused by inadequacies in the defendant's drainage systems. The House of Lords ruled that there could be no action in nuisance as Parliament had established a statutory framework of remedies for people who had been affected by the defendant's activities.

Prescription

A second defence is **prescription**. The defence is based on the idea of an easement, which is a land law concept giving one party rights over another's land, and its effect is that the defendant's activities become lawful if he has been carrying them out for at least twenty years to the claimant's knowledge. It was discussed, *obiter*, in *Lawrence* v *Fen Tigers* (2012) (see above), in the context of motor racing. The Court of Appeal felt firstly that an easement could exist for certain times of the day or certain days of the week or at certain times of the year, and secondly that an easement could exist with respect to transmitting sound waves – in other words, making a noise.

Non-defences: arguments not open to the defendant

By contrast, there are a number of possible arguments that the courts will not accept as a defence to a claim for private nuisance. The defendant, for instance, cannot rely on the fact that he was creating the nuisance before the claimant moved to the area and that the claimant knew of the activity before he arrived. In **Sturges v Bridgeman (1879)** a doctor was able to bring an action for private nuisance when he built a consulting room in his garden on land adjacent to a confectioner. The noise from the latter interfered with the doctor's ability to see his patients, and it was no defence that the confectioner had been established first.

It is also not a defence to say that the claimant could have helped himself – for instance, by shutting his windows. Neither is it a defence that the defendant was using reasonable care and skill, nor that the nuisance was partly caused by someone else.

Remedies in an action for private nuisance

A successful claimant in private nuisance might ask the court for an injunction, damages or both. In addition, he might be able to use the self-help remedy of abatement.

1 Injunction

An **injunction** is an order prohibiting or strictly controlling an activity. Frequently, a claimant will seek this remedy instead of, or as well as, damages because what he really wants is for the offending activity to stop. However, the courts will not grant an injunction for trivial matters or where it is in the public interest for the activity to continue. An injunction might impose a complete ban, or it might allow the activity to continue but within defined limits, as in *Kennaway* below.

In **Miller v Jackson (1977)** the claimants sought an injunction to stop cricket being played on a pitch adjacent to their house as occasionally a ball would land on their property, causing damage. The court refused because the cricket club was a focus of village life and it was in the interest of the community that the activity should continue. That interest outweighed the relatively minor inconvenience to the claimants.

In **Kennaway v Thompson (1981)** the defendant was a powerboat club that was organising an ever increasing number of races and other events with ever noisier boats. The defendant admitted that it was causing a nuisance to the claimant, who lived nearby, but argued that, because its activities were of great interest to the public, damages only should be awarded. The court disagreed, stating that, unlike *Miller* v *Jackson* (1977), the nuisance was substantial, and that it was not part of English law that a defendant could effectively turn an unlawful activity into a lawful activity by paying over a large sum of money. The court went on to impose a partial injunction limiting the number of races.

Key terms

Prescription: gaining a right to do something not otherwise permitted on the basis of the length of time which the activity was carried out unlawfully but without objection.

Injunction: court order (usually) forbidding a party to do something on pain of a criminal penalty.

Key cases

Sturges v Bridgeman (1879): defendant will not escape liability in private nuisance simply because he was there before the claimant.

Miller v Jackson (1977) and Kennaway v Thompson (1981): whether an injunction is granted to stop a private nuisance will depend in part on balancing the interest of the parties and of the community.

Study tip

In your exam, do not forget to conclude your answer with a discussion of possible remedies.

Key cases

Hunter v Canary Wharf (1997) and **Dennis v Ministry of Defence (2003):** damages for loss of use and enjoyment will be equivalent to the loss in value to the affected premises.

The Wagon Mound (No. 2) (1966): only damages that are reasonably foreseeable can be claimed.

Key terms

Abatement: claimant taking steps himself to remove or minimise a nuisance.

2 Damages

In the case of physical damage, damages are awarded for consequential damage to land, plants, buildings and goods. Note that damages cannot be awarded for personal injury. In the case of loss of use and enjoyment, the decision in **Hunter v Canary Wharf (1997)** makes it clear that damages should be equal to the loss in value of the land.

A good example is the decision in **Dennis v Ministry of Defence (2003)**, which we discussed above. The court refused to grant an injunction, because the training flights were necessary to the defence of the country, but it was prepared to award damages to reflect the reduction in the value of the land.

Finally, a claimant may only recover losses that are reasonably foreseeable. This is the same rule on remoteness as in negligence. In the case of private nuisance, the rule was set out in **The Wagon Mound (No. 2) (1966)** and was confirmed in *Cambridge Water* v *Eastern Counties Leather* (1994).

3 Abatement

Abatement is a self-help remedy and it means the right of a claimant to take reasonable steps to deal with any nuisance himself. Two examples might be chopping off the branches of a tree overhanging a boundary and unblocking a drain that is threatening to spill over.

In using abatement, the claimant must be careful not to overstep the limits of what is reasonable in the circumstances. For instance, if he needs to enter the defendant's land he should do so only having given proper notice or in an emergency, and if he needs to chop off the branches of any overhanging tree he should only do so from the point at which they overhang the boundary, and he should return any branches. The courts are wary of the remedy because of the possibility of confrontation and a resulting breach of the peace.

Topic illustration

Consider this scenario, taken from a past AQA exam paper:

> Residents living in the vicinity of the Johnsons factory had been complaining for some time of noise and vibration coming from the factory, especially at night. When an explosion occurred in the factory one morning, a thick cloud of smoke spread rapidly across the town, leaving a dirty, oily deposit on houses and other buildings.

Using the rules described in this topic, we can say that a discussion of any claim by the residents in private nuisance should identify the following elements:

▓ Many of the residents will own their properties, and thus qualify as claimants. Similarly, Johnsons, as the creator of the nuisance, will be the defendant.

▓ The damage suffered by the residents may be both physical loss (for instance, if the vibrations have shaken buildings) and a loss of amenity (for instance, sleepless nights).

▓ There are a number of factors relevant to any discussion on the unlawfulness of Johnsons' activities – for instance, locality, duration, degree of interference and social usefulness of the activity.

▓ On the facts, it is difficult to identify a relevant defence for certain, but remedies in the form of damages and an injunction are clearly relevant.

Activities

1 Consider whether you, your family or your friends have recently experienced anything, either at home, at school or in the workplace, that may amount to a private nuisance.

2 Consider this case study, which has been adapted from a past AQA exam paper:

Matt lived in a house with very substantial grounds. Once isolated, his property now backed onto newly built houses on an estate, from which it was screened only by a fence and a row of trees. Matt enjoyed a range of hobbies, including building and flying model helicopters. He was very eccentric, and often flew them late into the evening and early in the morning in the summer months. They were very noisy and disturbed the residents in their houses and their pet animals. His response to complaints seemed to be to fly them at even more unpredictable hours.

With reference to the tort of private nuisance, discuss the rights and remedies, if any, available to the residents of the estate arising out of Matt's pursuit of his hobby.

You should now be able to:

■ explain the nature of private nuisance

■ analyse the reasoning processes used in deciding whether an activity amounts to a private nuisance.

2 Public nuisance

Despite the similarity in name, private nuisance and public nuisance have little in common, although an unlawful activity on the part of the defendant can amount to both.

Definition of public nuisance

Public nuisance has very uncertain boundaries, and has been used to cover a wide variety of activities, many of which are now in fact covered by legislation. It is both a crime and a tort, and it seeks to protect the health, safety, morals and convenience of the public and to prevent the obstruction of any right held by every member of the public.

Case law examples of public nuisance include:

■ A pop festival causing noise, traffic congestion and general inconvenience: *Attorney-General for Ontario* v *Orange Productions* (1971).

■ Selling contaminated water: *AB* v *South West Water* (1993).

■ Obstructing a canal by mooring a boat across the navigation channel: *Rose* v *Miles* (1815).

■ Emitting large clouds of smoke so as to endanger the highway: *Holling* v *Yorkshire Traction* (1948).

■ Placing a golf tee so that players frequently hit golf balls onto the adjoining public road: *Castle* v *St Augustine's Links* (1922).

In order to establish a public nuisance, it is necessary to show that a class of people have been affected, and that the members of that class have suffered a common harm.

In this topic, you will learn how to:

■ explain the meaning of public nuisance

■ identify the elements needed for a claim in public nuisance.

Key terms

Public nuisance: an activity that interferes with the safety or convenience of a section of the general public.

Key cases

Attorney-General v PYA Quarries (1957): public nuisance is one which affects a class of Her Majesty's subjects.

Madden (1975): telephonist and a group of police officers and security guards do not amount to a class of Her Majesty's subjects.

Rimmington (2005): public nuisance requires a common injury – in other words, interference with a public right.

Lyons, Sons & Co. v Gulliver (1913): in an action for public nuisance, a court will consider the interests of the different parties.

Study tip

When considering a case study in an examination, do not forget the possibility of a liability in public nuisance. Ask yourself whether a large number of people have been affected by the activities of the defendant.

Key terms

Common law crime: crime whose elements are defined in case law rather than by statute.

Class of people

Unlike private nuisance, it is not enough that the defendant's activities affect a particular claimant. A public nuisance is any nuisance:

> which materially affects the reasonable comfort and convenience of life of a class of Her Majesty's subjects. (Romer LJ in Attorney-General v PYA Quarries (1957))

What constitutes a 'class of Her Majesty's subjects' is a question of fact, and has to be decided case by case. It should consist of a section of the public rather than individuals, and should involve a considerable number of people. In **Attorney-General v PYA Quarries (1957)** itself, a group of about 30 houses was enough to amount to a class, and consequently the noise, vibrations and dust thrown up by the defendant's quarry blasting were held to be public nuisance. In **Madden (1975)** a hoax bomb call was held not to amount to a nuisance because it only affected the telephonist who took the call, the police, and the security guards who spent an hour looking for the device before it was realised that it did not exist. The court in that case said that a public nuisance was one where 'a considerable number of persons or a section of the public, as distinct from individual persons, had been affected'.

Common injury

A public nuisance is one that affects a right, a protection or a benefit enjoyed in common by the members of the affected class. Thus, obstruction of a road is a public nuisance because it interferes with the public's ability to make use of a right of way. Conversely, the actions of the defendant in **Rimmington (2005)** in sending packages containing racially offensive material to a wide variety of recipients was not a public nuisance because, although the packages may have caused an injury to each individual's personal rights, there was no injury to a public right.

Actions and remedies for public nuisance

Public nuisance, like private nuisance, is about balancing the competing interests of different people. It is not public nuisance if a road or a pavement is partly and temporarily blocked by a vehicle that has broken down, or a van that is unloading goods outside business premises. However, it is different if the defendant is regularly blocking the highway for no good reason. In **Lyons, Sons & Co. v Gulliver (1913)** the defendant committed a public nuisance as he regularly allowed large queues of people seeking cheap seats to build up on the pavement outside his theatre, thus impeding access to the claimant's shop.

A case of public nuisance can reach the courts in one of three ways.

The first, and most common, is as a criminal case. Public nuisance is a **common law crime**, and will be investigated by the police and prosecuted by the Crown Prosecution Service like any other offence. Secondly, if a criminal case is not sufficient to deal with the problem, then the Attorney-General has the power (but not a duty) to seek an injunction in the civil courts on behalf of the public.

The third route into the courts is a civil action brought by an individual. This option is not open to a person just because he is a member of the class affected, as to allow all those affected to sue would lead to multiple cases from a single incident. In order to be able to sue, an individual must show that he has suffered a special or particular damage – in other words, a loss or injury over and above the rest of the members of the class. Examples include:

- In *Castle v St Augustine's Links* (1922) the defendant placed a golf tee so that golf balls regularly landed on the road, thus causing a public nuisance. However, the claimant was able to claim damages as it was his car, of all the cars on the road, that was hit.

- In *Halsey* v *Esso Petroleum Co. Ltd* (1961) the activities of the oil depot amounted to a public nuisance in that they affected the neighbourhood, but the claimant suffered special damage as it was the paintwork of his car that was damaged by acidic smuts.

- In **Tate & Lyle Industries v Greater London Council (1983)** the defendant caused a public nuisance by causing a river to become silted, thus interfering with public navigation rights. The claimant suffered special loss as it had to pay for dredging works to allow ships to reach its jetty.

Remedies, as in private nuisance, include damages and an injunction.

Comparing private nuisance and public nuisance

As we said earlier, private nuisance and public nuisance have little in common, although an unlawful activity on the part of the defendant can amount to both. Differences between the two include:

- public nuisance is both a crime and a tort, whereas private nuisance is actionable only in the civil courts as a tort

- private nuisance protects a claimant's interest in his land (remember that only someone with an interest in land can sue), whereas public nuisance can protect those without any relevant interest in land

- private nuisance may only affect a single individual, whereas public nuisance must affect an entire class

- public nuisance allows recovery for damages for personal injury, whereas private nuisance does not

- prescription can be used as a defence to an action in private nuisance, but not as a defence in an action for public nuisance, as a defendant cannot acquire the right to commit a crime.

Topic illustration

Consider again the scenario concerning Johnsons and their neighbours:

> Residents living in the vicinity of the Johnsons factory had been complaining for some time of noise and vibration coming from the factory, especially at night. When an explosion occurred in the factory one morning, a thick cloud of smoke spread rapidly across the town, leaving a dirty, oily deposit on houses and other buildings.

A discussion of public nuisance in relation to this scenario is likely to be briefer than any discussion relating to private nuisance, but we can probably identify the following elements:

- Given that the whole town is affected, there would appear to constitute a class of Her Majesty's subjects.

- Equally, there appears to be a common injury in the form, for instance, of a threat to health from the lack of sleep and the thick smoke.

- Concluding remarks would include a discussion of who could bring an action (probably only the Attorney-General in the absence of an individual householder suffering damage over and above everybody else) and what remedies might be granted.

> **Key cases**
>
> **Tate & Lyle Industries v Greater London Council (1983):** individual can sue for damages in public nuisance if his injury or loss is over and above the injury or loss suffered by the public.

	Activities

1 Given the wide definition of public nuisance, consider what events you have seen in the media recently that might give rise to such a liability.

2 Clara lives on a farm just outside a small village, and she runs an art studio in one of the barns. In each of the last several years, she has organised a country arts fair that has become steadily more popular and well attended. Last year's event attracted so many visitors that the road in the village was partially blocked by parked cars, and people were coming and going throughout the weekend. One of the villagers, Debbie, was particularly inconvenienced, as the normal access to her animal feeds business was blocked and she had to use an old farm track at great inconvenience and expense. Consider Clara's liability, if any, in public nuisance.

You should now be able to:

■ explain the nature of public nuisance

■ examine the differences between a claim in private nuisance and a claim in public nuisance.

In this topic, you will learn how to:

■ identify when the rule in *Rylands* v *Fletcher* applies

■ identify and explain the elements needed to claim under the rule in *Rylands* v *Fletcher*

■ identify defences and remedies appropriate to a claim under the rule in *Rylands* v *Fletcher*.

Key cases

Rylands v Fletcher (1868): defendant is liable if, on his land, he accumulates a dangerous substance during the course of a non-natural use of that land, and the substance escapes and causes damage.

Transco plc v Stockport MBC (2003): *Rylands* is a type of nuisance.

3 The rule in *Rylands* v *Fletcher*

The rule in *Rylands* v *Fletcher* originates in an 1868 House of Lords case of that name. It states that a defendant is liable if, on his land, he accumulates a dangerous thing in the course of a non-natural use of that land, and the thing escapes and causes reasonably foreseeable damage.

In **Rylands v Fletcher (1868)** itself, the defendant was the owner of a water mill who contracted with builders to construct a reservoir to guarantee a water supply to the mill. The builders sealed the bottom of the reservoir carelessly so that when it was filled, water leaked into the mine shafts below and from there escaped through connecting tunnels into the claimant's mines, causing considerable damage. The defendant was held liable for the escape.

There are two aspects to this liability that should be mentioned at the beginning. The first is that the rule in *Rylands* v *Fletcher* is one of strict liability. In *Rylands* v *Fletcher* itself, the defendant was liable for the actions of his independent contractors even though there was no fault on his part.

The second aspect is that the House of Lords confirmed in **Transco plc v Stockport MBC (2003)** that the rule is a sub-species (type) of nuisance. The significance of this is that a number of the rules that apply to private nuisance should therefore also apply to the rule in *Rylands* v *Fletcher*, and we will see this as we discuss some of the elements required to establish liability.

The Transco case itself involved a water pipe that was owned by the defendant and that supplied water to a block of flats. The pipe leaked, and the water washed away the earth supporting a gas pipe owned by the claimant, who then had to spend a considerable amount of money making the pipe safe. In the event, the claim in *Rylands* v *Fletcher* failed as the claimant, as we will see, was unable to show a number of the necessary elements.

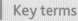

Bringing an action under the rule in *Rylands* v *Fletcher*

To establish liability in *Rylands* v *Fletcher*, a claimant needs to show each of the following elements:

1 claimant's legal position
2 accumulation
3 a dangerous thing
4 non-natural use
5 escape
6 reasonably foreseeable damage.

1 Claimant's legal position

Following the Transco case, discussed above, if it is the case that *Rylands* v *Fletcher* is a sub-species of private nuisance then a claimant should have a legal interest in the land affected by the escape. This follows from the decision in *Hunter* v *Canary Wharf* (1997), which we discussed under private nuisance above.

2 Accumulation

The defendant must voluntarily bring onto his land an **accumulation** of the substance that escaped. This requirement covers an artificial accumulation of material (whether the material itself is natural or not) but not a natural accumulation, such as a lake (unless the escape occurs because of non-natural processes, e.g. rock-blasting as against rock erosion). In **Giles v Walker (1890)** the defendant ploughed up his land, which then became self-sown with thistles, which in turn spread to neighbouring land. The defendant was not liable as the accumulation of thistles was natural and not artificial.

Liability exists only if the accumulation is on land the defendant controls, perhaps as an owner or a tenant. 'Land' has a relaxed meaning: various cases have suggested it can include the public highway, leaking pipes belonging to the defendant but running across the claimant's land, and a boat moored on a river that was being used for storing fireworks.

3 A dangerous thing

The substance accumulated must be dangerous – in other words, something likely to do mischief if it escapes. This includes obviously hazardous materials, such as chemicals and explosives, but also less threatening substances, such as water, if they are stored in bulk (as, of course, was the case in *Rylands* itself). Other case law examples include gas, electricity, oil. An unusual example is **Hale v Jennings Bros (1938)** in which the escaping object was a chair from a 'chair-o-plane' fairground attraction that had flown away from its moorings mid-ride.

An alternative definition of this requirement, discussed by the House of Lords in **Transco plc v Stockport MBC (2003)**, is that the accumulated substance should be something that poses an 'exceptional risk'. In that case, the water flowing through a pipe was not something that posed an exceptional risk should it escape and this was one of the grounds on which the claimant failed.

4 Non-natural use

A non-natural use does not mean a use that is artificial or man-made, but rather a use that is not commonplace. In **Rickards v Lothian (1913)** a tap overflowed in a part of the building leased by the defendant, and the water escaped to a lower level, damaging the claimant's goods. The defendant was not liable, as a tap supplied by a pipe was an ordinary and reasonable use of a building.

Key terms

The rule in *Rylands* v *Fletcher*: action available to a person who has suffered losses because of an escape of a dangerous substance from the defendant's land.

Accumulation: gathering together of a large amount of a material; in *Rylands* v *Fletcher*, any accumulation should be man-made.

A dangerous thing: something likely to do a mischief if it escapes.

A non-natural use: use which is man-made and which is unusual.

Study tip

Use the elements discussed in the text as a framework for an answer in an exam. Consider each in turn, citing cases where possible.

Key cases

Giles v Walker (1890): defendant is not liable for the escape of a substance that had accumulated naturally.

Hale v Jennings Bros (1938): 'dangerous thing' can consist of many and varied items, in this case the chair from a 'chair-o-plane' fairground ride.

Transco plc v Stockport MBC (2003): a 'dangerous thing' is one which poses an exceptional risk if it escapes.

Rickards v Lothian (1913): for the purposes of *Rylands*, a non-natural use does not include an ordinary use of the land.

Key cases

Cambridge Water v Eastern Counties Leather (1994): bulk storage of chemicals is the classic case of a non-natural use.

Read v Lyons & Co. (1946): there is no escape if the substance does not leave the land controlled by the defendant.

Cambridge Water v Eastern Counties Leather (1994): only loss or damage that is reasonably foreseeable as a consequence of an escape can be claimed.

Key terms

Escape: for the purposes of *Rylands* v *Fletcher*, an escape is when the dangerous substance leaves land controlled by the defendant.

The same point was made in *Transco plc* v *Stockport MBC* (2003) where some members of the House of Lords rephrased the requirement as a use that is 'extraordinary and unusual'. Thus, the claimant in that case failed to satisfy the requirement, as supplying water to a block of flats was an ordinary use.

An example of a non-natural use is provided by **Cambridge Water v Eastern Counties Leather (1994)**. The defendant was a long-established tannery. Chemicals from the process seeped through the concrete floor of the defendant's premises, and down through the earth until they reached a non-permeable layer of rock. At that point, the chemicals ran along the top of the layer, for about a mile and a half, until they reached the rock strata from which the claimant pumped water through a borehole. The chemicals contaminated the borehole, and the claimant was unable to use it and sued for substantial damages. The House of Lords stated that the bulk storage of chemicals to be used in an industrial process was almost the classic example of a non-natural use. (The claim ultimately failed on another ground.)

A recent example is *Harooni* v *Rustins* (2011) where the court felt that, while possessing a car with petrol in the tank or a can of paint did not amount to an extraordinary and unusual use of land, the storage of over 200,000 litres of flammable materials – including 25,000 litres of highly flammable materials – did amount to such a use. (The claim related to the spread of a fire, but failed on the ground that the fire had originated elsewhere.)

5 Escape

The claimant must show that the substance in question escaped, in other words it has moved from land the defendant controls to land that he does not. In **Read v Lyons & Co. (1946)**, the claimant was an inspector visiting the defendant's munitions factory. She was injured by an exploding shell, but her claim in *Rylands* failed, as she was still on the defendant's premises at the time and therefore there had been no escape.

6 Reasonably foreseeable damage

Only damage that is reasonably foreseeable is recoverable. This requirement was introduced by the House of Lords in **Cambridge Water v Eastern Counties Leather (1994)**, the facts of which we discussed above. The claimant's action in that case failed because it was not reasonably foreseeable that the defendant's activities would contaminate its springs.

As we have already said, the Transco case confirmed that *Rylands* v *Fletcher* is a sub-species of nuisance. Presumably, therefore, as in private nuisance, only damage to land and goods stored on the land can be recovered, and damage elsewhere and personal injury cannot be claimed. Not all of the older cases fit in with these ideas and in particular some of them, such as *Read* v *Lyons* (1946) (above), appear to assume that personal injury is recoverable.

Defences to a claim made under the rule in *Rylands* v *Fletcher*

There are a number of specific defences to a claim made under the rule in *Rylands* v *Fletcher*:

- act of a stranger
- act of God
- statutory authority
- further defences.

Act of a stranger

A defendant is not liable if the escape is caused by the deliberate and unforeseen **act of a stranger** – in other words, someone over whom the defendant has no control. In *Rickards* v *Lothian* (1913), discussed above, the defendant would not in any event have been liable for the damage caused by the overflowing water, because it was caused by the actions of a third party in turning on a tap and blocking the drain. Similarly, in **Perry v Kendricks Transport (1955)** the defendant was not liable for the consequences of an explosion caused by a third party placing a lit match in the petrol tank of one of the defendant's coaches.

Act of God

An **act of God** is a natural event so enormous that it cannot be either foreseen or guarded against. If an escape is caused by such an event, then the defendant is not liable as there is nothing he could have done to stop it. In **Nichols v Marsland (1876)** the defendant was not liable when water escaped from an artificial lake after a prolonged and violent rainstorm, the worst in living memory, caused the embankment of the lake to collapse under the pressure of the extra water.

Statutory authority

A defendant is not liable if the escape occurs during activities authorised by an Act of Parliament, provided negligence is not involved. In **Green v Chelsea Waterworks Company (1894)** the defendant was not liable when one of its water pipes burst and flooded the claimant's land. The defendant had a statutory duty to maintain a supply of water and, given that it was not negligent, it was not liable for the results of carrying out that duty.

Further defences

A defendant will avoid liability if the escape relates to something that was being maintained for the common benefit of the defendant and the claimant. A good example is a system of water pipes to different parts of a large building. A defendant will also avoid liability if the escape is due to the fault of the claimant. Finally, a claimant's damages will be reduced if the escape was partly his fault or if his damage is made worse because of the highly sensitive nature of his own property.

Topic illustration

Consider for a third time the scenario concerning Johnsons and their neighbours:

> Residents living in the vicinity of the Johnsons factory had been complaining for some time of noise and vibration coming from the factory, especially at night. When an explosion occurred in the factory one morning, a thick cloud of smoke spread rapidly across the town, leaving a dirty, oily deposit on houses and other buildings.

Clearly, there is the possibility of a claim under the rule in *Rylands* v *Fletcher*. Any discussion of this liability will probably cover the following points:

- As with private nuisance, many of the residents will qualify as claimants as they own their own properties. Similarly, Johnsons is the defendant, as it is its activities that caused the explosion.

- The elements necessary for a claim need to be identified: accumulation (although we do not know exactly what, something must have been brought into the factory to cause an explosion), a dangerous substance (it has exploded), a non-natural use of the premises, an escape (an oily deposit has been left on buildings) and reasonably foreseeable damage.

> **Key terms**

Act of a stranger: defence to a claim in *Rylands* v *Fletcher*, when the escape has been caused by the actions of a third party that the defendant neither foresaw or could control.

Act of God: natural event so powerful that precautions cannot be taken.

> **Key cases**

Perry v Kendricks Transport (1955): defendant is not liable if an escape is caused by the action of a third party who is beyond the foresight or control of the defendant.

Nichols v Marsland (1876): defendant will escape liability if he can show that any escape was caused by an act of God.

Green v Chelsea Waterworks Company (1894): defendant will escape liability if he can show that his activities were authorised by an Act of Parliament.

Finally, we need to discuss defences (it is not easy to identify one on the facts of this case) and remedies (damages, to put right any loss, but not an injunction as presumably the explosion was an isolated event that will not happen again).

■ Activity

Read this case study, which was taken from a past AQA exam paper, and then consider the rights and remedies of the owners of the cottages, including Irene, in connection with the problems caused by the leisure activities and the oil spill.

Previously a quiet lake overlooked by a few cottages, Greenwater has recently been developed by its owner, Highlife Sports, to provide extensive leisure facilities, including swimming and powerboating. In consequence, the owners of the cottages, including Irene, have experienced a large increase in noise, especially at weekends and during frequent competition weeks, when traffic and parking problems have also made it difficult for them to leave or return to their properties. Additionally, damage to a diesel storage tank owned by Highlife Sports resulted in a leak that caused extensive contamination of Irene's vegetable garden.

You should now be able to:

■ explain the nature of *Rylands* v *Fletcher* in relation to isolated escapes

■ identify and apply the requirements for a claim under the rule in *Rylands* v *Fletcher*.

19 Vicarious liability

Key terms

Vicarious liability: when one person is liable for a tort committed by another.

Strict liability: when a defendant can be held liable even though not at fault.

Joint liability: when two defendants are each liable for the whole of a judgement. The claimant can sue which he pleases, and the defendants can then apportion liability between themselves.

Introduction

Vicarious liability is when the law makes one person liable for a tort committed by another. In order for this to happen, there should be some sort of legal relationship between the two people, and the tort should in some way be connected to that relationship.

Examples of vicarious liability include business partners, who can be liable for each other's torts; and a principal, who can be liable for a tort committed by his agent. However, the most important example, and the only one required for the examination, is that an employer is liable for any tort committed by one of his employees during the course of employment.

Justification for vicarious liability

Vicarious liability is a form of **strict liability** because an employer remains liable for the actions of his employees even though the employer may not be at fault. This might seem harsh, but reasons for the existence of vicarious liability include:

- **Protecting the claimant:** an employer is much more likely than an employee to have the resources, including insurance, to meet any claim. In addition, a claimant may not be able to identify the precise employee involved, but this does not matter if he can sue the employer instead. One example is medical negligence, where it may be difficult to identify which hospital employee was to blame for an accident, but the patient can sue the hospital itself.
- **Protecting the employee:** as an employer is also liable if the person injured by a negligent employee is another employee, vicarious liability should encourage the employer to devise and enforce appropriate safety standards. In addition, vicarious liability ensures that an unscrupulous employer cannot escape liability by making his employees take any risks and then face any legal consequences.

Liability of the employee

Vicarious liability does not extinguish the employee's liability, and he remains **jointly liable**, with his employer, for his actions. In theory, the claimant can choose to sue the employee, but, as we have said, he is much more likely to sue the employer because the employer has the resources to pay any damages awarded.

In addition, an employer, having been sued, can sue the employee in turn under the provisions of the Civil Liability (Contributions) Act 1978. There is usually little point in doing this as, again, the employee does not have the personal resources to meet a major claim, but the employee may be subject to disciplinary procedures or even dismissed.

Establishing vicarious liability against an employer

To establish vicarious liability against an employer, a claimant must show three things.

The first is that the employee has committed a tort. The claimant must show the existence of the elements of whichever tort is alleged, as if he were suing the employee himself. So if, for instance, the claimant were

Study tip

When answering a question relating to vicarious liability, consider first whether the worker has committed a tort. Then go on to consider whether he is an employee and whether his act was in the course of his employment.

suing for negligence, he would need to show the normal negligence requirements of duty, breach and causation. Note that if the employee could have used a defence, such as contributory negligence, then the employer will be able to use the same defence.

Having established the relevant tort, the claimant must then show secondly that the worker concerned has employee status, and thirdly that the employee committed the tort during the course of his employment. We will now discuss these second and third requirements.

Topic illustration

Consider this scenario, taken from a past AQA exam paper:

> A year after Gita bought a new car, the manufacturer announced that the paint finish on certain models of that car would not maintain its desired appearance. The manufacturer offered, for three months, to fund the cost of a respray. The retailer from whom Gita bought her car was no longer in business and so she took her car to Frank. Frank asked Henry to find out whether Gita's model of car was affected. Henry consulted the manufacturer's list and decided that Gita's model was not affected. However, he had not realised that there was a more recent, amended list which did include Gita's model. By the time that the mistake was discovered, the manufacturer's offer had ended and Gita's car was worth £2,000 less than it should have been.

To work out if Gita is to make a claim against Frank in vicarious liability, you first need to establish the framework of the case:

- The first step is to identify the person who made the mistake, and to consider whether that person is liable. In this case, Henry gave wrong information to Gita, and this caused her a financial loss. To decide whether Henry is personally liable for his actions you need to apply the rules relating to economic loss in the context of a negligent misstatement.

- If Henry is liable, the issue is then whether Gita can sue Frank. This requires a discussion of whether Henry is an employee and whether he was acting in the course of his employment.

In this topic, you will learn how to:

- identify the difference between an employee and an independent contractor

- explain the approaches that are open to a court when identifying an employee and an independent contractor.

Key terms

Employee: worker who is employed and has a contract of employment.

Independent contractor: worker who is self-employed.

1 Who is an employee?

A worker is someone who performs services in return for payment. There are two types of worker: **employees** and **independent contractors** (those who are self-employed). The distinction is critical because an employer is vicariously liable for an employee but not for an independent contractor.

The basic definition is that an employee works under a contract of service (an employment contract), and an independent contractor works under a contract for services. In most circumstances, the difference between the two will be obvious – for instance, a teacher at a school and an assistant in a shop are employees of the school and the shop respectively, whereas a plumber and a decorator working in someone's house are independent contractors and are not employees of the householder. Equally, there is a clear difference between a freelance reporter (who contributes articles to various newspapers, and who is an independent contractor) and a journalist (who works full time for one newspaper, and who is an employee), even though both are performing the same service as reporters.

However, there are a number of awkward examples where it is less clear whether a worker is an employee or an independent contractor. Examples include casual workers (people who only work irregularly), those working on commission (who may therefore be working for themselves), consultants, freelance workers (people who work for a number of different employers) and agency workers (staff such as secretaries and cleaners who are supplied by an agency to a business which has a temporary shortage). In order to decide whether the employer is vicariously liable for such workers, the courts need to determine their status, but there is no single, simple test to decide this.

Employee or independent contractor – the traditional approaches

Originally, the courts used the **control test** to decide if someone was an employee or an independent contractor. This test states that an independent contractor is someone who is told only what to do, whereas an employee is told not only what to do but how to do it.

An example is **Walker v Crystal Palace Football Club (1909)** in which the court held that a professional footballer was an employee because his employer maintained a high degree of control over training schedules and procedures, play on the field and personal discipline.

Although this test works for many categories of worker, its major fault is that it does not deal adequately with professional or highly skilled workers. A lawyer employed by a local authority and a doctor employed by an NHS Trust are clearly employees, but as they were employed for their expertise they would not be told how to do their job.

One attempt to solve this problem raised by the control test was the **integration test**. It states that the more closely a worker is involved with the core business of the employer, the more likely he is to be an employee. The doctor employed by the NHS is clearly central to the purpose of the NHS, and therefore is an employee. However, the test has problems of its own, not least that it is not always certain who is integral to the employer's business and who is not – or even what the employer's business is.

Neither the control test nor the integration test therefore provides an answer to every case, but the courts still use both control and integration as factors when applying the multiple test.

Employee or independent contractor – the multiple test

The **multiple test** is the modern approach to classifying a worker, and it reflects the reality that there is no single way of telling employees and independent contractors apart. In those cases where it is not clear which a particular worker is, because some factors suggest that he is an independent contractor and some suggest that he is an employee, the courts weigh up the two sets of factors and decide which set outweighs the other.

Factors that the court may look at include:

- whether the worker is paid a regular salary or is paid on commission
- whether the worker pays income tax and national insurance contributions as an employee or as a self-employed person
- whether the contract describes the worker as an employee or not
- whether the worker has the ability to delegate his work to another without permission.

In addition, an independent contractor is more likely to work from his own premises, have his own equipment, hire his own helpers and be personally affected by his own investment and management decisions.

A good example of the business approach is **Ready Mix Concrete v Minister of Pensions (1968)**. The workers in question were lorry drivers for the employer. A number of factors suggested that they were

Study tip

A question may tell you that a worker is an employee. If that happens, do not spend much time discussing the rules in this section, but concentrate instead on the tort that the employee has committed and whether it was in the course of his employment.

Key terms

Control test: employee is a worker who is told not only what to do, but how to do it.

Integration test: employee is a worker who is closely involved with the main business of the employer.

Multiple test: approach whereby the court, having considered all the facts of a case, decides whether the overall picture of a worker is closer to an employee or to an independent contractor.

Key cases

Walker v Crystal Palace Football Club (1909): a worker is an employee if he satisfies the control test, in other words his employer tells him both what to do and how to do it.

Ready Mix Concrete v Minister of Pensions (1968): the multiple test involves the court considering all the facts of a case before deciding whether a worker is an employee or an independent contractor.

employees: they wore a company uniform; their lorries were painted in company colours; they had to follow instructions given by the company; and they could not work for anyone else. Against that, the drivers owned their own lorries, were responsible for keeping them repaired, paid the running costs of the lorries and could employ a substitute driver to carry out their deliveries. The court decided that the drivers were independent contractors because the fact that they owned their own major assets (the vehicles) and the fact that the amount of profit they made depended on their own decisions (e.g. where to buy petrol, where to get repairs carried out and whether to employ substitute drivers) effectively made them small businessmen trading for themselves.

The multiple test can be uncertain because each case is different and because the courts take a variety of factors into account, and sometimes it is difficult to predict the outcome of a case. However, there appear to be three factors that must exist before a worker can be classified as an employee, and if one is missing then a worker is an independent contractor. (The reverse, however, is not true: even if all three are present, the courts might decide that other factors indicate that a worker is nevertheless an independent contractor.)

The first is control. This does not mean the degree of control required by the old control test, but it does mean that the employer is, to some degree, in charge of the worker and the work being carried out.

The second is that under the contract the worker gives **personal performance** – in other words, he cannot delegate his job to someone else. In **Echo and Express Publication v Tanton (1999)**, therefore, the Court of Appeal decided that a van driver who was able to employ someone else to do his job if he were unavailable was an independent contractor.

The third is **mutuality of obligation** between the employer and the worker. This means that the employer has a legal obligation to pay the worker, and the worker has a corresponding obligation to be available to work within the terms of the contract. Neither can choose on a particular day not to be an employer or a worker. In **Carmichael v National Power (1999)** the worker worked as a tour guide at a power station. However, the company only contacted her when her services were needed, she was able to refuse to attend on a particular day, and she was paid by the hour for the work she actually did. Thus, neither side had a legal obligation to the other and, on that basis, the House of Lords decided that she was an independent contractor even though she wore a company uniform and was entitled to shares under the company's employee share scheme.

A final issue is a worker's written contract of employment. The courts are aware that an employer might word the contract in such a way that it appears his workers are independent contractors, thus allowing the employer to avoid the responsibilities he would have in respect of his employees. In **Autoclenz Ltd v Belcher (2011)** the Supreme Court made it clear that if this had happened, then a court should act on the true agreement between the two parties rather than the written agreement. In that case, the workers were valeters for a car-cleaning business. Their contracts of employments specifically said that they were not obliged to come in to work and that they could send along a substitute in their place. On the face of it, they would appear to be independent contractors. However, the Supreme Court decided that the workers were in fact employees, on the ground that the written contracts did not reflect the true contract under which the claimants worked, as they had never actually declined to come into work on a particular day, nor had they sent in a substitute.

Key terms

Personal performance: worker undertakes the promised services himself, rather than delegating them to someone else to do.

Mutuality of obligation: employer and the worker each have an obligation to the other in respect of a contract of employment.

Key cases

Echo and Express Publication v Tanton (1999): if a worker is able to delegate his duties, he is not an employee.

Carmichael v National Power (1999): if an employer is not obliged to offer work, and a worker is not obliged to undertake any work offered, then the worker is not an employee.

Autoclenz Ltd v Belcher (2011): when deciding if a worker is an employee or an independent contractor, a court will disregard a 'sham' written contract and will look to the true agreement between the parties.

Topic illustration

Consider again the scenario concerning Frank, Henry and Gita:

> A year after Gita bought a new car, the manufacturer announced that the paint finish on certain models of that car would not maintain its desired appearance. The manufacturer offered, for three months, to fund the cost of a respray. The retailer from whom Gita bought her car was no longer in business and so she took her car to Frank. Frank asked Henry to find out whether Gita's model of car was affected. Henry consulted the manufacturer's list and decided that Gita's model was not affected. However, he had not realised that there was a more recent, amended list which did include Gita's model. By the time that the mistake was discovered, the manufacturer's offer had ended and Gita's car was worth £2,000 less than it should have been.

Assuming Henry is personally liable for negligent misstatement, Gita needs to know whether he is an employee of Frank's before she can proceed against Frank for vicarious liability.

▓ Unhelpfully, if deliberately on the part of the examiner who set the paper, we are told nothing about the status of Henry. We have no information on, for instance, how he is paid or even if he is paid at all, how many hours he does and whether his work is regular.

▓ In these circumstances, we can only describe the rules relating to the identification of employees and independent contractors and explain the consequences of Henry being one or the other.

You should now be able to:

■ explain and discuss the control test, the integration test and the multiple test

■ identify factors which a judge might use when considering whether a worker is an independent contractor or an employee.

2 Course of employment

An employer is only liable for an employee acting in the course of his employment. This appears to include three situations:

▓ an authorised act

▓ an authorised act, even when it is carried out in an unauthorised manner

▓ an act that, while it is not part of an employee's job, is nevertheless so closely connected with the employment that it is fair and just to hold the employer liable.

We will look at each of these in turn, before considering the specific problem of road traffic accidents caused by an employee's negligence.

Authorised acts

An employer is vicariously liable for any **authorised act** of his employee that amounts to a tort.

An employer is not therefore vicariously liable if an employee undertakes an **unauthorised act** – in other words, an act that is not part of his job

In this topic, you will learn how to:

■ distinguish between authorised acts and unauthorised acts

■ consider the term 'course of employment' in relation to a variety of scenarios.

▓ **Study tip**

Even if you conclude that a worker is not an employee, you should nevertheless go on to discuss the rules relating to course of employment.

Key terms

Authorised act: act carried out by the employee on the instructions of the employer.

Unauthorised act: act carried out by the employee without instructions from the employer, either express or implied.

Key cases

Beard v London General Omnibus (1900): an employer is not vicariously liable for an unauthorised act on the part of an employee.

Harvey v RG O'Dell Ltd (1958): an employer can be vicariously liable for acts he impliedly authorised.

Century Insurance v Northern Ireland Road Transport Board (1942): an employee acts within the course of his employment even if he carries out his duties negligently.

Limpus v London General Omnibus (1863): an employer can be vicariously liable for an authorised act even when the employee has carried it out in a manner that the employer has expressly forbidden.

Lister v Hesley Hall Ltd (2001): an employer is vicariously liable for the criminal acts of an employee if those acts are so closely connected to what the employee was employed to do that it is fair and just to hold the employer responsible.

Mattis v Pollock (2003): an employer will be vicariously liable, even for actions strictly outside the place of work, if the sequence of events began at work and the employee had been encouraged to act in a particular way.

and that he was not unauthorised to do. In **Beard v London General Omnibus (1900)** the conductor of a bus took it upon himself to turn a bus around, during the course of which he injured a member of the public through his negligent driving. The employer was not vicariously liable as the conductor was not employed to drive, and his acts were therefore unauthorised.

Vicarious liability can exist for an act of an employee that is only impliedly authorised and that only benefits the employee rather than furthering the employer's work. In **Harvey v RG O'Dell Ltd (1958)** the employee had been sent out on a repair job that would last all day. At lunch time, he rode his bike into the nearest town to get lunch, but his negligence caused an accident during the return journey. The employer was vicariously liable for the employee's negligence, even though it happened at a time when the employee was not actually working on his tasks, because on a day-long assignment it would be necessary to travel out to find lunch.

Vicarious liability can even exist where the employee is carrying out an authorised act, but in a careless or incorrect fashion. A good example of this is **Century Insurance v Northern Ireland Road Transport Board (1942)**. The worker, a petrol tanker driver, was making a delivery to a petrol station when he lit a cigarette and discarded the match. This caused a fire, then an explosion, and there was considerable damage to property. The employer was vicariously liable for this damage because the employee was carrying out his authorised duties, albeit in a highly negligent way.

An unauthorised act using an expressly forbidden method

An employer is vicariously liable for an authorised act carried out by his employee, even when the authorised act has been carried out in a manner that the employer has expressly forbidden. In **Limpus v London General Omnibus (1863)** the defendant bus company had expressly told its drivers not to obstruct or race buses from rival companies. In contravention of this instruction, the driver in question manoeuvred his bus in such a way as to obstruct a rival bus, and in so doing injured one of the horses drawing the other vehicle. The employer was vicariously liable because at the time of the accident the driver was acting for his employer's business, and the fact that he was doing so in a forbidden way was irrelevant.

An act 'so closely connected' to the employment

Although the traditional approach is that an employer should be vicariously liable for an authorised act but not for an unauthorised act, this must now be considered in the light of the decision in **Lister v Hesley Hall Ltd (2001)**. The employee, a warden of a children's home, subjected a number of the boys in his care to systematic sexual abuse. Using traditional principles, the employer would not be vicariously liable as the abuse was clearly not an authorised act. However, the House of Lords introduced a new test: were the acts of the employee so closely connected with his employment that it was fair and just to hold the employer liable? Applying that test, the employer was vicariously liable for the abuse as the warden's job as a carer was inseparable from his acts as an abuser.

The House of Lords were probably influenced by a wish to make sure the boys received compensation, but the new test represents an extension of liability in this area, and it has been used in a number of subsequent cases. In **Mattis v Pollock (2003)** a doorman at a nightclub was involved in a heated and violent row with a group of customers including the claimant. The doorman escaped to his flat nearby and armed himself with a knife. Returning to the scene, set on revenge, the doorman stabbed the claimant several times, paralysing him. The nightclub was vicariously liable because it had encouraged the doorman to be aggressive and because the stabbing, although it took place outside the club, was the conclusion of a sequence of events that had begun in the club and that were closely connected to the doorman's employment.

The 'so closely connected' test was considered in a pair of cases heard together by the Court of Appeal: **Weddall v Barchester Healthcare (2012)** and **Wallbank v Wallbank Fox Designs (2012)**. In the *Weddall* case, the claimant was on duty at a care home and phoned another employee, who was at home, to ask for help. However, the second employee was drunk, was unable to help, and decided that the claimant was mocking him. He therefore went to the care home and violently assaulted the claimant. The employer was not vicariously liable for the assault because it was an independent venture, distinct from his employment and wholly unconnected with his role in the care home.

By contrast, in the *Wallbank* case the claimant, a manager at a furniture factory, reprimanded an employee for his uneconomical use of an oven. The employee promptly attacked him. The employer was vicariously liable for this assault as it was closely related to the attacker's employment in time and space, and it was an instantaneous reaction to something that had happened during the course of his employment. It was therefore incidental to, rather than unconnected to, the employment.

Road traffic accidents

A common example of vicarious liability is when an employer is liable for the negligent driving of one of his employees. Journeys to and from work are generally outside the course of employment, but road journeys made during working hours will normally be covered. Two specific issues commonly arise: giving a lift to an unauthorised person and making a detour. In both instances, whether the driver is acting in the course of his employment will depend on the individual facts of the case.

Dealing first with unauthorised lifts, an example is **Conway v Wimpey (1951)**. The defendant building company was a contractor in a major construction project, and its employees were driven around the site in the company's own lorries. However, there were notices in the cab of each lorry stating that drivers were not allowed to give lifts to employees of other companies, and the drivers had received verbal instructions to the same effect. On the day in question, the driver gave a lift to another company's employee, who was injured during the course of the journey by the driver's negligence. The defendant was not vicariously liable as the driver was carrying out an unauthorised act, an act that was not part of his job, namely giving a lift to someone he should not have.

A contrasting example is **Rose v Plenty (1975)**. The employer, a dairy, specifically forbade its milkmen, by means of prominent notices, to employ children when out making deliveries or to give them lifts on the milk floats. The milkman in question, in direct contravention of these instructions, employed the claimant, a thirteen-year-old boy, to help him make milk deliveries, and the claimant was injured through the milkman's negligent driving of his float. The defendant was held to be vicariously liable for these injuries because the court felt that, unlike *Conway*, the driver was carrying out an authorised act (delivering

Key cases

Weddall v Barchester Healthcare (2012) and **Wallbank v Wallbank Fox Designs (2012)**: whether an employer is vicariously liable for a violent employee will depend on how closely connected the assault was to the employment.

Conway v Wimpey (1951): an employer is not vicariously liable if his employee gives a lift to someone in circumstances where he is forbidden to do so.

Rose v Plenty (1975): an employer is vicariously liable if his employee gives a lift to someone while otherwise going about his duties, and the passenger contributes to those duties.

Key terms

A frolic of his own: unauthorised act on the part of an employee that is separate from his duties and for which the employer is not vicariously liable.

Key cases

Storey v Ashton (1869): an employer is not vicariously liable for an employee driver who embarks on a frolic of his own – in other words, undertakes a journey that is separate from anything the employer has asked him to do.

A&W Hemphill v Williams (1966): an employer is vicariously liable for a deviation by a driver from the normal route as long as the detour is connected to the employer's business and is not too great in extent.

milk) albeit in an unauthorised way (using a forbidden assistant). A further factor that influenced the court is that the claimant in *Rose* was effectively contributing to the defendant's business (by delivering milk) whereas the claimant in *Conway* was not.

The other issue is deviation from a set route. Whether the driver remains in the course of employment depends on the degree of deviation and whether he remains on his employer's business or is setting about something quite different ('on **a frolic of his own**' to use the Victorian phrase). In **Storey v Ashton (1869)**, for example, the driver and a clerk were asked to deliver wine, but on the return journey, they deviated significantly from the route in order to carry out a personal errand for the clerk. During the detour, a member of the public was injured due to the driver's negligence. The employer was held not to be vicariously liable as the detour amounted to a new and independent journey and was not made for the employer's business.

A different result was reached in **A&W Hemphill v Williams (1966)**. The driver of a lorry was transporting some boys back home after a camping expedition. At the request of the boys, the driver made a detour from the normal route home, and during the deviation an accident happened in which the claimant, one of the boys, was seriously injured. The employer of the driver was held to be vicariously liable because the driver was still carrying out his central task, taking the boys home, even though he had deviated from the proper route.

Topic illustration

Consider for a third time the scenario relating to Frank, Henry and Gita:

> A year after Gita bought a new car, the manufacturer announced that the paint finish on certain models of that car would not maintain its desired appearance. The manufacturer offered, for three months, to fund the cost of a respray. The retailer from whom Gita bought her car was no longer in business and so she took her car to Frank. Frank asked Henry to find out whether Gita's model of car was affected. Henry consulted the manufacturer's list and decided that Gita's model was not affected. However, he had not realised that there was a more recent, amended list which did include Gita's model. By the time that the mistake was discovered, the manufacturer's offer had ended and Gita's car was worth £2,000 less than it should have been.

At this stage, we are assuming both that Henry is personally liable for negligent misstatement and that he is an employee of Frank. Gita now needs to establish whether Henry's actions were in the course of his employment.

■ The first step is to ask whether Henry's acts were authorised. They would appear to be so, as Frank asked him to find out the position in relation to Gita's car.

■ There may be a place for a discussion of whether Henry carried out an unauthorised act but in an unauthorised manner, as Frank presumably did not mean Henry to use an out-of-date manufacturer's list.

■ However, one way or the other, Frank would appear to be vicariously liable as Henry's acts were authorised. We simply now need to explain the consequences for Frank, namely that he is liable for Gita's financial loss.

Activities

1 Do you think that it is fair that the employer in *Lister* v *Hesley Hall Ltd* should be liable given that it was unaware of the warden's activities?

2 Consider this problem, which raises the issue of vicarious liability:

Andrew was a historian engaged as a consultant by a national newspaper, *The Recorder*. He was shown diaries alleged to have been written in the 19th century by a famous soldier. The diaries were not previously known to exist. After extensive research, Andrew concluded that the diaries were genuine and *The Recorder* publicised his conclusions in a front page story. This was read by Beth who then bought the diaries at an auction for £50,000. Soon afterwards, Beth allowed other historians to examine them, and it was very rapidly discovered that the diaries were definitely not genuine and were, in fact, worthless forgeries. By that time, the forger had disappeared with the money. Consider the following questions:

a Which tort has Andrew perhaps committed? Do you think that he is in fact liable for that tort?

b Is Andrew an employee, and who is the employer? What reasons would you give for your conclusions?

c Was Andrew acting within the course of his employment? Give reasons for your answer.

You should now be able to:

■ identify the rules that govern when an act is part of an employee's course of employment

■ explain how the rules operate in relation to both negligent and criminal acts of employees.

Practice questions

Example question 1 (AQA, June 2012)

Read this scenario and answer **both** questions.

You should write in continuous prose, give reasoned answers, and make reference to cases, statutes and examples where appropriate.

Dale's friend, Imran, was an investment consultant and both of them were members of a tennis club. While they were at the club, Dale asked Imran for advice on the investment of £100,000. Imran advised Dale, free of charge, to invest all the money in Fortuna Co, which Dale later did. Without Imran's knowledge, Dale also told his neighbour, Mick, of Imran's advice. Mick then invested £10,000 in the company. Two months later, the company collapsed and Dale and Mick lost all their money.

Rocco, the manager of the tennis club, bought a TV set, manufactured by Goodview, for use by members in the club bar. When Dale was at the club, he switched on the TV, which exploded. Glass from the shattered TV screen cut Dale's face and damaged his clothes. The explosion was caused by a fault in the TV wiring circuit. The wiring circuit had recently been developed by Goodview, although research carried out by the company prior to manufacture had not detected this fault.

Ed was a lorry driver employed by Luigi. Luigi had told all his drivers not to use their mobile phones while driving. Ed was driving at speed on a busy road to make a delivery and was sending a text on his mobile. Ed lost control of his lorry, which swerved and crashed into the front wall of Mo's roadside cottage. As the wall collapsed, part of it fell on Mo. Jack, who had been driving behind Ed, ran into the cottage to help. He lifted the brickwork off Mo, who was screaming in pain from a broken leg and who was also covered in blood. Jack later suffered severe panic attacks.

1 **Consider the right and remedies, if any, of Dale and of Mick against Imran, and of Dale against Goodview.** *(25 marks)*

2 **Consider the rights and remedies, if any, of Mo and of Jack against Ed for their injuries. Consider whether Luigi may also be liable for those injuries.** *(25 marks)*

Example question 2 (AQA, June 2012)

Read this scenario and answer **both** questions.

You should write in continuous prose, give reasoned answers, and make reference to cases, statutes and examples where appropriate.

Rafa owned a small factory that produced equipment for hospitals. The factory was situated in a busy street with many shops, and it generated considerable noise, mainly in the afternoons. This annoyed Bob, the neighbouring owner of the only house in the street. He was particularly irritated if it interfered with his listening to music. The noise problem became even greater when Rafa, following a complaint by Bob, sometimes operated the factory at night. On one occasion, chemicals, which Rafa had purchased for use in his production process and stored near to the boundary of Bob's garden, leaked out of their containers. As a result, Bob's flowers and vegetables were ruined and the soil in his garden was contaminated.

Bob had recently considered raising the height of his fence because local boys had been entering his garden, but he had not yet done so. One night, Kurt, aged 15, scrambled over Bob's fence and climbed up his apple tree to steal apples. A branch gave way and Kurt fell to the ground on to the jagged edge of one of many bottles that Bob had thrown out. This caused Kurt to suffer a deep cut to his arm and severe bleeding. His wristwatch was also damaged. Shortly afterwards, Dr Weeks, a hospital consultant, injected Kurt with a drug to stop the bleeding. It was common medical practice to use this drug. However, some doctors disapproved of the use of this drug because, although it was very effective in stopping bleeding quickly, it occasionally caused the patient to suffer breathing difficulties. The following day, Kurt did suffer severe breathing problems due to the drug. As a result, he had to take several weeks off his Saturday delivery job, losing £200 in wages.

1   Consider the right and remedies, if any, of Bob against Rafa.

(25 marks)

2   Consider the right and remedies, if any, of Kurt against Bob and against Dr Weeks.

(25 marks)

Introduction

Chapters in this unit:

20 Law and morality

21 Law and justice

22 Judicial creativity

23 Fault

24 Balancing conflicting interests

1 The specification

The final section of Unit 4 is called 'Concepts of law'. This section requires you to review, from a different perspective, the areas of law you have already studied at AS and at A2. The AQA specification identifies five topics available for study. These are:

1 law and morality
2 law and justice
3 judicial creativity
4 fault
5 balancing conflicting interests.

2 Your study

The number of topics you study will be influenced very much by considerations of time, teacher preference, and your own interests and workload. You need to study a minimum of three topics to ensure that you can answer at least one question in the examination. The study of four topics will guarantee a choice of question, whereas coverage of all five topics will enable you to answer any question. Remember, however, that you are marked only on the question you choose to answer and not on knowledge of the other questions on the examination paper. Therefore consider carefully the appropriate number of topics to study and ultimately prepare.

In your coverage of these topics you will be drawing upon areas of law that you have already studied, as you will need them to illustrate your answer. It may be wise to draw the material from units that you are sitting at the same time, especially if you are resitting AS papers. There is no prescribed material that must be covered. Indeed, you may use illustrative material from outside the specification. The only requirement is that the material you use is relevant to the argument being developed.

You will find that the following five chapters contain a lot of information – too much for any individual student to be expected to cover. Don't worry. Select from these chapters the material that is relevant to your study. You will not be expected to cover all the material in every chapter in the examination.

3 The examination

In the examination, you will be asked to write one essay question from a choice of three. It is not possible to predict with any degree of certainty which three topics will appear on any one paper. The fact that a topic is not asked one year is no guarantee that it will appear on the paper the following year. The whole paper is two hours long, and you should have one hour to answer the Concepts of law questions. This means you will have time to reflect on the questions before deciding which one to answer. You will also have time to plan the answer for your selected question.

When planning and writing the essay, you should be conscious of the need to ensure that it contains some theory, usually by reference to the thoughts or writings of philosophers, academics and judges. Any law explained should be supported by reference to appropriate statutes and cases to illustrate the points being made. Refer to the facts of cases where these help to develop your discussion, but avoid merely writing detailed narratives of the cases without explaining their relevance. In addition, try to refer to other examples, not necessarily precedents, that you may have researched or discussed during your course. Finally, in your discussion do remember to address the particular question that is asked, and do not merely reproduce a prepared answer.

The essay will be marked according to

- the required explanation, and
- the quality of analysis or discussion.

It is possible to score highly under the first category by referring widely and in detail to relevant areas of law, and it may be possible to prepare most of this material with confidence as part of your revision and preparation. The quality of the discussion will be assessed by its relevance to the question, by its reference to theories of law that have been explained, and sometimes by your personal response to the issues posed by the question. It is possible that the question in the examination will be very different from any question you have already considered on the topic. Therefore, be prepared to take time to reflect on the particular nuance of the question in the examination.

In this topic, you will learn how to:

- explain theories of law and morality
- explain the characteristics of legal rules
- explain the characteristics of moral rules.

Key terms

Legal positivism: laws are valid where they are made by the recognised legislative power in the state; they do not have to satisfy any higher authority.

H.L.A Hart: leading 20th-century British legal philosopher and Professor of Jurisprudence at Oxford University; he developed a sophisticated theory of legal positivism, and wrote *The Concept of Law*.

Command theory of law: law is a command from a sovereign reinforced by a sanction.

1   An introduction to law and morality

Law

'Law' is not a word that lends itself to easy definition. For a start, the term is used in a general sense, in phrases such as 'English law', to mean 'all those rules of the state that govern our lives'. It is also used in a narrower sense to describe specific areas, such as 'the law of contract' which is concerned with agreements made between people, generally for the purchase and sale of goods or services. Another example is the law of tort which is to do with civil wrongs. However, these terms describe the substance, not the nature, of law. To discover what men believe law is, we need to look at two distinctive theories. These are legal positivism and natural law.

Legal positivism

The first of these theories is known as **legal positivism**. Positivists believe that a law is a legal rule which, if made in the manner recognised by the legislative power in the state, is valid – irrespective of its content. But each legal positivist has his own individual explanation of this theory, and these can diverge significantly – as we can see with the theories of John Austin and **H.L.A. Hart**.

Early in the 19th century, John Austin was appointed to the first chair of Jurisprudence at London University. He believed that once laws are made, or posited (put in place), they are binding upon people, whatever the morality of their content. In his words: 'The existence of law is one thing, its merit or demerit is another. A law which exists is a law, though we happen to dislike it.' Thus, we might find a law highly offensive, but that does not affect its validity.

Austin is perhaps best known for developing the **command theory of law**. He argued that a law is a command from a sovereign whom the population at large is in the habit of obeying, and it is reinforced by the availability of a sanction. Put simply, laws are orders backed by threats. In his view, a law is the expressed wish of the sovereign, and as such is distinguishable from other commands such as those from God or from an employer. The sovereign is the person or body whom others habitually obey, and who is not in the habit of giving obedience to anyone else.

Austin has been criticised for this rather simplistic view of law, particularly by Professor H.L.A. Hart, partly because it is difficult to identify a sovereign in many states but also because many areas of law such as contract law, which grant powers to people, do not fit neatly into such a definition. As a legal positivist, Hart insisted on the separation of law and morality, but he developed a much more sophisticated model than Austin's to explain the nature of law. There are, Hart argued, two categories of rules, called primary and secondary rules, which, in combination, form the basis of a functioning legal system.

Primary rules either impose legal obligations, as in criminal law, or they grant powers, as in the power to make a will, or the power to enter into a contract.

Secondary rules are concerned with the operation of primary legal rules. Hart identified three specific secondary rules. Firstly, the rule of recognition sets criteria for identifying primary legal rules. These criteria would include reference, for example, to Acts of Parliament and judicial decisions. Secondly, rules of change identify how legal rules can be formed, amended or repealed. For example, in the case of an Act of Parliament, reference would be made to the various readings in the House of Commons and the House of Lords, and to the need for royal assent. Thirdly, rules of adjudication enable the courts not only to settle disputes, but also to interpret the law.

Hart argues that a legal system is established by the union of these two sets of rules. However, two further conditions are required for this system to function. Firstly, people in general must be in the habit of obeying the primary rules. Secondly, public officials must accept the rules of recognition, change and adjudication.

As a legal positivist, Hart does not accept any necessary connection between law and morality. In other words, the validity of a law is not dependent upon its moral acceptability. Even a morally repugnant law may be legally valid. However, that does not mean we must obey laws that are morally repugnant. Obedience remains a matter of personal decision or conscience.

Natural law

Natural lawyers reject this: they believe that the validity of man-made laws depends upon their compatibility with a higher, moral authority, and where laws do not satisfy the requirements of this higher moral authority, those laws lack validity. There are, though, different views advanced on the precise nature of this higher moral authority. We shall explore two examples.

Thomas Aquinas was a 13th-century Catholic philosopher and theologian who devoted his life to scholarship, in particular to the study of Aristotle. His major work, the *Summa Theologica*, contains his explanation of four different types of law. The highest is eternal law: this governs everything within the universe, such as the law of gravity (although this was not known at the time of Aquinas), and includes general moral rules of conduct. Although we do not enjoy direct access to eternal law, we can acquire partial knowledge of it by reasoning upon the way that nature operates.

Divine law is concerned with the standards to which man must conform in order to attain salvation. These are revealed to mankind by inspiration or revelation, as, for example, the Ten Commandments contained within the Bible. Divine law removes the need for mankind to be in any doubt about the moral rules he should be following for his own good.

Natural law is derived from eternal law and deals with general rules of conduct that govern the behaviour of 'beings possessing reason and free will', i.e. humans. Natural law is implanted in us by God as part of our nature, and so we have a natural inclination to behave in a way that fulfils our purpose in life. This includes the inclination to preserve life, procreate, and live within society. By reasoning upon natural law, certain general rules of conduct can be developed. The first of these is to **do good and avoid evil**'. Some others are 'not to commit suicide', reflecting the inclination to preserve life; to 'rear and care for offspring', reflecting the inclination to procreate; and to 'develop our rational and moral capacities'.

Human law is derived by reason from natural law. It is the result of a process of applying the principles contained within natural law to particular geographical, historical and social circumstances. Thus, human laws may differ from society to society, but they should always conform to the spirit of natural law. Where they fail to achieve this, human laws are a perversion of law: they are laws in name only, and do not require obedience. In other words, human laws lack validity where they fail to conform to a higher authority – this authority being, for Aquinas, natural law. This illustrates a

> ### Key terms
>
> **Natural law:** higher authority to which man-made law must conform in order to be valid.
>
> **'Do good and avoid evil':** Thomas Aquinas's first and most important general rule of conduct derived from natural law.

Study tip

These notes provide detailed explanations of various philosophies. In the examination, identify and explain only the key points.

Key terms

Inner morality of law: describes the eight principles adopted by Lon Fuller. Laws must satisfy these eight principles, otherwise the legal system lacks validity.

key general point: posited law, human law in Aquinas's case, is dependent for its validity upon its conformity to a higher authority.

Lon Fuller (1902–1978) was Professor of Jurisprudence at Harvard Law School and wrote *The Morality of Law* in 1964, discussing the connection between law and morality. He is known as a natural lawyer in that he rejected legal positivism: he refused to accept the belief that law has no higher authority than that of a sovereign authority. Fuller, though, is not a natural lawyer in the tradition of Aquinas: for Fuller, law is earth-based.

Like Aquinas, Fuller views law as serving a purpose. In his case, that purpose is to 'achieve social order through subjecting people's conduct to the guidance of general rules by which they may themselves orient their behaviour'. For laws to be able to achieve this purpose, they must satisfy eight particular principles. These principles make up an '**inner morality of law**' which Fuller describes as a procedural version of natural law.

According to these eight principles, laws should be:

1 in existence, not ad hoc, i.e. only made to deal with a specific case
2 promulgated, i.e. published
3 prospective, rather than retrospective
4 clearly stated and comprehensible
5 consistent with each other
6 possible for people to obey
7 constant, i.e. relatively long-lasting and not constantly changing
8 applied and administered as stated.

Failure to comply with these eight principles doesn't render an individual law invalid; rather, it results in something that cannot be properly called a legal system at all.

Professor Hart, while not critical of the eight principles themselves, argued that Fuller was not justified in calling them a morality. He illustrates his objection by reference to the art of poisoning. Like law-making, poisoning is an activity with a purpose. The poisoner will develop principles to render his art effective. However, nobody would consider calling these principles the 'inner morality of poisoning'. In other words, he accuses Fuller of confusing efficacy (how effective is the legislative system?) with morality (is it good or bad?).

Morality

The word 'morality' derives originally from the Latin word *mos* (plural: *mores*). The standard meaning of this word is 'a custom, habit or usage that is determined by man's will rather than by law'. The Roman statesman and orator Cicero once wrote that law and custom (*mos*) must both be obeyed, illustrating their parity. Custom formed the bedrock of Roman society in Cicero's day, with duties and obligations balanced by rights and privileges. One example neatly illustrates this point: within the Roman patron–client system, leading men were regularly, often daily, attended by men of humbler origins. In return for assistance in humble matters, such as escorting them to the forum and voting for them when they stood for public office, these leading men would reciprocate by granting their attendants protection, advice and occasional acts of kindness. Often this relationship passed from one generation to the next, in this way forging strong family bonds between the leading families on the one hand and plebeians or freedmen on the other. This patron–client system was a significant factor in providing the integration between the social classes that gave the Roman Republic stability for many centuries.

This custom, like others, had a number of distinctive features. Firstly, it had no identifiable origin: rather, it developed into an accepted practice over a long period of time. Secondly, it constituted a course of conduct willingly practised by the majority. Thirdly, value was attached to it: it concerned not merely how people did behave, but also how they should behave. Fourthly, adherence to it was a matter for public judgement: reputations were damaged by failure to comply with its standards. Fifthly, being a custom it was not enshrined in law, but it was no less binding for that, even though enforcement was by social disapproval rather than by formal sanctions.

In short, this custom formed the basis of a code of conduct that reflected the expressed wishes of that society, and that members of the society accepted in large measure. It was therefore part of the morality of that age.

The Roman Republic was an example of what sociologist **Emile Durkheim** (1858–1917) would later refer to as a traditional society. In such a society, people had much in common. However, by Durkheim's day, society was becoming more fragmented. Firstly, labour was becoming specialised, with workers developing expertise in increasingly narrow fields, thereby becoming alienated from each other. Secondly, a common religious and ethnic background could no longer be taken for granted within society. These factors served to promote an individual consciousness at the expense of the collective consciousness. The speed of change, Durkheim argued, led to confusion in moral outlooks and to the breakdown of traditional norms of behaviour. Durkheim used the word 'anomie' to describe this result. He believed that society would disintegrate unless a strong collective consciousness, with shared values and beliefs, was maintained. One of the functions of education, therefore, is to strengthen the common morality and reduce individual consciousness. This can in part be achieved by a pledge of allegiance to the state, an idea promoted in 2008 for all school leavers in Britain.

Durkheim therefore identified a range of factors as potentially contributing to the breakdown of a common morality. These included the increasing specialisation of labour, the growing ethnic diversity within society, and the fading influence of religious belief. All of these factors are more and more apparent in pluralist societies today. Under Durkheim's analysis, therefore, we should not be surprised to discover a parallel growth in the diversity of moral outlook and in norms of behaviour in modern Britain.

Characteristics of legal and moral rules

Both legal rules and moral rules have certain characteristics that help to identify them and to distinguish them from each other. These characteristics relate not only to formal issues, such as how they are created and how they can be changed and enforced, but also to their nature and the extent of their influence.

Their origins

It is generally possible to trace legal rules back to a source. For centuries the most creative source of legal rules was the common law. This includes law, such as tort and contract, which have been developed incrementally by judges. For example, the principle that occupiers can owe a duty of care to trespassers came originally from the decision made by the House of Lords in *British Railways Board* v *Herrington* in 1972. During the 20th century, Parliament became increasingly active as a source of law. For example, following the decision in *Herrington*, in 1984 Parliament passed the Occupiers' Liability Act to establish new rules concerning the liability of occupiers for trespassers. As a result

Key terms

Emile Durkheim: regarded by many as the founding father of sociology, Durkheim explored a wide range of issues, including crime, law, suicide, education and religion.

Anomie: term used by Durkheim to describe the breakdown in society that can occur when traditional norms of behaviour disintegrate; this happens when collective consciousness is significantly weakened.

Study tip

In the examination, you do not need to cover all of these points in detail. You can either cover a wide range of issues in outline, or a more limited number in depth.

of parliamentary sovereignty, the law set by Parliament overruled the precedent and has become the cornerstone of this area of liability. In recent times, the European Union has become a major source of law-making in the UK through treaties, directives, regulations and decisions. For example, a 1993 directive established a 48-hour maximum working week and laid down requirements for rest periods. Another example is the requirement that workers be paid a minimum wage. This was put into force in the UK by the Minimum Wage Act 1998.

Moral rules are usually more difficult to trace back to a precise origin. For many, morality is based upon religious teaching: thus, holy texts – such as the Ten Commandments (which can be dated to 1513 BC) for Christians and Jews, and the Koran (which was written in the 7th century) for Muslims – will form the basis for their moral outlook. Codes such as these inform attitudes towards issues such as premarital sex, petty theft and the discovery of lost property. For others, morality is based upon upbringing, upon peer views, or upon the leanings of their own consciences.

Their date of commencement

Legal rules generally have a start date. Acts of Parliament come into force at a specific time – either at midnight of the day on which they receive royal assent, or at a specified later date. For instance, the Human Rights Act 1998 came into force on 1 October 2000, and provisions of the Equality Act 2006 have been introduced in stages. Similarly, European law becomes operative on a given date. Rules set by judicial precedent operate from the date of the final decision.

Moral rules are less straightforward. For example, western attitudes towards pre-marital sex have undergone significant change since World War II. However, it is not possible to attach a date to this change, as it is part of a wider change in social attitudes towards matters of sexual morality.

Their enforcement

Legal rules can be enforced. In criminal law, sanctions are available, ranging from a life sentence for those convicted of murder, to an absolute discharge where the court considers that no further punishment is required. In tort, damages can be awarded for those who have been injured. Damages are generally compensatory, and their purpose is to restore the victim to his pre-tort position, as far as money can do so. The equitable remedy of an injunction is available when the claimant seeks to stop the continuation of a tort – for example, to put an end to a neighbour causing a nuisance. In contract law, damages are the standard remedy sought by the claimant to put him in the position he would have been in had the contract been performed.

Sanctions may also be available for those who breach moral codes. A religious group might excommunicate a wayward member, and a member who uses offensive language may be excluded from a sports or social club. More often, though, moral rules are enforced through disapproval or social ostracism. For example, a young person who takes drugs within the family home may be required to leave to avoid harming his younger siblings. Often, however, moral rules are less enforceable than legal rules.

Their ease of change

In theory, legal rules are relatively easy to change. Parliament has authority to pass a law whenever it wants. This may be in response to a distasteful court judgement (e.g. the War Damage Act 1965), to a proposal from a law reform body (e.g. The Supply of Goods and Services Act 1982), or because of public pressure (e.g. the Dangerous Dogs Act 1991). In practice, however, Parliament is often slow to respond to change. Courts also have the power to change legal rules. The decision in **Williams v Roffey (1990)** limited the avoidance of obligations for lack of

Study tip

Note that examples are given to illustrate the points being made here. You should seek to do the same in your own essay.

■ Key cases

Williams v Roffey (1990): in the law of contract, an agreement must be supported by both parties giving something of value in exchange for the benefit they receive; this is known as consideration; carrying out an existing obligation does not provide consideration; however, following the decision in *Williams v Roffey*, the performance of an existing obligation may now be taken as consideration.

consideration; and the House of Lords in *G and R* (2003) reinstated the subjective test of recklessness for the offence of criminal damage.

Moral rules tend to change gradually, perhaps over decades or centuries. It is often only in hindsight that we become aware of such change. For example, it has taken decades for attitudes to cigarette smoking to become more negative. This has been encouraged by health warnings, by restrictions upon advertising, by bold 'Smoking kills' notices on cigarette packets, and by an increasing intolerance of the nuisance smoking causes to others. It is not possible to identify a particular date, or even a particular decade, when intolerance towards smoking became the dominant attitude but this approach developed over time. Since July 2007, when the ban of smoking in enclosed public places was introduced, the ban has become accepted by the majority of the UK population.

Their certainty of content

It is normally possible to discover the precise content of legal rules. For example, reference to s9 of the Theft Act 1968 will show the requirements for the *actus reus* and *mens rea* of burglary. Decisions of judges will be reported in law reports and newspapers. A measure of uncertainty may arise when an Act is amended. For example, following the Sexual Offences Act 2003, intent to rape will no longer provide the *mens rea* for a burglary conviction. Uncertainty may also arise where there are apparently conflicting precedents, or where a precedent has been distinguished. An example of this is found in the cases of *Brown* (1993) and *Wilson* (1996).

The content of moral rules may also be clear: for example, rules on etiquette and table manners are available in books; rules on sexual morality are often available within the written teachings of religious organisations; and rules on acceptable conduct within schools are often displayed on classroom walls. However, knowledge of the content of moral rules can often only be acquired informally through exposure to them in the setting where they are applied, whether that is the family home, the school playground, or the football pitch. Each setting will have its own mores, and strangers will take time to acquaint themselves with the rules and standards of what is acceptable conduct: what is acceptable at Glastonbury might not be tolerated at Buckingham Palace.

Application of the rules

Legal rules generally apply to everyone. Everyone in this country, including the prime minister, is required to follow road traffic rules such as driving on the left, stopping at red traffic lights and not parking on double yellow lines. It is true that diplomats enjoy a measure of immunity. Many embassies in London, for example, refuse to pay the congestion charge, claiming that they enjoy diplomatic privilege. However, this is a minor exception to the general rule that the laws of the country apply to all who live here, whether they agree with them or not.

The congestion charge aimed to relieve the pressure on London's roads

Moral rules, on the other hand, range in application from enjoying almost universal adoption to having only marginal acceptance. For example, the wedding guest wearing only a fig leaf would probably be quietly escorted from the premises, whoever the bride and groom were. However, perhaps only a small minority of people today are very strict vegans who will not consume, or even touch, any animal product. Other moral issues polarise public opinion: stem cell research, assisted suicide and gay adoption are all areas where it is possibly difficult to determine a prevailing public morality.

Activity

Read the following hypothetical situation:

Under their unwritten constitution the citizens of Brunetteland have always enjoyed freedom of speech. However, in 1984 the Parliament of Brunetteland duly passed a law declaring that all natural blondes are barred from voicing political opinions in private. The penalty for disobedience is a fixed five-year prison sentence. In 1988 Joe reported his wife, Marilyn, for criticising the government. She was given the mandatory five-year sentence. In 1995, the 1984 law was repealed. Joe was then charged with the common law offence of 'depriving an innocent person of his liberty'.

How might natural lawyers and legal positivists decide the outcome of Joe's case?

You should now be able to:

- understand the main distinction between different theories of law
- understand the key differences between legal rules and moral rules.

In this topic, you will learn how to:

- explain where legal and moral rules coincide
- explain the influence of legal and moral rules upon each other.

Study tip

As in the previous section, use examples to illustrate the points you are making. Try to think of some examples of your own to make your essay distinctive, rather than relying exclusively on those in the textbook.

2 The relationship between law and morality

The coincidence of legal and moral rules

Legal and moral rules, though distinctive, share certain characteristics. They are both concerned with setting standards, which are essential for governing the behaviour of individuals within society. For example, traffic laws require us to drive on the left. However, it is a long-established custom, that drivers give way to emergency vehicles to pass when their sirens are sounding and their emergency lights are flashing. Both rules are concerned with the behaviour of drivers and the saving of life.

Legal and moral rules employ similar language: they distinguish between right and wrong, and they speak of duties, obligations and responsibilities. For example, murder is regarded as wicked under both the legal and moral codes of conduct; parents have a legal duty and a moral duty to ensure that their young children are provided with shelter and nourishment; and getting emergency medical help for someone for whom you have responsibility is regarded as morally virtuous as well as legally binding.

Law and morality often coincide or overlap: for example, the Ten Commandments, given to Moses on Mount Sinai, continue to serve as a moral code for many today. The order 'Thou shalt not kill' is reflected in the common law on murder; the command 'Thou shalt not steal' 'is currently legislated in the Theft Act 1968; and the principle of the virtue of honesty, which lies behind the command 'not to give false witness', can be seen in the development of the law in areas such as fraud (crime), misrepresentation (contract), and defamation (tort).

Legal rules are strengthened by this convergence with moral rules, and their enforcement can more readily be justified. When legal rules are out of step with morality, obedience to them becomes more difficult to defend. Sometimes, though, legal rules possess no obvious moral content. Parking a car on a double yellow line in an empty town centre at four o'clock in the morning does not seem to infringe any moral code (other than the act itself of breaking the law).

It might be argued that strict liability offences are like this. In *Smedleys Ltd* v *Breed* (1974) the discovery of a caterpillar in a tin of peas does not seem to breach any moral rule. It is therefore not surprising that the principle of strict liability is controversial: legal rules are given greater validity by their moral content.

Conversely, there are many moral rules that are not enshrined in law. The commandment 'Thou shalt not commit adultery' was part of the Mosaic Law (i.e. the law of Moses) for the people of ancient Israel, and is the law in many countries of the world today. Indeed, such importance is attached to it in some countries that it is punishable by death. In Britain, however, there is no legal prohibition against committing adultery. The current law, the Matrimonial Causes Act 1973, provides that it is one of the grounds for applying for a divorce. This, though, does not reduce the possible moral outrage felt by some at its commission.

On a similar point, there is no liability in English criminal law for omissions, unless the failure falls within one of the recognised exceptions where there is a duty to act, such as a duty to children (*Gibbons and Proctor* (1918)), or a duty through a contract of employment (*Pittwood* (1902)). In other words, there is no requirement in English law to act as the 'good Samaritan'. Interestingly, this term is derived from a parable where a despised foreigner came to the aid of a man beaten and left for dead. The parable was designed to answer the question: who is my neighbour? Clearly, there is a potent moral argument that we should provide assistance to a person beaten and left to die, or rescue a child drowning in a pool of water, or prevent a blind pedestrian from being hit by a speeding lorry. However, although the fact that there is no legal obligation to assist our neighbour will enable us to escape criminal liability, it will not lessen the contempt in which we might be held for our failure to do so.

The influence of law and morality upon each other

Changing moral values can lead to developments in the law. In *The History of the Pleas of the Crown* (published in 1736), Sir Matthew Hale declared that 'a man cannot rape his wife'. This was based upon the doctrine of implied consent, i.e. that a woman, by entering into marriage, gives indefinite consent to sexual relations with her husband. This 'rule' was followed by judges until well into the 20th century, when judges succeeded in removing this immunity in certain situations. These included: where there was a legal separation order (*Clarke* (1949)), where a decree nisi had been issued as part of divorce proceedings (*O'Brien* (1974)), and where a non-molestation order had been imposed (*Steele* (1977)). In these decisions the courts were eager to limit the moral outrage that an acquittal would arouse.

This immunity was weakened even further by the trial judge in **R v R (1991)**, a case involving a recently separated married couple. Owen J declared: 'I find it hard to believe that it ever was common law that a husband was in effect entitled to beat his wife into submission to sexual intercourse.' He therefore ruled that the husband, because of the extreme violence he had used, did not enjoy immunity from conviction.

Before the case arrived at the House of Lords, on appeal, the Law Commission had produced a report recommending that 'the present marital immunity be abolished in all cases'. The House of Lords followed this recommendation. Lord Lane declared that 'the idea that a wife by marriage consents in advance to her husband having sexual intercourse with her whatever her state of health or however proper her objections

Key cases

R v R (1991): culmination of a series of cases in which judges attempted to avoid an outdated precedent generally regarded as morally repugnant.

is no longer acceptable'. In this way, the law eventually caught up with perceived public morality.

The Abortion Act 1967 represents an area of statutory reform introduced as a result of public concern over the existing law. Under s58 of the Offences against the Person Act 1861, abortion was punishable by a maximum of life imprisonment, even if performed for good medical reasons. The Infant Life Preservation Act 1929 allowed a limited exemption from this general prohibition in cases where the abortion was carried out in good faith for the sole purpose of preserving the life of the mother. In **Bourne (1939)**, however, Bourne, an eminent surgeon, carried out an abortion on a 14-year-old girl who had become pregnant as a result of a violent gang rape by soldiers. At his trial, Bourne argued that the operation had been necessary to preserve the mental health (but not the life) of the girl. The trial judge proved sympathetic to this argument. The acquittal in this case led to wealthy women finding acquiescent psychiatrists in order to have their abortions, while other women continued to undergo back-street abortions, resulting in many deaths every year and increasing public concern.

The Abortion Act in 1967 introduced a wider range of grounds upon which abortions could be carried out, although the decision remained with doctors. Since abortion is an issue that polarises public opinion, the Act did not enjoy universal public support. However, the law had changed in response to changing public concerns.

Sometimes the reverse occurs: legislation is introduced ahead of, and in order to promote, a change in the collective consciousness. Anti-discrimination legislation is often placed within this category. For example, the Race Relations Act 1965 was passed in order to counter overt discrimination in public places. Prior to this Act, colour prejudice, as it was then called, was widely practised in Britain, with signs such as 'No Blacks' seen on the fronts of guest houses, and non-whites turned away from some restaurants and public houses.

The 1965 Act, passed in spite of fierce opposition within Parliament, forbade discrimination 'on the grounds of colour, race, or ethnic or national origin'. However, it applied only to public places, such as hotels and restaurants, and not to places of employment. The powers of enforcement were also minimal: a Race Relations Board was empowered to listen to complaints and to attempt to negotiate with the parties to stop further discrimination. Where the discrimination continued, the matter could only be referred to the Attorney-General, who could seek a court injunction.

Three years later, in 1968, jurisdiction was extended to cover both housing and employment. Although these two Acts did not eliminate discrimination, they made a robust official statement about the values of British society. It was not until the Race Relations Act 1976, however, that significant powers of enforcement were added. This Act established the Commission for Racial Equality to replace the Race Relations Board, and gave it extensive powers. It distinguished between direct and indirect discrimination: direct occurring where a person is treated less favourably than another in similar relevant circumstances on the grounds of colour, race, nationality, or ethnic or national origins. Indirect discrimination is much more subtle, and occurs when a condition is applied equally to all employees, but one racial group is disadvantaged because it cannot comply as easily as other groups with that condition.

These provisions have done much to mitigate overt racism. On the 40th anniversary of the passage of the 1965 Act, Trevor Phillips, chairman of the Commission for Racial Equality, stated, 'The fact that we have strong anti-discrimination laws has led to the near disappearance of

---

■ Key cases

Bourne (1939): illustrates the willingness of judges to develop the law to avoid a conviction where the defendant is deemed to have acted morally.

■ Study tip

Referring to statements of legal commentators, such as Trevor Phillips, or of judges can help give authority to the evaluative part of the essay.

commonplace practices which disfigured our society. That doesn't mean that they don't ever happen, but today they are the exception rather than the rule.' Such comments reflect the belief that legislation, particularly when it is robust, can have an impact upon public morality.

Often it is difficult to assess whether changing attitudes or changes in the law came first. It is even possible that the two march alongside each other, though not necessarily in step all the way. One of the most heavily legislated areas in the last 50 years has been the law on homosexuality. In 1957, the **Wolfenden Report** recommended that 'homosexual behaviour between consenting adults in private should no longer be a criminal offence'. The committee further recommended that the age of consent be fixed at 21, which at that time was the age of majority in Britain.

Ten years were to pass before the Sexual Offences Bill was presented to Parliament, time enough for many to reflect on the principles underpinning Wolfenden. The Bill contained the two most significant recommendations of the Wolfenden Committee: first, that homosexuality be decriminalised for private consensual homosexual activity; and secondly, that the age of consent be set at 21.

A quarter of a century was to pass before the age of consent was reduced to 18 in the Criminal Justice and Public Order Act 1994, but only six years until it was further reduced to 16 under the Sexual Offences (Amendment) Act 2000, thereby equalising the age of consent for heterosexual and homosexual activity. This last reform attracted determined opposition within the House of Lords, and the powers of the Parliament Acts had to be invoked to secure passage of the measure. It is difficult to gauge whether those promoting or those opposing these Acts more accurately reflected public opinion on this issue, but what is evident is that the years since 1957 have seen not only substantial legislative activity, but also a major shift in public attitudes in this area.

> **Key terms**
>
> **Wolfenden Report 1957:** report of a 14-member committee appointed to examine the law on homosexuality and prostitution, and asked to make recommendations for law reform.

Activity

Consider the following hypothetical situations. What point about the relationship between law and morality would they illustrate?

1. After the First World War there was a shortage of men of marriageable age in Britain. As a result many young women's hopes of marriage were dashed. Parliament therefore passed an Act making polygamy compulsory for all men between the ages of 20 and 40.

2. Ivor Camm, a former member of the North Wales mountain ranger service, was scrambling over the ridge known as Crib Goch, when he met a party of inexperienced walkers. He ignored their pleas for help, as he was going to be late home for lunch. Two members of the party fell to their deaths.

3. As he was driving home, Robert failed to give way to an ambulance on its way to a traffic accident. The ambulance crashed trying to overtake him. As a result, a woman died in the accident. Evidence later showed that the woman would have survived if she had received emergency treatment and transfer to hospital.

You should now be able to:

- understand how legal and moral rules coincide, and how they influence each other.

In this topic, you will learn how to:

- ■ explain different theories about whether the law should be used to enforce morality, including the Hart–Devlin debate

- ■ discuss recent cases and legislation that reflect this debate.

Key terms

John Stuart Mill: 19th-century British philosopher, political economist and civil servant; Mill's idea of liberty justified the freedom of the individual as opposed to state control; he supported utilitarianism, a theory developed by Jeremy Bentham.

Tyranny of the majority: term used by Mill to describe the situation where the elected majority in government, or the majority within society as a whole, force their views upon others, thereby restricting their freedom.

Harm principle: Mill's belief that an individual's private conduct can be restricted only where it brings harm to other people. Otherwise, an individual is sovereign over his own mind and body.

3 The enforcement of morality

Britain is a pluralist society containing a diversity of moral views. This section explores the questions of whether, and to what extent, the law should seek to enforce any particular moral views. This is not merely a subject of academic debate: judges are often forced to consider these questions before determining the law. There are two starting points for this debate: the first is that the law, as the guardian of public morals, should intervene to ensure the continuation of the dominant morality within the state. The second is diametrically opposed: individuals should be left free to decide their own morality. In practice, both these positions are modified so that they tend towards convergence.

John Stuart Mill

In his book *On Liberty*, **John Stuart Mill**, a 19th-century philosopher, explored 'the nature and limits of the power which can be legitimately exercised by society over the individual'. He began by tracing the historical development of liberty as a protection against the rule of tyrants. Over a period of centuries, limits began to be imposed upon governmental power – first by the recognition of certain immunities, called rights or liberties, and secondly by the establishment of constitutional checks. Later, when tyrants were replaced by elected, temporary rulers who served as representatives of the people, the need for protection should have disappeared – as, in theory at least, people should not need protection against themselves. However, protection was still necessary against oppression by the elected majority: limitations on the power of the government were still needed to prevent the '**tyranny of the majority**'.

Mill went on to argue that such tyranny could be exercised by society collectively and not just by governments, and that this 'social tyranny' was more formidable than many forms of political repression. He therefore declared that it was necessary to protect individuals against the tendency of society to impose its own ideas and practices upon dissenters. There is, he asserted, 'a limit to the legitimate interference of collective opinion with individual independence'.

Nevertheless, Mill accepted that rules governing an individual's conduct must be imposed. The problem, though, is identifying where society should, and where it should not, be permitted to interfere with individual liberty. Mill developed the **'harm principle'** as the appropriate test to be used when considering this issue.

He wrote:

> The only purpose for which power can be rightfully exercised over any member of a civilised community, against his will, is to prevent harm to others. His own good, either physical or moral, is not a sufficient warrant .... Over himself, his own body and mind, the individual is sovereign.

Under this principle, an individual should be allowed to harm himself: society can only intervene where his conduct harms others.

Mill limits the application of the harm principle in one significant way: it does not apply to those who are not 'in the maturity of their faculties'. In other words, it does not apply to children, over whom society enjoys 'absolute power'. They must be protected against their own actions as well against the actions of others.

Mill provided a broad definition of harm. He argued that, as a general rule, harm will be caused by commissions rather than by omissions. However, he recognised that harm may also in certain circumstances be caused by a failure to act, such as a failure to give evidence in court, a failure to bear a fair share in the common defence, and a failure to save a fellow creature's life. In these and similar situations, an individual may rightfully be held accountable for his failure to act, and deserves society's disapproval. In the most severe cases, he also deserves to be punished under the law.

Mill recognised that others might refuse to admit this distinction between that part of a person's life which concerns only himself and that which concerns others. One such objector was the 19th-century judge, Sir James Stephen, who opposed the liberalism of Mill. Stephen argued that there is no distinction between acts that harm others and acts that harm oneself. He wrote: 'There are acts of wickedness so gross and outrageous that they must be punished at any cost to the offender'. He went on to argue that the prevention of wickedness and immorality is a proper end in itself and justifies state action. The law, Stephen argued, has a duty to proscribe behaviour condemned by society at large.

Mill answered such objections by making a distinction between the harmful act itself and its particular consequences. For example, society has no right to interfere with drunkenness itself. However, it does have the right to interfere where a man, through his drunkenness, is in breach of his duty to his family or his creditors, or if he is a soldier or a policeman on duty. In Mill's words: 'Whenever there is definite damage to an individual or to the public, the case is taken out of the province of liberty, and placed in that of morality or law'. However, where there is no such breach of duty to society and the damage affects only the individual himself, then 'the inconvenience is one which society can afford to bear, for the sake of the greater good of human freedom'. In other words, the liberty of the individual is too precious to be sacrificed merely to ease another's feeling of revulsion or repugnance.

The Hart–Devlin debate

This argument has endured. In the 20th century it blossomed in the debate between an eminent Law Lord, **Patrick Devlin**, and the academic H.L.A Hart. This debate was sparked by the publication in 1957 of the Wolfenden report on homosexuality and prostitution. The committee had concluded that the law has a role in preserving public order and decency, but 'it is not, in our view, the function of the law to intervene in the private life of citizens, or to seek to enforce any particular pattern of behaviour'. Furthermore, there 'must remain a realm of private morality and immorality which is, in brief and crude terms, not the law's business'. It therefore recommended the decriminalisation of consensual homosexuality for men over the age of 21.

In 'The Enforcement of Morals', published in 1965, Lord Devlin wrote that 'without shared ideas on politics, morals, and ethics, no society can exist'. Society, therefore, is constituted in part by its morality. In language reminiscent of Durkheim, Lord Devlin argued that the fabric of society is dependent upon a shared or common morality: where the bonds of that morality are loosened by private immoral conduct, the integrity of society will be lost and society will be liable to disintegrate. Society therefore has the right to defend itself against immorality. Even private wickedness and immorality may be punished because they are harmful to society. In Lord Devlin's own words, 'The suppression of vice is as much the law's business as the suppression of subversive activities.'

Study tip

References to the arguments of John Stuart Mill and Sir James Stephen provide context for the more recent Hart–Devlin debate.

Key terms

Patrick Devlin: Lord Devlin, a leading 20th-century judge and Law Lord, and opponent of the recommendations of the Wolfenden Report.

However, Lord Devlin recognised that there are limits to the right of society to interfere with private immoral conduct: 'There must be toleration of the maximum individual freedom that is consistent with the integrity of society'. He accepted that personal preferences, or likes and dislikes, should not form the basis for decisions about what immoral conduct should be outlawed. He therefore developed an apparently objective test, that of the reasonable or ordinary man, to help decide where the boundaries are to be drawn: only where immoral conduct is regarded by this ordinary man with 'intolerance, indignation or disgust', should it be prohibited by law.

It is worth noting that Lord Devlin's morality is based upon convention: in other words, it is based upon what is generally regarded by society at large as being the acceptable and desirable state of affairs. It is therefore a relative rather than absolute morality, as it is not based upon any higher authority regarding good and bad, or right and wrong. **Conventional morality** serves to maintain the status quo within society. Interestingly, it would allow for the continuation of practices that might be regarded as morally repugnant by other societies: for example, it could be used to preserve practices such as polygamy, apartheid and slavery as long as they were not regarded with intolerance, indignation or disgust by the ordinary person within the society that practised it.

Professor Hart proposed a more limited role for the law in the enforcement of morality. Whereas Lord Devlin started from the general principle that society has a duty to enforce its dominant morality, and then limited the application of this general principle to acts that the ordinary man regards with intolerance, Professor Hart started from the opposite end of the spectrum – that society should not interfere with private moral or immoral conduct. However, Hart then limited the application of this general principle by sanctioning the enforcement of morality in certain situations. First of all, he accepted that enforcement is permitted when one of society's dominant moralities is being eroded by a true threat to the cohesion of society. Such a threat, though, has to be more than merely a challenge to society's code of conduct: there must be evidence that it creates a genuine public nuisance.

Hart's discussion of the offence of bigamy illustrates this approach. He wrote that, in a country where deep religious significance is attached to monogamous marriage and to the wedding service, the law against bigamy should be accepted as an attempt to protect religious feelings from offence by a 'public act desecrating the ceremony'. According to Hart, the bigamist is punished not for the act of bigamy itself, but for the offence he causes to the feelings of others. Hart applied the same reasoning to public sexual intercourse between a man and his wife. The act of intercourse, he states, is not in itself immoral, but if it takes place in public it is an affront to decent people and, as a nuisance, deserves to be punished under the law.

Devlin accused Hart of being inconsistent. He challenged Hart, saying: 'Bigamy violates neither good manners nor decency. When committed without deception, it harms no one.' Although Devlin is not necessarily arguing here in favour of legalising bigamy, it is at least ironic that he seems to be adopting a more liberal stance than Hart on this issue.

Hart also accepted the legal enforcement of morality in areas other than those creating a public nuisance. On some issues, he adopted a **paternalistic** approach. The taking of drugs and consensual euthanasia are two areas where he believed people need to be protected against themselves. This stance seems less liberal than that adopted by Mill.

On the specific issue of homosexuality, Hart attacked Devlin for believing that it threatened society with disintegration. He argued that Devlin's

Key terms

Conventional morality: morality that is based upon a commonly agreed view of what is acceptable.

Paternalistic: when society is protective of its citizens and passes laws that restrict certain behaviours.

position was tantamount to declaring that any change in morality threatened the disintegration of society. Furthermore, he pointed out that Lord Devlin's approach would cause society's values to stagnate, to become permanently fixed at one point in time.

Some issues reflecting the Hart–Devlin debate

Judges and Parliament are often forced to confront complex moral issues. Parliament can choose whether to legislate. Judges have no choice. If a case comes to court they have to make a decision, and of course if a case reaches the higher appeal courts it becomes a precedent. In the following examples, judges had to confront 'new' issues affecting public morality.

In **Shaw v DPP (1962)** the case concerned a magazine advertising the services of prostitutes, and Shaw was convicted of 'conspiracy to corrupt public morals' – a previously unknown offence. The House of Lords confirmed the existence of this 'new' common law offence. Viscount Simonds declared: 'There remains in the courts a residual power to enforce the supreme and fundamental purpose of the law, to conserve not only the safety and order, but also the moral welfare of the State'. Lord Devlin would have approved of this paternalistic approach.

In **DPP v Knuller (Publishing, Printing and Promotions) Ltd (1971)** the Knuller company was charged with conspiracy to corrupt public morals and conspiracy to outrage public decency.

From 1 January 1969 to 30 May 1969 the company published, fortnightly, a magazine known as 'IT', the International Times. The defence claimed that the International Times was designed to give publicity to the views of those holding minority, and perhaps anti-establishment, views – for example, anarchists, squatters, those arrested for drug offences, schoolboys who were compelled by their headmasters to cut their hair, and all who felt themselves victimised and oppressed – including lesbian, gay, bisexual and transgender people. The circulation of the paper was said at one time to be about 38,000 copies. There were 54,000 copies printed of the last edition, which could have included as many as 10,000 schoolchildren and 20,000 to 30,000 students.

The magazine included adverts such as: 'Alert young designer, 30, seeks warm, friendly, pretty boy under 23 who needs regular sex, reliability and beautiful surroundings. If the cap fits and you need a friend, write.'

The majority in the House of Lords decided that the prosecution had established the existence of an offence of outraging public decency and it followed that there was also a common law offence of conspiring to outrage public decency. The Knuller company was found guilty of the offences with which they were charged. Again, it could be said that a paternalistic attitude was adopted by the senior judges.

In *Gibson* (1990) an artist was convicted under the common law offence of 'outraging public decency' for exhibiting earrings made from freeze-dried human foetuses. No doubt Devlin would maintain that this is exactly the type of immoral conduct that would arouse the intolerance, indignation and disgust of the ordinary person, and so should be subjected to the full rigour of the criminal law.

In the well-known case of **Brown and Others (1993)** the defendants were convicted under s47 and s20 of the Offences against the Person Act 1861 after engaging in violent sado-masochistic activities. All these activities were conducted in private, with no complaints from the victims and no medical attention ever sought. There were no permanent injuries. The activities came to the attention of the police as a result of a video recording the men had made of the event. The House of Lords declared

> ### Key cases
>
> **Shaw v DPP (1962):** illustrates the inherent power of the courts to establish a new common law offence to enforce public morality
>
> **DPP v Knuller (1971):** the House of Lords confirmed that a common law offence of outraging public decency existed.
>
> **Brown and Others (1993):** illustrates the tension that exists between the need to protect society at large against perceived immoral behaviour, and the right of individuals to conduct their private lives according to their own desires.

that consent is not available in cases of such serious injuries, subject to certain exceptions of which sado-masochistic behaviour was not one.

In the House of Lords, speaking for the majority, Lord Templeman declared that the issues of policy and public interest must be taken into account before deciding whether the defence of consent should be extended to sado-masochistic activities. Then, in words resonant of Lord Devlin, he expressed his own opinion: 'Society is entitled and bound to protect itself against a cult of violence. Pleasure derived from the infliction of pain is an evil thing. Cruelty is uncivilised.' He dismissed the men's appeal.

Lord Mustill, dissenting, declared, in words reminiscent of Professor Hart, that:

> the state should interfere with the rights of an individual to live his or her life as he or she may choose no more than is necessary to ensure a proper balance between the special interests of the individual and the general interests of the individuals who together comprise the populace at large.

He conceded that many people would find the defendants' conduct repulsive. Nevertheless, that feeling of repulsion did not, in his view, justify the men's conviction.

The defence of consent was also considered in the case of *Wilson* (1996). At his wife's request, Alan Wilson branded his initials ('AW') on her buttocks. Hearing the appeal against conviction for actual bodily harm, Russell LJ explained:

> Consensual activity between husband and wife, in the privacy of the matrimonial home, is not, in our judgment, a proper matter for criminal investigation, let alone criminal prosecution.

It is possible that the result would be welcomed by both Devlin and Hart, the former because consenting adults should be able to do what they want in the privacy of their own homes without the State interfering.

You should now be able to:

■ understand the main points in the Hart–Devlin debate

■ illustrate this debate by reference to various cases.

Study tip

The selection of material in this section is necessarily arbitrary. You may cover entirely different issues (for example, stem cell research, assisted suicide, anti-smoking legislation or internet pornography), all of which are equally valuable in exploring the issues raised in the Hart–Devlin debate. Whichever topic is discussed, it should aim to identify and discuss the issues on both sides of the debate.

In this topic, you will learn how to:

■ identify the requirements of the question

■ include in a discussion a range of information about the relationship between laws and morals and a discussion about whether law should reflect moral values.

4 Answering questions on the topic of law and morality

Essays on the topic of law and morality are extremely popular with students. The titles usually call for discussion of some or all of the following issues:

▥ an explanation of what is meant by the terms 'law' and 'morality'

▥ discussion of the relationship between law and morality

▥ consideration of whether the law should enforce morality.

To answer the first part successfully, you need to introduce some theory regarding what law is. For example, reference to the distinction between legal positivism (e.g. Austin and/or Hart) and natural law (e.g. Aquinas and/or Fuller) would satisfy this requirement. You also need to identify and explain the characteristics of legal and moral rules, with appropriate examples used to illustrate them.

To answer the second part successfully, you need to identify and discuss the common factors that unite law and morals, e.g. their concern with standards, and their use of similar terminology. You then must try to demonstrate how they influence each other, with examples of law promoting changes in moral attitudes, and vice-versa, or areas where such judgments are hard to make.

To answer the third part successfully, you need to refer to relevant theories. Discussion of the main arguments employed in the Hart–Devlin debate would satisfy this requirement. It is important that you then introduce some areas of law to illustrate how the points raised in this debate have been the subject of judicial reflection and parliamentary activity.

Although it is perfectly acceptable to refer to events of 60 years ago, such as the Wolfenden Report and *Shaw* v *DPP* (1962), try to show the relevance of the debate to current issues, such as assisted suicide.

Overall, the essay should contain:

- some theory (e.g. positivism v natural law; the Hart–Devlin debate)
- explanation of relevant material (e.g. characteristics of legal and moral rules)
- some relevant case authority
- some thoughtful discussion of relevant issues.

You should now be able to:

- understand what is required in an essay on the topic of law and morality.

Activity

This chapter is divided into three distinct topics. Reinforce your understanding of them by writing a 200–250 word summary of each.

21   Law and justice

In this topic, you will learn how to:

- explain and distinguish between various theories of justice

- provide material to illustrate these theories.

Study tip

In an examination, students are unlikely to be asked to describe particular theories, as the specification does not identify any by name. However, it would be useful to have the key ideas of a range of theories to provide a framework for the essay.

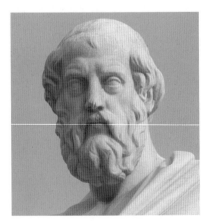

Plato

1   Theories of justice

Justice is a concept that can be described simply by a synonym such as fairness, equality or even-handedness. It is something for which we develop a 'feel' at a young age. It clearly includes treating like cases in a like manner, showing impartiality, and acting in good faith. However, the term 'justice' has occupied the minds of some of the greatest thinkers across the ages. As a result, there is a wide range of theories available to explain its meaning and application.

For the purpose of this chapter, the word 'law' refers not only to the substantive law – for example, criminal law, tort law or the law of contract, as developed in court decisions, by Parliament or through other sources, but also to procedural rules and principles by which the laws themselves are made and the legal system administered. For the most part, examples of substantive law are taken from the A Level syllabus.

Justice as harmony

Plato

Plato was a 4th-century Greek philosopher. In his major work, *The Republic*, he used Socrates as a mouthpiece to develop his own view of justice. Socrates begins by asking others what they think justice is. Cephalus, a wealthy man, suggests that justice is 'speaking the truth and paying one's debts'. Socrates quickly counters this view by asking whether it would be just to return a deadly weapon to a friend who has become insane. Clearly not. Polemarchus then proposes that justice is 'giving to each what is owed' – that is, to help one's friends and harm one's enemies, a popular Greek view. Socrates also rejects this, pointing out that harsh treatment of one's enemies makes them even more unjust.

After rejecting further suggestions, Socrates outlines his (i.e. Plato's) view of justice, both for the individual and for society. Dealing with the individual first: a man's soul has three elements, i.e. reason (the mind, responsible for decision-making), spirit (the human will, responsible for carrying out decisions made by the mind), and appetite or desire (the emotions, over which self-control must be exercised). A man is just when each of these three elements fulfils its appropriate function, and there is a harmonious relationship between them. If appetite/desire takes control, harmony and justice are lost.

Within society there are also three groups: the ruling class, made up of philosophers, corresponds to reason; the warrior class corresponds to spirit; and artisans, farmers and merchants correspond to appetite or desire, over which control must be exercised. Society is just when each class fulfils its appropriate function, and there is a harmonious relationship between them. Socrates compares an unjust city to a ship at sea that has a drunken captain and an unruly crew. The only way the ship will be able to reach land safely is by returning control to the navigator (the philosopher).

For both the individual and the state, therefore, Plato viewed justice as harmony between the warring elements.

Distributive justice

Distributive justice is concerned with the fair allocation of the benefits (e.g. money, property, family life) and responsibilities (e.g. taxes, civic duties) of life within an organisation.

Aristotle

Aristotle was a pupil of Plato. It is no surprise, therefore, that he also described justice as referring to individuals in their dealings with each other, and to the state in making and enforcing laws. He often stressed the need for proportionality, and for achieving the middle way, i.e. a proper balance between extremes.

Aristotle identified particular examples of justice that apply to different situations. Among these is distributive justice, which is concerned with the fair distribution of society's wealth. Aristotle argued that a just state will distribute its wealth on the basis of merit, giving to each according to his virtue and to his contribution to society. This is a proportionate system: the worthiest, rather than the neediest, receive the greatest share. To allocate resources on the basis of people's needs would be unjust, as it would reward the lazy at least as much as the hard-working. We might consider how this would apply today to paying for care for the elderly.

Aristotle (like Plato) did worry that a society in which there was a sharp division between rich and poor would not be 'just', almost by definition, and there would be a need to minimise the gap to some degree. Plato characterised such a society as really two societies in one, and because such a society would be dysfunctional (no harmony in the various 'parts') it would be unjust.

Corrective justice is needed to ensure that individuals can keep their entitlement. It is applied where one person, by his greed and self-interest, causes a loss to another person – for example, by stealing his property. The role of the court is to ensure that the gains and losses of each party are equalled out so that the offender doesn't benefit from his wrongdoing and that the victim doesn't suffer loss. In this way, balance – the middle way Aristotle so often sought – is achieved.

Thomas Aquinas

Thomas Aquinas, the 13th-century theologian, described justice in language similar to that of Aristotle. In general terms, justice governs our relationships with other people: it is the constant willingness to deal with other people as they deserve. The end result of justice is the common good, for the individual and for the community.

Aquinas identified particular forms of justice that govern our dealings with others, which help put into practice the general principle that people are given what is due to them. First of all, distributive justice concerns the fair allocation of goods and responsibilities throughout the community. This is governed by 'due **proportion**': people receive what they are due in accordance with their merit, rank and need. Concerning merit, it would be wrong to pay workers an equal amount for unequal work, or an unequal amount for equal work; concerning rank, people of higher social status will require a greater proportion of society's benefits; and concerning need, there is a moral obligation to look after the poor. Clearly these principles may conflict when put into practice.

Aquinas also spoke of commutative justice, which concerns the exchange of goods or services between people. This is governed by '**equality**': in a contract, for example, on the one hand the value of a product is what one should pay for it; on the other hand the vendor should receive the true worth of the goods.

Key terms

Distributive justice: concerned with the fairest way of distributing society's benefits and responsibilities.

Corrective justice: principle that the outcome ensures not only that the wrongdoer does not benefit from his wrongdoing, but also that the victim doesn't suffer permanent loss.

Proportionality and **equality:** two principles adopted by Aquinas for allocating society's benefits and responsibilities (proportionality), and for the exchange of goods and services (equality).

Aristotle

Thomas Aquinas

Aquinas based his doctrine on natural law. Natural law theories assume there is a higher order of law and that if the laws of a society follow this order, they will be just. Aristotle supported this view, and believed that the higher order came from nature. Aquinas thought that the higher order came from God.

Aquinas believed that a law that was contrary to human good was not true law at all. But such a law could still be obeyed if it would prevent social disorder. He also believed that a law that was against God's will, and therefore against natural law, should be disregarded.

Naturalists, such as Aquinas, believe that natural law principles are an inherent part of nature and exist regardless of whether government recognises or enforces them. Naturalists further believe that governments must incorporate natural law principles into their legal systems before justice can be achieved.

Karl Marx

Karl Marx, widely regarded as the founder of communism, developed a radically different model of distributive justice. This model was embodied in his slogan, 'from each according to his ability, to each according to his need'. This enshrines two principles of the ideal of communism: first, each will maximise his contribution to the common wealth by making full use of his abilities. Secondly, each will receive according to his need, irrespective of the personal contribution he has made to the production process. No doubt Aristotle would have regarded this model of distribution as unjust in that it has the potential for giving the greatest rewards to the least productive, and therefore least deserving, members of society.

The main criticism of Marx's views is that no country has so far been able to put them into practice with sufficient success to bring about the just society envisaged by Marx. However, capitalist societies that follow principles of distributive justice, closer to those held by Aristotle and Aquinas, are also criticised for endemic social injustice.

Marx

Chaim Perelman

The models of distributive justice described above are among those identified by Chaim Perelman, a Polish-born philosopher who lived in Belgium. In 1944, Perelman produced a study of justice, entitled *De la Justice*. He concluded that justice cannot be studied logically, as each attempt to define it is based upon a person's subjective values.

In *De la Justice* he discusses different understandings of justice. The first, 'to each according to his merits', is reminiscent of Aristotle: each person is treated in the manner he deserves. The good are rewarded, the bad deprived or punished. This view is consistent with the practice of the criminal courts, handing out punishment in the measure that is warranted by the offence committed. It is also consistent with many people's religious beliefs about life after death.

'To each according to his needs' is reminiscent of Marx's slogan. This approach is consistent with social democracy, in which a welfare system allocates resources such as social housing, tax allowances and benefits payments according to a means-tested system. Those in greatest need receive a proportionately higher share of the common wealth that is set aside for alleviating the most acute states of poverty. This was the dominant philosophy behind the development of the welfare state in the United Kingdom in the years following World War II, and still enjoys a significant measure of consensus among political parties today.

An alternative view of justice is 'to each according to his works', a liberal, individualistic approach favoured by supporters of the enterprise culture

Chaim Perelman

as it measures an individual's rewards according to the contributions he has made. Under this system, a highly skilled worker will receive considerably greater rewards than an unskilled worker. This approach is claimed to provide incentives for people to better themselves.

A fourth approach, 'to each equally', has a superficial attraction, and in some situations will be the fairest system of allocating scarce resources. For example, when food was in short supply during and after World War II, ration books were issued to each person. These contained tokens that had to be removed by the shopkeeper when scarce items of food and clothing were purchased. Even here, though, there were some exceptions: pregnant women were issued with more food tokens, and nursing mothers were allowed more milk. An equal distribution of resources would often be wasteful, and an equal sharing of burdens, such as tax contributions, would be unfair unless all resources were equally shared.

'To each according to his rank' may sound anti-democratic, but is widely practised. Rank may refer to social status: deference continues to be shown to members of the royal family and even to celebrities. It may refer to a position of authority: the quarters of army officers are superior to those of their troops. It may refer to age: the over 75s do not require a TV licence, irrespective of the ability to pay, and little sister is well aware that big sister enjoys more privileges.

Finally, 'to each according to his legal entitlement' is a rights-based system, and is not dependent upon merit. Thus, the vilest serial killer will be entitled to protection from attack by his fellow inmates in prison; and the most disloyal, undeserving child will inherit under the rules of intestacy. (Intestacy is when a deceased person leaves property but does not leave a will. The property is divided between the deceased's surviving relatives.)

Utilitarianism

Jeremy Bentham

Jeremy Bentham was a social reformer, inventor, wordsmith and philosopher who lived from 1748 to 1832. As well as designing a new type of prison, promoting animal rights and introducing new words to the English language, he developed the theory known today as **utilitarianism**. From observing that people act out of self-interest, pursuing happiness by seeking pleasure and avoiding pain, he developed the legal and moral principle of utility: what makes an action right or wrong is the usefulness, or value, of the consequence it brings. The more an action increases overall happiness, the more valuable it is; and the more it decreases happiness, the more reprehensible. For example, by visiting The Eagle pub tonight I can add to my own happiness by enjoying a glass or two of India Pale Ale. I will also be bringing pleasure to the landlord because of the boost I provide to his business. And if I help my team to win the pub quiz, I am adding immeasurably to the happiness of my colleagues. Clearly, I must go there.

Maximising happiness is the object of justice. To help measure this, Bentham developed a mathematical formula, known as the 'felicific calculus', which enables us to assess whether our conduct increases happiness. This formula identifies a range of factors concerning the pleasurable activity itself – for example, its intensity, its duration, and its extent. It then identifies and grades different types of pleasures – for example, those relating to the exercise of power, or to friendship, and different kinds of pain – for example, regret or grieving. These factors help to introduce some objectivity into what would normally be regarded as a subjective issue. Before deciding upon a course of action, a person is therefore able to judge whether it will add to or subtract from the sum of happiness.

The remains of Bentham on exhibition in University College, London

> ### Key terms
>
> **Utilitarianism:** doctrine that all actions should be judged in terms of their utility in promoting the greatest happiness for the greatest number.

One of the criticisms of utilitarianism is that the interest of an individual may be sacrificed for greater community happiness. For example, as a result of 'Sarah's law' the identity of an individual paedophile may be disclosed to the community in which he is living, causing him considerable distress and inconvenience. Under the felicific calculus, though, the greater happiness brought to the larger community by a conviction might outweigh the pain of a few individuals. Does this possibly make such an outcome just? John Rawls, a 20th-century political philosopher rightly criticises utilitarianism on this point.

Yet utilitarianism does at least attempt to provide a route to resolving difficult problems. For example, managers and doctors in the National Health Service have to prioritise resources. The felicific calculus will necessarily result in outcomes that are not pleasing to everyone; however, it will provide a rational justification for deciding priorities.

John Stuart Mill

John Stuart Mill was a 19th-century liberal, an ardent advocate of freedom of speech, a sponsor of Irish land reform and a supporter of equal rights for women. His pamphlet *Utilitarianism*, published in 1861, supported the basic principles of utilitarianism put forward by Bentham. In Chapter 2 of *Utilitarianism*, Mill wrote that actions are right 'in proportion as they tend to promote happiness, wrong as they tend to produce the reverse of happiness'. However, he focused upon the quality of happiness rather than merely upon its quantity. He wrote: 'Better to be a human being dissatisfied than a pig satisfied; better to be a Socrates dissatisfied than a fool satisfied'.

Mill also linked utilitarianism to justice. Justice, he explained, includes respect for people, for property and for rights, as well as the need for good faith and impartiality. All of these are consistent with the principle of utility, since their application brings the greatest happiness to the greatest number. It could also be argued that punishing wrongdoers also brings happiness to the greatest number. However, Mill argued that punishment is in itself an evil as it involves inflicting harm or pain, and can only be justified where it brings a greater benefit, such as public order.

Act and rule utilitarianism

The theory of utilitarianism has developed since Bentham and Mill. Under act utilitarianism, the rightness of an act is judged in isolation to see whether it adds to, or subtracts from, the sum of human happiness. For example, if I drive my Harley Davidson at 130mph on an empty motorway at three o' clock in the morning, I am considerably increasing my own happiness and causing pain to nobody else: the sum of human happiness is increased. According to rule utilitarianism, the rightness of an action is judged according to whether the sum of human happiness would be increased if everyone acted in the same way. Developing the example, if all Harley Davidson owners tried to drive along the same stretch of motorway at the same speed and at the same time, chaos would probably ensue, resulting in pain and misery: the sum of human happiness would decrease.

Social justice

John Rawls

John Rawls, a professor of political philosophy at Harvard, published *A Theory of Justice* in 1971. It sets out the concept of **social justice**. Rawls' starting point will be familiar to parents with only one bar of chocolate. They ask the first child to cut the bar, and allow the second to choose the larger piece. Fairness is guaranteed! Rawls described justice as fairness, and then presented a hypothetical society where each member would

John Stuart Mill

Key terms

Social justice: a key term used by John Rawls to describe a system where the burdens and benefits of society would be distributed in an equitable manner.

distribute its resources in a disinterested manner. To make this possible, nobody would know in advance what their position in that society would be, nor what stage of that society's development he would be born into: he would operate behind a 'veil of ignorance'. In Rawls' own words: 'No one knows his place in society, his class position or social status, nor does anyone know his fortune in the distribution of natural assets and abilities, his intelligence, strength, and the like'. Rawls believed that, on this basis, benefits and burdens would be distributed justly, i.e. fairly.

Rawls argued that two basic principles of justice would be evident within this society: firstly, each person would have 'an equal right to the most extensive scheme of basic liberties compatible with a similar scheme of liberties for others'. This would include certain basic freedoms, such as the right to own property, freedom of speech, freedom of association, and freedom from arbitrary arrest.

Secondly, social and economic inequalities may exist, but only: (a) where they benefit the least advantaged members of society; and (b) provided all offices and positions are open to everyone. In other words, under (a), it is acceptable for a neurosurgeon to earn four times the average wage, live in a large detached house, drive a Mercedes S class, and go to the Yorkshire Dales for his holidays because his work benefits disadvantaged members of society, and others are encouraged to imitate his example, further benefiting the disadvantaged. It is also acceptable under (b), provided that everyone with skills and abilities comparable to those of the neurosurgeon has a reasonable opportunity to pursue a similar path.

In employing the fiction of the 'veil of ignorance' to develop a society based upon consent, Rawls was promoting a rights-based system: basic rights such as freedom of speech and association are '**inalienable**': they can never be sacrificed for the common good. The state must always respect the autonomy of the individual. He wrote: 'Each person possesses an inviolability founded on justice that even the welfare of society as a whole cannot override. Therefore, in a just society the rights secured by justice are not subject to political bargaining or to the calculus of social interests.' This distinguishes Rawls from Bentham and the utilitarianists, against whom the final comment is directed, for utilitarians might allow individual freedoms to be sacrificed where this is considered necessary to promote wider benefits for the greater number.

Robert Nozick

Robert Nozick was a Harvard colleague of Rawls. In *A Theory of Justice*, Rawls had provided a philosophical basis for the welfare state and the redistribution of wealth to help the disadvantaged. In *Anarchy, State and Utopia*, Nozick developed an entitlement theory of justice, which consisted of three principles:

1 A principle of justice in acquisition, dealing with how property is initially acquired.
2 A principle of justice in transfer, dealing with how property can change hands.
3 A principle of rectification of injustice, dealing with injustices arising from the acquisition or transfer of property under the two principles above. This third principle would not be required if the world was entirely just.

Where a person obtains property in accordance with the principles of acquisition or transfer, he is entitled to keep that property. Where a person obtains property by fraud or theft or other unjust means, the third principle provides a remedy.

This is fundamentally different from Rawls, who argued that inequalities may exist only where they benefit the most disadvantaged members

> **Key terms**
>
> **Inalienable rights:** rights that cannot be traded-in or sold; for example, the American Declaration of Independence declared that 'every man hath an unalienable right to liberty'.

> **Study tip**
>
> Rawls and Nozick provide contrasting views on the meaning of justice. These provide a good basis for evaluating whether the law is just.

of society. Nozick places no such limits upon private ownership: property justly acquired may not be appropriated simply as a form of redistribution of wealth, to reduce inequalities. He wrote: 'No one has a right to something whose realisation requires certain uses of things and activities that other people have rights and entitlements over'. Therefore, those in possession of property have an inalienable right to keeping it, and no competing authority can justly deprive them of their property, no matter how just their cause may appear. This is a free-market, libertarian form of justice.

Following the publication of *Anarchy, State and Utopia*, Nozick became closely associated in people's minds with conservative economists such as Milton Friedman, who influenced the policies of the conservative government of Margaret Thatcher in Britain in the 1980s. However, unlike some other libertarians, Nozick did not restrict his principles to the field of economics: he also adopted a **libertarian** approach on social issues such as gay rights.

> ### Key terms
>
> **Libertarianism:** belief that all people are at liberty to do whatever they wish with their lives or their property, provided they allow other people the same liberty.

Activities

1 How would these philosophers react to the following situations?
- Plato and Bentham to: Tamsin eating a whole batch of chocolate muffins?
- Aristotle and Mill to: Mr Justice Soft, giving an absolute discharge to Robin Hood who is found guilty of robbing the rich to give to the poor?
- Rawls and Aquinas to: the Chancellor of the Exchequer withdrawing the 10 pence in the pound tax band, thereby disadvantaging the lowest-paid workers in the country?
- Rawls and Nozick to: a law introduced by the Government confiscating all private property that has lain derelict and unused for at least 20 years?

2 You have been appointed as chief executive of the Dunedinglas NHS Trust, with responsibility for deciding spending priorities for the next three years. Combatting the rise in obesity-related diabetes is your most urgent health-related issue, as it affects tens of thousands of people in your area, significantly reducing their quality and length of life. However, this will require diverting funds from existing programs, including the introduction of expensive equipment to enable the Trust to support the life-support systems of babies born at 22 weeks. How can you argue that it is just to deny vulnerable babies the equipment they need to survive, particularly when the money is to be spent on what some regard as self-inflicted ill health?

You should now be able to:

■ explain and illustrate various theories of justice.

2 Justice in procedural and substantive law

This topic will examine various issues and test the theories outlined in the previous topic, attempting to address this question: 'Is the law, and the legal system, just?' If you look at the law through the eyes of Plato, looking for justice in the form of harmony between the different groups in society, you may well be disappointed at the conflict between the legislature and the judiciary. This is seen in situations where judges are considered to uphold human rights of offenders or terrorists over the rights of society or of victims of crime. Alternatively, if you look at the law through the eyes of Marx, you will probably seethe with rage at the way society's benefits have been distributed, and at how the law is used to enforce inequalities. Or, if you put yourself in the position of Robert Nozick, you will be disappointed to observe how much the social justice model promoted by Rawls has influenced policy makers since World War II.

A distinction is often made between procedural law and substantive law. Hart referred to justice 'according to law' and justice 'of the law'. The former term relates to how laws are made and how the legal system operates; the latter to the laws themselves. It is a useful distinction upon which to base this topic. We will now examine a range of issues to help us to reflect on whether the law is just. Any conclusion reached may well depend on a personal view of justice.

Procedural justice

Social justice: legal aid

The Access to Justice Act 1999 established the Legal Services Commission (LSC), with responsibility for administering the annual **legal aid** budget of about £2.1 billion. The LSC set up the Community Legal Service, with responsibility for administering funding for civil justice; and the Criminal Defence Service, which provides professional advice and representation to those under investigation of, or facing, criminal charges.

Legal aid is regarded as an important element in promoting social justice. In a democratic society all citizens have a right to access justice, to receive a fair hearing, and to understand their legal rights and obligations. Many people need help to access and use these rights. Legal aid has been a significant vehicle through which this help is provided in both the civil and criminal justice systems.

However, for some time the budget for legal aid has not been demand led – that is, it does not pay for help and representation to everyone who needs it. The budget has been fixed by the Treasury. Managing a fixed budget inevitably places limits upon the operation of, and qualification to, legal aid. It cannot afford a comprehensive advice or representation service. Entitlement to legal aid in both civil and criminal cases is means tested.

Demand for the service continues to grow. The budget, however, does not. The LSC, therefore, is caught between a rock and a hard place. To meet this dilemma, the budget has to be divided between certain priority areas in both civil and criminal cases, to ensure that funding is being spent 'where it is most needed and can make most difference to people's lives'. This utilitarian approach will inevitably lead to many needs not being met.

Corrective justice: sanctions and damages

When judges or magistrates pass sentence upon an offender, they take into consideration a number of factors. These include the aim of the sentence: this may simply be to punish the offender for breaking the rules

---

In this topic, you will learn how to:

- recognise elements of the theories of justice in procedural and substantive law

- assess the extent to which procedural and substantive law are just.

Study tip

When assessing whether the law is just, try to examine it through the eyes of one or two philosophers, as well as through your own eyes.

Key terms

Legal aid: Government money made available to support people to assert or defend their rights in court; this is increasingly means-tested for civil cases.

Study tip

If the question asks you to consider whether the law is just, discuss a range of issues – issues of procedure and substantive law – as well as so-called miscarriages of justice.

or to deter others from committing the same offence. Balanced against these may be the desire to rehabilitate the offender. The court will also consider aggravating and mitigating factors relating to the offence and to the offender and will have to follow sentencing guidelines. As a result, the sentence should then be just. But in what way just? The sentence is more likely to be 'proportionate' to the offence committed and to the relevant surrounding circumstances.

This is a more sophisticated model than Aristotle's. He argued that the role of the court is to ensure that the gains and losses of each party are equalled out so that the offender doesn't benefit from his wrongdoing and that the victim doesn't suffer loss. This would be applicable to offences such as theft, but even then would not take into consideration the surrounding circumstances.

By contrast, John Stuart Mill did not accept the validity of a retributive approach, regarding all punishment as evil in itself. However, he did accept that imposing sanctions could be justified under the principle of utility if it corresponded to a greater benefit that measurably increased the happiness of others. Aims of sentencing such as rehabilitation, reparation and protection of the public would therefore fall within the utility model.

Compensation award for car crash girl sets personal injury record at £23m

A teenage girl paralysed in a car crash in which her mother was killed is to receive £23m compensation, thought to be record damages.

Agnes Collier, now 17, a pupil at Cheltenham Ladies' College, suffered spinal injuries 'at the very highest level of severity', which left her with no use of her legs and little function in her arms after the accident, on the A436 in Gloucestershire in March 2009.

Her mother, Karen Hood, 48, a teacher at Cheltenham College Junior School, was killed and her older brother, Rufus, suffered a serious head injury, from which he has made a good recovery.

Agnes's father, Dominic Collier, 57, an investment banker, and her stepmother, Jannene, were at the high court in London for the approval of a damages award against the insurers of Anthony Norton, the motorist who caused the accident when he pulled out of a side road, causing the family's car to be hit by an oncoming lorry.

In November 2009 Norton, 48, of Andoversford, Gloucestershire, pleaded guilty to causing death by driving without due care and attention. He was sentenced to six months' jail, suspended for a year, was banned from driving for 18 months and was ordered to do 300 hours' unpaid community work.

Norton, who worked for BMW, resigned from his job after the accident because he could no longer face driving. At his sentencing hearing, Collier and his daughter gave a statement saying they did not want to see him imprisoned.

After the hearing, the family's solicitor, Paul Paxton, of Stewarts Law, said the award would be worth £23m over Agnes's lifetime. Composed of a £7.25m lump sum plus annual payments of £270,000, it is believed to be the highest ever for personal injury, topping the previous record, of £12.2m.

He added: 'While it is a lot of money, Agnes's needs are great.' She would have those needs for the rest of her life, he said.

The Guardian, 19 November 2012

Key cases

Jebson v Ministry of Defence (2000): contributory negligence allows the court to apply the principle of proportionality, an aspect of justice.

Aristotle's model is probably more amenable to the award of damages in civil law. In the tort of negligence, the aim of compensation is to restore the claimant to his pre-tort position, in so far as money can achieve this. The award would include payment for any specialist medical treatment required, for future loss of earnings, for any loss of enjoyment of life, and for pain and suffering. To balance this, any contributory negligence on the part of the claimant will reduce his award. For example, in **Jebson v Ministry of Defence (2000)** 75 per cent of the claimant's award was deducted for his contributory negligence. The claimant had been with a party of about 20 drunken soldiers returning to their barracks in an army lorry after a night out in Portsmouth. He was standing on the lorry's tailgate when he fell out and was injured. This reduction is just because it is proportionate: it reflects that the claimant was largely responsible for his own harm.

In contract law, the basis of assessment of damages is loss of bargain: the claimant is placed in the position he would have been in had the contract been performed. However, only losses that are reasonably within the contemplation of the parties may be recovered. In **Victoria Laundry v Newman (1949)** the defendant had been late in fitting a boiler. As a result, the claimant had suffered not only normal business losses but also exceptional losses, through losing a special contract with the Ministry of Supply. As the exceptional losses were not within the contemplation of the parties at the time of the contract, they were not recoverable.

The judgements in the two cases above reflect the 'middle way' that Aristotle promoted. They also illustrate Aquinas's concept of due proportionality in that damages are awarded *pro rata* according to the merits of the claim, and not automatically in relation to the harm suffered. Under these tests the awards of damages are just.

The criminal process

The trial

Trial by jury enables the case against a defendant to be decided by his peers, who are free to apply their view of justice rather than adhere strictly to the rules of law. In **Ponting (1985)** a civil servant was charged with breaching the Official Secrets Act for releasing privileged information about the sinking of the Argentinian warship General Belgrano. The judge told the jury that any public interest in the information did not provide a defence. And yet the jury acquitted him. A jury does not have to give reasons for its decision. In this case, the jury must have felt that justice was best served, and it was in the public interest, to acquit Ponting.

The rules of evidence adopted in criminal trials seek to balance the interests of the parties to the action. In *Sang* (1979), Lord Diplock stated:

> A trial judge in a criminal trial has always a discretion to refuse to admit evidence if in his opinion its prejudicial effect outweighs its probative value.

For this reason, evidence of previous convictions is not generally admissible unless the facts are strikingly similar to those in the instant case.

On the other hand, even illegally obtained evidence may be admissible. In **Jeffery v Black (1978)** the police arrested a student for the theft of a sandwich, and then conducted an illegal search of his flat, where they discovered some drugs. The magistrates threw out the case after ruling the evidence inadmissible. However, the Divisional Court ruled that the illegality of the search did not justify excluding the evidence it had exposed. This may at first seem to be unjust. However, consider a situation where the police had discovered plans and materials to commit a terrorist attack. They would surely be justified in relying upon the material found in the 'illegal' search in court.

Appeals

In criminal cases heard in the magistrates' court, the defendant may appeal either to the Crown Court against conviction or sentence, or to

---

Key cases

Victoria Laundry v Newman (1949): where a contract is breached, the claimant may only recover damages for losses that were in the thoughts of the parties at the time of their agreement.

Ponting (1985): either illustrates the theory of jury equity, or serves as an example of a perverse decision, depending upon your point of view.

Jeffery v Black (1978): evidence will not be ruled inadmissible merely because it was obtained through an illegally conducted police search.

■ Study tip

Consider this point: is the criminal justice system 'unjust' because innocent people are sometimes, and perhaps inevitably, convicted of crimes that they did not commit? Or can it be considered 'just' because procedures exist to remedy such injustices? Discussion of these questions will lead to a more sophisticated level of evaluation.

the Queen's Bench Divisional Court, part of the High Court, by way of case stated on a point of law. In Crown Court cases the relevant appellate court is the Court of Appeal. Appeals can be made against conviction and/or sentence. Note that permission to appeal is first needed from either the trial judge or the Court of Appeal itself. The need for permission may seem difficult to justify: however, refusal is not an arbitrary decision. It is based upon realism: does the appeal have any merit? If not, why waste time pursuing it?

Under the Criminal Justice Act 1998, the prosecution may also appeal against 'unduly lenient' sentences. The numbers of such appeals is shown in the article below.

Unduly lenient sentence cases referred to the Court of Appeal for 2011

The Attorney General's Office has today released its unduly lenient sentence statistics for 2011. 117 sentences, from 78 cases, were referred to the Court of Appeal by the Law Officers. The Court considered 97 of them were unduly lenient (83%) and 94 sentences were increased (80% of the 117 referred).

Last year the sentences passed on 377 offenders were drawn to the attention of the Law Officers, compared to 342 in 2010 and 369 in 2009.

The Attorney General, the Rt Hon Dominic Grieve QC MP said:

'The unduly lenient sentence scheme allows anyone to refer a sentence to me for consideration. In the vast majority of cases judges impose sentences which are

appropriate to meet the justice of the case, but the scheme provides an important safeguard in those few cases in which the sentence falls significantly outside the proper range.'

The Solicitor General, Edward Garnier QC MP:

'Sentencing is not a precise science. It requires judgments to be made about a whole host of different factors, including any aggravating and mitigating features, and how any relevant guidelines should be applied.

'These statistics are only part of the story. Where there have been mistakes, in relation to the acceptance of pleas by the prosecution, these errors are followed up with the lawyers concerned to ensure they are not repeated.'

www.gov.uk, 5 July 2012

■ Key terms

Criminal Cases Review Commission: independent public body established under the Criminal Appeal Act 1995; there are 11 Commissioners, who review possible miscarriages of justice in the criminal courts of England, Wales and Northern Ireland; they refer appropriate cases to either the Crown Court or the Court of Appeal.

In addition, under the Criminal Justice Act 1972, the Attorney-General may refer a point of law to the Court of Appeal where he wishes to question the judge's direction that has led to an acquittal. For example, in *Attorney-General's Reference* (No. 2 of 1992) the Court of Appeal declared that the defence of automatism is not available where awareness is merely reduced: a total destruction of voluntary control is required. The defendant's acquittal was not affected.

Miscarriages of justice

In spite of this system of appeals, injustices arise: innocent men and women still serve long prison sentences for crimes they have not committed. The Birmingham Six, the Guildford Four, the Maguire Seven, Judith Ward and Stefan Kiszko are among those whose innocence took years to establish. The publicity of cases such as these led to the establishment in 1997 of the **Criminal Cases Review Commission** (CCRC), whose role is to review the cases of those they feel have been wrongly convicted of criminal offences, or unfairly sentenced.

Gerard Hunter, one of the Birmingham Six, released after being sentenced to life imprisonment in 1975 for two pub bombings on November 21, 1974; the justice decision was overturned by the Court of Appeal on 14 March 1991

Gerry Conlon, the best known from the Guildford Four, speaks to the media outside the Houses of Parliament; three decades after being falsely jailed for detonating IRA bombs at English pubs, the British Government apologised to 11 people in one of the nation's worst miscarriages of justice

Eddie Gilfoyle free after maintaining innocence for 18 years in jail

A man who spent 18 years in prison for murdering his heavily pregnant wife despite apparently serious flaws in the case uncovered by miscarriage of justice campaigners, has been released on parole but barred from discussing the matter.

Eddie Gilfoyle, 49, was freed from Sudbury open prison in Derbyshire yesterday.

However, a condition of his parole is that he does not directly or indirectly contact the media.

Gilfoyle's wife was found hanged in the garage of their home in Upton, Merseyside, in 1992. Prosecution evidence alleged that it would have been impossible for Paula Gilfoyle, who was eight-and-half months pregnant, to have strung the rope from a beam without assistance, and that her suicide note betrayed signs it had been written with her husband's help.

Gilfoyle insisted his innocence throughout. Forensic experts who supported him said it would be almost impossible to hang someone who was conscious against their will without leaving signs of a struggle. Police officers cut down her body before tests were carried out, meaning the time of her death could not be established, a crucial part of the case.

Despite the apparent gaps in the prosecution case, Gilfoyle lost two appeals.

A campaign group supporting Gilfoyle said it could not discuss the specifics of his release but indicated in a statement that his lawyers would appeal against the gagging condition, which reportedly includes his family, supporters and lawyers.

A spokesman for the parole board said he could not comment on individual cases but said a condition banning prisoners from talking to the media would be imposed to prevent further offending.

He said: 'Any prisoner who is released is released if we reach a judgment that he is safe to release and that he is not going to go on to commit another offence. It is sometimes the case that one of the licence conditions is that the prisoner being released doesn't get involved with the media. If that is the case, the only reason for that condition would be to prevent further offending.

'For instance, it might be the case that if a high-profile prisoner talks to the media after he has been released, there would be issues concerning the feelings of the victims.

'There might be concerns about the reaction of the general public to someone who has been released from a life sentence.'

The Guardian, 23 December 2010

The CCRC does not consider innocence or guilt, but whether there is new evidence or argument that may cast doubt on the safety of the original decision. Derek Bentley and Sally Clark are among those who have had their convictions quashed by the Court of Appeal following reference from the CCRC.

Cases such as these mentioned here involved gross miscarriages of justice, often where the evidence needed to prove the defendant's innocence was available at the time of the original trial. It is perhaps naïve to believe that some of these convictions would be less likely to occur today. Safeguards were introduced by the Police and Criminal Evidence Act 1984, and the separation of the investigation and prosecution of crime was introduced with the establishment of the Crown Prosecution Service. The only comfort in terms of justice is the fact that systems exist to bring miscarriages of justice to the attention of the appeal courts, even if in some cases a considerable period of time can lapse before the miscarriage is put right. Procedural justice relies very heavily upon the integrity of those responsible for the investigation and prosecution of crime.

Rules of natural justice

Natural justice is often described as containing two basic principles. The first is that the tribunal must not only be impartial, but also seen to be so. Judges should have no personal interest in a case. In the **Pinochet** case (1998), the House of Lords ruled that Senator Pinochet, the former dictator of Chile, could be extradited to Spain to stand trial for his alleged involvement in the torture and death of Spanish citizens in Chile.

One of the judges hearing the case was Lord Hoffman, subsequently found to be a director of Amnesty International, a human rights group that had been given permission to take part in the appeal. Clearly this infringed the principle of impartiality, a doctrine supported by Mill and others, and ignored the rule that a man should not be a judge in his own case (*nemo iudex in causa sua*). The decision in the House of Lords had to be set aside, and a further hearing before a different panel was arranged.

The second principle is that each party to the dispute must have a fair opportunity to present his own case and to answer the case of his opponent. In **Ridge v Baldwin (1964)** the House of Lords ruled that the decision by a police authority to dismiss its chief constable without a personal hearing contravened natural justice. In the words of Lord Hodson, the police authority 'had acted without jurisdiction'.

The rules of natural justice are designed to protect the interests of individuals against arbitrary decisions. In both the *Pinochet* case and *Ridge* v *Baldwin*, the original decision may have been correct. However, each was unreliable because of the breach of the rules of natural justice. In cases of judicial review, natural justice is not necessarily concerned with the rights and wrongs of a decision. Rather it is with the procedure followed in reaching the decision. The application of justice must be fair, and must be seen to be fair.

Key terms

Natural justice: generally refers to the rules that confirm the proper procedures have been followed; for example, those sitting in judgment must be free from bias, and each party to the dispute must have the opportunity to state his case.

Key cases

The **Pinochet** case (1998): illustrates the need for judges not only to be impartial, but also to appear impartial.

Ridge v Baldwin (1964): the rules of natural justice require that an accused has the opportunity to state his case.

Study tip

It is useful to provide some material from both procedural and substantive law to illustrate the operation of justice.

Substantive justice

Crime

The mandatory life sentence

The principle of proportionality, an attribute of justice under Aristotle and Aquinas, generally governs the sentencing practice of judges and magistrates. This satisfies our expectations that the more serious the offence, the harsher the sanction that will be imposed. Those convicted of murder are subject to a mandatory life sentence. The sentencing judge will then impose a tariff, this being the minimum term the murderer has to serve. The starting period for this tariff is generally agreed at 14 years, although for some particularly violent killers a whole-life tariff will be imposed. This means the killer will never be released.

Many agree that imposing a life sentence on a killer is just. Public opinion polls regularly show strong support for the return of the death penalty, to provide a degree of retributive justice. However, the majority of politicians regularly vote against its return, holding the view that such retributive justice is unnecessary.

Some murderers, though, are far less culpable than others: the setting of a tariff does not allow for proportionality, and so may lead to harsh decisions. In *Cocker* (1989) the defendant suffocated his wife, at her insistence, with a pillow; she had been terminally ill and in much pain. The trial judge denied the defendant the partial defence of provocation, leaving the jury with little alternative other than to convict him of murder. In such circumstances, a life sentence may seem a disproportionate punishment. However, the judge may be inclined to provide a measure of justice by imposing a reduced tariff period. For example, in the case of Frances Inglis the trial judge imposed a nine-year tariff period when the defendant was found guilty of murdering her son. She killed him because she believed that she was acting in the best interests of her son and did not want him to suffer any further. In the Court of Appeal, Lord Judge, the Lord Chief Justice ruled that the defendant's motive did not detract from the fact that she intentionally killed him. He commented:

> The law of murder does not distinguish between murder committed for malevolent reasons and murder motivated by familial love. Mercy killing is murder. Until Parliament decides otherwise, the law recognises a distinction between the withdrawal of treatment supporting life, which may be lawful, and the active termination of life, which is unlawful.

Describing the case as 'one of the most difficult sentencing decisions faced in this court', the judges reduced her tariff period from nine to five years. There appeared to be no outcry at the leniency of her sentence. Cases such as this show that, perhaps, justice is better served by allowing judges to pass the sentence they feel to be most appropriate, rather than have a system of fixed sentences.

Defences

Life is sometimes said to be our most valued possession. The premeditated killing of another human being must therefore be considered one of the greatest acts of injustice man can commit. And yet it is recognised that not all premeditated killing is equally culpable. The partial defences of loss of control and diminished responsibility were created to limit liability. The defences of self-defence and automatism will, where successful, excuse liability altogether. However, there are anomalies within the current law that have the potential for creating injustice.

Study tip

Howe (1987) and *Gotts* (1991) illustrate how the *obiter dicta* in an earlier case may form the *ratio decidendi* of a later one. Their facts may also be used to discuss whether the law operates justly.

Study tip

When considering justice in areas of substantive law, you can focus principally upon those areas of law studied in depth in Units 2, 3 and 4.

Key cases

Olley v Marlborough Court Hotel (1949): to be valid, an exclusion clause must be available at the point of agreement.

One of the generally accepted characteristics of justice is that like cases are treated in like manner. Yet the law gives more favourable treatment to those who kill while suffering diminished responsibility or while under provocation, than it does to those whose free will is overpowered by an external threat. The decision of the House of Lords in *Howe* (1987) clearly established that the defence of duress is not available on a charge of murder or attempted murder. Yet one feels much more sympathy for the defendant in *Gotts* (1991), a boy whose life was threatened by his own father, than one does for the defendant in *Byrne* (1960). The Law Commission has proposed adding duress as a defence that would attract conviction for second degree murder. This would introduce parity of treatment under the law, and satisfy a basic requirement of justice that like cases are treated in like manner.

Objective recklessness

In the famous case of Caldwell, objective recklessness was introduced as the appropriate test for recklessness for those charged under the Criminal Damage Act 1971. In *Elliot* v *C* (1983) a young girl of low intelligence was convicted of criminal damage for setting fire to a neighbour's shed. She had been playing with white spirit and matches, without realising the danger involved. The fact that she had not appreciated the risk was of no relevance, as the test was objective. Fortunately, the injustice of this outcome will not occur again, following the decision in *G and R* (2003). However, this could be considered unjust for those who were convicted with objective recklessness before the decision in 2003.

Contract

Exclusion clauses

Parties to a contract may try to limit their liability by relying upon exclusion clauses. The traditional rule of *caveat emptor* (let the buyer beware) could operate harshly against the interests of the weaker bargaining party. The courts have therefore sought to provide some measure of protection to consumers. In **Olley v Marlborough Court Hotel (1949)**, a fur coat belonging to the claimant was stolen from her hotel room. The hotel tried to disclaim liability, pointing to an exclusion clause on a notice on the door of her room. The court held that this exclusion clause was invalid: it had not been brought to Mrs Olley's attention when she booked in at reception. This would appear to be a just result for Mrs Olley, as the clause would not be immediately clear to her.

In *Spurling* v *Bradshaw* (1956) Lord Denning observed that some exclusion clauses were written in 'regrettably small print', and stated that the more harsh or unusual the term was, the more it needed to be brought to the attention of the person signing it – for example by being 'printed in red ink, with a red hand pointing to it'.

In 1977, Parliament passed the Unfair Contract Terms Act to restrict the use of exclusion clauses. Under s2(1) a person cannot exclude liability for death or personal injury resulting from his negligence, and other exclusion clauses are subjected to the test of reasonableness. This Act prevents those with strong bargaining power from taking unfair advantage of weaker parties, and provides a reasonable degree of protection to consumers. In this way, a fairer, more equitable balance is achieved between the bargaining parties.

Further protection is given to consumers by legislation such as the Unfair Terms in Consumer Contracts Regulations 1999, which implement the Unfair Consumer Contract Terms Directive into UK domestic law. If the courts think a term is unfair, then it is not binding on the consumer. In this context, an 'unfair' term is one that puts undue burdens on the consumer, or seeks to reduce his or her statutory rights. The Regulations set out that:

> A contractual term which has not been individually negotiated shall be regarded as unfair if, contrary to the requirement of good faith, it causes a significant imbalance in the parties' rights and obligations arising under the contract, to the detriment of the consumer.

This provision again offers justice to the consumer, who is perceived to be in a weaker bargaining position than a business.

Third party rights

Parliament has also intervened in protecting the rights of third parties to a contract. Traditionally, beneficiaries could not sue unless they were a party to the contract. Again, the courts tried to erode the injustice this caused. In **Jackson v Horizon Holidays (1975)** the Court of Appeal ruled that the claimant could succeed in seeking damages for himself and for members of his family after a package holiday failed to match the advertised description, even though only he, and not his family members, had signed the contract. In 1999, Parliament passed the Contract (Rights of Third Parties) Act, allowing third parties to make a claim where the contract expressly provided for this, or where the contract purported to confer a benefit on them. These provisions should avoid in future the obvious injustices caused in cases such as *Tweddle* v *Atkinson* (1861), where a man was not able to enforce an agreement between his father and father-in-law that conferred a financial benefit on him.

Frustrated contracts

Parliament again was responsible for legislating to ensure that, where a contract is frustrated through no fault of either party, a just outcome can be reached. Traditionally, under the common law the losses lay where they fell: thus, money paid in full in advance for a holiday was not recoverable. However, the Law Reform (Frustrated Contracts) Act 1943 enabled the courts to apportion the losses more fairly between the parties: the court may order 'a just sum' to be paid where either expenses have been incurred or a valuable benefit obtained.

Tort

Duty and breach in negligence

Within the tort of negligence, a duty of care will not be imposed unless it is fair, just and reasonable to do so. In *Hill* v *Chief Constable for West Yorkshire* (1988) the mother of the Yorkshire Ripper's final victim sued the police for damages for not preventing her daughter's death. The House of Lords decided that it would not be fair or just for the police to owe a duty of care to every potential victim of crime, as it could lead to defensive policing practices. This decision appears to be harsh on this claimant but could be considered just, as making the police liable could lead to defensive policing practices and lead the police away from their role of public protection and the detection of crime. However, where the victim is known to the police, such as in *Swinney* v *Chief Constable of Northumbria* (1996), it will be fair, just and reasonable for the police to owe a duty of care and to be liable for any loss suffered as a result of their negligence. This seems just, as the police in this case had accepted responsibility to the claimant.

The decision in **Nettleship v Weston (1971)** might also be regarded as unfair: a learner driver was judged according to the objective standard of a competent driver, and so was liable for injuries caused to her instructor. However, leaving an innocent victim without a remedy is probably the cause of an even greater injustice. In such situations, justice can only be achieved where the potential for injustice to each party is weighed in the balance. This could also be seen as just because the motorist's insurance policy could compensate the injured claimant.

Key cases

Jackson v Horizon Holidays (1975): in the interests of common sense and justice, the courts often seek to mitigate the harsh application of the law.

Nettleship v Weston (1971): learner driver is judged by the same standard as a competent driver; this principle applies to other dangerous activities, for example a surgeon performing his first operation.

It could be argued that an unjust verdict was arrived at in *Bolton* v *Stone* (1951). The innocent claimant was injured by a cricket ball hit out of a ground. Evidence showed that the cricket club had taken all necessary precautions to stop balls from hitting passers-by, as they had erected high fences around the perimeter. Evidence also showed that there was a low risk of harm, as balls had been hit to near where the claimant was only six times in the previous 30 years. It was decided by the House of Lords that the club had taken all necessary precautions to guard against the risk of passers-by being hit. In the words of Lord Normand, 'It is not the law that precautions must be taken against every peril that can be foreseen by the timorous'. This decision might be fair for the club but was unjust on the injured claimant, who received no compensation.

Occupier's liability

The decision in **British Railways Board v Herrington (1972)** illustrates how justice is achieved when the claims of the two parties to the dispute are weighed in the balance. Using the powers under the Practice Statement, the House of Lords ruled that an occupier may be liable for harm caused to trespassers. The fact that the victims were children was a significant factor: the railway company had 'failed to act with due regard to humane considerations' and owed a 'common duty of humanity' to its visitors, even trespassers. This result appeared to be just, as it compensated the injured boy. Also, social conditions had changed since 1929, when the previous leading case on the topic, *Addie* v *Dumbreck* (1929), ruled that the occupiers owed no duty to child trespassers. It was just for the court to decide that owners of land owed a responsibility to visitors, including trespassers.

Strict liability

In *Rylands* v *Fletcher* (1868) liability was imposed where the defendant was unaware of the danger. On the one hand, it seems rough justice to impose strict liability where the offending party may have taken all known precautions. On the other hand, it is arguably justifiable that individuals should be held responsible for the consequences of their actions, even when these consequences are unforeseen. Furthermore, potentially greater injustice is caused by the victim being left without a remedy. On balance, justice may have been achieved.

In *Abouzaid* v *Mothercare (UK) Ltd* (2000) the claimant used the strict liability provisions of the Consumer Protection Act to claim damages for personal injury. The claimant's mother purchased a sleeping bag, designed to be attached to a child's pushchair with elastic straps. Shortly after the purchase, the claimant, who was aged 12 at the time, helped his mother attach the product to his younger brother's pushchair. One of the elastic straps slipped and lashed back. The buckle attached to the elastic strap hit him in the eye, causing serious, permanent damage. The boy sued Mothercare, the supplier of the product, claiming damages in negligence and also under the Consumer Protection Act. This Act introduced strict product liability into UK law in 1987. In order to prove negligence, the claimant had to prove how and why the accident happened, and that it was the defendant's fault. Using a claim based on the Act, the claimant had to show that he was injured as a result of using a faulty product. This would make the claim easier to prove. Going against the trend of judgements in lower courts, the Court of Appeal found that although the product supplier was not negligent, the claimant had proved his strict liability claim and was entitled to damages. This result appeared to be just, as it compensated the injured boy.

■ **Key cases**

British Railways Board v Herrington (1972): changing social conditions may persuade the courts to depart from a previous binding precedent.

Activities

1 The payment of damages is the normal common law remedy for breach of contract. However, this will occasionally be unsuitable, particularly where unique goods or services are being provided. Equity therefore has provided the remedy of specific performance, forcing the defendant to carry out his part of the contract. However, the claimant must have acted in good faith. What do you think would be the just outcome in the following case (*Falcke* v *Gray*)?

An art dealer had agreed to buy a pair of vases for £20 each. However, the owner suspected they were worth much more, so consulted another dealer, and managed to sell them for £200. The original dealer now sought specific performance (i.e. to be awarded the vases for £20 each).

2 In the tort of negligence, a duty of care will be imposed where it is fair and just to do so. Why would it not be fair and just to impose a duty in the following case (*Ashton* v *Turner*)?

The claimant and defendant, after a night's heavy drinking, decided to commit a burglary. Using a borrowed car, they drove around until they came to a shop selling radios. They threw a brick through the window, helped themselves to some radios, and then began to drive off. Two taxi drivers tried to prevent their escape. While attempting to get away, Kevin Turner took a corner at high speed. The car crashed, and Philip Ashton was seriously injured. Ashton now sued for damages in negligence.

You should now be able to:

■ identify the requirements of the question

■ include in a discussion a range of information about theories of justice and examples when justice may or may not have been achieved.

3 Answering questions on the topic of law and justice

Essays on the topic of law and justice provide considerable scope for students to draw upon the areas of law that they have studied. The questions 'Is it fair? Is it just?' can be asked of any material studied throughout the course. Therefore, there is no prescribed content that must be included in an answer. Two equally deserving answers may contain no overlapping content.

Generally, a question will require you to provide:

■ an explanation of what is meant by the terms 'law' and 'justice', with some reference to theory

■ a discussion of justice within a choice of areas of procedural and substantive law

■ an evaluation that addresses the question set.

In the examination, you will have approximately 1 hour available for this section of the paper. This includes time to reflect on the specific issues raised in the question and to plan an answer.

As always, it is important for you to tailor your discussion of the material to the particular question that has been set, rather than to reproduce a prepared essay.

To answer the first part successfully, you need to introduce some explanation of what you understand by the terms 'law' and 'justice'. The focus of this initial part of the answer should be a discussion of what is meant by 'justice', with particular reference to some of the

In this topic, you will learn how to:

■ identify what material questions require

■ provide the required range of information and discussion.

theories explained in Topic 1 of this chapter. Some explanation of your understanding of the term 'law' is also required, as there will be reference made to considerable areas of law later in the essay.

To answer the second part successfully, you need to select a range of appropriate material, and to explain its relevance to the issue of justice. The selection of appropriate material is largely a matter of individual choice: you will be expected to draw it from your own specialised areas of study. It is not the choice of material, but rather the way that it is treated, that distinguishes between students in an examination. Whatever material is selected should be examined in the context of justice, with reference back to the theoretical framework provided earlier. Often it will be possible to identify a controversial area of law, where a matter would be regarded as just under one theory but unjust under another. The ability to draw such distinctions would show a welcome level of sophistication.

Needless to say, the evaluation should focus on the question that is set. This will be designed to stretch and challenge you, to force you to adapt your material to an unexpected slant. Credit is always given for the selection of appropriate material. However, the higher grades cannot be reached without evaluation of the material in the light of the actual issues addressed in the wording of the question. The evaluation ought to be personal: you, as well as philosophers, have different views of justice, and these should be reflected in your answers.

 Activity

Consider how the change of word in the following questions may influence the selection of material and focus of discussion.

1 To what extent does the law promote justice?

2 To what extent does the law achieve justice?

You should now be able to:

■ understand what is required in an essay on the topic of law and justice.

22 Judicial creativity

In this topic, you will learn how to:

- explain the operation of the doctrine of judicial precedent

- explain the scope for judicial creativity in the operation of precedent.

1 Creativity within the doctrine of judicial precedent

This topic deals with the role of judges when using judicial precedent and when interpreting statutes, material that is familiar from Unit 1 of AS Law. However, the emphasis here is on the degree of flexibility, or creativity, that judges enjoy. It therefore examines the extent to which judges are bound by existing rules on the one hand, and the extent to which they are free to change and develop the law on the other.

The operation of judicial precedent

The basic principles

When hearing cases, judges apply existing law from past precedents where they are available. However, they often have to develop past rules to fit new circumstances. This decision will add to the body of law, which can then be used by other judges in later cases. A decision will have greater authority when it is made by judges in either of the appeal courts – the Supreme Court and the Court of Appeal.

This policy is known as the doctrine of precedent (or as *stare decisis*, meaning 'standing by decisions') and it has certain key features:

- *Ratio deciendi* is 'the reason for the decision'. It is the legal principle upon which the outcome of a case is decided. This then sets a precedent for future judges to follow. Well-known examples are: the neighbour principle established in *Donoghue* v *Stevenson* (1932); the point in *G and R* (2003) that the test for recklessness in criminal damage is subjective rather than objective; and the decision in *Williams* v *Roffey* (1990) that the completion of an existing obligation on time, thereby avoiding consequential loss to the other party, can provide sufficient consideration.

- *Obiter dicta* means 'other things said'. This refers to all other legal arguments and comments made by a judge during a judgement, which were not central to deciding the case. For example, a judge might consider a range of possible outcomes had the facts of the case been different. It may be difficult to draw a clear line between the *ratio deciendi* and the *obiter dicta* contained within the judgement. It may depend on the interpretation of the judgement by lawyers and judges in later cases.

- A hierarchy of courts.

- A system of reporting decisions of judges.

Types of precedent

Precedents are described as original whenever the court addresses a point of law for the first time. For example, in **Re A (2000)** the court established a new precedent when it declared that the operation to separate conjoined twins was lawful, even though it would result in the immediate death of one of the girls.

Precedents are binding when they must be followed by a court in a later case. This will occur when the precedent was set by a higher court, particularly an appeal court when there will be three or four judges sitting.

Precedents are persuasive when they are not binding on future cases. Judges, however, are free to adopt persuasive precedents. There are many reasons why precedents are merely persuasive. They may have been set in a lower court; or were part of the *obiter dicta* of the case; or they were set by the Privy Council, such as the decision of a nine-man Privy Council in **Attorney-General for Jersey v Holley (2005)**.

Study tip

Explain the operation of precedent briefly, so that the main body of your answer focuses on discussing the flexibility of the system.

Key cases

Re A (2000): courts retain a residual power to establish new points of law.

Attorney-General for Jersey v Holley (2005): in deciding whether the partial defence of provocation is available on a charge of murder, the jury may consider characteristics of the defendant that relate to the gravity of the provocation, but not those that relate to his powers of self-control.

Key terms

Hierarchy of the courts: organisation of the courts into order of seniority.

Law reports: summaries of the details of decided cases.

The hierarchy of the courts

Judicial precedent operates within the **hierarchy of the courts**. Decisions of the Supreme Court are binding on all lower courts, including the Court of Appeal. Since issuing its Practice Statement in 1966, the (then House of Lords, now Supreme Court) may depart from its own previous decisions 'when it appears right to do so'. However, it will bear in mind the danger of disturbing retrospectively the basis on which contracts, settlements of property and fiscal arrangements have been entered into, and also the need for certainty in the criminal law. This freedom will therefore be used sparingly.

The Court of Appeal is bound by decisions of the Supreme Court, and it is generally bound by its own previous decisions. The justification for this is that the Supreme Court exists to provide a remedy in cases where the Court of Appeal cannot. The Court of Appeal has limited powers to depart from its own previous decisions. Both civil and criminal divisions may take advantage of the three exceptions identified in *Young* v *Bristol Aeroplane* (1944), and the criminal division is free to depart from its own earlier decision in cases where the freedom of an individual is at stake, as stated in *Gould* (1968).

Law Report

Badger cull lawful

Court of Appeal
Published December 14, 2012

Regina (Badger Trust) v Secretary of State for the Environment, Food and Rural Affairs

Before Lord Justice Laws, Lord Justice Rimer and Lord Justice Sullivan
Judgment September 11, 2012

The policy of granting licences to enable farmers and landowners, in areas said to be the worst affected by bovine TB in England, to carry out controlled culling of badgers was lawful.

The Court of Appeal so stated in an ex tempore judgment dismissing the appeal of the claimant, the Badger Trust, from a decision of Mr Justice Ouseley ([2012] EWHC 1904 (Admin)), which dismissed the trust's application for judicial review of a decision by the Secretary of State for the Environment, Food and Rural Affairs, to proceed with a policy of granting such licences pursuant to section 10(2)(a) of the Protection of Badgers Act 1992.

Mr David Wolfe, QC for the trust; **Mr Nigel Pleming, QC** and **Ms Kate Grange** for the secretary of state.

LORD JUSTICE LAWS said that the claimant sought to draw a distinction between the expressions "preventing the spread of disease" in section 10(2)(a) of the Protection of Badgers Act 1992 and "reduce the incidence of disease" in section 21(2)(b) of the Animal Health Act 1981.

It contended that (i) the former expression was a geographical concept, so that (ii) the section 10(2)(a) power was only to be used to prevent the spread of disease outside the area covered by the licence, while (iii) the secretary of state had not applied the section on that basis, proposing that licences under section 10(2) be used in effect for the distinct purpose that was given by section 21(2)(b) of the 1981 Act.

There was nothing in the language of section 10 of the 1992 Act to suggest that its purpose was limited to preventing the spread of disease outside the area of the licence and therefore the area of the proposed cull.

The verb "spread" might, no doubt, in some contexts indicate the occupation of or penetration into a greater geographic area. But in the context of disease it connoted, or might readily connote, an intensification or increase of the incidence of the disease, whether or not over a greater area, and in particular might connote, as it did naturally in the present context, the spread of disease from one species to another: from badgers to cattle.

In short it made very little sense to contemplate a provision concerned with preventing the spread of disease outside but not at all inside the area where action was being taken.

Lord Justice Rimer and Lord Justice Sullivan agreed.

Solicitors: **Bindmans LLP; Treasury Solicitor.**

A law report from The Times

Law reporting

Reports of the judgments of cases are required for the system of judicial precedent to operate successfully. Since 1865, **law reports** have been published by the Incorporated Council of Law Reporting for England and Wales, which is a joint society of the Inns of Court, the Law Society and the Bar Council. In 1953, the Council began publishing the Weekly Law Reports, which are available either weekly or in annual bound volumes. The All England Law Reports are another authorised series published weekly, by LexisNexis Butterworths. Some newspapers publish summaries of important cases, and online databases of law reports are increasingly available. Reports have to be authorised by the judge giving the judgement. Reports are generally written by lawyers, usually barristers, who were present in court when the judgement was delivered.

Means of avoiding precedent

At first sight, judicial precedent seems to operate restrictively, preventing judges from creative development of the law. The very term *'stare decisis'* implies rigidity and inflexibility, and the use of terms such as 'binding precedent' and 'hierarchy of the courts' reinforces this point. Furthermore, the fact that the Supreme Court is often reluctant to use its powers under the Practice Statement, and the fact that the Court of Appeal has only limited powers to overrule its own previous decisions, confirm the impression that judicial precedent straightjackets judges.

However, further examination reveals that judges are able to perform a delicate balancing act between the undoubted advantages of consistency and fairness on the one hand, and flexibility and creativity on the other. Within the operation of precedent, there are several ways in which a judge – even one in a lower court – can decide flexibly, enabling them to avoid a binding precedent that is deemed inappropriate. This flexibility also allows a judge to develop a new precedent when the situation requires it.

Distinguishing

A precedent set in one case should be followed in all later cases where the facts of the two cases are similar. However, where the facts in the second case are different from the binding precedent, the judge in the later case may choose not to apply the binding precedent by **distinguishing** the first case. For example, a contract is not formed unless the two parties intended to enter into a legally binding agreement. Where an agreement is made in a domestic setting, it is presumed that the agreement is not intended to be legally binding. In the case of **Balfour v Balfour (1919)** Mr Balfour agreed to pay his wife monthly maintenance while he was posted to Ceylon. Soon after, they separated, and the payments stopped. Mrs Balfour then took action to hold her husband to his promise. However, her action failed: the court decided that this was a domestic arrangement rather than a legally enforceable contract.

However, the presumption in favour of a domestic arrangement can be rebutted by evidence showing that the parties had intended to enter into a legal relationship. This occurred in **Merritt v Merritt (1971)**. After moving out of the family home, Mr Merritt made a signed, written agreement with his wife to pay her maintenance, and she would continue the mortgage repayments. Furthermore, he would eventually transfer the home into her name. When he later refused to do so, Mrs Merritt brought a court action to enforce the agreement. The court decided that the facts were different from those in *Balfour v Balfour* (1919). It was able to distinguish the facts of the two cases, and the presumption in favour of a domestic arrangement was successfully rebutted. The agreement became legally enforceable as there had been an intention to enter into a legal relationship.

The key differences between the two cases were that in *Merritt v Merritt* (1971) the husband and wife had separated before making their agreement, and that their agreement had been written down and signed. These points allowed the court to distinguish the precedent set in *Balfour v Balfour* (1919). Theoretically, at least, the power to distinguish offers judges unlimited discretion to avoid existing precedents. Another example of distinguishing is in the cases of *Brown* (1993) and *Wilson* (1996). As you have read in other chapters, in *Brown* a group of gay men carried out sadomasochistic acts of violence on each other. When charged with various non-fatal offences, the men argued that they had a defence of consent. The judge at their trial refused to allow the defence, and as a result the men pleaded guilty. The men then appealed against the judge's ruling and eventually the House of Lords established the precedent that the defence of consent could not always apply to cases involving offences of ABH and s20 OAPA.

In *Wilson*, Alan Wilson was encouraged by his wife to carve his initials onto her bottom as a sign of his love for her. He was subsequently charged with ABH and pleaded the defence of consent. The trial judge considered that he was bound by the precedent in *Brown* and refused to allow Wilson to use the defence. He appealed to the Court of Appeal, which distinguished the precedent of *Brown* on the facts of the case. The Wilsons were a married couple carrying out consensual activities in their own home. The facts of *Brown* were considered different as the defendants were a group of sadomasochistic individuals who carried out the activities on each other for their sexual pleasure.

Key terms

Distinguishing: court finds sufficient factual difference between two apparently similar cases that they are able to reach different decisions.

Key cases

Balfour v Balfour (1919); Merritt v Merritt (1971): where the facts of a case are materially different from those in the case establishing the precedent, the court may distinguish between them.

Key terms

Reversing: appeal court decides that the law was wrongly applied when the same case was heard in a lower court.

Overruling: court decides that the law was wrongly applied in an earlier, different case and the otherwise binding precedent established does not have to be followed.

Key cases

Kingston (1994): each appeal court is able to reverse the decision made by a court inferior to itself in the same case.

Addie v Dumbreck (1929): a duty of care was not owed by landowners to trespassers.

British Railways Board v Herrington (1972): where social conditions had changed existing precedents could be reviewed and overruled.

Lister v Hesley Hall (2001): previous decision could be overruled when it was felt the previous decision was wrongly decided.

Reversing

Sometimes, a higher court will decide that a lower court reached the wrong decision in a case. The higher court will then alter the decision made by the lower court in the same case. This is known as **reversing** the decision of the lower court. This famously occurred twice in **Kingston (1994)**. The defendant, who had paedophilic tendencies, went to the flat of another man, named Penn; unknown to Kingston, Penn intended to lure Kingston into a compromising situation in order to blackmail him. Penn drugged Kingston's coffee, and then took Kingston into a bedroom where there was a 15-year-old boy, also drugged. Kingston performed various acts with the boy and was subsequently convicted of indecent assault. Kingston appealed, and the Court of Appeal reversed the conviction, disagreeing with the trial judge's ruling. The appeal court ruled that a person cannot be blamed for acts committed only because of a drug surreptitiously administered. An appeal was then taken to the House of Lords, who reversed the Court of Appeal decision by ruling that a drugged intent is still an intent: involuntary intoxication might go to mitigation of sentence, but could not be a defence in these circumstances.

Another example is *Fitzpatrick* v *Sterling Housing Association (1999)*. Reversing the Court of Appeal, the House of Lords held that a gay man was entitled to take over the tenancy formerly held by his long-term male partner, now deceased, under the Housing Act 1988. Lord Slynn said the claimant could claim as 'a member of the family' living with the deceased at the time of his death. This would be equally true for an unmarried, co-habiting heterosexual couple in a serious relationship. The word 'family' is used in many senses, Slynn said, some wider than others, and if the claimant could show (as on the facts he could) the mutual inter-dependence, sharing of lives, caring, love, commitment and support that are presumed to exist between married couples, that would be enough to establish a family relationship.

Overruling

When **overruling**, the court decides that the point of law decided in a previous case was wrong and changes it. In **Addie v Dumbreck (1929)** a four-year-old boy wandered onto the defendant's land and was crushed in the wheel of a colliery machine. 'No Trespassers' signs were in place, but the defendant was aware that these were regularly ignored by children. The House of Lords decided that there was no general duty of care owed by the defendant to trespassers.

Forty years later, attitudes had changed. In **British Railways Board v Herrington (1972)**, the claimant was a six-year-old boy who suffered serious burns and injuries on an electrified railway line. He had stepped over a damaged fence running alongside the line. The House of Lords decided that, in the years since the decision in *Addie* v *Dumbreck* (1929), social and physical conditions had changed dramatically: in particular, the growth of towns had brought about a lack of play areas for children, leading to an increased temptation to trespass. Also, it was now expected that landowners should take responsibility for those coming onto their land, especially, as in this case, where boundary fences had been neglected. In view of this change in attitudes, it would now be right for an occupier to owe a duty of care to trespassers. The House of Lords used the 1966 Practice Statement to overrule the decision of *Addie* v *Dumbreck* (1929).

Another example is **Lister v Hesley Hall (2001)**. A number of former pupils sued in respect of sexual abuse by the warden of a residential school. Overruling the Court of Appeal decision in *T* v *North Yorkshire County Council* (1998), the House of Lords said there had been a close connection between the warden's acts and his employment at the school, and it would not be unfair or unjust to hold the defendant vicariously liable in this case.

When a higher court overrules a decision of a lower court, it does not (in theory) change the law, but says that the earlier case was decided wrongly. This is of more than academic importance, because it means that the law as declared by the higher court does not run only from the date of the decision, but has retroactive effect. But it does not alter the result of the earlier case, which remains as originally decided unless there is still time for it to be taken to appeal.

Activities

1. Review the case of *Sweet* v *Parsley* (1970). What was the basis for the House of Lords' decision to reverse the decision of the Queen's Bench Division?

2. In Units 1 and 2, you may have encountered the following cases. What point of law was overruled in each of them?
   Shivpuri (1981)
   Hall v *Simons* (2000)
   G and R (2003)
   Miliangos v *George Frank Textiles* (1976)

You should now be able to:

- explain how judicial precedent operates

- understand the scope for judicial creativity available within the operation of judicial precedent.

2 Creativity within statutory interpretation

The operation of statutory interpretation

The basic principles

The responsibility of Parliament for the legislative process has ended by the time that a Bill receives royal assent. Members of Parliament have no further influence over the law. Under the doctrine of the separation of powers, it is the role of the judiciary to interpret and apply that legislation. To ensure that they manage this responsibility effectively, judges have developed a range of approaches. Although many of these approaches are called rules, they are not necessarily binding upon judges: discretion exists in the selection of which approach to adopt, and the outcome of a case may depend entirely upon the approach selected.

The literal rule

Using this rule, judges follow the literal meaning of the words used in the statute, rather than seeking to discover the intention of Parliament behind the legislation. Lord Simonds argued that it is the duty of the court to interpret the words used and even if these words are ambiguous, judges should not go on a 'voyage of discovery' to find their intended meaning. In **Whiteley v Chappell (1868)** the defendant had voted twice in an election, first using his own name, and secondly masquerading as someone who had died. He was charged with impersonating a person

In this topic, you will learn how to:

- explain the operation of the doctrine of statutory interpretation

- explain the scope for judicial creativity in the operation of statutory interpretation.

Study tip

Any explanation of the rules of interpretation should be quite brief, so that the answer can concentrate the more important discussion of the opportunity for judicial creativity.

Key cases

Whiteley v Chappell (1868): adopting the literal rule can defeat the purpose of the legislation.

entitled to vote in an election. Using the literal rule, the court found him not guilty: he could not be guilty of impersonating someone entitled to vote, since dead people are not entitled to vote. This result would appear to be unfair as the defendant had clearly voted twice, which was against the rules.

The golden rule

The golden rule is used to mitigate, or reduce, the harshness of the literal rule. However, it is restricted to cases where the key word to be interpreted has more than one meaning. If one meaning would result in a 'manifestly absurd' outcome, another is to be preferred. Lord Reid once declared:

> You may not for any reason attach to a statutory provision a meaning which the words of that statute cannot possibly bear. If they are capable of more than one meaning then you can choose between those two meanings, but beyond that you cannot go.

This approach was adopted in **Adler v George (1964)**. Under s3 of the Official Secrets Act 1920 it was an offence to be found 'in the vicinity of a prohibited place'. The accused was arrested inside Marham Royal Air Force station, and argued that the phrase 'in the vicinity of' implied being 'outside of' a prohibited place. Lord Parker used the golden rule: 'in the vicinity of' could mean 'being in or in the vicinity of' the prohibited place. To have acquitted the defendant would have been a manifestly absurd outcome.

The mischief rule

A very different approach can be seen in the mischief rule. Here, the courts identify the mischief, or problem, with the old common law, and then examine the remedy provided by Parliament. They then try to ensure that they give effect to this remedy. This approach was adopted in **Smith v Hughes (1960)**. Under the Street Offences Act 1958 it was an offence for prostitutes to solicit in the street. In this case, the prostitutes were soliciting men from an open window of a house. Using the mischief rule, the courts identified the problem with the old common law (harassing people in the street), and looked at how Parliament tried to overcome this (by preventing soliciting in the street). They gave effect to this by finding the women guilty. It could have been argued under the literal rule that they were not 'in the street' when attracting the attention of passing men and so were not guilty of soliciting 'in the street'.

Lord Parker, giving the judgement of the court, said:

> Observe that it does not say there specifically that the person who is doing the soliciting must be in the street. Equally it does not say that it is enough if the person who receives the solicitation or to whom it is addressed is in the street. For my part, I approach the matter by considering what is the mischief aimed at by this Act. Everybody knows that this was an Act intended to clean up the streets, to enable people to walk along the streets without being molested or solicited by common prostitutes. Viewed in that way, it can matter little whether the prostitute is soliciting while in the street or is standing in a doorway or on a balcony, or at a window, or whether the window is shut or open or half open; in each case her solicitation is projected to and addressed to somebody walking in the street. For my part, I am content to base my decision on that ground and that ground alone.

The purposive approach

This approach is becoming increasingly popular in UK courts. Here, judges examine not only the words used on the pages of the Act, but also

Key cases

Adler v George (1964): where there are two meanings to the key word to be interpreted, the court can choose the one that will lead to the least absurd result.

Smith v Hughes (1960): the mischief rule may be used to ensure that effect is given to the remedy that Parliament was seeking to impose in the legislation.

the intention of Parliament when using these words. An example of this approach was seen in the case of **Jones v Tower Boot Company**, a case involving vicarious liability. The claimant had suffered constant racial harassment by fellow workers at the Tower Boot Company.

The Race Relations Act 1976 stated:

> Anything done by a person in the course of employment shall be treated for the purposes of this Act as done by his employer as well as by him, whether or not it was done with the employer's knowledge or approval.

The employers argued that the harassment was not authorised, and therefore not done 'in the course of employment' and that they shouldn't be liable for the actions of their employees.

The Court of Appeal adopted a purposive approach: the purpose of the Race Relations Act 1976 was to prevent, in the workplace, the discriminatory conduct to which the victim had been subjected. Therefore the employers were vicariously liable for the actions of their employees.

Creativity within the operation of statutory interpretation

Approaches that restrict judicial creativity

The literal approach is inflexible. It is argued in its favour that it promotes consistency and encourages parliamentary draftsmen to be precise. However, neither of these two arguments carries great weight. Firstly, consistency is not a virtue in itself: it needs to be allied to justice and fairness. Secondly, it is unreasonable to expect parliamentary draftsmen to be able to anticipate every conceivable interpretation, and misinterpretation, of their words. The argument in favour of the literal rule that carries most weight is that it respects a clear demarcation between the legislative function of Parliament and the interpretative function of the courts, thereby maintaining the doctrine of the separation of powers.

The main criticism of the literal rule is that it can defeat the legislative intention of Parliament. Clearly the defendant in *Whiteley* v *Chappell* (1868) was guilty of committing the very offence that Parliament had been mindful to outlaw. However, due to unfortunate draftsmanship and literal interpretation, he was acquitted. When Acts fail to meet their obvious and stated purpose, the law becomes discredited. Unfortunately, the golden rule provides only a limited safety valve, as its operation is restricted to cases where words have more than one meaning.

Approaches that promote judicial creativity

The mischief rule and the purposive approach both require judges to examine the intention of Parliament when introducing the legislation. To achieve a proper understanding of Parliament's intention, they seek to appreciate the circumstances leading to the introduction of the Bill. This is likely to mean that they refer to **Hansard** (the record of parliamentary debates) to read what the legislators said when the Bill was debated. This enables them to give effect to the declared intentions of Parliament. For example, in the case of *Jones* v *Tower Boot Company Ltd* (1997), if the Court of Appeal judges had adopted the literal approach, they may have agreed with the Employment Appeal Tribunal that racial harassment was not 'in the course of employment' as it was neither a wrongful act authorised by the employer nor an act, though authorised, carried out in an unauthorised way – the familiar definition used in vicarious liability in tort.

Key cases

Jones v Tower Boot Company Ltd (1997): by adopting a purposive approach, the court gave effect to the intention of Parliament when passing the Act.

Key terms

Hansard: edited verbatim report of proceedings in both Houses of Parliament; Commons Hansard covers proceedings in the Commons Chamber, Westminster Hall and Standing Committees; Lords Hansard covers proceedings in the Lords Chamber and its Grand Committees; both contain written Ministerial Statements and written Answers.

Rather than relying upon this interpretation of 'course of employment', the Court of Appeal adopted a purposive approach to the meaning of this phrase in s32(1) of the Race Relations Act 1976. This allowed a broader understanding of its meaning, and one that was more consistent with the natural meaning of the words. Furthermore, the Act was designed to prevent racial harassment at work: this was better achieved by holding employers responsible for the actions of their employees. Where employers had taken reasonable steps to ensure that such harassment did not arise, a defence would be available to them. Where they had not, it would not be reasonable to excuse them. The purpose of the 1976 Act could only be achieved by holding employers responsible for the conduct of their employees.

External aids

When the courts are seeking to discover the intention of Parliament, they are prepared to refer to external sources of information. Although this is time-consuming, it is necessary if judges are to give effect to the intentions of Parliament. Hansard is the record of parliamentary debates, and since the decision of the House of Lords in *Pepper* v *Hart* (1993), judges are able to refer to the speech of the government minister or promoter of the Bill in Parliament.

The Earl of Erroll: My Lords, I thought Pepper v Hart only applied if there was ambiguity on the face of the Bill or a conflict with European law? Otherwise, what is in the Bill applies and you cannot look at Pepper v Hart.

Baroness Hollis of Heigham: My Lords, as far as concerns Pepper v Hart, if there is any ambiguity or division of opinion as to what may be the situation, then, as I understand it, you may refer to the columns of Hansard in so far as they clarify the policy intent of Parliament.

Earl Ferrers: My Lords, before the Minister sits down, could she also clarify one point for me? It relates to what my noble friend Lord Tebbit said. He said that when you go down to inspect the register, if the birth certificate has been changed, why keep the original? The Minister says there are reasons for that, but does that not mean that there are then two birth certificates—the original one and the amended one? If so, what is the point of saying that nobody must refer to the original if it is still there?

Baroness Hollis of Heigham: My Lords, this is all about privacy and the right to privacy circumscribed by certain considerations—national security, crime, public health—that may impinge on that. There are indeed two birth certificates. People would have access to the acquired gender birth certificate. It would not be distinctive in any way. But the original one would exist in the same way as when studying the maps of Nottingham, I found that streets that later got called Corporation Street were originally known as Asylum Lane. I did not, as a result, suggest to my students that they got rid of the original maps. They kept both sets.

Lord Swinfen: My Lords, surely the birth certificate is a certified copy of the entry in the register of births. Is the Minister saying that that original entry is to be changed?

A Hansard report of a House of Lords debate

Key cases

Wilson v Secretary of State for Industry (2003): judicial access to Hansard should operate within narrowly defined limits.

Key terms

The Law Commission: statutory independent body created by the Law Commissions Act 1965 to keep the law under review and to recommend reform where it is needed.

However, clear limits have subsequently been placed upon reference to Hansard. In **Wilson v Secretary of State for Industry (2003)** the House of Lords ruled that Hansard may be consulted to discover the meaning of a word used in the legislation, but should not be consulted to try to unearth the reasons for the legislation. Warnings were also issued about the reliability of ministerial speeches as indicating the intention of Parliament. This judgment will reduce the 'fishing expedition' approach to the use of Hansard, and will limit reference to it in future cases.

Law Commission reports help judges to identify the thinking behind an Act. When Parliament legislates in response to their reports, the courts have ready access to a reliable critique of the failings of the previous law, and to the principles behind the proposed remedies. *G and R* (2003) illustrates this point well. The case concerned the *mens rea* for criminal damage. In *Caldwell* (1982) the House of Lords had introduced an objective test for recklessness. This had proved controversial. In *G and R*, Lord Bingham reviewed the historical development of the *mens rea* for criminal damage, starting with s51 of the Malicious Damage Act 1861.

He referred in detail to the initial working report of the Law Commission, in which it was stated:

> We assume that the traditional elements of intention, knowledge and recklessness (in the sense of foresight and disregard of consequences or awareness and disregard of the likelihood of the existence of circumstances) will continue to be required for serious crime.

Lord Bingham then referred to a Law Commission definition of recklessness produced one month before its final report on criminal damage. According to the first limb of this definition, a person is reckless if 'knowing that there is a risk that an event may result from his conduct or that a circumstance may exist, he takes that risk'. By reference to these proposals from the Law Commission, Lord Bingham was able to establish that the test for recklessness at the time of the 1971 Act was presumed to be subjective. In this way, he laid the foundation for overruling the decision in *Caldwell*, and reimposed a subjective test for recklessness in criminal damage. Other external aids, such as government White Papers, treaties, textbooks and dictionaries, may be used by the court in trying to discover the intention of Parliament when passing legislation.

Activity

Research the facts of the following cases. Identify the approach or rule adopted by the courts in each case. Consider the likely outcomes if different rules had been adopted.

a *Corkery* v *Carpenter* (1951)

b *Fisher* v *Bell* (1960)

c *Cheeseman* v *DPP* (1990)

You should now be able to:

- explain how the rules of statutory interpretation operate

- understand the scope for judicial creativity within the operation of the rules of statutory interpretation.

3 The creative role of judges

The constitutional relationship between Parliament and the judiciary

According to constitutional convention, Parliament is the supreme legislative authority in the United Kingdom, and no other body can challenge this position. In the words of Lord Radcliffe: 'It is unacceptable constitutionally that there should be two sources of law-making at work at the same time'. In recent years, however, Parliament has chosen to place some limits upon its own sovereign legislative authority, through membership of the European Union and through the passage of the Human Rights Act 1998.

Through membership of the European Union, Parliament has allowed primacy to be given to European law over conflicting national law, as seen in the series of cases known as *Factortame*. The law lords declared part of the Merchant Shipping Act 1988 invalid as it conflicted with European Union law, demonstrating not only the subordination of primary national legislation to European law, but also, and of more immediate relevance, the ability of the judiciary to set aside the clearly expressed will of Parliament.

In this topic, you will learn how to:

- explain the constitutional relationship between Parliament and the judiciary

- discuss the arguments for and against the exercise of judicial creativity.

Key terms

Relationship between Parliament and the judiciary: according to the unwritten constitution, Parliament is responsible for making law, and judges for interpreting and applying law.

The passage of the Human Rights Act 1998 also confers greater power on the judiciary. Where judges rule that part of an Act of Parliament has breached one of the human rights contained within the European Convention on Human Rights as enshrined in the 1998 Act, they have the power to make a declaration of incompatibility. This occurred in **A and Others v Secretary of State for the Home Department (2004)**. The House of Lords ruled that s23 of the Anti-Terrorism, Crime and Security Act 2001, in permitting the indefinite detention of foreign nationals without charge, was incompatible with article 5 of the European Convention of Human Rights. Parliament felt obliged to comply with this judgment, and so the Prevention of Terrorism Act 2005 was passed.

Subject to these two exceptions (European Law and the Human Rights Act), the judiciary is constitutionally bound to remain obedient to the expressed will of Parliament in its legislative capacity. In other words, the courts should not act in a way that frustrates the stated will of Parliament. It is worthwhile in this regard to examine parts of the speech of Lord Nicholls in the Privy Council decision in *Attorney-General for Jersey* v *Holley* (2005).

The case of *Holley* (2005) concerned the partial defence of provocation. In *Smith* (2000), the House of Lords ruled that psychological characteristics of the defendant could be considered when asking whether the reasonable man would have reacted in the same way under the same provocation. Lord Hoffman explained that a jury 'may think that there was some characteristic of the accused, whether temporary or permanent, which affected the degree of control which society could reasonably have expected of him and which it would be unjust not to take into account'. Following this guideline, it was thought that a jury could have been asked to consider whether a person with several characteristics could reasonably be expected to retain self-control under provocation.

This judgment significantly diluted the objective test, but it proved short-lived. In 2005, a nine-member Privy Council heard the appeal of Holley, a violent chronic alcoholic who had killed his girlfriend after provocation. Delivering the opinion of the majority, Lord Nicholls was critical of the approach of the House of Lords in *Smith*. The main target of his criticism was not so much the diluted test adopted in *Smith*; rather it was the attempt by the House of Lords to depart from the law as declared by Parliament in the Homicide Act 1957. In his words: 'It is not open to judges to change the common law and thereby depart from the law as declared by Parliament.' He then went on to explain how the judgment in *Smith* conflicted with the 1957 Act.

Underpinning this judgment is recognition by Lord Nicholls of the constitutional position of Parliament as the supreme legislative authority. Judges cannot develop the common law either to rival or to replace the declared will of Parliament in its enactments. Nor can they interpret statutes to the point of extinction by imposing their own judgment of what the law should be because of their distaste for what it actually is.

Public policy issues

As the supreme legislative authority, Parliament is responsible for determining issues of policy. The anti-discrimination legislation of the Labour government in the 1960s and 1970s, for example, clearly concerned significant policy issues about race and gender, and set new standards for employers, public bodies, service providers and others in their treatment of disadvantaged or minority groups. The Civil Partnership Act 2004 and the Equality Act 2006 extended earlier provisions, demonstrating a new policy direction.

According to convention, the judiciary leaves matters of policy to Parliament. Ronald Dworkin distinguished between principles and policy.

> ### Key cases
>
> **A and Others v Secretary of State for the Home Department (2004):** courts may rule statutes to be incompatible with human rights legislation.

Principles are concerned with rights, and with standards of fairness and justice – for example: justice is blind (impartial); people are equal before the law; defendants are presumed innocent until found guilty. These should always be applied by judges. Policies, on the other hand, are concerned with achieving social or political goals, such as the redistribution of wealth or the protection of the environment. These, Dworkin argues, are the responsibility of the legislature rather than of the judiciary. He condemns judges who stray from principles into areas of policy.

However, in some cases it is inevitable that judges stray into areas of policy. This is particularly seen when judges interpret statutes. For example, the case of **Royal College of Nursing v DHSS (1981)** involved interpretation of the Abortion Act 1967. Under the Act, abortions had to be carried out by a 'registered medical practitioner'. Since 1967, various drugs have been developed making it possible for nurses to carry out this operation. The court had to decide whether a nurse was a 'registered medical practitioner'. In a dissenting judgment, two law lords argued that the matter should be left to Parliament since it would be a significant policy change to allow nurses to carry out abortions. This argument failed to persuade the majority, who applied the mischief rule.

In developing the common law, judges also stray into matters of policy. In **Shaw v DPP (1962)** the House of Lords recognised the new offence of conspiracy to corrupt public morals. In the words of Viscount Simonds:

> there remains in the courts a residual power to enforce the supreme and fundamental purpose of the law, to conserve not only the safety and order, but also the moral welfare of the State.

In his dissenting judgment, Lord Reid argued that Parliament is the proper place for deciding whether the law should intervene further in the enforcement of morality:

> Some think that the law already goes too far, some that it does not go far enough. Parliament is the proper place, and I am firmly of the opinion the only proper place, to settle that.

This view was echoed by Lord Simon in *DPP for Northern Ireland* v *Lynch* (1975) where he argued that 'the collective wisdom of Parliament' is better suited to solving matters of social policy.

The third limb of the *Caparo* v *Dickman* (1990) test for duty of care in the tort of negligence encourages the judiciary to consider policy issues. In *Hill* v *Chief Constable of West Yorkshire* (1988) the House of Lords declined to impose a duty of care upon the police, as it would inhibit their judgment and encourage defensive policing strategies. In contrast, it was held in **Ashton v Turner (1980)** that a duty of care was not owed by one criminal to another while engaged in criminal activity.

Judges also engage in policy considerations when examining human rights under the Human Rights Act 1998. In *A and Others* v *Secretary of State for the Home Department* (2004) the courts declared existing counter-terrorism legislation to be incompatible with rights contained within the European Convention on Human Rights, as enshrined in the 1998 Act. Although the decision of the courts was based upon established principles such as *habeas corpus*, it has continued to have a serious effect upon the implementation of government policy.

In cases of judicial review where the decisions of government ministers may be in issue, judges inevitably have to consider matters of government policy. In **Council of Civil Service Unions v Minister for the Civil Service (1984)**, ('**The GCHQ Case**') the House of Lords upheld, on the grounds of national security, the ban on trade union membership imposed upon employees of the government surveillance headquarters in Cheltenham by the prime minister. This decision was seen by many

Key cases

Royal College of Nursing v DHSS (1981): a wide interpretation of the words used in an Act may be applied by the courts in order to give effect to the remedy devised by Parliament.

Shaw v DPP (1962): under common law, the courts retain a residual power to develop new offences.

Ashton v Turner (1980): where two parties are engaged in criminal activity, the law will not allow the first party to claim damages for harm suffered due to the negligence of the other party.

The GCHQ Case (1984); DPP v Hutchinson (1990): this combination of cases may be used to illustrate that the courts decide matters concerning public policy in an impartial manner, without due deference to the government of the day.

as pro-government and anti-trade union. However, it was based upon an interpretation of established law and not upon policy considerations.

In *DPP* v *Hutchinson* (1990) the House of Lords ruled that protesters at Greenham Common, a US airbase housing nuclear missiles, had the right to protest outside the base even though the Minister of Defence had banned them by issuing a bylaw denying them access to the land. Although this decision thwarted government policy, it was based upon existing principles of law and not upon policy issues.

Judicial attitudes

Judges openly acknowledge their law-making role. In the words of Lord Reid: 'We do not believe in fairy tales any more, so we must accept the fact that, for better or worse, judges do make law.' However, he recognised the demarcation between the judiciary and Parliament. In *Knuller* v *DPP* (1973), another case concerned with the offence of conspiracy to corrupt public morals, he declared:

> I said in Shaw's case and I repeat that Parliament and Parliament alone is the proper authority to change the law with regard to the punishment of immoral acts. Rightly or wrongly the law was determined by the decision in Shaw's case. Any alteration of the law as so determined must in my view be left to Parliament.

Other judges have proved to be more ready to embrace a creative approach. Lord Denning was driven by the basic principle: 'The judge should make the law correspond with the justice that the case requires.' In *Central London Property Trust Ltd* v *High Trees House Ltd* (1947) he developed the doctrine of promissory estoppel to prevent claimants going back on a promise on which the defendant had relied. In *Davis* v *Johnson* (1979) he ignored a binding precedent set by the Court of Appeal only days earlier, and extended the protection available under the Domestic Violence and Matrimonial Proceedings Act 1976. In *Schorsch Meier GmbH* v *Hennin* (1974) he ignored a binding precedent set in the *Havana Railways* case (1961) by the House of Lords. Lord Denning declared that damages may be paid in currencies other than sterling, and that the old rule had run its course.

In *Magor and St Mellons RDC* v *Newport Corporation* (1950) Lord Denning made the following declaration in support of this creative role:

> We sit here to find out the intention of Parliament and carry it out, and we do this better by filling in the gaps and making sense of the enactment than by opening it up to destructive analysis.

He expressed his criticism of the 'ultra-legalistic' interpretations that would deprive claimants of their rights. A cynic might conclude that this does more to give power to the judiciary than to carry out the intention of Parliament. Viscount Simonds described filling in the gaps as a 'naked usurpation of the legislative function under the thin disguise of interpretation'.

This tension within the judiciary is not novel. **Karl Llewellyn**, a leading figure in the school of **American Legal Realism** of the 1920s and 1930s and a keen observer of judicial methods, argued that the law is indeterminate: in other words, cases are capable of more than one possible outcome. Judges merely use legal rules and reasons to justify decisions they have already reached for non-legal reasons. Therefore, when interpreting statutes they may either stick closely to the text, or look beyond it, to justify their decisions. When considering precedents, they may either view them as loose (broad in application) and so follow them, or as strict (narrow in application) and so distinguish them. Lord Denning would clearly belong to the class of judges who looks beyond the text of the statutes, and who views precedents narrowly. Lord Reid and Viscount

Key terms

Karl Llewellyn: American legal scholar Llewellyn argued that judges are influenced by a range of factors that are unrelated to the law; he was therefore critical of those who viewed the law as something that operated simply as a system of objective rules.

American Legal Realism: legal realists believe that the outcome of cases is decided not by the law in the textbooks but by other factors. Jerome Frank once declared that a case might be decided by what the judge had for breakfast.

Simonds would belong to those who look at the text closely, rather than beyond it, and who view precedents as being broad in application.

Should judges make law?

The benefits

Judges are responsible for the development of the common law. Crime, contract and tort contain large elements of judge-made law. Even topics governed by statute, such as theft, occupiers' liability and consumer protection, have generated considerable case law as the legislation has been subjected to scrutiny in the courts. There is no doubt that judges play a significant role in creating and developing the law. The question arises: should they?

There are clear benefits to be derived from an active judiciary. First, it provides flexibility. Appropriate precedents may be followed, and inappropriate ones may be distinguished or overruled. *British Railways Board* v *Herrington* (1972), and **R v R (1991)** demonstrates the willingness of senior judges to adapt the law to changing social circumstances. *Attorney-General for Jersey* v *Holley* (2005) shows their readiness to recognise past errors of judgment and amend the law accordingly.

Secondly, the judiciary is able to provide practical solutions to real-life situations. The decision of the House of Lords in *R* v *R* (1991) provided an instant solution to the problem of the law on marital rape that had been festering for many years. In the Court of Appeal hearing in *Davis* v *Johnson* (1979) Lord Denning pointed the way to providing a remedy for a cohabitee, as opposed to a married woman, suffering domestic violence at the hands of her partner. Similarly, in *Jackson* v *Horizon Holidays* (1975) he sought to limit the strictness of the rule of privity of contract. In *Re A* (2000) the courts were faced with an application to sever conjoined twins in the sure knowledge that one would immediately die. And yet they were able to apply existing principles to establish a new point of law.

Thirdly, judges are able to address problems created by advancements in technology. In *Royal College of Nursing* v *DHSS* (1981) the House of Lords, in the light of technical advancements in drug-induced abortions, had to address the interpretation of a section of the Abortion Act 1967 and the use of the term 'medical practitioners'. In 2004, in the case of Natalie Evans, the Court of Appeal had to decide whether, under the terms of the **Human Fertilisation and Embryology Act 1994**, a young woman could have her frozen embryos implanted once her former boyfriend had withdrawn his consent.

Fourthly, judges are able to devote the required time to due consideration of a case. This contrasts with Parliament, which may see the need for legislation in a particular field, but not be able to prioritise it because of competing interests. For example, the need for wholesale reform of the law on non-fatal offences has been recognised for many years, with reports and draft bills being produced. However, Parliament has failed to provide the necessary time to introduce legislation. During the same period of time, the courts have been active in developing the law. In **Savage (1992)** the House of Lords overruled *Spratt* (1990) and reversed *Parmenter* (1991) in declaring that the *mens rea* for s47 occasioning actual bodily harm does not require intention or recklessness as to the harm caused. In *Chan Fook* (1994) the Court of Appeal declared that actual bodily harm includes psychiatric injury, and in *DPP* v *Smith* (2006) it was decided that cutting off a significant part of a person's hair satisfies the *actus reus* of actual bodily harm. Similarly, the *actus reus* of grievous bodily harm has been incrementally developed in *Burstow* (1997) to include serious psychiatric harm, and in *Dica* (2004) to include knowingly inflicting the HIV virus.

Key cases

R v R (1991): abandoned the long-held rule that a man cannot be guilty of raping his wife.

Savage (1992): the facts of this well-known case are as follows; while throwing some beer over another woman, the glass slipped out of her hand and broke; some shards of glass cut her victim's wrist.

Key terms

Human Fertilisation and Embryology Act 1994: as this Act (now amended) struggles to keep pace with developments in medical science, judges are forced to confront difficult ethical issues.

The problems

Leaving aside constitutional issues and the proper relationship between Parliament and the courts, which were discussed earlier, there are other problems with the judiciary exercising a law-making role. First, judges are not elected. Nor are they representative of society as a whole in terms of gender, ethnic origin, social class or age. In May 2006, Lord Falconer, the Constitutional Affairs Secretary and Lord Chancellor, issued a ministerial statement giving details of a strategy to increase the diversity of the judiciary. This was to include widening the range of people eligible to apply for judicial office, encouraging a wider range of applicants, and promoting an open and fair selection process. Meanwhile, the senior ranks of the judiciary remain predominantly white, middle-aged and male, promoting a suspicion, whether well-founded or not, that the judiciary lacks understanding and accountability.

Secondly, laws made by Parliament generally apply to the future. An Act of Parliament comes into force either at midnight on the day it receives royal assent, or at some specified time in the future. For example, the Human Rights Act was passed in 1998, but came into force on 1 October 2000. In contrast, judge-made law is by its nature **retrospective**: it applies to the past. This makes a person a criminal for an offence that, arguably, did not exist at the time it was committed. For example, in *R v R* (1991) the bar on marital rape was removed. However, the offence was committed before this bar was removed, when the old law still applied. The European Court of Human Rights has ruled that this does not contravene Article 7 of the European Convention on Human Rights, which states that no one should be found guilty of an offence which was not an offence when it was committed. Retrospective law prevents the law being used as a guide to future conduct, and therefore breaches one of the eight principles identified by Lon Fuller as essential for a valid legal system.

Thirdly, judge-made law can only be made when cases come to court. Therefore it is patchy, random, unstructured, and dependent upon the willingness and ability of the parties to pursue the matter on appeal. As a result, some areas of law remain unclear for many years. The decision in **Jackson v Horizon Holidays Ltd (1975)** clearly breached the doctrine of privity of contract, but to what extent and in what circumstances remained unclear. Further cases were needed before clarification could be provided.

The law on involuntary manslaughter is a prime example of judicial ping-pong, with subjective recklessness and gross negligence apparently striving for supremacy in those cases that are not suitable for unlawful act manslaughter. The elements of gross negligence manslaughter continue to attract debate, and the existence of subjective recklessness manslaughter is still questioned. In contrast, the elements of voluntary manslaughter are clear as they have been determined by statute, the Coroners and Justice Act 2009: it is only the interpretation of those elements by judges that has led to confusion.

At times, when a fundamental change in the law is necessary, judges may comment that the topic is an issue for Parliament to legislate on. This happened in *Clegg, C v DPP* when Lee Clegg appealed against his conviction for murder on the basis of legitimate self-defence. The House of Lords refused to interfere with the mandatory sentence for murder, commenting that it was for Parliament to decide if those killing when using unreasonable force should be convicted of murder and subject to the life sentence, or guilty of a form of manslaughter.

Finally, judges are often pressurised into making hasty decisions. In **Re S (1996)** an application to force a heavily pregnant woman to undergo a Caesarean section operation against her wishes was heard by the court

---

> ### Key terms
>
> **Retrospective law-making:** all judge-made law is necessarily retrospective; statute law is only occasionally retrospective; the War Crimes Act 1991 is such an example.

> ### Key cases
>
> **Jackson v Horizon Holidays Ltd (1975):** a remedy was provided to a claimant and to his family when their holiday had failed to live up to its advertised description, even though the claimant was the only member of his family to have contracted with the travel agent.
>
> **Re S (1996):** a declaration of the law by a higher court may arrive too late to prevent an injustice occurring.

within hours of its receipt, and the application granted. Later, at leisure, the Court of Appeal was able to give due consideration to the principles involved, and ruled that the woman's rights were paramount: the fact that her decision seemed unreasonable or bizarre was of no relevance. However, the Court of Appeal ruling was too late for the outcome to be changed.

Activity

Research the following cases. Consider whether there is a policy decision taken by the court in each case. Then consider why the court decided to make a policy decision rather than wait for Parliament to make the policy.

a *Hill* v *Chief Constable of West Yorkshire* (1988)

b *Hall* v *Simons* (2000)

c *Mitchell* v *Glasgow City Council* (2009)

You should now be able to:

- understand the constitutional relationship between Parliament and the judiciary

- provide a balanced discussion of the arguments for and against the exercise of judicial creativity.

4 Answering questions on the topic of judicial creativity

Questions on judicial creativity are centred on two topics covered in Unit 1: judicial precedent and statutory interpretation. However, the descriptive elements from AS merely provide the context for a more sophisticated level of discussion at A2.

Knowledge is needed of the operation of judicial precedent, and of the rules of statutory interpretation, with a range of appropriate examples to illustrate the points being made. Areas of flexibility within each of these processes should be identified and explained, with some evaluation of the significance and importance of each. Where possible, draw the illustrative material from across the syllabus, and not merely from one area of substantive law. It should be possible to reach a coherent judgment about the extent to which judges are able to develop the law within the parameters set for them.

The most challenging and interesting part of the topic is the discussion of the relationship between the judiciary on the one hand, and the legislature (Parliament) on the other. There is plenty of recent material upon which to draw to illustrate the tensions that exist here. Students should also be able to provide a thoughtful, balanced discussion of the arguments for and against judicial creativity.

This discussion should be informed by judicial comments taken from the judgments in cases, and by the opinions of academics. It is essential to be able to support this discussion with illustrative material, and to demonstrate how this material is relevant to the question being addressed.

You should not write out prepared answers. Although such an answer may score highly on Assessment Objective 1 (knowledge and understanding), it is unlikely to score highly on Assessment Objective 2 (evaluation). To gain a higher grade, you need to be able to consider

In this topic, you will learn how to:

- identify the material required in questions on judicial creativity

- provide the required range of information and discussion.

carefully the particular nuance, or shade of meaning, contained within the question. You will have most success if you take time to reflect on the wording of the question, and identify the particular issue being raised. Five or ten minutes spent in this way, and planning before embarking on the answer will usually be well rewarded.

For example, a typical question on this topic is: 'Critically analyse the extent to which judges are able to display creativity in the operation of judicial precedent and in the interpretation of statutory rules.'

An answer to this question is likely to require:

1 critical analysis of the development of common law rules

2 critical analysis in relation to the interpretation of statutory rules.

1 The critical analysis of the development of common law rules would need to include:

■ An explanation of the doctrine of precedent – the judicial hierarchy, the distinction between *ratio deciendi* and *obiter dicta*, binding and persuasive precedents.

■ The characteristics of flexibility in the system of judicial precedent, which provide the potential for legal development – distinguishing, flexibility available to the Supreme Court due to the 1966 Practice Statement, flexibility due to the possible vagueness of a *ratio*, overruling.

■ Identification and analysis of relevant examples and case law instances of judicial development in practice – the *mens rea* of murder, the duty of care in the tort of negligence (including areas such as negligent misstatements and psychiatric harm), judicial development of assault/ABH/GBH, aspects of formation of contracts.

■ Critical analysis (evaluation) of the extent to which judges are able to develop the common law – the Supreme Court only uses the Practice Statement when it is 'right to do so', judges often prefer to leave policy issue to Parliament (*Clegg*, *C v DPP*).

■ Arguments against judicial law-making – the haphazardness of the judicial process and the need for relevant cases and issues to arise, constitutional issues (e.g. the declaratory theory of judges), inappropriateness of the courts as a forum for law reform (e.g. lack of research material available to judges).

2 The critical analysis in relation to the interpretation of statutory rules would need to include:

■ Explanation of the approaches to statutory interpretation – the literal, golden and mischief rules, and the increasing importance of the purposive approach.

■ Analysis of the flexibility available to judges in statutory interpretation – any binding 'rules' of interpretation, the uncertainty of the meaning of language.

■ Identification and analysis of relevant examples and case law.

■ Critical analysis (evaluation) of the extent to which judges are able to display creativity in interpreting statutes – the greater scope for flexibility in the purposive approach as compared with the literal rule.

Activities

In the two questions below, consider the different issues that you might address in your answers.

1 How can judges display creativity in judicial precedent?

2 How can judges display creativity in statutory interpretation?

You should now be able to:

■ understand what is required in an essay on the topic of judicial creativity.

23 Fault

Introduction

The notion of fault covers a range of different thoughts. Firstly, it can indicate a blemish or imperfection, such as a scar on the skin or a character weakness. Secondly, it can refer to an error or miscalculation in a mathematical problem. Thirdly, in a legal sense, it can denote some form of wrongdoing. This could cover an offence in criminal law or being negligent in the civil law of tort. Lastly, again in a legal sense, fault is used to describe the idea of culpability or blameworthiness – in other words, legal responsibility. This topic examines the extent to which a person's liability in law is dependent upon fault – in other words, how blameworthy or culpable they are. It also examines whether a person can still be at fault even if the offence or action carried out is termed 'no fault'.

In this topic, you will learn how to explain elements of both civil and criminal law to show the relationship between fault and no-fault liability.

In this topic, you will learn how to:

- explain elements of criminal law where there is a close relationship between fault and liability

- explain elements of civil law where there is a close relationship between fault and liability.

Study tip

In this topic, you can introduce material from any part of the specification you have studied, whether AS or A2. Try to support your discussion with case examples.

Key terms

Voluntary *actus reus*: requires the defendant to be in control of his actions.

Key cases

Hill v Baxter (1958): Lord Goddard restated the general principle that no criminal liability is incurred unless the *actus reus* is voluntary.

1 Liability depending upon fault

Criminal law

In criminal law, there is a general presumption that liability is based upon fault. This is consistent with our sense of justice: a person should not be held liable for a criminal offence unless he is to some extent blameworthy, or at fault. The *mens rea* of a criminal offence is often thought to be the only fault element, since it examines the state of mind of the defendant at the time of committing the offence. Generally speaking, it is what is in a person's mind that distinguishes between a mere accident and a criminal offence. For example, breaking another's collarbone in a game of rugby will not normally incur criminal liability. However, breaking another's collarbone with an iron bar inside his home is probably a premeditated act, carried out with intention, and therefore rendering the offender liable for s18 of the Offences against the Person Act. The injury is the same; the defendant's mind frame is completely different. Further, the level of *mens rea* may vary between charges. For example, intention only is required for s18, but intent or recklessness to cause harm is required for s20. This is so even if the *actus reus*, the causing of the injury, is the same.

The *actus reus* and *mens rea* are not entirely disconnected concepts, as the *actus reus* may also contain elements of fault. As with *mens rea*, these elements also relate to the level of responsibility the defendant has for the outcome. There is a general rule that the *actus reus* must be voluntary, that it was willed by the defendant. The level of responsibility may then vary between a positive voluntary act and an omission.

Acts and omissions

The *actus reus* of the offence must be voluntary: in other words, the defendant must be in control of his actions. For example, a waiter might suffer a sudden sneezing fit and spill hot tea over a customer, or a crash of thunder might startle a child, causing him to step back and knock over an old woman. Or, to use the example quoted in **Hill v Baxter (1958)**, a driver might be attacked by a swarm of bees, and crash. In all of these examples, the *actus reus* would be involuntary as the defendant had no control over his criminal actions. He would not be regarded as being at fault. As a result, there would be no liability.

A positive voluntary act, such as a punch or kick, is generally recognised as having the greatest fault, as it was under the control of the defendant, and will carry the most severe punishment. However, liability can be imposed where the defendant omits, or fails, to do something – especially where a duty is imposed.

Examples of this have been seen in:

■ *Dytham*, when a police officer failed to perform his public duty
■ *Stone and Dobinson*, when a couple failed to care for Stone's sister
■ *Pittwood*, when a crossing keeper failed to do his job properly
■ *Miller*, when a man failed to call for help or to deal with a situation he had created.

Generally a failure, such as in these cases, will be punished less severely than where a positive voluntary action has been committed.

Causation

If it can be shown that the defendant caused the result, and therefore committed the *actus reus*, he will be criminally liable. In *White* (1910), the victim died from natural causes rather than from the poison fed to her by her son. Although morally at fault, White was not the cause of his mother's death and he was not legally at fault for her death. Contrast this with *Pagett* (1983), where the defendant started the sequence of events that led directly to the death of his girlfriend. He was responsible for her death, and therefore held at fault.

The defendant will not be at fault unless he was responsible in law for the outcome. Where the chain of causation is broken, the defendant will not be at fault. In *Jordan* (1956) the victim was recovering from his stab wound when he was given 'palpably wrong' treatment by doctors. He died from the treatment, not the original injury. It was decided on appeal that Jordan was not responsible for his death, and so was not at fault for the death; though, of course, he was at fault, and responsible for, the stabbing. By contrast, in *Smith* (1959) it was decided that the victim died as a result of the original injury. The subsequent poor medical treatment did not break the chain of causation. Smith was responsible for his victim's death, and was at fault. Finally, in *Cheshire* (1991) where the defendant shot the victim in the abdomen and leg in a fish and chip shop and the victim then received treatment in hospital, it was suggested that the cause of the victim's eventual death was due to the medical treatment. The appeal court decided that the medical treatment of the victim did not break the chain of causation to remove the defendant's fault.

Defences

The availability of a defence recognises that the defendant may have committed the *actus reus* of an offence, with the appropriate *mens rea*, but still not be at fault, or blameworthy. This may arise, for example, where he uses reasonable force to defend himself or his property. However, if the force used is considered to be unreasonable or excessive, the defence will not be available and the defendant will be fully at fault for the injury caused to the victim. This was seen in the cases of Tony Martin and Munir Hussain. In both of these cases, the defendants were legally at fault because the danger to them had passed and excessive force was used on the intruders. However, in 'the court of public opinion' neither was considered to be at fault, as they both acted to defend their properties.

Study tip

Using the facts of two contrasting cases (e.g. *Pagett* and *White*; or *Jordan* and *Smith*) can help to show real understanding in discussion of issues.

Using the defence of insanity, the defendant will not be guilty as he cannot form the *mens rea* due to a disease of his mind. Using the defence of automatism, the defendant will not be at fault, as he cannot form the *mens rea* due to the existence of an external factor. Using the defence of intoxication, the defendant will not be at fault for specific intent offences, as he cannot form the *mens rea* due to his intoxicated state.

Partial defences

Conviction for murder requires proof of intention to kill or commit grievous bodily harm. However, there are degrees of culpability, and these are reflected in the availability of special defences for murder, that, if successful, will reduce a conviction to voluntary manslaughter.

When pleading diminished responsibility, under the new rules introduced by the Coroners and Justice Act 2009, the defendant seeks to rely upon an abnormality of mental functioning that arises from a medical condition and provides an explanation for doing, or being a party to, the killing.

The classic case under the 1957 Homicide Act to illustrate diminished responsibility was that of *Byrne* (1960). The defendant had strangled a woman and mutilated her body. Evidence showed that he was a sexual psychopath who could exercise little control over his actions, which was judged to be an abnormality of mind. (It could now be considered to be an abnormality of mental functioning). He was found guilty at trial. The appeal court considered that this condition should have been considered by the jury at his trial, as they could have decided that it reduced his responsibility for his behaviour and reduced the level of his fault. Obviously, he was at fault for the unlawful killing, but the level of his fault could be reduced because of his mental condition. However, the appeal court decided that he still had a high level of fault as they considered he should still be sentenced to life imprisonment, the same sentence that he received at trial.

A further part defence to a charge of murder is loss of control (formerly provocation) as again introduced by the Coroners and Justice Act 2009. The part defence can be established where the defendant kills, but the killing resulted from the defendant's loss of self-control. This loss of self-control must have had a qualifying trigger, and it must be considered that a person of the defendant's age and sex might have acted in the same, or a similar, way. There have been few cases reported that have used this part defence since it was introduced. If used successfully, the defendant would again have been at fault for committing the killing, but the level of fault would be reduced due to the loss of self-control. A trial judge could then impose a sentence that fairly reflected the degree of fault.

Negligence in criminal law

Negligence is generally considered to be a civil concept that occurs where a person's act or omission falls below the standard of a reasonable person. This is an objective test that takes no account of the state of mind of the defendant. As mentioned previously, it occurs in the criminal offence of gross negligence manslaughter. The leading case is **Adomako (1995)** when an anaesthetist was on duty during an operation on a detached retina. One of the tubes supplying oxygen to the patient became disconnected. Adomako took six minutes to notice this, when evidence showed that a competent anaesthetist would have noticed it within seconds. The patient suffered a cardiac arrest and later died. The jury decided that the defendant was guilty of gross negligence manslaughter. On appeal, this conviction was upheld as the defendant's failure was so bad that it could be considered criminal. This level of fault by the defendant can be considered to be criminal, even though the defendant

> **Key terms**
>
> **Partial defences:** where a defendant uses a partial defence, his fault is only partially removed; for example, a successful plea of loss of control or diminished responsibility reduces murder to voluntary manslaughter.

> **Key cases**
>
> **Adomako (1995):** where the defendant owes a duty of care that results in the death of the victim, he can be criminally liable if his breach of duty (his fault) is so bad as to be considered criminal.

had no *mens rea* of intent or recklessness. This liability is partially mitigated by the fact that a defendant can only be liable where:

■ he owes a duty of care to the victim

■ his negligence, or level of fault, is gross; and

■ the jury considers his level of negligence to be so bad as to be criminal.

Mens rea

Mens rea is an essential element of all serious criminal offences. Unless the offence is one of strict liability, the absence of *mens rea* will result in an acquittal. For example, in *Clarke* (1972) a woman transferred some items from her shopping basket into her own bag before paying for them. She was able to show that she suffered from absent-mindedness due to depression. She therefore lacked *mens rea* for theft and was acquitted.

The two main forms of *mens rea* for serious criminal offences are intention and subjective recklessness. Direct intention is considered to have the highest level of fault, as the offence was deliberate. This is followed, in the level of fault, by indirect intent – where the result is virtually certain and the defendant appreciated this to be the case. The next level of fault will be subjective recklessness, where the defendant recognised a risk but still went ahead.

Generally, the more serious the offence, the higher the degree of *mens rea* that is required. In other words, crimes are graduated according to the level of fault in both the *actus reus* and the *mens rea*. For example, wounding or grievous bodily harm under s18, with a maximum life sentence, requires proof of intention to wound or cause grievous bodily harm; whereas s20, with a maximum of five years' imprisonment, requires either intention or recklessness, and only as to causing some harm.

Sentencing

Following a conviction, a judge or a magistrate has to impose a sentence. In most cases, judges are able to impose a sentence – up to the maximum allowed by law – that fairly reflects the fault of the defendant. For example, two defendants may have been separately convicted of grievous bodily harm under s20 of the Offences Against the Person Act 1861 and have received different sentences. The first may have been racially provoked, have acted on the spur of the moment, and without a weapon. Further, it may be his first offence, for which he has shown remorse, been co-operative with the police and pleaded guilty at an early opportunity. The second may have been part of a gang on the lookout for causing trouble, have hit his victim repeatedly and left him unconscious in the street. He may have previous convictions for similar offences, and threatened his victim with further violence later. The sentencing judge will take factors such as these into account when deciding upon a sentence. Clearly, it would appear that the first defendant has a number of **mitigating factors**, while the second defendant has plenty of **aggravating factors** present. The sentences imposed should reflect the different levels of fault of the two defendants.

A different approach is for the judge to reflect the level of fault in the offence. For example, for a conviction for an assault or battery, where the victim will suffer minor injuries not requiring medical attention, there is a maximum sentence of six months' imprisonment and/or a £5,000 fine. The more serious offence of assault or battery occasioning actual bodily harm, under s47, where the victim will require some medical attention, attracts a maximum sentence of five years.

Key terms

Mitigating factors: these are factors that can show reduced fault, and can result in a less severe sentence.

Aggravating factors: these are factors likely to show greater fault, and will result in a more severe sentence.

Sometimes, however, judges are obliged to pass a particular sentence that may not reflect the level of fault. The most obvious example is that of murder, where the life sentence is mandatory. Every defendant who is found guilty of murder has to be given a life sentence, whatever the motive or the mitigating factors.

However there is some flexibility, even in the mandatory life sentence. The sentencing judge is required to impose a tariff that the murderer has to serve, which will allow the judge to match the length of sentence to the particular circumstances of the killing. This can occur at two extremes. For example, Frances Inglis, who killed her son for compassionate reasons – 'with love in her heart' – was given, on appeal, a tariff of five years. By contrast, serial killers such as Peter Sutcliffe, Steve Wright and Levi Bellfield have been given 'whole life' tariffs, which means that they will never be released from prison. This tariff can therefore reflect the degree of fault in the killing, even when there is a fixed sentence.

Levi Bellfield gets life without parole

Levi Bellfield refused to leave his prison cell to hear Mr Justice Wilkie sentence him to life without parole and condemn him as a 'cruel and pitiless killer'.

His refusal marked him out as a man who lacked the 'courage to come into court to face his victims and receive his sentence', said Wilkie, who told the Old Bailey that the former club doorman would never leave prison.

He had robbed Milly Dowler, 13, 'of her promising life' and taken her from her family and friends. 'He treated her in death with total disrespect, depositing her naked body without even a semblance of a burial, in a wood, far away from her home, vulnerable to all the forces of nature thereby, as he clearly intended, causing her family the appalling anguish for many months of not knowing what had become of her.'

Milly had become his victim 'for no reason other than she was in the wrong place at the wrong time … a target of the unreasoning hatred which seem to have driven him,' said the judge.

The 'unreasoning hatred' evident from Bellfield's previous convictions appeared to be directed at women, and young blonde women in particular. His explosive and random attacks on lone women at night earned him the nickname the 'bus stop stalker' and made him one of the UK's most dangerous serial killers.

It also earned him a whole life sentence in 2008, when he was convicted of the murders of Amelie Delagrange, 22, Marsha McDonnell, 19, and the attempted murder of Kate Sheedy, 18. It is thought Bellfield is the first person to have received two whole life sentences.

Detectives believe he may have been responsible for around 20 attacks on women which were never solved, including rape.

The Guardian, 24 June 2011

Civil law

Civil law is concerned with weighing the interests of the two parties to an action and, where appropriate, providing the most suitable remedy. We will be looking particularly at tort law, where a civil wrong is committed. As a general rule, tort liability will only be imposed where a party is at fault. However, there are some torts where liability is strict, and fault does not have to be proved. Remember that in civil law, where fault is required it only has to be shown on the balance of probabilities. This is a lower standard than the criminal standard of beyond reasonable doubt. The most commonly used tort is negligence, and this is fault based.

The tort of negligence

For liability to be established in the tort of negligence, three tests need to be satisfied. It must be shown that:

■ a duty of care is owed to the claimant
■ there has been a breach of that duty, and
■ loss or damage has been caused to the claimant.

Firstly, the defendant must owe a duty of care to the claimant. **Caparo v Dickman (1990)** set out three requirements for this: the harm must be reasonably foreseeable; there must be proximity between defendant and victim, and it must be fair and just to owe the duty. In *Donoghue v Stevenson* (1932) a duty of care was said to exist between a drinks manufacturer and a customer, which allowed the customer to claim for the faulty manufacturing process that caused her physical and mental harm. However, in *Bourhill* v *Young* (1943) no duty of care was said to exist. The details of this case were that a pregnant woman heard a motorcyclist crash, and went to the scene to view the aftermath; on her arrival, she witnessed such a traumatic sight that she suffered a miscarriage. She sued the dead motorcyclist's estate. It was decided that the defendant (the dead motorcyclist's estate) did not owe a duty of care to her. The motorcyclist could not reasonably have foreseen the likelihood of the outcome that occurred (the miscarriage), nor was there a proximate relationship between him and the claimant. In *Watson* v *British Boxing Board of Control* (2001) it was decided that it was fair, just and reasonable for the Board to owe a duty of care to boxers who fought after obtaining a licence from the Board.

Secondly, the defendant's conduct must fall below the standard of the reasonable person. This part of negligence really shows the fault on the part of the defendant. In *Blyth* v *Birmingham Waterworks* (1856) it was stated: 'Negligence is the omission to do something which a reasonable man would do, or doing something which a prudent and reasonable man would not.' When deciding how the reasonable man would have behaved, the court will consider the size of the risk he was taking, the practicality of taking precautions, the likelihood of serious harm, and the social value of his activity. In **Bolton v Stone (1951)** the defendants had taken all reasonable precautions and the likelihood of the harm occurring was small. As a result, they could not be considered at fault, and so were not liable to Miss Stone for the injury she had sustained.

However, in *Nettleship* v *Weston* (1971) the defendant driver was liable to the claimant instructor even though she was inexperienced. She was judged according to the standard of the reasonably competent and experienced driver, and so was at fault.

Thirdly, the defendant must be the factual and the legal cause of the damage. In **Barnett v Kensington and Chelsea Hospital (1968)** a man died from arsenic poisoning. His widow claimed compensation against the hospital because the doctor had failed to treat her husband with due care. Her claim failed: it was the arsenic, not the doctor's breach, which killed her husband. Even if the doctor had acted properly, he could not have saved the man. Thus, liability will only be imposed where the defendant caused the outcome and was at fault. Even where the defendant was the initial link in the chain, liability will not be imposed unless the type of harm suffered was reasonably foreseeable and the defendant was therefore at fault (*The Wagon Mound* (1961)).

These general rules of **negligence** are developed further in claims of nervous shock and economic loss. In claims of nervous shock, the claimant has suffered mental injury due to the fault of the defendant in causing the accident. However, the defendant's fault is limited due to the restrictive

Key cases

Caparo v Dickman (1990): this case established the modern three-part test for establishing duty of care in the tort of negligence.

Bolton v Stone (1951): where the defendant has taken reasonable precautions against a small risk, he will not be in breach of his duty of care.

Barnett v Kensington and Chelsea Hospital (1969): even the most serious breach of duty will escape liability if the defendant did not in fact cause the damage suffered by the claimant.

Key terms

Negligence: 'negligence is the omission to do something which a reasonable man would do, or doing something which a prudent and reasonable man would not do' (*Blyth* v *Birmingham Waterworks* (1856)).

rules laid down in *Alcock* v *Chief Constable of South Yorkshire* (1992). The defendant is only liable to those who can satisfy the *Alcock* criteria:

- those having close ties of love and affection with the victim of the accident
- those who suffer the shock at the scene of the accident or its immediate aftermath, and
- those who see or hear the accident through their own unaided senses.

In cases of economic loss, the defendant is not liable, and therefore not at fault, to those who have suffered 'pure' economic loss (*Spartan Steel* v *Martin* (1972)). However, the defendant will be liable, and at fault, for a negligent misstatement to those who can establish a 'special relationship' with the defendant.

By developing these rules, the courts have limited the class of potential claimants. If a claimant can show he is in the class, he will succeed in a claim. If outside the class, he will fail. The defendant may have been at fault to those both inside and outside the class, but the number of claimants can be limited.

Damages in negligence

The award of damages is compensatory: damages are intended to restore the claimant to his pre-accident position, so far as money can do this. Following this idea, the defendant's fault is linked to the extent of harm or injury that has been caused. However, where the defendant contributes to his own harm or injury, the rules of contributory negligence will apply to reduce the amount of damages by such percentage as the court thinks just. This reflects the level of the defendant's fault in causing the harm or injuries. An example is *Jebson* v *Ministry of Defence* (2000).

A soldier had been in town drinking. At the end of the evening he rang the barracks, asking for a lift. A driver was sent with an open-backed van. The claimant fell out of the back of the van and was hurt. The driver clearly owed a duty of care to his passengers. However, in the circumstances, it was reasonable to reduce the damages because of the significant contribution made by the defendant to his own injuries.

The opposite may also arise: if the defendant has been particularly badly behaved towards the claimant, **exemplary damages** may be awarded. In *Treadaway* v *Chief Constable of West Midlands* (1994) the claimant had been tortured by the police into making a confession to a crime, and subsequently sentenced to 15 years' imprisonment. Exemplary damages were awarded against the police, as they had shown total disregard for the law. These rules seek to ensure that the actual compensation paid properly reflects the fault of the parties.

> **Key terms**
>
> **Exemplary damages:** awarded to punish the defendant and to serve as a deterrent.

Occupiers' liability

Liability under the Occupiers' Liability Acts 1957 and 1984 is also based on the tort of negligence, and the visitor will have to show that he is injured due to the fault of the occupier.

In order to make a claim as a lawful visitor, under the 1957 Act, the visitor has to show that the defendant broke the common duty of care. The defendant does not have to make his premises completely safe, just reasonably safe. The occupier's liability, or fault, depends upon his failure to take reasonable precautions to ensure the visitor's safety. In *Cotton* v *Derbyshire Dales DC* (1994) a walker was injured after falling from a path running along the top of a dangerous cliff. There were no signs to warn of the danger. In this case, there was no liability or fault on the part of the occupier, as the risk was obvious to any visitor exercising reasonable care; there was no need for the council to take any further steps to alert visitors to the danger.

As with negligence, it can be a defence for the occupier to argue that the claimant has been wholly (the defence of consent) or partly (the defence of contributory negligence) at fault, and as a result has suffered the injuries. By using the defence of consent, the occupier is saying that the claimant is completely at fault for his injuries. By using the defence of contributory negligence, the defendant is saying that the claimant is partly at fault for his injuries. In this way, the amount of damages will be reduced.

Claims as a trespasser under the 1984 Act require the claimant to show that the occupier was at fault due to a breach of s1 (3) of the Act. Under this section, the duty is owed when:

- the occupier is aware of the danger, or has reasonable grounds to believe it exists
- the occupier knows, or has reasonable grounds to believe, that the trespasser is near, or may come to be near, the danger; and
- the risk is one from which an occupier may reasonably be expected to protect visitors.

An example, from before the 1984 Act, was in **British Railways Board v Herrington (1972)** when a six-year-old boy stepped over a damaged fence and walked on to an electrified railway line. He suffered severe burns and injuries. The British Railways Board was at fault as they had known of the damaged fence, but had failed to take steps to prevent trespassers entering onto the railway line. They were held liable for the injuries suffered by the boy.

Key cases

British Railways Board v Herrington (1972): the principle of liability for trespassers established in the case became the main subject of the Occupiers' Liability Act 1984.

Activities

1 Compile a list of those recently convicted of murder. Identify the minimum tariff given to each. What are the distinguishing features that account for the range in the sentences given?

2 Consider how the House of Lords emphasised the need for subjectivity in criminal liability in their decisions in *B v DPP* (2000); *(Morgan) Smith* (2000); and *G and R* (2002).

You should now be able to:

- explain and illustrate the idea of fault-based liability.

In this topic, you will learn how to:

- explain elements of criminal law where there is not a close relationship between fault and liability
- explain elements of civil law where there is not a close relationship between fault and liability.

2 Liability not depending upon fault

There are many areas where a person can be held liable, and therefore at fault, in both criminal and civil law, even though he does not appear, at first sight, to have been at fault. This seems to be unjust, but often other considerations are taken into account to outweigh the interests of the individual involved.

Strict liability offences

Some offences, known as offences of **strict liability**, require no *mens rea*. It is said that liability is imposed without the need to prove fault on the part of the defendant. This 'no fault' liability is certainly true as regards the *mens rea*, but the offences are not completely without fault. This is because the defendant is still at fault as he has committed the *actus reus*.

These strict liability offences tend to be regulatory, dealing with matters of social concern, such as:

- food hygiene (*Smedleys Ltd* v *Breed* (1974))
- pollution of the environment (*Alphacell Ltd* v *Woodward* (1972))
- selling alcohol, cigarettes, lottery tickets, etc. to underage children (*Harrow LBC* v *Shah* (1999)).

In cases that are truly criminal however, *mens rea* is needed (*Sweet* v *Parsley* (1970)).

In *Gammon (HK) Ltd* v *Attorney-General of Hong Kong* (1985), Lord Scarman spoke of a presumption in favour of *mens rea*. The House of Lords has, in recent years, promoted subjectivity in criminal law. In other words, it is increasingly looking for the element of fault on the part of the defendant. In *B* v *DPP* (2000) a 15-year-old boy was convicted under the Indecency with Children Act 1960 of inciting a 14-year-old girl to commit an act of gross indecency with him on a bus. She had refused. There was no mention of *mens rea* in the offence. The Divisional Court ruled that no *mens rea* was required as regards the age of the girl. The House of Lords, however, decided that *mens rea* was required for this element of the offence, especially considering the severity of the punishment.

The boy's knowledge about the girl's age could be relevant, and the effect of the decision is that he could only be guilty if he knew she was underage. The decision does emphasise the link between fault and liability.

Strict liability offences are justified as generally a business will be prosecuted, the effect of them is to raise standards, and the punishments are generally relatively minor – normally a fine. Usually, there will be no defence to these types of offences. This may be unfair, especially if, as with Mr Shah, every precaution is taken to avoid committing the offence.

Absolute liability offences

We saw earlier the requirement that the *actus reus* be voluntary. However, where there is **absolute liability**, this requirement is waived: the defendant may be convicted even though he had no control over his conduct, and to some degree was not at fault. The case of *Larsonneur* (1933) illustrates this. It concerned a French woman. When her permission to remain in the UK expired, she travelled to Ireland. However, she was refused entry and brought back to Britain by the Irish police. On arrival, she was charged under the Aliens' Order 1920 with being 'an alien to whom leave to land in the United Kingdom had been refused'. The Court of Appeal decided that she had been rightly convicted, even though she had been brought into the country by force against her will.

A similar situation arose in *Winzar* v *Chief Constable of Kent* (1983). The defendant, who was drunk, was escorted out of a hospital by the police and then promptly arrested for 'being found drunk on the highway' contrary to s12 of the Licensing Act 1872. Clearly the *actus reus* was involuntary: the police had placed him on the highway.

Some may argue that Larsonneur gave insufficient thought to whether she would be allowed entry into the Republic of Ireland, and it could be argued that this showed some fault on her part. Winzar was reckless in becoming drunk, thereby exposing himself to the risk of committing criminal offences; again, it could be said that he was at fault for getting drunk. However, imposing liability for involuntary acts forced upon the defendants by the police seems particularly distasteful.

Key terms
Strict liability: where the defendant can be convicted by committing the *actus reus* alone; there is no need to prove any *mens rea*.
Absolute liability: where liability is absolute, the defendant may be convicted even though the *actus reus* of the offence was committed involuntarily.

The case of Harrow LBC *v* Shah *(1999) involved an employee in a corner shop selling a lottery ticket to a minor*

Offences of absolute liability have been introduced recently in the area of combatting terrorism. An example is s58 of the Terrorism Act 2000, where it is an offence to collect or make a record of information of a type likely to be useful to a person committing or preparing an act of terrorism, or to possess a document or record containing information of that type.

Civil law

Strict liability

Strict liability, or no-fault, also operates in tort. A good example of this is **Rylands v Fletcher (1868)**. In this famous case, a landowner decided to build a reservoir on his land. The contractors failed to seal the entrances to some disused mine shafts. When the land was flooded, water escaped through these shafts and into the claimant's mine. The claimant was able to succeed without having to show fault on the part of the contractors. In the words of Lord Cranworth, the defendant is liable 'however careful he may have been and whatever precautions he may have taken'. The liability is strict as no fault on the part of the defendant needs to be shown. No reason for the escape has to be given – the claim can be made by just showing that there has been an escape that has caused damage to the adjoining property.

Consumer Protection Act 1987

Claims can be made using the rules under the **Consumer Protection Act** 1987, which places strict **liability** upon 'a producer' for death, personal injury or property damage over £275 suffered by a consumer as a result of using a defective product. Unlike a claim for negligence, no fault is required to be shown. Therefore using this Act should make a claim by a consumer easier to prove. However, the harshness imposed by this strict liability is mitigated by defences that are available under the Act. These include the producer not being in business, the defect not existing at the time of manufacture, and the fact that the defect could not have been discovered under scientific or technical knowledge existing at the time.

Vicarious liability

Vicarious liability is another example of strict liability. This arises where one person is liable for the tort of another. This usually occurs in the field of employment: the employer may be liable for the torts of his employees, even where he has taken all reasonable steps to prevent their misconduct. In *Limpus* v *London Omnibus Co.* (1862) a driver of the defendants' bus company deliberately drove across the path of a rival company's bus, causing it to topple over. Although the bus company had issued strict instructions to its drivers not to drive dangerously, it was still held responsible for the damage caused. As a result, even the most cautious employer may find himself liable to pay damages for the wilful misconduct of his employees.

The employer can be vicariously liable even if the employee has been negligent (*Century Insurance* v *Northern Ireland Road Transport* (1942)) and if the employee has committed a crime during the course of his employment (*Lister* v *Hesley Hall* (2002)). The current test for deciding whether an employee's action is within the course of employment is whether there is a 'close connection' between the act and the work. In cases such as these, the employer will not be at fault but will still be liable for employee's actions.

Of course, it could be argued that the employer is at fault for employing that employee, or for not properly supervising the employee, but neither of these points has to be proved.

An employer will only escape liability where the employee was engaged in a 'frolic' of his own. In *Twine* v *Bean's Express* (1946) the driver had

---

■ **Key cases**

Rylands v Fletcher (1868): the original rule in this case is: 'the person who for his own purposes brings on his lands and collects and keeps there anything likely to do mischief if it escapes, must keep it at his peril, and, if he does not do so, is answerable for all the damage which is the natural consequence of its escape.'

■ **Key terms**

Consumer Protection Act liability: an alternative to claiming in negligence for a person who has suffered loss or damage as a result of using a defective product.

Vicarious liability: where a person who has not committed a tort is responsible for the fault of another – for example, an employer for the tort of his employee, provided the employee is acting in the course of his employment.

ignored his employer's instructions and given a lift to a hitchhiker. The employer was not liable for the driver's subsequent negligent driving, as it was outside the scope of his employment.

In a situation such as this, the employer will not have been at fault at all. The employee, who is at fault, has to bear full responsibility for his actions. Remember that an independent contractor cannot pass on any liability to another. He has to bear full responsibility for his actions. Further underpinning these decisions is an idea that those who run a business must be prepared to accept the risks, as well as the benefits, associated with that business.

Activities

1 Consider the use of implied malice in the *mens rea* of murder. Does it necessarily reflect a close relationship between fault and liability? How do the Law Commission proposals on homicide deal with implied malice for murder?

2 Consider the case of the terrorist who plants a small bomb in a busy shopping centre. He issues a warning to the police, but the bomb explodes prematurely, killing a policeman who was evacuating the centre. The terrorist will argue that he was trying to attract publicity for his cause, and not wanting to harm anyone, hence the warning. Most people would accept that he is morally more culpable than the defendant in *Cox* (1992). But does he have the *mens rea* for murder?

You should now be able to:

■ explain and illustrate the idea of non fault-based liability.

---

3 Should liability depend upon fault?

Arguments in support of liability not based upon fault

The arguments supporting no-fault liability may be summarised under the following three points:

1 Sometimes no-fault liability is essential in order to protect the public interest.
2 Individuals bear responsibility for the consequences of their actions.
3 It encourages businesses and property owners to exercise greater vigilance.

The public interest

The law seeks to protect and promote the wider interests of the public, and sometimes these are given priority over the requirement for fault in individual offenders.

Many strict liability offences concern the running of businesses. In **Smedleys v Breed (1974)** the producers of tinned vegetables were held liable for the presence of a caterpillar in a tin of peas. The House of Lords ruled that there was no defence of reasonable care: liability was strict. A similar principle operated in *Harrow London Borough Council* v *Shah* (1999), as seen above. It can be said that the reason for these decisions is the protection of the public, especially vulnerable members. In the case of *Smedley*, the focus is on consumers; in the case of *Shah*, underage children. This argument is also used to justify vicarious liability: just as an employer profits from the activity of his employee, so he should accept any risks. Additionally, businesses and employers are in a stronger

In this topic, you will learn how to:

■ discuss arguments in support of no-fault liability and fault-based liability.

Key cases

Smedleys v Breed (1974): in the interests of public health, producers will be held liable for contaminated food, even where all possible precautions were taken.

financial position either to insure against the risk or to meet claims made against them. Placing responsibility on businesses can also be said to raise standards of care, supervision and product quality.

Serious criminal offences require not only evidence of *mens rea* (and the more serious the offence, the higher the level of *mens rea* that is required), but also proof beyond reasonable doubt. In this way, the interests of the defendant are protected. However, the imposition of strict liability for less serious crimes may be justified on the ground that the public interest weighs heavily in the scales of justice. The public has an interest, for example, in road safety, in preventing pollution, in maintaining reasonable standards of hygiene, and in protecting children from the dangers associated with alcohol, smoking and gambling. It is argued that these public interests are better served by restricting liability to questions of fact (Was the driver speeding? Did the pollutant material come from the factory? Was the meat infected? Was the customer under age?), which are relatively straightforward to prove, and avoiding questions to do with what the defendant was thinking.

Additionally, no-fault offences tend to attract less serious penalties. Offences such as polluting the environment (*Alphacell Ltd* v *Woodward* (1972)), producing contaminated food (*Smedleys Ltd* v *Breed* (1974)), creating a public nuisance (*Shorrock* (1994)), and possession of cannabis (*Marriot* (1971)) are more likely to lead to a fine than to a custodial sentence. The guidelines issued by Lord Scarman in *Gammon (HK) Ltd* v *Attorney-General of Hong Kong* (1985) also point out that the presumption in favour of the need for *mens rea* is particularly strong in 'truly criminal' offences, these presumably being offences where the defendant is liable to be given a custodial sentence. Both **Sweet v Parsley (1970)** and *B* v *DPP* (2000) illustrate this point: the appellant's convictions were overturned by the House of Lords as the offences were so serious that *mens rea* should be required to be shown.

Strict and vicarious liability make it far less likely that an innocent victim will be left without a remedy in the courts. Supporters of no-fault liability argue that to leave a victim without a remedy is a greater injustice than to penalise a blameless defendant. For example, in *Limpus* v *London General Omnibus Co.* (1862), it was preferable to provide a remedy to the innocent claimant than to allow the equally innocent employer to escape liability for the wrongdoing of his employee. In **Rylands v Fletcher (1868)** it was preferable to grant the mine owners a remedy than to allow the landowner, albeit innocent, to escape liability for the harm he had caused.

However, in *Hilton* v *Thomas Burton (Rhodes) Ltd* (1961) the court decided that the innocent widow should be left without a remedy when the employers were not vicariously liable for the employees who were on a frolic of their own.

For many strict liability offences – for example, speeding, it would be almost impossible to prove a mental element in order to secure a conviction. Moreover, without vicarious liability it would often be difficult to secure compensation, because of difficulties in identifying the offending employee. No-fault liability clearly overcomes these problems. Where the claimant doesn't have to prove fault, the outcome of a claim is more predictable; and this in turn encourages defendants to admit their responsibility, thereby saving court time and costs. These are significant advantages.

Individual responsibility

There is a biblical principle that 'we reap what we sow'. No-fault liability promotes this principle in criminal and civil law. Strict liability in criminal law holds individuals or businesses responsible for the harm they cause, even where they are unaware of it. In *Howells* (1997) the defendant had failed to obtain a firearms certificate for his gun, falsely

---

Key cases

Sweet v Parsley (1970): where an offence is 'truly criminal', *mens rea* is more likely to be required.

Rylands v Fletcher (1868): a landowner will be held liable for the damage caused by the escape of a substance which he has stored on his land.

believing it was an antique and therefore not requiring a certificate. As an individual choosing to possess a gun, it was his responsibility to ensure that he complied with the necessary regulations. His failure to do so made him guilty: his belief in the licence requirement was irrelevant.

Civil law also provides evidence of the principle of **individual responsibility**. In *Rose* v *Plenty* (1976) a milkman allowed a 13-year-old boy to assist him with his round, even though this was expressly forbidden by his employer. When the child was injured due to the milkman's negligence, the employer was held liable: he bore responsibility for the conduct of his employees even if the employee was acting against orders.

Section 2(2) of the Consumer Protection Act 1987 contains a list of those who will be held strictly liable for death, personal injury or damage to property caused by a defective product. This list includes the manufacturers, those involved in the supply chain, any importer and the eventual retailer suppliers. Any or all of these may be sued as they all bear responsibility for the quality and safety of their products.

Deterrence

No-fault liability encourages higher standards of care among businessmen and property owners. In *Harrow LBC* v *Shah* (1999) the defendant shopkeeper was convicted of selling a lottery ticket to an underage boy. No doubt other shopkeepers would then take greater care selling age-limited products in the future. Students working in shops and supermarkets are no doubt aware of the greater vigilance being shown in selling a variety of age-limited products. In *Gammon (HK) Ltd* v *Attorney-General of Hong Kong* (1985) the defendants were held responsible for the collapse of part of a building, even though they were unaware that their plans were not being followed by the builders. Lord Scarman was convinced that strict liability would serve as a **deterrent**. He argued:

> Their Lordships are satisfied that strict liability would help to promote greater vigilance in the matters covered by the two offenders with which this appeal is concerned (the material deviation and the risk of injury or damage).

Arguments in support of liability based upon fault

There are two broad lines of reasoning adopted by supporters of fault-based liability. Firstly, they deny that it better protects the public, and that its deterrent value helps to raise standards. Secondly, they argue that it is inherently unjust to impose liability without establishing fault on the part of the defendant.

Rejection of claims for no-fault liability

First of all, it is not true to say that strict liability in criminal law is restricted to offences that attract fines rather than custodial sentences. In *Howells* (1997) the defendant was convicted under s1 of the Firearms Act 1968, which carries a maximum penalty of five years in prison.

Many driving offences carry points as well as possible fines, and if sufficient points have been placed on the driver, disqualification can result.

Secondly, no-fault liability cannot be justified merely to provide a way to compensate innocent victims. If priority should be given to ensuring that all victims of crime and tort are compensated, then it would be fairer and more efficient to introduce either wider insurance schemes or a no-fault government-sponsored compensation system. Victims could then be compensated according to their needs, rather than according to their ability to prove their claim.

If the difficulty in establishing *mens rea* is the main argument in favour of no-fault liability, then an extension of the *res ipsa loquitur* rule, or

Key terms

Individual responsibility: belief that people are accountable for their actions and for the harm they cause.

Deterrence: belief that imposing liability and punishment will make individuals and the public at large more careful in their conduct.

Key cases

Callow v Tillstone (1900): it is debatable whether the imposition of strict liability promotes higher standards of food hygiene.

Storkwain (1986): how may it be possible to justify the conviction of someone who is morally innocent of any offence?

Study tip

These arguments are enhanced by the inclusion of relevant illustrative material.

a reversal in the burden of proof, could serve as an alternative to the imposition of strict liability: there is no need to convict defendants merely on the basis of their actions.

Finally, there is little evidence to suggest that no-fault liability encourages the adoption of higher standards: how can shopkeepers or businesses prepare against unforeseeable outcomes? In **Callow v Tillstone (1900)** a butcher had some meat inspected by a vet to ensure that it was fit for human consumption. Unfortunately, the vet was negligent and passed the meat, even though it was unfit for humans. It was the butcher, though, who was convicted of exposing unsound meat for sale. Following this decision, butchers are probably less likely to have their meat inspected.

Vicarious liability is equally unlikely to promote higher standards. Where an employer has issued clear instructions to his drivers not to overtake competitors' buses (*Limpus* v *London General Omnibus Co.* (1862)), or to carry children on their milk floats (*Rose* v *Plenty* (1976)), it is hard to see how imposing liability on him will alter his employees' conduct.

Justice

The view that individuals and businesses may be held responsible for the unforeseen, or even unforeseeable, consequences of their conduct conflicts with our sense of justice and fairness. In criminal law it seems morally offensive to punish a person who is blameless, and in civil law it seems distasteful to impose liability upon a person who has taken all reasonable care to prevent an undesired outcome. This is because the notion of fault is central to people's idea of justice and fairness.

The law enforces society's rules and values. The conviction of blameless people fosters a sense of grievance within the offender, and promotes a more widespread lack of confidence in the fairness of the criminal justice system. It reflects badly upon the values of a free society that people may be punished, even deprived of their liberty, when they are morally guiltless. In **Storkwain (1986)** a pharmacist was the victim of fraud, yet he was convicted of supplying prescription drugs. People may even be convicted where the offence was procured by the police: in *Winzar* (1983) the defendant was removed by the police to the place where he was committing the offence. Even if it were true that no-fault liability offences attract only minor penalties, it is still unjustifiable that blameless people should be punished at all.

A conviction has lasting consequences: not only does the offender undergo the immediate sanction imposed by the court, but he also has to suffer society's condemnation, a point recognised in *Sweet* v *Parsley* (1970). A criminal record might act as a barrier to much employment, tarnish the offender's reputation, and expose him to suspicion and prejudice. Such consequences should not have to be endured by the blameless.

Finally, one of the functions of law is to serve as a guide to behaviour, enabling people to amend their conduct to comply with society's requirements. No-fault liability does not allow for this: a defendant who has not been malicious, negligent, or even careless cannot avoid reoffending no matter how much more care or thought he applies. The pharmacist in *Storkwain* (1986) could be duped a second or even a third time by a convincingly forged prescription, but would be no more culpable than on the first occasion. The law requires public trust. This cannot be achieved where no distinction is made between the blameless and the blameworthy.

You should now be able to:

■ understand and discuss arguments relating to fault-based and no-fault liability.

Activity

List the cases in this chapter where you think that the wrong decision was reached. By looking at your reasons for criticising the decisions in these cases, you will be able to work out where you stand on the issue of fault-based liability.

4 Answering questions on the topic of fault

Questions on the topic of fault will inevitably require you to explore the relationship between fault and liability, and to provide some evaluation of the importance of fault in establishing liability. Usually, this will require you to begin by providing some definitions of what is meant by the term 'fault'.

In providing an explanation of the relationship between fault and liability, a balanced discussion is expected, identifying areas of fault-based and non fault-based liability. It is important that appropriate examples from the law are used throughout this part of the answer. Often you will be allowed to choose between criminal and civil law, or both. In Unit 2, you will have covered both criminal and civil liability: this should provide a range of material to illustrate your discussion, in addition to the more specialist topics studied at A2.

Sometimes, the question will invite students to focus upon fault-based or no-fault liability. This reduces the scope of the question. Even here, however, you might feel that your argument could be enhanced by some reference to the other side of the argument. If the question were on no-fault liability, it could still be useful to point out the general expectation of the need for fault to prove liability, supported by some illustrative material. Clearly, though, the main focus would then be on no-fault liability.

The evaluation is often the most challenging part of the question. It will usually have a specific focus. You should 'think on your feet', rather than a prepared answer. You should concentrate your arguments on a particular focus, and avoid simply repeating the whole range of arguments to which you have been exposed. Evaluation also needs to be supported by reference to relevant case authority. It can be productive to develop the facts of cases to illustrate the point being made.

The topic of fault contains a lot of balanced discussion. You should show an awareness of this in your evaluation. It is not a black-and-white topic that lends itself to easy solutions. The arguments are complex, and involve conflicting principles. An awareness of this complexity will be reflected in better-quality answers.

In this topic, you will learn how to:

- identify what material is required in questions on fault and non-fault liability

- provide a range of information on fault and non-fault liability, and discussion based on this.

Activities

1. Consider the appropriate content for addressing the issues identified in the following statement.

   'It is a principle of fundamental importance in English law that there should be no liability without fault.'

2. Consider how far fault is an essential requirement of liability in English law, and discuss the suggestion that fault should be an essential requirement.

You should now be able to:

- understand what is required in an essay on the topic of fault.

24 Balancing conflicting interests

In this topic, you will learn how to:
- describe some theories about the nature of legal interests
- illustrate these theories with examples.

Study tip

This topic has less theory than other topics. Nevertheless, there is a need to identify and discuss what is meant by the term 'interests'.

1 Theories about interests

Rudolph von Jhering

Rudolf von Jhering, a 19th-century legal theorist, saw law as a means of ordering a society in which there are many competing interests. These interests cannot all be satisfied, and the battle between them would lead to chaos and anarchy if it were not regulated. The law therefore acts as a mediator, assessing the value of each of these interests and deciding the proper balance between them. In particular, an individual's interests may conflict with the interests of the wider society, so the law redresses the balance by attaching rewards to some forms of conduct, and penalties to others, until the individual's interests (after taking into account these rewards and penalties) coincide with what is best for society.

Roscoe Pound

The American jurist Roscoe Pound (1870–1964) was greatly influenced by von Jhering's work. He suggested that the 'claims or demands or desires' seeking legal recognition could be classified as:

- individual interests, such as personality, privacy, reputation, owning property and domestic relations
- public interests asserted by individuals, including the interests of the state, such as public order and security
- social interests, such as safety, health, security of property, security of family, general morality, conservation of resources, free speech, free trade, economic and political progress, and the ability of each individual to live a human life according to the standards of society.

Pound insisted then that competing interests could only be balanced if they were interests on the same plane: individual interests can only be weighed against other individual interests, and social interests likewise. Otherwise, individual interests would be in danger of always being subordinated to social ones.

Wesley Hohfeld

A Professor of Law at Yale during the early 20th century, Wesley Hohfeld tried to introduce some intellectual rigour into the language used when discussing interests or rights. He distinguished between rights and liberties. A right can be claimed as an entitlement, and can therefore be viewed as a 'claim-right': this imposes a corresponding duty on the other party to honour it. For example, if X has a claim-right to freedom of speech, then Y has a duty to allow X to exercise that right. Y cannot, for example, put a gag on X, or rip up all X's letters to the local newspaper, or drown X's opinions with deafeningly loud music. Note this point, however: the existence of a large number of rights, with their corresponding duties, limits other people's freedom to act as they choose.

A liberty (or privilege), on the other hand, is the freedom to act in the way that one chooses. It ensures that individuals have control over their choice of action. Unlike a right, a liberty enjoyed by X does not impose any duties upon Y. For example, X is at liberty to catch the number 12 bus from Eastbourne to Brighton. However, if there is only one place left on this bus, Y is under no obligation to give up her place to X (unless perhaps X is aged and Y is sitting in a priority seat). Note this point: if all legal interests were regarded as liberties rather than as rights, then there would be greater freedom of choice available to people in their legal relationships with others.

Activity

Identify the interests of the parties in the following cases. Which interest do you think should take priority, and why?

1. A development company built a tower block to provide office accommodation. Unfortunately this interfered with the television reception in nearby homes.

2. A doctor ran his practice from a smart London street. He later built an extension at the bottom of his garden, adjoining a factory with heavy machinery. As a result of the noise he couldn't use his new consulting rooms.

3. When Bill sold his car, he accepted a personal cheque in payment. When the cheque bounced he discovered that the car had been sold on for cash to Ben. Bill sued Ben for the return of the car.

4. Two sailors deserted ship. The captain promised to share their wages among the remaining crew, to complete the remainder of the journey. When the ship arrived home, he refused to pay the extra wages.

You should now be able to:

- explain and illustrate different theories about the nature of interests.

2 Balancing interests in procedural law

Throughout the criminal and civil processes, attempts are made to ensure that the parties' respective interests are given due consideration.

Section A: The criminal justice system

Criminal law provides citizens with a code of conduct to guide their behaviour. Where individuals are accused of breaking that code, that accusation will be tested before an impartial tribunal of the defendant's peers, either lay magistrates or a randomly selected jury. There is a burden of proof on each charge on the prosecution. Due to the consequences of a conviction, the defendant's guilt has to be proved beyond reasonable doubt and the defendant is able to put forward a defence. Trials are held in open court and are often reported in the media. The following examples illustrate this balancing exercise.

The right to legal advice

Under s58 of the Police and Criminal Evidence Act 1984, a person arrested and held in custody has a right to legal advice and consult privately with a solicitor, and to have a solicitor present during interview. The Police Code of Practice requires the custody officer to inform the suspect of this right as soon as he is 'booked in', to issue him with a written notice with the arrangements for obtaining legal advice, and to invite him to sign the custody record to acknowledge receipt of this notice. This would be classified as a claim-right under Hohfeld's analysis as it imposes a corresponding duty upon others, particularly the custody officer.

In this topic, you will learn how to:

- explain how the criminal and civil justice systems balance the interests of the opposing parties

- illustrate with a suitable range of cases.

In the case of a serious arrestable offence, access to a solicitor may be delayed for up to 36 hours if agreed by a senior officer. This is allowed where there are reasonable grounds for believing that contact with a solicitor will:

- lead to interference with the evidence, or interference with other people
- lead to alerting other suspects still at large
- hinder the recovery of stolen property.

The Act and the Codes of Practice strive for a fair balance between the need to enable the police to investigate crime and question suspects, and the right of suspects to be free from undue influence in an intimidating environment. Where the right to legal advice is unfairly delayed, the proper balance between the interests of the parties is temporarily lost, introducing scope for considerable injustice.

Samuel (1988) concerned a man who had been arrested and interviewed four times over two days. He was denied access to a solicitor on the ground that it would lead to the alerting of other suspects. At his fourth interview, he confessed to two offences of burglary, and was charged with these. He continued to be denied access to his solicitor. He was then interviewed a fifth time, and confessed to a robbery. The Court of Appeal quashed his subsequent conviction for robbery. It described the right to legal advice as 'one of the most important and fundamental rights of a citizen'. This fired a warning shot across the bows of the police, who had acted in breach of their duty in denying the suspect his legal right.

Bail

The police and the courts perform a similar balancing of interests when deciding whether to grant **bail** to a suspect while further enquiries are made or while awaiting trial. The custody officer can refuse to grant bail if he does not have the suspect's name or address, if he doesn't believe the name or address given, or if any of the conditions of the Bail Act 1976 applies. Where bail is refused, the suspect must appear before magistrates at the first available opportunity. The magistrates will then decide whether bail should be granted. Appeals against refusal of bail may be made to a Crown Court judge.

Under the Bail Act 1976, there is a presumption that the accused should be granted bail. However, a person can be refused bail if:

- he is charged with an offence for which he could be imprisoned if found guilty, *and* the court believes that he would not turn up, commit an offence while on bail, or interfere with witnesses
- he is already serving a custodial sentence
- he needs to be kept in prison for his own safety, or, if a juvenile, for his own welfare
- he has already been bailed during the same proceedings, but has absconded.

Where bail is granted, conditions may be attached. These include:

- sureties (a fixed payment that is forfeited if the suspect absconds)
- reporting to the local police station at regular times
- a residence order
- restrictions such as a curfew, or a ban on speaking to a certain person who may be a witness.

The Act seeks to protect the right to liberty of suspects, but balances this against the need to ensure that victims are not intimidated, the public is protected, and the criminal process can operate without undue interference. Each application for bail, therefore, is determined on its merits. Bail is awarded or denied once the court has performed this balancing act.

■ **Key terms**

Bail: conditional release of a suspect until trial.

Hearsay evidence

Once a case arrives in court, the judge must decide what evidence can be admitted and used in the trial. Evidence of previous convictions, for example, is generally not admissible as it is prejudicial, and is not in itself evidence that the defendant committed the offence in question. Another type of evidence generally not admitted is **hearsay evidence**. For example, X tells Y that he saw A hit B with a frying pan. X can give first-hand evidence in court of what he saw. But Y's evidence would be second-hand: it is hearsay, as she is stating what X told her. Traditionally, the courts have barred hearsay evidence, as it prejudices the interests of the defendant, whose counsel cannot cross-examine Y to test the truth of her claim.

However, the Criminal Justice Act 2003 enables judges to admit hearsay evidence where the interests of justice require it. This shifts the balance between the interests of the defence and prosecution. In *Maher* v *DPP* (2006) the appellant reversed her BMW into an Astra in a supermarket car park, and drove off. An eye-witness saw the incident and placed a note of the BMW's registration on the windscreen of the damaged vehicle. The owner of the Astra reported this to the police, who recorded it in the incident log. The original note was then lost. The prosecution was allowed to rely upon the log as evidence of the contents of the note, even though this was 'multiple' hearsay, as the information had passed through various hands before being recorded in the log.

Multiple hearsay evidence may be admitted where 'the court is satisfied that the value of the evidence in question, taking into account how reliable the statements appear to be, is so high that the interests of justice require the later statement to be admissible for that purpose'. Few, other than the appellant, would probably argue against the justice of this decision: the interests of the injured party should not be sacrificed on the altar of technical rules of court.

Sentencing

Before passing sentence, magistrates and judges consider a range of issues. These include **aggravating and mitigating factors** relating to the offence as well as to the offender. The following diagram illustrates aggravating and mitigating factors that might apply to a conviction for one of the non-fatal offences of the OAPA 1861.

> **Key terms**
>
> **Hearsay evidence:** evidence contained in an out-of-court statement made by someone, and now offered in court to prove the truth of its contents.
>
> **Aggravating and mitigating factors:** aggravating factors increase the seriousness of the offence and lead to a more severe sentence; mitigating factors have the opposite effect.

Aggravating and mitigating factors that could relate to a conviction for one of the non-fatal offences under OAPA 1861

	Aggravating factors	Mitigating factors
Factors relating to the offence	1 Serious injury caused 2 Use of a weapon 3 Planned attack 4 Sustained attack with multiple blows 5 Racial motive 6 Vulnerable victim	1 Minor injury caused 2 No weapon 3 Spur of the moment attack 4 Single blow
Factors relating to the offender	1 Resisting arrest 2 Previous conviction 3 Pleading not guilty 4 No remorse	1 Handing yourself in to the police 2 First offence 3 Early guilty plea 4 Showing remorse/offering compensation

The magistrates or judge may also take into account one or more of the aims of sentencing. These include retribution, deterrence, threat to the public, rehabilitation and reparation.

Where magistrates or a judge fail to achieve an appropriate balance in relation to either sentencing aims or factors, the defendant – or, when an unduly lenient sentence is imposed, the prosecution – may appeal. An appeal court may agree with the original sentence or vary it upwards or downwards. Therefore, eventually, an appropriate balance may be achieved.

Section B: The civil justice system

The civil justice system seeks to ensure that those who believe that their rights have been infringed may test their claim before an impartial tribunal, and that the opposing party may reply to that claim. The claimant will seek some form of remedy, ranging from a declaration of the law to injunctions and damages. Throughout the civil justice process, the law considers the interests of both parties to the dispute.

The burden and standard of proof

In the civil justice system, the burden of proof falls upon the one who makes the assertion. The civil standard of proof required is 'on the balance of probabilities', or 'more probable than not'. This is easier to establish than the criminal standard of 'beyond reasonable doubt'. The reason for this is that civil sanctions of injunctions or damages are considered less severe and can have less effect on a person than criminal sanctions, particularly in the area of loss of liberty.

■ Activities

1 When considering bail, remember that the magistrates or judge weigh up the competing interests of the state and the defendant. Is bail likely to be granted in the following situations?

  a Donald had badly beaten his wife, Mavis, before leaving the country. When he voluntarily returned two months later, he handed himself in to the police. He has been charged under s20 of the OAPA 1861.

  b Angela's car ran out of fuel when she was shopping. As she tried to siphon some petrol from another car in a supermarket car park, she caused it to ignite. Twenty other cars were badly damaged, one of which had a baby sleeping in the back seat. The baby suffered minor burns. An angry crowd is waiting outside court.

2 Julie has been sentenced to three years in prison under s18 of the OAPA 1861. Identify the competing interests present in the case. Consider whether she or the prosecution should appeal against her sentence. The facts are as follows:

Julie works from home. She had been married for six years when her husband began a series of affairs with women from his work. After rows, he twice left home, but both times Julie accepted him back. However, he became increasingly uncommunicative and violent towards her. Whenever Julie questioned him about staying out late, he threatened her. This behaviour continued for some time. One evening, while drunk, he smashed her computer and threw it at her when she protested. Later that evening, when he fell asleep in an armchair, she threw a pan of boiling chip fat over him, blinding him in one eye and causing very serious burns to his face, neck and arms.

You should now be able to:

■ explain and illustrate how opposing interests are balanced in the criminal and civil justice systems.

3 Balancing interests in substantive law

1 Criminal law

As with the criminal justice system, areas of substantive criminal law seek to provide a balance between the interests of the prosecution and defence. However, this balance can shift. Recent examples of this shift include the development of the defence of duress of circumstances, and the increasingly subjective approach adopted by the House of Lords in cases such as *B v DPP* (2000) and *Gemmell and Richards* (2003), which leans towards the interests of the defendant. By contrast, the introduction of mandatory life sentences for repeat serious offenders can be said to encroach upon a defendant's interests.

In a criminal trial there is a high standard of proof placed on the prosecution to prove all elements of the offence because of the effect of a criminal conviction. The following examples illustrate this point.

'Belonging to another': theft

For someone to be guilty of theft, the property appropriated must **'belong to another'**. In *Turner* (1971) the defendant took his car to a garage for repairs, to be paid for later when he picked up the car. However, seeing the car on the road next to the garage, he used a spare key and drove it away without paying. When charged with theft of the car, he argued that it belonged to him. The Court of Appeal, however, upheld his conviction for theft: the garage had a proprietary interest in the car that was protected under the law.

In this case, the court did not seek to balance the interests of the two parties in the same property, or to discover which party had a stronger interest in it. It merely asked: did the garage have an interest in the property? Since it did, it was irrelevant that the defendant might have a stronger claim on the car.

'Belonging to another': criminal damage

Section 1(1) of the Criminal Damage Act 1971 creates the basic offence of damaging or destroying property belonging to another. A person cannot be convicted of damaging or destroying his own property. Clementine Churchill attracted notoriety, rather than criminal charges, for destroying the 1954 portrait of her husband, Sir Winston, by the artist Graham Sutherland.

However, under the aggravated offence of endangering life under s1(2), and under arson in s1(3), the defendant can be convicted even where he damages or destroys his own property. This can be said to be logical. The basic offence is simply concerned with safeguarding people's interest in protecting their property. Where people damage or destroy their own property, they are merely setting aside this personal interest. Others may regard this as perverse or tasteless, but their interests are not affected. However, a powerful new interest is introduced under the aggravated offences: people's interest in their very lives. When this is placed in the scales, it is rightly adjudged to outweigh the interest of the owner in dealing with his property as he chooses.

Self-defence

The private defence of self-defence protects the interest of a defendant who justifies the use of reasonable force against another person. This can be to defend himself or another person, or property. Further, the public defence under the Criminal Law Act 1967 states that reasonable force may be used to prevent crime, or to assist the arrest of offenders or those unlawfully at large.

> **Key terms**
>
> **Belonging to another:** s5 of the Theft Act 1968 defines 'belonging to another' as belonging to 'any person having possession or control of it, or having any proprietary right or interest' in it.

To succeed, the defendant must first have believed he needed to use force. In *Williams (Gladstone)* (1987), the defendant made an honest mistake about the need to use force. In the Court of Appeal, Lord Lane made allowance for this: the defendant, he explained, 'must be judged against the mistaken facts as he believes them to be.' On the other hand, no such allowance is made if the mistake was induced by alcohol (*O'Grady* (1987)).

Secondly, the force used must be reasonable. In *Palmer* (1971), Lord Morris conceded that 'a person defending himself cannot weigh to a nicety the exact measure of his defensive action.' However, this would not extend to using a gun on burglars already heading towards an exit, as in Tony Martin's case; or if an intruder had left the premises, such as in the case of Munir Hussain. There have been a number of widely reported cases where householders have been arrested after injuring, or sometimes killing, intruders. It appears that the balance has moved against the householder, as the first reaction of the police is to arrest the householder. Many argue that this balance between the interests of the householder and of the burglar needs to be realigned, allowing the householder to decide the appropriate degree of force to be used when confronting burglars.

Consent

Where the victim consents to an assault, the defendant may escape liability. Two cases illustrate how the courts balance the interests of the defendant against those of their victims. In *Wilson* (1996) the defendant, at his wife's request, had branded his initials on her buttocks. His appeal against conviction for ABH was allowed: the Court of Appeal decided it was not in the public interest for the courts to interfere with consensual activity occurring between married couples in the privacy of their own homes.

By contrast, in *Brown* (1993) the defendants were convicted under ss47 and 20 of the OAPA 1861 after engaging in sadomasochistic practices. These were consensual and conducted in private. The House of Lords decided that consent is not available in cases of serious injury, subject to certain exceptions, of which sado-masochistic sexual violence was not one.

The main distinction between these two cases is circumstantial. On the one hand a married couple were engaging in a form of tattooing, where the pain was incidental to the desired outcome. On the other hand, a group of sado-masochists were engaged in inflicting pain upon others in their group. In *Brown*, Lord Templeman spoke of the need for issues of policy and public interest to be weighed in the balance. Lord Mustill, however, spoke of the rights of an individual to live his life as he chooses. Clearly, these judges had different views about which considerations should form part of the balancing exercise they were performing.

■ Study tip

Using cases in pairs can be a useful way to draw out contrasts that highlight how the law operates in balancing different interests.

Lord Templeman   Lord Mustill

As shown in Brown *(1993), different judges may have different attitudes when it comes to the balancing of interests*

2 Contract law

In contract law, the courts are often confronted with the interests of two innocent parties, both of whom believe they have a plausible legal argument. The following issues illustrate the problems that the courts have faced when balancing the interests of the parties.

The postal rule

For a contract to be formed, A makes an offer to B, which B then accepts. In *Adams* v *Lindsell* (1818) the defendant wrote to the claimant offering to sell him some wool, and asking for a reply by post. Due to postal delays, the letter of acceptance sent by the claimant arrived later than expected. By this time, the defendant had sold the wool to another party. The question arose whether a valid contract had been formed between the claimant and defendant: if it had, the claimant was entitled to the wool; if not, the defendant had been free to sell the wool to someone else.

The court decided in favour of the claimant: a valid contract was formed at the moment the letter of acceptance was posted. This decision appears to tip the balance in favour of the buyer, which seems to be unfair as the seller has no idea of the buyer's intention until he receives the letter. In arriving at this judgement, the court recognised that the offeror could redress the balance and protect his interests by insisting that the acceptance must be effectively communicated to him personally by a stated date.

Third party rights

In *Tweddle* v *Atkinson* (1861) the father and prospective father-in-law of the claimant contracted to provide the claimant with a future payment. When the father-in-law defaulted, the claimant sued. The claim failed: as he was not a party to the contract, he had no legal interest in the case. The rigidity of this rule was recognised in *Jackson* v *Horizon Holidays* (1975). The House of Lords awarded the claimant damages on his own behalf and on behalf of his family for their disappointment over a package holiday that failed to match the advertised description. This award was made even though Mr Jackson was the only member of his family who was a party to the contract for the holiday.

The Contract (Rights of Third Parties) Act 1999 gave wider recognition to the interests of third parties, allowing them to make a claim where a contract expressly provides for them (as it had in *Tweddle* v *Atkinson* (1861)), or where it purports to confer a benefit on the claimant. This recognises that the traditional approach unfairly disadvantaged the legitimate interests of innocent parties, and shifts the balance of power in the relationship between the defaulting defendant and the intended beneficiary. As a result, there is now formal legal recognition of set circumstances in which the interests of third parties become what Hohfeld would call 'claim-rights'.

Remedies for frustration

A contract becomes **frustrated** when, due to the fault of neither party, it becomes impossible to fulfil. In *Taylor* v *Caldwell* (1863) a music hall burned down, making it impossible for Caldwell to hire it to Taylor as promised. As Taylor had spent money advertising a programme of concerts, he sought damages from Caldwell. The court decided that the contract was frustrated, and both sides were therefore released from their obligations under the contract.

This decision does nothing to remove the potential for injustice. In *Chandler* v *Webster* (1904) the claimant made full advance payment for

> **Key terms**
>
> **Frustration:** contract is frustrated when it becomes commercially sterile, when an intervening event makes performance impossible, or when performance becomes illegal.

a room to watch the coronation procession of Edward VII. This could not be recovered when the coronation was cancelled and the contract frustrated. In *Krell* v *Henry* (1903), however, no money had been paid in advance, so the property owner bore the full loss when the contract was frustrated.

A better balance in apportioning losses between the parties was introduced in the Law Reform (Frustrated Contracts) Act 1943. This allows for the recovery of money paid in advance of a contract, and for the payment of a just sum for either expenses incurred or benefits obtained. This enables the court to apportion the losses fairly between the parties, and not simply allow the loss to remain where it happens to fall. In this way, the interests of both parties are afforded some measure of protection.

Mistaken identity

In frustration, the courts may arrive at a compromise decision, where the interests of both parties are to some degree protected. In cases of 'mistaken identity', however, this is not possible: the courts must decide in favour of one party. In reaching their decision they attempt to balance the legal interests of the two parties, but in their judgment there will clearly be a winner and a loser.

'Mistaken identity' cases arise where a rogue, R, pretending to be someone else, buys (perhaps with a stolen cheque) an item of value from A. By the time A realises that R is a rogue and is not going to pay, R has already sold the item to B. A has no alternative than to try to recover the item from B. To succeed, A must prove that the contract he signed with R was void from the start, and so title in the goods never transferred to R.

In *Shogun Finance Ltd* v *Hudson* (2003) a rogue obtained a new car from a dealer by paying a ten per cent deposit and signing a hire purchase agreement under a false name. The credit company, Shogun Finance Ltd, conducted a credit search of the name they had been given before releasing the car. The rogue then sold the car to the innocent Mr Hudson. The House of Lords ruled that the contract between the credit company and the rogue was void, and therefore the credit company was entitled to the return of the car from Mr Hudson.

This was harsh on Mr Hudson, an innocent third party. The court was not prepared to develop the law to split the loss between the innocent parties by financial adjustment. Compromise was impossible: a car cannot be split into two. The court, therefore, balanced the weight of legal argument of both parties, but the decision was one-sided.

Activity

Look at the facts and judgments in *Poussard* v *Spiers* (1876), and in *Bettini* v *Gye* (1876). Identify the interests of the parties in the two cases. Explain why the courts reached different outcomes even though the facts and interests were so similar.

3 Tort

Tort law is concerned with obligations or duties owed by one party to another. It seeks to provide a remedy, usually damages, for the harm that is caused by the wrongdoing of one person to another. Often it is difficult to decide which party's interest should take precedence. The following issues illustrate the courts' concern to find the appropriate balance between the interests of the claimant and defendant.

Negligence: breach of duty of care

In negligence, the fictional 'reasonable man' is used to establish whether a duty of care is breached. A variety of factors will be considered. One of these is the likelihood of harm. In *Bolton* v *Stone* (1951) a woman was struck by a cricket ball hit out of the ground. The club had erected a high fence, minimising the risk. Evidence showed that balls had been hit out of the ground only six times in the previous 30 years. The House of Lords decided that, although the risk was foreseeable, the likelihood of injury was so small that the defendants had taken all reasonable precautions and were not negligent. The balance here was in favour of the cricket club at the expense of the innocent victim. The Lords believed there were policy implications in terms of the message of what liability would have meant in creating restrictions in what we can do in our everyday lives in an urbanised modern society.

Contrast this decision with *Haley* v *London Electricity Board* (1964). Workmen had dug a trench in a London pavement. They had positioned a pick and shovel at the far end, and a long handle with a weight attached at the near end. This handle sloped up from ground level on the road side, to two feet high on the inside of the pavement. The claimant, a blind man, tripped over the handle. He fell forward, and cracked his head on the pavement, causing deafness. The House of Lords held that the precautions taken were sufficient for able-bodied pedestrians, but not for blind ones. The likelihood of harm to someone blind was high and the LEB was liable. Here, the balance was in favour of the claimant.

Both claimants suffered harm. Both had a similar interest in pursuing a claim. However, one claim was successful while the other was not. The balance in these two cases depended on the likelihood of harm occurring.

Contributory negligence

Prior to 1945, a person who was partly responsible for harm done to him could not recover damages in tort. In the light of this injustice, the Law Reform (Contributory Negligence) Act 1945 was passed. This allowed a claimant who contributed to his own injuries to succeed in his claim, but have his award reduced to the extent of his own contribution. For example, a passenger injured due to the driver's negligence will have his award reduced, by a certain percentage, if he was not wearing a seat belt.

Jebson v *Ministry of Defence* (2000) concerned a soldier who was injured returning to camp after a night out in Portsmouth. He had fallen out of an army truck while attempting to clamber over the tailgate and onto the canvas roof. The MoD, as the provider of the vehicle and driver, owed a duty of care to the soldier. Furthermore, since it was reasonably foreseeable that drunken soldiers might engage in dangerous activities, the MoD had breached their duty of care by not providing adequate supervision. However, in the words of Potter LJ, the claimant was 'largely the author of his own misfortune. On any view his actions were foolish and dangerous in the extreme'. As a result, the Court of Appeal upheld the trial judge's ruling that the claimant should receive only 25 per cent of his damages. This apportionment fairly reflected the contributions of each party to the injuries, and a balance was achieved.

Vicarious liability

When vicarious liability is proved, the defendant is responsible for the actions of another party. This is usually seen where an employer is liable for the actions of his employees. The employer may be liable even if the employee acts against orders. In *Limpus* v *London General Omnibus Co.* (1862) the employer was held liable for the dangerous driving of his employee. In *Rose* v *Plenty* (1976) the employer was similarly liable when his employee allowed a boy to ride on its milk float, the boy was subsequently injured. In both of these cases, the employee was doing his job, even though acting against orders, and the employer was receiving a benefit from the employee's actions.

However, in *Twine* v *Bean's Express* (1946) the employer was not liable when his employee gave a lift to a hitchhiker and negligently injured him. Again the employee was ignoring clear instructions given by his employer. In this case, the forbidden activity conferred no benefit upon the employer: it was totally outside the scope of his employment. The interests of the employer therefore outweighed those of the innocent, injured claimant.

Where vicarious liability is proved, the balance can be said to be weighed in favour of the claimant, who will receive compensation for his injuries, perhaps from an innocent employer. If the claimant is unsuccessful in proving vicarious liability, the balance will be in favour of the employer. The claimant will have suffered injuries but will be unlikely to be able to receive any damages from the person primarily liable.

Nuisance

Nuisance is defined as an unlawful interference with a person's use or enjoyment of land. It generally deals with the conflicting claims of neighbours. The courts expect neighbours to tolerate a measure of inconvenience from each other, but will intervene where the interference becomes unreasonable.

In nuisance claims, the court has clearly to balance the interests of the two neighbours. They take account of factors such as the time of day the conduct takes place, the duration, whether the behaviour is repeated, whether there is a social benefit from the activity, and whether malice is present.

In *Christie* v *Davey* (1893) the claimant used his home for private music lessons, to the annoyance of his neighbour, the defendant, who retaliated by banging on walls, beating trays and shouting during the lessons. The court granted the claimant an injunction. The malice behind the defendant's behaviour was a critical factor in the decision. The court decided that the music lessons were a legitimate use of the claimant's house and they refused the defendant an injunction to stop or limit those lessons.

The situation was different in *Miller* v *Jackson* (1977) as the parties' interests were different. The claimants, Mr and Mrs Miller, bought a house adjacent to a long-established cricket ground and subsequently discovered that balls were regularly hit into their garden during the cricket season. The club made various offers to the Millers to deal with the situation, but to no avail. The Millers sought an injunction to stop cricket being played. The fact that the Millers had 'come to the nuisance' was no defence. The court had to weigh up the claimants' private interest to peacefully enjoy their own home against the defendant's enjoyment of a valuable recreational activity. There was, in addition, the interest of the local community in enjoying the open space. Roscoe Pound had warned against this balancing of a private with a social interest.

Two of the Court of Appeal judges accepted that there was a nuisance, but refused to grant an injunction as there was a strong community interest in the playing of cricket. Lord Denning MR dissented from the finding of negligence and nuisance, holding that 'the public interest should prevail over the private interest'. Lord Justice Cumming-Bruce said that the court had to 'strike a fair balance between the right of the (claimants) to have quiet enjoyment of their house and garden without exposure to cricket balls occasionally falling like thunderbolts from the heavens, and the opportunity of the inhabitants of the village in which they live to continue to enjoy the manly sport which constitutes a summer recreation for adults and young persons'. It was considered that the Millers had bought a house with the benefit of an open space adjacent to their land, and had to accept that the innocent and lawful use of the open land could restrict the enjoyment of their garden. The Millers were merely awarded damages for the inconvenience and damage to their house. The effect of the decision was that the public interest of the cricket club and the local community outweighed the right of the individual householder to enjoy their property.

A different result came in the case of *Dennis* v *MoD* (2003). In this case, Mr and Mrs Dennis owned and occupied an estate about two miles from RAF Wittering, an operational and training base for Harrier Jump Jets. They claimed that they suffered severe noise disturbance every time the Harrier pilots carried out training circuits: an average of 70 times a day. They alleged that the noise nuisance constituted a very serious interference with their enjoyment of their land, and amounted to a violation of their fundamental human rights. They sought a declaration that the flying was a nuisance and damages amounting to £10,000,000, representing the loss in value of their land.

Although the MoD accepted that operations at the air base caused noise and disturbance to the Dennis's, it argued a defence that the Harrier training was undertaken for the public benefit. So, again, the private interest of the Dennis's had to be balanced with the public interest of the MOD.

As we saw with *Miller* v *Jackson*, where the interests in dispute are on a different level it is more likely that the public interest will prevail. In Dennis's case, the court refused to grant the declaration sought but awarded the defendants damages of £950,000, representing loss of capital value, past and future loss of use and past and future loss of amenity. It decided that the noise from the Harriers amounted to a nuisance and constituted a serious interference with the private interest of the Dennis's to enjoy of their land. It was decided that although there was a public benefit to the continued training of Harrier pilots, the Dennis's should not be required to bear the cost of the public benefit. In contrast to *Miller* v *Jackson* the private interest outweighed the public interest.

4 Human rights

The European Convention on Human Rights (ECHR) was signed by the Council of Europe in 1950. The United Kingdom government ratified the ECHR in 1951, and it came into force in 1953. In 1966, the United Kingdom government allowed 'individual petitions' to be made to the European Court of Human Rights in Strasbourg. Finally, in 1998, the Human Rights Act was passed, allowing individuals to seek redress under the ECHR in UK courts. The following examples illustrate the fine balancing act in which the courts must engage when considering claims under the ECHR and the HRA.

Article 8 and the rights of prisoners to IVF treatment

Under Article 8 of the ECHR, every person has the right to respect for his private and family life, his home and his correspondence. The case of *Dickson* v *UK* (2007) concerned a prisoner serving a life sentence for murder for kicking a drunk to death. While in prison, he met and married his wife. Upon his earliest release date his wife would be 51 years old, and too old to conceive a child naturally. The couple had been refused their application for IVF treatment on the grounds that the relationship had yet to be tested in a normal environment, that there was insufficient provision for the welfare of any child, and that it was inconsistent with the public's expectation of how a violent killer should be punished.

The couple applied to the European Court of Human Rights under Article 8, arguing that the refusal of IVF treatment contravened their right to family life. The court upheld their complaint: prisoners did not forfeit their rights under the convention. The court stated that the wife was able to look after any child until her husband's release, and that the interest of the state in wishing to avoid giving offence to public opinion was not a relevant consideration. Key to the decision was the fact that UK policy placed an impossible burden upon the complainants: they could not under any circumstances meet the criteria for IVF treatment. This prevented the secretary of state and the domestic courts from properly balancing the individual and public interests. The European court, by its decision, was able to balance these interests.

This case was heard in Strasbourg. The following two cases were heard before British courts using jurisdiction granted under the Human Rights Act 1998.

Article 5 and the prevention of terrorism

Under Article 5, everyone has the right to liberty and security of person. This is subject to certain exceptions, including lawful detention after conviction by a court, lawful arrest or detention for the purpose of bringing someone to trial, and lawful detention pending deportation. In the case of *A and Others* v *Secretary of State for the Home Department* (2004) the House of Lords was asked to consider the case of foreign nationals who were being held indefinitely under the Anti-Terrorism, Crime and Security Act 2001. The House declared that s23 of the Act, in allowing the men's indefinite detention, was incompatible with Article 5 of the ECHR.

Lord Bingham, one of nine judges who heard the case, recognised the nature of the threat imposed by terrorists. However, he argued that if the threat presented to the security of the United Kingdom by UK nationals suspected of being terrorists could be addressed without infringing their right to personal liberty, then why did the same not apply to foreign nationals resident in the United Kingdom? He continued:

> Since the right to personal liberty is among the most fundamental of the rights protected by the European Convention, any restriction of it must be closely scrutinised by the national court.

As a result of this judgment the government, in the Prevention of Terrorism Act 2005, limited the detention of foreign nationals to 28 days. However, there is continuing debate about the extent to which civil liberties should be subordinated to the need to fight the threat of terrorism.

The European Convention on Human Rights

The Convention is divided into sections, with s1 listing the rights as Articles. These include:

Article 2 Everyone's right to life shall be protected by law. No one shall be deprived of his life intentionally save in the execution of a sentence of a court.

Article 3 No one shall be subjected to torture or to inhuman or degrading treatment or punishment.

Article 4 No one shall be held in slavery or servitude.

Article 5 Everyone has the right to liberty and security of person.

Article 6 In the determination of his civil rights and obligations or of any criminal charge against him, everyone is entitled to a fair and public hearing within a reasonable time by an independent and impartial tribunal established by law.

Article 7 No one shall be held guilty of any criminal offence on account of any act or omission which did not constitute a criminal offence at the time when it was committed.

Article 8 Everyone has the right to respect for his private and family life, his home and his correspondence.

Article 9 Everyone has the right to freedom of thought, conscience and religion.

Article 10 Everyone has the right to freedom of expression.

Article 11 Everyone has the right to freedom of peaceful assembly and to freedom of association with others, including the right to form and to join trade unions for the protection of his interests.

Article 12 Men and women of marriageable age have the right to marry and to found a family.

Article 13 Everyone whose rights and freedoms as set forth in this Convention are violated shall have an effective remedy before a national authority.

Article 14 The enjoyment of the rights and freedoms set forth in this Convention shall be secured without discrimination on any ground.

The European Convention on Human Rights (ECHR)

Article 6 and witness anonymity

Under Article 6 of the ECHR, everyone is entitled to a fair and public hearing within a reasonable time by an independent and impartial tribunal established by law. Included within this is the right to examine or have examined witnesses against him.

In *Davis* (2008) the House of Lords was asked to consider whether this right was breached in the case of Iain Davis, who had been convicted in 2004 for murdering two men at a party in Hackney. The trial judge had granted **anonymity** to seven witnesses, three of whom identified Davis as the gunman. It was argued that this prevented defence counsel from performing an effective cross-examination of the witnesses, as they could not ask any questions that might lead to disclosing the witnesses' identity.

The House found in favour of Davis. Lord Bingham declared that the protective measures adopted by the trial judge 'hampered the conduct of the defence in a manner and to an extent which was unlawful and rendered the trial unfair'. He ruled that anonymity should not be granted where the testimony is the decisive evidence in a case, or where it prevents the defence from effectively cross-examining the witness.

> ### Key terms
>
> **Witness anonymity:** in an attempt to persuade members of the public to come forward with evidence that will help to secure the conviction of violent offenders, courts allow witnesses to remain anonymous in court; these witnesses are hidden behind a screen, visible to judge and jury, but not to the defendant or to the public gallery; their voices are electronically distorted so that their race, age and gender cannot be told.

What is the balance to be struck here? On the one hand, the granting of witness anonymity promotes the public interest in securing the conviction of violent offenders who resort to intimidation. Without the promise of anonymity, many cases will never reach court. On the other hand, the granting of anonymity increases the risk of people with ulterior motives 'setting-up' innocent individuals as part of a campaign of vengeance, and lying or exaggerating in order to achieve their purpose. Also, the mere presence of a screen and electronically distorted voices is prejudicial to the defendant.

Following the decision in this case, the Justice Secretary declared that 'there is a difficult balance to strike here, between giving witnesses who fear for their safety the confidence to give evidence in court, and ensuring that innocent people are not convicted'. However, Article 6 grants the defendant an absolute right to have witnesses examined. This cannot be balanced against other considerations. Should any legislation impose restrictions upon the operation of this right, doubtlessly the House of Lords will declare it incompatible with the defendant's rights under Article 6. Other solutions will have to be found to counter the problem of witness intimidation.

> ### ■ Activity
>
> Read through the details of the following case and consider how you would weigh the interests of the two parties in this claim.
>
> Under Article 3 of the Protocol to the ECHR, member states 'undertake to hold free elections at reasonable intervals by secret ballot, under conditions which will ensure the free expression of the opinion of the people in the choice of the legislature'. Three prisoners, one serving ten years for importing drugs, another life for committing arson with intent to endanger life, and the third life for manslaughter, used this Article to challenge the Home Office ruling that prisoners are barred from participating in elections. They argued in addition that having the chance to vote would help them to become responsible citizens and increase their chances of going straight when released. The Home Office argued that prisoners forfeited their right to vote while in prison.

You should now be able to:

■ explain and illustrate how opposing interests are balanced in some cases of substantive law.

In this topic, you will learn how to:

■ identify the material that questions on balancing conflicting interests could include

■ provide a range of information and discussion.

▪4▪ Answering questions on the topic of balancing conflicting interests

Questions on this topic call for less theoretical background than other topics. However, it is useful to make some reference to theories about the nature of interests and to intersperse later discussion with reference to these. It is also worthwhile to focus upon the meaning of the word 'balance'. There are different ways in which the term may be used. In procedural law, it means giving equal consideration to the interests of the different parties to the action. This can be seen in criminal and civil trials where both parties are granted the opportunity to state their cases and to influence the tribunal.

Substantive law may also provide balance in reflecting the competing interests of the parties. The defence of self-defence, for example, provides a measure of protection to both parties: the defendant is not denied the defence if he was honestly mistaken about the need to use force. In this way, the interest of the defendant is recognised. However, if the mistake was alcohol-induced, the defence is not available. In this way, the interest of the victim and of the prosecution is recognised.

Judges also perform a balancing act when applying civil law. Only rarely will the two sides be in perfect equilibrium. A judge may not attach equal weight to the opposing arguments. In cases such as *Miller* v *Jackson* (1977) they may come down clearly on one side of the argument; in this case, in favour of the public interest.

The question on this topic will require you to introduce a lot of illustrative material as the basis for discussion. It is probably more open than any other topic for you to use such illustrative material as you and your teacher have considered during your course.

You could refer in your answer to either procedural or substantive law, or both. When dealing with the former, you could refer to either the criminal or the civil justice system, or both. When dealing with substantive law, you could successfully use contrasting cases such as *Miller* v *Jackson* and *Dennis* v *MoD*. Try to ensure, when using a case, that you do more than set out the facts of the case. Try to analyse the competing interests in the case (for example, the public and private interests) and try to consider whether the result of the case has successfully balanced the different interests.

Activity

Select six decided cases that you might include in an essay on this topic. Refer briefly to the relevant facts, identify the interests of the parties, and explain the outcome. An example is provided below:

Case:	*Miller* v *Jackson* (1977)
Facts:	The Millers bought a house adjacent to a long-established cricket ground. Balls hit by the cricketers regularly came into their garden. The cricket club tried several ways to deal with the situation. The Millers brought an action for nuisance to stop the club playing cricket.
Interests:	The Millers: private interest, loss of enjoyment of their property;
	The cricket club/local community: public interest in playing sport and having an open space for recreation
Outcome:	The public interest prevailed over the private interest: the Court of Appeal decided that the club's activities were not a nuisance requiring the grant of a prohibitory injunction;
Balancing of interests:	The cricket club and the local community were able to continue to use the recreation ground. Their interests outweighed those of Mr and Mrs Miller, who were unlikely to be able to enjoy the use of their garden (particularly on summer weekends).

You should now be able to:

■ understand what is required in an essay on the topic of balancing conflicting interests.

Practice questions

You should write in continuous prose, give reasoned answers, and make reference to cases, statutes and examples where appropriate. It is recommended that you spend 15 minutes planning your answer.

▨ Example question 1: Law and morality (AQA, June 2011)

Consider the view that there is a close relationship between law and morality. Examine the debate as to whether the law should reflect moral values, and discuss issues that show the continuing importance of that debate.

(30 marks + 5 marks for AO3)

▨ Example question 2: Law and justice (AQA, June 2011)

Discuss the meaning of justice. Critically analyse the extent to which the law is successful in achieving justice, and discuss the difficulties that it faces in seeking to do so.

(30 marks + 5 marks for AO3)

▨ Example question 3: Judicial creativity (AQA, June 2011)

Analyse the extent to which judges are able to develop the law through the operation of the doctrine of judicial precedent and in the interpretation of statutes. Discuss whether judges should be allowed to develop the law.

(30 marks + 5 marks for AO3)

▨ Example question 4: Fault (AQA, June 2012)

Briefly explain what is meant by 'fault', and discuss the extent to which liability is based on fault. Consider the arguments for and against fault-based liability.

(30 marks + 5 marks for AO3)

▨ Example question 5: Balancing conflicting interests (AQA, June 2012)

Explain what is meant by 'balancing conflicting interests'. Discuss the extent to which English law balances conflicting interests and briefly consider whether it is important to do so.

(30 marks + 5 marks for AO3)

Index

Key terms and their page numbers are in **bold**.

A

abatement **298**
abnormality of mental functioning 14–17
abortion 328, 365, 367
absolute liability 379–380, **379**
acceptance 84–87, **85**, 97, 106, 151–154
accidents 313–314
accord 89
accumulation **303**
act of God **305**
act and rule utilitarianism 340
act of a stranger **305**
action taken by the victim 5–6
actual bodily harm 3, 35–37, **35**, 55, 70–71, 334, 367
actual breach 137
actus reus
  assault 31–33
  battery 33–34
  blackmail 184
  burglary 325
  criminal damage 193–195
  duress 225
  false representation 200–203
  fault 371–372
  murder 2–3, 28–30
  non-fatal offences against the person 31–40
  robbery 181
  self-defence 226
  theft 167, 168–174, 179
adequacy 88, 154
advertisements 82, 97, 152
agency exceptions 93
aggravated offence of criminal damage 195–196
aggravating factors **374**, 389
alcohol dependency 16–17
'all or nothing' approach 78, 245
amenity loss 246–247, **246**, 293
American Legal Realism **366**
anomie 323
anonymity 399–400, **399**
anti-discrimination 364–365
anticipatory breach 136–137, **136**
appeals 345–346
apprehend 32
appropriation 167, 168–169, **168**
Aquinas, Thomas 321, 337–338
Aristotle 337, 344
arson 196–197
assault 31–33, **31**, 35
  balancing conflicting interests 392
  fault 374
  mens rea 33
assault occasioning actual bodily harm 35–36, **35**
assessment of damages 143–145, 163, 344

assisted suicides 53, 77, 326, 334, 335
auctions 82, 85, 101, 112, 121, 153, 262
Austin, John 320
authorised acts 311–313, **312**
automatism 44, 46–48, 372
avoiding payment 198, 201–202, 204–211
avoiding precedent 356–359

B

badger culls 356
bail **388**
balancing conflicting interests 318, 386–401
  civil law 390
  contract law 393–394
  criminal justice system 387–390
  damages 390–397
  human rights 397–400
  negligence 395
  procedural law 387–390
  self-defence 391–392
  substantive justice 391–400
  theories 386–387
  tort 394–397
  vicarious liability 395–396
basic intent 50–51, 75, 214–215
battery 31, 33–34, **33**
  actus reus 33–34
  fault 374
  mens rea 34
Bellfield, Levi 375
belonging to another 167, 172–174, 194–195, **391**
benefits of judicial creativity 367
Bentham, Jeremy 339–340
bigamy 332
bilateral contracts **81**
blackmail **181**, 184–187
blood tests 55
breaches
  discharge of contracts 136–139
  duty of care 237–240, 248–252, 270–271, 351–352, 395
  implied contract terms 109
  remedies 137–138
building or part thereof 190
burden of proof
  balancing conflicting interests 390
  insanity 73
  self-defence 59, 229
  voluntary manslaughter 13, 17
burglary 188–192, **188**, 211, 325
Burstow, Anthony 38
business contract arrangements 95, 96
business efficacy 99
but for tests **240**
Butler Committee 74
bystander tests 99

C

causation
  assault 32
  defective goods negligence 271

fault 372
involuntary manslaughter 25–26
murder 3–4
occupiers' liability 284
tort of negligence 240–243, 251
caveat emptor 350
CCRC (Criminal Cases Review Commission) **346**
certainty of content 325
characteristics of law and morality 323–326
children 68, 284
circumstances
  duress 223–226
  frustrating events 132–133, 139
civil law 375–378, 380–381, 390
claimants, **private nuisance** 292–293
claiming damages 103–109, 123–126, 130–131, 136–148, 157–165, 246–247, 256, 344–345, 352
class of people 299, 300–301
clinical negligence 247–252, **247**
close tie of love and affection **256**
codify 63
coincidence, law and morality 327–328
collateral contracts 93–94
Collier, Agnes 344
command theory of law 320–321, **320**
commencement of law and morality rules 324
commercial contract arrangements 95, 96
common injury 300
common law 102, 110–112, 158
common law crime **300**
communication
  contract acceptance 85–87
  contract offers 83–84
compensation 344–345
concepts of law
  balancing conflicts of interest 318, 386–401
  fault 318, 371–385
  judicial creativity 318, 355–370
  law and justice 318, 336–354
  law and morality 318, 320–335
conditional intent 177
conditions, contracts **100**, 107, 136, 138
conflicting interests 318, 386–401
  see also balancing conflicting interests
consent
  balancing conflicting interests 392
  defences 53–56, 76–77, 244–246, **244**, 285–286, 290
consequences
  breaching duty of care 248–250
  murder 4, 6–8, 11
consequential economic loss **261**
consideration 83, 88–92, **88**, 93, 97, 154–155
constitutional relationships 363–366, **363**

constructive manslaughter 19, 23–27
consumer protection 86–87, 152,
   156–158, 165, 234, 268–279, **274**,
   352, 366, 380–381, 383
consumers 113–118, **113**
contract law 80–165, **146**, 345
   balancing conflicting interests
      393–394
   damages 106–107, 123–125, 130,
      136–138, 140–145, 147, 162–164
   discharge of contracts 128–139, **128**
   exclusion clauses 100–101, 110–118,
      158–159, 286, 290, 350–351
   express contract terms 99–100
   formation of contracts 81–98
   frustrating events 128–129, **128**,
      132–135, 138–139, 351–352
   goods 100, 102–107, 113,
      157–158, 165
   implied contract terms 99–100,
      102–110, 157–158
   injunctions 146–147, **146**, 164
   law reforms 134–135, 138–139,
      151–165
   misrepresentation 119–127, **119**,
      159–162
   mistaken identity 394
   performance 129–131, 138–139, 147
   postal rule 85–86, **85**, 152–154, 393
   rejection 146, 157, 165
   remedies 105–107, 109, 123–126,
      131, 134–135, 137–138, 140–148,
      162–165
   repudiation 106, **134**, 158, 165
   rescission 123, 125, 126, 146–148
   satisfaction 89
   specific performance 147, 164–165
   substantive justice 350–351
   terms of contracts 99–118,
      157–159, 165
   third party rights 94, 126, 265,
      351, 393
   validity 157
   vitiating factors 119–127, 159–162
contractors 285, 308–311, **308**
contributory negligence **244**, 251,
   278, 285, 290, 378, 394
control tests **309**
controls, terms of contracts 100–101,
   110–118
conventional morality **332**
Cooke, Gary 21
corrective justice **337**, 343–345
cost of precautions 239
Cotterill, James 54
court hierarchy **356**
covenants 94
creativity *see* judicial creativity
crime prevention defences 57–59
**Criminal Cases Review Commission
   (CCRC) 346**
criminal damage 193–197, 215, 362
criminal law 1–79
   balancing conflicting interests
      387–390
   blackmail **181**, 184–187
   burglary 188–192, **188**, 211, 325
   criminal damage 193–197, 215, 362
   defences 9–17, 42–59, 212–229

fatal offences against the
   person 2–30, 62–69
fault 371–375
fraud 198–210, 217
involuntary manslaughter 3, 19–30
murder 2–30, 62–68
non-fatal offences against the
   person 31–41, 69–79
offences against property 166–231
robbery 181–184, **181**, 211
substantive justice 349–350
theft 167–184, **167**, 188–192, 217
voluntary manslaughter 2–18, 62–68
criminal processes in law and
   justice 345–346
custom, terms of contracts 99

D

damage
   criminal damage 193–197, 215, 362
   liability in tort for defective
      goods 232, 268–279
   medical damage 232, 233–252
   occupiers' liability 282, 286–287, 290
   physical damage 232, 233–252, 293
   psychiatric damage 232, 253–267,
      253, **255**, **256**
   remoteness of damage 163,
      240–243, **241**
   tort of negligence 232, 233–267
damages
   assessment 143–145, 163, 344
   balancing conflicting interests
      390–397
   claiming 103–109, 123–126,
      130–131, 136–148, 157–165,
      246–247, 256, 344–345, 352
   contract law 106–107, 123–125,
      130, 136–138, 140–145, 147,
      162–164
   corrective justice 343–345
   fault liability 376–378
   fraudulent misrepresentation
      123–124
   implied contract terms 106–107
   law and justice 343–345, 351–352
   misrepresentation 119, 123–126
   negligence 125, 246–247, 377
   negligent misrepresentation 125
   occupiers' liability 286–287,
      290–291
   private nuisance 297–298
dangerous act 24–25
dangerous thing **303**
debts 89–92
defamation, tort 326
defect **275**
defect of reason 43
defective goods 232, 268–279
defences
   automatism 44, 46–48
   consent 53–56, 76–77, 244–246,
      244, 285–286, 290
   criminal law 9–17, 42–59, 212–229
   defective goods negligence 272–273,
      277–279
   duress **212**, 217–226
   fault 372–373
   force 57–59

insanity 42–45, 73–74, 75
intoxication 48–52, 74–76, 212–217,
   219
mental responsibility 42–45
murder 9–17
occupiers' liability 285–286,
   290–291
offences against property 212–229
prevention of crime 57–59, 226–229
private nuisance 296–297
provocation 9–13
self-defence 57–59, 77–78, 226–229
substantive justice 349–350
tort of negligence 244–246
tort of nuisance 296–297, 304–305
defendants, **private nuisance** 293
degree of interference 295
dentistry 55
departing without payment 206–211
destruction 193–194
deterrence **383**
development risks defence **277**
Devlin, Patrick 331–334, **331**
diminished responsibility 14–18, 45,
   59, 66–68
discharge of contracts 128–139, **128**
   anticipatory breach 136–137, **136**
   breach 136–139
   definitions 128–129
   divisibility 129–131, **129**
   frustrating events 128–129, **128**,
      132–135, 138–139
   partial performance 130
   performance 129–131, 138–139
   remedies 131
   substantial performance 130
discharging duty of care 289–290
discretionary sentences **65**, 68
disease of the mind 43–44
dishonesty
   fraud 198, 199, 203–207
   theft 167, **175**, 177–179, 180
distance selling 86–87
distinguishing **357**
distributive justice 337–339, **337**
divine law 321
divisibility 129–131, **129**
do good and avoid evil **321**
doctrine of allurement 280
domestic contracts 95, 96
1998 draft Bill **71–72**
duration, **private nuisance** 294
duress **212**, 217–226
Durkheim, Emile **323**
'Dutch Courage' 215
duty 34, 77–79, 90–92, 97, 120–124,
   154, 159–162, 233–267
duty of care
   breaches 237–240, 248–252,
      270–271, 351–352, 395
   defective goods 268–274
   gross negligence manslaughter
      20–21
   law and morality 327
   occupiers' liability 282–284,
      288–291
   tort of negligence 233–267, **233**,
      351–352, 395
Dworkin, Ronald 364–365

E

earnings 247
ECHR *see* European Convention on Human Rights
ECJ (European Court of Justice) 277
economic loss 232, 253, 260–267, **260**
ejusdem generis rule 170
electronic commerce 86
embryology 367
employees 307, 308–311, **308**
employers 307–308, 311–315
employment 307–315
enforcement of law and morality 324, 330–334
entry 189–190, 280
equality 328–329, **337**, 338–339, 361, 364–365
equitable remedies 146–147
escape 5–6, 24–26, 220, 223–224, 238, **304**, 312
EU (European Union) 363–364, 368
European Convention on Human Rights (ECHR) 53, 74, 364–365, 368, 397–400
European Court of Justice (ECJ) 277
European Union (EU) 363–364, 368
euthanasia 76–77, 332
exclusion clauses
    contract law 100–101, 110–118, 158–159, 286, 290, 350–351
    occupiers' liability 286, 290
exemplary damages 377
existing duty 90–92
expectation losses 143–145
express contract terms 99–100
expressly forbidden methods 312
external aids in statutory interpretation 362–363
external factors, automatism 46

F

Factortame 363
factual causation, murder 4
failure to pay 207–211
fairness, contracts 154–155
fatal offences against the person
    involuntary manslaughter 3, 19–30, 68
    manslaughter/murder 2–30, 62–68
    voluntary manslaughter 2–18, 62–68
fault 318, 371–385
    absolute liability 379–380, **379**
    actus reus 371–372
    causation 372
    civil law 375–378, 380–381
    defences 372–373
    dependency debate 381–384
    justice 384
    liability dependency debate 381–384
    liability depending on fault 371–378, 381–385
    liability not depending on fault 378–385
    mens rea 371, 374–375, 378, 382–384
    occupiers' liability 377–378
    strict liability 378–380, **379**
    tort 375–378
    vicarious liability 380–381, **380**

faulty manufacturing processes 270–271, 273, 376
fear of serious violence 11, 65–66
first degree murder 68
flexibility, contracts 154–155
force
    assault 32
    battery 33–34
    defences 57–59
    robbery 181–184
    self-defence 78, 227–229
foreseeable risk 133
foresight of consequences 6–8
formation of contracts 81–98, 152
    acceptance 84–87, **85**, 97, 151–154
    business arrangements 95, 96
    commercial arrangements 95, 96
    consideration 83, 88–93, **88**, 97, 154–155
    domestic arrangements 95, 96
    intention to create legal relations 95–96
    legal relation creation 95–96, 97, 156–157
    offers 81–84, **81**, 87, 97, 151–154
    postal rule 85–86, **85**, 152–154
    privity of contract 93–94, 97, 155–156
    social arrangements 95–96
fraud 203
    criminal law 198–210, 217
    false representation 198–207, **198**, 200–203, 217
    misrepresentation 123–124, 127
freedom of contract 152
frustration/frustrating events 128–129, **128**, 132–135, 138–139, 351–352, 393–394, **393**
Fuller, Lon 322
future earnings 247

G

gains, **blackmail** 187
Ghosh test 175, 178–179, 180, 203
Gilfoyle, Eddie 347
golden rule 360
goods
    contract terms 100, 102–107, 113, 157–158, 165
    fraud 209
    liability in tort 232, 268–279
Graham test 217, 218
grievous bodily harm 37, 38–39, 40
gross negligence manslaughter 19–23, 26–27, 373

H

habeas corpus 365
Hansard 361–362, **361**
harm principle 330
harmony 336
Hart, Herbert Lionel Adolphus 320–321, **320**, 322, 331–334
hearsay evidence 389
Hemming, Christine 171
hierarchy of the courts 356
hierarchy of seriousness 70–71
Hillsborough football disaster 53, 254
Hohfeld, Wesley 386–387

homicide
    reclassification 68
    see also murder
homosexuality 329, 333, 358
horseplay 55–56, 75
human rights 397–400
Hussain, Munir 78, 372, 392

I

identity issues 126, 202–203, 205, 264–265, 340, 394, 399–400
illegality, **frustrating events** 132
immediate aftermath 257
immediate violence 32
implied contract terms 99–100, 102–110, 157–158
implied malice 64
impossibility, **frustrating events** 132
inalienable rights 341
incitement 11
incorporation, contracts 110–112
independent contractors 285, 308–311, **308**
indeterminate terms 100, 107
indirect battery 34
individual freedom 76
individual responsibility 382–383, **383**
inflict, non-fatal offences against the person 70
influences on law and morality 327–329
information requests 85
informed consent 76–77
Inglis, Francis 65, 349
injunctions 146–147, **146**, 164, 297
inner morality of law 321
innocent misrepresentation 125–126
innominate terms 100, 107
insanity 42–48, 68, 73–75, 372
integration tests 309
intent
    intoxication 50–51, 75, 214–215
    murder 62–64
intention to create legal relations 95–96, 97, 156–157
intention to permanently deprive 167, 175–177, **175**, 180
interests, conflict balancing 318, 386–401
interference, **private nuisance** 293–296
intervening acts, murder 5
intervening cause 242–243, **242**
intoxication 358
    defences 48–52, 74–76, 212–217, 219
    law reforms 75–76
    mens rea 48–52, 213, 214–215
    voluntary manslaughter 16–17
invitation to treat 82
involuntary act 46
involuntary intoxication 48–52, 74–76, 212–217
involuntary manslaughter 3, 19–30, 68
    gross negligence manslaughter 19–23, 26–27
    mens rea 22, 26–27
    unlawful act manslaughter 19, 23–27
IVF treatment rights 398

J

von Jhering, Rudolf 386
Johnson, Laura 221
joint liability 307
judges
  law-making 367–368
  role in judicial creativity 363–368
judicial creativity 318, 355–370
  benefits 367
  judges role 363–368
  Parliament 363–366
  precedents 355–359
  statutory interpretation 359–363
justice 318, 336–354, 384
  see also law and justice
justification 307

K

knowledge 101, 369
known users/purposes 264–265

L

labels 82, 104, 112, 168, 270–271,
  276, 278
language 69–70
Law Commission
  judicial creativity 362–363, **362**
  murder 63–64, 65
  non-fatal offences against the
    person 69, 71–72, 74–77
  voluntary manslaughter 66–68
Law Commission Report 1993 69,
  71–72
law and justice 318, 336–354
  damages 343–345, 351–352
  procedural justice 343–348
  substantive justice 343, 349–351
  theories 336–342
law and morality 318, 320–335
  characteristics 323–326
  coincidence 327–328
  enforcement 324, 330–334
  influences 327–329
  relationships 326–329
law reforms
  consent defence 77
  contract law 134–135, 138–139,
    151–165
  frustrating events 134–135,
    138–139
  insanity 74
  intoxication defences 75–76
  law and morality rules 324–325
  non-fatal offences against the
    person 71–72, 74–79
  self-defence 78–79
  voluntary manslaughter 66–67
law reports 356
law-making 367–368
lawful visitors 232, 280–281, **280**
legal advice rights 387–388
legal aid 343
legal causation 4
legal interests 292–293, **292**
legal positivism 320–321, **320**
legal relation creation 95–96, 97,
  156–157
lenient sentences 346

liability
  dependency debate 381–384
  depending on fault 371–378,
    381–385
  fault 371–385
  not depending on fault 378–385
  occupiers' liability 232, 280–291,
    352, 378
  in tort for defective goods 232,
    268–279
  vicarious liability 232, 307–315,
    307, 352
libertarianism 342
life sentences 64–65, 68, 349
likelihood of injury 238–239
limitation clauses 100–101, 110–118,
  158–159
limits, occupiers' liability 281–282
liquidated damages 145
literal rule 359–360, 361
Llewellyn, Karl 366
locality factors 294
loss
  of amenity 246–247, **246**, **293**
  of bargain 143–145
  blackmail 187
  of control 9–14, 17, 65–67
  to property 246

M

main purpose rule 112
makes off from the spot 209
making off without payment 206–211
malice 64, 295–296, **295**
malice aforethought 2, 6, 64
maliciously 36, 39–41, **39**, 70
mandatory life sentences 64–65, **64**,
  68, 349
manslaughter
  fatal offences against the
    person 2–30, 62–68
  involuntary 3, 19–30, 68
  voluntary 2–18, 62–68
Marx, Karl 338
material fact 120–122
medical conditions 14–17
medical damage 232, 233–252
medical negligence 247–252, **247**
medical procedures 55
menaces 184–187, **185**
mens rea
  assault 33
  battery 34
  blackmail 184
  burglary 325
  criminal damage 194
  duress 225
  fault 371, 374–375, 378, 382–384
  fraud 203
  intoxication 48–52, 213–215
  involuntary manslaughter 22, 26–27
  murder 6–8, 28–30
  non-fatal offences against the person
    33, 34, 36–37, 39–41, 69, 71
  robbery 181
  self-defence 226
  theft 167, 175–180
mental responsibility 14–17, 42–45,
  67–68

Mill, John Stuart 330–331, **331**, 340,
  343
miscarriages of justice 343, 346–348
mischief rule 360
misrepresentation
  contract law 119–127, **119**, 159–162
  damages 119, 123–126
  fraud 123–124, 127
  innocent misrepresentation 125–126
  negligence 124–125, 127
  negotiations 121–122
  remedies 123–126, 161–162
  silence 122
  types 123–126, 160–161
misstatements 262–267, **262**
mistaken identity 394
mitigating factors 374, **389**
morality 318, 320–335
  see also law and morality
Mosaic Law 327
multiple tests 309–310, **309**
murder 2–30, 62–68, 349
  actus reus 2–3, 28–30
  defences 9–17
  fatal offences against the
    person 2–30, 62–68
  intent 62–64
  involuntary manslaughter 3,
    19–30, 68
  mens rea 6–8, 28–30
  voluntary manslaughter 2–18, 62–68
mutuality of obligation 310

N

natural justice 348
natural law 321–322, **321**
nature of act 44–45
nature of breach 136–137
necessity of force 57–58, 227–229
negligence 376
  balancing conflicting interests 395
  claiming damages 246–247
  criminal law 373–374
  damages 125, 246–247, 377
  defective goods 268–274
  fault 375–377
  misrepresentation 124–125, 127
  product liability 268–274
  tort of negligence 232, 233–267
negligent misstatement 262–267, **262**
negotiations 121–122
neighbour tests 233–234
nemo iudex in causa sua 348
nervous shock 232, 253–267
Nizzar, Farrakh 200
no-fault liability 378–385
non-defences 297
non-fatal offences against the
  person 31–41, 69–79
  actus reus 31–40
  assault 31–33, **31**
  battery 31, 33–34, **33**
  Law Commission 71–72, 74–76, 77
  law reforms 71–72, 74–79
  mens rea 33, 34, 36–37, 39–41,
    69, 71
non-natural use 303–304, **303**
non-pecuniary loss 144–145
Norton, Anthony 344

notices, contracts 111
Nozick, Robert 341–342
nuisance 232, 292–306, 396–397

O

obiter dicta 350, 355
objective recklessness 350
objective tests 12–13
obtaining services dishonestly 204–207
occasioning 3, 35–36, **35**, 367, 374
occupiers 232, 280–291, **283**, 323, 352, 377–378
occupiers' liability 232, 280–291, 323, 352, 377–378
offences against property 166–231
  blackmail 181, 184–187
  burglary 188–192, **188**, 211, 325
  criminal damage 193–197, 215
  defences 212–229
  fraud 198–210, 217
  robbery 181–184, **181**, 211
  theft 167–184, **167**, 188–192, 217
offerees 81
offerers 81
offers 81–84, **81**, 87, 97, 151–154
officious bystander tests 99
omissions
  battery 34
  duty of care 235–236, 248–252
  law and morality 327
  murder 2
'on a frolic of his own' 314
oral statements 112
origins of law and morality 323–324
overriding oral statements 112
overruling 358–359, **358**

P

pain, suffering and loss of amenity 246–247, **246**
Parliament 363–366, **363**
part payments 89–92
partial defences 42, 67, 78, 349, 355, 372–373, **373**
partial performance 130
party to the contract 93, 121–122, 156, 164, 351, 393
past consideration, contracts 88–89
paternalistic approaches **332**
payments
  contracts 89–92
  fraud 198, 201–202, 204–211
Perelman, Chaim 338–339
performance, contract law 129–131, 138–139, 147
personal assistance 247
personal injury damages 246–247
personal performance 310
physical damage 232, 233–252, 293
physical damage to land 293
Pidgley, Oliver 208
piercing (human body) 55
Plato 336
postal rule 85–86, **85**, 152–154, 393
Pound, Roscoe 386
precedents 355–359
premises 283
prescription 296–297, **296**
prevention of crime 57–59, 226–229

prevention of terrorism 398
previous course of dealing 111–112
primary victims 255–256, **255**, 259–260
prisoners' rights to IVF treatment 398
private defences 57–59, 227–229
private nuisance 292–299, **292**, 293, 301
  defences 296–297
  interference 293–296
  remedies 297–298
  unlawfulness 293–296
privity of contract 93–94, 97, 155–156
Privy Council 355–356, 364
procedural law 343–348, 387–390
product 275
product liability 232, 268–279
promissory estoppels 89–90, 154–155, 366
property 167, **168**, 169–172, 194
proportionality 59, **337**
prosecution 3
provocation 9–13
psychiatric damage 232, 253–267, **253**, **255**, **256**
public defences 57–59, 227–229
public interest 381–382
public nuisance 299–302, **299**, 382
public policy 364–366
pure economic loss 261
purposive approaches 360–361

Q

quality of act 44–45
quantum meruit **130**, 135

R

racial equality 328–329, 361
radical changes in circumstances 132–133, 139
rape 65, 75, 183, 187, 189, 325, 327–328, 367–368, 375
ratio decidendi 355
Rawls, John 340–341
reasonable action 59, 229
reasonable fortitude 258–259, **258**
reasonable manufacturer tests 270
'reasonable person in being' 2, 3
reasonable person test 237–240, **237**
reasonable reliance 265
reasonable time 83, 103, 106–107, 109, 113, 275, 281, 399
reasonable warning 283
reasonableness of force 58, 78–79
recklessness 191, 350
reclassification of homicide 68
rejection, contract law 146, 157, 165
relationship between Parliament and the judiciary 363–366, **363**
relationships, law and morality 326–329
remedies
  breach 137–138
  contract law 105–107, 109, 123–126, 131, 134–135, 137–138, 140–148, 162–165
  discharge of contracts 131
  frustrating events 134–135
  implied contract terms 105–107, 109

misrepresentation 123–126, 161–162
  occupiers' liability 286–287, 290–291
  private nuisance 297–298
  public nuisance 300–301
remoteness, occupiers' liability 284
remoteness of damage 163, 240–243, **241**
repeated visits 280
representations, terms of contracts 101
representee 119
representor 119
repudiation 106, **134**, 158, 165
requests for information 85
res ipsa loquitur **249**, 383–384
rescission 123, 125, 126, 146–148
rescuers 255–256, **255**, 259–260
restrictive approach **253**, 361
restrictive covenants 94
retrospective law-making 368
reversing 358
risk
  of death 22
  frustrating events 133
road traffic accidents 313–314
robbery 181–184, **181**, 211
Roman Republic 322–323
Rooney, Coolen 185
Rothko, Mark 194
rule of recognition 320–321
rule in *Rylands* v *Fletcher* 302–306, **303**
rules in acceptance of contracts 84–87

S

sanctions 343–345
satisfaction, contracts 89
satisfactory quality 104
second degree murder 68
secondary victims 256–258, **256**, 260
self-control 9–14, 17, 65–67
self-defence
  balancing conflicting interests 391–392
  defences 57–59, 77–78, 226–229
  law reforms 78–79
  voluntary manslaughter 11
self-induced duress 220–222
self-induced frustration 133
self-service displays 82
sensitivity, **private nuisance** 295
sentences/sentencing 64–65, 68, 349, 374–375, 389–390
seriousness of consequences 239
seriousness hierarchy 70–71
services
  contract terms 100, 103, 107, 108–110, 113, 157–158
  fraud 204–207, 209
sexual activities 55–56
sexual infidelity 11–12, 66
shop window displays 82
signatures 110
silence 122
Simpson, Jacqueline 22
skill of the party 101
social contracts 95–96
social intercourse 54

social justice 340–342, **340**, 343
social utility 295
Socrates 336
special knowledge 101
special relationships 263
specialist visitors 284
specific intent 50–51, 75, 214–215
specific performance 147, 164–165
sports activities 54
spot payments 206, 209–211
stalking 38–39
standard of proof 390
statements, **misrepresentation**
119–127, **119**, 159–162
statutory authority 296
statutory law aspects
judicial creativity 359–363
occupiers' liability 281
terms of contracts 102, 113–117,
158–159
strict liability 307, 352, 378–380,
379, 381–382
strict rule 129, 138
subjective recklessness 36, 70, 191,
368, 374
subsequent illegality 132
substantial cause of death 25–26
substantial impairment 16–17
substantial performance 130
substantive justice 343, 349–351,
391–400
sudden shock 257–258, **257**, 260
suffering and loss of amenity
246–247, **246**
sufficiency 88, 154
suicide 53, 77, 326, 334, 335

T
'taking the victim as he finds him' 4
tattooing 55
termination of offers 82–83
terms of contracts 99–118, 157–159,
165
terrorism 398
theft 167–184, **167**, 188–192, 217
actus reus 167, 168–174, 179
balancing conflicting interests 391
definition 167–168, **167**
mens rea 167, 175–178, 179–180
theories in conflicting interests
386–387
theories in law and justice 336–342
third party rights 94, 126, 265, 351,
393

Thomas, Brian 47
Thompson, Gordon 197
threats 181–184, 217–222
time of the essence 130
tort 232–317
balancing conflicting interests
394–397
defamation 326
fault 375–378
liability in tort for defective
goods 232, 268–279
occupiers' liability 232,
280–291, 352
product liability 232, 268–279
rule in *Rylands* v *Fletcher*
302–306, **303**
substantive justice 343,
349–351
vicarious liability 232, 307–315,
307, 352
tort of deceit 123
tort of negligence 232, 233–267, 344
balancing conflicting interests 394
causation 240–243
damages 232, 233–267
defences 244–246
duty of care 233–240, **233**,
237–243, 248–267, 351–352, 395
economic loss 232, 253, 260–267,
260
fault 375–377
medical damage 232, 233–252
medical negligence 247–252, **247**
nervous shock 232, 253–267
physical damage 232, 233–252
psychiatric damage 232, 253–267,
253
remoteness of damage 240–243,
241
tort of nuisance 232, 292–306,
396–397
defences 296–297, 304–305
private nuisance 292–299, **292**,
293, 301
public nuisance 299–302, **299**
vicarious liability 232, 307–315,
307, 352
trespassers
burglary 190–191
occupiers' liability 281–282, **281**,
287, 378
tort of negligence 259
trials 345
tyranny of the majority 330

U
unauthorised acts 311–313, **312**
unconditional acceptance 84–85
'under the Queens peace' 3
unilateral contracts 81
unlawful act manslaughter 19, 23–27
unlawful homicide *see* murder
unlawful physical force 33–34
unlawful violence 32–33
unlawfulness, **private nuisance**
293–296
untrue statements 120
unwarranted demand 184–187, **184**
utilitarianism 339–340, **339**
'utmost good faith' 122

V
validity, contract law 157
value of conduct 239
vicarious liability 232, 307–315, **307**,
352, 380–381, 395–396
visitors 232, 280–281, **280**
vitiating factors in contract law
119–127, 159–162
volenti non fit injuria 244
voluntary *actus reus*, fault 371–372, **371**
**voluntary assumption of
responsibility** 263–264, **263**
voluntary intoxication 48–52, 74–76,
212–217
voluntary manslaughter 2–18, 62–68
defence of provocation 9–13
diminished responsibility 14–18,
66–68
law reforms 66–67
loss of control 9–14, 17, 65–67
self-control 9–14, 17, 65–67
von Jhering, Rudolf 386

W
warning labels 270–271, 276, 278
warnings, occupiers' liability 283–284,
283
warranties 100, 107, 136, 138
wild animals 171
wild food 170–171
Wilkinson, Aaron 15
withdrawal of offers 82–83
without lawful excuse 195
witness anonymity 399–400, **399**
Wolfenden Report 1957 329
wounding 37–38, 70
written agreements 96, 310, 357